MW00610737

# LATINOLAND

## A PORTRAIT OF
## AMERICA'S LARGEST AND
## LEAST UNDERSTOOD MINORITY

## MARIE ARANA

**SIMON & SCHUSTER**

NEW YORK   LONDON   TORONTO   SYDNEY   NEW DELHI

*Certain names and characteristics have been changed to protect five individuals'*
*privacy. Those instances are identified in the Notes section.*

1230 Avenue of the Americas
New York, NY 10020

First Simon & Schuster hardcover edition February 2024

Simon & Schuster: Celebrating 100 Years of Publishing in 2024

For information about special discounts for bulk purchases,
please contact Simon & Schuster Special Sales
at 1-866-506-1949 or business@simonandschuster.com.

The Simon & Schuster Speakers Bureau can bring authors to your live event.
For more information or to book an event, contact the
Simon & Schuster Speakers Bureau at 1-866-248-3049
or visit our website at www.simonspeakers.com.

*Interior design by Ruth Lee-Mui*

Manufactured in the United States of America

5   7   9   10   8   6   4

Library of Congress Cataloging-in-Publication Data has been applied for.

ISBN 978-1-9821-8489-6
ISBN 978-1-9821-8491-9 (ebook)

*For Jorge Enrique Arana Cisneros,*
*who passed me this torch, and*


*For Aidan, Ryder, Max, Grayson, Julian,*
*who carry it now*

I know who I am, and what I might be.

—Miguel de Cervantes,
Spain, 1605

You mind your own business
And I will not ask you
Any personal questions aside
From how the hell did you get here

—Pedro Pietri, poet,
Nuyorican, 2015

# CONTENTS

# AUTHOR'S NOTE

## We of No Name

We are not a race, a nation, a state, a language, a culture; we are the simultaneous transcendence of all these things through something so modern, so unknown, that we still have no name.

—José Carlos Mariátegui, Peruvian journalist, 1929

To tell the truth, we have no name. We never did. When we proliferated through these ancient lands in our countless varietals, we were simply tribes of this hemisphere, inheritors of a natural world, progenitors of a breed. We gave ourselves a multitude of names. Thousands of years later, when we were invaded and conquered, first by Spain, then by a battery of occupiers and usurpers, we became colonies to power—united by the boot, the sword, the crown, the cross, and the Spanish language. As time went on and history raveled, we became citizens of nineteen independent republics, admixtures of a crush of skin colors and cultures; we began to call ourselves by the names of our separate nations. Finally, when we found ourselves in the United States of America—some of us finding ourselves here without ever having left our native land—we ceased calling ourselves anything at all. We were amorphous, we were everyone, we were no one, we were invisible. We were chameleons, reflecting every color of man. When asked, we reached for the last turf we had occupied and the last label we had worn: we were Mexicanos, *Boricuas, cubanos, colombianos, dominicanos, peruanos*. Although we were no longer anything of the kind.

We were Americans long before the founders dreamed of a United States of America. Our ancestors have lived here for more than a half millennium, longer than any immigrant to this hemisphere, and still we come. Indeed, although we arrived long before the pilgrims—and although we account for more than half of the US population growth over the last decade and are projected to lead population growth for the next thirty-five years—it seems as if the rest of the country is perpetually in the act of discovering us. When they do, they give us unfamiliar and puzzling names. President Richard Nixon called us "Hispanics," hoping to unify us as a political force that could be counted, organized, and influenced. Yet, though we may speak Spanish, only a fraction of us have "Hispanic"—or Spanish—blood in our veins. And, if we do, the blood quantum itself is but a portion of the whole. That said, many of us accept the name Hispanic, and worthy institutions that support us go by that name.

The term *Latinos* was subsequently imposed on us, although it seemed alien, artificial, an appellation that ancestors in our origin countries would have found odd two hundred years ago, even laughable. It derived from the term *Latin America*, "*América Latine*," a contrivance fashioned by the French of the Napoleonic era (1799–1815), who aimed to colonize Mexico and associate the general region with the southern republics of Europe that speak Romance languages (derived from the Latin language) and distinguish us from the northern origins of the United States. It was a controversial label, smacking of colonialism, but held out, ironically, as an anti-imperialist moniker, specifically against Anglo-Americans. Surprisingly, América Latina or Latinoamérica became widely adopted throughout the Central, South, and Caribbean Americas in the twentieth century, and over time the term *Latinos* stuck, particularly in the western United States and especially in the mass media.

More recently, activists seeking to render our name gender neutral, out of respect for our LGBTQ members, have devised yet another name for us: *Latinx*. They have done this, although gender in languages is grammatical, not sociological or sexual, and found in linguistic families throughout the world, from French to Russian to Japanese. When I ask the distinguished LGBTQ activist and writer Cheríe Moraga whether she uses Latinx to refer to herself, she tells me, "I worked too hard for the "a" in Latina to give it up! I refer to myself as Xicana." Of our accumulated ethnic population, only a third use *Hispanic* to identify themselves, a mere 14 percent use *Latino*, and less than 2 percent recognize *Latinx*. A good number of us choose not to use any identifying term at all. As the prizewinning novelist Junot Díaz tells it: "We have yet to find a name that isn't enforced by a third party"—by the academy, the government, the fad-mongers, the institutions—"a name that gets us where the people live."

We are truly Americans of no name. And yet upon arrival in this country—or if we are indigenous and have been here all along, or Mexicans whose lands were stolen from us in America's "Westward ho!" expansion—we accept the denominations we are given. We will respond when called. For purposes of simplification, this book uses *Latino/ Latina, Hispanic, or Latinx* interchangeably, and yet it will seek to explain our grand diversity that defies any one label.

This book strives to be a sweeping, personal portrait of our cohort in this country. LatinoLand is populated by a vast citizenry—a multitude of classes, races, historical backgrounds, and cultures. Currently, we number sixty-three million, or 19 percent of the United States whole; the US Bureau of the Census predicts that, by 2060, Americans of Hispanic descent will total 111.2 million—almost 30 percent of the people in this country. The great majority of us are American born, speak English as well as any native, are employed, obey the law, work hard. It would take a monumental library to capture the grand totality of who we are. So I begin with a deficit, and I ask my reader's indulgence, because one book cannot possibly capture the whole.

*LatinoLand* is meant to address, at least in an impressionistic way, stories that go ignored; lives not often seen. Frequently we are characterized by the famous or the notorious: glamorous Hollywood luminary

Eva Longoria, for instance; or incarcerated drug lord Joaquín "El Chapo" Guzmán; or the great, inimitable labor leaders Cesar Chavez and Dolores Huerta; or baseball giant Roberto Clemente. Our libraries are filled with countless admirable works that portray the good and the bad to perfection. In contrast, this book follows an old entreaty by British historian Edward P. Thompson, who sought to rescue ordinary human beings from "the enormous condescension of posterity," the selective amnesia of history, and the arrogance of the "great man theory." It is not meant to be a comprehensive work, nor an academic treatise, nor is it intended to lay claim that one canvas can possibly capture the breadth or grandeur of our numbers. We citizens of LatinoLand hail, after all, from twenty-one origin countries; we are sixty-three million on a planet that counts more than a half billion Spanish speakers. It is an impossible task.

Perhaps more aptly described, this book is the result of a lifetime of reflection about where we came from, who we once were, what we've become, and what we bring to the United States of America. Many of us identify by the countries from which we emigrated: we are Mexicans, Puerto Ricans, Cubans, Salvadorans, Venezuelans—itinerants from the soil on which our ancestors were born. We only become Latinos, or Hispanics, or Latinx upon arrival, when the US Census asks us to declare; when America stamps us with a name. But whatever the label, it offers a precious unity that Spain, in all its perverse efforts to separate its conquered minions, never did. My own instinct—and that of most of the hundreds of people I interviewed for this book—is to embrace these labels. To get at what it is that unites us. To make the classification truly ours.

And so, this is meant to be a journey through the variegated universe of American Latino identity. I mean to stop at its various stations and point out its humanity, its grand array, its surprising connections, its shared sense of otherness. I am grateful to the scores of individuals from different national and ethnic backgrounds, representing wildly diverse stations—from domestic servants to university presidents, from grape pickers to corporate executives—who participated in this book via generous and candid interviews. To understand the measure of who we are, I have needed to dig down and study the history of our presence in this country. The centuries we have been here. The randomness of our arrivals. The thousands of years of history that our indigenous populations represent.

We may not have a single narrative, but we are united by a number of commonalities: By the fact that we are still considered newcomers, although our ancestors were the first inhabitants of this hemisphere. By being marginalized, virtually unseen, although we are a burgeoning, exuberant population. By being remarkably upwardly mobile, successful, yet trammeled by prejudice and poverty. By cherishing our collective reverence for family, work, and joy—whatever our origin or station. By being a mind-boggling labyrinth of contradictions that is joined by a single tongue. Even if we don't speak it very well anymore.

The nineteenth-century Venezuelan paladin Simón Bolívar, liberator and founder of six South American republics, dreamed of creating one strong Pan-American nation—a consolidation of all the newly independent, Spanish-speaking countries. His hope was to unify the region, cement the ties, and create a bulwark against a predatory world. He never achieved that vision. The colonies Spain left in its wake were too divided, too infantilized, too suspicious of one another, and too accustomed to reporting to Madrid much as separate spokes connect to the hub of a wheel. The region's postindependence euphoria quickly spun into chaos, territorial wars, grasping caudillos (warlords), and a rigid caste system, and the divisions only grew. All the same, I've come to believe that Bolívar's dream lives on in us, the United States Latinos—in this largest, fastest growing minority that hasn't quite realized that it is legion—a cohort that has yet to understand its past, its bonds, its inherent power. Here in LatinoLand, in this wildly diverse population, in our yearning for unity, in our sheer perseverance, lives a vibrant force. A veritable engine of the American future.

# PART I

# ORIGIN STORIES

Origin stories matter. They inform our sense of self, telling us what kind of people we believe we are, what kind of nation we believe we live in. They usually carry, at least, a hope that where we started might hold the key to where we are in the present.

—Annette Gordon-Reed, American historian, 2021

# 1

# ARRIVALS

We are on the bus now / that is all.

—Juan Felipe Herrera, poet, Mexican American, 2015

I can sense the anticipation and frenzy. The unfamiliar bustle of a way station. I have slept through the journey and awaken now to a vast and alien arcade, pulled from my father's shoulder and set resolutely on my feet. There are lines of bright, eager faces to the left of me, lines to the right. They are shouting to hear one another over the din, shoving their bags across a mud-streaked floor, sweeping the rain from their shoulders. A downpour pummels the hulking machinery in the distance. The buses are gray, glistening, cyclopean, like the boulders that litter the rugged shore of my seaside home. I look around for my mother and see her at a counter, parlaying our transit. She shakes her golden mane emphatically, clutching the papers in her fist. My father stands uncharacteristically apart with the children, taking no role in the negotiation. He is Peruvian, dark skinned, black haired; a lively man rendered suddenly mute in this raucous American ambit. He lights up a cigarette and takes in a long, deep drag. I reach up to grasp his hand. I am six years old.

It was the first of my arrivals. I would not stay long; a more permanent ingress would come years later, when I was nine. But this was Miami before the Cubans. America before the wave. There were a scant four million Latinos and Latinas in the country—barely 2 percent of the overall population. The overwhelming majority were Mexican Americans in the Southwest and West, with roots that had been in place for generations, centuries, preceding the arrival of the Spanish conquistadors or the British colonists. But we were not alone on that Eastern Seaboard. Over the course of the previous fifteen years, three-quarters of a million Puerto Ricans—full-fledged Americans from the US Commonwealth of Puerto Rico—had landed in New York City. They, too, were Spanish-speaking newcomers who claimed roots of their own, quite apart from the Mexican Americans. In the course of my lifetime, that overall population of four million Latinos would soar to more than sixty-three million, from 2 percent to 19 percent, from two major ethnicities to twenty, and Puerto Ricans would be calling Mexicans their brothers. *Compadres*. Today one in five souls on American soil claims Hispanic heritage, checks the box, joins my tribe: *la familia*. Whatever *mi familia* means to any one of us. We are not a unified people. And yet, in so many ways, America makes us so.

The bus station was jarring, riveting, frightening. I had come from the bosom of a warm and insular family in Peru to a clamor of strangers. Only my father, brother, and sister were speaking my native tongue. I had never heard so much chatter in English, a purr I associated with the bedtime hour, when, having me all to herself, my mother would sing to me in her language: Stephen Foster, Robert Burns, George and Ira Gershwin, Gilbert and Sullivan.

She flew toward us now, a triumphant smile on her face. She had been the only American—the only gringa—I had ever known in our tiny village on the faraway coast of Peru. I had heard indigenous Peruvians whisper about pale strangers like her, *pishtacos*, white ghouls, hungry ghosts who needed the grease of *indios* to run their gargantuan machines. Mother had been an immigrant to Peru, a casualty of love, following my father home after his two-year sojourn in the United States. For fourteen years, she had been an ill-fitting cog in my staunchly Peruvian family. The Arana-Cisneros clan was a tight, self-contained band of criollos—who claimed to be descendants of Spaniards—that had inhabited the South American continent for more than four hundred years. It had not been an easy migrant crossing for Mother. But the tables were turned now. She was in charge, on her turf. As she came, she waved the fistful of tickets that would take us from Miami to Detroit, and then from there to her parents on Elk Mountain, Wyoming. Her joy was so infectious that my father couldn't help but grin back. He would not smile often in the months to come.

When *la familia* arrives in this America, if we haven't inhabited this land before Christopher Columbus's time, we step onto a dock or the grit of a tarmac. Or we scoot under fences, swim in the black of night, scud across seas in improvised rubber rafts. For me, all I recall is that bus station on the outskirts of Miami, a site of more than one awakening. I have no memory of the airport or the airplane that carried me there and ushered me to that moment. I had dozed through the winged pageantry of it—the mad, incoming rush of it—the rumble of touchdown, the spectacle my mother had promised to deliver when she stepped from the plane, got on her knees, and kissed that sainted land. "Home of the brave and the free! Cradle of liberty!" she'd say of her country. "You can drink straight from the rivers!"—something she would never let us do in the land we had left behind. "You can lick the pavement if you care to!" But the jittery depot, with its popcorn stink, greasy fumes, steaming hot dogs, and gimcrack souvenirs was all I could see of her United States of America. For five full days until we reached the Rocky Mountains, bus stations and an endless ribbon of gray asphalt between them would be all I could see of my future home. As we made our way across the continent, those bustling halls of itinerants, those nervous nodes of transit, made a deep impression on me. They were harbingers of an American restlessness to come.

My sister, brother, and I followed our parents through that alien wonderland, gawking at gewgaws, jabbering in Spanish happily, until my mother decided that I—being the youngest and most unreliable—should avail myself of the facilities. She pulled me toward a plaque with the words "Public Bathrooms." Below it, thick black arrows pointed to opposite sides of the hallway. The door on the left said "Whites Only," the one on the right, "Colored." Instinctively, remembering the stories about

America's white ghouls, I headed to the right, but my mother's hand jerked me in the opposite direction. Sitting alone in the stall, I looked down at my legs. They were dark like my father's: "*Café con leche*," he would say with an approving pat of my knee. You're milk infused, coffee brown. There was no way I was white. I was no *pishtaco*. But suddenly I wasn't sure. I had never been made to reckon what color I was. It was the beginning of my American education.

. . .

For Latinos like me, the question of skin color has always been a complicated one, crazed by five hundred years of promiscuous history. We are the products of a racial alchemy that began the moment Columbus's men came ashore and conjugated with indigenous women. The Spanish were already a stew of ethnicities, born of a mingling of Moors and Jews and ancient Christian Iberians. We were manifold from the beginning. When black slaves arrived in the Spanish colonies in the mid-1500s, we mixed with them freely; they became part of our DNA. As major waves of Chinese poured into the continent in the nineteenth century, they joined our bloodline, too. When race-obsessed governments welcomed large-scale European immigration to whiten their populations, we became Italians, Eastern Europeans, Germans, Jews. How can we know what color or ethnicity we really are? How can we be reduced to a common denominator? A multitude of shades defines us. My own DNA tells me I'm every race of man: indigenous, European, Asian, black African. We have been multiracial for more than a half millennium. Simón Bolívar, the Venezuelan-born general and statesman of the early nineteenth century, put it best when he said:

> Our people are nothing like Europeans or North Americans; indeed, we are more a mixture of Africa and the Americas than we are children of Europe. . . . It is impossible to say with any certainty to which human race we belong. Most of our Indians have been annihilated; Spaniards have mixed with Americans and Africans; their children, in turn, have mixed with Indians and Spaniards. . . . we all differ visibly in the color of our skin. We will require an infinitely firm hand and an

infinitely fine tact to manage all the racial divisions in this heteroge-
neous society.

"An infinitely fine tact." *"La chica parece media chinita"*—"the girl
looks a little Chinese"—I remember my aunt's boyfriend smiling and
saying whenever he picked me up and set me on his knee. He was curly
haired, pecan skinned, and my aunt called him *turco*. "Turk." There was
a sliding scale in our world, a continuum so rich and broad that a society
parsed in black and white—a society so binary as to adhere to a "one-
drop rule" and ask that we choose one color or the other, as I was asked
to do in that long-ago Miami bus station—seems harsh and alien to us.

It's not that we're unfamiliar with the uses of race. Spain's über-
masters of the colonial era tried their hand at a taxonomy of our color.
They drew up a chart of possible race admixtures in the Americas and
then attempted to administer accordingly. There were sixteen possible
combinations, each with its caste name. The first was a New World child
born of two Spaniards—a criollo—the luminous ideal. White-on-white
children, in Spain's reckoning, would be the happy few in the Americas,
the aristocrats, even though conquistadors were seldom truly "white"
and seldom of noble bloodlines. In second place was a child born of
a Spaniard and an Indian—resulting in a mestizo—a more preferable
blend, to be sure, than a child tainted with both Indian and mulatto
blood, which resulted in a Morisco. But the sixteenth category, the very
last entry, addressed the issue of a marriage between a man who carried
all races—Asian, black, white, and indigenous—and an Indian woman;
this was a *toma-atrás*. A "backslider." A slip on the wheel of fortune.
That was in the 1600s, when crossbreeding was beginning to be so commonplace in the Americas of the southern regions that a vocabulary for
it had become necessary.

By then, race mixing was wild, unmanageable—despite Spain's ob-
sessive attempts to record it—and Spanish America had become an experiment in rampant multiracial breeding, a brand-new world that had
no equal on the planet. In truth, it wasn't difficult for interracial marriages to be approved, despite the feverish codification; all the Church

required was proof of Catholic baptism and a pledge of faith. And so mixed marriages were actually facilitated by the Church, and newborns' races became details to be determined and recorded by the priests. Did she look a little Chinese to the friar? Then she might be a *toma-atrás*, a "leap-back." Was she Indian, perhaps? Mulatto? A note would be made of it diligently, alongside the birth date and the parents' names. By the 1700s, as Dutch, Portuguese, English, and Spanish slave ships undertook the vast and lucrative enterprise of hauling twelve million brutalized Africans to market in the Americas (90 percent of whom—more than eleven million—went to South America, the Caribbean, and Mexico), the Latin American bloodline had become so interbred that no one was counting anymore.

Unraveling the Latino identity is perhaps a bit like trying to piece together the rubble of the Tower of Babel. As the biblical story goes, God, in a moment of fury, smashed the edifice that was being erected by the last dregs of humanity—survivors of the Deluge—because they were speaking a single language. Fractured suddenly into countless cultures and a multitude of tongues, the people dispersed over the face of the earth, unable to understand one another and powerless to communicate.

Projected onto the many diverse nations of Latin America, the story takes on a different twist. The irony is that we all speak the same language. Spanish, in spite of its many dialects, is the very system that unites us. We are a monolingual Tower of Babel, from the fisherman at the southernmost tip of Argentina to the Salvadoran migrant worker in North Dakota. What Spain's harsh colonial system wrought, in its effort to play God, was a single language from a multitude of indigenous tongues. But it also destroyed any possible sense of unity. Separated by grim colonial strictures that did not allow intra-colonial travel or trade or communication, Latin America became a slew of cultures with distinct national characters. But the looming tower of Spanish still stands, even if our children don't speak it as well as our ancestors. Even if our grandchildren don't speak it at all. Spanish is the umbilical that connects us, along with myriad more subtly shared experiences: our fierce sense of family, our tireless work ethic, our rituals of music and dance, our inability to fully exorcise the ghosts of a crushing colonial past.

To me, our story begins with Álvar Núñez Cabeza de Vaca, the first European to reside on this continent and to live with, serve, and understand its native population. There were others who may have touched feet to these shores but sailed away; adventurers who skimmed the coast but never truly walked it. The rich, dapper Juan Ponce de León, for instance, who—looking for more treasures—chanced upon Florida in 1513, named it, then sailed alongside it, hugging the coast until he reached the Bay of Biscayne and the Keys. His first visit was cursory, fleeting; and it included an African conquistador shipmate, very possibly the first black to ever tread this ground. When Ponce de León returned to Florida in 1521 with every intention of establishing a colony, he was felled by a poison-tipped arrow from the deft bow of a Calusa warrior and was carried off to Cuba to die. There was Alonso Álvarez de Pineda, another Spaniard, who circumnavigated the Floridian peninsula, sailed up the Gulf coast and entered the Mississippi waterway in 1519, even as Hernán Cortés was conquering the Aztecs. Spanish slavers, too, very possibly conducted earlier raids along North American coasts—killing, capturing, and being killed—in a frenzied effort to make their fortunes by shackling Indians. In 1524 Giovanni da Verrazzano, the intrepid Italian explorer who sailed for France, famously crawled up the coast from Cape Fear and anchored briefly in the Narrows between Staten Island and Brooklyn. But none of these instances of First Contact was as sustained or meaningful as the bizarre, decade-long American residence of Cabeza de Vaca. I offer it here as the potential dawn of the Latino presence.

# THE FIRST WHITE (AND BLACK) INHABITANTS OF AMERICA

All of them are archers, and, since they are so strongly built and naked, from afar they look like giants.
—Álvar Núñez Cabeza de Vaca, Spanish conquistador, 1528

Four hundred and thirty years before that rain-pummeled spring of my arrival in Miami, another traveler made landfall in Florida and marveled at the alien wonderland into which his ship had blown. It was April 12, 1528—the Thursday before Easter Sunday—and, having prevailed against tempests, torrential rains, and a churning sea, he heard a voice call, *"Tierra!"* looked out, saw land, and thanked God for his deliverance. He was Álvar Núñez Cabeza de Vaca, the royal treasurer of Spain's Narváez expedition and a veteran of the Spanish conquest. His commander, Pánfilo de Narváez, a slick speculator and fast talker, had persuaded the ambitious young Holy Roman emperor and king of Spain, Charles I, that there were gold-rich empires to be won north of the Aztecs. Indeed, Cortés's breathtaking conquest of Montezuma II's empire seven years before had inspired a flurry of gold-hunting expeditions bent on seizing and subjugating ever more civilizations in the New World. Never before had Columbus's accidental foray into indigenous waters looked so promising.

There were rumors, for instance, of a "White King" and a vast empire of silver somewhere to the south of Hispaniola—the Caribbean island that later was divided into Haiti and the Dominican Republic—where Columbus had established his foothold in the Caribbean. More than one tribe in those island-flecked waters had pointed south to indicate the general direction. Within four years, Francisco Pizarro would sail along the rugged Pacific rim of South America, find that realm, fool and foil its emperor, Atahualpa, and wrest the Inca Empire for Spain. So it had been that another silver-rich territory—as long as the United States is wide—fell into the Holy Roman Emperor's eager hands.

Other legends beckoned Spaniards in the opposite direction. One in particular told of a glittering chimera somewhere to the north of Mexico known as the Seven Cities of Cíbola. A Franciscan friar, spreading the word of Jesus and wandering beyond the frontiers of his known world, claimed to have stumbled upon that fabled megalopolis. The priest reported that, seen from a faraway promontory—presumably in the hazy shimmer of dawn—the enchanted cities seemed built entirely of gold. Dreams such as these were fueled by a raw metal hunger, and Narváez and Cabeza de Vaca were not immune to them. Indeed, as starry-eyed fortune hunters in a rambunctious age, they had concocted as many fool's paradises as they had pursued. They were medieval men in a medieval time, with primitive notions about swarthy pygmies who walked on their heads, thought with their feet, and inhabited lands where gold and emeralds grow. Surely God would favor the Christians and make the pagans' riches theirs. With such illusions and convictions, Narváez, Cabeza de Vaca, and six hundred adventurous souls—women and Africans among them—set sail on five ships from the beaches of Sanlúcar de Barrameda, where the dun-colored waters of Spain's Guadalquivir River spill into the open sea.

By the time their flotilla arrived off the island of Hispaniola, the ships had been at sea for more than a month in wretched, overcrowded conditions. One hundred forty members deserted the expedition. Narváez and Cabeza de Vaca moved quickly to repopulate and restock the ships, and by October, in the height of hurricane season, they moved on from Hispaniola only to face battering storms and devastating losses at sea. That was only the beginning of their troubles. The crews dropped anchor in Cuba in time to behold a colossal, wildly erratic hurricane rip up the coast at sunset and roar overhead into night. Venturing out the next morning, they found sixty of their men dead, twenty horses lost to the sea, and two ships reduced to flotsam. It seemed God himself was determined to scuttle the expedition.

But Narváez's charge from the king had been a clear imperative—an *adelantamiento,* a promise of a lucrative governorship—more compelling, perhaps, than God's own hand. Narváez was to conquer and govern the land between Cortés's prized colony in Mexico and the enigmatic territory of La Florida, which the explorer Juan Ponce de León (the conqueror of Puerto Rico) had fleetingly identified and claimed for Spain fifteen years before. There was little known about the vast middle-earth that separated the Aztecs from Florida, only scant information gleaned from slavers who had strayed into the forbidding swamps of Florida during those reckless years. There was, too, another incentive: Narváez's extreme hatred of Cortés—a rivalry and envy that stretched back many years—and the fear that, given the ravenous scramble of exploits in those early days of colonization, Cortés's forces might sweep up through northern Mexico and take that middle ground for themselves. It wasn't out of the question: Cortés had conquered the Aztecs by defying the king's orders and invading Mexico without an official *adelantamiento* from the Crown. But Narváez and his lead man, Cabeza de Vaca, were following their charge to the letter: their expedition would cross the Caribbean from east to west—from Cuba to Mexico's mainland, where the Rio de las Palmas enters the sea, just north of Cortés's domain. That, and everything between it and Florida, was to be theirs. For Cabeza de Vaca, this was no passing assignment. As the expedition's royal treasurer and head clerk, he was sworn to defend it with his life.

On that bright spring day of arrival, as the royal treasurer looked out at the tangle of green before him, he could not have known that he was seeing land Ponce de León had seen fifteen years before—the "island" the late conquistador had named La Florida, claimed for Spain, and died trying to settle. The leaders of Cabeza de Vaca's expedition had assumed they were somewhere in Mexico and had sailed the nine hundred miles it took to reach it. The timing of their arrival certainly suggested they were correct: it would have taken the flotilla that number of weeks to travel that length of sea. But these were men who had never sailed those waters. They had no way of knowing that their frail vessels had been struggling against the gyre of the powerful Gulf Stream. They had been pushed back as much as they had advanced. Blinded by fog and a storm-whipped brume, they had lost all sense of direction. They believed they had pressed west against the winds, but for countless weeks they had been thrust north. They had plied only the mere three hundred miles that separate Cuba from Tampa Bay.

In time, seeing that the sun was setting on sea rather than on land, the leaders understood that they were nowhere near the land of the Aztecs. But there was little else they understood as they skimmed along the mangrove that snarled Florida's inhospitable coast. Certainly Cabeza de Vaca could not have imagined that he would spend the next nine years making his way over that terrain, or that he would be the first white man to survive America's hazards and live to tell the tale. His chronicle *La relación* (1542), describing that mysterious continent and its tribes, stands as an early and unparalleled witness of what, more than three centuries later, would become the United States of America. No work by an English "pilgrim" in those lands can match it. In the course of Cabeza de Vaca's 2,500-mile journey, he would meet an extraordinary diversity of indigenous peoples, from the Calusa, Muskogee, and Seminoles in the east, to the Apache, Comanche, and Navajo in the west.

Soon after their arrival in Florida, the Spanish adventurers met the chief of the Timicua: the naked, dark-skinned, and strongly built natives they had glimpsed fleetingly along the shore. Heartened by the Indian's apparent courtesy, the conquistadors ventured on land to learn more. Within weeks, the expedition split, with half of its ranks, including Cabeza de Vaca, traveling overland in search of the Apalachee, a chiefdom that, according to the locals, overflowed with spectacular riches. But the trek seemed endless, menaced by bellicose tribes and a harsh, unyielding landscape. When at last the detachment reached the Apalachee, the fabled empire turned out to be little more than a cluster of villages with ample stores of corn. The Spaniards were grateful to sate their hunger, but the reality was inescapable: Apalachee was no Montezuma's empire and corn was no substitute for gold. As Narváez's men ransacked the villages, searching for any redeeming bangle, taking hostages as they went, it must have occurred to them that their futures were now in peril. They had abandoned their ships; they had been conned by false promises. A once mighty expedition had been reduced to a fearful party of strays.

The Spaniards now undertook a disastrous march back to the sea.

Desperate, disillusioned, exhausted, they waded through chest-deep waters, endured brutal Indian attacks, and lost shipmates along the way. As time passed and starvation forced them to eat human flesh, their hunt for imagined gold became less urgent than life itself. They were trespassers in a hostile land; nothing was more evident than that. Their ready conquest of Caribbean souls had not prepared them for the more truculent tribes of the North. Chastened, they stumbled their way back to the bay, hoping their ships would be there to meet them. They were not. The flotilla was gone, never to be seen again. All the survivors could do now was kill their horses for sustenance, build crude rafts from surrounding pines, and brave their way on a fickle sea.

In November, seven months after their landing in Tampa Bay, 250 survivors, fewer than half of the original Narváez expedition, set out on five improvised rafts. The majority did not ride out the journey. As winter overtook them, as tempests raged and corpses mounted, the living endured by feeding on the dead. The very argument that Catholic Spain had used to justify its conquest and enslavement of the New World—that Indians were cannibals, abominators, less than human—was suddenly turned on its head. Cannibalism was being practiced by agents of the Christian word.

As desperation grew, Narváez spun into demented denial, refusing to scavenge the land for food, preferring to ride hungry on a perilous sea. Hunting on shore would only invite disease, he claimed, or, worse, spur a murderous ambush. But the few who remained were dog-hungry, increasingly contentious, and they began to rebel. Losing all patience now, Narváez told them it was each man for himself. All rules were over; his orders, meaningless; the expedition, finished. As the clutch of desperados spilled onto land to scavenge for their salvation, Narváez's raft floated off into the Gulf's swirling waters and disappeared into the horizon. In the end, Narváez would die, not because of contagion or a well-dispatched spear, but because of a failure of courage. A mad abdication of mission. As fate unfolded, he drifted into the great expanse of the Gulf of Mexico, surrounded by the enormous *adelantamiento* that might have been his prize.

The few who had gone ashore and found some modicum of nourishment now pushed west on their fragile rafts. But as they rounded the Mississippi Delta, rough waters dashed them against the rocky shoals of what was probably Galveston Island, sundering the logs into a thousand pieces. Only four survived the wreckage: Cabeza de Vaca, two of his cohort, and the black Moroccan slave Estebanico, who became the first black in recorded history to reside in the continental United States. Naked, covered only by loincloths, and shod with improvised sandals of twine, the four undertook a punishing overland odyssey that would last another eight years. In the course of that harrowing trek, the indigenous would overpower them, enslave them, and put them to work as rank chattel. If they escaped one master, they were soon captured by another. So it was that the castaways were the first Spanish speakers—the first speakers of any European language, for that matter—to inhabit the American continent. Almost a century would pass before the *Mayflower* landed at Plymouth Rock.

As years went by, the Indians discovered that the four vagrants wandering their lands—the *barbudos*, as they came to be known, or "bearded ones"—seemed to have surprising shamanic powers. Cabeza de Vaca, especially, proved skilled at healing the sick or wounded. Praying fervently in Spanish, improvising manically, and employing the most rudimentary knowledge of Western medicine, he extracted spearheads from fallen Indians, treated mortal diseases, and—miraculously, it seemed—raised the presumed dead. Cabeza de Vaca's renown grew, and, as he moved from encampment to encampment, making a hallucinatory pilgrimage across the continental Southwest, he became revered as a miracle worker, welcomed by one tribe after another. In the course of those nine years, Cabeza de Vaca and his three companions would live among dozens of clans, from the Muskogee, Seminole, and Alabama, to the Apache, Comanche, and Navajo. They would live as those Indians lived, dress as they dressed, hunt and eat as they hunted and ate. They would be given rare gifts in exchange for their miracles: emeralds, or amulets of coral and turquoise, or buffalo hides—even six hundred hearts of deer. Saved by an uncanny aptitude for foiling death, the four shipwrecked conquistadors finally crossed the Rio Grande onto land that was being hunted by a vanguard of Spanish slavers.

Sometime in April 1536, while passing through a native village, one of the four Spaniards spied an Indian wearing a necklace hung with a European belt buckle and the iron nail of a horseshoe. When asked where he had found them, the tribesman pointed south and said that a *barbudo*, a bearded Spaniard like them, had given him the baubles. And there it was. Almost a decade after the expedition had sailed from Spain—after almost nine years of an erratic peregrination that would prefigure America's restlessness—Cabeza de Vaca understood that he was nearing the destination he had been meant to reach all along. They were clearly on the Mexican mainland, somewhere north of Cortés's conquest. Filled with expectation now, Cabeza de Vaca, Estebaníco, and eleven braves marched ahead to where the Indian had pointed until, one morning, in the far distance, they spied a posse of Spanish slavers on horseback. Even at that remove, the business at hand was unmistakable: a line of chained Indians shuffled alongside the horses, steel collars around their necks; their women and children were bound fast with ropes.

From the perspective of the distant conquistadors on horseback, the thirteen strangers approaching must have seemed like typical Indians—bronzed, naked, strongly built, armed with bows and arrows. Except that they were walking unafraid toward the slavers. As they drew closer, the men on horseback could see that one of them had black skin; another, a knotted beard that hung to his chest. When Cabeza de Vaca addressed them in Spanish, they were momentarily confused.

## NATIVE BORN

> And when Columbus discovered America, where were we?
>
> —Ignacio Ek, Mexican farmer, 1970

Cabeza de Vaca may have been the first European to truly inhabit the American landscape and tell of his adventures, just as Estebaníco was the first Black African known to roam that ground, yet these are but two in a long string of migrations that have defined this country. If the United States is a nation of immigrants, as the old chestnut claims, it has been so for thousands of years.

Contrary to what contemporary textbooks teach us, the American origin story does not begin with white Protestant settlers—"saints," as they liked to call themselves—who arrived in Jamestown or Plymouth Rock for the betterment of all. Indeed, they forced out the natives, established a white-male-dominant culture and government, and began a lucrative commerce of African slaves. Nor does it begin with the Genovese mercenary Christopher Columbus, who, finding fewer treasures than he'd promised his Spanish queen, captured and abducted thousands of Caribbean Indians, sold them into bondage wherever he could, and began a slave trade that eventually displaced five million indigenous souls. History hardly exists before Columbus in the American mind, and the 128 years that separate Columbus from the pilgrims don't seem to exist at all. As absent as this larger narrative is from US schoolbooks—as erased as it is from our collective memory—the American story begins with an indigenous past. And that past may be fragile elsewhere, but it is still vibrantly alive in Latino neighborhoods today.

If Latinos are the largest minority in the United States of America—close to 20 percent and growing—they are also the largest population that can claim an indigenous heritage. Ironically, according to US Census Bureau statistics, in 1990 almost ten million American Latinos identified as mestizo or indigenous; thirty years later, in 2020, that number soared to more than forty-five million. It wasn't that Latino indigeneity (or its half brother, *mestizaje*) had grown exponentially in the course of three decades, it was just a matter of claiming it: a matter of owning one's ancestors. For a multitude of reasons, largely imposed and political, our indigenous roots are still not fully counted. No one calls us Native Americans, for we do not belong to tribes (as indigeneity in the North requires) and only a tiny percentage of our ranks checks that box on the census, but if our DNA tells us anything, it is an ancestry many of us can claim. The exuberant diversity of tribes that Cabeza de Vaca encountered on his trek from Tampa Bay to Mexico City is certainly part of our larger, more ancient clan.

So, it should not be surprising that an overwhelmingly large percentage of Latinos in the United States carries the blood of the original peoples of the Americas: the Nahua, Maya, Arawak, Taíno, Caribs, and Quechua, among countless other ethnicities that once thrived in this hemisphere. Much as the first people of North America were killed, reduced, and driven off at the whims of an expansionist government, the first people of Central and South America were similarly obliterated. First, by three hundred years of harsh, racist Spanish colonial rule that annihilated 90 percent of their population and enslaved the rest; and then, if they happened to have ended up in this country, by a predominantly white Anglo culture that has rendered Latino indigeneity invisible. The United States of America was born seeing white; it has now been made to see black. But it doesn't yet see its brown.

When it comes to the Latino population, brown is a veritable melting pot in itself. From the very start of the conquest, the Spanish mated promiscuously with Indians. Having brought no women to these shores, they appropriated native females at will, conjugating with them freely and creating a new breed of human: the mestizo, the mixed-race child of a conquistador and an Indian. All that Catholic Spain required of its freewheeling, freelancing conquerors was that if and when they married indigenous women—which they rarely did, preferring to take them at will and by force—the prospective bride would be brought to Jesus.

And yet the conquistador himself was a stew of ethnicities; a "mestizo" of a different order. In January 1492, the very year that Columbus would sail toward his fortunes, the Spanish Crown sealed its victory against the Arabs and announced that it would purge Spain of all infidels. With a raging will to Christianize their peninsula, Queen Isabella I and King Ferdinand V offered Jews a choice between Christian conversion, expulsion, or being burned alive in an auto-da-fé. As for the Moors, who by then had occupied the southern province of Granada for eight hundred years, no choice was offered: all Muslims would either be killed or be driven from Spain's shores once and for all. So it was that the

Inquisition kicked into high gear, bringing new bloodlust to an already belligerent nation. But by then, after centuries of intermarriage, the typical Spaniard headed for these latitudes was himself a miscellany of creeds and colors. For all the Catholic queen's insistence on the old Castilian precept of *limpieza de sangre*, or "purity of blood," she would have been hard-pressed to find a Spaniard who didn't have a strain of Arab, Jewish, or African blood in his veins. "White," in other words, was a precarious notion to begin with when Spain invaded the New World, much as it is a precarious notion among Latinos today. A US census form becomes a conundrum; an existential exercise. What color are we, anyway?

As more and more Spaniards arrived to settle the Indies in that feral first century of conquest, the mestizo breed multiplied wildly. Much is made of the claim that Spanish colonizers were kinder to the natives than the English would be, and less racist. At least they mixed with them—so the argument goes—lived among them, married them. But that calculus masks a wider, more sinister history. Indian women were rarely married to their Spanish masters; they were abducted, enslaved, raped, abandoned. This was done on such a massive scale that mestizo numbers soared, making "miscegenation" one of the most violent assaults on the native population apart from outright killing. For even as indigenous women were forced to breed with Spaniards, indigenous men were denied the ability to propagate their race.

By 1600, a mere hundred years after Columbus's arrival, a combination of war, disease, and a failure to multiply had slashed the indigenous population by as much as 90 percent. The vibrant race of sixty million that once inhabited this hemisphere had been reduced to a scant six million. It was a genocide of historic proportion. Contemporary scientists call that period from 1492 to 1620 "the Great Dying," an eradication so vast that the air's carbon dioxide levels fell markedly, lowering global temperatures by 0.15 degrees Celsius. Spain didn't need scientists to tell it that something was drastically awry. Eventually the Spanish Crown, dimly coming to terms with the social consequences of the conquistadors' rapacity, began to insist that colonizers take their white women with them to "the Indies." But by then, a mixed-race, Spanish-indigenous population was in the Americas to stay. Bringing white women to the New World would change things, but not in a way that the indigenous could have anticipated. The children of Spanish marriages became a new caste in the colonial firmament: the ruling criollo aristocracy—the ever-tiny, rabidly racist, and self-perpetuating white elite. It would be centuries before the indigenous, the lowest rung of humanity, recovered their original numbers.

Within a century of Columbus's arrival, then, the mestizo—a new, totally unique breed of humanity—was proliferating throughout the hemisphere. And they, in turn, bred with blacks during the four hundred years of a brisk Atlantic slave trade that brought more than ten million African slaves to Spanish America: a staggering figure, twenty-seven times more than the 388,000 Africans shipped to plantations in the American South. By the nineteenth century, the crossbreeding in Latino origin countries would add Chinese and Japanese infusions, as Asian laborers and merchants began to arrive, seeking New World opportunities. In five hundred years of race mixing, as a consequence, Latin Americans—and we, their US Latino descendants—have come to represent every possible skin color. Nearly two-thirds of us are mixed race. Nowhere else on earth has a people of such ethnic complexity been wrought in such a short span of time. We are, as one philosopher called us, *la raza cósmica*—the cosmic race. We contain multitudes. And we are, in ourselves, a microcosm of the diverse nation the United States is gradually becoming.

But the indigenous remain at the heart of the Latino story. Even if we are phenotypically white. Even if we hail from the tiny, alabaster-skinned European elite who still reign south of the Rio Grande. If Latin American whites do not carry indigenous (or black, or Asian) blood, it is because their forebears have subjugated it, or disappeared it, or stood idly by in its demise. (As the nineteenth century Cuban poet and liberationist José Martí said famously, "To gaze idly at a crime is to commit it.") Or, if Latin American nations lack indigenous populations, it is because governments have actively sought to replace the colored races, as Argentina did when it instigated—even institutionalized—white supremacy by calling for large-scale European immigration in a separate article of its 1853 constitution. Or as Chile did in the nineteenth and twentieth centuries by systematically purging its indigenous roots and welcoming immigrants from Switzerland, Germany, England, and Yugoslavia. Or, for that matter, Uruguay, which celebrated its declaration of independence in 1831 with a sweeping genocide that killed all but five hundred of its native people, then spun around, flung open its ports, and vigorously transformed itself into a nation that is now 90 percent white. Every country in this hemisphere bears an indigenous past, even if, in some countries, few natives remain to claim it. As the Mapuche Indians of Chile say, the ghosts live on. There is no washing the indigenous from our hands in the Pan-American experience.

Our arrival on this American land, in the form of its original people, goes back thousands of years. Twenty thousand years, to be precise, according to paleontologists. The first arrivals appeared 180 centuries before the birth of Christ—long before their descendants, the Calusa, Muskogee, Maya, and Nahua greeted the shipwrecked Cabeza de Vaca on his trek from Florida to Mexico City. Our progenitors were Asian by origin, descendants of a great migration, survivors of a freak environmental disaster. They had made their home in Beringia, a remote strip of grassland between Siberia and Alaska. When the Bering Sea rushed overland, flooding their villages, they had no choice but to migrate south. As the waters rose behind them, the Beringians were separated from the rest of humanity for almost twenty thousand years. Spilling into what are now the Americas, these newly indigenous proceeded to be flung far and wide by necessity and a pioneer spirit. It was a teeming, effervescent, highly diversified population, and it multiplied, adapted to terrain, moved ever south, then surged—via war, famine, or conquest—in every direction to become a profusion of cultures with strong tribal identities. Developing their own idiosyncrasies, they have become as different as a tundra Inuit can be from a rainforest Yanomama. But they are essentially ancestral brothers, and the blood ties run deep. These, then, are the original peoples of the Americas, the true discoverers—progenitors of the Latino—who roamed and worked this hemisphere long before its five-hundred-year Europeanization. If twenty thousand years of human history were collapsed into a week, the indigenous Latino has been here the entire time. The conquistadors arrived on this American continent within the last four hours. The English settlers, a mere one hundred minutes ago.

## THE ANCIENTS WHO WALK AMONG US

*What shall I be called when all that remains of me*
*is but a memory, upon a rock of a deserted isle?*
—Julia de Burgos, Puerto Rican poet, 1943

When ancestors come to call, their voices can be irresistible. At least this was so for Sandra Guzmán when she learned that her origin story reached deeper into the past than a childhood voyage from Puerto Rico to New Jersey might suggest. She was, on the face of things, a young Afro-Boricua—a black Puerto Rican—immigrating with a single mother and four siblings to a struggling, largely immigrant community in Jersey City. But as is often the case among Puerto Ricans, skin color is an elusive gauge, and race is a wild variable. Even within the confines of her immediate family, there were pronounced phenotypical differences.

Sandra's father, a cane cutter and Korean War veteran who had separated from the family years before, was a descendant of enslaved Africans. Her mother was a strong, copper-skinned woman—a seamstress by occupation—who had packed up her children and sailed to America, determined to find a door out of poverty. Life in Puerto Rico may have been lucrative for American corporations, but it had been calamitous for most Puerto Ricans, and Sandra's mother was determined to give her children more than the island could offer. Even so, there were aspects of their Caribbean past that she refused to leave behind. Intent on preserving her traditions, she continued to practice the ancient rituals with her family and friends, or alone, beyond the gaze of censorious whites. She would greet mornings with a prayer, praise the ancestors, sing to the plants, bless the children, and celebrate each phase of the moon with a ceremony. These were deep-rooted Boricua customs and she made sure her children valued them.

Sandra and her siblings went their own ways, forging their own identities, trying to make sense of the faces that stared back at them from the mirror. "Color was the elephant in the room," recounts Sandra, and each seemed to belong to an entirely different ethnicity. Some had a profusion of tightly coiled hair, others soft, wavy curls; some were dark caramel, others creamy white; some had wide, Nubian noses, others, high-bridged Roman. But, although one or two of them could pass for white, all saw themselves as *negras* or *negros* and, so, fell in comfortably with other blacks in their Jersey City neighborhood.

Skin color was as defining and political a touchstone under Sandra's own roof as it was on the streets of Jersey City. To be light skinned was to be more fortunate, more successful, more welcome in the world. And, in the United States of America, as had been made clear every day since their arrival, a white immigrant was more desirable than a dark one. But as Sandra soon began to learn, nothing—not skin, not kinky hair, not being short or tall—would define her so much as Puerto Rico's colonial history. It was there that ultimately she would find who she was.

Puerto Rico joined the United States as war booty at the close of the Spanish-American War, just before the turn of the twentieth century. American soldiers had fought Spain for the Caribbean and Philippines and won, and Puerto Ricans, including Sandra's forebears, had been traded to the victors in the bargain. The treaty, signed in Paris in 1898 with no Puerto Ricans in sight, had made the island a US territory, meaning that when Sandra and her family arrived in New Jersey more than seventy-five years later, they weren't really immigrants at all. Officially, their papers were in order; they could travel the United States freely. But, given the terms of the treaty, they were second-class nationals, both at home and on the mainland. This was nothing new. Puerto Ricans had been provisional citizens for centuries, beginning with Columbus's claims on the island in 1493, Ponce de León's settlement in 1508, and almost four hundred more years of unimaginably violent colonial rule, as Spain proceeded to avail itself of the island's gold, sugar, and tobacco.

That was until Cuba, rising up in a rebel fervor, decided to oust its Spanish masters. Even as the Cubans engaged in a grueling guerrilla war against Spain—even as they began to win hearts and minds in the United States—the US Navy began blockading Havana's harbor as a means of pressuring Spain to release her colony. When a mine detonated aboard the USS *Maine*, one of the blockade's ships, and killed two-thirds of its American crew, the public response in the United States was fierce and unequivocal. Although there was no proof that Spanish forces had planted the mine, newspapers reported otherwise and Americans rushed the streets, placing all blame on Madrid. "Remember the *Maine*, to hell with Spain!" became their outcry.

Seizing the moment, President William McKinley made a grab for one of the last Spanish strongholds in the Western hemisphere. On April 25, 1898, in the heat of Cuba's revolution, the United States declared war on Spain. A mighty fleet of eighty-six American ships sailed for the Caribbean, Theodore Roosevelt and his Rough Riders rushed Cuba's San Juan Hill, and, within weeks, a *New York Times* columnist suggested: While we're at it, why don't we take Puerto Rico? "There can be no question to perplex any reasonable mind about the wisdom of taking possession of the Island of Puerto Rico and keeping it for all time," he insisted. The rationale was stunningly, blatantly imperialistic: Appropriating the island would provide a strategically placed naval station, a "commanding position between the two continents," and the geography and people could be forced to serve American economic interests as well. Besides, a labor force that "had never been half utilized under Spanish rule" could be a productive US asset. "There are many blacks, possibly a third of all the people, and much mixed blood, but the population is not ignorant or indolent or in any way degraded," the editorialist concluded, placing a firm white supremacist seal on his opinion. Two weeks after the article's publication, eighteen thousand US troops invaded Puerto Rico to claim the island for all time.

Spain, consumed by its colonial revolutions, hardly had a chance against America's formidable naval power, and the United States quickly emerged victorious, heralding its emergence as a world power. Soon after, US forces occupied Cuba until it could establish its independence and Puerto Rico found itself traded to Washington as spoils, along with Guam and the Philippines. So it was that the archipelago was handed off from loser to victor, from master to master, so that the colony of one empire became the pawn of another. In less than four months, without any ability to determine their own fate, Puerto Ricans went from being provisional Spaniards to being provisional Americans. Less than two decades later, in 1917, although they had advocated passionately for their independence, they woke up one day to discover they had been declared US citizens, not because of their invader's sudden largesse but because the United States needed soldiers to feed the ravenous maw of World War I and, as President Woodrow Wilson put it, make the world safe for democracy.

Puerto Ricans continue to fight for self-determination, but they have no constitutional rights, no representation in Congress, and cannot vote in presidential elections, although they pay US taxes and are subject to US military service. Many Puerto Ricans, Sandra among them, consider Puerto Rico a sovereign nation that has labored under foreign military occupation for more than five hundred years. There is good reason why. Having been wrung dry of metal, crops, slaves, and soldiers, Boricuas, as they call themselves, have not had the luxury of self-determination since Columbus abducted the first Boricua from Puerto Rican shores. Other nations' appetites have always defined them.

Indeed, after World War II, Puerto Rico's governor, craving a stronger relationship with the US government, installed Operation Bootstrap to scrap the island's ancient agrarian roots, transform its economy to a new industrial model, and attract more mainland businesses to its shores. Sugar plantations were shuttered; factories offering American corporations cheap labor and untaxed profits were opened; whole populations were uprooted, displaced; and, although factory jobs became available for many islanders, just as many found themselves disenfranchised and afloat. La Gran Migración—the Great Migration—was the result: a tidal wave of humanity that, over the course of three decades, from 1950 to 1980, ended up bringing twice as many Puerto Ricans to this country as the total population of Puerto Rico itself. Arriving in the 1970s, at the tail end of that migration, Sandra's family struggled to adapt to America's ways and language. Culturally, they were Boricuas; linguistically, they were Spanish speakers; economically, they were impoverished. They were nominal US citizens, but they were as disconnected as any bewildered immigrant from the global south. And yet, to them, America seemed to shimmer with possibility.

The Jersey City to which Sandra came in the 1970s, like its sister city New York at the time, was shimmering with nothing so much as panic. Its municipal systems were in free fall. Despite the welcoming Statue of Liberty and historic port of entry at Ellis Island, there was little to greet an aspiring immigrant family of six. The city teetered on bankruptcy. An oil slick surrounded Lady Liberty. Skyrocketing prices, a petroleum crisis, and rampant unemployment had gutted the economy. The municipality's police force, like its firefighter crews, had been drastically downsized to make ends meet. Theft, rapes, and murders proliferated. Fires ravaged the tenements. Nature reclaimed construction sites that had been halted when the money ran out; grass grew over the railroad tracks. Populations of color seemed the only asset that was booming in Jersey City. In the course of Sandra's childhood, Latinos would triple their numbers; blacks would grow by 10 percent. Whites, in turn, terrified by plummeting real estate values, headed for whiter neighborhoods. By the time Sandra was in high school, the city's Caucasian population had shrunk by half. It hardly mattered. She was a black Latina comfortable among blacks, and beguiled, inexplicably from time to time, by the ancient rituals her mother continued to practice.

It wasn't until her mother had gone back to live in Puerto Rico and Sandra had left Jersey City, graduated from Rutgers University, and gone on to a highly successful, prize-studded career as a journalist, that she discovered that her mother's rituals had been conjuring a very different island from the one she had left behind. Sandra was half black—of that she was sure. It was an identity she could see in the mirror; one she could trace to the brutal slave trade that had forced her father's ancestors across the seas. She knew through her paternal uncle, an elder griot—or oral historian—that she was the great-great-granddaughter of a run-away slave, a woman who had managed to escape the sugar plantation where her race had labored, cut cane, died young. Or, if they were lucky, escaped to *maroon* villages—runaway slave settlements—in the rainfor-est. But as Sandra subsequently learned from a geneticist, her mother came from a long line of indigenous people whose dominion over the island predated Columbus's landing by thousands of years. Which is to say, history had come knocking on her door.

Looking back on it, she was just doing her job. In 2009, Sandra, a features editor for the *New York Post*, had been assigned to be one of four subjects of a story on ancestry that focused on the genetic makeup of Latinos. A geneticist was engaged to conduct DNA tests and explore the subjects' roots beyond what they knew to be true. One of the partici-pants had been born in Argentina, another in Cuba, the third in Colom-bia, and Sandra in Puerto Rico. When the scientist secured and analyzed Sandra's results, he informed her that her mitochondrial DNA indicated that all her dominant maternal ancestors were ancient, pre-Columbian women specific to the Caribbean. More precisely, they were native to the southwest corner of Boriken, as the island of Puerto Rico was then called. The scientist had not been told that Sandra was born there; he did not know that her maternal great-great-grandparents had claimed to be from that ancient corner of Boriken called Guainía.

He informed her that she was certainly Taíno but that her DNA suggested an even more ancient line—the Igneri, a tribe of traders, ar-tisans, and farmers who, scholars tell us, migrated from the Orinoco River, deep in the heart of Venezuela, to settle in Boriken, more than a thousand miles away. Though the United States does not recognize any native peoples in Puerto Rico, a full 60 percent of contemporary Puerto Ricans have been found to carry genes of civilizations that may have thrived as many as nine thousand years ago. Ironically, because of large-scale migrations like that of the Igneri, the current population may contain more of this ancient DNA than it did in 1491, before Columbus's arrival and before the genocide unleashed by the conquest. The tribes may be said to be extinct and the political and social structures may be gone, but the genes are not. The bloodlines are not. And families like Sandra's have never stopped practicing the ancient traditions. Even here, in these United States.

When Sandra called her mother in Puerto Rico to relay the findings, her mother responded that neither she nor Sandra needed any test to tell them who they are. "We are Boricuas *de pura cepa*"—Puerto Ricans of the purest stock—she told her daughter. Sandra, too, had intuited that history all along, had felt it in her bones. As it turned out, her maternal lineage hailed from the land of the great cacique Aguëybana, the powerful chieftain who had greeted Columbus, welcomed Ponce de León with sumptuous feasts, and then led his people in a war against the Spaniards when their motives became clear. Sandra was the descendant of a proud clan that lived by the lunar cycles, sang to the trees, passed power through matriarchal lines, and planted placentas deep in the earth to tether future generations to the land. They didn't need blood tests to know these things.

"It was humbling, thrilling, a revelation to hear my mother's response," says Sandra. "All my life, I had been under the spell of colonization," a world wrought by a half millennium of conquest and occupation. "I did not recognize who I was. It was then, as a mature adult, that I saw clearly—and for the first time—what had been in front of me all along: my indigenousness." Sandra's ancestors had been citizens of the hemisphere before the conquistadors, before the slavers, before the American invasion and the further humiliation and infantilization of her people. "Colonization robs you of sight, but my DNA test was like being slapped from a deep slumber," she said. It was an arrival of a very different kind.

# 2

# THE PRICE OF ADMISSION

The question of where we began is the secret heart of our anxiety and anguish.

—Octavio Paz, Mexican poet, 1950

**M**y mother had been an immigrant to Peru. As so many stories of rapt love go, she had fallen under the spell of a lover, traveled across the seas in a warship, and shucked her language, her traditions—everything she knew—to suffer whatever indignities might come her way. Many would follow. There were a multitude of reasons why she was a misfit in Lima's intensely insular family life, why she felt a captive in that unfamiliar system. To begin, there was history. It was the mid-twentieth century in Peru, and Europe was ablaze in the Second World War, but it might as well have been two hundred years before, when other, older belligerences held sway. The seventeenth-century wars between Britain and Spain had been long, brutal, costly—taught punctiliously in Lima schoolrooms—and two centuries later, in 1945, when my father took my mother home to Peru on an Argentine battleship, the animosities still smoldered. All that could be considered Anglo, including the English language, remained inimical to anyone who counted himself a criollo, a Peruvian-born descendant of Spaniards. As for Peruvian sentiments toward the United States, there was a love-hate dynamic at work: an intense reverence for America's power and prosperity, and an equally intense indignation against its predatory habits, its strut, its greed. It was clear to many Peruvians that the United States wanted what Spain had once had: The continent's riches. The fruit of its orchards. Gold.

My grandmother, the proud Peruvian matriarch of a large, united clan, was immediately suspicious of the tall, blonde, blue-eyed American who moved into the rambling family house in the quiet suburbs of Lima. Everything she did seemed wrong: her manner was brash; her dress was too free; her skin too visible; her Spanish, preposterous; her Protestantism, unacceptable; her disregard for the hierarchy, shocking. A casual racism fell into place: the lumbering Yankee my father had married without her consent was an embarrassment. She was scorned at the dinner table, mocked by the kitchen help, ridiculed in the streets, relegated to silence. To an introspective life. To books.

Fifteen years later, after birthing three thoroughly Peruvian children, my mother demanded to go home. My father, deeply in love with his wife, capitulated. Once our long bus trip from Miami to Wyoming was done and the visit to her family was over, my parents returned to Peru and imagined making a new life in New Jersey. As the reasoning went, it was close to New York, where Jorge Arana could continue his career as an engineer and work on Latin American projects for American corporations. Within two years, we had moved to a small apartment in the über-white, tony suburban town of Summit, New Jersey—a bedroom community of New York City—where the public schools were said to be excellent. Apart from us, there seemed to be no Hispanics as far as the eye could see.

Now it was my Peruvian father who struggled to fit in. A spirited, highly intelligent man accustomed to quick-witted banter and a room full of friends and family, he was suddenly alone. At bay. Mute. Joining the lonely crowds as they clambered onto trains, making their way up the American Dream, he commuted to the concrete bristle of Manhattan. There he strained to make his heavily accented English understood, scoured Spanish Harlem for fleeting tastes of home. From our dining room table, he wrote endless letters home in a neatly disciplined hand. We could see the measure of his disquiet: there was the unremitting sting of gringo disrespect; the thinly veiled references to his short stature, his brown skin, his thick accent. There were, too, the more stark undercurrents of bigotry: "Oh, so you work in an office?" "You went to college, did you?" "Peru is a very poor country, isn't it?" "Do you wear a poncho when you're there?" Trapped on an endless treadmill that seemed to want nothing from him but work—and a household that demanded larger and larger paychecks—he turned to spending weekends alone in his garage workshop, listening to wistful Peruvian valses on his portable record player: *"Todos vuelven a la tierra en que nacieron."* "All return to the land where they were born!" To its inimitable sun. To remembering. To drink.

In both my mother's and father's cases, the engine of immigration had been love. For the rest of their lives, they would move on a restless bridge from one country to the other, never quite putting down roots. They hadn't forsworn governments or abandoned untenable political systems. They hadn't fled poverty or violence or bedlam. On the contrary: they had sacrificed homelands they both held dear. Nor did they hold the slightest animus for the countries they had adopted. They respected the other's culture, admired its fundamental character; they simply didn't feel entirely welcome in it. As a result, I, their bifurcated child, became destined to shuttle between two irreconcilable worlds that I loved beyond expression and that, taken separately, could never truly be called "home."

That is not the case for immigrants who are dissidents, fugitives from repressive regimes or from governments whose political convulsions put their lives in peril. That was certainly not the case, for instance, for Ralph de la Vega, a Cuban boy from a reasonably well-to-do Havana family who found himself in the fiery crucible of history at the tender age of ten. In the course of his young life, Cuba had become progressively unrecognizable. It all came to a climax on December 31, 1958, when a company of eighty-two raggedy Marxist revolutionaries swept from their strongholds in the Sierra Maestra mountains to take possession of the Cuban capital, where much of Ralph's family lived. The next day—New Year's Day, 1959—Fidel Castro's forces declared a resounding victory and began to dismantle the venal, Mafia-ridden, US-backed military dictatorship of Fulgencio Batista, who had fled the island along with its wealthiest landowners, sugar magnates, and corporate titans. The revolutionaries had promised to decontaminate Batista's Cuba, "the brothel of the Western hemisphere." It was, at first, a welcome objective. Many hardworking members of the middle class—like Ralph's parents—were galvanized, even thrilled at the prospect of ridding Cuba of the corruption that had gripped it for so long. They'd had their fill of Batista: of his flagrant 1952 election coup; of his capricious and arbitrary rule; of the mercenary US interests that had sustained him. Filled with hope, they worked feverishly for the revolutionary underground, trusting that Castro would soon liberate Cuba of its sycophantic predators. When the rebel forces made a triumphant entry into Havana, they rushed down the streets to welcome them.

In truth, Cuba had been one of the most advanced, successful countries in Latin America, though much of it was indeed beholden to American interests. After winning Cuba in the Spanish-American War, the United States had demurred in taking it over completely. According to one historian, the reason was simple enough: the voluble, peremptory Colorado senator commanding the debate didn't want Cuban sugar competing with his state's beet sugar crop. The US military proceeded to occupy Cuba until 1902, at which point it ceded control to an independent Cuban government that was subject, at any point, to American override. Indeed, the United States didn't need to own Cuba outright: within a few decades, it would own 90 percent of its telephone and electric services, half of its railroads, and 40 percent of its enormous sugar business. By 1950, one-quarter of all Cuban wealth was held by American banks. It was, in many respects, a puppet nation.

All this would change overnight. But not the way many Cubans thought it would. At first, Fidel had promised a very different country: "We are fighting for the beautiful ideal of a free, democratic, and just Cuba. We want elections, but with one condition: truly free, democratic, and impartial elections." Once in power, Castro revealed his new government for what it was: it would be more autocracy than democracy, and it would entail a single party, a secret police, a firm grip on all media and communications, and the end of civil society. With every day, as the machinery of change advanced, the goals became clearer—as did the perceived enemy. "Our hardest fight is against North American monopolies," trumpeted Che Guevara, El Comandante's second-in-command, signaling that one of the core objectives of the revolution was to purge Cuba of American ownership. "We'll take and take," Castro said, putting a finer point on it, "until not even the nails of their shoes are left."

## DISSIDENTS

> Look David. How the last few horses fret. How they bolt at the triumphant shriek of the trumpet. They tell us we must flee. It doesn't matter where.
>
> —Maria Elena Cruz Varela, Cuban poet
> and anti-Castro activist, 1953

On January 2, 1959, the second day of his administration, Castro announced that he would nationalize all utilities, distribute all arable land to tenant farmers, share 30 percent of any factory's profits with its workers, modernize the country's infrastructure, and begin huge rural housing projects that would alter the face of the Cuban poor. At the time, Ralph's father was managing a wholesale grocery business that supplied retail shops across the island with fruit and vegetables. It was a profitable enterprise not far from the capital, in the bucolic fields of Artemisa, where the earth was fertile and banana and papaya trees flourished. Ralph had spent much of his young life in that paradise of green, but El Comandante's New Year's proclamation was the herald of how profoundly Ralph's universe would change. Within days, his father lost his business to the revolution's central offices.

By the second week of Castro's rule, other correctives—even more troubling to Ralph's family—went into effect. It became evident that for anyone who had risen too high in Batista's Cuba, life itself was in peril. Hundreds of Batista's operatives as well as anyone who could be identified as a counterrevolutionary were herded into fortresses or stadiums and summarily shot by firing squads. Thousands were taken into custody and imprisoned. Priests and nuns were banished. Churches were shuttered. Airplanes were suddenly filled with frightened members of the clergy. Successful businessmen, including Ralph's father, were persecuted, stripped of all status, hounded, humiliated, and sent to the bottom of the social order. Schools were commandeered, reorganized: some for the better, as student populations were desegregated; some for the worse as a strict system of indoctrination was established. Military barracks were converted into classrooms, signaling the importance of Castro's reeducation initiative. It was rumored that children would soon be separated from their parents, their legal status reassigned, and then—as wards of the revolutionary state—they would be shunted to faraway camps to be educated in Castro thought. Or perhaps sent to the Soviet Union, where their pre-Castro identities would be erased entirely.

By the time Ralph was nine, those rumors had indeed become law: Raúl Castro, Fidel's brother, declared that, henceforward, the 26 of July Movement—Cuba's governing party—would control every concept and idea taught in schools so that young, budding revolutionaries would all think alike. Che Guevara, eager to transform Cuba into a Communist state, emphasized the centrality of that plan and the importance of starting with the children. "We will create the man of the twenty-first century!" he exclaimed. "The fundamental clay of our work is the young." To his parents' dismay, Ralph was shuttled off to a rural school to be indoctrinated; he was ordered to report to his teacher any negative comments his mother or father had ever expressed about the government; and, indeed, as rumored, children his age began to be sent to Young Pioneer camps on the shores of the Black Sea. There was no denying it: children had become targets—and agents—of revolutionary change.

News soon reached Ralph's family that Cuban boys, all of them slated for service in the Revolutionary Armed Forces, would be forbidden from leaving the country once they reached the age of fifteen. In sum, time was short. By 1961, Ralph's mother and father had begun to plan their escape, although leaving Cuba was no simple matter.

Nearly a million and a half had already fled the country in 1959, shortly after Castro had taken up the reins. These were largely the rich, the anti-Communists, the American company workers, the Batista collaborators, the anti-Castro dissidents. But dissidence itself had now taken a surprising turn. Some of the very people who had worked underground against Batista began to have second thoughts about the government they had helped usher in. With Cuba's new realities hardening by the day, it was clear that Castro's reforms were leading the country in a radically different direction. The entire infrastructure of Cuban society was being turned on its head. A jolt of panic shot through the country once more, unnerving a large portion of the middle class. Warriors who had fought alongside Castro in the forests of the Sierra Maestra now began fighting against him in the Escambray Mountains. They spoke of "the revolution betrayed."

The revolutionary government would have none of it. Leaving the country was tantamount to sedition. Only *gusanos*—worms, maggots, the lowest form of life—would dare. But cash was short, Castro was desperate to raise funds, and, soon, immigration could be had for a price in the new Cuba: anyone wanting to leave would simply sacrifice every material possession, every centimeter of property, every *peso* he or she owned to the state.

On the morning of Monday, July 1, 1961—two months after the calamitous failure of the CIA-backed Bay of Pigs invasion—Ralph, his parents, and his baby sister made their way to the airport in Havana. Their request to travel had finally been approved; they would fly to Miami. Their home had been duly inspected to ensure that all property had been left behind. The family's plan seemed to be going smoothly: their documents were official; they had advised relatives of their departure. Indeed, they were escorted to the airport by one of Ralph's aunts. But as they were waiting to board their flight, a solemn man in uniform approached Ralph's father. Watching his father's jaw harden, the boy sensed that something was gravely wrong. There are irregularities, the airport official told him. Your family's documents are not in order. Except for Ralph's. "Only the boy can go," he said.

Ralph's parents were momentarily flummoxed. How could they possibly let their ten-year-old travel to a foreign country alone? And yet, in their eyes, it was precisely their son who was in the most immediate danger. Ralph's aunt suddenly remembered that she had an acquaintance in Miami, a young couple who had fled Cuba years before. Placing a call to them from the airport, miraculously, she was able to reach them. They agreed to meet Ralph at Miami Airport and house him until his parents could follow. Boarding the plane with nothing more than a boy's trinkets in his pocket, Ralph cast one last look back at his family. We'll come soon! his mother called. Don't worry! Ralph waved nervously, turned, and walked on. He would not see their faces again for another four years.

## FLYING

> Mothers of Cuba! Don't let them take your children! The new law of the Revolutionary Government will be to take them when they turn five . . . and when they return, they will come back to you as Marxist monsters.
>
> —Radio Swan, CIA broadcast, Cuba, 1960

Ralph de la Vega was not the only child traveling from the Havana airport alone. By the day of his departure, thousands of Cubans had already sent their unaccompanied children to safe havens in the United States. The exodus had begun more than eighteen months earlier, and Ralph's parents were fully aware of it, although the initiative was highly secret. Operation Pedro Pan (Peter Pan), as it would eventually become known, was the brainchild of James Baker, principal of the Ruston Academy, an American school in Havana, and Monsignor Bryan O. Walsh, an Irish-born priest ordained in Florida. But it was eventually carried out as a cooperative agreement between the US government and Catholic Charities of Miami. Financed largely by Washington, it had the full support of the Eisenhower, Kennedy, and Johnson administrations. Its goal was to organize and conduct a massive evacuation of Cuban youngsters between the ages of four and sixteen, precisely the cohort that Che had identified as the "fundamental clay" of the revolution. Started in December 1960, just as Castro's reeducation program was cranking into high gear, Pedro Pan managed to fly thousands of unescorted children from Cuba to Miami, and place them in camps, fitted-out airbases, orphanages, and foster homes throughout the United States. Visa waivers for the young were facilitated by the American government, processed by Monsignor Walsh, and distributed to Cuban families with the assistance of the Ruston Academy. Throughout, the shroud of secrecy was sacrosanct; the discipline, rigorously maintained.

Remarkably enough, some of the covert organizers of the operation were not new to this type of work. One had helped resettle one thousand unaccompanied teenagers after forces from the Soviet Union cracked down on young revolutionaries in the 1956 Hungarian Uprising. Another had honed her skills in the brilliantly conceived and executed Kindertransport, the removal of nearly ten thousand Jewish children from Nazi Germany during World War II. Ever present in the organizers' minds were the vast and thorny issues that accompanied such enterprises: when a similar operation had evacuated four thousand Basque children to England after the Nazi bombing of Guernica, Spain, Britain's conservative government was none too pleased about the influx of young refugees. But the English public was more sympathetic: they sent a clear message to their government that saving children's lives was an urgent imperative.

A similar sense of urgency now drove the American mission to save Cuba's young from falling prey to Communist groupthink or from suffering the consequences of their parents' sedition. Not only did that mission galvanize a Catholic network that sprang to action in the United States, but also the operation likely became a pet project for Central Intelligence Agency (CIA) personnel focused on Cuba. A gift of sorts. After all, the business of rescuing children offered the CIA a rich source of anti-Castro, anti-Communist propaganda. Who would be unmoved by the sight of a tiny child, surrendered to fortune by loving parents and making her way across a tarmac alone, a note pinned to her chest: "My name is Carmen Gómez. I am five years old. Please be good to me." It was not the first time in history the plight of children had been put to potent political use.

The operation quickly established a pretext to justify the youngsters' travel: the children had been accepted to and were enrolled in American schools. At least ostensibly, and for a time, the ruse worked with Cuban officials. However, in October 1962, less than two years into the evacuation, the entire operation was brought to an abrupt halt by the Cuban Missile Crisis. The Americans had confronted Cuba with photographic evidence that the Soviet Union was in the process of deploying an arsenal of nuclear warheads to the island. President John F. Kennedy ordered a naval blockade of Cuba—a clear provocation—and for thirteen harrowing days, the superpowers hovered on the brink of nuclear war. With the White House and the Kremlin going eyeball to eyeball in a hair-raising political and military standoff, all commercial flights out of Cuba were blocked, and Operation Pedro Pan's "underground railway in the sky" came to a full stop.

But in the interim, Pedro Pan had become the largest recorded mass exodus of child refugees in history, a spectacular rescue operation that brought more than fourteen thousand Cuban children to these shores. In the course of those twenty-two months, the airport in Havana had become accustomed to a prodigious river of schoolchildren flowing through its system. It was probably why the airport official decided that Ralph, who fell precisely into that age group, could board the airplane. Perhaps Ralph's name had been identified by a Pedro Pan operative. Perhaps a high-level airline executive had waved the boy through. It was not out of the realm of possibility. Indeed, Pan American World Airways agents in Havana had long been assisting the rescue efforts and producing visa waivers for children. Ralph's family would never know the exact details.

It is a crushing, heartbreaking decision to part with a child as young as ten—much less a child of four—and surrender him to the hazards of fate, but fear was running high among members of the anti-Castro underground, and faith in the United States was strong. Many parents believed the new Cuban government might imprison, even execute them for treason. Others were convinced that any separation from their children would be brief: a few weeks perhaps; a month or two at most. Surely Washington would drive Castro from Cuba; surely President Kennedy—good Catholic that he was—would not allow a Communist regime to thrive a mere ninety miles from American shores. It was just a matter of time. Even the Bay of Pigs fiasco had not succeeded in dashing those hopes; if Americans had tried it once, they would try it again. El Comandante would be deposed, just as President Dwight Eisenhower had deposed Jacobo Arbenz's Socialist regime in Guatemala in 1954 (for that matter, just as President Lyndon B. Johnson later would topple Juan Bosch's left-leaning presidency in the Dominican Republic in 1965). Or perhaps the United States would begin a clandestine rescue of the parents, too. Families were bound to be reunited within a short time, and, until then, the little Pedro Pans would be safely ensconced in commodious American homes or schools, their every care abated, their English steadily more fluent, their minds free of Marxist cant.

The stark realities of what became of the Pedro Pan children would emerge gradually as years went by. The more fortunate were met on arrival by family members who had fled to America in the first wave of immigration at the close of the revolution—familiar faces that now awaited them at Miami Airport. Fortune also favored those whose parents joined them a few months later. Others, however, would cry into their pillows night after night, separated from their families for as many as eighteen years. A number would never see their parents again.

The children with no family members to greet them—those who were met at the airport by the Catholic Welfare Bureau—embarked on a roulette of possibilities: shuttled to receiving facilities—mass shelters known as Kendall, Florida City, Matacumbe—some would spend anywhere from months to years in makeshift quarters until a relative could claim them. Others would be flown to foster homes in far corners of the United States. Some flourished happily in those homes for years until their parents could collect them (a few grew so distant from their families that they refused to rejoin them); some were treated like chattel and made to work; some were sexually abused. Many who were sent off to orphanages or homes for delinquent youth emerged with lifelong psychological scars. Mistreatment by sadists, neglect in shoddy institutions, the cruel sting of displacement and abandonment—these figured along the way to varying degrees. In Miami, it was reported that some Cuban children even appeared to have escaped the facilities and were wandering the city streets, begging for handouts and a place to sleep. One thirteen-year-old was bounced from Miami to Costa Rica and then on to the Dominican Republic, eventually graduating from high school in Colombia years later; he did not see his parents again until he was thirty-four.

But the great majority went on to joyful reunions as airplane loads of white, middle- and upper-middle-class Cuban exiles continued to pour into the United States, beneficiaries of a US-government-approved preferential status. The Golden Exile, they called it, and from January 1959, when it began, until October 1962, when it was over, 248,100 Cuban immigrants had flooded into the United States, and the Miami area proceeded to become one of the most prosperous Latino communities in the country. Indeed, the prevailing narrative about the Pedro Pans is that their solo journeys strengthened them, taught them resilience and independence. Many grew up to be driven, successful, outstanding leaders in their fields.

How is it that Castro's Cuba allowed such an exodus to happen? Why did officials look the other way as a firehose of Cuban children clambered aboard aircrafts day after day, month after month—a veritable brain drain—headed for the United States? Some have conjectured that the flight manifests, a virtual list of Cuba's dissidents, were a dead giveaway; they made for a handy guide to identify the very population that was active in the anti-Castro underground. Others speculate that Castro, anxious about his cash-poor country, decided that he wanted to be free of agitators as long as they took nothing with them; as long as they left all possessions and currency to the state. *Escoria*, he called them. Scum. Bourgeois, capitalist worms. The country would be better off without them.

When Ralph stepped off the airplane that sweltering Monday afternoon in July, he looked around anxiously for his aunt's acquaintance; for

some identifying feature. He had only the most rudimentary description: young, Cuban, friendly. We can imagine a small boy's bafflement
in that chaotic airport—the adults clamoring at the gate, the unaccompanied children straining to find a familiar face, the sheer confusion and
terror of arrival. A quick, tight fear rose in Ralph's throat as he reckoned
the possibility that no one would be there for him. But Ada and Arnaldo
Báez were indeed present. They worked their way to the front, holding a cardboard sign with his name. They were young, fresh faced, a
recently married couple in their late twenties. Ada had worked in an
Artemisa dress shop with Ralph's aunt. Arnaldo, active in the anti-Castro
underground, had been charged as an enemy of the revolution. Granted
asylum in the Venezuelan embassy, he had escaped to Caracas and then
made his way to Miami, where he arranged for Ada to join him. She had
arrived only months before.

Ralph had expected that his stay with the couple would last only
a few days, but weeks went by, then months, until October came, and
the Cuban Missile Crisis put a hard stop to the flow of refugees. It was
clear that his parents would not be arriving anytime soon, if ever. Ada
enrolled him in the local elementary school, where he struggled to get
by. There were other jarring cultural adjustments. Overnight, Ralph had
been stripped of his family, his friends, his native tongue. Even the food
seemed unwelcoming. As Cuban refugees, the cobbled little family were
given government-issued tubs of processed lunch meat, blocks of cheddar cheese. It was a far cry from his mother's table; from the charmed
green fields of Artemisa.

To make matters worse, Miami's overwhelmingly white, English-
speaking population did not welcome the newcomers. Cubans were
considered loud, pushy, and—worst of all—they spoke in Spanish. Signs
in establishments' windows began to appear, confirming the animus:
"No children. No pets. No Cubans." County officials complained to
Congress that the large influx of refugees was ruffling the status quo,
"changing the complexion of the city." According to them, not only had
Cubans become a threat to the local balance of power, but also, worse,
the day would come when they actually demanded the right to vote. At

about this time, a number of newspapers began to report that the growing number of Cuban children had put a severe strain on Miami schools;
some noted that a full third of all passengers arriving on Pan American Airways were minors. In short, by 1961, Cubans weren't wanted in
Miami. A campaign was being organized to get the Pedro Pans out of
the area, out of state, to wait for their parents elsewhere. It was a tension
that even a youngster could sense. But there was something else afoot
for Ralph: a plucky, no-nonsense energy that he was beginning to learn
from his minders; an attitude that brooked no pessimism; and, most important, a firm refusal to see himself as a victim.

The Báezes lived in a rented room in a multifamily house. They
had no money, no apparent prospects, and they spoke no English. But
they were as resourceful as they were generous, and they were fierce
disciples of the timeworn, rags-to-riches American Dream. In the course
of Ralph's four years in their care, Arnaldo and Ada found work in a
furniture factory, learned the trade, and set out to establish a business
of their own. Starting with little more than a hammer and a saw, they
eventually opened a furniture shop, raised a family, made a good living for themselves. They seemed the very personification of something
Ralph's grandmother had always said to him: let no one place limits on
what you can do.

By the time Ralph turned fourteen and his beleaguered parents finally set foot in the United States, he had learned to negotiate the city,
the culture, the obstacles. He spoke fluent English. He was able to trans-
late for them, lead them through the tinned meat and cheddar of refugee life, show them the ins and outs of the American way. They didn't
know it then, but they would never go home, never again see the island
on which they were born. Not for all the tears they would shed; not for
all the Christmases they would welcome with the cry, "Next year in Havana!" This, then, would be the price of admission.

In time, his parents went to work in a shoe factory, while Ralph took
his grandmother's advice to dream big. Almost exactly fifty years later,
Ralph's career would reflect the grace and grit of those early childhood
days, when he learned what it meant to press on, keep going. Pushing

himself beyond his high school teachers' expectations, beyond his parents' ability to pay for higher education, he went on to earn degrees in engineering and management, and finally arrived at the very portals of the American Dream: in 2016 the man who had once been a worried little boy stepping into the hullaballoo of a way station—the Pedro Pan who disembarked without a penny to his name—was made a top executive of one of the most dynamic telecommunications corporations on the planet. He became chief executive officer of Business Solutions and vice chairman of AT&T.

## DEVIL'S HIGHWAY

> I thought I was done with borders; I didn't know there would be more to be crossed—cultural borders, language borders, legal borders, gender and career borders . . .
>
> —Reyna Grande, author, Mexican American, 2021

To this day, Julia Mamani is not entirely sure of the name of the American state into which she crossed. What she does remember is the Mexican coyote—pulling her across the Rio Grande by one foot. What remains in memory, vivid as a fresh scar, is a wet, panicked crawl up a steep escarpment, the pitch black of a starless night, the searchlights suddenly flashing, a deranged sprint across a busy highway, and then the vultures wheeling overhead in the morning. It was her third attempt to cross into the United States. It had taken her three months and $10,000—more time and money than she had ever imagined—to achieve it. It was March 2005, and ten million undocumented immigrants like her had come to live and work north of that river, chasing the American Dream. Unlike most of them, she was not Mexican, nor a refugee from the violence-torn Northern Triangle that spanned Guatemala, El Salvador, and Honduras. She was from a tiny village in Peru, a half hemisphere away.

Julia was but one in a steady stream of fugitives from the Colca Valley, a deep river canyon that splits the Peruvian landscape—a geologic exuberance whose striking beauty and vaulting vistas belie the rank poverty of its inhabitants. The area's exodus had begun in the 1970s, just as the glaciers began to disappear, water became scarce, and a truculent red wave inspired by Castro's Revolution consumed much of the South American continent. The Communist promise had played well in that nervous precinct of inequalities. Governments were unstable, economies corrupt to the core; societies, among the most discriminatory in the world. These were countries conceived in conquest and held captive by exploitation, racial divisions, rampant poverty, the degradation of the vast majority, and the entitlement and wealth of a tiny elite. It was at that jittery juncture, as the seventies slipped anxiously into the eighties, that the Maoist-inspired guerrilla group called the Shining Path began slashing its bloody way through rural Peru, murdering the village elders, forcing the young to enlist at knifepoint, vowing to dismantle Peru's precarious socioeconomic structure and begin the country afresh.

Julia's people, the citizens of Cabanaconde, a mud-poor pueblo in the heart of the Colca Valley, were hungry, desperate, and terrified. They fled first to Peru's coastal towns of Majes and Camaná—a mere hundred miles away—hoping to find work, but they found little relief there. They moved on to the historic city of Arequipa, filling the wretched barrios to bursting. They continued to Lima, seeking security in the capital and huddling in newly created *"pueblos jovenes"*: heartbreaking, disease-ridden ghettos that ring the periphery of that chaotic metropolis. Eventually they began to flee to the United States.

In the 1970s, the first migrants to make the 3,500-mile trip from Cabanaconde to El Otro Lado—the coveted "other side," as they call the United States—undertook a long, complicated passage through a chain of countries, crossed the rugged US-Mexican border with the aid of coyotes, and, as fate would have it, arrived in the burgeoning suburbs of Maryland, where they were welcomed as landscapers and menial workers. They were an ancient race of Quechua people, indigenous mountainfolk with an inborn respect for the principle of mutual assistance and reciprocity, or *ayni*: do first for others, and they will do for you. They had no intention to stay, only to make enough money to send home to their families and, perhaps, return to Cabanaconde in better times.

Universally undocumented, they worked as kitchen help, construction hands, nannies, house cleaners, janitors, gardeners, day laborers, and—as years went by—they bought homes, paid taxes, birthed American children, and helped one another survive. And they stayed.

If one Cabanacondino—one fellow villager—in this new, growing cluster in the United States became widowed, or ill, or the victim of a crippling accident, the entire group followed the Andean custom of gathering forces to help. They cooked, sewed, or donned their elaborate native dress and danced the Wititi—and peddled those goods and entertainments to raise funds for the afflicted. Attuned to the poverty from which they had come, they wired a steady flow of remittances to their struggling families in the Colca Valley. Their loyalty to their village—and to Pachamama, the Mother Earth, where their umbilical cords lay buried—was so strong and their generosity so large that eventually others were motivated to try their hand at the Dream. A veritable river of Cabanacondinos began to head north, traveling three thousand miles, shunting from airport to airport to reach Mexico. Braving the perils of homicidal border towns, and the bleak, blood-soaked trail the conquistadors named El Camino del Diablo—the Devil's Highway—they crossed the desert, swam the river, scooted under barbed wire. They poured silently into Arizona, New Mexico, Texas, California, and then pressed eastward, confident that the fellow villagers who had preceded them would receive them as brothers and sisters. By 1984, hundreds of Cabanacondinos had formed a tenuous little colony of largely undocumented immigrants in the bustling Maryland neighborhoods of North Potomac, Silver Spring, and Rockville, serving American families and enterprises in myriad ways. It was then that the community's leaders decided to incorporate the group as a nonprofit organization. They called themselves Cabanaconde City Colca USA (CCC-USA).

By 2005, when Julia decided to risk the crossing, the Maryland population of Cabanacondinos—which included some of her distant relatives—had burgeoned to well over a thousand, a third of the population of Cabanaconde itself. By then, many of the first arrivals had successful small businesses; their children had graduated from high school, gone to college, maybe even had families of their own. They had formed mutual help groups, organized soccer teams, raised up lawyers, American soldiers, teachers, musicians. If their fellow countrymen had homes to remodel, they remodeled them together. If there were young athletes to coach, fathers banded together and took to the schoolyards. If families couldn't afford food, other mothers provided. If there were recent arrivals to house, they were welcomed.

In July 2021 CCC-USA bought a picturesque, million-square-foot parcel of land in Poolesville, Maryland. It is an open, grassy field reminiscent of the wide pampas that punctuate the Colca Valley. A stately stand of conifers, poplars, and oaks separates it from the road that leads to town. Here on this land where the Underground Railroad once ushered slaves to freedom, where Civil War soldiers once marched to fight bloody battles to the death, the Cabanacondinos intend to hold their ancestral festivities, honor their faith, raise their youngsters, dance. Highly motivated and culturally minded, the Cabanacondinos have already planted baby pines circling the property—one for each family in their current army of two thousand. They are determined to maintain ties to their beloved corner of the Colca Canyon, even in this exurban American milieu—this mecca of pickup trucks, strip malls, and a predominantly white population. Those fortunate enough to hold green cards or US passports will return to Cabanaconde year after year for the five-day fiesta that honors the Virgin Carmen. Wearing magnificently embroidered capes and highly adorned costumes that signal their newfound status, they will dance the Wititi, the Chukchu, the Chullcho, savoring their rank as prodigal village heroes. When all the drinking and revelry are done, they will fly back to rejoin the American labor force.

In turn, the village of Cabanaconde, enriched by a constant infusion of dollars, is no longer the dusty, destitute pueblo of Julia's childhood. It has been transformed from a haphazard jumble of stone huts to a tourist destination with three-story hotels, thriving restaurants, round-the-clock wireless services, and English-speaking tour guides. Migrant workers from as far away as Lake Titicaca come there to fill the ranks of workers who have immigrated to the United States. American and European thrill-seekers throng the area in summer months, eager to hike the scenic Colca Valley—an earthly fissure twice as deep as the Grand Canyon—where the Inca built vertiginous terraces and where mighty condors reign. As one Cabanacondino put it, "Imagine! The gringos are swarming our old stomping grounds, and we are now here, in theirs." For the thousands of members of Cabanaconde City Colca USA, however, the journey to the Dream has been far more arduous than any trekker's junket to Peru. The great majority, like Julia, marked their American arrival with a terrifying scramble up a thorn-studded riverbank.

•   •   •

Julia's story begins in the slums of Lima, where she had fled at the age of fifteen to find work and quell poverty's perpetual hunger. She started as a lowly maid in a house that had posted a promising sign on the front door—"Girl wanted. No education preferable"—but she was scared off by her master's overt sexual advances. By seventeen, she had become a sweatshop seamstress in Gamarra, the "informal," lawless district where young women hunch over sewing machines in cramped, airless quarters, fashioning designer knockoffs for a few dollars a day. Making her home in a squalid shantytown on Lima's rim where a number of Cabanacondinos had gathered, she found herself courted vigorously by her own uncle, also a fugitive from the valley. He was aggressive, insistent, far older; eventually she gave in to his sexual demands. According to Julia, once they were married, and even as she birthed each of their three children, he became progressively more abusive. Jobless, drinking himself into a stupor, he would beat her, filch money from her purse, menace her with a knife.

In desperation, Julia invited her younger sister to come live with them and help fend off his abuses. But as time went by and the maltreatment continued, as she recounts it, she discovered that her husband was paying nightly visits to her sister's bed. Repelled and humiliated by the compound infidelity, Julia decided to desert the shack, make a clean break of it, join her fellow villagers in the United States. For years, she had heard that her cousin and niece had found work in Cabanaconde

City Colca USA; they were living in a high-rise building, enjoying an American abundance, prosperous enough to send dollars home. She had dreamed of it, longed for it, and furtively set aside money, planning for just such an escape. Eventually, in her dreams, she would bring her children, too. It was 2004; she was forty-five. Her children were five, eighteen, and twenty-two. She had endured her husband's depredations for more than twenty-five years.

In December 2004, Julia took her secret savings, borrowed more from relatives in Maryland, and signed a contract with an unlicensed operator who was known to arrange illegal crossings from Mexico to the United States. "La Señora," as her clients called her, ran a "travel agency" from a ramshackle building in a rough neighborhood in Lima, tapping into a mammoth network of illegal brokers that fanned up South America to the American Southwest. Visiting her makeshift office in a shuttered garage in the La Victoria district, Julia heard La Señora tell of the many Cabanacondinos whom she had successfully guided to El Otro Lado, the longed for "other side." She asked for $10,000 up front, with no stipulations and no assurances. The understanding was that however many attempts it would take—whether Julia crossed successfully on her first try or her fifth—the advance would cover the entire transaction: all airplane flights, ground transportation, stays in safe-houses, the aid of coyotes and subagents, any necessary clothes, food. Remarkably, Julia was able to raise the cash. It was more than she would have earned in three years as a garment factory worker, but she had been shrewd and frugal. She had stashed away funds precisely for this purpose for two decades. And she had been enterprising in cajoling others to lend her the rest. One month later, in January 2005, she departed Lima for Mexico City.

Julia had barely stepped off the plane in the Mexico City airport when she was taken into custody. Of the four Peruvians traveling with La Señora's counterfeit documents, she and two others were seized, kept under surveillance for ten hours, and then flown out to Chile as "*secados*"—"quick-dried"—apprehended criminals. Within twenty-four hours, they were back in Peru. Days later, La Señora put her on another flight to Santa Cruz, Bolivia, where she spent fifteen days holed up with a constantly changing cast of transients in a shabby, airless hostel. On the sixteenth day, she was picked up by a stranger and driven for two and a half days to Brazil's border with Paraguay. By then, weeks had passed; it was March, and seven other Peruvians had joined her. On March 15 the band bound for the paradise of El Otro Lado was shuttled to São Paulo, where they boarded a flight to Guadalajara, Mexico; but even before the flight could lift off, a pair of Brazilian security officers boarded the airplane and removed them all.

Impatient with her now, La Señora decided Julia needed a total transformation: better clothes, new hairdo, makeup, high heels, perhaps another personality entirely. She gave Julia money to buy an outfit at one of Lima's department stores, have her face and hair professionally done. She coached Julia on how to keep her lipstick on, her chin up, her stride confident. Flying directly from Lima to Mexico City this time, Julia passed through customs handily, waved along as if she were any businesswoman. Switching documents as La Señora had instructed, she boarded another flight to Monterrey with a new name and a Mexican identity. Just as planned, she was met on arrival by her first coyote, who took her to an empty house. There she spent thirty hours alone, wondering where she was and what to expect. At sunset on the second day, another coyote fetched her and took her to another abandoned house, where a gruff, no-nonsense truck driver gave her curt instructions. "We leave after I've had my dinner. You get in the tractor and lie on the pallet behind my seat. If a police or anyone else stops us, you are my wife. Do not get up. Do not open your eyes. I'll tell them you are resting."

The trip in his hulking semi was uneventful. At midnight, he dropped her off at a taxi stand in Nuevo Laredo, directly across the border from Laredo, Texas, with hastily scribbled instructions to take a taxi to a hotel in a rough part of town. The hotel manager turned out to be part of the ring that worked closely with the cartels and the coyotes. After a few hours, she was met again and taken to a far corner of the city. By now, she understood that she was little more than freight in a dizzying chain of agents, subagents, couriers, merchants, and young, hardened coyotes—all in the service of the infamous Gulf Cartel, alias "La Mano"

(The Hand), or their rivals, the criminal syndicate Los Zetas; cogs in the billion-dollar business of trafficking souls and illegal drugs across the US border. The owners of the houses in which she had stayed along the way had vacated their premises for just this purpose: to warehouse the human cargo as necessary and to profit from the spirited cash flow.

Days later, toward the end of March, she was ushered into a room filled with Peruvian immigrants—fourteen in total, men and women in their early twenties who, like Julia, had been funneled into Mexico the week before. They were told they would be crossing the river that night. What was not said—what they would not hear until much later—was that they had already survived a hair-raising peril, *la carretera de la muerte*, "the highway of death," the 136-mile artery connecting Monterrey to Nuevo Laredo. For decades, that singularly nondescript thoroughfare had been the backdrop for kidnappings, rapes, young girls sold into sexual slavery, robberies, "disappearances," and outright murders. The vast multitudes of desperate refugees moving up through the heart of Mexico had become easy prey for the drug cartels: objects of further extortion, pawns in a long trail of tears. If the *desperados* had raised enough money to get this far, surely their relatives could be squeezed for more.

The coyotes in the immediate vicinity of the border—most of them lackeys of La Mano—are known to regularly beat, hold captive, or starve itinerants in their care. They take unbridled risks that too often go awry. They have been known to cause accidents that drown, suffocate, or mutilate whole payloads of migrants. Once, on a bridge to Laredo, US border agents peeked into an empty tanker trailer reeking of gasoline and found fifty men crammed inside. La Mano was—and still is—responsible for much of the border violence on the Mexican side. By 2005, when Julia was in their hands, evidence of the carnage was everywhere: in the burned bone fragments that lay scattered in the brush, or the hastily dug graves that littered the roadside. She didn't see it. She didn't know it. But disappearances had been so common since 1964 that local officials no longer bothered to answer inquiries. Chance discoveries of clandestine crematoriums had become so routine that police stopped recording them.

That night, after midnight, a young, wiry coyote in an unmarked van came to collect the northbound travelers. Piling them all in, he drove them to a grassy embankment on a narrow part of the Rio Grande where two other coyotes awaited. The travelers were instructed to strip completely and stuff all their clothes into a single garbage bag. They obeyed, too terrified to be anxious or shy about their nakedness. Julia, who confessed instantly she didn't know how to swim, was assigned to ride a rubber tire that was rolled down to the river's edge. Clutching the garbage bag to her bare breasts, she clambered onto the tire, draping her legs over the side as the others waded into the foul, sewage-laden river. They swam silently through the black of night—a coyote pulling Julia along by one foot—until they finally arrived at the opposite bank. The American side. El Otro Lado. They crawled up the grassy bank into Texas. They had made it. But they had yet to run the gauntlet of border guards, barricades, and guns that separated them from the Dream.

Clothed again, the group moved swiftly along the river's edge until they came upon a stone trail that led up an escarpment and onto a clearing. The coyotes explained that once they reached the top, they would need to watch for the sweeping searchlights and cameras. "Run when the field is dark," they cautioned them. "Head straight across that open range and hit the ground whenever the lights swing toward you." The group obeyed, following the coyotes' whispered shouts, racing across what appeared to be the wide, open pasture of a very large ranch and throwing themselves belly down whenever the blazing eye swept by. Too old at forty-six to keep up with the rest, Julia tried to cling to the hand of a young woman as she ran, but the woman begged her to let go. Panicked and out of breath now, Julia stumbled ahead but quickly fell behind. Suddenly she lost hope, slowed to a walk, barely bothering to crouch when the searchlights spun her way. A coyote shot through the night and pulled her to safety.

Once they had passed the lights and rejoined the others, the group pressed on, weaving in and out of the mesquite for what seemed like a quarter mile before they were confronted with another hurdle. This time it was a towering chain-link fence festooned with razor wire. The coyotes showed them a spot where they had cut a hole into the steel and painstakingly reattached the piece so that it was not easily detected. The fragment came away to reveal a gap large enough to allow a human to pass through. The Peruvians were told that, on command, each should jump through the hole and run as fast as humanly possible until they reached Interstate-35, a multilane highway some one thousand yards away. Time was of the essence now. The moment they breached the fence, they would be traversing a hot zone stalked by border patrol, police, and self-appointed, gun-toting vigilantes. Militias from as far away as Wisconsin were known to hunt migrants for sport. But once they crossed I-35's busy asphalt, they would be on safer ground. There they would be met by a pickup truck and transported to a house somewhere in Laredo.

Being the slowest of the lot, Julia knew she would need time to get as far as the rest. She asked to go first. The coyotes agreed and indicated that the others should follow immediately. But when one of them gave her the signal, "Now, señora! Run!" she bounded into the dark, tripped over the loose patch of wire, and fell face down in front of the opening. The others, keen to get through the gap as quickly as instructed, ran over her, leaping off her legs, her arms, her back. When the coyotes lifted her up, she had lost all feeling in her feet.

The men urged Julia to stand. She could not. They rubbed her legs, her back, until, after about a half hour, she was able to bring herself to a wobbling stand. The older coyote ordered the younger one, a gangly, callow boy of nineteen, to do whatever was necessary—pull, drag, carry—but get her to the highway as best he could. "Señora," the boy commanded her, "you are going to stand behind me. I'm going to grab you by your arms, and we are going to run." She did as he said. All she recalls today is a sensation of running on air, flapping like a banner behind him, her feet barely touching the ground.

Indeed, there was a truck waiting on the other side of the highway. The driver switched off its headlights and sped them over a dirt road until they reached a box of a house behind a thick stand of elm. The rooms were tiny, littered with dirty clothes—on the cots, the floor, the furniture. The Peruvians were told to wash them, set them in the sun to dry, and wear them on the next leg of the journey. A T-shirt, a pair of pants, sneakers—these were all the property they were allowed, nothing more. They would need to pass undetected through a US Border Patrol checkpoint, and they would need to be free of body odor. No sweaty clothes, no fragrance whatsoever, nothing on their breaths. There would be dogs.

Julia stayed in the house for a week, long enough to become attached to a shy, young woman, roughly the age of her oldest child. She was Mirta, a pretty thing, large eyed, small boned; it was remarkable that she had survived the crossing at all. It was also instantly clear to Julia that one of the new coyotes was eyeing Mirta hungrily. When he took the girl aside and demanded she go to one of the bedrooms with him, Julia took it upon herself to shield Mirta, try to talk the man down. At first, he would have none of it, but eventually he relented. Julia would soon learn why. Come dawn, the coyote announced that Julia would be the first to brave the checkpoint. She was to accompany three others who were housed elsewhere. Julia tried to persuade him to let the girl come with her, but he only snarled and pointed her to the door. As she walked toward the car that had come to fetch her, she looked up into the great dome of American sky. A pair of black vultures was wheeling lazily into the blue.

At the next house, Julia was given fresh clothes and instructions for the last leg of her journey. She would be smuggled through the patrol station with three men. A young family of Mexican Americans—man, woman, and baby, all of them US citizens—would ferry them in the trunk of their station wagon.

The car had clearly made such trips before. Its trunk had been ripped out, hollowed, reconfigured to fit human cargo under its tidy, carpeted floor. The four stowaways, including Julia, were told to lie next to one another, face down. When they came to the checkpoint, they would hear two sharp raps on the passenger's door: the signal to hold their breath so that the canine team would not hear them. The dogs might detect their hearts, too, if they beat too loudly, so it was imperative that they remain calm. Although they were in the United States, there was every chance they would be caught, impounded, and sent back.

The ride to the checkpoint was surprisingly quick and not uncomfortable; the three youths on either side of Julia were reed thin, hardly bigger than she. Despite the roar of the car's engine, they were able to say a few words, comfort one another, grow calm. Their lives were knit together tightly now; a slip from one could sacrifice the rest. As the car pulled up to the front of the line and a guard strode up to ask the man for papers, the wife rapped the signal "Do not breathe."

It was at that point that the couple's baby, a strapping boy of eighteen months, began to wail, sending ear-splitting screams into the Texas morning. The stowaways held their breath as the border police reviewed the documents and the child continued to shriek and howl; furiously, unconsolably. The police, clearly unnerved by the child's misery, spoke impatiently in English. Julia could hear their disquietude, but did not understand a word. Before long, she heard the woman shout over the baby's desperate cries—"Colic!" "Emergency!"—words close enough to Spanish to understand. The policeman in charge snapped shut his log and shouted, "Okay! Go!" and then again, "Go!" The engine roared to life, and the station wagon barreled out of the station onto the freeway.

Hours later, on a dusty road somewhere in central Texas, the stowaways scrambled out of the trunk and into the back seat, and Julia—a mother herself—asked after the child. Was he all right? Why the heartwrenching cries? The woman turned to her and answered, "Those cries are why you are here, señora. You owe my baby your life. I told the police that he was sick with colic, probably a serious intestinal obstruction, and that we were taking him to an emergency room, but, in truth, I was pinching him. Hard. All the while."

By evening, Julia had been handed over to "a guide" in Boston, Texas. Two days later, she was in Maryland, delivered safely to her relatives, yet another postulant to the American Dream. She had been ferried to Rockville in a church van adorned with the image of praying hands. She was told that if they were stopped, she and the three migrants with her were to say they were members of an Evangelical church, on their way to meet brothers and sisters of their faith.

Within a week, she had a job minding American youngsters in a capacious house in one of the wealthiest suburbs of Washington, DC, cleaning their messes, cooking their lunches, walking them to school. She had spent three harrowing months crisscrossing Latin America in an odyssey she had never fully comprehended. She had surrendered her children, her destiny, and her life savings to fortune. But, for all the cost of admission, she had arrived. She was now one of America's ten million "illegals," a classification she has yet to shed. But she had work, a decent wage, and she had Cabanaconde City Colca USA—a support system of souls that shared her birthplace, now almost four thousand miles away. It would be sixteen more years before her children would begin to join her.

# 3

# FORERUNNERS

I live *al reves*, upside down. Always have. Who called me here? The spirits maybe.

—Sandra Cisneros, author, Mexican American, 2013

Julia Mamani could not have known it, but she had stumbled into the United States very near to where the conquistador Cabeza de Vaca—naked but for his loincloth—had wandered south to Mexico after almost a decade of living among the origin peoples of the North. There, almost five hundred years apart and on lands serially claimed by Karankawa Indians, Spanish settlers, and American expansionists, Cabeza de Vaca and Julia had shared a common purpose: to reach the other side, to stay alive. Neither had thought they would stay long.

If the United States–Mexico border seems a permeable boundary, it is because it always has been. Before Columbus's arrival, tribes crossed the Rio Grande freely, to trade if not to raid villages or wage war. By the end of the eighteenth century, Spanish settlers had penetrated both continents of the Western Hemisphere and claimed territories from southernmost Argentina to Wyoming, and from westernmost California to Missouri, making the mighty Rio Grande just one more topographic hurdle in Spain's dominion. Today forty indigenous tribes continue to straddle the existing border, and many have age-old traditions of crossing it as they please, since their ancestral lands do not hew to modern legal limits.

The English settlements at Jamestown and Plymouth—in 1607 and 1620, respectively—would drastically erode Spain's preeminence in the hemisphere. The Britons' expansionist glee in the Americas, like the Spaniards' before them, began from the moment their ships met shore. An assumption of infinite land, all of it for the taking, was uppermost in the pilgrim imagination, and nothing would stand in their way—not Indians, not sovereign nations, not previous boundaries, and certainly not the Spanish, who had been England's archenemy for as long as anyone could remember.

As the colonies developed and political differences ensued, the simple solution to any vexation was to move out, move on, find the requisite elbow room—"extend the sphere!" as congressman James Madison had exhorted his countrymen to do as early as 1787. But this was no American invention. The white Anglo-Saxon spirit of expansion and colonization had been present even before the founders dreamed of independence, and it was a force to be reckoned with—a formidable engine of perpetual unfurling. A century and a half before, the English philosopher Thomas Hobbes had described that British impulse as driven by an "insatiable appetite, or Bulimia, of enlarging dominion." The immediate problem, of course, was that the continent already had its masters. For all the colonists' propaganda that they had arrived in "a wilderness," confronting the subjugation of nature itself, the human population that preceded them was their constant impediment, the chronic annoyance that hampered the way.

Once the American Revolution was done and the United States established, the prevailing view was that it wasn't enough to push out the native tribes—or "foreign nations," as one secretary of war called them. The indigenous needed to be eradicated, disappeared. Even the mild-mannered Thomas Jefferson offered that history "will oblige us now to pursue them to extermination, or drive them to new seats beyond our reach." In other words, mass murder was the only solution. As for the Spanish and Mexicano settlements, which soon became as inconvenient as the Indians had been, Jefferson imagined that his infant nation would nibble away at Spain's jurisdiction, snatching the whole of Latin America "piece by piece." Extortion, murder, lynching, outright conquest—all of these tactics of intimidation would become viable strategies in that effort. And all would have their uses in the pursuit of Manifest Destiny: the belief that Anglo-Americans were destined by God to expand their dominion and spread their notions of exceptionalism throughout the North American continent, including Mexico.

But being more bound to the land than the nomadic, warrior tribes of the North, the Mexicanos were not so easily herded and expelled. Even as American imperialism ate its way into Spanish America either by purchase, incursion, or war—even as President James A. Polk forced the American frontier west and south, redefining it at will, driving Native Americans from their ancestral lands and arbitrarily making the Rio Grande the new limit—souls continued to move back and forth across the border. Indeed, for more than a half century after the United States pushed its way into Mexico, appropriated more than half of it in the Mexican-American War, and imposed the 1848 Treaty of Guadalupe Hidalgo (a treaty negotiated at gunpoint even as US troops occupied Mexico City), the border remained wide open and undefended. Anyone could move across it as freely as Cabeza de Vaca once had and as deliberately as Julia Mamani subsequently would. Grandparents visited their grandchildren in El Otro Lado; workers crossed, boosting the American economy in factory and field; students scurried back and forth to school. It wasn't until 1904 that fifty mounted guards were posted in El Paso, Texas, to watch for Chinese arrivals, the only incomers officially designated as illegal by the rabidly racist 1882 Chinese Exclusion Act. And it wasn't until 1924 that immigration laws were put in place to keep Mexican American communities in the United States from growing. Although their land had essentially been stolen from under their feet, Mexicans became the unwanted masses, the pariahs, those whom one white governor of New Mexico described as the apogee of "stupidity, obstinacy, ignorance, duplicity, and vanity." "The meanest looking race of people I ever saw," one US Army captain leading the expansion trumpeted. "Dirty, filthy-looking creatures."

Never mind that Spanish Americans had inhabited that land long before Anglos had set foot in the Americas—that they had built shining cities, universities, judicial systems, public institutions, places of worship, and a thriving commerce. Never mind that, before them for thousands of years, the Maya, Nahua, Yaqui, O'odham, and Kumeyaay—a veritable multitude of tribes—had claimed it, governed it, worked its fields. If roots had any meaning, as Mexican American writer Sandra Cisneros once put it, ancestral spirits would summon their descendants from one side to the other, regardless of any barriers raised to foil them.

• • •

As fate would have it, my own grandfather crossed into the United States through Mexico. He had come, as many have, because he was summoned. It was 1898, and the United States was waging yet another war for expansion, this time in the Caribbean, with the expulsion of Spain as the goal and Cuba and Puerto Rico as the prizes. Abuelito was a teenager at the time, a gifted student in a Catholic school in Lima, with a fine future before him. His father was a senator, shuttling busily between his jurisdiction in the sierra and the nation's capital, looking to give his son a more ample view of the world. Providentially enough, The University of Notre Dame had just thrown its doors open to Latin American students. Its vice president, Reverend John Augustine Zahm, an avid explorer of South America, had sailed the mighty Orinoco River, which cuts through the heart of the Venezuelan rainforest, trekked the vertiginous Andes, and was looking to infuse Notre Dame with young, Catholic South Americans. The major universities of the day were largely Protestant institutions with decided prejudices against the Catholic faith; he wanted to instill in his students a more worldly view. There was also the question of the university's finances, which had become catastrophic under the flamboyant explorer's charge. Notre Dame needed my grandfather's tuition. My great-grandfather obliged. Like any laborer lured to El Norte's vineyards or any steelworker called to the mills, my sixteen-year-old abuelito answered the American demand. He sailed up the Pacific coast on a series of ships—large and small—stopping in Ecuador, Colombia, and Panama, then finally arriving in Veracruz, Mexico, at which point he ran out of pocket money. This is where I lose him. Family legend has it that, being a boy in a strange land, he did what any boy would do. He hitchhiked his way to the border and then on to South Bend, Indiana, as the beneficiary of many kindnesses. Upon graduating from Notre Dame in 1902 with a degree in engineering, he taught for a while in a university in Maine and then he did what migrants did after answering a seasonal need: he returned to his native country.

Remarkable as it may seem, this story repeats with my father. Almost a half century later, in December 1941, when my father was a twenty-two-year-old engineering student in Lima, the Japanese dive-bombed Pearl Harbor, catapulting the United States into World War II against Japan, Nazi Germany, and Italy. Young men and women in American universities answered the nation's call, emptied the classrooms, and joined the war effort. The US State Department rushed to enlist young Latin Americans to fill those lecture halls and allow universities to stay open. Urged by his father, Papi met the demand, accepting a place in the master's program at the Massachusetts Institute of Technology. In early 1943, just as General George Patton was strategizing a breathtaking leap from Africa to Europe, Papi flew to Panama City, intending to fly to Miami on his way to MIT. But civilian travel to the United States had been halted. Panama was crawling with American soldiers, and flights from the isthmus had been preempted for military use. For seven days, Papi began each morning with a horde of other Latin Americans at the airport, awaiting an open seat. On the eighth day, an official announced that the US mail plane to Miami was running one sack light. One hundred twenty pounds. Did anyone fit that profile? My father, a stringy man, a tight bundle of energy, sprang up to volunteer. He was weighed, checked in, and allowed to scramble in with the freight.

Like any migrant riding a boat, a tire, a tanker truck, or the hollowed-out trunk of a car, my father came to America as cargo: even as a letter might, with no more than a scribbled destination and a sliver of hope. Two years later, after earning his degree from MIT and staying on briefly to produce turbines for the American war machine, he would do what any Mexican laborer answering a seasonal demand did, and what his father had done: he returned to his country, but with a slight modification. Along with his American degree, he brought home an American wife. It would take my family a third generation of itinerants to the United States—my generation—to come to America to stay.

## THE IN-BETWEEN PEOPLE

> Mexicans who live in the borderlands, north and south, have a word
> for that liminal space between languages, cultures, and mentalities.
> They call it *nepantla*.
>
> —Sergio Troncoso, author, Mexican American, 2021

Staying is the crux of the Latino immigrant's dilemma, which is why homeland umbilicals are never quite severed in first-generation arrivals. There is always the chance that you will want to go home. "Go back where you belong!" a red-faced schoolmate shouted at me on my first day of school in Summit, New Jersey. What about me could possibly have made her so angry? I can still remember the pang of it; the longing to go home. But there is also the chance that you will be shooed back to your country of origin, without recourse or explanation. And that is a very Mexican story.

The pattern of summoning Mexican workers when needed and deporting them arbitrarily began at the turn of the twentieth century, and then ballooned with every major American war. It persists today as agricultural seasons come and go. Mexicans lured to our fields during the First World War—some as young as twelve years old—were often lied to, swindled, and corralled in miserable conditions only to be deported when the Great Depression arrived. They had become an inconvenience. Americans balked at the prospect of including Mexicans in New Deal welfare programs. Not only were they shunned and vilified as a race, but also they were scapegoated for allegedly having produced the economic disaster in the first place. The prejudice made for rank cruelties.

Employers who didn't want to pay field-workers for a season of backbreaking work simply forced them onto deportation wagons and sent them away. It is estimated that police, local officials, and the FBI rounded up and deported nearly two million Mexicanos during the 1930s, 60 percent of whom were fully documented American citizens. The authorities called it "repatriation" to give it the gloss of a voluntary program. But it was uniformly coerced, and it was harsh. It happened throughout the country.

One Idaho farm family was just sitting down to breakfast when local sheriffs burst into their house, placed everyone under arrest, and piled them into police cars, refusing to let them bring any belongings with them. They left home with no identification, no birth certificates, no savings—nothing. Only the clothes on their backs. The father of the family, who was out working the fields, was rounded up later. All were put in jail for a week and then herded onto a train bound for Mexico. They were assured their belongings would follow, but they never did. Among the items left behind: documentation that showed they owned property, that the head of the household had worked in the country legally for twenty-five years, and that his siblings and children had been born in the United States and were American citizens. "We all know about the internment of 145,000 Japanese," a United States senator has said about these dire violations of citizens' rights, "but 1.8 million Mexican deportees dwarfs that size, and most Americans know nothing about this topic."

It didn't stop there. During the Second World War, with a desperate need for workers, the US government installed the Bracero Program, which invited in as many as a half million Mexicans a year. Four and a half million workers streamed across the border in rotating cycles from 1942 to 1964, toiling in menial jobs that allowed the country to function. Once the Korean War was over, however, the Eisenhower administration implemented Operation Wetback, an initiative executed with the zeal and precision of a military rout, terrorizing the very population that had been ushered in to feed and build America. As many as 1.3 million people—once again, some of them native-born American citizens—were snatched from their homes or workplaces, shoved unceremoniously onto buses, boats, and airplanes, and dumped into random, unfamiliar cities in Mexico. Staying had become an inconvenient option, both for the United States, which had beckoned them in, and for labor-starved Mexico, which now wanted them back. Never mind that, in the interim, they'd had American children; never mind that those youngsters may never have learned Spanish. Indeed, in the fanatical eagerness to purge the Southwest of anyone who was brown, local governments took law-abiding Mexican Americans whose families had inhabited that land for generations, thrust them into vans, and ferried them away. Constitutional rights be damned. As one politician put it, "It was about the color of their skin."

But attitudes toward staying or repatriating are as various for Latinos as are their countries of origin. Staying had not been the goal of the overwhelming majority of Cubans who fled the Communist Revolution in the 1950s and 1960s. But as Castro hung on year after year, and US presidents proved powerless to oust him, Cuban exiles found themselves progressively wed to this country and increasingly intent on cementing their domain.

Puerto Ricans, too, did not necessarily intend to stay when they flooded into the New York area in the 1950s. Ready-made citizens by virtue of the US takeover a half century before, they had been displaced by a sudden and radical transformation of the economy at home. That redefinition, which would convert an ancient sugar-producing nation into an industrial model, had been encouraged in large part by American corporations eager to take advantage of Puerto Rico's cheap labor. The metamorphosis ended up turning the job market upside down and putting Puerto Ricans out of work. Hundreds of thousands—a full fifth of the island's entire population—poured into the New York area and beyond to work, eat, and claim their due as American citizens. But many had every hope of returning.

Unlike the Mexicanos, by far the largest group of Latinos in this land, the Cuban and Puerto Rican communities began relatively modestly in 1950 but ballooned quickly: Puerto Ricans in the United States numbered one million in 1960; twenty years later, their numbers had doubled. Today, given natural population growth, approximately six million Americans identify as Puerto Rican. Cubans, on the other hand, amounted to a mere 163,000 US residents in 1960, and fewer than a million by 1980, even after three major waves of immigration. Today there are two and a half million Americans who identify as Cuban. Taken together, these two Caribbean Latino ethnicities represent eight and a half million people—more than 2 percent of the American whole—a population equal to that of Virginia. They are, respectively, the second and third largest communities of Latinos in the country, and by far the most dominant population of Latinos on the East Coast. They differ racially—almost half of all Puerto Ricans in the United States identify as nonwhite, while the overwhelming majority of Cuban-Americans are white. But they also have distinct reasons for being here: the first arrived as US citizens, the second arrived as refugees. And both are very much here to stay.

•   •   •

I do not think there was ever a more wicked war than that waged by
the United States on Mexico. I thought so at the time, when I was a
youngster, only I had not moral courage enough to resign.
          —Former president Ulysses S. Grant to a journalist, 1879

The question of staying is far more monumental for Mexicanos. After all, for many of them, this is their ancestral land. In 1848, after hundreds, maybe thousands of years of habitation on this continent, they suddenly found themselves on foreign soil by virtue of a treacherous Anglo-American incursion across their borders. They were victims of an organized onslaught, a bitter war, a hastily concocted treaty, and the massive land grab of an area that became Texas, California, New Mexico, Arizona, Utah, and Nevada, as well as parts of Colorado and Wyoming. It was as cynical and brash an invasion as the Nazi lunge for lebensraum, Adolf Hitler's infamous march across Europe to gain Germany more elbow room. Eventually, to make clear the conviction that Americans were the indisputable masters of the hemisphere, the commanding general of the US Army, "Old Fuss and Feathers" Winfield Scott, executed the largest amphibious landing in history, invaded

Mexico's port of Veracruz, captured the federal capital of Mexico City, and killed thousands of Mexicans along the way. Ironically enough, a striking number of American soldiers involved would later find themselves fighting one another as adversaries in the Civil War: Ulysses S. Grant, George Meade, and George McClellan went on to become Union generals, whereas Robert E. Lee, Stonewall Jackson, and George Pickett would become leaders on the Confederate side. One of the chief generals in the hostilities, Zachary Taylor, would ride his fame as war hero—and as uncontested champion of Manifest Destiny—to be elected the twelfth president of the United States.

The bald offensive that usurped a landmass as large as southern Europe would have its critics: Congressman Abraham Lincoln of Illinois, galled by the sheer impudence of invading a neighboring nation, railed against it on the floor of Congress. It was a clear violation of international law, according to Lincoln, hardly worthy of a great nation. Abolitionists rose up in fury, claiming the push into new territory was a ploy to add more slave states to the Confederacy. As the fierce, bloody battles unfolded, the Saint Patrick's Battalion—a unit of two hundred Catholic American soldiers, most of them beleaguered Irish immigrants who knew the sting of discrimination all too well—ended up sympathizing with their fellow Catholics and defecting to the Mexican side. The few members of the battalion who survived were either hanged in perfunctory executions or branded as traitors.

Quite aside from the human drama of that perfidious history are the sheer numbers it entails: in 1848, at the close of the Mexican-American War, there were twenty-five thousand dead Mexicans (twice the number of American casualties) and a scant population of one hundred thousand Mexican survivors still clinging to their ravished lands. Many more had fled south across the Rio Grande, fearing the expansionist fervor with which the whites had invaded their territory. In a strange arc of justice, within a century, that same territory would become home to three and a half million Mexican Americans—a population thirty-five times greater than that which had stood firm and stayed. Today, on that once furiously disputed expanse, there are more than thirty million people of Mexican origin. Not only had the tenacious held their ground, but a biblical tide had come back to join them. Mexican Americans now represent a full third of the population that inhabits those American states. As a whole, they are thirty-seven million, or more than two-thirds of the country's Latino population. The numbers alone tell a vivid tale.

The human side of the Mexican American drama is perhaps captured most strikingly in the origin stories of Linda Chavez and Arturo García, two individuals who hail from radically different backgrounds yet share ancient roots in that quarrelsome history. Chavez is a Republican commentator and public intellectual, a descendant of an old and illustrious Spanish Mexican family; García, an undocumented Mexican laborer living and working as a handyman in Austin, Texas. One's family has owned land in New Mexico since 1600, long before the United States was even an idea. The other is an Acoma Indian of the Pueblo nation, whose ancestors inhabited New Mexico for millennia only to be forced out, first by Spaniards and then by Americans. He would drift back—almost as a rebuttal—centuries later, in 2015.

## TO HAVE AND HAVE NOT

> We took the liberty of removing his right foot on behalf of our brothers and sisters of Acoma Pueblo. We see no glory in celebrating his fourth centennial.
>
> —Graffiti at the foot of the mutilated statue of
> conquistador Juan de Oñate, New Mexico, 1998

Among Linda Chavez's earliest memories is moving from one dingy motel room in Denver to another with her mother and baby sister as they searched for a place to live. As time went on, they rented rooms in basements and attics in a largely white neighborhood, where her mother—of Irish Anglo descent—had enrolled Linda in school. They had fled Albuquerque, leaving behind her father after one too many of his drinking binges and a string of alcohol-fueled calamities. Her mother, Velma McKenna Chavez, had loaded as many belongings as she could manage into their 1954 red and white Ford convertible, sat her two little girls—ages seven and eighteen months—where she could, and headed to Denver to make a new life.

They were speeding down a highway in the middle of the night at some distance from Albuquerque when Velma fell asleep at the wheel. The ear-splitting bray of a truck horn woke Linda in time to see a semi tractor-trailer's headlights barreling toward them. Her mother jerked the steering wheel to the right, flipping the Ford onto a grassy bank and propelling the children and a multitude of boxes through the open windows. When Linda regained her senses, she was making her way barefoot across the dirt, headed toward her sister's cries. The baby was unharmed, but when Linda carried her back to the overturned car, she saw that her mother was crumpled inside, unconscious, blood streaked across her face and neck. Linda could also see that somehow, in her own hypnopompic stupor, she had managed to pull her crisp, white First Communion dress from a box, wad up the hem, and thrust it into a gaping hole in her mother's head. She didn't remember doing it. Panicking now, she tried waving down passing cars, but they flew by in the dark, oblivious to the desperate child on the side of the road. Finally, a family in a jalopy with all their possessions wobbling on top pulled up and immediately grasped the gravity of the situation. An ambulance was summoned and the damage assessed. Velma had shattered her vertebrae, broken a shoulder, acquired a one-inch hole in her skull, and mangled her ankle so badly that it had to be reassembled with metal screws.

Linda's father, Rudy Chavez, was a tall, devilishly handsome man—a good-time Charlie—whose innate intelligence, curiosity, and charm were his prime assets. He had been a staff sergeant in the US Army, serving in the Pacific during World War II. A high school dropout, his prospects for work had never been good, and when Velma took off for the highway, he had been trying to make a living as a housepainter. But life had never been easy for Rudy. The son of a bootlegger, he had suffered the humiliation of seeing his father, Ambrosio Chavez, hauled away in handcuffs and chains to serve eleven years in Leavenworth Penitentiary. His father was college-educated and nothing if not charismatic, but he had thrown the family into desperate poverty just as the country was emerging from the Great Depression. The rest of the family wasn't much help: Ambrosio's brother, a casino owner in Mexico, had been killed by irked Mafia investors. Being the eldest, Rudy was suddenly responsible for the health and welfare of his four younger siblings. He did what he could, suffering the double mortification of want and disgrace. As he grew older, he served time for writing bad checks. Swinging fecklessly between sprees of misconduct and bouts of remorse, he found solace in strong drink.

Velma, alabaster skinned, blonde, and beautiful, had wild impulses as well. She never explained why, but she had fled a husband before Rudy, abandoning two young sons somewhere in Wyoming. Meeting Rudy by chance in a bar in Albuquerque, she struck up a romance with the winsome, spirited young Mexicano, and, a few months into their affair, she learned she was pregnant. She soon learned something else: Rudy was married. After his service in the Pacific, he had brought home an Australian wife, Cecily. Their daughter, Pamela, had been born just months before. Linda would be Rudy's second child.

Remarkably enough, Velma moved in with Rudy, Cecily, and their infant daughter. She found work as a waitress, gave birth to Linda on a balmy June evening, and lived with her lover and his family briefly, until he could extricate himself from his marriage. Years later, once the two little girls had grown close, even inseparable, Cecily asked Rudy for permission to give up Pamela for adoption; clearly, she had no interest in being a single mother. Rudy agreed reluctantly, disappearing for days thereafter on a doleful, drunken binge. Crushed to lose her big sister, Linda began to understand that—in her world at least—families were tenuous propositions, easily formed and just as easily discarded. Children in families such as hers were little more than accessories: tentative, disposable casualties of love's fickle fortunes.

It hadn't always been so. As she grew older, Linda learned from her grandparents—the thrill-seeking Ambrosio Chavez and his imperturbable wife, Petra Armijo—that she was actually descended from a long line of illustrious conquistadors. Her ancestral line, the Chavez and Armijo families, had once enjoyed a formidable place in the history of the Americas and the founding of New Mexico. In 1599 Linda's direct ancestor Captain Pedro Durán y Chaves—a native of Spain, province of Estremadura, where half the village was named Chaves—had joined the Oñate expedition, a large-scale initiative to settle the land north of the vanquished Aztec Empire. Ironically enough, it was the very land that the Narváez expedition, including Cabeza de Vaca, had intended to settle almost seventy-five years before. Within a year, Durán y Chaves, "a well-built" midlife widower "with good features" had headed for the region that would be called Nuevo México. Chaves became one of the founders of Santa Fe, a city planted very near the heart of Acoma-Pueblo Indian territory.

The history of that occupation was nothing short of murderous. Although the Acoma often assisted in the Spaniards' settlements, offering food and labor, very soon after Oñate's arrival, they grew enraged with the conquistadors' arrogance and casual violence. Historians offer a slew of reasons for the rebellions that ensued. Some claim that the Acoma had abducted a Spanish priest and invited a ruthless crackdown, or that Spanish soldiers had gone on a rampage and raped young Acoma girls, or that Spaniards—driven by hunger—had raided the Indians' stockpiles and stolen their food. When the Acoma rose up against the expeditionary forces, murdering Governor Oñate's nephew, the governor retaliated with devastating brutality. Many Acoma were taken prisoner and simply slaughtered, their bodies thrown off the high cliffs of the mesa at Sky City, the tribe's ancient, towering capital. Oñate then ordered his soldiers to amputate the right foot of every surviving Acoma male older than the age of twenty-five and put them into servitude. The women were condemned to slavery for twenty years. All female children were to be assigned to serve in Franciscan missions; the boys, trained as soldiers.

Moving constantly between New Mexico and Mexico City, Pedro Durán y Chaves eventually brought a young wife to join him. So began the dynasty that would found Albuquerque and govern the area for 250 years. In time, the clan would drop the name Durán and change the *s* in *Chaves* to a *z*. When the Chavezes intermarried with the wealthy Armijo bloodline in the 1700s, they consolidated much of the power in

Nuevo México, leading one historian of the time to write, "[T]he families of Armijo, Chávez, Perea and Ortíz are par excellence the *ricos*"—the
wealthiest—"of New Mexico." They lived in palatial mansions with opu-
lent furnishings, married their own cousins to preserve their whiteness,
and subsisted on the brisk trade of goods and provisions that dominated
that area for hundreds of years. Later, when the fever of Manifest Destiny lit American ambitions and Zachary Taylor's army invaded New
Mexico, Linda Chavez's ancestor Governor Manuel Armijo surrendered
that hard-won territory without so much as a single shot being fired.
"I've always been proud of [Armijo's] role in New Mexico history,"
Linda wrote in her memoir *An Unlikely Conservative*, "without which I
might not be an American today."

Indeed, within a scant generation after Nuevo México was absorbed
into the United States along with half of the Mexican landmass, the
Chavez and Armijo families were so comfortably assimilated that they
began to lose their Spanish. Linda Chavez does not speak Spanish, nor
did her father or grandfather. According to her mother, the family has
spoken English primarily since the 1870s. Which would explain why, one
hundred years later in the 1970s, after dabbling in Hispanic studies and
working for the American Federation of Teachers union, Linda began to
be convinced that the quickest road out of poverty for the spiraling Latino population was to focus on English proficiency, and—like any other
twentieth-century European immigrant—fully embrace their American
identity. In time, Linda's strong convictions about the importance of
English and the perils of affirmative action led her to become active in
politics. She supported California legislation to repeal bilingual education and subsequently became president of U.S. English, an organization
dedicated to making English the official and mandated national language. In this, she might well have agreed with Theodore Roosevelt's famous assertion, "Every immigrant who comes here should be required
within five years to learn English or leave the country." In progressive Latino circles working to preserve their language and culture and to make
Latinos more visible—the National Council of La Raza, for instance,
and the League of United Latin American Citizens (LULAC)—she was

becoming, as she made very clear in the subtitle of her memoir, the *Most Hated Hispanic in America*. But she was also becoming a darling of the political Right.

In 1985 those firm conservative convictions led President Ronald Reagan to appoint Linda as his administration's director of public liaison. As such, she became the highest-ranking woman in the Reagan White House. One year later, she left that post to run for the US Senate seat vacated by Maryland's liberal Republican Charles Mathias but lost to Democrat Barbara Mikulski. Her star rose again in 2001, when President George W. Bush selected her to be his secretary of labor, making her the first Hispanic to be nominated for a cabinet position. But when it was revealed that she had been sheltering an undocumented Guatemalan and paying her to do some housecleaning, but had failed to divulge that fact to the White House and the Federal Bureau of Investigation, she was forced to withdraw her name from consideration.

Since then, Linda has made a successful career as a conservative commentator on the Fox television network and the Public Broadcasting System. Although she is called on to speak to Latino issues—and although she draws on her modest working-class roots to do so—she feels little attachment to the Latino population of this country. And certainly none to Latinos who would hesitate to move into the mainstream; who prefer to portray "Hispanics as permanently disadvantaged victims of a racist society." Her position on her *Latinidad*—her Latina identity—seems to have been sharply defined by childhood experiences: On the one hand, she recalls the six-year-old playmate in Denver who once said he could no longer see her because his mother had forbidden him "to play with Mes'cans." On the other hand, she was shunned by Mexican youngsters because she didn't speak Spanish. In point of fact, despite her obvious Mexican features, she didn't feel Mexican at all. As she grew older, given her New Mexican family's solid, traceable roots in the conquest, she considered herself attached more to Spain than to Mexico. "I don't feel affiliated to the Latino community," she tells me for this book. "I'm interested in immigration, but more as a general question of assimilation—as part of the American democratic process."

As it turns out, the Chavez and Armijo families—for all their consanguineous marriages with cousins in order to preserve their bloodline—could not avoid the race mixing that is so common to the Latino story. A deeper probe into her family's history offered Linda a surprise. Selected in 2012 to be featured in Henry Louis Gates Jr.'s genealogical PBS series, *Finding Your Roots*, she learned that her ancestors were actually conversos: Jews who had converted to Catholicism and decided that they would rather be shipped out to conquer the New World than be burned alive in the bonfires of the Spanish Inquisition. They were even willing to settle the remote hinterlands in order to put distance between them and the Inquisition's offices in Mexico City. There was good reason her forebears had joined the Oñate expedition into the wilds of Nuevo México.

Linda also learned that, in the Pueblo Revolt of 1680, when thousands of Pueblo Indians, including the Acoma, finally rose up successfully against their colonial masters, the Armijo and Chavez families were driven from those lands, along with most of the Spaniards. That rebellion effectively ended Spanish rule in Nuevo México for twelve years. However, in the mayhem of killing, not all Spaniards fled the area. Some stayed, either by choice or because they were taken prisoner. Linda's seventh great-grandmother, a woman named María, was one of these. Spanish documents from the returning colonial army meticulously recorded what had become of her: in their absence, María had given birth to a daughter by a nameless Acoma Indian (Linda's seventh great-grandfather). So, in spite of all of the Chavez-Armijo efforts to prevent an indigenous stain on the family—and in spite of her clear affiliation to Spain rather than to Mexico—Linda is genetically part Acoma. She is as much a descendant of the New World as she is of the Old. As much the heir of an indigenous slave with a hacked-off foot as the progeny of conquistadors who would inflict such a punishment.

# THE BOOMERANG OF HISTORY

The U.S.-Mexican border [is an open wound] where the Third World grates against the first and bleeds. And before a scab forms it hemorrhages again, the lifeblood of two worlds merging to form a third country—a border culture.

—Gloria Anzaldúa, Chicana, South Texas, 1987

Just as Linda Chavez is part indigenous, part Spanish, part Anglo, with ancestors who represented opposing forces in this hemisphere's past, I carry that history, too. Victims and victors in our part of the world are often joined by blood, as the Nobel Prize–winning Peruvian writer Mario Vargas Llosa once said. But posterity's pages are seldom written by victims, and so victors rule on, even in the telling. After Napoléon Bonaparte's defeat at the Battle of Waterloo in 1815—after he was ousted from power, forced to flee, and then exiled for the rest of his life to a dismal island in the middle of the South Atlantic Ocean—the defeated French emperor is said to have complained bitterly that history was little more than a string of agreed-upon lies.

Perhaps not quite lies, but the American historical narrative is so dominated by prevailing trends and polarized points of view that it comes as no surprise that historians disagree. David McCullough has praised American pioneers as noble souls, pressing west "not for money, not for possessions or fame, but to advance the quality and opportunities of life—to propel as best they could the American ideals." Yale University historian Greg Grandin, on the other hand, takes issue with that perspective. He writes: "No myth in American history has been more powerful, more invoked by more presidents, than that of pioneers advancing across an endless meridian." The ruthless expropriation of Indian and Spanish lands, Grandin contends, was nothing more than a greedy enterprise with bloody consequences: "a horizon where endless sky meets endless hate."

I never knew my Anglo family as well as I have known my Peruvian one. Perhaps because they were a diaspora unto themselves, flung to

far corners of this country as so many American families can be. Unlike
my close-knit Peruvian clan, which has inhabited one city for almost
five hundred years, my Americans were rootless by nature, independent, less possessive about their children. No one made a point of introducing me to my kin in Louisiana, Kansas, Colorado, Nebraska;
no one made an effort to tell me who and where they were. Much
later, when my mother's generation was dead and gone, I began to
research the family history and learned that I have pioneer blood in
my veins. My first ancestor to arrive on these shores was Dr. George
Gilson Clapp, a colorful individual, passionate traveler, and itinerant
physician who, it is reported, spent twenty years healing the sick in
Palestine, Egypt, the Turkish Empire, and Northern Africa. Born in
Deptford, England, in the mid-1600s, he reached the strip of land that
would become Charleston sometime before 1700. The area did not sit
well with him, perhaps because of the climate; perhaps because his
impulse was to move north, where five Clapp brothers, his cousins, had
planted stakes in Scituate, Massachusetts, many years before. Or perhaps there was a third possible reason: having served as a medical doctor in the global south—in India and Africa—he may have had strong
antipathies to the slave commerce that had begun to define plantation
life in the Carolinas.

He soon moved to Westchester, New York, where his descendants—
my forebears—established themselves for many generations. One of
those offspring did go back to Carolina, it seems. But when westward
expansion spiraled into high fever one hundred years later, the majority of my Clapps joined the pursuit of Manifest Destiny—to carry the
"great experiment of liberty" into a boundless horizon and avail themselves of the land in between. They settled in Ohio, then pushed west to
Kansas, Colorado, and, ultimately, to Elk Mountain, Wyoming, where,
as a six-year-old Peruvian, I wended my way down Rattlesnake Pass to
meet my maternal grandparents. They seemed as different from my
Lima *familia* as anyone I had ever met: I was struck by their immediate
ease and friendliness; their spartan lives, their love of nature; their cozy
cabin with its blazing fireplace; their horses, cattle, sheep; the wide, wild

prairie that beckoned from their front door. The thrill and shock of that encounter has never left me.

My grandfather, James Bayard Clapp, apart from being a rancher, was a medical man, much as his ancient progenitor George Gilson Clapp had been. He was a strapping, big-shouldered, generous-hearted soul. Grandpa Doc, as we called him, became known for offering Native Americans his services free of charge, and they came from far and wide to his office in the Ferguson Building in Rawlins to receive them; he welcomed his Peruvian son-in-law and Spanish-speaking grandchildren with an equanimity rare for Wyomingites of the time. I know this because I soon felt the full sting of racist venom from his neighbors.

Looking back, there was nothing to suggest that my Clapps were land-grabbers, usurpers, chest-pounding victors of the American story. But as sure as the sun snuffs its fires on Elk Mountain every evening, they were trespassers—"adverse possessors," as law books now put it— pioneers with a grand sense of entitlement, who had pressed ever west to claim lands not their own. Call it courage, as McCullough has; call it arrogant fecklessness, as Grandin has. Call it answering a government's vision and mandate; or call it simple thievery, as indigenous people of both the North and the South long have. However you choose to define the "Westward ho!" spirit, the troubles that vex the American border began then and there.

One individual whose past is intricately wound into the complicated fabric of this story is Arturo García, an undocumented Mexican laborer in Austin, Texas, whose ancestors, the Acoma Pueblo, once inhabited a picturesque mesa just west of Albuquerque, the very land expropriated by Linda Chavez's conquistador clan. Arturo insists on his Pueblo ancestry; a strong sense of kinship that has furled down his family's generations for almost 175 years. He is deeply aware that his ancestral roots are planted firmly in that preconquest desert seven hundred miles away, even though his people fled south across the Rio Grande long ago, after the American pioneers swept in to take half of Mexico.

Arturo is small of stature but sturdy and muscled of frame. His sharply chiseled face is deeply tanned by endless hours working in the swelter of a Texas sun: laying concrete, laboring at construction, hauling hay, tending yards, grilling fajitas for garden parties. So dark is his skin—*tan prieto*—that, wherever he is, it's as if he were standing in the shade of a densely leafed tree. He is, as one friend has described him, the epitome of rural Mexico—as courteous in speech as he is in demeanor. He is a Mexicano to the core: gentle, polite, deferential; yet resolute, fearless, and manly. Not yet forty, he has been on this side of the Rio Grande for eight years. When he arrived, making his way north with a tourist visa, it was to visit his brother, who had found work in Texas. It was not a casual visit.

For decades, Veracruz had been a hub of criminal activity in Mexico, a pivotal port city where corruption reigned. But in 2010 it was revealed to be a white-hot locus of rabid violence—a result of an unholy bond between the government and the cartels. Eleven state governors in Mexico had come under investigation for their complicity in the country's skyrocketing violence; among them, Veracruz was the most flagrant.

By 2014, the year that Arturo decided he and his little family needed to leave, the killings had catapulted into high gear: organized crime had mutated from the buy-and-sell of narco-trafficking into extreme, predatory crime: suddenly every neighborhood seemed vulnerable to extortion, kidnapping, rampant disappearances, gangland executions, and human trafficking. As one crisis group put it a few years later, "In Veracruz, an alliance between criminal groups and the highest levels of local political power have paved the way to an unbridled campaign of violence." Mass graves were unearthed. Thousands of murders and disappearances went unresolved. Veracruz had become the medulla of almost 95 percent of all unreported crimes in Mexico.

Making things worse, the region was waging an all-out war on transparency: it had become the most lethal area for journalists in all of the Americas. For Arturo, immigration was urgent and the only option. He had a young wife, Josefina; an infant daughter, Rosita. As a young, physically fit man, he could expect only to be pressed into criminal service or be killed. He had no choice but to seek refuge elsewhere.

That he had an older brother in Austin became a godsend. His visit became a job hunt. Eventually, wiring Josefina the money he was able to earn through odd jobs, Arturo brought her and three-year-old Rosita out of the hellhole of Veracruz. So it was that in mid-2014, Josefina and Rosita joined Arturo's pilgrimage to safety. Josefina now works part-time at a bustling neighborhood taqueria, where working-class Mexicanos like them can afford to eat. Rosita is so precocious, so fluent in English—and so outstanding a student in the local public elementary school—that she routinely occupies the top of her class.

Arturo had not been as fortunate as his daughter; he had forfeited school as a boy to join the workforce. By twelve, he was running errands at the dockyards. By twenty, he began longing for a better life. He had been born in Veracruz, the intemperate port city on the Caribbean where Cortés had launched the conquest of Mexico and where my own abuelito had come ashore at sixteen and begun his overland journey to college. But the city had more than a Latin American past—it had a complicated history with the United States. In 1848, during the Mexican-American War that would win America more than half of Mexico, President James Polk ordered a massive amphibious invasion of Veracruz that would lead to the US occupation of Mexico City. Sixty-six years later, in 1914, in the full heat of the Mexican Revolution—a devastating civil war that was catalyzed, in part, by American interference—President Woodrow Wilson ordered the occupation of Veracruz because, in his estimation, the repressive and corrupt military regime he'd helped install had become unruly. So it was that the American flag had flown over Arturo's birthplace not once, but twice.

If it is true that we are all children of disorderly, unpredictable histories, the same can be said for Arturo and his antecedents. That stretch of time, 1848 to 2014—from his great-grandparents' exile to his own—is filled with calamities that pushed borders, moved populations, shifted the nexus of power, and affect us to this day. Although it is unclear how Arturo's people made their way from Pueblo country to the faraway shore of Veracruz, more than 1,500 miles away, it is not as confounding a displacement, perhaps, as any in the teeming sociopolitical cauldron that is Latin America. The Acoma diaspora was certainly not as far removed a pilgrimage as that undertaken by Julia Mamani, who saw her first light of day in an Andean valley and traveled 3,500 miles, with no little determination, to escape extreme poverty and domestic abuse, and start a new life in Rockville, Maryland.

What we do know is that Arturo's immediate kin were citizens of Veracruz for at least one hundred years—since shortly after the turn of the twentieth century, when the Mexican Revolution ripped through the republic with its wholesale deracination and killing. The effects of their dislocation would rattle down generations of Garcías with crippling consequences. No male in Arturo's family boasted more than a fifth-grade education. When his own studies were cut short so that he could contribute to the family coffers, his classroom became the dining table, where his grandparents and great-grandparents held forth about their ancestors in El Norte and the ancient claims they held there. They were Acoma, period, and, as far as they knew, their people had lived in El Otro Lado since the beginning of time. He was convinced he would go back someday with all the confidence of a tribesman going from one corner of his stomping grounds to another.

He has yet to get himself there. In 2014, when Arturo arrived in Austin—seven hundred miles from his ancestral land—he held only an ordinary six-month tourist visa. His goal was to visit his brother, who had been toiling there for several years, and see if there might be a future for him in the American labor force. He set to work immediately, hustling jobs as menial help. Hardworking, punctual, affable, Arturo didn't lack for periodic or seasonal employment. The American hunger for unskilled, cheap labor seemed boundless. But there was the question of his dwindling legality. Before long, on the advice of fellow Mexicanos, he sought help from an old, public-minded gentleman, Juan Antonio "Sonny" Falcon, "king of the Austin fajita," a friendly, larger-than-life, second-generation Mexican American with a rich Texan drawl and a seemingly endless network of allies. For years, Sonny and his wife, Lupe, had been beloved fixtures on the Mexican side of town, renowned for their warmth and generosity. Sonny had begun his career as a butcher in Lupe's parents' popular Latino food market. While there, he gained fame for inventing the classic Austin fajita: skirt steak, flash-grilled then sliced into juicy strips, tucked into tortillas, drowned in tomatoes, onion, serrano peppers, and cilantro. But he was equally known for lending a hand to hardworking, young, upstanding Mexicanos in difficult circumstances. That was all Arturo's brother needed to hear. He took Arturo in tow, walked across town, and knocked on the Falcons' front door.

The old couple immediately opened their home to the young wayfarer. Before long, they installed him in one of their garages, which they had transformed into a modest but pleasant apartment. Every evening at nine o'clock, after Arturo's backbreaking, fifteen-hour workday, they greeted him with a hot dinner. In return for their kindnesses, Arturo performed chores around the house—small tasks any son would do for his elderly parents: he mowed their front yard, took out their garbage, fired up the grill, minded repairs. As Sonny and Lupe grew fonder of Arturo and saw how intent he was to provide for his family, they encouraged him to bring Josefina and Rosita to the United States. He deserved to have them near, they told him, and they merited more comfortable, secure lives. There was room enough for them. When Arturo's wife and daughter finally arrived—on tourist visas—Lupe introduced Josefina to the neighborhood, enrolled Rosita in school, and incorporated the family as a whole into their community of friends. Arturo now had more part-time work, a convivial nexus of acquaintances, and a clear opportunity for a better future. A half year later, when the family was agreeably settled and all the visas had run out, Arturo opted to stay.

Arturo is certainly not alone in overstaying the expiration date of his visa. The primary mode of entry by undocumented immigrants in the United States today is not a furtive slip across the border, as many Americans believe, but a breach of a legally issued document. Currently, the undocumented population in the United States is holding at about eleven million. It has remained at that number for many years, although, over the course of the last decade, the population of undocumented Mexicans—once the largest group—has plummeted by a remarkable one and a half million. That is to say, in recent years, Mexican departures have exceeded arrivals. The overall number of undocumented has not changed because people of other nationalities—Salvadorans, Hondurans, Asians, South Asians, and sub-Saharan Africans—have been violating their visas in unprecedented numbers.

Since 2010, two-thirds of the country's unauthorized immigrants have been travelers who flew into US airports comfortably, passed through customs legally, and then ignored the expiration dates on their credentials. Analysts for the Pew Research Center estimate that for every person apprehended at the border with Mexico, thirty more let their visas expire and join the illegal population. In 2019, five years after Arturo arrived, seven-hundred thousand tourists like him—a little more than 1.2 percent of all fifty-six million visitors to the United States—overstayed their visas. The great majority of them were Canadians.

Arturo and his family lived with the Falcons for more than seven years. It wasn't long before Rosita, who adored them as any child might adore a grandparent, was calling Sonny and Lupe Abuelito and Abuelita. Josefina cooked for them, accompanied them wherever they needed to go, and minded them as they became increasingly incapacitated. As long as he could, Arturo assisted Sonny with the upkeep of the house and his signature fajita fiestas in the front yard. When the old couple died—Lupe first, Sonny soon after—and the COVID pandemic swept in to paralyze the living, the young family stayed in the house for another two years. In 2022 they finally moved to a modest apartment nearby, their undocumented status continuing to bind them to danger.

By now, Arturo has laid more concrete, built more streets, helped erect more buildings, and assisted the financial viability of more rancheros than anyone might think humanly possible in a short sojourn of eight years. Still, he fears that the deportation officials might knock on his door at any moment. This is his predicament, even though his ancestors were rightful inhabitants of the Southwest for centuries before the conquistadors rode in, before the pioneers took over, and long before Texas existed. Of such stories are Latinos made.

# PART II

# TURF AND SKIN

"If we could light up the room with pain, we'd be such a glorious fire."
—Ada Limón, United States Poet Laureate,
Mexican American, 2015

# 4

# WHY THEY LEFT,
# WHERE THEY WENT

*I'm going to sing America!*
*with all América*
*inside me:*
*from the soles*
*of Tierra del Fuego*
*to the thin waist*
*of Chiriquí*
*up the spine of the Mississippi*
*through the heartland*
*of the Yanquis.*

                    —Julia Álvarez, author, Dominican American, 2015

The first Latino to live in what would become New York City was Juan Rodriguez, a Dominican who sailed up the Atlantic coast and stepped onto the verdant shores of Manahatta Island in the spring of 1613. He would become the first person of African descent, the first free black—indeed, the first non-Indian—to settle in the future United States of America. Half black, half European, he had been pressed into service by a Dutch captain intent on buying coveted furs from the tribes that ruled the perimeter of that enigmatic continent. Juan had been born of an African woman and a Portuguese sailor in the bustling, culturally diverse settlement of Santo Domingo—the capital of Hispaniola, established by Christopher Columbus's brother Bartholomew in 1496—the polestar of Spain's grip on the Caribbean, now known as the Dominican Republic. Raised speaking three languages, Juan had the rare ability to learn native dialects effortlessly. The Dutch captain, Thijs Mossel, an ambitious speculator, understood that the young linguist's peculiar skills were indispensable to his expedition's profits.

Juan, however, was not enamored of the captain, nor of the Dutch, nor of the ways the enterprise was being run on board the *Jonge Tobias*. It isn't clear whether the disaffection was because of Juan's status as a black man or because of a quarrel with the crew, or perhaps it was just the lure of Manahatta's "sweetness of Air," its exuberant woods and fields—its riots of fragrant, wild roses. Whatever the reason, when trade with the Lenape Indians was done and Captain Mossel prepared to return to Holland with his precious pelts, Juan Rodriguez opted to stay.

By then, he had fallen under the spell of a Lenape woman, learned her Munsee tongue, and decided that her land and people were far more agreeable than the Netherlanders on the *Jonge Tobias*. His argument to the captain was that he would be more useful as a broker for any future visits to the richly endowed Manahatta than he would be on the cobbled streets of Amsterdam, where his brand of linguistic virtuosity would be moot. Captain Mossel mulled over the proposition, agreed grudgingly, and left Juan behind, along with a store of eighty hatchets, an array of knives, a few muskets, and a sword. With these in hand, Juan established his own trading post among the natives, emerging from time to time to offer his services to other Dutch captains who began dropping anchor, one after another, along that increasingly busy frontier.

I like to think of Juan's weapons bazaar as the first Latino small business in the rustic wonderland that prefigured New York City. Certainly he was the first non-native merchant. His name may be forgotten by the rest of the world, but it lives on today, emblazoned on New York street signs all the way up Broadway from 159th Street to 218th Street—best known as Washington Heights—the most heavily Dominican square mileage in the country. In time, Juan was likely joined by other Dominican blacks employed by the Dutch of New Amsterdam, the island's moniker before the English captured it and renamed it New York. In other words, the "Spanish Negroes," as the Dutch called Juan and his cohort, became the first free "African American" population of Manhattan. And, if we allow a little imagination, Juan's business of assorted ironware represented the first Latino corner store—the ubiquitous New York bodega: open late hours, stocking your every little need, with a cat in the corner and plenty of friendly advice. More than four hundred years later, Dominican-style mom-and-pop bodegas are still there. Thirteen thousand of them.

## DOMINICAN AMERICANS

*We are a Dominican-ass family, quite superstitious.*
*Pennies on our foreheads to stop nosebleeds.*
*Sacraments to guarantee entry to heaven.*
*My mother still believes dreams tell us when someone is going to die.*
                    —Elizabeth Acevedo, poet, Dominican American, 2009

We don't know what became of Juan Rodriguez's children—surely among the first black/white/indigenous issue on that soil—apart from the fact that he had several, perhaps by more than one woman. But a vast population of Dominicans followed him to Manhattan. Today Dominicans are the fifth largest population of Latinos in the United States (after Mexicans, Puerto Ricans, Salvadorans, and Cubans), and more of them live in the New York metropolitan area than in any other city on this planet, except for the capital of the Dominican Republic, Santo Domingo. Indeed, one out of every three Latinos living in New York is Dominican. There are more than two million in this country overall, most of them clustered in urban centers, with the great majority occupying a tidy crescent that stretches from the Bronx to Paterson, New Jersey. There is a strong representation of Dominicans, too, in Latino neighborhoods of Florida, Massachusetts, Pennsylvania, Rhode Island, and

Connecticut. They are an East Coast breed. They are also overwhelmingly mixed race, with three-quarters of them identifying as black or part black. Taken as a whole, they are our brownest brothers.

They may also be one of the most segregated Latino groups in the United States. Comfortable in black neighborhoods, they nevertheless prefer to live in Dominican communities, marry one another, and have Dominican children. If they do marry outside their immediate cohort, they typically choose Puerto Ricans. Which is entirely understandable, since Dominicans and Puerto Ricans often live side by side in vibrant urban enclaves along the Eastern Seaboard. But as compatible as they can be, differences do arise.

Michelle Rodriguez, the Latina actress best known for her fearless, rough-and-tumble roles in action films such as *Girlfight* and *Fast & Furious 7*, tells of the tension between her father's Puerto Rican family and her Dominican mother, who was considerably darker skinned. As Michelle learned eventually, generations of her Puerto Rican ancestors had gone to great lengths to keep the bloodline white—even marrying their own cousins, a not uncommon practice among elite white Latin Americans in general. Suddenly being forced to accept a black Dominican bride into the clan and break that chain of whiteness was too much for Michelle's Puerto Rican family, and the marriage eventually collapsed. Michelle had been born in San Antonio, Texas, but her mother then took her to live in her grandmother's neighborhood in Santo Domingo, where, as an impressionable eight-year-old, she saw rampant poverty up close and for the first time. Before long, her grandmother and mother decided to emigrate. They tried Puerto Rico for a few years but finally moved to the predominantly black neighborhoods of Jersey City.

The irony is that for many Dominicans, race is a sliding scale. The novelist Julia Álvarez tells me of a moment at one of her book signings when two dark-skinned Dominican American girls—enthusiastic fans of her books—were taken aback by her whiteness and whispered to Álvarez's agent, "That's Julia Álvarez? But she's not a Latina!" In their view, she couldn't be one of them; her skin was too porcelain, too European looking, too fair. "It's possible to be too white in the Dominican

Republic," Álvarez says wistfully. And yet what passes for white on that island may very well be black in our one-drop-rule United States. A child with three white grandparents and one black would likely be seen as white in the Dominican Republic but black in America. Another Dominican novelist, Junot Díaz, puts it this way: "We Dominicans in the United States have the highest rate of claiming blackness of any Latinos in the country. In the DR, it's the opposite. Most people there hedge and describe themselves as 'other' when they fill out a form, but here in the United States, we find the freedom to claim our black roots."

There are plenty of reasons for Dominicans to deny blackness in their home country. Under the infamous dictatorship of Rafael Trujillo—"El Jefe," a US-trained and -backed caudillo who held the country in a vicious reign of terror for thirty years, from 1930 until his assassination in 1961—it was manifestly dangerous to be black. This was so even though Trujillo's own grandmother was a black Haitian; and this was so even though it was clear that the great majority of Dominicans, over the course of five hundred years, had acquired at least some African features. El Jefe himself was known to wear a thick layer of pancake makeup to appear several shades lighter than he truly was. All the same, Trujillo insisted on a thoroughly nonblack nation; one "racially superior" to the Haitians next door. Openly inspired by Adolf Hitler's racist theories, he framed his paranoid mania about skin color as a paternal act to save his people from being "defiled" by their black neighbors. "Other" became an imperative description for oneself in the Dominican Republic, a fluid racial identity that was neither black nor white but something else. Something undefinable. It was as if the whole country was in thrall to Trujillo's lie.

Trujillo had begun his career as a lowly sugarcane plantation guard and small-time criminal. But his stars aligned when he joined the National Guard just as the United States invaded the Dominican Republic on May 5, 1916, subverted a leftist coup, and established control of the country. The US Marines occupying the island offered him the opportunity to train for the municipal police force. Within five years, Trujillo was its commander in chief. To the Americans in charge, he was a useful figure in a precarious era, and their support for him was unequivocal. With their help, Trujillo rose quickly through the ranks and became head of the armed forces by the time they departed in 1924.

He didn't stop there. Come 1930, Trujillo ousted an aging president, threatened to torture or murder anyone who dared support the opposing candidate in the national elections, and so—quite logically—took the presidency in a landslide. In a dictatorship marked by decadence and corruption, he proceeded to arrogate all profits to himself and eliminate enemies through outright force or intimidation. To keep his countrymen under his thumb, he introduced martial law, established a secret police, censored the press, and killed all dissidents. He also renamed the capital after himself, transforming the ancient, historic city of Santo Domingo into Ciudad Trujillo, in the event anyone had doubts about who was in command. But he continued to be peeved by the race question and what he saw as a growing negritude in his people. In September 1937, just as he was reading Hitler's autobiographical manifesto *Mein Kampf*, fretting about blacks, and pondering the German chancellor's theories about white superiority, he welcomed a Nazi delegation, prompting toadies in the official press to crow, "Long live our illustrious leaders!"—by which they meant El Jefe and the Führer.

One month later, in October 1937, in a breathtakingly brutal move to *mejorar la raza*—whiten the population—Trujillo ordered a mass genocide of all black-skinned residents occupying Dominican borderlands with Haiti; this, despite the fact that not only were Haitian migrant workers the lifeblood of the Dominican economy but also many Haitians had offspring who were legal citizens of the Dominican Republic. As far as the dictator was concerned, there were too many Haitians on his side of the island, and they were sullying the country's racial profile. In the newly installed "pigmentocracy," a Dominican could be "white," or "*trigueño*" (light-skinned Indian), or even "*indio oscuro*" or "*moreno*" (a dark-skinned Indian or light-skinned black), but to be truly black—*tan negro como un teléfono*, "as black as a telephone"—was to be Haitian, and Trujillo made it very clear he didn't want any more of those.

Given the order, Trujillo's generals went about pressing known criminals into service and rounding up tens of thousands of "Haitians"—even those who had been born in the Dominican Republic and lived there for generations. Within the course of one week, the military butchered tens of thousands. They bludgeoned them with machetes, dispatched them with bullets, tossed them into shark-infested waters. Holding up sprigs of parsley and asking, *"Cómo se llama esto?"*—"What's this called?"—Dominicans would force the corralled blacks to say the Spanish word *perejil*. If they couldn't pronounce "parsley" properly, if it was uttered with a Haitian accent or a distinct inability to trill the *r*, the machetes would fall.

The killing was rampant, merciless. Heaps of corpses were thrown unceremoniously into improvised mass graves or left to rot in the sun. Dominicans of all walks—be they intellectuals, politicians, businessmen, or ordinary farmers, even clerics—were too cowed by the terror to object much. They went along with the pogrom dutifully, without mounting protests or displaying outrage. They simply cleaned up the carnage and carried on. Trujillo had learned Hitler's lesson well: in the face of genocide, self-preservation will always trump outrage. By the end of *"El Corte"* ("The Harvest"), when El Jefe's countrymen finally straightened up and looked around, nearly thirty thousand blacks had been slaughtered. It was wise, at the end of the bloodbath, for a largely dark-skinned Dominican population to identify itself as "other."

Having become a monster to his own people, Trujillo began to embarrass the Americans who had supported him in the first place. Franklin Delano Roosevelt reputedly had said, "I know he is an SOB, but at least he is *our* SOB," which had been the prevailing American attitude for thirty-one years of Trujillo's rule. But though the strongman had come to power via US muscle, he would be undone via American pragmatism. The CIA, finally, due to pressure from Washington, began maneuvering to oust him from office and relieve the United States of an increasingly awkward affiliation.

The assassination of Trujillo in 1961 prompted an era of disorientation and unrest. El Jefe's death led to the election of a liberal intellectual, Juan Bosch, who was despised by the powerful military machine that had mushroomed under the Trujillo presidency. A cabal of generals overthrew Bosch summarily in 1963, casting the government into turmoil, as factions wrestled for power and the country lurched into civil war. The chaos was such that the United States government began to fear that another Cuba was in the making; one more Communist threat to American dominance in the hemisphere. Just as Theodore Roosevelt had asserted that the United States could deploy "the exercise of an international police power" in the Caribbean, leading Washington to interfere in Dominican affairs in 1905—just as Woodrow Wilson had taken gunboat diplomacy to a higher level by ordering the US invasion of Veracruz and ousting a Mexican president in 1914—President Lyndon Johnson now decided to intercede yet again in that grand "American Lake."

On April 28, 1965, just months after issuing the Gulf of Tonkin Resolution that effectively launched the Vietnam War, Johnson ordered twenty-two thousand US Marines and paratroopers to invade the Dominican Republic, occupy the nation by force, and facilitate the installation of a conservative government more in line with US interests. President Bosch was summarily toppled, and Joaquín Balaguer, Trujillo's loyal vice president, was installed in his place.

It is here that the wider story of Dominican American immigration begins. A CIA official might file this story under "Blowback," the unintended effects of US political actions abroad. Or, as at least one American historian observed: the chickens were coming home to roost. After all, the Dominicans had seen "their independence destroyed, their affairs and their property taken over and made subject to the president of the United States. . . . Yet, who among us seems noticeably to care?" Indeed, nobody seemed to give a damn in those years; and they didn't for many more. President Ronald Reagan, who traveled to Latin America seventeen years later in 1982, would say with genuine wonder on his return, "You'd be surprised! They're all individual countries!"

And so it was that after a long history of American interventions in that fragile nation's internal affairs, a great wave of Dominicans began to arrive on these shores. Many were forced to leave for urgent political reasons; others, because the economic noose had grown intolerable.

Others took advantage of the gates thrown open by Lyndon B. Johnson's Immigration Act of 1965, which changed the face of America by welcoming more than just Northern Europeans to our shores. Until then, the United States had made no secret of favoring whites as its immigrants of choice. With a single legislative act, however, Johnson—a champion of Hispanics since his days as a young, callow teacher in Texas's Mexican schools—transformed the largely white, European infusion (85 percent of America's immigrants) into a firehose of races from formerly restricted parts of the world.

As a result, between 1960 and 1980, the population of Dominicans residing in the United States soared from a mere twelve thousand immigrants to seven hundred thousand. A full 85 percent of those new arrivals crowded into New York's metropolitan area, on the very ground that Juan Rodriguez had settled 352 years before with his Lenape wife, his steel bodega, and his multiracial children. Two generations later, the Dominican population in the United States would triple to more than two million, and its ranks would begin to spill out of New York to more remote enclaves along the Eastern Seaboard, from Miami to Portland, Maine.

It was during the initial surge in the 1960s and 1970s that novelists Julia Álvarez and Junot Díaz, both of whom have written vividly about the Trujillato—the Trujillo era—left the Dominican Republic for the United States. Their fathers had been caught in the political cross fire of the Trujillato for very different reasons, and yet both opted to flee, revealing the peculiar ways that chaos can bring diametrically opposed actors to the same decision. Álvarez's father, a physician, had been working in the anti-Trujillo underground, devising a plot to derail the dictatorship, when he was informed that Trujillo's goons were preparing to arrest him, or do worse. The Álvarez family fled the country immediately; it was 1960, and little Julia was a sweet-faced, impressionable girl of ten.

Junot Díaz's father, on the other hand, was an avid legionnaire, a loyal soldier to the despot. As Díaz puts it, "I had a father who was in the post-Trujillo military apparatus, a father who grew up *inside* of the Trujillato, and was very supportive of it. . . . He had a very romantic vision of who Trujillo was." Indeed, his father—a "crypto-fascist," according to

Díaz—"fought on the side of the Americans during the 1965 invasion," putting US interests in the Caribbean ahead of those of his struggling republic. When he left the country for work in Paterson, New Jersey, the family soon followed. Arriving in 1974, six-year-old Díaz grew up in a midsize city of tough-guy Puerto Ricans, Cubans, and blacks—a *macho*, "hypermasculine world" that would inform his bracingly wild and gritty stories. Today more than one-third of Paterson's residents are Dominicans, and Dominicans as a whole represent the second largest population of Latinos in the Northeast.

Julia Álvarez and Junot Díaz are dazzlingly gifted representatives of the Dominican American experience. Their novels *How the García Girls Lost Their Accent* and *The Brief Wondrous Life of Oscar Wao*, respectively, are great literary achievements, veritable atlases of the Dominican soul. But these writers are hardly representative of most first-generation Dominicans, who are less likely to be educated than the average Hispanic and more likely to live below the poverty line. More than half are more proficient in Spanish than English (only 5 percent are English dominant), and 45 percent are bilingual. Keeping their Spanish alive—a rapid-fire, distinctly casual, and colorful version of Spanish—is of utmost importance to them. Almost 90 percent speak it at home, well above the 73 percent average for Latino families. In the second generation, those characteristics change: a full 21 percent of the children of Dominican immigrants go to college, considerably higher than the Mexican American average (14 percent) and the Puerto Rican (9 percent) cohort. What accounts for that impressive leap in the second generation? Surely some credit must go to public schools in the Northeast and Southeast, where these populations congregate. But much of the advancement is due to simple spunk and ambition.

All the same, for most Dominicans who identify as mixed race, navigating a white-majority nation is not an easy business. Dominicans say they bear the brunt of discrimination in more ways than most: for having African features, for being Latino, for insisting on preserving Spanish in their homes, and for coming from a land about which many Americans are patently ignorant. In 2006, Jefferson B. Sessions II, the

Republican senator from Alabama (who would later rise to attorney general of the land), argued on the Senate floor that "Fundamentally, almost no one coming from the Dominican Republic to the United States is coming here because they have a provable skill that would benefit us and that would indicate their likely success in our society." And yet, over the years, like Julia Álvarez and Junot Díaz, many Dominican Americans have risen from humble circumstances to reach *el sueño americano*—the American Dream—and to lend considerable skills to this country.

Take Shirley Collado, a Dominican who was born and raised in Brooklyn, the child of a New York cab driver and a clothing factory seamstress. Although Collado started work as an eleven-year-old—and although her father had no more than a fourth-grade education—school was a priority in her household. Her mother insisted on it. A serious girl with high expectations for herself, Collado announced to her parents early on that she wanted to go to college. It seemed a far-fetched fantasy for a family that was struggling financially. Nevertheless, in 1989, when she turned seventeen, her academic excellence won the attention of the Posse Foundation, a newly founded organization whose mandate was to identify and train young leaders from diverse backgrounds and support them with full-tuition scholarships. Before long, she was on a bus to Nashville to attend Vanderbilt University—one of the few blacks, and even fewer Latinos, in that bastion of whiteness.

Collado went on to earn graduate degrees in clinical psychology from Duke University, although she was the only nonwhite person in her department, the only Latina. Thirty years later, she was named president of Ithaca College, the first person of color to serve as head of that institution and the first Dominican in the United States to lead a four-year college. Today Collado works to bring other youngsters along that route to success in her capacity as chief executive officer of College Track, a foundation that equips promising students to overcome systemic barriers, earn college degrees, and rise to positions of power.

The same could be said—although from a completely different perspective—for Mario Álvarez (no relation to Julia), who grew up in his grandmother's shack in Villa Vásquez, in the far northwest corner of the Dominican Republic, near the border with Haiti. Mario is a genial, round-faced young man who responds to questions meticulously, pausing as his eyes search the ceiling for the precise and constructive answer. When I ask what he remembers about that childhood home, he is patient with me. It was a typical home in a poor, rural precinct of the Republic, he says: no running water, no toilets or latrines. "We relieved ourselves in the backyard, like dogs," he adds matter-of-factly. His father and mother, in desperation, had deposited him with his grandmother and taken off for the United States in search of work, a roof, a brighter future.

There were strong reasons to leave: Trujillo's toady, President Joaquin Balaguer, the doddering, mentally enfeebled, autocratic eighty-four-year-old who continued to be boosted by Washington policymakers, had just reclaimed the Dominican presidency after an election riddled with accusations of fraud. Mario's father, an accountant, was intent on getting out from under the rampant dysfunctions. In time, he eventually found work as a superintendent of a residential building in New York City's bustling midtown. The job came with an attractive perk: a small basement apartment. It was cramped, dank, and infested with rats and roaches, but it meant a roof overhead and no rent to pay. Mario would spend the next ten years in those quarters before the family moved to another building uptown, in Washington Heights, where to this day his father continues to work as superintendent. But it was in that inhospitable underground space that everything changed for Mario's prospects. The agent of his upward mobility was a simple test, administered to eleven-year-olds in New York public schools. Undocumented, from a family with little or no English skills, Mario performed brilliantly, scoring among the highest in the city in a student search conducted by an institution called Prep for Prep.

The idea of Prep for Prep was to be disruptive: in the wake of the landmark 1954 *Brown v. Board of Education* ruling, in an era committed to desegregation, the very opposite was happening: New York City's schools had become more segregated than ever. Prep for Prep aimed to identify highly intelligent students of color and inject them into the most exclusive and competitive private schools in the Northeast: Dalton, Choate, Brearley, Groton, Andover, Exeter, Deerfield, Hotchkiss, among scores of others. Now in its forty-fourth year, Prep conducts a citywide talent search for high-achieving Latinx, black, and Asian students, then administers a battery of exams and interviews. The children who are chosen spend summers before and after sixth grade in intensive remedial classes five days a week, as well as evenings and Saturdays. In exchange, Prep secures seventh-grade spots for them in dozens of participating private schools.

In 2002 Mario was selected to prepare for one of the coveted places at Horace Mann, an exclusive establishment founded in 1887 and alma mater to American lights such as William Carlos Williams, Robert Caro, Gertrude Weil, Jack Kerouac, Rockwell Kent. When Mario turned thirteen, he entered those halls, spending his days in glittering classrooms alongside members of the privileged white establishment—among them sons of bankers, diplomats, aristocrats—then returning to his family's underground burrow in the evening. "The rich white kids laughed when I identified myself as a Dominican. They told me I was black. Until then, I had no idea," Mario says now. There was open disrespect for his economic status, his skin color, his ignorance of elite habits and tastes. "Coming home to my broken-down apartment every night, hearing my parents speak in broken English, listening to my mother worry about my being deported, I learned about American privilege. It wasn't easy. I became an angry kid." But he learned, persevered, and, six years later, was accepted into Columbia University.

Eventually, in 2021, having completed his courses at Columbia, he graduated with high honors from New York University's School of Law. But instead of accepting a job in a white-shoe law firm, he joined a fellowship that would take him to Arizona—to the US border with Mexico—to defend the rights of undocumented migrants rounded up by the US Border Patrol. "I could have joined the majority of my fellow graduates who flooded into the corporate world," Mario tells me. "My family wonders why I didn't. Instead, I began to think about me, the brown kid in an elite white school—the kid with all the self-doubt—there for no other reason than that the school needed some colored faces in its brochure. I guess this is all to say that I have a tortured relationship with my own success. I wanted to do something other than make money, get rich. I wanted to do something that might contribute directly to someone's life." That is precisely what this Ivy League graduate does today in a gray, austere office thirty miles from the border: contributing to lives directly, shepherding the potential, counseling the bewildered survivors of a harrowing passage. He now administers prep for prep of a different order: an orientation class for those who have sacrificed all for a chance at the American roulette.

Indeed, one could point to any number of Dominican Americans who have contributed mightily to different aspects of this country's culture: fashion luminary Oscar de la Renta; retired baseball star Alex Rodriguez; award-winning actress Zoe Saldana; Hollywood's "Queen of Technicolor," María Montéz; New York congressman Adriano Espaillat; New York City Ballet star Francisco Moncíon; comedian The Kid Mero; hip-hop poet Elizabeth Acevedo; jazz pianist and composer Michel Camilo; US assistant attorney general for civil rights Thomas Pérez. In short, former attorney general Jeff Sessions would do well to look around.

## HONDURAN AMERICANS

> The history of Honduras can be written on a gun, or on a bullet, or better yet, in the viscera of a drop of blood.
>> —Roberto Sosa, author, Honduras, 1985

Raymundo Paniagua is a marine biologist, a native of Honduras, which in 2011 reached the inglorious state of being the most murderous country on earth. That year, the homicide rate climbed to eighty-seven per hundred thousand, almost twenty times higher than that of the United States. The skyrocketing killings had begun in 2004, the very year that Raymundo decided to book a flight to Washington, DC, let his visa expire, and take his chances as an undocumented alien. He has been here ever since.

There were myriad reasons to seek refuge, but the first had emerged a decade before, in the early 1990s, when he was a chief biologist for a foreign company that farms tilapia and shrimp for American supermarkets. It was then that Raymundo began to worry about the company's rampant use of pesticides and the damage being done to the algae that fed the coral reefs. As a scientist who had studied at Georgetown and Texas A&M Universities, he was well aware of the dangers of excessive use of herbicides, insecticides, and fertilizers. He could see for himself that the mangrove forests along the coast had been contaminated and that the marine life in general was at risk. The company was growing fish larvae in laboratories precisely to elude the harmful effects of its own spoliations, and it was using hormones to induce growth in its farmed shrimp.

The cumulative dangers to the environment, workers, and consumers concerned Raymundo. But there were other preoccupations: the company was paying its Honduran laborers a pittance for a backbreaking workday, and it was terminating them before the end of the sixty-day probationary period in order to avoid having to pay benefits. Raymundo didn't know it then, but sharing these apprehensions casually with his brother, Alex, a lawyer just starting his career in civil service law, initiated the process of a broad-based, class-action legal investigation. As years passed, he would learn how a tangled web of bribes, graft, illegal alliances, and convenient murders tied Honduran politicians to foreign businesses as well as to the all-powerful drug cartels.

It was precisely as these things were becoming clear in 1994 that his life changed irreversibly in what was meant to be a night of harmless frivolity. It began in El Crucero del Sabor, a nightclub in a hip neighborhood of Tegucigalpa, the capital of Honduras. After a pleasurable night celebrating his birthday with salsa music and friends, Raymundo left the bar at four in the morning and hailed a passing taxi. He had just slid into his seat and given the driver his address when a black Toyota Land Cruiser with a concealed license plate swung in front of them, screeched to a halt, and blocked their exit. A group of young men sporting flashy clothes and gold jewelry tumbled out of the car, laughing. Raymundo's driver honked his horn, signaling for the offending car to move, but it didn't budge. Infuriated, he sprang out of the car to confront the men. Raymundo, equally annoyed, stepped out and shouted, "Hey! Let's go!"

Before he knew it, a battery of gunshots filled the air. One bullet entered the taxi driver's chest and killed him instantly. Others sprayed the street indiscriminately, felling ten bystanders. Within seconds, Raymundo was aware of a pistol at point-blank range, saw the grin of the man behind it, and then the rest vanished. The bullet tore into his left cheekbone just below his eye, sent splinters of bone into his skull, skimmed his brain, and lodged itself in the hard mound of his zygomatic bone, which forms the cheek and outer portions of the eye socket. To this day, the bullet remains embedded in his skull, too near the brain to remove. Raymundo was bounced from one overwhelmed hospital to another, fell momentarily into a coma, but, miraculously, survived. When he regained his senses, he learned that the party of revelers in the shiny black car was commandeered by none other than the son of Juan Ramón Matta Ballesteros, the most notorious narco-trafficker in Honduras—the man who had forged the link between the Colombian and Mexican drug cartels and was now serving time in a high-security federal prison in the United States. Although there were witnesses willing to testify about the shooting, no investigation was undertaken. To be Matta's son was to be feared, untouchable. No charges were pressed.

Three years later, Raymundo was dozing in the passenger seat of his brother's car as they drove along a winding country road on a sun-drenched afternoon. Suddenly, as they rounded a tight curve, a 4x4 vehicle with a heavy grille guard flew into view and plowed headlong into their hood. Raymundo was flung forward, smashing the very place on his cheekbone where the bullet was lodged. His brow was cut and his eyeball ruptured, requiring its removal, yet once again he weathered the injury. All the same, his brother's car was wrecked, irrecoverably so, as was a fruit farmer's truck behind them. And yet, for all the police who gathered to take note, no official report was made.

With good reason. The driver turned out to be Juan Antonio "Tony" Hernández, one of sixteen siblings of then congressman Juan Orlando Hernández, future president of Honduras. Twenty-five years later, president and brother would be brought to justice in the United States for decades-long careers as drug kingpins and weapons smugglers. In April 2022, just after completing his second term in office, President Hernández was arrested in his house, led out in shackles, and extradited to the United States to face charges of drug and firearm trafficking. Brother Tony would be sentenced to life in prison for transporting 185 tons of cocaine to the United States and for possessing stores of machine guns to further that trade. Under President Hernández's auspices, it was reported, five hundred tons of cocaine from Honduras had entered the bloodstreams of American users. Shortly after his arrest, the US Justice Department had conceded that throughout his career, from congressman to president, Hernández had been paid millions of dollars in cocaine proceeds, which he used to enrich himself and commit voter fraud, even as the vast majority of Hondurans were living in poverty and enduring unimaginable carnage. The director of the US Drug Enforcement Agency (DEA), Anne Milgram, was emphatic in her censure: "The former president of Honduras was a central figure in one of the largest and most violent cocaine trafficking conspiracies in the world," she said. "Hernández used drug trafficking proceeds to finance his political ascent and, once elected president, leveraged the government of Honduras's law enforcement, military, and financial resources to further his drug trafficking scheme."

As has been the case in US–Latin American affairs, Washington was reluctant to admonish or prosecute leaders who had minded US interests in the region, but by 2013, it was clear that corruption in Honduras had proliferated to such a degree that the powerful Sinaloa Cartel and its notorious Mexican leader, Joaquín "El Chapo" Guzmán, had a firm grip on the highest offices of the land. Raymundo—and hundreds of thousands of his countrymen—didn't need to wait that long to know something was gravely wrong. By 2001, a massive exodus had begun. A drought had impoverished subsistence farmers, hunger had reached epidemic proportions, and drug gangs and paramilitary forces had cut a bloody path through city and countryside. It was only a matter of time before the head would begin to consume the tail, Raymundo reasoned; before the country, like Cronus of Greek mythology, would devour all of its sons.

He needed to get out. The excruciating throb in his skull could mean only that he needed urgent medical help. But even more pressing to this marine biologist was the glaring fact that his country's waters were being poisoned by his own employer; and, finally, there was no future in a land where drug traffickers and corrupt politicians were exempt from the law. Many years later, sitting in his modest quarters in a Latino neighborhood in Virginia, Raymundo watched telecasts of his native country plunging into incomprehensible truculence. Rampant butchery and political assassinations had made Honduras the most homicidal country in the world. Environmentalists and journalists working on exposing the ecological depredations were being gunned down in the streets. Berta Cáceres, an indigenous activist working to halt the construction of a potentially devastating dam on her ancestral lands, was shot dead in her bedroom. It was later learned that the assassination had been ordered by Roberto David Castillo, a West Point–trained intelligence officer and president of the powerful corporation DESA (Desarrollos Energéticos SA). A few years later, in 2020, as two hurricanes and a pandemic roared into Honduras, battering the long-suffering population, Raymundo's brother, Alex, and a cohort of civil rights lawyers brought legal action against Standard Fruit de Honduras SA, accusing it of contaminating banana orchards and sickening farmworkers with toxic pesticides. Not long after, Alex ended up dead in a Tegucigalpa hospital. According to his biologist brother, he had died from poisoning. The official cause, however, was cited as COVID.

## THE NORTHERN TRIANGLE

H.R. 3524, A Bill: To support the people of Central America and strengthen United States national security by addressing the root causes of migration from El Salvador, Guatemala, and Honduras.

—US Congress, 116th Session, 2019

The Northern Triangle, which includes Honduras, El Salvador, and Guatemala, a triad of Central American countries crazed by crime and gangland desperados, is the source of a boom in immigration that began in the 1980s, grew exponentially in the first decade of this millennium, and is now one of the largest engines of Latino migration to America. The fuel that drives it is fear. That the Triangle claims the highest murder rate in the world is due in no small part to its geography. It is the narrow, intensely green funnel of land through which the ubiquitous drug trade must pass—a traffic that represents more than $150 billion annually in the United States of America. It is a colossal enterprise, exceeding the GDPs of the vast majority of countries on the planet.

The commerce of illegal drugs in this hemisphere—a product of the ravenous US appetite for recreational highs—has become increasingly more powerful in these lands of the ancient Maya. So much so, according to a report from the Brookings Institution, that the power of a drug lord in the Northern Triangle can surpass that of a president. This otherwise tropical paradise is now the functioning nozzle for a firehose of cocaine, heroin, marijuana, meth, and fentanyl that floods into the United States every year. Little wonder that the lawlessness—the violence, corruption, protection rackets, and human trafficking—propels a massive exodus to safer ground, to the perceived tranquility and security of the North: El Otro Lado, the other side.

But drugs and crime aren't the only catalysts driving migration from the Northern Triangle. The region swings from drought to deluge, from privation to poverty, from iron fist to all-out civil war. The United States has not been innocent in this: the political instability of these three countries is, in some measure, a result of generations of American interference in their internal affairs. But in the past three decades, even the wind, the water, and the ground beneath one's feet have proven to be calamitous. Since 1990, devastating hurricanes, earthquakes, and floods have spiked by 500 percent in this slender umbilical of the hemisphere. In 2020 alone, tropical storms ripped through it and displaced a whopping six and a half million people. The destruction and uncertainty have become so prevalent, so catastrophic, that parents surrender to fortune what is most precious to them: one out of every six migrants who fled the Northern Triangle in 2021 was an unaccompanied child. Of the two million souls who headed for the United States between 2014 and 2021, more than three hundred thousand have been minors from ten to seventeen years old, traveling alone, risking the perils of starvation, kidnapping, and human trafficking.

The overall numbers are staggering. In the last three months of 2022, the US Border Patrol apprehended an average of 240,000 unauthorized migrants crossing the southwest border every month, which translates to about 360 fugitives per hour, six per minute, one every ten seconds—most of them from the Northern Triangle, a stretch of land no larger than the state of Wyoming. Add to this the many thousands of evacuees who, like Raymundo Paniagua, fly into American airports and let their tourist visas expire, and you begin to understand the magnitude of displacement.

As a result, although only a half million of these Central Americans lived in the United States thirty years ago, today that figure has shot up to almost five million—a population roughly equivalent to that of Los Angeles. Migrants from Honduras, Salvador, and Guatemala make up one of the fastest growing segments of the Latino community, mostly inhabiting cities and towns that cling to America's periphery: the metropolitan areas of Texas and California, as well as the suburbs of New York, Miami, and Washington, DC. The newcomers fill every niche of the blue-collar American workplace: construction crews, assembly lines, service jobs, maintenance teams, agricultural fields, childcare establishments, domestic employment. But the flight of young, motivated laborers from the Northern Triangle is a liability to the region itself: a formidable loss of human capital.

Like any other immigrants in the history of the United States—such as the Irish fleeing the potato famine, or the Germans avoiding religious persecution, or the Swedish escaping poverty—Central Americans come to work, find a better life, send money home. Eventually, like those of their European predecessors, their labors become a lifeline for the families they leave behind. In 2017 alone, Northern Triangle migrants sent home $16 billion in remittances, staving off hunger and destitution in their countries and stimulating their economies. This precinct of the globe may be losing human capital, but its fugitives make up for that loss with a deeply ingrained work ethic and a profound reverence for family. Whole villages in their native countries have been transformed by their labor. In 2019 the funds sent home by Salvadorans living and working in the United States boosted El Salvador's GDP by nearly 22 percent.

What is most striking about migrants from the Northern Triangle is how close their ties are—culturally, genetically, historically, gastronomically—to our vast population of Mexican Americans. And yet this should not be surprising, given that they are a mix of the same ancient peoples, including the Nahua (Aztec), the Maya, the Lenca, the Paya, and the Miskito, among others. Overwhelmingly, they are mestizos, the product of a half millennium of exuberant crossbreeding between European colonizers and indigenous peoples, which, themselves, experienced long histories of conquest and hybridization. Finally, immigrants from this part of Central America, like Mexicans, can range across a broad spectrum of phenotypes. Although they may be perceived as brown, on census forms they generally identify as white.

But Central Americans feel a kinship to Mexican Americans for yet another reason: for three centuries under Spanish colonial rule, they were treated as one people. From 1521 until 1821, the Viceroyalty of New Spain had jurisdiction over Mexico, and eventually it spread its dominion to the northernmost reaches of California. But its gubernatorial powers also reached south, embracing much of Central America. Even after the wars of independence, that area was annexed briefly to Mexico until it pulled away to become the Federal Republic of Central America—which included Panama, Costa Rica, Nicaragua, Belize, Honduras, El Salvador, Guatemala, and the Mexican state of Chiapas—before ultimately breaking off into separate republics. There is good reason for Mexicano writer Dagoberto Gilb to say, "I feel no bond with a Cuban or an Argentine, not really. But a Salvadoreño or a Guatemalteco? Yes. Oh, yes."

# SALVADORAN AMERICANS

*I am what comes after the civil war*
*after the dismembered corpses*
*the burnt sugar cane fields*
*the mango tree strung with a single hanging body . . .*
*take this, my story*
*eat it and remember me.*

—Yesika Salgado, poet, El Salvador, 2019

Tanita is a small, energetic Salvadoran with a wild shock of black hair framing her pixie face. She is fifty-four years old and has spent almost half of her life in this country but has yet to command more than a polite salutation in English. That said, her three sons—ages sixteen, eighteen, and twenty—are native English speakers, strong performers in the Maryland public education system. Her youngest, Alejandro, is an award-winning science student known by his teachers for his good study habits and his bright future prospects. Tanita's husband, Genaro, is sixty-nine, more than fifteen years older, a laid-off printshop worker who managed to find work briefly as a janitor, but was let go and is now unemployed. The family survives on Tanita's labors: office sanitation and housecleaning. They live in a modest cluster of apartment buildings on a busy highway in Maryland, along with hundreds of Ethiopian, Haitian, and Vietnamese aspirants to the American Dream; the boys share a room no larger than a ten-foot cube.

This last is nothing new. Tanita and Genaro are accustomed to meager circumstances. They hail from the same pueblo in the southeastern corner of El Salvador: Chilanguera, a dirt-poor village of no more than a few thousand souls, nestled between a rushing river and the towering Chaparrastique, an active volcano whose flying rock and fiery intemperance have kindled writers' imaginations since the 1500s. The town of Chilanguera is so inbred, so closely knit, and so thoroughly connected by a single road, that Genaro remembers Tanita waving to him as a little girl, as he bicycled past her front door on his way to work.

Tanita's father, aged 102 today, is a subsistence farmer who grows his own corn, beans, and cashew trees in a small plot adjacent to his cement house. Tanita's late mother was a baker who fired bread and tortillas in an outdoor kiln and peddled them in the nearby market. If the average wage of a local schoolteacher is less than $10 a day, the daily income for Tanita's family when she was growing up was a fraction of that. They never went hungry, given the effluence of their little plot, but hurricanes had been known to level their world, progress took a back seat to survival, and grinding poverty was all they knew.

Magnifying the family's penury were a number of scourges that swept El Salvador after the 1970s—both political and ecological. At the heart of the political troubles was the country's five-hundred-year-old caste system, which kept power in the hands of a very few and shackled a vast population to an endless cycle of privation. Compounding El Salvador's woes were the predatory practices of a number of American businesses—not least the United and Standard Fruit companies—that had helped themselves to the country's cheap labor and rich soil.

By 1910, Central America was firmly under the thumb of Washington and Wall Street and had even reached, by every rational definition, semicolonial status. Some of the countries had been occupied by American military forces for decades; but in all five, at least one government had been removed or installed by direct US pressure. Most radicalizing for leftist rebels in the early 1960s was Washington's willingness to use force to keep Central America's despots in power and install *democracias de fachada*: governments that painted themselves as pro-democracy but kept citizens under relentless dictatorial rule. "I used to believe in democracy," says Honduran biologist Raymundo Paniagua, "but democracy has been employed as a Trojan horse in our countries, and the embassy of the United States is our real government. Just as conquistadors would give Indians little mirrors in exchange for plundering their gold, the Americans give us baubles and help themselves to everything else." By the end of the twentieth century, for all the US investment and interest in the region, the poor had become poorer and the divisions extreme.

Civil injustices became so acute in El Salvador that rebellion began to electrify the collective imagination, especially since grassroots Socialist revolutions had already overtaken its neighbors Guatemala and Nicaragua. A many-tentacled proxy war soon gripped the region—the United States locked horns with Soviet expansionism—and the Cold War superpowers began pouring billions of dollars and a torrent of killing machines into existing civil wars. From Jimmy Carter's to Ronald Reagan's to George H. W. Bush's, one administration after another plied strong-arm governments with rifles, ammunition, grenades, and helicopters, allowing military juntas to kill tens of thousands of men, women, and children as the wars ground on. In turn, revolutionaries did their share of the carnage as Soviet hardware and money flowed into war zones through the auspices of nations in Moscow's thrall: Nicaragua, Cuba, North Korea.

In El Salvador, moderate politicians tried to mitigate the tension by proposing a land reform program that redistributed acreage to the poor, but the fourteen families that controlled the vast majority of the country's wealth balked at the idea. Within a few years, the elite and the military closed ranks and, via a US-supported coup, installed a junta that defended their interests.

But by then, the revolution was enlisting young Salvadorans as vigorously as the army generals. Come the 1980s, a series of destabilizing events would tip the scale: the flagrant shooting of Archbishop Oscar Romero, El Salvador's beloved activist priest, even as he stood at the altar, administering communion wafers in the chapel of a hospital; the outright execution of four American women—two nuns and two missionaries—whom the military suspected of fomenting political unrest; a spate of bank robberies and high-profile kidnappings by radicals intent on funding their revolution; and a brutal retaliation by American-trained soldiers of the Atlácatl Battalion, who descended on the village of El Mozote, leaving hundreds of villagers dead, largely by decapitation. Even as the ranks of the Left grew, right-wing death squads combed the countryside, forcing the young to join the army or die. To drive home their point, they left a trail of human body parts in their wake, strewn on the landscape like expendable dross. Genaro, by then twenty-three and a trained accountant, decided to leave Chilanguera rather than be forced at gunpoint to serve either side of an increasingly feral civil war. He slipped from Mexico into the United States in late December 1981, making his way north toward the East Coast. One-third of the Salvadoran population would soon abandon their country and join him.

By then, the entire Northern Triangle, along with its neighbor Nicaragua, was in flames. Indeed, one-quarter of the population of Nicaragua, battered by the US-supported war against the Sandinistas—a fiercely anti-American socialist party—had been rendered homeless. In Guatemala, the government's large-scale obliteration of entire villages had graduated to a full-blown genocide of the Mayan people that would result in two hundred thousand dead and missing. And Honduras was now a staging area for the Reagan administration's response to the region's "Communist menace," as US troops and intelligence officers trained and equipped tens of thousands of Central American soldiers to maintain a fierce, authoritarian grip on the isthmus.

Meanwhile, Tanita was a mere girl of eight, growing up in the shadow of a looming crater and the mounting dead. As she tells me now, shaking her head in disbelief at how her American sons take their tranquility for granted, "Not us! We lived under the ire of a volcano and a war, and every day the earth rumbled and bucked beneath us. We grew up thinking that every sunrise might be our last." Her village of Chilanguera was sporadically raided by rebel guerrillas or army troops, sweeping through city and hamlet to force boys as young as twelve into service or to execute anyone they suspected of helping the other side. Her parents would welcome the fighters without prejudice: feed them, give them clean pallets to sleep on, wash their clothes, bandage their wounds. From time to time, children at play would find grenades, bullet clips, even toe-popper mines tossed under a bed or into the cornfields nearby. What side they belonged to, they never knew. Tanita learned to avert her eyes when strangers with machine guns burst through the door looking for food, drink, women, or a fight. Her brothers, like Genaro's, had all made their way north and scooted under barbed wire into the relative safety of Texas.

When the civil war finally drew to a close in 1992, seventy-five thousand Salvadorans were dead and a million displaced; the nation had been at war for twelve long and frenzied years. Leaders of both sides gathered in Mexico to sign the Chapultepec Peace Accords, but the violence was hardly over. That was when the gangs emerged. And, surprisingly enough, they emerged first on the streets of Los Angeles, not the alleys and byways of El Salvador.

The US Immigration and Naturalization Service under President Bill Clinton's Department of Justice had blamed the spiraling rise of crime in American streets on "criminal aliens," and its officers were arresting tens of thousands of immigrants and American citizens—largely young Hispanics—for minor offenses, herding them onto buses and airplanes, and shuttling them arbitrarily to their countries of origin. In the Los Angeles area alone, federal and local authorities organized the deportation of thousands of young Salvadorans—the very youths who had fled the Civil War—to a country they hardly knew anymore. Within a few years, those angry young renegades, all too familiar with US gang culture and adrift in a country awash with guns, had cemented gang ties, rounded up a multitude of out-of-work soldiers, and transformed the notorious Mara Salvatrucha (MS-13) into a veritable army.

Gangs, or *bandillas*, took over entire neighborhoods, entire towns, recruiting youths with three simple words: "Join or die." Using violence, extortion, threats, sex trafficking, kidnappings, and outright murder— and financing their operations by facilitating the drug trade—the gangs proliferated. Soon MS-13 would forge alliances with Mexican and Colombian cartels, take over the trafficking of the burgeoning cocaine and marijuana trade, and become the largest employer in the country. Which is to say that young boys, schooled and hardened on America's mean streets, had returned to become the very brokers of violence they'd fled Central America to escape.

It was at about this time, as human barbarity resurfaced in Tanita's ambit, that nature unleashed an additional scourge. A deadly, Category 5 hurricane, Mitch, descended on the Caribbean one sultry October afternoon in 1998, cutting a ferocious path through the Northern Triangle, razing whole towns with its 185-mile-per-hour winds and taking more than eleven thousand lives as it went. The devastation was mind-boggling: more than one and a half million people were suddenly uprooted and homeless. Chilanguera did not go unscathed. Tanita's brother's family, whose house verged on the banks of the river, was swept into the moiling waters and drowned. One of Tanita's nephews, overtaken by a rushing flood, was gasping desperately for air when he suddenly felt something hard graze his leg. It was a bull: alive, massive, but floating by helplessly in the deluge. The boy latched onto its back, clung to its horns, and rode the animal for what seemed an eternity before he could grab hold of the branches of a tree and clamber its heights to safety. Tanita, who, along with her parents, had found safety on high ground near the volcano, returned after the rains to find their house, her mother's stone oven, the animals, and their precious vegetable plot totally submerged in a lake of mud.

When Genaro came back to the village to visit his parents the following year, he looked for the little girl he had known so many years before. She was now twenty-five years old; he was forty. When he proposed marriage and a future in Maryland, she did not hesitate.

• • •

Although America's immigrants from this part of the world are fugitives from present dangers, fleeing a homicide rate that is 500 percent higher than what the World Health Organization considers epidemic proportions, many are turned away at our borders, prompting them— in desperation—to send their children across the Rio Grande alone. In 2018, defying the harsh strictures put in place by the Trump administration, the great majority of unaccompanied minors crossing the border were from Guatemala, sprinting their way through cactus and mesquite, two thousand miles from home. In 2021, despite urgent circumstances, nearly four hundred thousand aspirants from Honduras and Guatemala were summarily expelled in the course of a single year.

That said, since 1990, the United States government has granted certain civilians from El Salvador, Honduras, and Nicaragua (among other strife-torn nations) entry under a classification called Temporary

Protected Status (TPS), which acknowledges that they are fleeing real
and life-threatening perils. Such fugitives are generally classified as refugees, but the US government hesitates to use that term with Northern Triangle immigrants, since Washington is so obviously implicated
in their wars. And so, a special category was devised for such circumstances. Although TPS is not a legal status and can readily be rescinded,
it has been a lifesaver for these immigrants, allowing its holders to apply
for work permits and driver's licenses, which make them eligible to open
bank accounts and buy homes.

Which is why there is a large, ever increasing number of Central
Americans in this country, even as Mexican immigration has slowed
down and Mexicanos in the United States today are more likely to head
south rather than north. When I arrived in Miami as a child, there were
fewer than ninety thousand Central Americans in the United States,
sprinkled across the agricultural fields of California and Texas; today,
more than a half century later, there are almost four million—forty-four
times that number—scattered throughout the land. And the spike has
been most pronounced in only the last fifteen years. That demographic
boom would be equivalent to taking a modest town the size of Kokomo,
Indiana, and transforming it into a megalopolis the size of Detroit in the
course of just two generations.

The overwhelming majority in that immigrant surge are Salvadorans, who—like Genaro and Tanita—did not want to leave home but were
driven north by fear, hunger, and desperation. Salvadorans represent the
third largest Latino community in the United States, after Mexicans and
Puerto Ricans. Today, four decades after Genaro's anxious flight to the
suburbs of Washington, DC, there are even more Salvadorans among us
than there are Cubans. They may be less concentrated geographically
than the *cubanos* in Miami, the Boricuas in New York, or the Mexicanos
in the Southwest—and they are less educated and less affluent than their
Latino cohort in general—but Salvadorans are a vibrant, ever-morphing
community and, like the blue-collar Tanita with her three fledgling,
white-collar "Salvi"-American sons, they occupy every ring of the American social order.

## THE DEPARTMENT OF SECOND CHANCES

This country is the mother of second chances.
—Jorge Ramos, news anchor, Mexican American, 2015

When Raymundo Paniagua finally managed to find a room to rent in Arlington, Virginia, and a temporary job to pay for it, he realized quickly that he had more ailments to contend with than a bullet in his skull and an empty eye socket. Among the many attendant conditions he had brought with him on his flight from Tegucigalpa were an acute case of post-traumatic stress disorder, a daily flurry of sudden and terrifying panic attacks, and a debilitating battery of narcoleptic collapses—the product of a proclivity to extreme and chronic fatigue. His Honduran friends in the area were able to help with the immediate logistics of work and lodging, but they were at a loss as to how to navigate the complicated, expensive grid of American health care.

What became quickly apparent was that he had landed in an ideal place to address his myriad aggravations. First, his neighborhood in Arlington was flush with Hondurans, Salvadorans, Guatemalans—precisely the cohort that had abandoned the perilous straits of the afflicted Triangle to find safe harbor near the seat of government of the United States. It was not the community itself that was helpful in negotiating life in this country, it was the proliferation of services—run mostly by "gringos," according to Raymundo—that had cropped up in that area to support the influx of Latinos in need: state government offices, nonprofit organizations, charitable organizations, and two entities that were battling for his soul and would end up helping him most of all: the local Catholic and Mormon churches.

Within a few years, Raymundo was able to pay for the surgery he needed as well as the acrylic eyeball necessary to keep the bony structure of his face from collapsing. The funds were provided by the Lions Club of Virginia and the St. Charles Catholic Church. The surgery for the ocular implant was performed at a drastically reduced price by a generous Johns Hopkins University surgeon who took pity on his circumstances and the horrifying events that had produced them. The prosthesis was a gift from the Mormon Church. Before long, Raymundo found temporary work keeping books for a corps of Honduran painters, construction workers, street pavers, and handymen doing work in the vicinity. Eventually he was offered employment as a maintenance man in a church of Latter-day Saints whose staff was infinitely patient with his intermittent bouts of incapacitating fatigue. In exchange for his labors, social workers there helped Raymundo with his debts and assisted him with his needs. Cleaning and maintaining a place of worship is a far cry from work as a marine biologist, but, for Raymundo, the association has been a lifesaver. In the end, Raymundo and Tanita may be Latinos from separate countries, discrete conflagrations, and very different walks of life, but they share a single, unwavering view of the United States of America. They call it their "sanctuary of second chances."

# 5

# SHADES OF BELONGING

Imagine having to constantly tell people that you're made of two colors: blue and yellow, but all that the people see is green, and you constantly have to go into the light and show them that you are made of both.

—Cindy Y. Rodriguez, journalist, Peruvian American, 2014

For Latinos, it seems the rest of the world is constantly trying to tell us what color we should be. Brown, some want to call us, although we are often shades of beige, yellow, or mahogany. Given the standard American binary choice—memorialized in the 1790 census when the newly minted US government decided to count slaves—we are squeezed into a black-white taxonomy that feels all wrong. I'm reminded of the long-ago moment when, wandering around a Miami bus depot on the day of my arrival in the United States, I was confronted with the all-too American dilemma of choosing between two races. Should I go into the washroom labeled "Colored"? Or should I choose the one marked "Whites Only"? And what did those labels mean exactly? I had never been made to ponder the precise color of my skin.

Not so for Mexicans on the other side of the country. When the Mexican-American War was over, and their first US census came around in the 1850s, Mexicanos whose lands had been hijacked by "Westward ho!" invaders pluckily decided to be on the side of privilege and identify themselves as "white." But they were treated like blacks anyway. They were beaten, lynched, forbidden from entering restaurants, shops, movie houses, schools, and any Anglo establishment that declared it didn't want them. Signs on storefronts reminded them of their status: "No dogs. No Negroes. No Mexicans." Latinos in those days were, for all intents and purposes, black. That's what a deeply ingrained binary system will do to a nuanced population. Even now, in the current parlance, Latinos are called people of color, when in truth, we are a people of many colors. A rainbow of colors. Give us a skin color, and we can produce cousins who wear it. We can fit any phenotype. Even under a single roof and within the same nuclear family.

For a highly racialized country like the United States of America, which struggles to codify us and put us in neat, categorical boxes, that infinite range can be hard to absorb. When Hollywood decided to produce the film *West Side Story* in 1960, Rita Moreno—the only Puerto Rican in a movie portraying Puerto Ricans—was made to wear dark pancake makeup many shades deeper than her skin. Puerto Ricans, at least in the Hollywood mind-set of the time, were expected to be uniformly brown. They were also expected to loathe their motherland, its customs, its weather—and ultimately themselves. (The lyrics said it all: "Always the population growing! And the money owing! And the sunlight streaming! And the natives steaming!" There it was: the presumed self-hatred a Puerto Rican must feel. The brazen sneer of rank revulsion.)

And yet, for all the purported progress in racial awareness in the sixty years since, when Disney unveiled Lin-Manuel Miranda's high-spirited, supposedly more ethnically aware film about Dominicans, 2021's *In the Heights*, it drew far less of an audience than expected. Instead, a hue and cry went up from some Afro-Latinos. The largely Latino cast, they complained, was not Dominican enough, not dark enough, not black. The pendulum had swung. But the message was very much the same: you can't talk about Latinos as a uniform ethnicity or race—someone is bound to feel left out. Nor can you assume that any one of us can represent the whole: the Dominican writer Julia Álvarez, who is phenotypically white, may look worlds apart from the retired Dominican baseball player Juan Soto, who is phenotypically black. And yet, in some families, they might be siblings. It is a complicated business. It has been so for more than five hundred years.

I remember being in my childhood home in the coastal hacienda of Paramonga, Peru, and sitting in my Tía Chaba's lap as she turned the pages of a family album she had brought from Lima. One after another, the photographs made me put out a finger and ask, Who is that? And that? I had never seen a Negroid or Asian face before—we lived largely among the indigenous—and it was the distinct architecture of the facial features that made me curious. Oh, she would say, that is our aunt Tía Eufemia; we called her la Negrita (the little black one). And that one over there is your grandmother's cousin, China. And that was the end of that. No explanation. Only the glaring brazenness of racial diminutives, as if that would be elucidation enough. And then silence. Many years later, as a young woman, I asked my grandmother—who, as far as I was concerned, was the fount of family truth—about those faces, but she just waved me away. *"Somos blancos, Marisi. Puro blancos. Criollos de hace mucho tiempo."* We're white, Marisi. Pure white. Peruvian-born Spanish from all the way back.

It was a lie. My family, like families of the majority of American Latinos, had been mixing with indigenous and Africans for a very long time. Despite the strict laws of *limpieza de sangre* (racial purity) that had operated for centuries in the Spanish colonies—not to mention the bizarre loophole allowing a mulatto to purchase "whiteness" and access "white" privileges if he paid the Spanish Crown enough money—race mixing had accompanied the conquest from the very beginning. It had existed from the moment a ship full of concupiscent men landed on New World shores and violated native women. For our family, it had been 480 years of multiraciality, to be exact; since 1542, when my first Spanish ancestor in this hemisphere pulled ashore somewhere in the Caribbean and wended his way south to Peru, launching twenty-four generations of commingled offspring in a multitude of latitudes and provinces. I would come to learn that phenotypical surprises like the ones I was seeing in our family album were not rare in the broader world of Latino families.

What was rare was to talk about it. Babies were awaited with a certain tension. And all along, epithelial folds, hairless bodies, and Nubian noses continued to make appearances in the Arana Cisneros family. "Ay! Salió quemadita!" a jolly uncle might exclaim. "Oh, she came out a little over-baked!" But after that, silence.

Javier Lizarzaburu, a Latino BBC correspondent in Europe and the United States for many years, wrote about this eloquently in a series he produced about his own voyage of racial discovery:

> According to family legend, I was one hundred percent white. But I am not. My face is, let us say, a typical Peruvian face. A face that declares an undeniable history of race mixing—something we never spoke about in our house. And if something as obvious as my face weren't proof enough, what of the legion of unspoken histories in our family? It's very possible that no one lied. It's very possible that what happened is what happens all too often in [Latino] families. You stay silent. Because there are histories and origins about which, very simply, you must never speak.

You must never speak about those origins because the stakes are too high. To be less than white in Peru (and most Latin countries, for that matter) is to inhabit a great, unruly mass historically barred from the front halls, the quality educations, coveted careers, high echelons of government, desirable marriages. In Javier's case, he never suspected he didn't belong in the front halls: his education had been superb; his journalistic successes—in London, Washington, DC, and Madrid—enviable; his social world, rich and full. That was until he recalled an incident he experienced when he was twenty years old, and a classmate in his Spanish university said to him casually as they were heading out the door one day, "Ven, indio. Vamos." Come on, Indian. Let's go. It had felt like a joke at the time.

Many years later, pondering his DNA results, Javier was reminded of that moment in Madrid. The memory became a sudden epiphany. Just as a passing comment had been for young Dominican American Mario Álvarez when, one day in the grand, baronial halls of the Horace

Mann School in New York, he was told he was black—thoroughly and unequivocally black. Javier took a good look at the mirror: ebony hair, deep brown eyes, tawny skin, slight physique. It seemed ridiculous that he hadn't seen it before. But that is precisely how lies passed down through generations can twist a person's self-perception. The picture was in sharp focus now: everyone in his family was white, except him. Being a journalist, Javier began a scrutiny of his family's past that would launch not only a BBC series on little white lies of racial classification but also, eventually, a full retrospective of the identity of Lima itself, positing the notion that white elites had perpetuated the big lie of their inherent superiority and, so, erased the rich indigenous civilizations that had defined the city for millennia. The reckoning with his racial identity was now complete. "*Salí del Peru blanco*," he wrote—I left Peru as a white—"*y regresé indio*"—and I came back as an Indian.

Javier's maternal grandmother had told him that she had been born in Spain, with an English father and a fair-skinned, northern Italian grandfather. It made sense: she had porcelain-white skin, bright blue eyes, blonde hair; she was clearly a northerner. But she also made a habit of repeating constantly to Javier, "*Hay que blanquear la raza.*" We need to whiten the race; improve it. Which meant that Javier was obliged to marry whiter, reproduce whiter, cleanse the blood. It was a general mantra that I had heard in childhood, too, especially because my Peruvian father had married an Anglo. According to the elders, at least racially he had done well to marry my mother; his nut brown would—in me—become *café con leche*. And it did. It was the Latin American obsession with eugenics that, by the early 1900s, verged on madness, with whole governments—Argentina, Chile, Uruguay, Paraguay—encouraging Europeans to immigrate to their countries and erase the *indio* in them. We are creating a cosmic race! as one Mexican educator described it; *un gran mestizaje*—a great mixing— where we would all gradually lighten our skins generation after generation until we were all the color of conquistadors again. Well into the twentieth century, that impulse was still in force.

Javier had to ask himself: why would his grandmother, his whitest relative, insist on whitening the race, if—as she maintained—the family was 100 percent *blanca*? Mind you, hers wasn't the race obsession that forces people to declare whether they are black or white—that unequivocal, binary choice asked for, not so long ago, in some American public places. *Hay que blanquear—o mejorar—la raza* was a slipperier notion: an admission that, in a varicolored country traumatized by a brutal, racist colonial past, a lighter shade of skin—*un blanqueamiento*, a whitening—would make your children's lives better, easier. It is a systemic racism of another kind. The Latino kind. And it took it for granted that races would cross the line and procreate with one another willy-nilly.

*Blanqueamiento* was the rule, although whitening for us is a fickle and arbitrary scale, because "conquistador white" is hardly Scandinavian white, preserved and maintained in isolation for centuries. Spanish white is a slapdash alloy of European, Arab, Mediterranean, and Jew. And when it's in this hemisphere a while, it can even include a little indigenous and black as well. As the sixteenth-century English poet Edmund Spenser, a hater of Spain and promoter of the fierce, anti-Spanish Black Legend so popular in Britain, once wrote, "Of all nations under heaven, I suppose the Spaniard is the most mingled, most uncertain and most bastardly." A few hundred years later, a French intellectual put a finer point on it: "Africa begins in the Pyrenees"—which means at the border with Spain. So, the "purity of race" Spain demanded of its colonial offspring in the Américas was ridiculously impossible to achieve from the start.

At the time, Javier's friend's casual, derogatory allusion to Javier's brownness prompted him momentarily to question everything he had been told. He wrote to his mother: "So, which of my ancestors is the Indian?" The letter she wrote back was filled with tenderness, but it reinforced the secrecy: "Don't worry, you are intelligent. Just dress well and don't think about such things." In time, and with some research, the truth would come tumbling out: Javier's father, said to be of Basque extraction and therefore presumably white, was actually from a long line of Lizarzaburus who had been in the Americas since the fifteenth century. Who knew what carnal alliances had been made in the generations since? On his maternal side, the blue-eyed grandmother who claimed to have been born in Spain had actually been born in Moyobamba, in the

Peruvian jungle. Her whiteness—not her grandson's brownness—had been the family fluke. Moreover, the grandfather whose memory she treasured was not Italian, nor was he northern; he had been born in an outpost near Chachapoyas, high up in the rural Andes. The lies had been meant to mask a local, browner ancestry, but looking around at his fair-skinned family, he had believed everyone was white as the flesh of a coconut, including himself.

Studying the results of his DNA test, Javier came to understand that his color was no accident; he was almost 50 percent indigenous. The blood of native American civilizations coursed in his veins, a heritage going back twenty thousand years. His particular genetic cocktail included a dollop of Southeast Asian; not surprising in an immigrant from Peru, whose population had received infusions of Asian blood in the form of slaves and merchants over the centuries. Ultimately, the quest for his identity showed him that brownness—embedded in the cellular memory of his skin—was testament to an ancient narrative, a fusion of all mankind's phenotypes common enough among Latinos but unique in the history of the world.

## SHADES OF INVISIBILITY

We didn't cross the border, the border crossed us.
　　　　　—Chicano activist chant, American Southwest, 1960s

Whereas Javier had convinced himself he was white via a lie, Mexican Americans became white via the law. In the last half of the nineteenth century, after Americans had pushed their way into Mexico, created a massive immigration problem there, waged war, and then taken half of the Mexican landmass, Mexicanos who suddenly found themselves on this side of the border demanded to be considered full American citizens. They'd had no such ambitions before. Although a number decided to accept Mexico's offer to resettle on its side of the new border, others struggled to preserve the land and possessions that had belonged to their families for hundreds of years. It had seemed disorienting, if not hallucinatory, to be asked to leave behind all their worldly properties to join their country of origin.

Mexicanos are largely mestizo, a blend of indigenous and Spanish, sometimes with doses of black African as well, but in 1848, when they looked around at the race-obsessed, binary society into which they had been absorbed—when they saw American ranchers and farmers flooding into their lands, bringing their slaves with them—they wanted no part of the "colored" label. Indeed, those fears had been stoked long before: an 1839 article in *La Luna*, a Chihuahua newspaper, warned that if Americans were indeed to invade, Mexicans would be "sold as beasts" because "their color was not as white as that of their new conquerors." It was an alarming prospect because a reverse one-drop rule had long operated among Mexicans and would eventually operate among Mexican Americans: if they had any Spanish blood at all from a distant ancestor, they considered themselves classifiably and justifiably white. To be anything else in the United States—to be black, mulatto, or Asian—was to have no votes, no access to property, no rights at all. By demanding citizenship, they were demanding whiteness. When the Treaty of Guadalupe Hidalgo was finally signed in 1848, they were granted it. And so, as America approached the turn of the century, in the midst of government efforts to sharpen the census and determine exactly who was who in the American populace, Mexicans preferred to disappear into the white majority. They chose not to be counted as Mexicanos at all.

But in time, the Great Depression got in the way. As the stock market tanked and unemployment skyrocketed, Anglos began to blame Mexicanos for taking their jobs—an age-old accusation, and entirely unfounded. To mitigate white anger, the United States forcibly removed as many as two million people of Mexican descent—up to 60 percent of whom were American citizens. Then, in 1930, the word *Mexican* suddenly appeared on the census questionnaire as a separate race—a cynical attempt to count them for discriminatory purposes. But Mexicans rose up and rejected the designation, mistrustful of a government that had treated them badly in the first place. They continued to mark "white," insisting on disappearing into the plurality, although it was becoming clear that, against America's entrenched racism, true assimilation was little more than a hollow hope. Even so, that instinct to mark the white box would prove prescient a few years later when President Franklin D. Roosevelt signed Executive Order 9066, and the 1930 census was used to round up Japanese Americans and force them into internment camps.

The story of Rubén Aguilar—a US citizen by birth—presents a striking cameo of the extreme anti-Mexican racism of the time. Herded onto a truck in 1933 and forcibly deported along with his family when he was only six years old, Rubén has strong memories of the moment. "What I remember," he says, recalling the FBI officials who invaded his Chicago home, "is the way that the agents crashed into the house: 'Okay, people, line up against the wall!'" Rubén soon found himself in a country that seemed entirely foreign, in an area that his parents did not know. He spoke no Spanish; and without citizenship, an American child in Mexico could not receive health care or attend public school. Twelve years later, in 1945, just after his eighteenth birthday, he received a letter from the United States Selective Service ordering him to report for military service. There was a war on. He was a US citizen. He was obliged to serve. Dutifully, he took a bus to Chicago, where he was to be inducted into the army and shipped out to fight the Japanese. On the way, the bus driver stopped in Laredo, and Rubén asked where he might find a washroom. "Right around the corner," said the driver. "So, I go around the corner, and I see a big sign: 'No Mexicans or Dogs.'"

•    •    •

To appreciate the acute sense of a shared past among Mexicanos—a sense that has only grown with time—one has to imagine the magnitude of the Mexican land grab, an appropriation of five hundred thousand square miles and every resident on it. As one American professor who set out a few years ago to travel Mexico's original border put it, "One thing that we found really fascinating was going to places like Medicine Bow, Wyoming, which would have been a border town. People have no concept of the fact that Mexico stretched that far north." Today it's hard to comprehend that those original 2,400 miles of border were shoved so far south that much of what was once the newly independent republic of Mexico is now California, Utah, Nevada, Texas, New Mexico, Arizona, Oklahoma, Colorado, and Wyoming. If the Mexican American segment of the US population represents our largest ethnic minority (forty million strong, which is to say that more than one in nine Americans are of Mexican extraction), it is because many have been here all along. If they weren't here from the very beginning, by 1940, the lion's share of Mexican Americans were native born.

Today, three generations later, more than 70 percent of Mexican Americans are US born, and yet a full third say they face racism every day. That racism, so present since the United States' earliest days, eventually found its backlash in the Chicano movement of the 1960s, a short-lived but fierce campaign of young radicals committed to rejecting their parents' assertions of whiteness, embracing their "Mexicanness," and reclaiming their rights to their ancestral lands. Young Chicanos had taken a hard look at their place in American society and become infuriated by what they saw: not only had they been unilaterally denied the land grants the US government had promised them in the Treaty of Guadalupe Hidalgo, but also they now had the lowest per-capita income in the country, a spiraling unemployment rate, a 50 percent high school dropout rate, minimal numbers in higher education, no political representation to speak of, *and* young Mexicanos were dying in Vietnam at nearly twice the rate of any other ethnic group. Spurred by the civil rights movement and the growing antiwar fervor, they refused to be silent anymore. They took on a name that had once been a racial slur and, in a burst of youthful idealism, gathered as many as 150,000 demonstrators at a time, stoking fervent, often violent rallies and provoking stern—even covert and illegal—oversight by the FBI.

Inspired by a growing number of supporters, Chicanos announced they would now rebuild and populate Aztlán, the mythical homeland of the Aztecs that allegedly had stretched from northern Mexico into the American Southwest. To these leaders, Aztlán represented self-determination, a return to roots, racial pride. "We were driven by a hot, passionate anger. It's what sparked us. People had sat on that anger for years. Once it exploded, we didn't have the tools to sustain it," said Richard Martinez, a Chicano activist who went on to become state senator, attorney, and retired judge. Indeed, within fifteen years, many of the movement's "revolutionary" leaders—such as Martinez—had joined the establishment as lawyers, business executives, college professors, and bureaucrats. They were proving their point by entering the mainstream. Others turned their radicalism into hard-nosed realism, as did the Chicano William C. Velásquez, who, after years of leading protest marches, saw that the fundamental problem of Mexican American marginalization was a systemic, discriminatory exclusion from the democratic process. "Willie" Velásquez, as he was known, set out to educate young Mexicans about the power of the ballot box, register eligible voters, and persuade all Hispanics to make themselves heard at the polls. *"Su voto es su voz!"* he exhorted them—Your vote is your voice!—and his massive, grassroots effort to correct Latino invisibility would prove more powerful than any act of civil disobedience.

By 1983, the movement that had ushered so many young Mexicans to greater participation in corridors of power—a movement that had come into its own on the shoulders of renowned union organizers such as Cesar Chavez and Dolores Huerta of the United Farm Workers of America—was largely forgotten. Half the Latino population of Los Angeles had never even heard the term *Chicano*. Just two generations after the census had written "Mexican" into its taxonomy of skin colors, the group that would have adopted that racial category with gusto was gone. And yet no one can deny that the Chicanos had greatly advanced the full, activist embrace of Latinidad that would finally come in the twenty-first century.

## THE CENSUS AND LATINIDAD

The Constitution's original sin was that apportionment of "the people" did not mean counting all people the same. . . . "We the people"
did not include everyone.

—Laura E. Gómez, law professor,

Mexican American, 2020

In the 1890s, the very decade that my sixteen-year-old abuelito sailed
up the coast from Peru, traveled overland, and crossed the border into
the United States, at least three watershed moments were taking place.
First, the US Army would invade Indian territory, engage the Lakota
people in the Battle at Wounded Knee, in South Dakota, and massacre as
many as three hundred men, women, and children, including Chief Sitting Bull, virtually ending armed Indian resistance to white pioneer encroachment. Second, the US Census Bureau, by then one hundred years
in operation, would declare the frontier closed and the borders defined,
obliging my grandfather to present papers and an official letter of invitation as he crossed into American territory. Third, that US territory, con-
flicted and disputed for so long, now occupied the continent from sea to
shining sea. The census stopped tracking adventurers pushing westward,
proclaimed the "unsettled" frontier to exist no longer, and, since many
Mexicans had fled south to safety, conveniently decided to ignore the approximately one hundred thousand who had opted to stay behind.

It had other things to do. As fickle as the census has always been—as
sporadic its progress—it is best to see it as an evolving instrument. It was
born of Article 1, Section 2 of the Constitution, and it was largely meant
to be a decennial (ten-year) inventory to decide "apportionments"—that
is, the number of congressional representatives each state would be allowed. But very quickly, it seemed to have other political uses. In 1850,
a landmark year, clerks began to register more than just the male heads
of every white household and the number of slaves he owned. Women,
children, and slaves were now recorded by name; and churches, rates
of poverty, and crime went into the calculus, too. Most remarkably,

the questionnaire now specified three choices of race: white, black, or mulatto. All the same, judging race was an entirely subjective exercise. White male clerks documented skin color as they perceived it, much as Spanish priests had done throughout the colonial Americas since 1493— by eyeing the person in front of them and arbitrarily assigning them a color. Naturally, their opinions on race were random and arguable.

Ten years later, in 1860, perhaps reflecting white fears of an angry Native American backlash, the census began to tally Indians. And given the whites' alarm over the growing influx of "yellow hordes" now streaming into America to pan gold and build the country's railroads and byways, the census began to count Chinese as well. Indeed, in that perfect storm of racist anxieties, the United States would ban Chinese women from entering the country, claiming that it needed to control the birth rate, prevent prostitution, and halt the perceived yellow infestation; a few years later, the infamous Chinese Exclusion Act barred all immigration and inspired the US Border Patrol, since it was feared that Asians would land in Mexico and pour unseen across the border. For all the arguments that the count was a purely demographic, scientific exercise, singling out Chinese, "Hindoo," Japanese, and other racial distinctions had clearly become, as one legal scholar put it, "a form of surveillance, a mechanism for imposing order and racial clarity on the proliferation of an ambiguous alien." White Europeans, on the other hand, would not be subjected to that kind of scrutiny.

Then again, every census seemed to have its racial controversies. It had begun in 1797, with a debate that resulted in counting slaves to determine apportionments, but registering them as only three-fifths of a human being—an inclusion without which Thomas Jefferson might not have won the presidency in 1800. Similarly, the Indian inventory in 1860 recorded a mere forty thousand Native Americans—and only those who were willing to renounce membership in their tribes and be taxed; the more accurate number was almost ten times greater. In the 1870 census, the first after the Civil War, its gross underestimation of America's blacks was controversial. African Americans, so recently enslaved and so thoroughly tyrannized, refused to cooperate with the Census Bureau, understandably afraid of how the information might be used against them. Throughout the end of the nineteenth century, there were active lobbies to control apportionments, not to mention manipulate information on America's races. At times, the system seemed to take on a blood calculus reminiscent of the Inquisition, measuring not only Indian, Chinese, Hindu, Korean, and Japanese, but also black, mulatto, quadroon, and octoroon.

By 1900, when there were already a minimum of a half million people of Spanish American origin in the southwestern United States, the government was blithely ignoring the numbers. Any records we have of the size of that population are taken from informal surveys of Spanish-sounding surnames, which can be misleading. People can change their names, and a Márquez can become a Marks as easily as Ralph Rueben Lifshitz became Ralph Lauren. Or a household with an English surname might actually be overwhelmingly mestizo through the unrecorded female line. In my own Peruvian family, we have O'Connors, Koehnes, and Barclays, who are blended with mestizo stock, are culturally Latin American, consider themselves thoroughly Peruvian, and have done so for many generations.

In its methodical determination to count Hispanics, the census has come far since 1930, when it suddenly posited "Mexican" as a racial category. The outcry against that categorization was immediate; in fact, it anticipated the process itself. It began when the League of the United Latin American Citizens (LULAC), a Mexican American organization formed in Corpus Christi, Texas, became aware of the pending "Mexican" category and organized to purge it from the census. They protested: We are white; we have always been white; look it up; we are Americans.

Even the Mexican government complained, reminding Washington, DC, that when the US government had confiscated Mexican territory, it had signed a treaty that accepted all Mexicans on that land as full American citizens. At the time of that signing—in 1848—a US citizen had to be white, so, by association, LULAC argued, Mexican Americans had been white for more than eighty years. Why change their racial status now? The Census Bureau eventually relented and, by the time the next census came around, "Mexican" had been struck from the questionnaire.

The government conundrum about what to do with America's Mexicans was complicated by Mexico's Revolution, a long and brutal killing machine that devastated the country from 1910 to 1920 and propelled anywhere from six hundred thousand to more than a million Mexicans north to safety. Now, with the "Mexican" race designation gone, those immigrants, too, proceeded to register as white, following the example of their Americanized *hermanos*. As a result, the 1940 census portrayed an America that was 90 percent white (the remaining 10 percent, black), although a population bomb of Latin American indigenous and mestizos had detonated in the Southwest, virtually unseen.

What does it say about a country that a whole demographic of its people should be ignored by its official demographers, and that the neglect would go on decade after decade for more than 120 years? As the historian Kenneth Prewitt has written, "It would of course be an exaggeration to attribute the racialization of American politics to the census. But the availability of a racial taxonomy—counting and sorting by race—was handmaiden to the politics of race that continue to the present." It is clear that between the Civil War and the end of World War II, the demographic of the United States was changing willy-nilly, and a rigid racial hierarchy was being cemented—indeed, the census information was the glue—and yet Hispanics continued to remain invisible.

In 1960 the official number of people "of Spanish surnames" in the United States counted less than a million—and only in the Southwest—an under-reckoning that illustrated the census's patent failure to tally the burgeoning multitudes. By then, Puerto Ricans and Cubans had begun to arrive, and they, too, marked "white" on the census, although only the wealthier Cubans escaping Castro's Communist Revolution fit the phenotype. And so, despite the fact that the 1960 census began asking the populace to self-identify their race, the charade continued: Latinos became officially white because they called themselves white, but socially they were "colored"—most of them segregated in ghettos, barred from public places, and relegated to a racial limbo. "I grew up in a black and white America, which had no place to put brown," author Richard Rodriguez wrote of those baffling boyhood days.

## BIRTH OF "THE HISPANIC"

*Nixon* found us. He made us known and famous.
—Henry M. Ramírez, politician, Mexican American, 2014

Come the 1970s, one man would know where to put America's "brown." His name was Richard Milhous Nixon. When President Nixon began his first term in 1969, one of his first objectives was to address a population he had come to know well in his hometown of Whittier, California. In them, he saw a segment of America that had gone ignored, unregistered—one that might have great political capital if it was courted, acknowledged, and unified. He was, after all, the son of a failed lemon farmer turned grocer, a boy who had seen Mexicans up close, not only in the fields of Yorba Linda, where he had been born, but in his father's grocery business in Whittier. He had observed their strong work ethic, their binding family traditions, their abiding faith. At twelve, working elbow to elbow with them, loading fruit and vegetables onto trucks, he grew comfortable in their company. "I know who you Mexicans are," he said when he gathered a group of them in the White House to talk about the future of his administration.

By September 12, 1969, Nixon had signed a proclamation dedicating the week of September 14 to a nationwide celebration of American Hispanics; Congress baptized it National Hispanic Heritage Week. Eventually the festivities would stretch to a month. At no time had an American president been so praiseful of the wider population of Latino people, so sanguine about their future and their potential. His declaration a year later was near panegyric:

The Hispanic culture is one to which this nation is particularly indebted. Men of Hispanic origin were among the first Europeans to explore this hemisphere. For four centuries, men and women of

Hispanic descent have provided distinguished leadership in our country and in other New World countries, both in government and in other walks of life.

Today the people of the United States are reminded of this rich heritage in many ways. Millions of our citizens speak Spanish, and Hispanic names and traditions grace many parts of our landscape, including both the town where I was born and the place where I am making my new home.

This country's Hispanic heritage is particularly important because it reminds us of the great traditions we share with our neighbors in Latin America. . . . The culture is one of depth, excitement, and beauty. It has crossed borders and mountains and oceans, and has made its influence felt in all parts of the globe. In honoring it, we give strength to that international understanding which is indispensable to world order.

That same year, Nixon called for the formation of a Cabinet Committee on Opportunities for Spanish-Speaking People, whose charter would be to ensure that his government programs reached every Spanish speaker in the country. But the committee, chaired by Henry M. Ramírez, would accomplish far more. When Nixon asked how they might improve the 5 percent support from Mexican Americans that Nixon had received in the 1968 presidential election, he was told without hesitation: Count us. Invest in us. We are a faithful people, so make one of us a bishop. We serve enthusiastically in the military, so make one of us a general. We are an economic force, so make one of us the United States Treasurer. Give us documentation—most of us who arrived in the diaspora fleeing the Mexican Revolution still don't have papers—make us legal, allow us to visit Mexico one last time before we come home to die in the United States. Nixon's response was immediate: Let's do it. All of it. Start the paperwork, make it happen.

And so it was that Nixon invented Hispanics, a hitherto unknown and invisible category of Americans, a mulligatawny of many hues, habits, and tribes. It was utter fabrication. There was never a category so

shambling, so vague. No color so undefinable. And yet, there it was—
"Hispanic"—telling us that those of us formerly from the southern part
of the hemisphere, now living north of the border, were one classification of humanity. One ethno-racial group.

All of what Ramírez pointed out was done. Mexican American bishop
Patricio Flores was consecrated; Richard E. Cavazos was identified as the
first Mexican American four-star general. The first Hispanic US Treasurer,
Romana Acosta Bañuelos, was appointed—a US born citizen who had
been deported as a child during the 1930s anti-Mexican backlash and re-
turned as a seventeen-year-old single mother; over the years, a run of
Latina treasurers would follow. Not least among his efforts on behalf of
Hispanics, Nixon established the Office of Minority Business Enterprise
(OMBE) to invest in "brown capitalism" as well as black businesses—it
had been a central theme of his presidential campaign. In the end, Nixon
selected more Hispanics to high positions than either John F. Kennedy or
Lyndon B. Johnson—or any American president in history, for that matter,
until Bill Clinton in the 1990s. And the White House began immediate
pressure on the Census Bureau to count "people of Spanish origin."

In 1972, when he ran for reelection, Nixon created the first comprehensive campaign to win the "Hispanic vote" that the country had ever
experienced. "Amigo buses" with bands of musicians roamed the Southwest, playing mariachi to appeal to Mexican Americans; in the East, they
played salsa and *cumbia* to win over Puerto Ricans and Cubans. The Democratic Party had never attempted anything quite like this. JFK's 1960
campaign had formed the Viva Kennedy clubs, but they were largely to
win the Mexican American vote. And even though Lyndon Johnson was
acutely aware of Mexicanos in Texas—though he had begun his professional career as a teacher in impoverished rural "Mexican schools,"
and though his administration would accomplish enormous advances
on their behalf, not least the Immigration Act of 1965—Johnson had not
envisioned a national constituency of Hispanics, nor imagined them as
a potentially powerful political bloc of their own.

When the 1972 election was over, with Nixon winning in a landslide, he had increased his Hispanic vote from 5 percent to 40 percent.

Singlehandedly, a Republican had given Hispanics a name, put them on the map, and been rewarded for it. Never mind that he had sought to dismember Johnson's Great Society and all the anti-poverty programs that might have benefited the Hispanic poor. For the first time, a president had seen them as a potentially powerful political base.

But the Watergate scandal ensued, climaxing with Nixon's resignation in 1974, and so Ramírez's last item—the bill to grant amnesty to two million undocumented Mexican Americans—was stranded in Congress and ultimately vanquished by a Democratic Senate. In 1986 it was resuscitated by President Ronald Reagan and passed handily, allowing three million undocumented immigrants from a variety of countries to be "legalized." By then, the Latino population had diversified and proliferated, not only in the Southwest but along the East Coast. In the intervening seventeen years between Nixon's pledge to count "people of Spanish origin" and Reagan's hammering home the last item of the "Nixon Hispanic Strategy," the population of Latinos had more than doubled from nine million to nineteen million.

But as far as Latinos went, the Census Bureau remained an imperfect statistician. The government agency had kicked off the effort haltingly in the 1970s, testing a tiny percentage of homes. But it did so in English, thereby missing the magnitude of the population. By 1980, when the agency set out to do a full enumeration, it offered a box labeled "people of Spanish origin," which was thoroughly confusing to a majority that saw itself not as Spanish but as mestizo, indigenous, black, or Asian. It had also missed Nixon's clear grasp of Latino phenotypes. "Look at the color of your skin," he had told his appointee, Henry M. Ramírez. "Vanilla. The Mexicans I knew all had vanilla skin." He meant the skin of a Spaniard infused with indigenous blood—the color of a vanilla bean, which is brown.

"Those Mexican judges and lawyers and movie stars," Nixon pointed out to Ramírez, "they all look like me. They look Anglo. I'm not talking about them. I'm talking about Mexicans like you." He told Ramírez that he wanted to promote "real Hispanics," not the white ones. His goal was to reject the century-old gloss, sanctioned by the Treaty of Guadalupe

Hidalgo, that it was safest for Hispanics to pass themselves off as white. Instead of the Hollywood-inspired white faces seen constantly on Mexico's television screens, billboards, and corporate boardrooms, he wanted to focus on those he had seen as a boy in the fields: the darker ones. Race was very much a part of the "Nixon Strategy." But the US Census was making no such distinction. Just as it had gone from offering a generic black box to the prodigious banquet of black/mulatto/quadroon/octoroon—only to retreat to the old one-drop version again—the Census Bureau would wrestle with the business of Hispanic pigments for years to come.

## UP FROM A STEEL-TOWN BASEMENT

> She made history this afternoon. And she is the first person of color, the first Latina in the history of our country to write speeches for the president.
>                     —President Bill Clinton, White House, July 19, 1995

Carolyn Curiel, a third-generation Mexican American whose family was rooted in Mexico, Kansas, and California but moved to Indiana in the 1930s and 1940s, recalls the deep and systemic racism that informed her childhood. Carolyn can pass for white, but she grew up in a brown family and so was a collateral victim to the policies put into place by communities experiencing large inflows of Mexicano laborers. "In East Chicago, Indiana, where my father worked in the steel mills," she tells me, "my first educational experience was segregated. My classmates and I were not allowed to attend classes with our white neighbors. My first classroom was in the basement of a Catholic school for Poles and Eastern Europeans. We Mexicans were literally relegated to the bowels of the building, where there was little fresh air or sunlight. The blond kids were upstairs, the Mexicans below. I didn't know the word 'segregated' at the time, but I knew what was going on. White nuns from the same religious order taught upstairs and downstairs. The only difference among the students was color and culture. We were treated as inferior."

Perhaps the most crucial lesson Carolyn learned in that school was
the value of fighting back, not allowing the racism to cow her. When, for
no ostensible reason, a hefty nun came at her from behind and slammed a
well-aimed fist into her back, she folded, winded, hardly able to breathe.
She was asthmatic, shy, fragile, and totally bewildered by the assault, as
were her classmates. When her mother heard of it, she stormed onto
the school's playground, called out the nun for all to see, and reduced the
woman to tears. "That," says Carolyn today, "was the most important
lesson I learned in that school."

On the other hand, when the white kids misbehaved, their punishment was to be sent down to the brown kids in the basement for a day.
"One boy stayed for a few weeks. We befriended him. He cried—and we
cried—when he finished his 'sentence' with us. We were not allowed to
play on their pretty playgrounds either. We entered our school from a
side door, and we played on a city street."

Her maternal grandmother and grandfather had been orphans, surviving by their wits in a Mexico bludgeoned by famine and deadly cycles
of typhus, and then terrorized by a merciless revolution. "My mother's
mother was fair skinned, with some real Spanish in her; her father, on the
other hand, was pure indigenous—small, muscular, dark." They found
each other in Michoacán, where they married and lived until American
companies began recruiting Mexicans to come north and build the railways that crisscross Kansas. Between 1900 and 1930, tens of thousands
of Mexican workers flooded into the state to lay tracks, erect stations,
and create some of the most prominent railroad junctions in the American Midwest. In time they brought their families. "So, my mother was
born in Kansas, delivered by her own father in a boxcar where they made
their home. She was the tenth of their eleven children."

Eventually Carolyn's grandfather would fall victim to the punishing work of laying track. One day, he was found doubled over with
what seemed to be a hernia; the company doctors decided to perform
exploratory surgery immediately. They did so without anesthesia, simply strapping him to a table, butchering him, and leaving him there to
die. "Mexicans would do much of the work to build Kansas," Carolyn

recounts sadly, "but they were not regarded as fully human." Widowed now, her grandmother left Kansas and moved with her troop of children to East Chicago, where her sons found work at the steel mills. Carolyn's mother, a mere teenager, soon married Carolyn's father, a steelworker, and they proceeded to raise a family in that relentlessly gray boom-town whose factory walls screamed the company trademark—Inland Steel—and whose towering stacks pumped fat spires of endless black into the sky.

Carolyn's father had been born in California, but by the time he was four, a fire had consumed the house and the family was suddenly home-less. With no choice but to leave, they landed in East Chicago, where an aunt with spare rooms took them in and the steel mills welcomed their labor. Come the 1929 Depression, however, the Curiels—along with nearly two million other Mexicans, including American-born citizens like Carolyn's father—suddenly found themselves back in Mexico. Most had been banished by force, ripped from their homes and sent back with nothing; Carolyn's grandfather, most likely anticipating that indignity, took his wife and children away before the trucks could come for them.

But life in Mexico soon became intolerable. Circumstances were such that as soon as Carolyn's father reached five, he was put to work. At twelve, he would be made to labor in the silver mines in the mountains that ring Puerto Vallarta, or deliver mail by burro to houses in nearby villages. Years later, as a teenager, when he tried to join the Mexican army, he was summarily ordered to renounce his American citizenship; he decided to return to the United States instead. He had received word that the steel mills had resumed hiring Mexicans, and so he made his way to Brownsville, Texas, where employment ads lured him back to Indiana.

By then, East Chicago had enjoyed a long romance with Mexican workers. It had begun at the very beginning of the twentieth century, when workers' unions began making demands for higher wages and bet-ter conditions, and Inland Steel—the largest steel mill in the world—let it be known that they would seek Mexicans to fill the jobs. Thousands responded, rushing to Indiana to apply for the openings, eventually making Inland the largest employer of Mexicans in the nation. With little or no command of the language, the new hires were unaware that they were "scabs," and didn't learn it until they were in the factories, having crossed picket lines and invited a blistering white anger. Some of them walked off when they understood why they had been called to the factories; most, desperate for work and far from home, stayed.

Inland managers would stand at the company's portals, admitting only the lighter-skinned applicants, aiming to blur the color line and ease racial tensions among the workers. One of the managers was reported to have said, "When I hire Mexicans at the gate, I pick out the lightest among them. No, it isn't that the lighter-colored ones are any better workers, but the darker ones are like the niggers." Meaning that they weren't wanted in the community. Meaning that skin color had become a job qualification and whiteness a desirable skill. All the same, light skinned or no, the Mexicans were put in segregated housing, their children made to attend "Mexican schools."

The segregated school that Carolyn attended as a child was like any of a legion across America. Most were in California and Texas, but they proliferated throughout the Southwest, mainly in agricultural areas, with a smattering in the industrial towns that laced the Midwest. Carolyn's school, Our Lady of Guadalupe, was run by nuns and consisted of four basement rooms, accessed via a steep staircase. There, a Mexican child would be given a sobering view of her place in the caste system. These were improvised schools, organized for shifting populations and subject to local prejudices, and there is little documentation on them beyond personal memories such as Carolyn's—or the lawsuits tenacious Mexican American parents would bring to seek a way out of the suffocating injustices.

Most Americans are familiar with the movement that produced *Brown v. Board of Education* in 1954 and the steady, determined struggle to end segregated schooling for blacks. The images of six-year-old Ruby Bridges in New Orleans and the Little Rock Nine in Arkansas, quietly bulldozing the racial barriers thrown up by the likes of Alabama governor George Wallace ("Segregation now, segregation tomorrow, and segregation forever!"), are vivid and indelible in the collective American memory. But few history books tell of the compelling case that actually preceded and influenced that ruling: *Mendez v. Westminster*, filed in a US District Court in 1946, in which five Mexican American families, led by Gonzalo and Felicitas Mendez, sued the school district in the Los Angeles suburb of Westminster, California, for segregating their children and relegating them to a substandard education in wretched conditions.

Sylvia Mendez, the child of a Mexican father and a black Puerto Rican mother, had been all of nine years old when she told her parents that she wished she could play on the pretty playground for white children. Every day, the community school bus would drop her off at the white elementary school in Westminster—a handsome building with manicured grounds and a beautifully appointed playground—but she was not allowed to access it. Instead, she would walk down the street to her Mexican school, two hastily constructed wooden shacks on a dirt lot next to a cow pasture. When Sylvia told her parents that she longed to play where the white kids played, they listened. But when Mr. Mendez's sister—a light-skinned Mexican with a French surname—managed to get Sylvia's cousin into that white school, they were stunned by the brazen inequity. Sylvia's father, Gonzalo, a reasonably well-off restaurant owner who had leased a nearby vegetable farm, soon hired a lawyer and took the Westminster school system to federal court.

At the time, California laws expressly allowed the segregation of certain racial groups—blacks, Chinese, and Japanese, for instance—but Mexicans were not listed among them. School officials argued that segregation for Mexicans was not racial but linguistic, for purposes of remedial learning. It was a flimsy defense, since children were not being herded into "Mexican schools" depending on any assessment of their individual language abilities, but by surname and skin color. There were plenty of youngsters in those classrooms who spoke English as well as any white child. And yet the white opposition in Westminster was fierce; they wanted no dark-skinned, Mexican–Puerto Rican youngster sitting next to their children, regardless of ability. Similar cases fighting this hidebound racism had been brought and tried in Colorado, Texas, and California from 1914 through 1931, and each time, school districts had maintained precisely what the school officials in Westminster were arguing: that the segregation was not being carried out in contravention of any law but for the good of the Mexican children. The school superintendents and their boards simply knew what was best for their community. It was segregation by custom (de facto), not by sanction (de jure), and so a court case was moot, they had claimed.

But to Gonzalo Mendez, who was determined to do right by his daughter, the precedents were compelling. In the 1914 case in Alamosa, Colorado, a town with deep Mexican roots, for instance, Mexicanos had argued that segregating their children was against the law, since Colorado's constitution prohibited schools from classifying children according to race. In a patently disingenuous response, the Alamosa School Board countered that, in fact, the children were white, which meant that the separation couldn't possibly be based on race. Even so, the presiding judge declared the discrimination to be flagrantly racist and illegal. But the win had little effect on other school boards in the region.

Instead, in 1930 in Corpus Christi, Mexican American taxpayers moved to halt the construction of a school that would perpetuate the segregation of their children. But officials argued that Texas law granted Texas authorities the power to construct schools as they deemed necessary and to manage students according to their "pedagogical expertise." A sympathetic judge ruled on behalf of the Mexicans, emphasizing that educational institutions should not separate youngsters from their peers, whatever their color. However, an appellate court soon reversed the decision, upholding the whites' desires.

It was hardly surprising. Texan officials had been barring Mexicanos from public facilities, eating establishments, theaters, churches, and cemeteries for nearly a century. They prohibited military burials for the remains of decorated war veterans. They denied active soldiers entry to pool halls. To add insult to injury, during the hot Texan summers, Mexicanos were allowed to use public swimming pools only for a few hours at the end of a week—after which the pools would be drained and refilled for the whites. Even into the 1960s, long after the days when

Texas Rangers would maraud Mexican properties, murder the residents, and fight an undeclared war that historians have called "tantamount to state-sanctioned terrorism," the silver-screen image of the noble white Ranger and the "dirty Mexican" persisted. Why would they treat schools any differently?

Another important case would emerge in 1931, in Lemon Grove, California, a small community outside San Diego. As with the Corpus Christi proceedings, a community of Mexican Americans rose up to protest the plan to build a segregated Mexican school for their families. The official arguments were the same: the children would be better off; remedial language training was necessary; they would "Americanize" sooner if they were shuttered away to work on it. But the judge disagreed, this time paying no attention to the "pedagogical expertise" of the superintendent and school board. For him, it was manifestly obvious that a Spanish-speaking child would acclimate faster and more completely in an English-speaking classroom; and besides, many Mexican youngsters had a strong command of the language already. It was a resounding victory, but it was a local one, with no influence beyond the immediate community.

*Mendez v. Westminster* was entirely different. Bringing the case before a federal court, the Mendez family's lawyer filed a class-action lawsuit against four Orange County school districts in California, seeking an injunction that would force the schools to integrate. The school boards argued that children's public education was the business of the state, and federal courts had no jurisdiction over it. They brandished the old, threadbare claim that the object of a Mexican school was to segregate young Mexicanos for their own good. On March 18, 1946, the judge ruled that separating Mexican students was, in fact, anything but good for the children; he held that the rank insult of segregation had done little more than "foster antagonisms in the children and suggest inferiority among them where none exists." It was the first federal ruling to declare the segregation of Latino children unconstitutional. One year later, the ruling was upheld in a federal appeals court.

The message was now crystal clear and unequivocal: Sylvia's

wood-shack school was a travesty no child should have to suffer. By then, Governor Earl Warren—who would go on to be chief justice on the United States Supreme Court and lead the court into one of its most liberal periods—had pushed his state legislature to repeal any legal provision that permitted school segregation in California. The future towering Supreme Court justice Thurgood Marshall, then chief of the segregation-busting National Association for the Advancement of Colored People's Legal Defense and Educational Fund, helped write the NAACP's official letter supporting *Mendez*, and he would resuscitate it eight years later when arguing the historic 1954 *Brown v. Board of Education* case before the Supreme Court, with Chief Justice Earl Warren presiding. In a unanimous decision, the nine justices ruling on *Brown* would declare school segregation and the sham of "separate but equal" classrooms to be un-American and unconstitutional for any child, regardless of race.

And yet, in 1962, eight more years after that emphatic repudiation of racism, seven-year-old Carolyn Curiel would still be descending the steps to her basement classroom in Indiana, never to reach the pretty playground of the white students upstairs. It would take time for the segregation of Mexicans to truly be struck from the habit of the land. What Carolyn did reach eventually, though—given her drive, pluck, and mental acuity—was far prettier than a swing on a forbidden playground. The seats she would come to occupy speak to the industry of a little girl who dared to dream big in the shadow of a steel mill's smokestacks. Graduating from Purdue University, she went on to a successful career as a journalist, a seat on the editorial board of the *New York Times*, a job in the White House as the first Latina speechwriter for an American president, and, finally, to the honorific "Her Excellency" in her capacity as the United States ambassador to Belize.

# THE VIRUS OF LATINO COLORISM

> When we understand that none of us is pure, that we are all made of
> desire and imagination as much as of blood and bone, and that each
> of us is part Christian, part Jew, part Moor, part Caucasian, part black,
> part Indian, only then will we understand both the grandeur and vas-
> salage of Spain.
>
> —Carlos Fuentes, Mexican author, 1992

It needs to be said: Carolyn Curiel is proud of her Mexican roots and her
ability to rise above the scars of prejudice, but in a crowd of whites, she
would not stand out. In the strict American binary, she is white; but even
in the more fleshed-out spectrum of Spanish colonial *castas*, she would
be read as *blanca*. As social scientists tell us, we are not just the race we
see in the mirror or the race insisted on in our family legends; we are the
race people see when they pass us on the street. If this seems too fluid
and elusive a calculus, it is because it is. Self-perception is deceiving, particularly when it comes to skin color, and Latinos historically have been
unsure how to classify the color of their skin. Sometimes we need for
others to tell us what we are, as was the case with Javier Lizarzaburu of
Peru and the indigenous declaration imprinted on his face, or Mario Álvarez of the Dominican Republic and the black assertion telegraphed by
his skin. "We are all men of La Mancha," the eminent Mexican author
Carlos Fuentes once wrote, using a word—*mancha*—that signifies a region of Spain, but also means "blemish." We are people of the stain. Or,
as the old joke goes, like bananas, we Latinos eventually show our black
spots. We are mutable, uncertain creatures, protean in our very selves—
the bewildered offspring of centuries of cross-fertilization and chance.

Take this simple contradiction: in 2010 more than 50 percent of all
Latinos responding to the US Census claimed they were white; 80 percent
even described their skin as occupying the lighter side of the spectrum—
from ivory to wheat. One-third said they were "some other race," an
"opt-out" category that has begun to have serious data-processing consequences for social programs constructed to benefit specific ethnicities.

And yet, only ten years later, in the 2020 census, Latinos changed their minds completely. Suddenly only 20 percent of us were white. The majority had decided to switch their color, now claiming they were "some other race." Not only that, but a third major category had emerged for Latinos: "two or more races." A full third of all Latinos, including those who had once registered as fully black, now identified themselves as being varying admixtures of white, indigenous, and black. Millions abandoned the fully "white" or fully "black" categories for more comfortable, more representative—and more ambiguous—sides of the ledger. In the course of a mere decade, the number of mixed-race Latinos had increased by almost 600 percent. Which is to say that we are beginning to register the mongrelization of races we truly represent.

Somehow, registering our own individual heterogeneity doesn't begin to fix the misapprehensions about us. Or even the delusions of our own. Start with the fact that the US Census Bureau depends on what *we* think our racial affiliation is, whether or not that self-perception has any viability in the wider world and the way others see us. There are plenty of us, like Javier Lizarzaburu, who arrive to this country thinking we're white until someone tells us we're not. Or, as the Dominican American poet Chiqui Vicioso has written: "Until I came to New York, I didn't know I was black." Then there are the misconceptions bandied about in the press or in halls of government, treating us as if we are a shared and measurable race—one human family—when, in truth, we are a multi-chrome ethnicity consisting of every conceivable shade of man. "The internet was bypassing blacks and some Hispanics as whites," the *New York Times* reports, "and Asian Americans were rapidly increasing their use of it." And yet Hispanics may very well count themselves white, black, or Asian American, so the *Times*'s numbers about the internet in this report are doomed from the start. Similarly, Fox News will announce that "Achievement gaps between white and black and Hispanic students remain," ignoring the fact that we can be either white or black, so any attempt to measure "Hispanic achievement" with any accuracy is bound to yield flawed results. Adding the singularly uninformative "other race" to a questionnaire only clouds the issues further: what can a pollster or social scientist possibly conclude from such information? The most egregious, and all too common practice is to lump us all under the rubrics "brown" or "people of color," which muddies the reality completely.

Marco A. Davis, now the president of the Congressional Hispanic Caucus Institute in Washington, DC, and a New York–born Afro-Latino himself, tells me that he has begun to wonder why we don't simply go ahead and call ourselves a "race" on the US census, even if, categorically speaking, we are not. There is a certain logic to what he says: if—as Davis reasons and science corroborates—the concept of race is a social construct, distilled into a one-drop rule and utilized by the United States to further racist policies, one sees how arbitrarily the designation has been employed. There is no comprehensive scientific data behind "blackness" or "Asian-ness" or "whiteness," and yet these labels continue to be used in government polls. So why couldn't Latinos be a "race" just as the others are (arbitrarily) designated "races" in the census? The effect of diluting us to an "ethnicity," complicating the process of self-identification and forcing the population to define itself under other labels, has very real, societal effects: any statistics involving law enforcement, police brutality, the criminal justice system, educational attainment, discrimination, economic success or peril, among many others are not tracked for Latinos. (Asian Americans do not have the same issue and are tracked as one race, although there are equally stark phenotypical differences between, say, a Pakistani, a Filipino, and a Han Chinese.) The end result of these misperceptions and misallocations is that Hispanics vanish from the picture entirely. "We become erased from the American experience," says Davis, when, in truth, we represent a massive population with important statistics of our own.

Today, as the largest and most diversified ethno-racial group in the United States—as the very essence of the American melting pot—we are positioned to reshape the meaning of human color, or perhaps the relevance of racial benchmarks at all. As Junot Díaz said to me, "We're here to forge a new path, fight the binary." Or as one prominent Latino historian once put it, in our singular dynamic of race inclusion and absorption, we "will inevitably change America from within." To be Latino, in other words, may be to serve as a transformational template for the whole society.

But any celebration of our racial mix is often fraught with nuances of racism itself. When José Vasconcelos, the 1920s philosopher, called Mexicans *la raza cósmica*—the cosmic race—he meant it as a compliment, an advantage, even a grand and manifest destiny. As the thinking went, a largely mestizo population was a national virtue, quintessentially Mexican. If Mexico were to continue its five-hundred-year experiment in multiraciality—fusing brown with black and white and creating what Nixon might have called a "vanilla" people—eventually the colored masses would rise to a higher rung on the dreaded ladder of *las castas*, and racism would be rendered moot, inconceivable.

But there was a problem with this "progressive" thinking. It was in perfect alignment with the old racist trope, *"hay que mejorar la raza"*: we need to whiten the race. *Mejorando la raza* had already had a bad start in the conquistadors' rape and pillage of the indigenous and the enslavement and ravishing of blacks. In striving to lighten the generations, the unmistakable message of the Latin American elite was clear: white was better, white culture would prevail, and, in time, blackness and indigenousness would recede and disappear completely. The 1895 census in Argentina encapsulated that thought in a chilling few words: "It will not take long for the population to be completely unified into a beautiful new white race!" More than a century later, there are still many Latin Americans who think that way. Were Vasconcelos alive today, he might be shocked to learn just how gripped by colorism his beloved Mexico still is.

## THE COLOR OF LANGUAGE

> My father made the decision to deprive me of a language (Spanish) in
> a sense to cut out my tongue. But he was not stupid. He understood
> this country, he respected the weight of its racism.
> —Cecile Pineda, novelist, Chicana, 1996

For many scholars who study the question, the business of pursuing full *mestizaje*—a complete blending of the races—carries the veiled stench of white supremacy. And yet, more blending is precisely what is happening to American Latinos. Not only do Latinos begin to lose their Spanish language proficiency by the third generation in this country, but also they begin to lose themselves in the general population of whites. By the fourth generation, only half of the people with Hispanic ancestry say they are Hispanic. Whereas in the 1980s and 1990s Latino numbers were rising because of a veritable tsunami of Latin American immigrants, by the 2000s, it was US-born Latinos who were the dominant drivers of growth. American Latinos were simply begetting more Latinos. Between 2000 and 2010, almost ten million Hispanic births were recorded, while the number of newly arrived immigrants from Latin America declined; during that decade, only six million entered the country. The overall immigrant numbers are still falling. Which is to say that the majority of Latinx today are American-born citizens. And within this vast majority, Latinos are increasingly likely to marry across ethnic lines. Perhaps because of our long history of *mestizaje*, we are the Americans most disposed to mix it up. A full 40 percent of Latinos born in this country marry non-Latinos. Those who have earned a college education are even more likely to do so; half of all Hispanics with a bachelor's degree marry outside the cohort. And the overwhelming likelihood is that they will marry whites.

To put it bluntly, little has changed since the conquest. It is now as it ever was and seemingly ever will be: in these Americas, a fierce colorism persists, and whitening the race continues to be concomitant with upward mobility.

I am reminded of an afternoon when I was in my parents' house, puttering about their kitchen, preparing some favorite *plato criollo*—Peruvian dish—for my father, when he suddenly asked me: "Why aren't you whiter? *Cómo llegaste a ser tan morena*, so dark?" It was more than forty years after we had moved to the United States; he was eighty-four years old and a great deal darker than I. He had never said anything like that to me in my life. I turned to look at him in surprise, but he only shook his head in disbelief. "I look at your mother with her porcelain skin and her light-blue eyes, and I wonder where all that went in you."

It is quite true; I am unmistakably Latina. Like 75 percent of foreign-born Hispanics, I am certain that anyone walking past me on the street would recognize me as such. Indeed, I am constantly stopped by people addressing me in Spanish and wanting directions or simply offering a polite greeting. People see me and call me María, even though it is not my name. But by the time more generations of my descendants roll around—my grandchildren, for instance, all of whom have Anglo surnames—it is very likely that my all-too-obvious Latino genes may not hold their ground. According to the Pew Research Center, third-generation Latinos are not convinced that anyone on the street will guess their ethnicity correctly. Only half believe they display physical manifestations of their Latinidad. And, although almost 20 percent of all people in this country identify openly as Hispanic, there is another 11 percent of Americans with Hispanic ancestry who, for one reason or another, are reticent to wear the mantle. My daughter, who is as fair as my mother and never learned Spanish, tells me she feels like an impostor claiming Latinx roots on a questionnaire. I wish my brown father were still alive, still sitting at his kitchen table, still blissfully unworried about his genes disappearing into a white slipstream, so that we could talk about that.

# 6

# THE COLOR LINE

There are green-eyed Mexicans. The rich blond Mexicans. The Mexicans with the faces of Arab sheiks. The Jewish Mexicans. The big-footed-as-a-German Mexicans. The leftover-French Mexicans. The *chaparrito* compact Mexicans. The Tarahumara tall-as-desert saguaro Mexicans. The Mediterranean Mexicans. The Mexicans with Tunisian eyebrows. The *negrito* Mexicans of the double coasts. The Chinese Mexican. The curly haired, freckle-faced, redheaded Mexicans. The Lebanese Mexicans. Look, I don't know what you're talking about when you say I don't look Mexican. I *am* Mexican.

—Sandra Cisneros, author, Mexican American, 2002

## WHITENESS

The perennial question I face: "You're Hispanic? But you don't *really* think of yourself as Hispanic, do you?" White Hispanic Americans like me remain an anomaly to North Americans. We just don't fit the mold.

—Don Podesta, journalist, Chilean American, 1997

Almost a year after the article appeared in *Variety*, Valeria Meiller was still outraged by the reporter's characterization of the subject at hand. Anya Taylor-Joy, the prodigiously talented, alabaster-skinned, blonde, Latina star of the silver screen had just won a Golden Globe Award for her role in the television miniseries *The Queen's Gambit*, and the writer's depiction of her was nothing short of jaw-dropping. "Argentinian Taylor-Joy is the first woman of color to win this category since Queen Latifah in 2008," the reporter declaimed breathlessly, "and only the fifth woman of color to win overall since 1982, when the category was introduced." It was an astonishing blunder, a strikingly tone-deaf description of one small niche of Latino ethnicity. For the Argentine Tailor-Joy is, in any sane reckoning, white.

White Latinos—descendants of 100 percent white European stock—are not people of color. And they certainly cannot be compared to Queen Latifah or Diana Ross or Whoopi Goldberg, or any of the other icons of diversity who had won the award in the past. *Variety* was forced to make a hasty correction, and Taylor-Joy herself seemed to apologize, "I'm aware of the fact I don't look like a typical Latin person, and that it's not fair." As if that weren't enough, she added that she hadn't been comfortable auditioning for Latina roles because, being as white as she is, the casting never seemed right. She didn't feel she could represent the ethnicity. In other words, the gaffe had thrust her into an existential bind: not only had *Variety* gotten her DNA wrong, but also it had made her doubt her legitimacy, period.

For Valeria Meiller, the mistake was personal. Like Taylor-Joy, she had grown up in Buenos Aires, a descendant of British ancestors, yet raised in a Spanish-speaking ambit. Like the actress, she had spent her youth in a lavish family hacienda, riding impeccably groomed horses, a child of privilege. Both hailed from white Argentine families, whose lineage—like the majority of their fellow citizens—is overwhelmingly European. Like Taylor-Joy, Valeria is blonde, alabaster skinned, in her twenties, and enchantingly warm and effusive. Like her, she is a US Latina building a successful career in this country. And, like her, she arrived speaking perfect "U," or "upper-class" London English.

Valeria's great-grandfather immigrated to Argentina in the late nineteenth century, just as hundreds of thousands of white Europeans were being welcomed to populate, transform, and "civilize" the country. Eventually one hundred thousand British immigrants would join the influx of Swiss, Italians, and Germans who were disembarking daily on the docks of Buenos Aires. In the century that separated 1850 from 1950, six million Europeans would pour into Argentina—among them the parents of the first Latin American pope, Jorge Mario Bergoglio—and be met with generous civic assistance in finding work, lodging, medical care, and enviable tracts of land. They were wanted.

In order to clear space for them, General Julio Argentina Roca, a beloved national hero and statesman, ordered a cold-blooded genocide of the Mapuche people in the Rio Azul Valley, the very valley where Valeria's family would establish their grand estancia: a handsome, sprawling, profitable cattle ranch and farm. Argentines persist in calling the purge "the Campaign in the Desert," a sorry euphemism for the murder and exile of an entire people. Indeed, schoolchildren have been taught to see Roca's "campaign" as the dawn of Argentina's metamorphosis into a modern world power. Genocides of similar proportion were carried out in Chile and Paraguay in the 1800s, two more countries whose indigenous populations were "reduced" to make room for white immigration. There are fewer than five hundred thousand Latinos from these countries inhabiting the United States; a tiny 0.5 percent of the vast mixed-race population of Latino Americans. And yet they occupy the very highest rungs of our middle class.

Valeria didn't learn the truth about what she calls her "whitewashed country" until she began college in Buenos Aires. Today Valeria is married to a half-Anglo, half-Jewish American and looks back at her coddled childhood in Argentina with a cold eye. "I've come to terms with it," she tells me. "We are a white supremacist culture." And, indeed, 97 percent of her fellow Argentinians are white (compared with the 75 percent of all Americans who identify as white in the United States); the millions of indigenous who once inhabited that region are now reduced to 2 percent; and, although in the early 1800s blacks represented one-third of the denizens of a brimming Buenos Aires, today they amount to less than 1 percent of the population of the entire country.

"Whatever happened to them?" Valeria asks. "There is zero aware-ness of the erasure. The scholars doing the work of resuscitating that history are people of color from other countries. In Argentina, we're simply taught that the indigenous all died of yellow fever," she says. "So few are doing the work of unearthing the real truth. Maybe it's because all our intellectuals are sent off to be educated somewhere else: England, France, Spain, Italy. They don't want anything to do with Latin Ameri-can culture. You know the old joke that Argentines are Spanish-speaking Italians who believe that they're really French? It's so true." And thus, as far as Valeria is concerned, for the American media to consider Anya Taylor-Joy—a blonde, white Hollywood star from Argentina—a person of color seems a sick joke of hallucinatory proportions. But she does not laugh. As the Guatemalan American novelist and journalist Hector Tobar writes in his deeply perceptive memoir, *Our Migrant Souls,* "Our relationship as Latinos to whiteness is the tragedy and comedy of us."

• • •

In a time when "minority representation" in the workplace is a high pri-ority, being white and Latino has become a favorable combination. An-other Guatemalan American who works at an employment agency tells me: "It's a win-win situation. Administrators get to check the diversity box, but they get a white person, just like them." For decades, brown His-panics have watched the prize jobs, the top Ivy League spots, the fancy apartments, and choice artistic opportunities go to their whiter broth-ers and sisters. As one educational consultant observed when he was asked whether Hispanics were admitted to Yale University: "Of course Yale accepts Hispanic Americans. The reason you don't 'see' them is be-cause you're looking for brown people." Certainly, light-skinned Latinos are preferred in Hollywood, too: Antonio Banderas, who is Spanish and white, is cast as a murderous Mexican in *Desperado,* his skin darkened for the role. And it is the preferred skin tone in the corridors of power: Mexican American Carolyn Curiel recalls that when she served tempo-rarily on the editorial board of the *New York Times,* "the only other La-tino at the table was a blond, blue-eyed Argentine." But nowhere is this colorism more evident than in negotiating ordinary life: Carolina Santa

Cruz, a successful, white Latina businesswoman, leaves her Afro-Latino husband behind when she goes looking to rent a house, lest they be told that the place is no longer available.

Whiteness has been a winning ticket in American ports of entry, too. For fifty years, from 1966 until 2017, border officers processing incomers gave white Cubans special privileges. Immigration officials would hurry them past the Central Americans or Caribbean blacks. Whereas the darker aspirants were packed in detention cells and deported, or ordered to appear in immigration courts, the Cubans moved through effortlessly, most of them in less than an hour. After weeks of grueling travel through Panama, Costa Rica, and Mexico, some were stunned by the ease with which they were whisked into the United States. If they were "dry foot" (those who entered on land), they were waved through; if they were "wet foot" (apprehended at sea), they were returned to Cuba. Once past the gates, they were welcomed by special advocacy groups and—if they had walked in from Mexico—given free airfare to Miami. They were offered federal welfare benefits, English lessons, and financial assistance for a minimum of nine months. After a year, they could apply for permanent residency, the golden gateway to American citizenship. Once they were citizens, they advanced handily into the American middle class. Why? Border officials explained routinely that it was because Cubans were fleeing a broken, totalitarian state. But so were the brown people. The only plausible explanations were because they were walking proof of Fidel Castro's failures—and because they were white.

•  •  •

Lissette Méndez's American beginning was a chaotic voyage over a wind-tossed sea, yet she weathered it to become one of the pillars of Miami's cultural life. She was eight years old when her widowed mother pulled her from bed in the black of night, hurried her to the seashore, squeezed her onto a crowded boat, and brought her to America in the Mariel boat lift. It was April 1980, and when all was said and done, 125,000 desperate, sun-scorched Cubans had stumbled through Florida's ports of entry with Lissette.

Her maternal grandparents had been humble, door-to-door tailors

in Havana, immigrant Jews with ancestral roots in Belarus; her deceased
father's family were Cubans of Spanish origin who had inhabited the
island for many generations. Now she and her mother were leaving that
history behind to be met by an uncle and deposited in a hard-knock
neighborhood of Miami Beach. Somehow they found the mettle to survive. "We were poor," Lissette tells me. "The white Cuban establishment in Miami didn't want anything to do with us. We were white, but
we weren't like them—affluent, entitled, with their big houses and cars.
They had bought into the propaganda that we Marielitos were undesirables, jailbirds, mental cases. There were only six or eight kids in my
school who spoke Spanish, and we were regularly beat up on the playground."

Lissette's mother eventually found work in a supermarket. She
cleaned buildings, took odd jobs, did what she could. It wasn't long before Lissette decided to change her persona entirely, inhabit her new
American identity, leave Cuba truly behind. "I did everything possible
to strip away my *Cubanidad*," she says. She had been raised a Marxist
and a Jew, two creeds scorned by the overwhelmingly conservative,
anti-Communist Cubans of Miami. Her scant eight years in Havana had
infused her with Socialist values—a painstakingly taught rhetoric of
equality, fairness, and racial justice. It was that sympathy for the under-
dog, perhaps, that led her to feel utterly disconnected from the prosperous Miami Cubans—she wanted to cut all emotional ties with the exile
community and shuck the identity altogether. If she felt any affiliation
at all, it was as a newly minted American; or it was with the Haitians,
the truly marginalized in her newly adopted city. There was something
about them that reminded her of the playful precincts of Cuba where
creole was spoken, voodoo was practiced, and music was an agent of
freedom.

All the same, once she dropped out of high school and entered the
workforce, Lissette got a strong dose of reality about her whiteness. She
had passed her GED equivalency exam and, somewhat miraculously,
been hired as a secretary at an international bank catering to rich Latin
American moguls. Her goal was to pay her own way through college.

The bank's managers hired her on the spot. "In my gut, I could see that they liked me because I was white." She hadn't been particularly equipped for the job; her skin struck her as her only true qualification. Listening to her say this, I can't help but object. I suggest that she might have been hired for her youth, her beauty, her effervescence, her natural intelligence, her easy command of Spanish. "But more than anything," she shoots back firmly and without hesitation, "it was the *whiteness*. That rankled me."

Like Lissette, a full 85 percent of Cuban Americans in Miami are white. And they are more European white than "Mexican white." When the first wave of fugitives began to arrive in the late 1950s—even before Fidel Castro's revolution could claim victory—they were chiefly upper class, fleeing the Red scourge, in fear of imminent, anticapitalist retributions. The Cuba that has remained after three subsequent waves of migration is now largely black, although Havana claims otherwise. According to Cuban census officials, the island is 65 percent white. To give those officials the benefit of the doubt, light-skinned mulattos may well register as white because they don't consider themselves black—Latin American perceptions of skin color can be very fluid. But the US State Department, judging from a more American (and, so, strictly binary and one-drop) frame of reference, flips that percentage completely. By its reckoning, Cuba is two-thirds black. Some scholars posit that the share is probably closer to 72 percent. One thing is sure: in the course of the past seven decades, the country has undergone a "white flight" like none other. Even the postapartheid white abandonment of South Africa can't compare.

The brain drain and financial runoff that accompanied Cuba's white flight was swift and ruinous, but there is little doubt that it allowed for a sweeping Communist overhaul and enormous opportunities for humbler citizens. As the historian Ada Ferrer has documented, of the six thousand doctors who were practicing in Cuba just before Fidel Castro marched into Havana in 1959, about half fled to the United States. As did a full seven hundred of Cuba's two thousand dentists. And, in a country that had so famously subsisted on its sugar, rum, and abundant farmlands, all but thirty of its agronomists took off for other pastures. By 1961, more than two-thirds of the faculty at the University of Havana had settled in Miami, and a mere seventeen professors of medicine stayed behind. The adjustment to American life was not always easy for this expatriate elite. Sacrifices had to be made. But America, as we all know, was built by freelancers. To keep food on the table, doctors become hospital orderlies, architects labor as gardeners, teachers as janitors, pharmacists as milkmen. Those who once luxuriated in majestic mansions in Havana or Santiago had to squeeze themselves into apartments in the down-and-out, mean streets of a district that eventually became known as Little Havana.

Black Miamians were not happy about the invasion. Overtown, the historic black district, sat just across the river from Little Havana, and its citizens could witness firsthand as Cubans, no matter their skin shade, began to be given privileges that were forbidden to blacks. As if, by some miracle, they had all become lily white. There were the vouchers for all-white hotels. Or the free access to Miami beaches. White-only schools began to choke with the influx of Cuban youngsters. The advantages would make for difficult relations between blacks and Cubans, perhaps not because of the arrivals themselves but because of the preferential treatment given them by the local government. "We're not angry at the Cubans," the head of the Miami Urban League insisted, "but at a system that will do more for outsiders than for its own citizens."

But the Cuban will to prevail was strong. Overnight, it seemed, the run-down streets of Little Havana began to see renewal. Soon small businesses, like the furniture store of Ralph de la Vega's childhood, began cropping up here and there. Strivers adapted to new trades. Businesses put out new signboards: there were coffee shops, photography studios, knickknack shops, domestic workers' agencies—a flurry of brand-new enterprises. By 1980, when Marielitos like Lissette rushed in, whole areas of the city would be transformed and the white Cuban presence established.

The Mariel boat lift was unlike any other Cuban exodus in that it did not bring a chiefly white, overwhelmingly upper-middle-class immigrant. Aboard those rickety, burdened fishing boats, there were no bosses with ready cash and heady connections. The Marielitos came as Lissette Méndez did: with only the shirts on their backs, some even without shoes. They were markedly poorer—the island's "human detritus," as Castro called them—uniformly shunned by Cuba's Communist brass. They were also blacker; up to 40 percent were Afro-Cubans. One Miami resident recalled how this new chapter of the exodus reframed his sense of who he was and where he had come from: "We had invented a Cuba in which everyone was white," he said. In other words, white like them. "When the Marielitos came, we were forcibly reminded that Cuba is not a white island but largely a black one."

Today there are about two and a half million residents of Cuban origin in the United States, the vast majority of them clustered together in Florida. They amount to more than a quarter of the population of Cuba itself: 250,000 souls more than all of Havana. By now, about half are native-born US citizens, and those who are function comfortably in any American setting and speak English fluently. But they are also passionate about maintaining the language of their homeland; almost 80 percent speak Spanish at home—a higher percentage than most segments of the Latino population. As such, they often serve as bridges between north and south business interests. Even after the Mariel infusion, Cuban Americans represent the wealthiest, most successful, most educated, and certainly whitest agglomeration of Latinos in this country. Many are established professionals and, as a whole, own more businesses than any other subset of Latinos. Almost 40 percent of those born here have a college or graduate school degree. Because they are congregated so densely in a geographical area, they tend to live in Cuban neighborhoods, shop in Cuban stores, buy Cuban products, and consume Cuban media. That solidarity makes for strong ethnic pride; it also serves to maintain the racism and sense of exceptionalism that Lissette Méndez has long repudiated.

But it cannot be denied: Cuban Americans have contributed much to the country's economy, culture, and civic life. Many have risen to considerable stature in the American wheel of fortune. From Jeff Bezos, the adopted son of a Cuban shop owner who became one of the richest men in the world, to Ralph de la Vega, the Pedro Pan boy who grew up to be a chief executive officer of AT&T, the stories of grit, ingenuity, and determination are legion. But business acumen is not these Latinos' only forte. They have met success in any number of professions: there are entertainers (among them, Gloria Estefan, Sammy Davis Jr., Desi Arnaz, Cameron Díaz, Eva Mendes, Andy García), literary figures (Cristina García, Oscar Hijuelos, Piri Thomas, Mirta Ojito, Carlos Eire, Nilo Cruz), television personalities (Soledad O'Brien and Cristina Saraluegi), athletes (Yordan Álvarez and Gilbert Arenas), and politicians (Florida senator Marco Rubio, Texas senator Ted Cruz, New Jersey senator Bob Menendez, Housing and Urban Development [HUD] Secretary Mel Martinez, Homeland Security Secretary Alejandro Mayorkas).

To this catalog of distinction, we can add feisty, determined Lissette Méndez, the eight-year-old sprite who braved a tempestuous sea, took her shots on the playground, paid her way through college, found her true calling as a serious reader, and rose to become the lead organizer of one of the most successful cultural events in the country. Today, in her capacity as the literary director of the Miami Book Fair, Lissette revels in bringing together English-, Spanish-, and Creole-language authors in an internationally recognized, annual celebration of diversity in books. If whiteness did indeed win her that first job, she has since offered the stage to a virtual spectrum of human color.

## BLACK LIKE US

> According to media by us or for us, dark-skinned Afro-Latinos do not exist, and if they do, they aren't Latino. Not *really*.
> —Karla Cornejo Villavicencio, author,
> Ecuadorian American, Connecticut, 2021

When Antonio Delgado was sworn in as lieutenant governor of New York on May 25, 2022, Governor Kathy Hochul declared him to be exactly what the state needed, an Afro-Latino who could combine the two largest

minority communities and help her address their needs. One in five New York-
ers, after all, is Latino. There was, at first, immediate joy among Latinos at his ascendancy—until the question arose: Sure, he's black, but just
how Latino is he, exactly? He had defeated two Latina candidates, and
people wanted to know. It didn't help that he didn't have a pat and ready
answer. His African American father had ancestors in Cape Verde, he explained, a Portuguese-speaking island nation off the west coast of Africa,
a former hub of the transatlantic slave trade. His grandmother's surname
was Gómez, but she had actually never met the father who gave her that
name, and he was Delgado's only apparent connection to Latino ancestry.
That long-departed, mysterious great-grandfather, according to Delgado,
was a vague combination of Mexican, Venezuelan, Colombian; no one
really seemed to know. Antonio Delgado may well have been a Harvard-
educated Rhodes scholar with a solid law degree and an unblemished stint
as a US congressman, but did he truly have the credentials to represent
Latinos? And so would it be correct to claim that he was the first Latino to
hold a statewide office in the great state of New York?

"I find it curious that those of us with black skin often have our Latino identity questioned," offered Representative Ritchie Torres of the
Bronx, who supported Delgado. "As an Afro-Latino, I have been told
repeatedly that I do not look Latino, whatever that means, and therefore,
I must be less authentically Latino than those with lighter skin." But an
Afro-Latina professor of Caribbean Studies stepped up to say she understood the questions about Delgado's bona fides and his ability to speak
for Latinos: representation was about "authentically" living and understanding his constituents' experiences and needs, she told the *New York
Times*, not about "checking a box" just because your name is Hispanic.

Such are the complications of being Afro-Latino in a binary world.
By imposing "black or white" shibboleths of belonging and a strict one-
drop rule—false binaries unique to this country—all nuance goes missing. If Lieutenant Governor Delgado identifies as Latino, if he wants to
own that ancestral past however faded and forgotten it may be, shouldn't
he be allowed to? On the other hand, can an Afro-Latino boy be blamed
for a country that—given its long, violent history of racism—doesn't see

culture, only sees color, and pushes him to identify as black exclusively? Who gets to judge how Latino we are? As the novelist Junot Díaz puts it, "We've been laboring too long under 'elite capture' of who we are. We need to decolonize ourselves from their binary. I'm not here to play into anyone's categorical anxieties."

For all the assumptions about what it takes to "look Latino," of the sixty-three million Latinos who inhabit this country, six million identify as Afro-Latino. These *hermanos* and *hermanas* tend to be concentrated on the East Coast or in the South—New York, California, and Florida—and are more apt to be born on other shores, especially in Puerto Rico, the Dominican Republic, or Cuba. They are less inclined to have college educations and more likely to have lower incomes. "Double discrimination"—both as blacks and as Hispanics—is experienced by more than two-thirds of their number, and they are far more likely to be stopped by police than their nonblack Latino friends. And yet many have gone on to command extraordinary careers: musical superstar Mariah Carey, for instance, whose father is Afro-Venezuelan; the late television news anchor Gwen Ifill, whose father was Panamanian; New York Mets shortstop Francisco Lindor, a Puerto Rican; and Harlem Renaissance historian Arturo Schomburg or activist poet Felipe Luciano, both of whom were also Puerto Rican.

But to call oneself Afro-Latino is not necessarily to identify as black. Paradoxically, when it comes to pinpointing race, the great majority describe themselves as white or scribble into the margin "Hispanic," even though, according to the US Census Bureau, Hispanic is not a racial category. Only one in four Afro-Latinos actually call themselves black, embrace the full race, and check that box. In real numbers, that boils down to a scant 2 percent of the entire American population. And, given the pressures imposed by America's strict binary on race—pressures felt, perhaps, by Lieutenant Governor Antonio Delgado and his parents—more than half choose to live as black Americans and not stress their Latino identity at all.

For some, this is the frightening specter of erasure. In 2000, for instance, only 12 percent of Puerto Ricans registered as black, even though the vast majority has roots in African ancestry. Eight out of ten called themselves white. "Based on the current rate," one Puerto Rican scholar lamented, "Afro-Puerto Ricans will statistically disappear at the end of the current century. This has happened in Argentina and Mexico, where leadership in both countries publicly stated that they have no black populations despite the presence of very active black organizations fighting for political inclusion. We are witnessing the beginning of statistical genocide." The organization Colectivo Ilé was formed precisely to arrive at a more granular count of Puerto Rican blacks and battle that erasure. Don't let the feds cancel you, they exhorted Boricuas, whether they were on the mainland or in the Caribbean. How can we fight institutional racism—how can we rectify the obvious injustices—if we don't even identify as black? Claiming to be "a little bit of everything," as Puerto Ricans do, was causing serious sociopolitical consequences. Twenty years later, in 2020, despite the aggressive campaign mounted by Colectivo Ilé and other activist institutions, the black count dropped dramatically among Puerto Ricans, but the category of "other" jumped from 3 percent to 50 percent.

The surprising data on how we Latinos perceive ourselves are reflections of the complex histories we carry. It is why census forms can be so bewildering. How to be honest or accurate? Very often, like Javier Lizarzaburu, who left Peru as a white man and returned as an *indio*, the color we feel ourselves to be is not the color we are. Very often, like chameleons, we take on the ambient color of our immediate surroundings. "When I'm in the Dominican Republic, I'm white," says Mario Álvarez, shaking his head, "and when I'm in the United States, I'm black."

It shouldn't be surprising that a full quarter of us claim a blood quantum of blackness, given that the overwhelming number of black Africans abducted by the transatlantic slave trade were dispatched to Latin America or the Caribbean. Of the ten million captives who survived the journey, 97 percent were delivered to points south of the Rio Grande. The greatest number—a staggering five million—were sent to colonies in the Caribbean; 3.5 million were pulled off boats in Brazil; and 650,000 souls were force-marched to servitude in Spanish South America— largely Venezuela, Colombia, and the Guyanas. As for the United States, a mere 366,000, or 3 percent, were sold in slave markets scattered along the North American coasts, from New Orleans, to Charleston, North Carolina, to Newport, Rhode Island. So, the sheer magnitude of the calamitous slave trade in the Spanish colonies accounts for the generous fraction of Afro-Latinos here today. Most Latinos were (if we study the phenotypical evidence and look at the long scourge of history) raped into being at some point in their ancestral past. To quote Junot Díaz once more: "What brought me to the New World was my blackness. As my grandfather in the DR used to say, '*Hijo*, look out at those sugar fields. That's why we're here.' No one in my family didn't wield a machete."

The Puerto Rican author Esmeralda Santiago sees it from another perspective. Clearly, she is one of the Afro-Latinos who doesn't pigeonhole herself as black. "The United States is so obsessed with labels," she tells me. "My dad was black, my mom was white, but I think of myself as Puerto Rican. A Boricua. I don't think of myself as a skin color." But the history fascinates her all the same: the earliest document the family can produce is a Spanish *lista de esclavos*—a list of slaves. (The Spanish were nothing if not meticulous about colonial records.) Her paternal great-grandfather's name is memorialized there: Juan Díaz, a slave whose family toiled on a Puerto Rican sugar plantation for generations. Black is not all they were; Esmeralda's paternal grandmother was part indigenous, descended from a Taíno Indian. "They called him *el indio salvaje*." As capricious as Latino histories can be, Esmeralda's mother's family hailed from the other side of servitude. Her grandparents arrived in Puerto Rico from the lush, green, mountain coast of Asturias, Spain. They were flush with wealth, ambitious, Catholic. How a girl—the descendant of a rich, urban family from Spain—married a boy—the offspring of slaves from Puerto Rico's outback—is the story of our Latin American ancestry in a nutshell. As Mario Vargas Llosa once described that seemingly farfetched admixture: "The conquest of America was cruel, violent, as all conquests have been through time, and we must level a critical eye on its legacy, without forgetting that the perpetrators of those crimes and plunder were our own grandparents and great-grandparents." We are, in other words, inheritors of that collision, children of opposing legacies. And, so, a multitude of pigments courses through our veins.

## ASIAN LATINOS

> Sometimes Asians feel free to say derogatory, racist things about Latinos to me. That hurts.
> —Isabella Do-Orozco, college student, Wichita, Kansas, 2021

Isabella Do-Orozco, born in Wichita, is an undergraduate at the Massachusetts Institute of Technology (MIT), where my father did graduate work during World War II. Jorge Enrique Arana was at MIT because the university needed to fill classrooms emptied by a sweeping, rigorous wartime draft. The students who had gone off from MIT to battle, or to labor for the American war effort, were mostly white New Englanders. When V-J Day finally arrived in August 1945, and the hostilities were over, the white Americans returned, and all the Latin Americans—the "nonwhite" imports, like my father—took their degrees and went home. Today, however, three out of four MIT undergraduates are nonwhite Americans. One out of every three is of Asian extraction; one out of six is Hispanic. A universe of transmutation has transpired in the seventy-seven years that separate Isabella's college experience from my father's.

Isabella counts herself as neither entirely Latina nor Asian. She is both. Like 1 percent of the Hispanic population—a tiny subset amounting to a scant six hundred thousand people—she is Asian Latina, the child of a Vietnamese father and a Mexican mother. Her father was born in war-torn Vietnam in 1971, just as the Communist Vietcong were making startling advances against American and South Vietnamese forces. The US military decided to "Vietnamize" the war and hazard a gradual withdrawal, intensifying antiwar sentiments among the troops and bankrupting morale. The commanding American general on the ground had just warned that, given Washington's declining financial support for the conflict, the United States might as well "write off South Vietnam as a bad investment and broken promise."

Four years later, with Saigon having fallen and the Communists in full command of the country, Pat Dinh Do's parents snatched him from his bed and fled into the night, determined to smuggle their little family out of the grim detritus of war. Pat's father, a civil engineer, had compromised himself by providing detailed plans of Vietnam's cities to American military officers; he had no choice but to leave or face the Vietcong's notorious retributions: to be buried alive with his family or clubbed to death by a marauding brigade. With a retinue of eighteen relatives, the Dos made the long trek to the city of Da Nang, where they joined a massive exodus that became known as the Vietnamese boat people. It was a harrowing journey. More than a million desperate souls were abandoning South Vietnam to toss their fortunes to the vagaries of the South China Sea. Preyed upon by pirates and buffeted by tropical storms, thousands of flimsy wooden fishing boats—some no more than thirty feet long and laden with dozens of panic-stricken refugees—braved the hundreds of miles to imagined safe havens on the neighboring shores of Malaysia, Thailand, or Hong Kong. Many were summarily turned away. Forced to roam those rough waters, the rusty boats became easy targets for Thai pirates, who overtook the fugitives, murdered wantonly, raped or abducted the women, cast screaming children overboard, and stole what little was on board. As many as four hundred thousand Vietnamese died in the transit.

But Pat Dinh Do's little boat met with a miracle. After several agonizing days adrift, the crew of a US Navy ship skimming those waters caught sight of the frantic exiles and—in spite of the fact that the navy had received no military orders to save Vietnamese who were found adrift on high seas—lifted them to safety. The Dos were soon delivered to California's Camp Pendleton, where they joined tens of thousands of bewildered fugitives in "Tent City," until an American family—members of the Church of Latter-day Saints—decided to sponsor them. The Mormons swept Pat Dinh Do's little family of five to Irvine, California, set them up in a mobile home, and enrolled the children in school. Four-year-old Pat grew up American. Excelling in school and college, he went on to medical school to become an orthopedic surgeon. As he was completing his internship in Dallas, he met a pretty nurse determined to expand her ambitions and become a full-fledged doctor. She was larger than life, bold, feisty, with a hearty, infectious laugh. Her name was Sylvia Orozco, a Mexican immigrant from Chihuahua.

Sylvia's family comes from a long line of Mexicans—half Spanish, half Nahua or Aztec. Family lore has it that they are direct descendants of Cuauhtémoc, the last Aztec emperor. And indeed, a DNA test confirms her indigeneity; her regal bearing and robust self-confidence infer the lineage. Since girlhood, Sylvia had always wanted to be a doctor, but her father, a former US Air Force recruit and old-school *machista*, was against it. He maintained that women—especially his own daughters—were meant to stay at home, not strut about recklessly in universities and workplaces. Sixteen years old and disheartened, Sylvia was about to run off and join the Air Force herself (her father's service had conveyed US citizenship) when she had a better idea. She decided to consult an aunt who had defied her own father and brothers, gone to college in the United States, studied biochemistry, married a Swede, and now was head of research for a large pharmacological company in California's Silicon Valley. Before long, Sylvia was living with that aunt in Cupertino and enrolled in the nearby high school; eventually she went on to study nursing at San Diego State University.

Upon graduation, however, she noted that San Diego hospitals seemed to have strong biases against Mexicans. It was 1994, and California had just passed Proposition 187, which was meant to curb a surge in the undocumented population. Schools and workplaces began interrogating Latinos and reporting noncitizens to the local authorities. Anyone who looked Mexican or answered to a Hispanic surname was required to prove his or her legal bona fides. Sylvia had naturalization papers—she was not at risk—but she was outraged by the overt discrimination. Looking around at places where she might apply for a job, she could see that the doctors and nurses in San Diego hospitals were almost entirely white; the only Hispanics on staff were the cleaning crews. Whenever she inquired about a position, she was told straightaway that it had already been filled. Proposition 187 was effectively killed in 1999, although bits and pieces of it lived on in policy until 2014, but the experience was enough to persuade Sylvia that she did not want to spend another day in California. She soon moved to Dallas and accepted an offer from a hospital that hired people of color. There she made two life changes she would never regret: one was to pursue her dream and study to be an internist, a fully certified MD; the second was to marry an immigrant from the opposite side of the planet, Pat Dinh Do. The result was their firstborn, an Asian Latina: Isabella Do-Orozco.

Isabella spent the first few years of her life in El Dorado, Kansas, where her parents initially established their medical practices. But by the time she was three, the little family had moved to Wichita permanently, and her parents were on their way to successful careers and financial security the likes of which neither had enjoyed previously—in Mexico or Vietnam. Isabella was able to attend the most prestigious private school in Wichita and, excelling in her studies, easily win a place at MIT. She is studying to be a cancer researcher.

This is not an unusual story. And yet that trajectory of success in immigrant Latino families isn't acknowledged by the American public. The prevailing American myth holds that the whites who flooded Ellis Island at the turn of the twentieth century and went on to settle the prairies or propel the Industrial Revolution are the heroes of America's success story, while today's nonwhite immigrants arrive without skills, looking for handouts, and burdening the country's socioeconomic infrastructure. Recent genealogical research shatters that racist notion. Data now show that the immigrants who arrived here from 1997 to 2015—the two largest influxes being Asian and Latin American—have assimilated and succeeded at virtually the same rate as European immigrants did a century ago. At the very top of the prosperity charts are the Chinese and Vietnamese, who, by the second generation, enter the country's 65th income percentile. Mexicans are not far behind. Which is to say that the children of Asian and Latino immigrants catapult handily from poverty to the middle class—from the bottom of the economic ladder to vigorous financial viability. "Mexicans today are just as upwardly mobile as the English and Norwegians of the past," report economists from Stanford and Princeton Universities. And "children of immigrants from Mexico and the Dominican Republic today are just as likely to move up from their parents' circumstances as were children of poor Swedes and Finns a hundred years ago."

Many Asian Latinos like Isabella Do-Orozco—"Lasians," as some call themselves—are children of interracial marriages that were sealed in this country. But Latin America has a long history of Asian immigration, and a family might well have forged their Asian Latino identity generations ago and elsewhere. The first Asians to inhabit the New World were Filipino sailors, *chinos de manila*, who settled in Mexico in the 1500s, a consequence of the exuberant gold and silver trade that traveled the Pacific from Acapulco to Manila. The Filipinos arrived on Spanish galleon ships so plagued with vermin and disease that half of them died en route. When the survivors reached colonial Mexico, they vowed never to cross the Pacific again. They established themselves in Acapulco and married the local women, giving rise to the hemisphere's first Asian Latinos.

But the greatest influx of Asians in Latin America came in the nineteenth century, when Chinese "coolie" and Japanese "issei" labor—all male—supplanted slave labor in Brazil, Peru, Mexico, and Cuba, as they eventually would do in the United States. Those populations went on to thrive, even grow, as they intermarried with the locals and scaled the economic ladder to the comfortable classes. In Cuba, nineteenth century plantation owners imported so many coolies to work their sugar fields that a considerable population of Cuban-Chinese sprang up as a result; when Castro ascended to power, many immigrated to New York City, generating a proliferation of *chino-cubano* restaurants and climbing handily to the higher rungs of small business owners. Today there are more than six million Latin Americans of Asian descent, one and a half million of them in Peru, the only nation outside the Far East that has elected an Asian president. The eastern influence is so present in Peru that the national cuisine is a fusion of Chinese, Japanese, and the rest of our genetic jumble. As a child in Lima, I was raised on *arroz chaufa* (fried rice), *lomo saltado* (stir-fry beef), crisp shrimp *wontones*, and *ceviche* (citrus infused sashimi); and, for me, the *chifas*, the ubiquitous Chinese restaurants that punctuate the Lima neighborhoods, were obligatory gathering places for sprawling family lunches on Sundays.

That is certainly the case for the family of Kelly Huang Chen, an industrial engineer at California Polytechnic State University who was born to Chinese parents in Mexico and immigrated to Los Angeles when she was ten. Kelly doesn't think twice about starting her day with dim sum and ending it with tacos. Or Amalia Chamorro, a Chinese Peruvian education specialist in Washington, DC, whose family emigrated from China to Peru so long ago that no one can remember what their last name was before they changed it to a Spanish one in order to better adapt to their new home.

But to be Asian-Latino is to live under an ample umbrella. The descendants of Valentina Álvarez and Rullia Singh, a Mexican Punjabi couple who met and married in Holtville, California, in 1917, are Asian Latinos, too, according to this country's discriminatory legal definitions. Thousands of Sikh men like Rullia had immigrated to the United States in the early 1900s in order to join California's labor force, but they were soon met with a law that prohibited them from returning to India to bring back brides. The starkly racist and punitive Asian Exclusion laws had slammed shut the country's gates to Chinese in 1882 and then, in 1924, "to preserve the ideal of American homogeneity," added Japanese, Koreans, and Indians to the list of undesirables. Apart from criminalizing the incoming traffic of slaves in 1808, the United States had never prohibited the entry of migrants from any part of the world until Congress decided to outlaw allegedly "subversive" or "loathsomely diseased" or "morally" unfit aspirants from Asia.

The "Asiatic Barred Zone," as it was legally called by the Immigration Act of 1917, soon became no-man's land, its people inconvenient and unwelcome. Bhaghat Singh Thind, an American Sikh like Rullia Singh—and a US Army soldier who had fought honorably in the First World War—balked when he was advised that his citizenship would be revoked because he was "racially ineligible" to be a citizen. Thind's case went all the way to the Supreme Court, where he argued that he deserved to keep his citizenship because he was Aryan—part of the Indo-European breed—and, therefore, a "white person of good character," as the 1790 US Naturalization Bill required all citizens to be. But the justices dismissed his case on the grounds that the "great body of our people instinctively . . . reject the thought of assimilation" of South

Asians. In other words, despite his service to the country—despite his being sworn in as a citizen just days before—the American people simply did not want Thind in their country. He was inadmissible, unwelcome, a pariah.

At the foundation of the intolerance was the worm of resentment that always crawls into the immigrant story, be it against the Irish, Chinese, Muslims, or Latin Americans. The start of the gold rush in 1848 had inspired buoyant, untrammeled growth in the West and, as hundreds of thousands of Chinese poured in to erect California's cities and construct the transcontinental railroad, the anti-Asian sentiment became shrill. Few white workers had applied for the backbreaking, hazardous work, but whites nevertheless complained that the Chinese were robbing them of jobs, undercutting their wages, getting rich. It wasn't the first time that immigrants had been accused of these things, but this time it carried an ugly, racist spin. Asians became the country's first illegal immigrants, the only race blatantly to be barred from entering the United States. A torrent of ire had been unleashed, and it had been long in the making. In 1871, a decade before President Chester Arthur signed the Chinese Exclusion Act, a murderous mob had descended on—and hanged—seventeen Chinese men and boys in Los Angeles, culminating in the largest mass lynching in American history. Before long, agents known as "Chinese catchers" were dispatched to the border with Mexico, which had become the preferred route of entry for Asian immigrants. Even after a devastating civil war, even after the promise of an Emancipation Proclamation, here—in all its mulish stubbornness—was the nettlesome predicament of the twentieth century: the problem of the color line.

The country's gates were tightly shut against the Chinese for sixty years until 1943, when President Franklin D. Roosevelt made an impassioned plea to correct this "historic mistake," and Congress moved to repeal and restructure the laws. But, at least in the public mind, the message had been sent, the damage done, the prejudice ingrained. For as long as anyone could remember, Asians had been the cause of all of America's ills—from plagues to penury—an easy scapegoat for a multitude of woes, and their punishment was not only being barred from entry: if

East Asians or Southeast Asians had to depart the United States for any reason, they would not be allowed to return. Nor could their kin become naturalized citizens. Those who already possessed citizenship, summarily and without explanation, were stripped of it. So, any Chinese, Japanese, Indian, Korean, Vietnamese, Cambodian, Hmong, or Filipino who had fled cruelty and calamity at home soon learned that the United States was not a beacon of freedom for them as the Statue of Liberty assured, but a nation contaminated by race hatreds. Racism became the unifying factor in the Asian American experience, merging twenty-four distinct immigrant groups and a veritable Babel of languages from far-flung regions of the world. If there is any unity among Asian America today—and its members profess that there is—it is because banding together has served as a useful bulwark against a centuries-old systemic racism.

Ironically enough, although President Franklin D. Roosevelt initiated the repeal of the exclusion laws, almost simultaneously he signed Executive Order 9066, prompting one of the darkest chapters in American immigrant history. It was the early 1940s, World War II was in full fury, and, just about the same time that the US State Department decided to ship my father north to fill an empty seat at MIT, thousands of Latin Americans—among them, 1,800 Peruvians—were forced onto US transport ships and ferried to the United States for a very different reason. They were Japanese Latinos, many of them citizens of South America for generations and a good portion of them successful business owners and professionals. Roosevelt's executive order to round up and incarcerate all Japanese in the United States had produced a ripple effect. Citing "hemispheric security," US government officials now demanded that twelve Latin American countries arrest, deracinate, and deliver all resident Japanese Latin Americans on their soil to the bleak, highly guarded internment camps in the American Southwest, where 120,000 Japanese Americans had been corralled behind barbed wire.

Peruvian police stole into homes, arrested whole families, impounded their possessions—even burned down their houses, schools, and businesses—and deported them against their will to the United States. The five-year-old Japanese boy who would someday be president of Peru, Alberto Fujimori, was among them. Once the war was over, half of those hapless Latin American families were refused reentry to their home countries. Many survived the indignities to take up residence in the Southwest and harbor bitter memories about the arbitrary cruelty of their adopted country. If it had been perilous to be a Chinese laborer in Los Angeles or a Punjabi immigrant in Holtville, it had turned out to be downright terrifying to be Japanese Latin American anywhere south of the Rio Grande. Especially if the United States government had anything to do with it. The message had been unequivocal: Asians were not to be trusted, no matter their citizenship. Not until 1988, when President Ronald Reagan apologized for the injustices, were any reparations attempted: any Japanese American who had been forcibly interred during World War II was offered $20,000 for his or her trouble. On the other hand, each Japanese Latin American whom the US government had subjected to the same suffering would count as substantially less than a whole soul. They were offered $5,000 instead.

•   •   •

There is no question that the long history of racist legislation in this country has played havoc with immigrant lives, sometimes propelling whole communities in unanticipated directions. Given the punitive legal strictures imposed on Sikh laborers in 1924, virtually blocking their ability to return to Punjab to seek their brides, the Sikhs did what they could. They married Mexican women instead. Like Punjabi women, the Mexicanas were brown, family oriented, respectful of their men, loyal. Today the descendants of those marriages may dine on curry enchiladas or vindaloo frijoles, but they seldom identify as Latinos. The Punjabi Mexicans are a fading community, their numbers diminishing from one generation to another as they intermarry with other Indians, dropping their Latino identities entirely. In this way, whole histories of a Latino past can disappear into the ether, casualties of the American impulse to assign one race and erase all others. "I'm proud of my Mexican heritage, says Amelia Singh Netervala, the daughter of a Mexican Indian marriage who grew up on an alfalfa and cotton farm south of Phoenix. "But if I had to choose, I would identify as an Indian."

Twenty-year-old Isabella Do-Orozco takes an opposing view. Raised speaking Spanish yet manifesting distinctly Asian features, she is determined to preserve both sides of her bifurcated reality. The work hasn't been easy. "Visiting my mother's intensely Mexican family in El Paso, I was well aware we were the outsiders," she tells me. "We weren't as closely bound to them as they were to each other." All the same, she felt closer to Hispanic culture than to Vietnamese, perhaps because she had been raised in a Spanish-speaking environment. With her Vietnamese family in California, however, the dynamic was entirely distinct. "I don't speak Vietnamese, and neither do my Vietnamese cousins. There's a wall between generations there that doesn't exist in my Mexican family." Other cultural differences got in the way. "Mexicans tend to be lively, forward, and loud," she says, smiling, and these are traits you aren't likely to find in a Vietnamese.

In fact, there was much about Latinos that made her Vietnamese relatives uncomfortable: our inclination to hug and kiss even the most distant acquaintances, the unbridled way we share our emotions, the unselfconscious way we dance. But the real source of frustration for Isabella was physical rather than social. "People take one look at me and assume I am Asian. They don't recognize the Latina in me. My sister definitely looks Latina. My brother is racially ambiguous; in the summertime, he might even be half black. I, on the other hand—the one who identifies most as a Mexican—get spoken to in English when I'm being introduced to Spanish speakers. It never fails to surprise me. I take pride in my mixed identity, my fluent Spanish, so it's hard when people don't see it in me. Sometimes Asians even feel free to say derogatory, racist things about Latinos to me. That hurts." If she ever longed to share these feelings with a sympathetic, commiserating ear, she'd be hard pressed to do so. She's never known another Asian Latino apart from her siblings.

Being Asian Latino can certainly be a complicated, lonely affair. Mekita Rivas, a contributing editor for *Cosmopolitan* magazine, describes it this way: "As an Asian Latina, I've struggled with not feeling Asian or Latina 'enough,' especially in predominantly Asian or Latino communities.

For much of my life, I thought that being one-half Mexican and one-half Filipina suggested some type of shortcoming. If I wasn't 'whole' in either community, did I really belong?" Was half of her identity an encroachment on the other? Was she appropriating identities she couldn't fully own?

Then there is Lisa Murtaugh from Atlanta, who—like Isabella—is Vietnamese Mexican and sees nothing but strength in the mix. "I'm not gonna lie," she says. "Being an Asian Latina can be tough and confusing and lonely to navigate, especially if you're also an American. But I think it's worth it because there's so much power in it. There's so much beauty. And there's so much damn good food."

Today, with a half millennium's legacy in the Americas, Asian Latinos represent not only a coupling of antipodes but also a unique, living link between the two largest and fastest growing immigrant groups in the United States. A fledgling fusion of these gigantic populations, they may yet be sparse in number, but they have made names for themselves in a variety of fields, from pop music to plasma physics. The prizewinning novelist Sigrid Nunez is a child of a marriage between a German American mother and a Chinese Panamanian father. The wildly popular singer Enrique Iglesias is the naturalized American son of a Spaniard and a Filipina. Wallace Loh, the descendant of prosperous Shanghai business magnates, fled Communist China with his family and grew up in Lima, Peru, only to immigrate to the United States and become president of the University of Maryland. And then there is the American scientist Franklin Chang-Díaz, son of a Chinese immigrant and a Costa Rican mother. Chang-Díaz has been celebrated widely as "the first Latino astronaut." But, in fact, he is the first *Asian Latino* astronaut; the first of that ilk in the history of space exploration to float free from a spaceship and glance back at Earth to see what a very small world we actually are.

# PART III

# SOULS

The Latina in me is an ember that blazes forever.
—Sonia Sotomayor, Supreme Court justice,
Puerto Rican American, 1996

# 7

# THE GOD OF CONQUEST

God exists. And if not, it ought to. As an aspiration, a necessity, and as
the deepest, inviolable bedrock of our being.

—Octavio Paz, Mexican poet, 1914–1998

**A**s wildly different as Latino phenotypes can be—as variegated the
skin colors—our spiritual lives, too, are manifold. The easy assumption is that we are all Roman Catholics, as Spain certainly forced
its American colonies to be and as the Vatican has been struggling to
cement for centuries. But today, in the mercurial, quickly evolving Latino present—with new, biological ways to explore our roots, with the
discovery of traces of Spain's eradicated Jewry in our veins, with massive
decampment to Protestant churches or our inclination to merge Christianity with indigenous beliefs, not to mention a growing trend to abandon church participation altogether—making pat assumptions about
Latino spirituality is a hazardous business.

All the same, when asked, the majority of Latinos will say they are
religiously observant. Compared with the broader American public, we
are more likely to declare a faith and attend religious services, even if we
have discarded one faith for another. Believing is the inviolable bedrock
of our being, as the poet Octavio Paz once wrote. We are a resolutely
religious breed. So much so that sometimes we combine faiths and rituals in order to cover our spiritual bases. According to surveys, more than

90 percent of Latinos say they believe in God. Little wonder that Simón Bolívar, the nineteenth-century liberator of six republics, claimed that religion was Latin America's glue, Catholicism its rock. According to him, the two traits that brought his Americas together as a unified body politic—from the Caribbean to the Antarctic, and from Panama to the far reaches of the Andes—were faith and the Spanish language. For this, we have Spain to thank. We are most closely joined, it seems, by the two codes forced on our ancestors during colonial rule: by the strictures of Rome and by the tongue of Cervantes.

Bolívar, who hated Spain's dominion over the colonies yet knew something about the chaos his revolution had left behind, was convinced that a common faith and language could bind South America fast, resolve petty divisions, create unity, and make of the continent a great Pan-American nation—a mighty, sovereign force. Bolívar's dream might have been realized but for the hidebound, small-minded tyrants who got in its way. After the unimaginable violence of the wars of independence, the victors emerged with no singleness of purpose, no spirit of collegiality. Rather than join hands to create a great nation, warlords clung tight to their petty fiefdoms, forging undersized dreams from their undersized visions. Little by little over the centuries, Latin America's spiritscape shifted. Indigenous myths crept into the Christian sacrament; republics emerged with their own varieties of worship; liberation priests acquired warrior mentalities; Protestant evangelists swarmed into the region evincing a tangible appeal. And once Latinos arrive in the United States of America, their spiritual allegiances can morph completely. Second-generation immigrants are being lured away by new religions; third-generation immigrants may choose not to be affiliated with religion at all. This last is becoming more and more evident with the years: Latinos (especially the US born) are on a par with other Americans in drifting away from houses of worship entirely. In 2009, 15 percent were "nones"—polled as having no affiliation whatsoever. By 2022, that figure had risen to 30 percent.

"I was raised Catholic," young Latinos will answer when I ask them about their beliefs, and then their voices trail off, leaving open the question of whether they still practice or how they will raise their children. As Olga, a university student, tells it, "My mom's *really* Catholic, [and so] I went to Catholic schools." She describes how, as a child, she practiced the faith to please her parents, "but now," she says bluntly, "I just don't." Later on, she elaborates: "I didn't question it until I came to the States, because in Mexico everybody was Catholic. People there didn't ask you, 'What is your religion?' Everybody just assumed you were Catholic. But when I came to the States, I encountered so many different racial and religious backgrounds. . ." That's when she became more reflective, more aware of her cultural background and her religious training—the catechization of her girlhood. She was also struck by the very American notion that faith might be a matter of choice, and she began to have a clearer picture of how peremptory Catholicism had been in the world from which she had come.

## HOW THE CATHOLIC CHURCH CONQUERED THE NEW WORLD

With the faith, the scourge of God came into the country.
—"Jesuit Relations," New France, North America, 1653

The road to Latin American—and, therefore, Latino—Catholicism is a long and twisted trail. It begins on January 2, 1492, with the consolidation of Spain under Queen Isabella I and King Ferdinand II and their fierce expulsion of the peninsula's Muslims and Jews. Seven centuries before, in AD 711, the Moors had swept up from their conquests in Africa, crossed the Strait of Gibraltar, and swallowed Hispania whole, making the Umayyad Caliphate one of the great empires of the world. Over the centuries, Christian armies continuously repulsed the Muslim occupiers, pushing them ever south but leaving them in control of a swath of land that straddled the southernmost part of Iberia. Ferdinand and Isabella, intent on recapturing that land and ridding the peninsula not only of Muslims but also of its wealthy Jewish merchants, unleashed a relentless, decade-long war against the "infidels." Their burning ambition was to establish a muscular, Catholic Spain that would champion the Church and its pope, and act as a knight protector in its evangelizing wars.

Spain had emerged from centuries of foreign domination with a crusading spirit, a passionate commitment to forge a powerful nation, and the truculence to achieve it. By the end of the hostilities, one hundred thousand Moors were dead, two hundred thousand more had fled, and the two hundred thousand who remained were subject to strict laws of conversion. The Jews, too, were offered the choice to convert or leave, and when the Spanish Inquisition—blessed by a papal bull—began in earnest, more than half the Jewish population would be expelled and several thousand savagely executed. Open atrocities—burnings at the stake, autos-da-fé, hangings—took place in city squares with royalty present and an almost festive air. Europeans who visited Spain at the time were appalled by the public's enthusiasm for these executions. Less visible were the Jews' hasty conversions, the rush to hide one's traditions, the sudden, passionate claim that Catholicism was the true faith and Jesus the only prophet. Denial and recantations ruled the day. A granddaughter of Jews converted and became Saint Teresa of Ávila, the famous Carmelite mystic. The ancestors of Miguel de Cervantes, the author of the quintessentially Spanish masterwork *Don Quijote de la Mancha*, are said to have been Jews, and *"la mancha,"* or "the stain," is said to refer cryptically to Cervantes's Jewish heritage. Very likely, the forebears of Christopher Columbus—Spain's "Admiral of the Ocean Seas"—were Jews. And, as irony would have it, the first inquisitor general appointed by the Crown, Cardinal Tomás de Torquemada, was born into a Jewish family and, fired by zeal that only a radical conversion can bring, went on to lead the most bloodcurdling era of the Inquisition and prosecute chilling cruelties against his own people.

By April 1492, Isabella "La Católica" had finally persuaded her husband that, in order to finance their ambitions, they needed to reach beyond the confines of the known world—beyond the legendary Pillars of Hercules—and make a bid for distant conquests on far-flung, uncharted continents. The monarchs soon signed the Capitulations of Santa Fe, investing Christopher Columbus with the additional title Governor of the Indies and granting him the authority to launch an expedition that promised legions of new Christian souls, an abundance of gold, and funds sufficient to engage more holy wars.

Columbus may have opened the door to the Americas, but he ended up encountering more meek, destitute Indians than gem-studded princes; more wild, uninhabited terrain than royal palaces; more parrots than gold. It would take a half century—it would take Hernán Cortés's dizzying triumph in Mexico and Francisco Pizarro's even more profit- able victories in Peru—to bring Spain the vast stores of lucre it craved. Meanwhile, the Catholic queen's insistence that evangelization be at the core of the conquest went all but ignored. Religion wasn't the imme- diate order of business for the ravenously ambitious freelancers who joined the ranks of the conquistadors; gold was. Every soldier and sailor in every expedition to the New World understood this. There were bo- nanzas to seize, fortunes to be made. One of Cortés's faithful adjutants wrote that he and his cohort had come to America "to serve God and His Majesty and to get rich." Even the priests could see that personal wealth was at the heart of the mission—and indeed some acquired their own measure of it.

Greed among the religious wasn't anything new. By the 1500s, the Catholic Church had morphed into a bureaucracy, a sales operation, a vast and insatiable financial network. At precisely the time that Cortés was cutting a bloody path through the Yucatán Peninsula, Pope Leo X, a member of the powerful de' Medici family, was presiding over the sale of two thousand church offices a year for the round sum of 500,000 ducats ($100 million a year today), an astounding figure for its time. Violations abounded, proceeds were pocketed. Priests learned to look the other way. Once they became fully enlisted in the business of conquest, friars accompanied conquistadors to every rout. The lockstep of church and state, cross and sword, priest and soldier was established, and it would march ahead boldly for another half millennium.

But in that covenant to "serve God and get rich," the Church would lose a far greater opportunity. The New World had actually represented a chance for the faith to redeem itself, return to its roots, serve a tabula rasa of fresh souls and separate itself from the debauched and corrupt institution the European Church had become. There were religious orders—the Capuchins, for instance, founded in 1209 by Saint Francis of Assisi—that were sickened by the corruption of the Age of Discovery and broke away to return to a more rigorous observance of their original vows. Or the Dominicans, who objected to the cruel direction the conquest was taking. Or friar Bartolomé de las Casas, who decried the cruelties that were being visited on indigenous Mexicans. But, as a whole, representatives of the Church in the New World joined the invaders' routine, making Christianization an armed spiritual conquest— part combat, part biblical salve to assuage their queen.

It began with the *requerimiento*, a declaration read out in Spanish to uncomprehending natives, spelling out Spain's divinely ordained right to appropriate any territory it encountered, subjugate and enslave its inhabitants, and, if necessary, wage war and kill. The pronouncement prefaced every attack, sometimes shouted into a crowd of faces, sometimes mumbled from distant hilltops with not a soul in sight. A priest would hold high a cross, and a conquistador would launch into a seemingly innocuous preamble citing angels and holy men, including Saint James and Saint Peter, but the pronouncement would end with an unmistakable threat: "If you do not comply—if you pit yourself against me—I swear that with God's help I shall engage all my powers against you, make war on you wherever and however I can, subject you to the yoke, force you to obey the Church and his Highness, and I will take you, your women, and your children and make you all slaves to sell or dispose of as his Highness sees fit, and I will take all that you own, and inflict every ill and possible harm."

To the indigenous who heard it, the words were mere sounds, incomprehensible babble, as baffling as the yapping of dogs. Some surrendered to the cross and sword peacefully; others resisted violently. In the end, in the face of superior armaments—guns, cannons, galloping horses, salivating dogs, and a raging, genocidal disease—field after field fell to the soldiers of Jesus. And so it was that the Word arrived in the Americas.

Not only did priests become accessories to the invasion, but also they became an integral part of the law inasmuch as bishops were appointed by kings, priests were appointed by viceroys, and monks were keepers of the official registers. Even as conquistadors continued to forge bold paths of exploration, the Church imported the Inquisition, transforming it into a reign of terror in the New World. The magnificent cities of the Inca, Aztecs, and Maya were viewed as vast kingdoms of Satan, and, so, gutted and razed. Just as the Romans had routinely leveled the temples of their enemies fifteen centuries before, the invaders now proceeded to dispatch what was formerly holy into oblivion. Idols were smashed, holy relics torched, books burned, soaring pyramids reduced to rubble, their stone repurposed as cathedral walls. To make the triumph absolute, churches were built directly on top of the temples' foundations, appropriating the very holiness of the ground. Once the sacking was complete and colonial settlers streamed in to make their fortunes, priests mobilized whole communities of the indigenous into forced settlements of labor called *reducciones*, and went about the business of Christianization. Franciscan and Jesuit missions dedicated themselves to evangelizing the multitudes; toward that end, they created Latin America's enduring machine for instilling the faith: the Catholic school.

As remarkable as it may seem, within a century of Columbus's having dropped anchor in Hispaniola, the Catholic Eucharist was being offered at altars all the way from the swamplands of La Florida to the pampas of Argentina. Indeed, no sooner had Cortés crushed Montezuma's empire than a flurry of baptisms began. Within a decade, five million Indians were baptized in Mexico. The New World's Christianization and Hispanicization were as fleet and relentless as its rout. It beggars the mind to consider the speed with which Spain won the hemisphere's souls. The only religion in recorded human history that adopted converts as quickly is probably Islam, although Mohammedans did not force conversion, nor did they require believers to abandon faiths as they took on the new.

All the same, it wasn't a seamless, uniform style of Catholicism. The Church didn't serve people equally, nor did it intend to. It employed a different tone and demeanor with the darker races, and the people of the darker races understood this. Although the work had begun modestly, with Franciscans, Dominicans, and Jesuits focusing their attentions on the conquered and tending to the lower castes, it soon assumed the posture of conqueror and coercer. The evidence was everywhere: in the pomp, the accoutrements, the marshaling of the lower castes, the pandering to the aristocracy—and, ultimately, in the churches' sheer wealth and magnificence. The result was that many of the converted in the humbler classes repudiated the religion on its face and were Roman Catholic in name only. Many others embraced the religion in earnest but embellished it with "pagan" practices from their ancient pasts. Christian saints had corresponding native deities. Catholic rituals and dances had roots in beliefs that had gone before. The Church, in other words, was gradually being conquered by the New World as much as it had conquered it. The result was an altered, mutt form of worship: a syncretic faith, as heterogenous as the people of the Americas.

With time, many followed Catholicism's teachings scrupulously; they crossed themselves when passing a church, built shrines in their homes, hung crucifixes over their beds, filled their pockets with amulets and rosaries. But, for just as many, Catholicism was a fluid, flexible faith—distinct from the Catholicism of Europe. It could be shot through with indigenous or African influences: an Andean Catholic might erect an altar to Pachamama; a Yoruba Catholic might recite Holy Marys before a favorite orisha or African deity. Others might burn incense or splash liquor at the foot of the crucifix without really knowing why. A Bolivian might pray to the Virgin painted in the shape of a mountain; a Dominican might place an image of Jesus alongside that of a voodoo spirit; a Mexican will cherish the Virgin of Guadalupe for her brownness. Even the strictest Catholic believers may find themselves reaching back to touch the faith of the ancients—return to the gods that presided over this hemisphere before the hellfire of forced conversion.

But the Church has also been a builder; an energetic force in establishing order in the wild chaos of conquest and colonization. It was undeniably the single most important institution in the colonial world. Because it counted everyone in the vast New World as a nominal member, it went about busily organizing its flock. In the process, it controlled and documented every aspect of human life, from birth to marriage to the grave. Along with its mandate to convert the natives, it began fashioning a groupthink for everyone involved. The Church was now the principal educator of the masses, the entity that saw to the uniformity of doctrine and the curation of knowledge and, therefore, the institution that could guarantee conformity of thought, along with a basic education. But that was not all. As its power accumulated, it became the preeminent source of capital, the banker, the largest employer, and the largest property owner in Latin America, augmenting its considerable influence with a vast empire of real estate tracts and magnificent edifices, not to mention thousands of sheep ranches, textile businesses, and agricultural farms.

That kind of clout could not have been achieved without the strong arm of the Crown. Throughout Spain's colonial hold on the Americas, the Church remained a handmaid to political power. In every major plaza, a cardinal's house would be built next to the cathedral, and the cathedral would be built next to the governor's palace. The message was clear: no other sect was admissible; no other god allowed. The elite, white, Americas-born descendants of Spanish settlers—the criollo aristocracy—maintained a fervent loyalty to the faith, serving as another leg of that power structure. As twilight descended on the colonial era, the naturalist Alexander von Humboldt remarked that, in Mexico (New Spain, at the time), mine owners and merchants may have had a vice's clamp on the commerce, but no less than half of Mexico's real estate and fungible assets belonged to the Church, which controlled all the rest through mortgages. Serving the Spanish Crown had proven to be highly remunerative for the holy orders.

Even during Latin America's wars of independence, from 1808 to 1833, the Church continued to support Spain, fearing that if rebels gained power and ousted Spain altogether, the Church's authority would be shucked along with the viceroys and governors. But things didn't turn out that way. After independence was won, the whites immediately took command of the halls of government and wrested power from the liberating armies, which were largely colored, and churches continued to hold their pride of place as protectors of the elite status quo. The Church had so thoroughly dominated hearts and minds for three hundred years that the faithful simply marched on as before. Spain may have been evicted, the loyalist priests sent home, but Catholicism continued to rule. The wealthy whites moved into the colonial palaces, while the more commercially inclined appropriated the haciendas. And although slavery had been eliminated in principle, in practice it was very much in play. Those who had been poor and enslaved before would be poor and enslaved thereafter. Scripture's assurances that the meek would inherit the world—that they would be rewarded in the kingdom of heaven—would have to do for now.

For a while—at least until the dust of revolution had settled—the Holy See refused to recognize the new republics, and churches staggered ahead, rudderless, without a central command. But, to the Church's surprise and delight, although some fledgling nations moved to separate church and state, Catholicism continued to be the institution most revered by the newly independent citizens. The colossal educational system the Spanish priests and nuns had built remained a force in forging young Catholic minds and hearts. Governments could come and go, power might swing from tyrant to rebel, people might weather feast or famine, but the Church would always be there—a rock for the mighty, and the meek would simply totter along.

Even so, at this most critical turning point in Latin America's history, the Church did not temper its role in any substantive way. Much as it had glossed over the sixteenth-century Dominican friars' pleas for social justice, and much as it had turned a deaf ear to Bishop Bartolomé de las Casas' outrage about cruelties visited on the indigenous, it now ignored an opportunity to shape a new reality for itself. It accepted the white elite power structure as surely as it had aligned itself with the colonial masters. It had blessed serfdom and slavery in the old days, and it would bless classism and racism now. Indeed, the Church would continue to turn its back on its darker-skinned adherents for 150 more years. Even among members of the clergy, race discrimination had been barefaced and rampant: to serve as a priest in Mexico, an aspirant had to prove that more than three-quarters of his ancestors were Spanish. So it was that an entire hierarchy of blood quantum was devised, and those who could count themselves *castizos*—more Spanish than Indian—would regard those who bore greater quotients of mixed blood with flagrant contempt. This calculus would operate into the twenty-first century.

It wasn't until 2002, just before the canonization of Juan Diego Cuauhtlahtoatzin—the humble sixteenth-century Mexican who claimed to have seen a vision of the Virgin of Guadalupe—that the Church decided to recognize "Indians as peoples." But it had taken more than five hundred years for that institutional pat on the head. For many of the Indian congregants who gathered in Mexico to mark that historic moment, the portrait of Juan Diego that was unveiled was infuriating: what they saw before them was a light-skinned, fully bearded man—more a sword-wielding conquistador than a Chichimeca Indian. Even so, the Church proceeded to reproduce that white man's likeness on millions of posters, stamps, and prayer cards, since it was clear that no one in the Church's hierarchy really minded: at the time, not one of Mexico's 132 bishops was indigenous. And why worry anyway? For hundreds of years, the Church had enjoyed unopposed spiritual and political power in every Latin American republic it had helped conquer. The Vatican had demanded blind faith, and its flock had dutifully provided it. Until 1960, more than 90 percent of all Latin Americans counted themselves Catholic believers. The same was doubtless true for all American Latinos. But when the winds of liberation theology blew into the Americas, and Protestant evangelizers followed, that flock began to stray. Today the region's population is only slightly more than 50 percent Catholic. The urge to find salvation in other houses of worship has found its way into Catholicism's fortress: the Latin American soul.

# THE SOUL DRAIN

Latin America is a Catholic region, but there's no reason to assume that this need always be so. I believe that if Guatemala becomes the first predominantly Evangelical nation in Latin America, it will have a domino effect.

—Church growth planner, Evangelical,
Overseas Crusades Ministries, 1984

The history of the Latino Catholic church in the United States began in earnest in 1848, when the United States first flexed its imperialist muscle by appropriating half of the Mexican republic. Things didn't go well for those crossed by the border and swallowed into the American maw. For them, the business of faith—like the concept of homeland—would undergo an earthshaking redefinition. Newly minted Mexican Americans were now forced to become part of a white, largely Irish Catholic Church that was patently unprepared to serve them. Until then, American Catholics had comprised a tiny segment of the overall US population—a mere 5 percent—and they represented an amalgamation of outcasts: Irish, Germans, Poles, and Slavs. But for all that seeming diversity, there was one unifying feature that served this larger Catholic laity well. They were white. The US government had officially labeled Mexicans white for voting purposes, but, in the American eye, they were decidedly not. Just as the Anglos had shunned the Irish for their poverty, the Irish now shunned Mexicans for their "race."

Mexican priests who had served congregations in what had once been Mexico were summarily evicted from the churches, sent south unceremoniously, and replaced with Irish and German clergy. In the same manner that Americans had swept in and taken possession of the land, Irish-German Catholics now swooped in and took possession of the churches. Signs directed Mexicans to the rear of establishments—relegating them to a subspecies of worshiper, a breed of untouchables: "Last Three Rows for Mexicans," the large print declared to anyone who cared to enter the house of God. "By every rational standard, they should have left the church right then," says Father Virgilio Elizondo, a church historian. Many did, but their faith prevailed. They simply built shrines and altars at home, where they could worship in private with their families. As generations passed and the numbers of Latinos in the country burgeoned, the American Catholic Church began to understand that its future might very well depend on them. And why not? The Church in Rome had certainly banked on Latinos' homelands for centuries.

But Catholicism in those home countries was beginning to change. In the 1920s in northern Mexico, rich entrepreneurs campaigning to adopt American practices—many of them Protestant converts—created a movement to transform Mexico, divorce it from its Catholic past, and convert it into a rich, secular state—a vibrant center of economic expansion. Mexican president Plutarco Elías Calles, the movement's most passionate advocate, placed rigid regulations on Catholic churches, initiated the oversight of priests, and issued an order to close church schools. Outraged, the Mexican Church mounted a strike and ceased all religious services. The people—especially the rural, marginalized poor—reacted with panic, their fury bursting into a full-scale rebellion. Calling themselves Cristeros, the insurgents mobilized a guerrilla war to overthrow the government. The result was a bloody, protracted three-year battle between militant believers and the Mexican army, which United States arsenals were only too glad to supply with rifles, ammunition, aircraft, even pilots. In time, the hostilities ravaged the Mexican heartland, razed whole villages, disrupted the farms, created a famine, and claimed the lives of one hundred thousand people. US ambassador Dwight Morrow, who had enjoyed a friendly relationship with President Calles, stepped in to broker the peace. The Mexican government was persuaded to loosen its grip on the Church and make amends, but in the rest of a very Catholic Latin America, the stain of betrayal would hold fast. Mexico became known as a nation that dared set itself against God.

One might consign the Cristero Rebellion to local history, all of it unfolding in one very confined precinct of Mexico, but that would be wrong. Like the Mexican Revolution before it, and the Central American wars that would follow, the belligerence pushed its way into the

United States of America, filling Mexican barrios across this country with a deluge of refugees. By 1928, tens of thousands of displaced laborers and more than two thousand exiled nuns and priests had surged across the border, creating a diaspora that maintained absolute loyalty to the Church. The new émigrés threw themselves into the business of cementing a network, supporting the Cristeros at home, and consolidating a powerful sense of unity around their faith. Some even engaged in arms smuggling, military recruitment, espionage, and armed border revolts in order to topple a president that had presumed to oppose the Word. Today the American children and grandchildren of that diaspora are scattered across the United States, attending churches, embodying that history. It is no surprise that, among Latinos, Mexican Americans are the most ardent supporters of Catholicism. Six out of ten say they hold strong ties to the Church.

•   •   •

Forty years later, in the late 1960s, violence would emerge again as a wave of Marxist activism, inspired by the Cuban Revolution, swept Latin America and rocked the very foundations of the Church. Latin American priests, weary of the social injustices that had gripped the region for centuries, began to preach a more muscular defense of the oppressed—many of them willing to fight for it with guns, if necessary. Priests divorced themselves from the halls of power, even from their own bishops and Rome, to lead congregations against the forces that persecuted and exploited them. They called it liberation theology, a vigorous campaign for social justice—a "Preferential Option for the Poor," a kind of affirmative action for a whole segment of the socioeconomic order—and the stern, ascetic, conservative minders of the Holy See met it with arch disapproval. But there was little they could do to stop it. The fight for civil liberties was in full flower, and it energized the clergy every bit as much as it did the civil rights leaders. Priests began to be seen and heard at political gatherings, marching with Dr. Martin Luther King Jr., protesting the Vietnam War, calling for justice for people of color. Latinos soon turned that attention to injustices in their origin countries, and, before long, American Catholics rose to join them. Like a row of clacking dominos, other denominations followed. Mormons and Evangelicals streamed down to the most squalid and miserable neighborhoods of Latin America to save lives and win souls. Wherever the nuns and Catholic missionaries went, Evangelicals followed. Down the street from a tumbledown church near the wild, lawless, poisonous gold mines of La Rinconada, Peru—the highest human habitation on earth—a sign was nailed precariously on the door of a shack: "Come on in, friend. We are Leaving Footprints. We are the Assemblies of God."

The proliferation was nothing short of viral: from 1960 to 1970, Evangelical churches preaching liberation in some areas of Latin America grew by 77 percent. Come the 1970s, the growth reached an astonishing 155 percent. By then, Latin American military governments had seen enough. Liberation theology had become such anathema to elites and the American interests supporting them that extermination seemed the only solution. Army generals and their death squads began targeting and murdering priests and nuns. *"Haz patria, mata un cura!"* ("Be a patriot, kill a priest!") became the battle cry for Salvadoran right-wing extremists. On March 24, 1980, the beloved Archbishop Óscar Romero was gunned down while administering the host in a chapel in San Salvador's Hospital of the Divine Providence. A sharpshooter emerged from a red Volkswagen wielding a .22-caliber rifle, took aim at the chapel's open door, and fired a single shot down the center aisle to meet its mark in the holy man's heart. News of the execution sped through Latin America, inflaming the faithful like a lit wick. Whole cities rose up in outrage. What could the archbishop possibly have done to deserve such a cold-blooded extermination? "Romero's sin," a newsman posited, "was to have sent off, a few days before his death, a letter to President Jimmy Carter, pleading with him to stop shipping military aid to El Salvador's reactionary government." Worse, on the day before his death, the good bishop had beseeched soldiers to disobey their generals, put down their guns, and heed the fifth commandment: do not kill.

But the killing didn't stop. In October of the same year, five Salvadoran National Guard soldiers kidnapped and raped three American Maryknoll sisters and a lay missionary, and then executed all four at

gunpoint, tossing their corpses into a shallow grave. Death squad killings of clergy proliferated throughout Latin America, from the Northern Triangle to the Andes. And all too often, it was discovered that the
executioners had been trained and armed by the United States. In Nicaragua, three nuns and a bishop were attacked by American-backed con-
tra rebels on a highway on their way from Managua to the town of La
Rosita; the contras blew up their car with a rocket-launched grenade
and killed two of the women, pounding them with rifle shot. In Bolivia,
an activist priest who had joined a hunger strike against the ultra-right-
wing government of Hugo Banzer was kidnapped, tortured, and then
dispatched with seventeen bullets, his naked corpse flung to the side of
a road in a remote corner of the Andean cordillera.

In Guatemala—whose genocidal president, Efraín Ríos Montt, was
a Reagan White House favorite—the military descended on the leftist
Guerrilla Army of the Poor, slaughtering rebels and priests as well as
thousands of indigenous villagers. In that nation's war against itself, 626
villages were destroyed, one and a half million people were displaced,
forty-two thousand were disappeared, and two hundred thousand were
killed, most of them rural Maya. But a special death sentence was issued
against pastors who were visiting villagers from house to house, praying
with the faithful, and suspected of serving the rebel spirit. In Quiché, a
death squad murdered three Spanish activist priests, then tortured and
massacred seven Mayan religious workers, including a boy of twelve. The
message was clear: in joining liberation theology, the priests had betrayed
their historical allegiance to power, the lockstep their forebears had joined
when men of the cloth had walked with conquistadors. So it was that Ríos
Montt's generals, with the help of millions of dollars in military aid from
Washington, embarked on a concerted campaign to wipe out the holy
men along with anyone else suspected in the slightest of harboring a Socialist thought. Meanwhile, the American military, accustomed to partner-
ing with Latin American dictators and hellbent on eradicating Marxism in
the hemisphere, now found itself engaged in an uncomfortable proxy war
against the rebel clergy, training military juntas in targeted assassination
techniques at the School of the Americas in Fort Benning, Georgia.

To be perfectly clear, the US military and the CIA were not doing the killing, but they were facilitating the genocide, subsidizing the annihilation of a people. According to the Peruvian founder of liberation theology, Father Gustavo Gutierrez, the United States had become Latin America's bogeyman. In his electrifying and seminal book, *A Theology of Liberation*, Father Gutierrez explained that a light had switched on in Latin American minds and illuminated the reality: there could be no "authentic development for Latin America" as long as it was dominated by "the great capitalist countries, especially by the most powerful, the United States of America." Naturally, the millions of migrants who had spilled into El Norte precisely because of the region's instability were drawn into the debate. Was it right for family members they had left behind to hoist guns in defense of Jesus? Was it justifiable for relatives recruited into armies to suddenly find themselves hunting priests? Fiery arguments ensued among stateside Latinos who struggled to make sense of this new warrior faith that liberation priests were demanding in their homelands and that Rome had unilaterally reviled.

In 1989, when an elite commando unit butchered six Jesuit priests on the campus of a university in San Salvador along with their housekeeper and her teenage daughter, something seemed to snap among the region's faithful. The bloodletting had gone too far. Catholics, afraid to enter the churches, now started to look elsewhere for safe communities of worship. And the Protestant churches were there, in their very neighborhoods—all the way from Utah to Paraguay—ready to welcome them with open arms.

•  •  •

Today in Brazil, which boasts the largest Catholic population of any country on the planet, the Church has been losing adherents at accelerated rates. In the span of two generations, it has lost a full third of its flock to Protestantism. The pace has been startling, particularly for a religion that has held a monopoly for more than five hundred years. The bleeding of adherents, which had begun as a barely perceived trickle in the 1980s, grew so wildly that, by 2005, the newly inaugurated Pope Benedict XVI decided to make Brazil his first papal visit. Something had to be done to stop the hemorrhage. All the same, despite the pope's visit, Brazil's Catholic population plunged and its number of Protestant Evangelicals doubled. Today one-third of Brazil's population is Evangelical. By 2032, Brazil is projected to be a majority Protestant nation.

The seismic shifts in Latin America's spiritual life have been so swift in recent years that it is difficult to report them with any precision. But the most important began, interestingly enough, with a very earthly tectonic event: the devastating 1976 earthquake that rocked Guatemala, killed twenty-three thousand, injured another seventy-five thousand, razed dozens of villages in the highlands, and left tens of thousands homeless. Evangelical churches rushed in to assist the victims and gained many grateful converts in the process. When the civil wars began a few years later, and Catholic priests became politicized, many took comfort in the politically neutral Evangelical promise of a better life. Today the trend is clear. In Nicaragua, El Salvador, Honduras, and Guatemala—countries racked by bloodshed for decades—one out of three residents has abandoned Catholicism in favor of Evangelical rebirth. In 1990 Guatemala inaugurated the first democratically elected Evangelical president in Latin America, and, sure enough, by 2020, the first domino had fallen: between its seven million Evangelicals and additional Protestant denominations, Guatemala had effectively become a majority Protestant nation.

A Protestant or Evangelical conversion would have been unthinkable in most Latin American families just thirty years ago, but today it's a rare family that doesn't count an Evangelical at the dinner table. Indeed, nearly 40 percent of all Pentecostals are estimated to live in Latin America. Nearly all began life as Catholics. Nearly all come from the humbler classes. It is no surprise that US Latinos with strong ties to these countries are leaving the Church and joining other denominations. Their reasons for doing so are not always war or violence. Like their Anglo counterparts, some have fled Catholicism because of simple disillusionment: either a growing disgust with mounting cases of corrupt and pedophile priests, or the Church's resolute stand against abortion and same-sex marriage. But the proof is in the calculus: among

Latinos—for whom oppression, poverty, and racism are the rule—an astonishing number are taking a cue from their origin countries and finding refuge in Evangelical megachurches. This is not an aberration but part of a larger trend, particularly in the global south. In the 1990s only 6 percent of the world's Christians claimed to be Pentecostalists; a generation later, that figure is more than 30 percent. Today the majority of Christians on this planet are either Pentecostal or Evangelical.

Whatever belief system they choose, there is no question that Latinos gravitate to religious life. Three out of four claim to be good Christians and attend church regularly. Some even attend services every day. But less than half (47 percent) of the entire Latinx population in the United States is Catholic—a radical drop from the majority (67 percent) the Church held just ten years ago. Throughout the hemisphere, from North Dakota to the southernmost tip of Chile, believers are being born again in breathtaking numbers, prompting Evangelical temples to sprout by the thousands even as Catholic churches sell off properties to survive.

The most stubbornly Catholic among us, it seems, are the Mexican and Dominican Americans, perhaps because their countries of origin were among the first to be conquered and evangelized by Spain: 60 percent are loyal members of the faith. And yet the overall Latino numbers tell a very different story: 25 percent of all Hispanics in this country have converted to Evangelism or Protestantism. (One in three Salvadorans is an Evangelical.) Among these figure the Baptist Latinos, whose burgeoning accumulation of seven thousand churches is scattered to every corner of the United States. If the numbers seem imprecise, it is because some of the congregations choose the shadows. Many start as basement prayer gatherings. Others meet at night, in shuttered shops. They congregate in private homes, open fields, parking lots. Rather than websites, they have Facebook pages or YouTube channels. Sometimes the only way to find them is by a handwritten sign planted in a front yard or taped to a streetlamp.

According to Richard Land, a former executive of the Southern Baptist Convention, "If you left Washington, DC, and drove all the way to LA, there wouldn't be one town you'd pass that doesn't have a Baptist church with an *Iglesia Bautista* [a Spanish-language affiliate] attached to it." There is, by now, a ritual to the recruitment: When a Latin American appears in town, a Baptist missionary is sent out to greet her. He knocks on her door, shares the Gospel, courts the family, assists them with their transition to a new life, and, before long, new church members are born. These fledgling, improvised congregations are meant to be a deliberate departure from whatever faith went before, a way of assuming a new American identity, and yet they have a distinctly Hispanic twist. Prayer services feature salsa music, fragrant heaps of *pan dulce*, strong coffee, and that family-friendly, bear-hugging, ebullient Latino warmth that Anglo churches just don't offer. These rapidly sprouting little assemblies "don't look or sound anything like the megachurches," according to one observer. They are intimate, human, contagious, breeding wildly from town to town. "And they are hiding in plain sight."

But the choice isn't just between Catholicism and Evangelism. It can mean choosing no faith at all. One out of five Latinos—generally young and US born—is unaffiliated with any religion, even though they were raised Catholic, a fact that surely scandalizes grandparents and sets Vatican teeth on edge. One out of twenty-five is an avowed atheist. And one out of a hundred is a practicing Mormon, Jew, or Muslim, although that number, too, is currently in flux. The population is, without a doubt, as willing to adjust matters of the soul as it is to forfeit its past and wager its future.

## A FRIAR'S TALE

As my Father hath sent me, even so send I you.

—John 20:21

Father Emilio Biosca is a tall, commanding presence with a clipped gray beard, broad shoulders, and a bull chest. In his flowing brown robe, a cord circling his waist (its three tidy knots signifying poverty, chastity, and obedience), and large pointed hood, he might be a medieval monk wandering the narrow cobblestone streets of Umbria eight hundred years ago. He is a Capuchin, a spiritual companion of Saint Francis of Assisi. He is a fool for God—a *Jongleur de Dieu*—as Saint Francis liked to call his priests. Sworn to poverty and to carry out Christ's work as Christ himself might have done, Father Emilio is a Cuban American who first saw earthly light in Colorado Springs, grew up in the leafy suburbs of Virginia, served the Capuchins as far away as the rainforests of Papua New Guinea, and has come to minister the largely Hispanic flock that worships at the Shrine of the Sacred Heart in the very bosom of the nation's capital, twenty blocks north of the White House.

His parents had witnessed Fidel Castro's revolution in the late 1950s and, like the majority of Cubans at the time, welcomed the fresh wave of hope that the regime promised. But when the executions began, it became clear that they had no future under Castro. Emilio's father, a young dentist with a pregnant wife and two small daughters, had been told by the new government that, given his valuable skills, he could not emigrate; but his baby girl had developed a rare form of childhood cancer, and he and his wife were determined to give her the best medical attention they could find. When officials informed them that the child would be sent off to Communist Czechoslovakia for treatment, it was time to go—illegally, if need be. Come 1964, Dr. Biosca secured the necessary counterfeit documents, packed up his older daughter, and left Havana for good. He traveled through Mexico, crossing into the United States alongside a multitude of others who were fleeing the chaos of that island. He had already smuggled his pregnant wife and ailing baby out of Cuba via the Bahamas and arranged for the child to be seen at a hospital in Colorado Springs. When he finally arrived there, his wife greeted him with an American-born son, Emilio, and the news that their little girl had begun the urgently needed treatment.

In Marxist Cuba, the Bioscas had been people of faith, but not necessarily among those who chose a high profile in the church. They were not alone in this. Before the revolution, Catholic churches had focused on serving the rich, and so, once Marxists assumed power, the faithful were not inclined to attend Mass and expose themselves as members of the former oligarchy. For those who struggled to survive those harsh

years of Communist indoctrination, the Church's halls were more hazard than sanctuary. Some of the Bioscas who remained on the island ad-
hered to the faith; others joined the Communist Party and turned their
attentions to altering the highly divided society Cuba had become.

All that changed when Dr. Biosca moved his family to Colorado and
then to Kansas to attend medical school for the second time, and then
to Arlington, Virginia, where he would open his practice. As his patients
and family grew in number, the young father, hungry for camaraderie,
rejoined the Agrupación Católica Universitaria, a Cuban organization he
had known as a young man. *The agrupados* championed the development
of young professionals and advocated Jesuit principles of faith, family, educational excellence, and mutual support. The *agrupados* met officially in
"houses" scattered along the Eastern Seaboard as well as informally—on
camping trips or at barbecues—where they bantered in Spanglish and established lifelong bonds over *cafecitos* and *pan con lechón*. With a growing
family and shouldering all the expenses of his education, Dr. Biosca was
virtually penniless, but he made ends meet by stocking shelves at his local
Woolworths or pumping gas at a nearby station. Fortunately, he also had
the fraternal support of priests and young professionals of the Agrupación.

In time, with seven children in tow—six girls and Emilio—Dr. Biosca
began to take Emilio on father-son outings with the *agrupados*, and a
firm seed of spirituality was planted in the boy. Emilio never told the
priests who were recruiting in the Catholic school he attended, but by
the time he was fifteen, he longed to pursue life as a missionary. It was an
unusual step for a Latino boy. Even today, out of the tens of thousands
of Catholic priests in the country, only 8 percent are men of Hispanic
descent. But Emilio was determined, and that ambition gradually sharp-
ened. Not only did he dream of serving abroad, wanting no easy as-
signments, but also he longed to pursue his mission on a faraway island
"beyond the structural order of things." Perhaps even in Communist
Cuba, the land his parents had abandoned to bring him to America.

In 1994 young Emilio was ordained into the Catholic ministry at
the Shrine of the Sacred Heart in Washington, DC, the very church he
would come to lead twenty-five years later. He had pledged himself to

the Capuchins, a Franciscan order that had been founded in 1525 with the firm purpose of renewing Saint Francis of Assisi's original, highly rigorous vows of poverty, devotion, and service. Almost immediately, Emilio was sent on a mission that certainly qualified as one beyond the structural order of things. It was to be on a faraway island. But it wasn't Cuba. He was to replace an elderly priest who had just returned from his mission severely pummeled not only by disease but by a battery of rocks flung by tribesmen in the bush. Emilio was dispatched on a ten-year mission to the rainforests and highlands of Papua New Guinea.

In 1955 the Pittsburgh order of Capuchins, which had identified the remote, un-contacted Papua New Guineans as a population ripe for evangelization, sent its first priests to begin the mission. They had decided to Christianize the islanders after World War II, when American airplanes flying over the Pacific had looked down and seen that Papua New Guinea—the second largest island on earth—was swarming with tribal settlements heretofore unknown to the civilized world. There seemed to be no end to the clusters of villages below, and, indeed, when the first Capuchins arrived, they learned that two million souls who belonged to thousands of tribes and spoke more than eight hundred languages inhabited that dense tangle of green.

As the Capuchins descended from boats and, later, from twentieth-century aircraft, they understood they were dropping into a world of Stone Age aboriginals. Throughout this wild, stormy, and uncharted territory—from its towering, snow-capped peaks to its tropical rainforest valleys—lived a people still locked in tribal wars, practicing age-old polygamy, devoid of the most basic tools and health education. By the time Father Emilio stepped off an airplane in 1994, the population had more than doubled to five million. It would double again in the course of his ten-year stay. Brought briskly into the modern day by a multitude of Christian churches that followed the Capuchins and filled the island with missionaries, Papua New Guineans would leap ten thousand years in the course of a single lifetime.

More than anything, young Emilio was struck by what Christianity was bringing to this isolated landmass. His mission seemed an uncomfortable mirror on the past—a surreal facsimile of the Franciscan vanguard that had penetrated the New World in the fifteenth century with the fevered aim of winning souls to Jesus. He found Papuans close to the earth, warm, approachable, highly perceptive, with an appreciation for community that was rare. He began to reflect on their earthly experience, so different from his own: an attenuated lifespan of forty years; a mind-set in which one's only known horizon is the next row of trees; the absence of any notion of a nuclear family, or central marketplace, or place of learning; the gaping social gulf between men and women, with tribesmen inhabiting a single, large, central house while women lived on its perimeter.

In time, his long treks into the bush to find Christian prospects became a singularly gratifying experience. There were dazzling successes: Emilio found most Papuans opening themselves eagerly to Western knowledge—to mathematics, science, reading, writing, and the basic tenets of Christianity. The receptive ones learned rapidly and well. "In an American context," he conjectures, "they might have gone on to become physicists or poets." But teaching the principle of individual independence in a culture that prized tribal allegiance was a thorny business. And preaching monogamy to a polygamous society became a revelation. Emilio found himself teaching the meaning of adultery—even the concept of sin itself. The Christian covenant of marriage—one man, one woman, one family—as "the original cell of human society," and the Christian taboo of bigamy, much less polygamy, seemed anomalous and bizarre to the Papuans. After all, multiple marriage was not about men enjoying sex with an assortment of women; it was about tribal relations: about the use of a river, the establishment of diplomatic relations, the ability to walk safely from one territory to another. When a man took a wife from another tribe and propagated with her, wars were ended, treaties forged, alliances made. Take that away from this ancient tribal culture, and what might be the ramifications? Take war from a warrior nation, and you could end up with a population of unemployed men. Such were the conundrums this young Latino from the suburbs of Virginia was made to contemplate about the evangelization of the world's peoples. And yet the dividends were rich: a soaring population of believers, a vigorous rise in their lifespans, a safe passage into modernity.

When his Papuan mission ended ten years later in 2004, Friar Emilio was drawn to study the centrality of the Christian marriage more deeply. He spent two years in Washington, DC, devoting himself to the Pontifical John Paul II Institute for Studies on Marriage and Family. Returning to an American setting was jarring, disorienting. So much had changed in the course of ten years: America seemed louder, shriller, ruder, and more frenetic. The Bill Clinton–Monica Lewinsky sex scandal and the president's subsequent impeachment had rocked the land. Then there was the bitterly contested 2000 election of George W. Bush, followed a year later by al Qaeda's ruthless attacks on Manhattan's World Trade Center. The terrorist actions set the stage for two protracted wars overseas, in Afghanistan and then, senselessly, in Iraq. The cacophony made Emilio long to be back in the Papuan bush, tending to hungry souls, serving their spiritual needs, bringing them to Jesus. But not much later, in 2007, he was called to serve on an island that was experiencing the opposite of Papua New Guinea's Christian efflorescence. He was sent to Cuba, where Catholicism effectively had been purged from the map.

The Catholic faith was hardly in evidence in Havana, Santiago, or Santa Clara. It seemed nonexistent. When Friar Emilio arrived, there were only four Capuchin Franciscan friars serving the entire country, and they were all from Spain. Certainly, the survival of the order was in peril here. But even more pressing, as far as Emilio was concerned, was the fact that, although 60 percent of the Cuban population self-identified as culturally Catholic, less than 0.5 percent attended services, and some were using the Church as a stepping stone—to leave Cuba entirely.

Cuba's Communist Party, clearly opposed to the restoration of any vestige of Catholicism, monitored the foreign clergy closely; once priests were admitted to the island, they were watched, their every action followed. If that weren't challenge enough, there was the rising prevalence of Santería. This folk religion—a syncretic blend of West African Lukumí and Catholicism—had been strictly forbidden by both Church and government before the revolution, but it was flourishing now in Cuba, especially Havana, and it was being practiced at home by more than 70 percent of the island's residents.

Based on myths of Yoruba gods, rituals of animal sacrifice, and a deep connection to nature, Santería had been firmly planted by the slaves of the Middle Passage: the hundreds of thousands of Africans who had been shackled, shanghaied, and impelled to labor in the sugar fields of the colonial lords. Wildly popular, it infused the music, the art, the very culture of Cuba, and Fidel Castro's government could do little to stop it, other than intimidating, threatening, criminalizing, and detaining the priests who ministered to the faithful—the *babalawos* and *olorishas*. For twelve long years, Father Emilio did what he could, exorcising those who wanted to release themselves from Santería, striving to win souls to the Christian fold, and working feverishly to offset the constant drain of practicing Catholics who, year after year, abandoned Cuba for friendlier shores. But these were lean times for evangelization, and when he departed the island, Emilio felt he had left much work behind.

His reward would come in his next mission, an opportunity to lead the Shrine of the Sacred Heart, a church and school that served the Hispanic neighborhoods of Washington, DC: Mount Pleasant and Columbia Heights. These were communities that, for years, had received an open fire hose of Salvadorans, Hondurans, and Guatemalans, refugees from the wars and calamities that continued to grip the Northern Triangle. Unlike the feeble congregations of Cuba, here was a church replete with passionate believers, lined with the shining, expectant faces of those who had heard of Sacred Heart even before crossing the border to El Norte. *"Vayate al Sagrado Corazón"*—"Get yourself to the Sacred Heart"—desperate aspirants were advised as they fled their native villages to make the long trek north. It's there, in the very bosom of the American capital. *"Te ayudarán."* "They will help you."

After Father Emilio's improvised missions in the bush of Papua New Guinea and the dilapidated neighborhoods of Cuba, his work in this splendid Byzantine shrine, modeled after the cathedral in Ravenna, Italy, seemed almost too effortless. The church and its companion school are humming hives of activity, well-oiled machines that run themselves. Ninety percent of Sacred Heart's parishioners are first- or second-generation Central Americans, and they are committed, energetic, engaged in every possible chore. They lead prayer meetings, cook for the hungry, serve any pilgrim who appears at the doorstep, clean the facilities, tend the garden, build the furniture, fix whatever breaks. The church offers Mass in English, Spanish, Vietnamese, Portuguese, and Haitian Creole in dozens of services every week. And it does all this with funds provided by the most humble of devotees, donated several times a day via the collection plates. Not one penny of support comes from the greater Church. When I expressed surprise at this, given the ample bank accounts of Protestant churches that court Latinos, Father Emilio only smiled. He was a Capuchin, after all, pledged to a life of privation.

Sacred Heart hadn't always been a church for Hispanics. It began as one for the rich. But it was also a church for the city's marginalized. It had been built and founded at the turn of the twentieth century by prosperous Italian Americans, families that, despite their mounting successes, were sneered at by the Anglo American elite. The Italians sought a suitable place to worship, a place to thank God for their good fortune, and they quickly decided to do so on one of the grandest avenues of all: Sixteenth Street, the elegant promenade that leads from the White House to the magnificent Tudor mansions of northwest Washington.

Toward that objective, they bought a large tract of land that straddled Sixteenth Street and made for a conspicuous Catholic presence in the very heart of the city. But leaders of Anglo congregations that worshiped in the stately churches lining that boulevard, all of them Protestant, objected. Prejudice against Catholics was so widespread in the nation's capital at the turn of the twentieth century—as it was throughout America—that Catholic churches were forbidden from being built on that coveted stretch of real estate. According to detractors, Catholics were papists, "garlic eaters," partisans of "rum, Romanism, and rebellion," and certainly not to be trusted. So, to mollify the Protestants, Sacred Heart's foundation was dug slightly to one side, with a narrow sliver of a lane—essentially a driveway—separating the structure from the avenue.

By the 1940s, Spanish-speaking members of Washington's international diplomatic corps, finding Catholic establishments few and far between, began attending the church, and, to accommodate them, Mass began to be offered in that language. But the tide truly turned in the 1970s, when a massive wave of Central Americans, largely Salvadorans, began to flow into the capital's "Spanish" neighborhoods, producing a proliferation of bodegas, taquerías, and dance halls in the heart of the city. By the 1980s, 90 percent of Sacred Heart's parishioners were Latinx, a good number of them undocumented. The Sacred Heart School, which had been founded in 1905 to serve the children of European ancestry, quickly became a bilingual Spanish establishment—the only Catholic school in the city offering a bilingual curriculum and, eventually, the winner of many accolades and prizes. Today, more than forty years later, it is not unusual to see three generations of a Latino family at the church's Spanish-language Mass or the breakfast that follows—the wholly American children chattering freely in both languages. The English-language services, too, are filled to capacity with worshipers straining to comprehend and absorb the language of their new home.

It is in moments like these that raw statistics come to life. If Catholicism is slipping away neglected among American whites (one in ten of all American adults is a former Catholic), those dwindling congregations are being more than offset by the constant influx of Hispanic and Asians who arrive on our shores every year. A full third of America's Catholics today are foreign born and more than likely nonwhite. Indeed, Catholicism the world over has become more brown and yellow. The trend is fully observable in geographic terms: in 1910 two-thirds of all Catholics lived in Europe; a century later, only a quarter live there and two-thirds live in the global South. While parishes in Europe and the United States are watching attendance spin into free fall, Catholicism is enjoying its greatest expansion in history: in the last one hundred years, its believers have more than quintupled their numbers from 267 million in 1900 to 1.36 billion today. This is due, in no short measure, to the evangelizing missions of priests such as Friar Emilio, who have focused on winning souls in places like Papua New Guinea—or sub-Saharan Africa, or the Asia-Pacific. It stands

to reason that America's Catholic clergy are gradually coming to the realization that their future depends on congregations that look exactly like
Father Emilio's in the Latino barrio of Washington, DC.

If Emilio, one of Saint Francis's chosen "fools for God," had begun
his priestly charge by rescuing a godless flock in a faraway rainforest
only to move to re-Christianize souls on a postlapsarian island, he now
arrived at the third test of his missionary prowess. This time it would
turn out to be a stock American challenge. He had been brought to
Washington, DC, to the very church in which he had been ordained a
quarter century before, to succeed the parish's leader—a much-loved
Capuchin priest who, for all his merits, had failed to chastise a friar accused of molesting girls. It was a thorny crisis, scandalizing the city yet
prompting some to rise to the accused's defense, and it required a calm,
just, and conciliatory hand. As the investigation deepened, six accusers
came forward, two women and four girls between nine and fifteen years
old with various claims of sexual abuse against the accused friar, from
inappropriate kissing to outright groping of "private parts." The head
priest, having neglected to report these allegations to the archdiocese
in a timely manner, was removed from his post and relocated to Puerto
Rico. Emilio was to take his place.

For Father Emilio, a man of God who had grown up wanting to
serve in the most challenging parts of the world, this was a test of a
different kind. There were no tribespeople to educate, no Communist
atheists to lure home to the faith. He was not expected to wander blind
into the bush or knock on strangers' doors so much as to tend to a congregation of refugees who had flocked to the Shrine's portals seeking
nothing but safety and found danger instead. Not from the known perils
of the past—rampant hunger or civil wars—but from a libidinous priest.
From the church itself.

A few months after Emilio's arrival to this spiritual nadir, the COVID
virus descended like a scourge, robbing the lives of many a parishioner
at the front lines of the pandemic: hospital orderlies, sanitation workers, nannies, eldercare providers, kitchen help, truckers, food factory laborers, field-workers. But out of that vortex, and by virtue of Emilio's

steady guidance, a kind of order emerged: the offending priest was sent to prison, his superior was transferred to a faraway post; Sacred Heart teachers rallied to serve the children; humble volunteers undertook to scour the premises, lead the prayer groups, double the number of services, and reach out to others in need. Mario Andrade, a Guatemalan who had arrived in the United States twenty years before, rose at five in the morning on Sundays to make his way to that century-old temple, disinfect its pews after every service, cook the food, scrub the floors, and assist any pilgrims who knocked on the door, looking for sanctuary. Like everyone else, he did what was needed. Nobody left the fold.

"The people have made this house," Father Emilio tells me. "In all my experience with the church and its missions, I've never seen a commitment so total." This congregation of displaced souls, this army of fierce believers—and their thoroughly American children—are his flock now. When I ask about the prospect of going back to the harder work of evangelizing the faithless, he corrects me. "Not faithless. Human beings are never entirely faithless. They are inherently believing," he says with conviction. "When they say they don't believe, they are simply doing violence to themselves." Preventing that self-immolation and making the spirit whole is this friar's work—wherever his God might take him.

# 8

# THE GODS OF CHOICE

If there are two religions in the land, they will cut each other's throats;
and if there are thirty, they will dwell happily in peace.

—Voltaire, *The Philosophical Letters*, 1733

For the first four years of my life, I had no religion. I had been born
into the world a disputed soul. My Episcopalian mother had refused
to capitulate to Peruvian custom and baptize me Catholic. She was still
livid that my grandmother Rosa—my beloved abuelita—had whisked
off my older sister, Vicky, to be baptized in the clinic's chapel just hours
after her birth, even as our Lima family was in the lobby, drinking champagne and toasting my father. My brother, George, on the other hand,
had been born during Mother's visit to her parents in Wyoming, and so
he was baptized Protestant in St. Thomas's Episcopal Church in Rawlins, establishing a full-blown war with my abuelita. Mother was only too
happy that before I was twenty-four days old, our little family had moved
far from Lima—far from her mother-in-law—to the sugar fields that
rimmed the raging coast of the Pacific, just north of Trujillo. Mother
decided to hold out on my baptism, keep me on neutral ground, all too
sure that my soul would be the next battlefield.

To my abuelita's dismay, years passed with my tiny spirit in limbo.
As far as she was concerned, I was a pagan, barred from heaven, and, indeed, from a Catholic point of view, I suppose I was. Any truly religious

education I received was from the humble Peruvians around me, the ordinary villagers who came and went from our house, tending the gardens, peddling their fruit, feeding us, minding me when my parents were out and about, partying with their friends. It was those Quechua Indians who taught me about our earthly cosmos, its pantheon of gods, its natural wonders, its nocturnal demons. From them, I learned about the munificence of Pachamama, our bountiful earth mother, and the all-seeing *apus*, powerful gods that looked down from their mountain perches, heralding my mornings with shimmering, sunlit crowns. From time to time, my father would drive us into Trujillo to sit in the pews of its majestic seventeenth-century cathedral, light candles, and have our heads patted by gentle-eyed monks. But I was learning more about Inti, the great god sun, or Ai-Apaec, the vengeful decapitator, than about God, the Son, or the Holy Spirit. Whenever my grandparents made yearly visits from Lima, tottering out to our sand-blown, seaside hacienda in their city finery, Abuelita would fume to my father that time was passing me by, I was bound for hellfire, and what kind of mother would do that to her child, anyway?

Abuelita eventually would have her way when I was four years old. One fogbound winter's day, my parents sped down the coastal highway to deposit me on my grandparents' doorstep to go off for a four-month holiday with my sister and brother. Not an hour went by before Abuelita started plotting the salvation of my eternal soul. During my stay, she taught me prayers, cut my hair to a tidy bob, took my chubby measurements, and fashioned a smart white suit with a neatly pleated skirt. She ferried me to the center of Lima, shooed me through the splendid cathedral, told me all this would be mine, and bought me a pair of gleaming patent leather shoes to hallow the moment. On the appointed day of my baptism, she scrubbed me down, dressed me, and pinned a white lace doily on my head, and then we all went off to La Virgen Milagrosa, the imposing, gray stone church on the Miraflores plaza, where I was blessed, anointed with holy water, and brought to the arms of Jesus.

When my parents returned, flushed with the ruddy glow of an American summer, I greeted them with the happy news that I was now

Catholic. My mother was furious, but I thought I spied my father giving Abuelita a conspiratorial wink. Eight years later, when I was already an immigrant to the United States of America, Mother had the final victory in that unrelenting war of the spirit: she signed me up for confirmation classes at Calvary Episcopal Church in Summit, New Jersey, making me not only bilingual and bicultural, but bi-theist—cleft to my very soul.

## BORN-AGAIN LATINOS

He said to me, "Selena, hold on, I hurt when you hurt. I cry when you cry, but I will *never, ever* leave your side. Work with me, walk with me, and watch how I do it."

—Selena Gomez, singer, Mexican American,
conversation with Jesus, 2019

I had been confirmed in the Episcopal Church, but as years went by, I remained a bifurcated soul. I was Catholic, I was Protestant. I sensed my heart was large enough—open enough—to hold the faiths of the two women who had most shaped the adult I had become. As a result, today I attend both churches and feel at home in both. It is not the usual way. Most Latinos who have fled the Catholic Church to become Protestants or born-again Evangelicals put loyalty to Rome firmly aside, and they do so with considerable conviction. Their numbers are impressive: by 2007, almost half of all Latino seminarians in the country identified as Evangelicals; researchers project that, by 2030, half of the entire population of American Latinos will identify as Protestant Evangelicals. Combine that with the projected growth expected in the overall Hispanic population, and, in less than a decade, we may see forty million Latinos—a congregation the size of California—heading to American Evangelical churches every Sunday. The Catholic Church may no longer serve them, but they remain resolute Christians—a people of faith, first and foremost.

Today the overwhelming majority of these newly minted Protestants are millennials or Generation Xers. Statistics tell us they are mostly female. The lion's share are also foreign-born immigrants with less than a high-school education, and they live in households that subsist on less than $30,000 a year. This working-class, born-again cohort of Latinx join Evangelical churches largely because they are attracted to the warmth of the embrace and the built-in lure of economic advancement—the promise that, once they ascend the money ladder, they can redraw themselves as not poor, not inferior, not objects of prejudice, but as inheritors of the beautiful "reset" that is implicit in the American Dream. They believe that if they reach that Evangelical promised land of rebirth, they will reap the elusive—and entirely mythological—American reward of being a member of a truly egalitarian democracy. They don't necessarily care to assimilate and join the mainstream, mind you, since many Latino immigrants choose to retain their Spanish, reside in Latino neighborhoods, and preserve their cultural traditions; they simply aspire to have what they believe every other American has: affirmation and opportunity.

To put it simply, Latinos are depending on Evangelicalism to fulfill its promise of vertical mobility. Often, the most persuasive models of success are the leaders of churches themselves, chief executive officers such as Samuel Rodriguez, the galvanic, high-profile CEO of the National Hispanic Christian Leadership Conference (NHCLC), the largest Latino Evangelical Christian organization in the world. "Pastor Sam," as he is called by his hundreds of thousands of followers, was a convert not from Catholicism but from science. His grandfather had been a pioneer for the Pentecostal church in Puerto Rico, the island's first Evangelical chaplain for the Assemblies of God, and the old man was known for taking the parable of the Good Samaritan seriously. He would bring home strangers who needed a hearty meal or a safe place to sleep, and if anyone in the house objected, he would roar out the pertinent verses of Luke 10 to shush them. As a boy, Sam was familiar with the basic tenets of Pentecostalism and attended services every Sunday with his parents, but he doubted everything he heard. He was more interested in physics than in parables, more likely to pursue life as an agnostic than follow in his grandfather's footsteps.

He had been born in the old, legendary steel town of Bethlehem,

Pennsylvania, to working-class Puerto Rican immigrants whose ancestors carried every phenotype of the island's tempestuous colonial past. Sam was a naturally gregarious boy with racially ambiguous features—not entirely white, not indigenous, not black—and he made friends across racial lines easily. His father was a Mack truck driver, his mother a homemaker. They were bred-in-the-bone Pentecostalists, faithful members of Bethlehem's Central Assembly of God. The Assemblies had established roots in 1914 as white offshoots of an African American church, but they and their Pentecostalist spinoffs mushroomed rapidly and purposefully over the years, their vigorous proliferation virtually unnoticed. From the start, Pentecostalism had been conceived as a muscular, evangelizing faith and its overriding goal was to "plant" as many churches around the world as possible. The name itself comes from *Pentecost*, which refers to the moment—fifty days after Jesus's death on the cross—that the Holy Spirit appeared and granted Christ's apostles the ability to speak in foreign tongues, enabling them to go forth anywhere in creation and bring converts to the faith.

And so it was. In 1980 only 6 percent of the world's Christians were Pentecostalist, but those few went forth and brought in converts, as the faith required. As a result, a mere generation later, one in four of the world's Christians was a member. With each evangelized recruit becoming an evangelizer, the mission continued its powerful algorithm for exponential growth. Today, every twenty-four hours, the Pentecostal church adds another thirty-five thousand born-again faithful to its ranks. Pentecostals now represent some six hundred million believers worldwide, twenty million of them in the United States, with an overwhelming majority in Latin America and Africa. Clearly, this is the fastest growing religion on God's good earth. It counts a tidy third of the two billion Christians on the planet. By 2050, it aims to count a billion. So, it is no surprise that, if Latin Americans are converting so enthusiastically, American Latinos are following suit. The rate of conversion among this contingent is astonishing, and Reverend Rodriguez is a premier agent of that change: one out of every three Latinos who leaves the Catholic Church in this country joins Pastor Sam as a Pentecostal.

For Pentecostalism, a physical church—some the size of an airport—
is vital to the mission. They are villages unto themselves: part music sta-
dium, part hall of worship, part school, part way station for any conceivable
need. The programs they offer are often education oriented, focusing on
the young. They provide remedial tutoring for flagging students, music
classes for toddlers, English-language learning for immigrants, speed-
dating events for young professionals, financial advice for small business
owners, counseling for troubled teens, even addiction cures. For those
who need assistance reading a legal document in English, or applying for
a green card, or even finding the right childcare, the church becomes a
one-stop destination. The network of support alone is a powerful magnet. Latinos are courted, welcomed, invited to come find whatever assistance they need. And come they do. As their numbers burgeon, so does
the faith's political power. If it surprises anyone that Latinos—a segment
of American society once assumed to be liberal—have recently begun to
identify more and more with conservative doctrine, one only need study
the religious migration to Evangelicalism to understand why.

The reasons for those conversions abound. Latino immigrants arrive
in this country weary of corruption, violence, and the lack of opportunity in their homelands. They come here with a hunger for a better
economy, heightened security, a more controlled society, a more governed self, a system that demands principles and opens the door to a
better life. The Evangelicals are offering just that. As Pastor Sam puts
it, "We have all heard the old song—the song of hatred, sin, racism, intolerance, division, strife, brokenness. It's time to sing something new."
Worshiping in their ranks, they argue, offers a direct conversation with
God, fewer intermediaries between man and his Creator. Whereas in a
Catholic Mass the congregation is made to sit and listen, the Evangelical
Church urges theirs to speak, shout, share the faith, hug a stranger, join
the family. "You can't do that in Catholic churches," says Pastor Sam.
"We offer Latinos greater equity in the moment. Greater unity."

It is this sense of participation and advancement that Evangelical
churches promise and many Latinos crave. Not only are the codes of
ethics rigorous, they are often spartan: in many churches, a convert is

expected to attend religious services regularly, bond with neighbors, reject homosexuality, prohibit drinking, spurn sex before marriage, condemn abortion, decry racism, and place a man as the bedrock of his family (although women are valued as church equals). For a culture steeped in machismo yet weary of violence, the appeal is obvious. But there are other inducements. To reach salvation, for instance, there is no need to confess to a priest or travel via a crucis of self-blame: conversion and baptism alone can win it. Neither is there a need to die poor in order to inherit the earth; life can be better right here, on this very ground. Evangelicals call it spiritual rebirth, instant regeneration, the grace of being born again. Most alluring in the missionary's message, perhaps, is the sheer practicality of these religions. Pentecostalism—which touts itself as "prosperity theology"—promises a road to upward socioeconomic mobility. There is nothing wrong with wanting the good life in the here and now, its pastors say. Never mind that Jesus preached that you cannot serve both God and mammon. For blue-collar Latino immigrants struggling to feed their families, keep a roof over their heads, and shoulder a Sisyphean rock up the proverbial slope, it is a tantalizing invitation.

Not all Evangelicals count themselves in the struggling classes, however. Some are Hollywood stars such as pop rock singer Selena Gomez, who was—until scandals of infidelity rocked her church's leadership— a regular worshiper at the Hillsong Church in Los Angeles. Gomez, a third-generation Mexican American once rated by Instagram as the most popular living person on the planet, has not been shy about attaching her faith to her public persona. Her social media posts, her interviews, even her songs are filled with euphoric references to God, Jesus, and the Bible. "I'm literally just laying down and thanking Jesus," she wrote one late-night moment on Twitter. "Where my Father has taken me . . . is exactly where I am meant to be." Naturally, the quarter million ardent fans who "loved" that tweet might have been tempted to follow their doll-faced heroine to Hillsong the following Sunday, especially since Selena has counted Hillsong's pop rock band—and its silk-throated singer-songwriter, Brooke Fraser—as one of her all-time listening favorites. Star promotion such as this can have an exponential effect on recruitment. Hillsong is nothing if not a celebration of upbeat, singularly engaging pop Christian music, and its message of welcome to young, phenomenally successful professionals has met with remarkable success, attracting the likes of Justin Bieber, Kourtney Kardashian, U2's Bono, and former NBA basketball star Tyson Chandler, not to mention Selena's upwardly mobile Latinx fans.

In the last thirty years or so, a flurry of high-end megachurches like Hillsong have sprung up, especially in the West, and the Evangelical movement has emerged as a slick, highly commercial, multimedia leviathan. In the Los Angeles congregation of the Mosaic church, for instance, its founder and leading pastor, Erwin McManus, born in El Salvador, emerges onstage in skinny black jeans, black leather high-top sneakers, hair slicked back in a trendy undercut, looking for all the world—as one observer put it—like a pop star swanning into the Chateau Marmont. He is a self-described "cultural thought leader," part entrepreneur, part fashion designer, filmmaker, and futurist. Only rarely does he refer to his Latino roots, but when he does, he is blunt. "I'm an immigrant from El Salvador," he tells an interviewer, "and Spanish was my first language. I learned English here in the States. I never knew my real father and my mother remarried someone who was involved in what I would call creative underground economies."

The name McManus, he admits, is an alias. His real name as a boy was Irving Rafael Mesa-Cardona, and in that very real childhood, growing up wasn't easy. Arriving in the United States, he felt unstrung, confused; his teachers classified him as "retarded." But if his climb to success was hard, he doesn't talk about it much. His sermons are light-hearted, filled with pop references. He compares conversations with God to the information-sharing network of Waze: click on God and He can always tell you the easiest way to get there. He wonders why Picasso and Mozart are called geniuses, but Christ is not. He talks about being an imperfect man who had to encounter Jesus before he could dig down and find the valuable human being within his own skin. His congregation, which consists largely of prosperous, white, millennial urbanites—from starlets to engineers—finds strong connection to his story. Mosaic's message of self-resurrection is contagious, and, for the moment at least, is making inroads among ambitious young Latinx not only in California, but farther south in Ecuador and Mexico.

On the opposite side of the continent, in Orlando, Florida, another megachurch with a similar name has sprung up to serve an entirely different clientele. Ironically enough, it is called—in an almost peremptory tone—*This* is Mosaic. One of its pastors, Javier Antique, a Venezuelan army veteran who works as an emergency room nurse during the week, is committed to spreading the gospel on Sundays. Not to rich, young millennials, but to working-class Latinos who struggle to make a living laboring in the giant amusement parks and tourist hotels that have sprung up around them. Perhaps because there is no system of ordination or any true governing body, Evangelical churches like This is Mosaic spin off from other churches and mushroom ad hoc, according to the whims of their founders. It is this ease in formation and leadership that have made Latino pastors more and more common in the Evangelical universe.

This is Mosaic grew from modest prayer gatherings in a Clermont, Florida aerobics gym to massive music extravaganzas in the reconfigured shell of a former appliance megastore in Winter Garden, Florida. Within a few years, the church had raised enough money to purchase another colossal building near Orlando's Walt Disney World. On any given Sunday when rock bands ramp up the speakers and the church walls begin to shake, thousands of worshipers crowd into these venues to share God's love. Pastor Antique began his connection to Evangelicalism in Venezuela as a translator for Team Mania Ministries, a worldwide, youth-oriented Evangelical mission committed to "raising up a young army who will change the world for Christ." When he immigrated to Tyler, Texas, in 2001 and began work there as an urgent-care nurse, Team Mania found him. Antique was immediately identified as a potential leader and, as he made friends in the Texan circuit of Evangelicals, he was recruited by This is Mosaic. Called to grow the newly planted church in Orlando, he is now responsible for drawing Latinos to the flock—anyone who needs help adjusting to American life and work—particularly the dazed, disoriented, and godforsaken who stumble in from troubled countries like his.

"They come with nothing but two hands and a desire to work," says Antique. "We need to help them. The church alone can't do it. Eventually we learn to live this work, reach out to them ourselves. We are the body of Christ, are we not? I try to be loving and kind, so that people can see Jesus in what we do." His church's credo agrees. "We are like a mosaic," its website states. "A broken, shattered people redeemed and brought together to display God's beauty to one another." Indeed, brokenness is key to the message that reverberates throughout the Evangelical world. Emerging from a shattered world is at the very core of the faith's explosive growth generally, and the image resonates deeply with the Latino experience. When Reverend Samuel Rodriguez says, "The size of our praise is directly proportional to the magnitude of the hell that God took us out of," Latinos know exactly what he means.

There is little doubt that Reverend Rodriguez's thundering rhetoric is responsible for the Evangelical church's meteoric rise among the Latino population in the United States—perhaps even the rising numbers in Javier Antique's cohort in Orlando. As chief executive officer of the National Hispanic Christian Leadership Conference (NHCLC), Rodriguez leads a network of more than forty-two thousand Evangelical churches that cater to Hispanic Americans. Between the Americas north and south, there are more than one hundred million souls in his flock. Pastor Sam, who bases his ministry on the teachings of Dr. Martin Luther King Jr. and Billy Graham, has served as advisor to three distinctly different United States presidents on both sides of the political aisle: George W. Bush, Barack Obama, and Donald Trump. He has spoken at presidential inaugurations as well as at the White House, and he has enjoyed the singular honor of being the first Latino invited to deliver keynote remarks at Martin Luther King Jr.'s memorial services. This is no easy high-wire act to negotiate: Reverend King to President Trump represents a breathtaking leap of ideology, not to mention oratorical style.

A dynamo of energy in his network as well as behind a podium, the sunny, baby-faced Rodriguez is, at least for the moment, the most ecumenical, apolitical—and sought-after—Evangelical preacher in the country. He is popular in both spiritual and secular circles. The *Wall Street Journal* identified him as one of America's seven most influential leaders. In 2013 *Time* magazine nominated him one of the one hundred most influential people in the world. He has held forth in passionate and eloquently inspirational sermons at Princeton, Yale, and the halls of the United States Congress. He has spoken on every major broadcast medium in the nation. He has produced films replete with his brand of Evangelicalism. His message? Latinos are Christians first, and we are a microcosm of a progressively diverse America. Yet we are misunderstood, underappreciated, and overlooked to the country's detriment. The political ramifications, he tells us, are bound to surprise us all.

But politics aside, Pastor Sam's message is overwhelmingly positive. Since the age of sixteen he has been preaching a message of reconciliation. Inspired as a child by the stirring oratory of Dr. King and the optimism of Billy Graham, he became convinced that, united spiritually, the Latino population could become a force for good in this country. For him, it wasn't so much an epiphany of the spirit as one of the mind. Strangely enough, having turned away from God as a boy, he found Him—all of a sudden—in the physics lab as a young man.

"My conversion came in an entirely nonreligious setting," he recounts. "I was a science guy. To me, the Webb Telescope was the greatest thing I'd ever heard of. But studying mathematics and the probability of chance at Penn State—as well as studying the complexities of what it took to create the Big Bang—there was no doubt in my mind that a higher intelligence had to be at work. How did we go from a mitochondrial level to sentient beings? When I broke down that equation, we had zero chance of being here without some greater design. It was math that revolutionized me. My belief in God is undergirded by calculus."

He was a star student, moved along so quickly through high school and college that, by the time he was nineteen, he had married his high school sweetheart and was teaching history at Liberty High School in Bethlehem. The day after he and his new bride moved into their all-white neighborhood, he woke up to see their house pounded with rotten eggs.

"White supremacists were marching through the streets of Pennsylvania in those days," he says. "It was clear that we—the only people of color in that neighborhood—had walked into hostile territory." But racism was not new to him. He had encountered it on the streets of Bethlehem, the schoolrooms, the playing fields. Even so, staring at his egg-slimed front door, he decided this was something he could use. Some good would come of it.

That single act of race hatred convinced him to focus on Hispanics. He wanted to fashion a mechanism that legitimized them, raised them up, not one that pleaded for special treatment. "I have always refused to see us as victims," he tells me. "We want no handouts. We work. We lead. We are the head, not the tail. I want Latinos to thrive, move on. I want them to go from waiter to owner, day laborer to boss. Come to my church, I tell them, and be empowered." Even as a teacher, he began speaking to large groups—to a massive congregation of ten thousand Texan Latinos on Thanksgiving Day in San Antonio, for instance, or massive audiences of popular television shows in Mexico. His language—be it English or Spanish—was spirited, human, powerful. "Why don't you reference Cesar Chavez?" he was asked, when he drew on the sermons of King and Graham. But he was determined to follow his own vision of interracial sympathies. "There is a divine order in this," he says, acknowledging his reliance on King's spiritual leadership. "We Latinos are deeply connected to the Black community. We have to get away from these mono-chromatic silos, away from the cognitive dissonance of the American binary, the artificial color line—the black versus white thing. They're nothing but echo chambers. A fight for social justice in this country can't be parsed by color. Your struggle is my struggle, pure and simple."

His passion for racial reconciliation is easily visible in the gargantuan hall of the church he personally calls his own, New Season Worship, in Sacramento, California, where worshipers gather in an auditorium much as they might gather for a rock concert. There, Pastor Sam serves a vibrant, multiethnic congregation of many ages. "My church looks like heaven to me," he says. And indeed, it is a phenotypically diverse representation of God's children. Unlike his massive, world-wide accu-mulation of Latino worshipers, New Season's followers are 40 percent white, 40 percent African American, and 20 percent Latino and Asian, spread across two campuses. They enter the hall jubilantly, greet one another with warm embraces, and jump from their seats when a band of rock musicians sporting baseball caps and crucifixes roar into their open-ing song, "Wake Up Sleepers!" Hands suddenly fly overhead and the entire assembly begins to sway and sing along with the band as words scroll on a jumbo screen, "Do you see what I see? He is risen! We are risen with him! Wake up, sleepers! If you see what I see, anything is pos-sible!" There is thunderous clapping, cheering, dancing in the aisles—a wild exultation—what Pastor Sam calls the Holy Spirit, rising from the floorboards, surging through the crowd.

At this particular service, a full hour of revelry goes by before Pastor Sam appears onstage and brings forward one of the singers, and then another; one is Ukrainian, the other Russian, and for at least a brief mo-ment in that electrified hall, a war is no more. The hostilities are paused. The Ukrainian turns out to be the daughter of Christian evangelist pas-tors in Kyiv. The Russian is a dewy-eyed beauty born far from Moscow. The women embrace, and Rodriguez proclaims that God's power is alive in the room. When he finally launches into his message for the con-gregation, it is impassioned, real, stirring, based entirely on Scripture, which he quotes book by book, verse by verse, and entirely by heart. He walks his mesmerized audience through passages phrase by phrase, putting each in context. When Jesus speaks with the Virgin Mary, he is "talking with his mama"; when Jesus gathers his disciples, he says, "Hey, guys, now that you know who I am, I need to tell you . . . I'm gonna die." By now, Rodriguez is pacing the stage in his workaday jacket, blue jeans, and sneakers, punching the air, looking every bit like any vigorous young man walking the streets of Sacramento. The effect is galvanizing. The crowd begins to chant, "Jesus! Jesus!" Pastor Sam's sunny babyface lights up with an infectious grin. "Say it again! Shout it again!" he tells them. When the members leave the hall, they are elated, slapping one another on the back, propelled by soul fire into a bright California morning.

Pastor Sam is so well known by now that he preaches to those of every stripe, from white Southern Baptists to African American civil rights groups. But he believes something unique is taking place among Hispanic believers. "Wherever you see a wildfire of spirituality, you see a Hispanic presence. The Latino community is a passionate community," he asserts, and here he uses the visual aid of the crucifix itself: We Latinos, he tells me, tend to reach across to one another, laterally, from person to person, group to group, like the horizontal bar in Jesus's cross. "But vertically," he points out, "God moves through the Hispanic church by the power of the Holy Spirit"—that is, up and down, from the Creator to the individual directly, just like Michelangelo's painting that dominates the ceiling of the Sistine Chapel. A godly reach. One by one.

The wildfire to which Reverend Rodriguez refers is all too evident in the thousands of Latino Pentecostal congregations cropping up every year in urban and rural landscapes alike. Across the United States, more Latino pastors with an eye on US Census predictions are energetically "planting" churches than ever before, winning Latino souls one at a time. After all, the Census Bureau has projected that, by 2060, Hispanics will number 111 million, nearly a third of this country's entire population, and white Evangelicals are not blind to the promise of growth inherent in that calculation. In fact, since 2006, white Evangelical churches have experienced a precipitous drop in their numbers, shrinking from 24 percent of the American population in 2006 to 14 precent in 2020. Pastor Sam fully understands the meaning of this. "We Latinos are not extending our hand to primarily white denominations and asking, 'Can you help us plant churches?'" says Pastor Sam. "We're going to them, saying, 'You all need *our* help.' This is a flipping of the script." It is surely as clear to white Evangelicals as it is obvious to him that Latinos represent the future of the church.

Indeed, according to Rodriguez, were you to group Pentecostals and Charismatics together (since both believe in direct, animating encounters with the Holy Spirit), you would be looking at half the entire Latino population in the United States. It is a stunning figure, attesting to the

Evangelical message's phenomenal success with this ethnicity. "We are people of the Holy Spirit," Rodriguez says. "I mean—based on sheer numbers—we are arguably the most Holy Spirit–centered community on planet Earth. So, if you're a Latino in this country, in all probability, you've had a direct encounter with the power of the Holy Spirit. That's pretty crazy, isn't it?"

## THE MORMONS

> I know that a lot of people coming here from Latin America are coming for a purpose. We are building a New Jerusalem here.
> —Bishop Saul Bramasco, Mormon, Chicago, 2022

In the sprawling periphery of Mexico City, in a district called Chimalhuacán, a bright-red two-hundred-foot statue—more evocative of an outsize, flamboyant nutcracker than a proud Aztec warrior—towers over one of the most destitute barrios of that grand metropolis. Built to the tune of $1.5 million, the *Guerrero Chimalli*, or "Warrior with a shield," overlooks neighborhoods that proliferate willy-nilly atop Mexico's largest landfill—a bawdy, scarlet affront to those who live in rank poverty below. The titan's shield, a monstrous metal plate that measures approximately fifty feet across and dominates the structure, is more a celebration of conquistador steel than Aztec valor. Almost five hundred miles away, nestled in a mountainous exuberance in the state of Jalisco, is Chimaltitán, the forgotten village where the genuine fifteenth-century shields were actually fashioned. They were not forged of gaudy red steel, to be sure, and they were not produced anywhere near Montezuma's shining city. They were sturdy escutcheons of plaited palm—highly ornamented and adorned with riotously colored feathers—built to repel the keenest spear, and they were manufactured in the busy workshops that once studded these hills. Today, except for random artifacts in museum windows, these armaments no longer exist. The village is a sleepy little agricultural town of six hundred, and it bears a crest bestowed by its conquerors: there is a cow, a row of corn, and a crucifix.

It is here in Chimaltitán—maker of shields—that Saul Bramasco was born into a family of eleven children, to a father who once dreamed of becoming a Catholic priest. Instead, his father married, became the village schoolteacher, and young Saul—filled with his own aspirations—made the long walk to California, then Utah, and eventually realized his father's dream. With a peculiar twist. He was baptized into the Mormon faith and ordained a bishop of the Church of Latter-day Saints.

Even as a boy, Saul doubted the stories he was reading in the family Bible. "I can't believe any of them," he told his mother in confidence one day as they walked to church. "I just don't think the Catholic Church is *true.*" Señora Bramasco was taken aback, horrified. "Don't say those things!" she told her son. "They will only bring you trouble." Life was hard enough even for the believers; how hard would it be for a child who bucked the faith? They were poor; dirt poor. That was worry enough for any mother. What was needed was not a rebel son, but hands to put on a plow, food to put on the table. Like the conqueror's crest, the landscape of Chimaltitán had been dominated by cornfields for five hundred years, and Saul's grandparents—as well as his ancestors of dozens of generations past—had labored in them. In 1985, with more than a dozen hungry mouths in his family, young Saul decided to leave, make his way north for a little while, and see what a future in El Norte might bring. Perhaps he would be more useful to his family there. He was little more than sixteen years old.

So it was that Saul crept across the border one night not far from San Diego and soon found himself three hundred miles away, picking cherries, grapes, lemons, and oranges in the farmlands that dominate Fresno County. Working his way along the Fresno Fruit Trail as a day laborer, he could see American pleasure-seekers enjoying the seasonal festivals: the pick-your-own-fruit farms, the stone-fruit jubilees, the bus tours that spilled smiling visitors onto the fertile fields. They were happy families, ordinary people, and the vision they cast of his American future was tantalizing. Saul decided to stay. After all, President Reagan had just passed the Immigration Reform and Control Act of 1986, which granted residency to farmworkers who could prove they had labored in the United States for at least ninety days. He applied, was accepted as a permanent resident, and eventually was lured away to Idaho to work in the lucrative potato industry, where the pay was better and opportunities more plentiful.

It was in Idaho Falls that he met the itinerant Mormon missionaries. One handed him the Book of Mormon in Spanish and asked nothing more of him than to read it, familiarize himself with its story, and let him know what he thought. Saul had already confessed to the man that he had studied the Old and New Testaments and not believed a word of them. The missionary nodded with understanding, but insisted. And so the young man read. On the night he turned the last page, he went out into the potato fields alone. It was near midnight, and the moon was full, resplendent with a glow Saul had never seen before, the land shimmering with a rare effulgence. He raised his eyes to the vaulting sky, its ink-black dome glistening with a thousand stars, and asked God if what he had just read was true. "It was like a spiritual rebirth," Saul tells me. "At that moment, a feeling of goodness shot right through me. The Lord Himself was bringing me to the Gospel." Saul was overwhelmed by the sense that the book had spoken to him directly. It had explained that people like him—Mexicans and other Latinos from even farther south—were especially blessed. They were the rightful descendants of the House of Israel, and, one day, legions of them would be drawn over the border and onto the American side—their ancient, ancestral terrain—and there would be little the Anglo-Saxons could do to stop them. They would flow home, back to the land they had always inhabited, back to where they had always belonged.

Saul was baptized into the Church of Latter-Day Saints in Idaho Falls, and, later that year, as per custom, he went on a mission to Mexico to recruit more Mormons. Stopping in Chimaltitán, he told his father, "Papi, I have found the true church." His father simply gazed into his eyes, searching for the boy he had once known. "Come home," was all he said. But the faith was too strong now. "My daddy is my earthly father," Saul says simply, "but I had found my Heavenly Father. That was never going to change." After his missionary sojourn in Mexico, he returned to Idaho Falls, took and passed the GED exam in Spanish, and decided to apply to Brigham Young University, the citadel of Mormon education, in order to finish his education. Saul hardly knew English well enough, but he entered a special plea on his application: "I am a convert to the church, I am here alone, I have served my mission, I pray you will consider me." He was accepted with a full scholarship.

He was not the first Latino soul the church had courted. As early as 1920, Mormon missionaries were aggressively pursuing Hispanic converts, but, since 1990, the campaign has intensified to a fever pitch, due to the general "crucial need" among Protestant faiths to attract the rapidly burgeoning Latino population. For the Church of the Latter-day Saints, however, the need goes deeper: its missionary efforts seek to return an entire people to a service and worship to which, according to the church, they always belonged. Mormon teachings claim that the Native Americans of today (and their mestizo offspring) are descendants of Israelites who migrated to the North American continent in 600 BC. Eventually, after centuries of war, they split into two groups: the Nephites, who were destroyed; and the Lamanites, who survived but lost their faith in God. Mormons believe that until all remaining Lamanites are converted to the faith, the millennial kingdom of Christ cannot begin. They are so convinced of this that when the church was organized in 1830, the elders considered what the Lord had in mind for the remnants of the Lamanite population. In 1948 one elder put a firm stamp on the Lord's desires:

> I see the Lamanites coming into this Church. Instead of coming in small groups of tens and hundreds, they will be in thousands. I see them organized into wards and stakes [congregations of three to five thousand believers] with Lamanite people comprising these stakes. I see them filling temples and officiating therein.

So, despite damning, racist passages in the Book of Mormon that rail against "the dark skins" of the Lamanites—a mark "set upon their fathers . . . a curse upon them because of their transgression and rebellion against their [white] brethren"—the drive to recruit the presumed descendants of the Lamanites, the Latinos—the indigenous people of the Americas—has become a key objective in Mormon churches from coast to coast.

It is not an easy objective. Whereas Latino Evangelical churches have experienced explosive growth in the last half century, mirroring the enormous success they have had throughout the global South, the same cannot be said for the Church of Latter-day Saints. Today Mormons are far more numerous in Latin America than they are in the United States. Indeed, although the faith was born here, 60 percent of all Mormons in the world live outside this country. There are almost six million in South America—a "bastion of Mormons," as one bishop puts it—with the great majority of them found in Mexico and Brazil. But in the United States, Latino Mormons represent a mere 1 percent of the Hispanic population—about six hundred thousand faithful—far fewer than the number of Mormons in either Mexico or Brazil, or even Peru. Still, the drive is on, and for all the challenges, American Latinos have become the fastest growing group in the church. When Bishop Bramasco says that Mormons like him are coming here from Latin America to build a new Jerusalem, he means it. Many of the Latino Mormons in the United States are transplants from Mexico or Peru, and, once here, their goal is to bring other Latinos into the temple.

By 1999, when Saul Bramasco had long since graduated from Brigham Young and begun his missionary work in earnest, the Mormon campaign to win more Lamanites was in full swing. He was on his way to visit a college friend in Washington, DC, when he stopped halfway across the country to visit the imposing temple in Chicago. Recruiting and baptizing a new member while he was there, Saul was persuaded to stay a little longer. When he met his future wife at a meeting of the temple's Young Single Adults program, he decided to put down roots and pursue a career and a family in Chicago. In time, he and his wife—who had joined the church in Guadalajara, Mexico—would have six children, all of them active Mormons, all of them bound for college. Today, during office hours, Saul works as a caseworker for the state of Illinois, determining which Latino applicants are eligible for public aid. It is cherry-picking of a different order. On off-hours and weekends, he is an active bishop of the church, bringing more Hispanics into the faith, specializing in the critical role of sealer: the priest who "seals" marriages, joining together a man and woman for all eternity, beyond the throes of mortal death.

By now, Saul has baptized his parents, grandparents, and friends into the church, not to mention all his ancestors into the seventh generation. "It is my plan of salvation," Saul says, affirming the Mormon tenets. "Before we were born, we lived with our Heavenly Parents. But our souls were sent to earth with bodies of flesh and bone, away from that celestial realm, to be tested in all things. We don't come to get rich, we come to be tested." And yet the Latino Mormons do prosper. When Saul last returned to his poor little village of Chimaltitán, he was amazed by what he saw there. "Everyone baptized a Mormon was becoming an engineer, a lawyer, or a doctor! My nieces are all professionals in New York!"

Unlike Father Emilio Biosca's Shrine of the Sacred Heart in Washington, DC, which survives on whatever its impecunious members from the Northern Triangle can place in its offertory baskets, the Mormon network has what Bishop Barry Olsen of Virginia calls "sacred funds," gathered from the strict tithing practices of all its constituents—rich and humble alike. Often those funds will pay for a promising young Latino's college tuition, or a family's emergency medical need, or to stock the shelves of a "Bishop's Storehouse," meant to feed a penniless immigrant family and set it on its feet.

Bishop Olsen, the college friend Saul Bramasco started out to visit before he stopped in Chicago and never left, is a strapping Scandinavian American who speaks Spanish like a native. Standing among his flock of Latino Mormons in Virginia, Bishop Olsen is hard to miss, towering over them with hair as yellow as flax. His wife, Julieta, is a Mexican American who was baptized into the church well before she came to Utah to join relatives in Provo, and before she decided to try her hand at landing a place at Brigham Young. Her father's family in Mexico is almost entirely Mormon and has been for generations; in fact, they were brought to the faith by American missionaries in the late nineteenth century. At the time, a new law in the United States had just made polygamous marriage illegal, and the church experienced a historic split over that injunction. A sizable contingent of American Mormons fled over the border to Mexico, where laws against polygamy did not exist. Miles Romney, for example—the great-grandfather of US presidential candidate Senator Mitt Romney of Utah—had four wives and, so, was forced to seek refuge in a Mormon colony on the other side of the Rio Grande; indeed, Senator Romney's father was born in the colony they established, the Colonia Dublán. Like the ancestral Romneys, Mormons brought their multiple wives to the hinterlands of Mexico, set up successful colonies and haciendas, and began evangelizing the natives.

As a result of that reverse migration and the church's campaign to win more souls, the Republic of Mexico now boasts 220 Mormon "stakes," or clusters of churches, almost two thousand congregations, thirteen full temples, and more than a million and a half Mormon believers. It is a larger representation of Latino faithful than hardworking bishops like Saul Bramasco and Barry Olsen have been able to muster in total in this country. And yet Latinos represent the fastest growing community of Mormons in the United States. From 2010 to 2020, for instance, the number of Spanish-speaking wards across the nation doubled their numbers. One in ten Mormons in this country today is Latino. But success has come with growing pains: although numerous LDS wards count a substantial enough population of Spanish-speaking Mormons (three thousand church members or more) to warrant full stakes of their own with properly elected Latino presidents, the church has been slow to grant them. As of this writing, it boasts but one—in Santa Ana, California—where the numbers are so overwhelming that it would have been blatantly insulting to install an all-white leadership. Which is to say that, although the church is fully aware that the Latino population holds the most promise for Mormon recruitment, it has yet to embrace Latinos fully.

This is a prejudice in the church that many, such as Bishop Olsen and his Mexican wife, Julieta, in Falls Church, Virginia—and surely Bishop Bramasco in Chicago—are struggling to counter. But as one Latino Mormon intellectual who remains faithful to the church tells it, the unspoken, underlying bigotry remains. Not all his white brothers and sisters feel comfortable with his color, he claims, and there is a vexatious top-down, white-to-brown hierarchy that nettles the church. He describes it this way:

> Mormonism has always had a way out of its racial dilemmas because the "solution" is given in the Book of Mormon where it affirms that the "colored" righteous will someday become "fair and delightsome" [when they reach heaven]—or "turn white" as we used to say when I was growing up a brown Mormon. . . . When a Peruvian brother says he wants the Resurrection to come quickly because he wants to arise tall, blond, and blue-eyed, he reflects the fundamental default position of many Latinos who have bought into a white theology that, as uncomfortable as it might be to discuss, remains unchallenged at its core. . . . Few white Mormon leaders realize how insidious this default position is. And they fail to understand, at least from the standpoint of Latino Mormons, that if the explanation of our final destination is unequal, then all that the Church believes of the present and of its history is suspect, unfair, discriminatory, or, God forbid, a true reflection of a celestial pecking order which cannot be (collectively) avoided no matter our faith and our works.

And indeed, when I attend the Hispanic Heritage Fiesta at a local church near where I live, there is not one brown face in the greeting party. The polite young Mormons welcoming us in the parking lot, bringing us through the door, and showing us to the festivities are all white—blond as a lit tungsten filament—and though they speak perfect Spanish to us and smile brightly, this is clearly their house, their domain. Even a cursory glance at the Mormon leadership from the lowliest stake to the President and his Quorum of the Twelve Apostles (the church's highest governing body) reveals the deeper truth: the church's patriarchs are just that—patriarchs. All male, all white, all nabobs of a certain age. Unlike the Catholic and Evangelical parishes led by the likes of Catholic Father Emilio Biosca or Pentecostal Reverend Samuel Rodriguez, there is not one brown face at the big table. When I ask the public relations office in Salt Lake City for the exact numbers of Latino members, Latino bishops, and Latino stakes, I am told "We don't track race" at the Church of Latter-day Saints. A disingenuous response, since it is clear that this demographic (which is not "a race") is one they are hotly pursuing. Yet there is one defining feature that Catholic and Mormon houses of worship do share: whereas women serve crucially as essential workers, as of this writing, no woman sits in a governing chair.

## LATINO JEWS

Living, as many of them do, with no religious or ceremonial customs to remind them of their ancient heritage and traditions, they yet keep their Jewishness alive.
—Harry O. Sandberg, historian, *The Jews of Latin America*, 1917

"Our America"—*Nuestra América*—Claude Lomnitz's account of his family's flight from the Jewish shtetls of Romania to the Andean cordillera during the fractious days of the twentieth century, is a triumph of historical record. In it, he tells the story of three generations of Eastern European Jews and their struggles to adapt and thrive in the radically different worlds of Chile, Peru, Colombia, and Mexico. As the story unfolds, it serves as a detailed description of the diaspora that deposited whole communities of Jews throughout Latin America, especially during that harrowing time.

Between 1880 and 1925, hundreds of thousands of Jews fleeing the cruelties and depredations of anti-Semitism in Europe or the socioeconomic turbulence in the Middle East and North Africa, crowded onto boats headed for the Americas and scattered themselves from Cuba to Argentina, and from Rio de Janeiro to the Yucatán. This was especially true after 1920, when the United States restricted immigration rigorously and Jews had little choice but to change course for more welcoming shores. As the Lomnitz family memoir unfolds, seven-year-old Claude journeys from Chile to Berkeley, California, on the coattails of his professor father, a scientist and geophysicist. Before long, the family is displaced again, and Claude spends his boyhood in Mexico City before returning to the United States as a college student. Supplanting one's hearth, tongue, and identity was nothing new for the Lomnitzes. War, bigotry, and exile had forced generations of the family to scatter to far corners of South America. They had shunted from Old World to New, and then headed north to the United States, adapting as they went, reinventing themselves on every shore.

Lomnitz writes in one especially moving passage that the Jews and indigenous of Latin America have this in common: they have survived displacement, trauma, and brutal conquest, and yet their pre-Christian faiths have managed to endure. This is, to some extent, true; but not entirely. Latin America is filled with those whose ancestors were once Jewish, but—given Spain's relentless fifteenth-century expulsion and the hard-bitten prejudice that followed—many Jews had no choice but to capitulate to the Church, convert to Catholicism, and bury their ancestral pasts for good.

What does this have to do with Latino Jews in the United States? A great deal. From the very beginning of the Age of Discovery, the Americas were a haven for Europe's persecuted Jews. Indeed, in 1492, the year that Columbus sailed into the Caribbean believing that he was in Asian waters, the Spanish Inquisition reached its fullest frenzy. Thousands of Jewish *conversos* to Catholicism as well as crypto-Jews—forced to practice their faith in secret—fled to the Americas, joining the conquest as adventurers, sailors, or servants, and bypassing the "laws of purity of blood" (*limpieza de sangre*) that were imposed so meticulously on Spain's colonial leaders. Some, like Pedro Arias Dávila (Pedrarias), a scion of one of the most influential Jewish families in Castile—and married to an intimate friend of Queen Isabella—masked his Sephardic roots, joined the conquest with abundant relish, and rose to ruthless prominence in the New World. Other *conversos,* such as the Chaves and Montoya families—Mexican ancestors of Linda Chavez, the highest ranking woman in the Reagan White House—managed to evade officialdom completely by moving as far away from the offices of the Inquisition as possible, transforming themselves into Christians, and establishing prosperous haciendas on the North American continent. For the Chaves-Montoya clan, home became the patch of New Mexico we now call Albuquerque. Three hundred fifty years later, Linda was born on the very same ground to which her forebears had come, totally unaware that they had headed there to put the Sephardic stain behind them. She is not alone. Genetic research shows that almost a full quarter of all of us who call ourselves Latinos or Hispanics have significant Jewish DNA but may not know it. Many may have vestiges that date back a half millennium. My own genetic tests manifest a trace of Ashkenazi blood, probably from Spanish ancestors who arrived in the Americas in the early sixteenth century.

Today Latino Jews populate countless spheres of American culture and a multitude of professions. The entertainer Sammy Davis Jr., son of a Cuban mother and African American father—and surely one of the twentieth century's most famous religious converts—claimed he evolved into the truest version of himself when he became a Jew. The journalist Gigi Anders, on the other hand, did not convert but was born Jewish in Havana; she wrote about that collision of cultures in her irrepressible memoir *Jubana!: The Awkwardly True and Dazzling Adventures of a Jewish Cubana Goddess*. Then there is the celebrated Guatemalan American Francisco Goldman, whose winning autobiographical novel *Monkey Boy* echoes his childhood between Boston and Guatemala City and probes the protean nature of his Jewish identity. Or the Chilean American novelist and essayist Ariel Dorfman, author of *Death and the Maiden*, whose profoundly astute insights about inhabiting multiple cultures pervade everything he writes.

Lucas Cantor Santiago, the composer son of Puerto Rican novelist Esmeralda Santiago, speaks frankly about being Jewish Latino in a largely white, male profession. "If you look at me," says Lucas, "you don't see white. But I don't speak Spanish. I don't write salsa music. I don't wear the Puerto Rican flag. I'm the wrong kind of Latino for a lot of quotas. People just can't place me. I make them uncomfortable." It is true. Lucas is all-American yet phenotypically hard to place: he could be Middle Eastern, or even part black, or Caribbean Hispanic, like his mother.

This strain of Jewishness didn't enter the American bloodstream in any perceptible way until Latino Jews began to arrive in stronger numbers in the late twentieth century. Before that, of the three million Jews who streamed into the United States between 1880 and 1940, 94 percent were from Eastern Europe and the great majority, Ashkenazi. While the Ashkenazi had been ostracized as nonwhite in Europe, in America—given the country's black-white fixation—they easily passed as white. By now, Jews with Eastern European roots are considered solidly white, a phenomenon described amply in Karen Brodkin's *How Jews Became White Folks and What That Says About Race in America.* That isn't necessarily so for Jews who hail from points south and carry Latin American DNA. Latino Jews tend to be darker skinned, largely Sephardic, originally from Spain, Italy, Portugal, and the Arab world; or Mizrachi, with roots in Northern Africa, Turkey, Greece, and Syria. They are, as some scholars label them, "Jews of color." They have little in common with the Ashkenazi from Argentina or Chile—Europeans who were invited in by those countries' governments specifically because they promised a salutary white infusion. (In Argentina, Jews are called *rusos*—Russians—precisely because of their lily-white skin.) They hardly would be confused with Jews who descend from mixed Caribbean or Central American ancestry—Latinos like Lucas Cantor Santiago.

Latino Jews tend to have roots in Latin American countries where Jewish populations thrive: Argentina, Mexico, Venezuela. They are generally an urban breed, migrating from Buenos Aires, Mexico City, or Caracas to the similarly sprawling cities of Miami, Los Angeles, or New York. When they arrive, they are surprised by the lack of kinship their new Jewish American communities offer; Jews are far more united in Latin America than they are in the United States. It is difficult to escape being a Jew in Buenos Aires or Mexico City. And yet, when these immigrants do come north, they are eager to melt into the great American cauldron of whiteness, as so many Jews have done before. Overwhelmingly, they identify as white on US census forms, rarely as Hispanic. "Hispanic?" one Jewish immigrant from Argentina exclaims to me in alarm. "Why would I mark Hispanic? That word refers to Puerto Ricans or Mexicans, not me."

They are also often from well-off, highly educated, politically liberal families, and if they do not enjoy a high economic status when they arrive, they find it soon enough. One survey concluded that 67 percent of Latino Jews earn three times more than the nation's median income, much more than the typical Jewish household in America. But there are other measures of success than money: 92 percent have earned a bachelor's degree, and 68 percent have gone on to graduate school; on average, they enjoy considerable business and professional distinction, not only here in the United States but also, in the past, in the countries from which they emigrated. Speaking broadly, they are comfortably removed from the discrimination felt by the overwhelming majority of Latinos in America.

• • •

We are no longer a homogenous minority; we come in all colors and from all corners of the world.
    —Ilan Stavans, cultural critic, Mexican American, 2016

Ilan Stavans, a prolific author, publisher, and distinguished scribe of the Latino experience, is also a tireless scholar—in the most Talmudic sense—of what we Latinos bring to America. He is best known for his tireless tracking of the multiplicity of strains we carry, the amorphousness of our so-called Latino identity. Born Ilan Stavchansky Slomianski in Mexico City to second-generation Mexicans whose ancestors had fled Poland and Ukraine in the early twentieth century, Stavans was raised in a hermetic Jewish community within that vast and exuberant city. "I went to a Jewish school in Mexico City," he recounts. And then, almost in wonder: "I learned Mexican history in Yiddish."

It was an insular life in which Jewish immigrants from Eastern Europe did not know much about the Sephardic history that had transpired on that very ground—the fact, for instance, that Sephardic Jews had once been burned alive on the picturesque plaza across the street, the pretty square where their children frolicked and lovers went for strolls. Indeed, for many Ashkenazis, encounters with Sephardic Jews were as baffling as those with the local *campesinos* in Mexico. Nor did they know much about Mexico itself. Stavans's father eventually broke with that self-sequestration and became an actor—first in experimental theater, later in television soap operas and feature films. His mother had been raised in a rabbinical family but left behind its strictures in order to marry his father, and it was through her that Stavans became steeped in the very rich tradition of Hasidic stories.

"I grew up as a Mexican Jew, or—better said—as a Jew in Mexico," he recalls. "I was in a small minority there, in some way ghettoized, living not quite in the present tense." All that changed when he graduated from high school in the late 1970s and went on to the Universidad Autónoma Metropolitana, the public university where Subcomandante Marcos—Rafael Sebastián Guillén Vicente, the flamboyant, pipe-smoking, masked rebel leader of the far-left, militant Zapatista Army of National Liberation—was teaching graphic design with a touch of political philosophy thrown in for good measure. The experience was galvanizing for Stavans, revelatory, and it was here that he began to learn what it meant to be living in Mexico; to truly inhabit his birthplace and take part in a political moment. But nothing was so defining, perhaps, as when Stavans took off to Israel, where he intended to taste what it meant to be "a happy Jew"—to live among those who were comfortable in their Jewishness, surrounded by people with a shared history and established traditions. It was there he understood that he was a child of a greater diaspora—one who would forever wander the outskirts, a quintessential outsider, ever the immigrant—and it was there that he forged the conviction that he would write about the mercurial condition of being a Latin American Jew.

He decided, too, that he would come to the United States—a capricious choice, because although he knew Spanish, Yiddish, and Hebrew, he spoke no English. Sitting down with a copy of *Moby-Dick* and a dictionary, he forced himself to learn the language. In New York, he got a job reporting on the United States for a Mexican newspaper, which obliged him to get out and speak to the American people, learn their ways. After the familiarity of Mexico City and Jerusalem, New York City was oddly disorienting. No one there seemed to care that he was Jewish, an unsettling sensation, given the circumscribed, locked Jewishness of his life in Mexico and the very open Jewishness of his experience in Israel. New York seemed to shrug at that aspect of his identity, registering him only for his language and culture. He was a Mexican—a Hispanic. "In Mexico, I was a Jew," he says, still marveling at the shift in classification. "I became a Mexican when I came here to the United States. And I became interested in the business of being Mexican in a way that I couldn't possibly have been in Mexico."

In his career as writer, critic, and professor at Amherst College in Massachusetts, Stavans has been an indefatigable producer of anthologies on Latino culture. Called "the czar of Latino literature," he is both impresario and referee, offering up the many ways one can be a Latino writer—pointing to the richness of our diversity—and passing judgment as he goes. He has taken withering potshots at the idols, questioning the fame of Sandra Cisneros, for instance, the beloved Chicana author of *The House on Mango Street*. He has accused Pablo Neruda, the revered Chilean poet, of producing "cheap Red propaganda." He has dismissed Gabriel García Márquez as an "outrageous" political activist, a high-living pretender, a champagne revolutionary. In the process, Stavans has irritated many Latinx intellectuals who consider him a poser, an outsider who "doesn't come from within the culture"—a Jew in Mexican clothing who passes judgment on Latinidad without truly living inside its skin. As one reviewer for the *Times Literary Supplement* said of one of his anthologies, "Why Oxford University Press, which used to pride itself on publishing reliable anthologies, should have sponsored this particular collection, edited by a nonspecialist, must be left open to question." Such are the perils of being a canon maker for an ethnicity that is, in itself, a stew of manifold parts. But Stavans's retort to his critics is equally pointed: "I think you can know enough," he says, proud of his status as an outsider. "Because you live in two or three worlds doesn't mean that you don't live in any of them."

That business of being judged for being more Jew than Latino resonates with Ruth Behar, a Cuban American writer and anthropologist who teaches at the University of Michigan. She was born in Havana but is the child of an Ashkenazi mother and a Sephardic father—a hybrid of European and Middle Eastern tribes, each of which has its own language, operates with its own traditions, and evinces its own markedly identifiable phenotypes. Her mother's people are descendants of Poles and Russians, whereas her father's family has roots in Turkey. But, like Stavans, she also struggles with the authenticity crisis imposed by those who would ask: which are you more, a Jew or a Latina? In academic circles that involve Latinos, she is often questioned. Is she a real and legitimate Latina? A genuine representative of a minority? Or is she a diaspora Jew, an interloper, who really has no claim to Latinidad? How many generations has her family lived in Cuba anyway?

"It is a backward notion of identity," she tells me. "A this-or-that election—a black and white choice—when, in fact, so many of us have far more complicated histories. Thank goodness we are coming to have a better understanding of the intersectionality involved in being an American Latino."

Being a Latino and a Jew, as Stavans tells it, or as Behar has lived it, is to have clung to one's faith fiercely for generations, in isolation or in secret, despite the constant tides of unrelenting prejudice. The unexpected outcome for many is how much easier it is to live as a Jew in the United States than anywhere else in Latin America.

But there are also those Latinos who become Jewish after arriving in this America; who, weary of the assumption that a Hispanic must be a Catholic, have traveled the opposite course of the *converso* to become a convert to the Torah. Jews can be made as well as born, after all, although Judaism does not make a business of recruiting new souls; it is not a proselytizing faith. At least not like Christianity, which—from the very beginning—was built on the concept of spreading the gospel and redeeming the heathen. According to historians of religion, Latino Jews, like Latino Muslims (also a rapidly growing minority), are more often forged in this country, and of their own free will. An estimated five thousand to ten thousand people become Jews by choice each year in North America, a healthy portion of them Latinos. The rate is even higher for Latino Muslims, whose numbers skyrocketed from thirty-five thousand to a quarter million over the course of a single decade, half of them converts from Catholicism. Those converts can hail from anywhere: from Mexico, Central America, and the Caribbean to the furthermost reaches of Argentina. Such is the case for Rabbi Eli Rafael de la Fuente, a Latino who was born to a traditional Catholic family in Peru, immigrated to this country as a graduate student, fell in love with American Judaism, and abandoned all else in its pursuit.

Rabbi Eli does not use the word *Latino* when he speaks of his identity. He sees himself as an American Jew who happens to speak Spanish. "I've never identified with Latino culture," he tells me. "I don't dance the *cumbia*. I don't eat *frijoles*. I am an American from Latin America, yes. But more than anything, I am a Jew."

Rabbi Eli was raised in Arequipa by a devout Catholic mother. A child of divorce in a Catholic country that frowns on broken families, he nevertheless followed the pope's faith, matriculating from the Catholic University of Peru with a degree in finance. Somewhere along the way, in his late teens, he began to be fascinated by Judaism; perhaps it was the romance of its history, its exoticism, its enigmatic Hebrew letters, its values; or perhaps it was simply the beautiful young Jewish Peruvian he was dating at the time. In any case, he began looking for books about Jewish history and traditions. He taught himself the Hebrew alphabet. In university lectures, he took notes in Hebrew script even though his professors were speaking in Spanish. Seeking more information on Jewish religious practices, he nevertheless was discouraged from sitting in on Shabbat services. The only synagogue in Peru—La Sinagoga 1870, which occupied an old mansion in a sleepy district of the capital—was a strictly conservative Ashkenazi institution that did not welcome strangers, nor, for that matter, anyone not born of an Ashkenazi mother. He would leave behind another twenty years—as well as a Catholic marriage—before changing his life many times over in the United States.

He had been living in Columbus, Ohio—a divorced father and "displaced person"—working in a bank, when he found himself thinking about Judaism again, about the religion that had once fascinated him for its ecumenicalism, its ancient history, and welcoming temper. "Judaism is not based on dogma but on action," the rabbi explains. "It does not focus on beliefs per se, but on how you employ them. It is based on books, tradition, on making this world a better place. The Catholic faith, on the other hand, promises you a better world in the next life. I was attracted to Judaism because of its openness to accept you as you are, now." Not much later, as a forty-something yearning for a more meaningful life, Rafael de la Fuente finally converted to Judaism and began calling himself by another name: Eli. "That was my second reinvention," he tells me, "after coming to America and adopting an American way of life." The following year, he searched for the Jewish beauty he had dated decades before, found her in Israel, and proposed marriage. "So you see, I reinvented myself all over again as a Jewish husband." Ten years later, he would reinvent himself a fourth time by discarding his career as a banker, going to rabbinical school, and donning a rabbi's tallit.

Today Eli de la Fuente is the head rabbi at a hospice in the suburb of a sprawling American metropolis. He is expert at handling extreme cases because—as he argues—having worked with elite professionals the world over, he knows how to study people, read them. "I now work with human beings in dire situations," he explains. "People with erased memories, Alzheimer's, the physically damaged, the old, the dying. And their families." Among all the doctors and nurses who serve the hospice, Rabbi Eli is the only Spanish-speaker and so is called on regularly to minister to Dominicans, Puerto Ricans, Mexicans. "The Spanish language reminds me all the time who I am," he says, "which is strange. While I was working in finance, Spanish seldom came up. It was the language of my house, not my work. In those days, if I had been asked to use Spanish in the workplace, I would have felt I was being asked to jump up and down with a banana on my head. Now, as a rabbi, Spanish has become a daily instrument of my work. If I can console the dying in Spanish, I am happy to do it." But Spanish isn't the only language that he, his wife, and children speak at home: their house is generally abuzz with a dizzying conglomeration of Spanish, English, and Hebrew.

"Could any of this have happened in Peru?" he asks rhetorically, then answers himself: "I don't think so. Only here. Only in America. Land of reincarnations." And indeed, young Paco de la Fuente, one of the rabbi's children by his first marriage, has reinvented himself as an altogether different breed of American. A bright-eyed, black-bearded, highly philosophical Hispanic like his father, he has opted to don dreadlocks and identify as Afro-Latino. His circle of friends who, like him, are immersed in identity studies, are African American and Afro-Latino, as are the children of his Latina partner. "Paco sees himself as black," the rabbi says, shaking his head and shrugging amiably. "Black is his theme. Jewishness is mine. My America is not his America. We have our own Americas."

# PART IV

# HOW WE THINK, HOW WE WORK

You are the storyteller of your own life, and you can create your own legend, or not.

—Isabel Allende, author, Chilean American, 2002

# 9

# MIND-SETS

If we are to be heard and, more importantly, be effective, we must define what we stand for. This task will not be accomplished in one day or even a generation, but we must be bold enough to begin the discussion.

—Raul Yzaguirre, founder of National Council
of La Raza, Mexican American, 2004

**M**y Peruvian father was something of a Republican, even when he wasn't yet a citizen of this country. For the first fifteen years of my parents' marriage in Peru, his views vis-à-vis US politics were hardly the subject of family conversation. He was more concerned with the careening allegiances of his own countrymen: the gaping divide between the elites and the poor; the wild, destabilizing vacillation between right wing and left wing in Latin America; the perpetual pendulum swing between oppression and revolution. But when my parents immigrated to this side of the Americas, looking for better opportunities for their children, a sea change was afoot in this country. The United States had drifted away from its rose-colored complacency of the 1950s. It was no longer the gold-paved, sparkling Arcadia my American mother had promised. The country we encountered in the 1960s had embarked on a Cold War, committed civil rights atrocities that made a mockery of the American Dream, endured a slew of grisly assassinations, and experienced a radical change in the color of its immigrants. The gaping divide between the two political philosophies in the gringo mind-set now became a regular theme at our dinner table in Summit, New Jersey.

"What exactly is the difference between a Republican and a Democrat?" my father asked, as well he might have when the country had whipsawed from Eisenhower to Kennedy to Johnson, and now seemed to be lurching in a different direction. For him, a man who had lived through the vicissitudes of Peruvian politics, the divide that separated liberals from conservatives in his own mind was stark—more likely the difference between a Communist revolutionary and a hidebound military dictator. "Well," answered my mother, a descendant of generations who firmly believed in American exceptionalism, "a Republican believes in family, education, hard work, opportunity, individuality, the freedom to succeed on one's own, the freedom from government interference, and the conviction that a sturdy belief in God makes the rest possible."

That was all it took. My father may have been conservative by way of Latin American Catholicism and the region's carefully inbred colonial mind-set, but he was not, by any means, a ready-made Republican, which is where the story turns. Jorge Arana Cisneros had always been a lover of scientific progress and its allies: individual curiosity, group commitment, chance. He had come from a culture that believed in education, hard work, and faith in a supreme being: the conviction that talent could supersede any social barrier; the notion that intelligence, skill, and drive—no matter a person's rank—might be a person's salvation. Like W. E. B. Du Bois, the African American sociologist and civil rights activist of the early twentieth century, he believed in a talented tenth that might lead the rest into a brighter future. He had championed those principles in far-flung corners of South America by building factories, improvising solutions, bringing along the talented but less fortunate, founding whole towns dedicated to making something from nothing: cane fields from an arid strip of desert, sugar from cane, paper from sugar's refuse, bioplastics from paper's dregs, electricity from whatever was left. This was the world he knew, and these were the values he brought with him to America. When my mother described a Republican's sense of individualism and self-reliance, he was convinced that described him completely. Education? Work? Faith? Being left alone to do what an individual needed to do? He was sold.

It took many more years—more than a quarter century of living and working in these United States to be exact—before he became a citizen, but when he did, he voted a Republican slate for the rest of his life. My mother finally broke ranks to vote for Barack Obama in 2008, by which time my father had decamped this mortal coil. I, on the other hand, had left the ranks of Republicans as a child, in that heartbreak year of 1968, when Martin Luther King Jr. and Bobby Kennedy were assassinated. My parents did not object. A few years later, repelled altogether by the rigid binary of two parties, two racial categories, and the with-us-or-against-us polemic of Vietnam War defenders, I became a registered independent—a not unusual choice for Hispanics like me, impatient with the system's lack of nuance. We may be social conservatives with a progressive streak; or, the other way around, progressives with a conservative streak. And why not? Even Hillary Clinton, confessing her defection from Nixon to antiwar Democrat Senator George McGovern in 1972, crowed, "I'm a heart liberal, but a mind conservative." So are Latinos. Or the other way around: a liberal thinker with a conservative core. Often, they shun party allegiances altogether and vote issue by issue, candidate by candidate. As Manny Díaz, the former mayor of Miami and chair of the Florida Democratic Party, once said, "Party is not an issue. We can think Democrat until we register Republican. We transcend political affiliation."

That tendency for Latinos to shift between blue and red has become more and more prevalent in the last few decades. In 1960 John F. Kennedy received the vast majority of the Hispanic vote; after his assassination, Hispanics remained loyal to his vision with 90 percent of the Mexican American and 86 percent of the Puerto Rican vote giving successor Lyndon Johnson a pass to reelection in 1964. Likewise, in 1968, Hispanics favored Johnson's vice president, Hubert Humphrey. But, in 1972, a good many reversed course, with almost 40 percent putting their faith in incumbent Richard M. Nixon. That love appears to have been mutual: in the course of his first term, President Nixon had named some fifty Spanish-speaking civil servants, mostly Mexican Americans, to top positions in his government. Nixon seemed to understand what Latinos truly wanted. When he reached out to them, he talked about the issues that mattered most to them: education, health care, small businesses, work.

As years went by, Latinos remained largely faithful to Democrats, but the Nixon seed had taken root, and the Republican numbers continued to multiply. Four in five Latinos in Florida (mostly Cubans) voted to give Ronald Reagan the presidency in 1980. George W. Bush, too, won over the Hispanics of Florida, but he also won a large share of Mexican Americans in Texas—although he garnered only a smattering in the (largely Puerto Rican) Latino population of New York. Bill Clinton's charm, on the other hand, won him a Latino landslide in 1992, picking off the hearts of 65 percent of us; Barack Obama continued that trend, racking up 67 percent of the Latino vote when he ran against Republican senator John McCain in 2008, then increasing that to 71 percent against Mitt Romney four years later.

Nevertheless, over the years, the attraction of the Democratic ticket has eroded somewhat, and roughly one-third of Hispanics now seem to vote consistently for Republican candidates. That said, I am quite sure that if my father had been alive when Senator Obama ran for office, he would have abandoned Republicans for the Democratic ticket, as my mother did, to vote for the first black president of the United States. In fact, many a Latino Republican changed course to support Obama. And so, for all the conjecture about Latinos' party leanings and the assumption that we are natural-born Democrats or deep-down Republicans, there is little predictable about our politics, just as there is little predictable about our race, class, or beliefs. Gallup Polls indicate that we are weak Democrats and shaky Republicans at best, with more than half of us claiming to be independents at heart. Increasingly, we are an unclassifiable, protean agglomeration of Americans—a web of contradictions—adrift in a purple sea.

# THE MYTH OF THE LATINO VOTE

Hispanics are Republicans. They just don't know it. Love of family,
hard work, patriotism, faith in God. All you have to do is communicate
the message.

—Ronald Reagan, 1978

And so, we come to the storied enigma that is the "Latino voter." For
many decades now, the press as well as "political elites" who campaign
for office or dedicate themselves to promoting Latino interests have
depicted us as a unified political community. And indeed, for the past
half century, Latinos as a whole have tended to vote Democratic. But
analysts have observed, too, that we are also more apt to have lower
voter turnout than any other bloc, which means that any projections
about the Hispanic population as a whole are inherently flawed. Half a
populace does not represent a unified voice, a robust political engine, or
even—as some pundits imagine—a reliable swing vote.

In some counties in Texas, for instance, where Hispanic populations
are sizable, voter turnout has been as paltry as 17 percent. Even as recently as the 2020 presidential election, only half of all eligible Hispanic
Americans went to the polls, well below the overall 72 percent national
average and far less than the ratios of African Americans and Asian
Americans who marked their ballots. Which means, of course, that half
of all Latinos in the country are choosing to forfeit their rights to the
democratic process, fail to make their voices heard, and, thus, receive
less public services than would otherwise be due them. Eventually this
lack of civic participation threatens to deepen the cycle of systemic barriers that have plagued too many Hispanics over the years: rank poverty,
poor health, inferior housing, substandard education, lack of opportunity, marginalization, and—ultimately—invisibility.

For many, a lack of interest in the voting process is simply a by-
product of disillusionment or distrust. Those who fail to participate may
have emigrated from a country in which voter suppression is common.
Or they are afraid to vote, reveal their addresses, and call attention to the

status of someone in their household. Or they may feel that neither the red team nor the blue team represents them exactly; that a two-party system with no room for nuance doesn't serve their slice of the American pie and never has.

Come 2022, however, Hispanic voter registration rallied, especially among women. Suddenly, in anticipation of the midterm elections, Latinos added five million voters to their ranks, the largest increase in any sector of the country. Perhaps it was due to the Supreme Court's historic decision to dismantle *Roe v. Wade* (74 percent of Latino voters are pro-choice); or perhaps it was because younger Hispanics decided to jettison their parents' complacency and take power into their own hands. (The average age of a Hispanic voter today is thirty-nine, more than ten years younger than the average US adult voter.) Or maybe the surge in interest was due to the steady stream of Latinos who join Evangelical churches every day and are encouraged to take their faith to the polling place. "Don't just pray," says Reverend Samuel Rodriguez to his congregation of millions, "register all the people in your church to vote life, liberty, and biblical justice"—be a political force, in other words, a catalyst of change. Clearly, something galvanized the Latino population.

Make no doubt about it: the Evangelical movement in American politics has had a profound effect on the Hispanic population and is acting as an efficient spur. For all his chameleonlike ability to serve presidents' platforms and constituencies on both sides of the party divide, Pastor Sam's rhetoric has become markedly conservative. When asked about his leanings in the countdown to the 2022 midterm elections, he was blunt: "It's not that I embrace the values of the Republican Party. It's that the Republican Party embraces more of my values, while the Democratic Party is not only against my values but vehemently opposed to who I am as an Evangelical." Evangelical churches such as Pastor Sam's insist they aren't beholden to any party, but they routinely espouse conservative positions on core issues such as abortion, same-sex marriage, religious liberty, and family values, and, increasingly, they are effective in driving the electorate to the voting booths. Most recently, Pastor Sam's forty-two-thousand-strong network of churches (the National Hispanic

Christian Leadership Conference) launched a campaign called "El Voto Hispano" to muster Evangelicals to get out and vote.

Whatever the cause, from 2010 to 2020, Latino voter registration climbed from 50 percent to more than 60 percent, with the vast majority of registered Hispanics actually heading to booths and depositing their ballots. It is clear that American Latinos—currently 15 percent of this country's voters—now represent the fastest growing racial and ethnic group in the electorate. Even so, Latinos continue to lag behind other groups in making themselves heard. As of this writing, of the sixty-three million who reside here, only thirty-five million are eligible to vote in the next election. Some cannot because they are not citizens; some demur because they are intimidated by the registration process or by the risk of racial harassment at the polls; and others, because they simply don't feel they are part of the democratic process. But what seems to baffle non-Hispanics most of all (and bedevil advocacy groups that claim to speak for American Latinos) is this: the ones that do manage to vote do not represent a tidy, unified bloc.

There is solid history for this. For the past century at least, Latino allegiances to the party system have been erratic. Indeed, there once was a time when most Latinos were Republicans like my father. As the distinguished scholar Geraldo Cadava describes in his book *The Hispanic Republican: The Shaping of an American Political Identity, from Nixon to Trump*, political conservatives have been a part of the Hispanic community for a very long time. A century ago, when Hispanic Americans numbered little more than a million and were overwhelmingly of Mexican extraction, they were, like most African Americans of the era, almost entirely Republican—that is, they were loyal to Abraham Lincoln's party, the party of Emancipation. That was until the Great Depression and Franklin Delano Roosevelt's New Deal—with its bold rescue of the poor—began to change minds. By 1964 and the increasing ferment of the civil rights struggle, the transformation was vigorously underway: The Democratic Party, which had been pro-slavery, began to be liberalized by Roosevelt's initiatives. As African Americans took flight from the Republicans to join the Democratic side, the number of Hispanics voting for Republicans began to rise. The reason for this was simple: Republicans had gone to work on them. Recognizing that they were losing African American voters by the legion, the party avidly turned its attention to the burgeoning population of Latinos. By now, it was the early 1970s, after all—the Mexican American population had boomed; Puerto Ricans and Cubans were pouring into the East Coast—and Republican hopefuls like Nixon and Reagan pricked up their ears and began to contemplate the utility of a Latino voting bloc.

It was then that the concept of a "Hispanic" was born; and it was then that, from an ungainly and wildly dissimilar mass of immigrants and their offspring, the illusion of a unified political community was created. And so, during the volatile 1970s, even as rebellious Chicanos championed the idea of dropping out of the American experiment altogether and disgruntled Puerto Ricans advocated the abolition of their colonial status via independence or statehood, a shift occurred in Latino affiliation. The GOP's concerted, decades-long effort to recruit Hispanics began to show results, and, starting in 1972, a hefty chunk of the Latino electorate—from 30 percent to 40 percent—began to vote for Republican candidates. These growing citadels of Latino Republicanism were largely in the Southwest, principally among Mexican Americans and migrants from Central America, and in Florida, among fiercely conservative, anti-Communist, anti-Castro Cubans. On the other hand, Puerto Ricans and Dominicans, whose communities dominated the New York–New Jersey corridor all the way to Boston, have seldom strayed from the Democratic flock.

The landscape these mercurial loyalties paint can be confounding, especially to operatives in the political sphere. Sometimes that picture can be downright contradictory. For example, despite Donald Trump's outrageous remarks about Mexicans on day one of his campaign for president (accusing them of being "criminals, drug dealers, and rapists") and despite his austere anti-immigrant policies (caging migrant children and separating their families), he racked up almost 30 percent of the "Latino vote" in 2016 and actually expanded that count in his failed 2020 run for re-election. The numbers astounded Democratic operatives, who had relied on aggrieved Latinos to reject the incumbent president and deliver a foolproof majority. Instead, almost two million rallied to Donald Trump's support, many of them in full agreement that taxes and illegal immigration had spiraled out of control. The Democrats' fevered hope that Hispanics would finally kill the Republican Party never came to pass; instead, the elusive "Latino vote" was keeping the Republicans alive. Nevertheless, in that election year, that same vote also helped Joe Biden flip states that Trump had won in 2016, including Wisconsin, Michigan, Pennsylvania, and, most remarkably, the conservative bastion of Arizona. The Latino electorate had made itself heard, but the cacophony its voice had produced was jarring.

## WHAT DO LATINOS WANT?

> Overall, these groups do not constitute a political community. They clearly agree on some key questions, but they disagree on others. Indeed, sometimes a particular group more closely resembles Anglos than any of the other populations.
>
> —Latino National Political Survey, University of Texas, 1992

Cristina Beltrán, a deeply thoughtful political theorist who thinks well beyond the confines of any partisan strategy, has characterized the Latino population as nearly impossible to view as a single entity, either socially or politically. According to her, we have long been portrayed as a community on the cusp of political power, a power we never quite seem to reach. As a result, we are seen as a stubborn breed: politically passive, difficult to mobilize. We are, to put a finer point on it, a sleeping Leviathan—a narcoleptic colossus—that, from time to time, stirs ever so slightly and squints out into the world only to fall back into hapless obscurity. And yet the very image of a giant waiting to flex its electoral muscle and redefine the social and political landscape of this country presumes a collective consciousness, a uniform identity.

To be sure, there are a few realities we share. It is true that all Latinos come from somewhere near or south of the Rio Grande. It is also true that most of us claim the mantle of Latinidad and say so on the census, whether or not we call ourselves Hispanic, Latino, Latina, Latine, or Latinx. Sometimes we even speak alike. Often we celebrate "our heritage," "our culture," "our music." Which might lead some to believe that we think alike. But, as Beltrán points out, we do nothing of the kind.

There is no Latino mind-set. Apart from the fact that language shapes our brains to some degree, or a Catholic childhood might inform our hopes and fears, or the rampant mistrust engendered by our colonial past may bubble up to haunt us—there is no unifying philosophy. There is no credo or group-think that binds a Cuban American to a Mexican American, or a Dominican to an Argentine. And there are no collective ambitions that drive a shared perspective, aside from the purely human, obvious ones of survival and generational advancement. Indeed, there often are stark differences of opinion between the major groups of origin: Mexican Americans and Cubans are less approving of affirmative action quotas than Puerto Ricans, for instance. But alliances shift when considering abortion: the majority of Mexican Americans and Puerto Ricans oppose it, whereas most Cubans would permit it for any reason. Defying widely held stereotypes, all three groups, as dynamically different as they are, do not necessarily support traditional roles for women; all three are more likely than Anglos to agree that a woman is better off if she has a career.

What do Latinos want? The Democrats say we want a firm safety net. They say we want our immigrant families protected, our children educated, our less fortunate plucked out of poverty, our ills managed by the state. The Republicans say we want the freedom to make our own way. They say we value strong families, individual liberties, religious choice, safety, and a shining stair to economic prosperity. Clearly, some of what each party says is true: Latinos who lean to the Democratic side do feel secure in the knowledge that their party sympathizes with the less fortunate, while Latino Republicans are very sure that their party will pave the road to a better life. Neither side is wrong in its assumptions. We may not want exactly the same things from our government—making us fair game for both parties—but, from the surveys, at least, our priorities are fairly clear. At the moment, according to the Pew Research Center, the cardinal concern of Latinos who lean toward the Democratic Party is affordable health care; their other top priorities are, in descending order: economic security (jobs), education, gun safety, and the need to address climate change. On the other hand, the hot topic for Latinos who lean toward Republican candidates is economic security; and, in descending order, violent crime, education, immigration, and the nation's voting policies. These priorities, for the most part, agree along party lines—Democratic candidates, and the Latinos who vote for them, tend to prioritize health care; Republican candidates, and the Latinos who favor them, prioritize economic security. But they are also the basic, everyday issues we all care about as Americans. As Ritchie Torres, a Latino congressman from New York's poorest district, suggests, Hispanics in the South Bronx essentially want the same thing as Hispanics in Arizona: we are, like most populations struggling to clamber onto the next rung, "practical rather than ideological. The concerns are bread and butter, health and housing, schools and jobs." Latinos want, in other words, what every other American wants.

The Republicans seem to understand this better than the Democrats. Although Latinos have been largely faithful to the Democratic ticket, there is no question that the party has been taking them for granted. The assumption has been that if they are immigrants and poor, they are surely in need of social services, and, so, they must be liberals; they must be hard-core Democrats. Some years ago, Harry S. Reid, the Senate majority leader from Nevada, summed up this attitude when he blurted to a crowd of Hispanics in Las Vegas, "I don't know how *anyone* of Hispanic heritage could be a Republican, okay? Do I need to say more?" The editorial page of the *Las Vegas Review-Journal* snapped back, "They all think alike, right, Senator Reid?" The journalist went on to say, "Indeed, how could the concepts of limited government, economic freedom, and individual liberty have any relevance to Hispanics?" The head of a conservative Latino organization gleefully joined in the drubbing: "Hispanic voters don't have a 'herd mentality.' Their vote cannot be taken for granted by any party."

The senator's remark had been ham-handed, even clueless. But it was also revealing: Democrats have felt entitled to the Latino vote for some time. Not without reason: most Latinos do indeed believe that liberals care more about them than conservatives do. And yet Republicans are eagerly taking advantage of a growing segment of Latinos who are disenchanted with that presumption. As Oscar Pollorena, a US border patrol agent attending a GOP "law enforcement appreciation" barbecue in Laredo, Texas, describes it, the Democrats—in whom his forebears have invested their votes for decades—were supposed to take care of Mexican Americans, whereas conservatives were perceived as prosperous gringos oblivious to their needs. "People here have grown up believing that the Democratic Party is the one for lower-income families. It's the way the party sells itself: 'Vote for us, and we'll give you free food, free health care, free everything.' And then they never actually come through." That disillusionment led a considerable percentage of Latinos, particularly in the poorer precincts of the Southwest, to conclude that the party of Franklin Delano Roosevelt wasn't for them after all. More to the point, if elections were not gaining them any traction in the real world, why bother with them at all?

The very fact that almost half of all Hispanics stay home on Election Day has proved galvanizing for Republicans. With such a low turnout rate, the population becomes fair game for potential recruitment. As a result, conservative funders have poured money into an organized effort to lure Latinos to their side. In the past decade particularly, the Republican outreach has been more than purposeful; it has been assertive, dedicated, strategic, massive. One of the most energetic enterprises doing this work is Libre, an initiative funded by conservative billionaires Charles and David Koch and committed to persuading millions of Latinos to vote Republican. The *New York Times* describes Libre's efforts as "guided by an app powered by i360, a Koch-affiliated data-analytics company that draws on consumer data and voter information to predict voters' behavior. The app divides neighborhoods into 'books' that can be canvassed in a single outing." In the course of a weekend, canvassers can cover thousands of households in a single district, millions of houses across the country. Libre's staff and volunteers set about their work not only in the way that a pop-up political committee might—by ringing doorbells to muster support for a specific, upcoming election—but over time, for the long haul, and it does so by providing English-language education, GED courses, financial advice, tutoring for children—taking its lessons from the enormous success of Evangelical churches who have courted Latinos in exactly the same way.

According to Daniel Garza, the winsome, hardworking, Evangelical president of Libre, "GOP ideas are better" because they are "pro-growth, pro-energy, pro-parent, and pro-advancement." In contrast, when Democratic campaigners knock on Latinos' doors, they dwell on issues that many Latinos regard as less urgent: voter suppression, diversity, right-wing disinformation, abortion rights. These issues may seem compelling to liberal elites, but they are quite secondary on Hispanic priority lists. If polls have it right, Latinos across the board want a booming economy, abundant jobs, better education, higher wages, and more health options, as well as opportunities for advancement and the ability to support themselves and their families. So, the Republican message can be appealing. Somehow, Libre, which claims to be nonpartisan, manages to sidestep the fact that Koch money is working to defeat any hike of the minimum wage or further implementation of the Affordable Care Act—two outcomes most Latinos want. Instead, it makes headway by seeking out needy Latino neighborhoods, giving away millions of dollars in food and services, taking down citizens' personal information for future promotional uses and mobilization, and then, quite incongruously, giving them the news that good conservatives do not rely on handouts or government services. Latina Senator Catherine Cortez Masto (D-NV), who accuses Libre and the Kochs of "hijacking democracy for their own benefit," has this to say about the organization and its masters:

"There's no such thing as a free lunch." But what about other things? What about free Spanish-language driver's education classes? Free backpacks, notebooks, pencils, and school supplies in the month before school starts? Free financial wellness workshops? Free turkeys on the week before Thanksgiving? These things were all given away at events hosted by the Libre initiative, a self-described grassroots organization dedicated to a "free and open society." The events were held in Latino communities throughout the country. . . . If you follow the money just one step back, you learn that Libre is a shell organization funded by Charles and David Koch, two of the most powerful men in American politics. . . . The Kochs believe in a world with no Medicare; no Social Security; no federal minimum wage; no public programs that support families when they fall on hard times; and no rules preventing Koch Industries from polluting our air, drinking water, or our public lands. . . . The Koch brothers think they can buy the Latino vote, just like they've bought the votes of the House Freedom Caucus and so many Republican politicians. But despite what their ads say, the Koch brothers are not advocates for the Latino community. They are advocates for more money in their own pockets. Nothing more.

In short, there appears to be an all-out war for the hearts and minds of American Latinos, and, on the battlefield, the Koch purse has become a formidable arms dealer. It's as if a vast, richly equipped conservative army has been quietly hard at work in the trenches for more than a decade, and the Democrats are just waking up, rubbing their eyes, and learning about it. "We need to quit taking a policy book to a fistfight," says one liberal political analyst, voicing a growing concern that the Democratic approach has been too lackadaisical, its ideas too flabby; that the losses will only grow worse; that liberals will continue to bleed Latinos in the way that the Catholic Church has bled them to Evangelical megachurches. Most worrisome of all to Democrats is the mounting realization that Republicans may indeed have a better script and that they will use it to chip away at a constituency that is now—and should always be—rightfully theirs.

# HISTORY LESSONS

My greatest strength is knowing who I am and where I come from.
—Oscar de la Renta, fashion designer,
Dominican American, 2002

As Latinos take a larger role in the American collective and begin to make clear what it is we want—as individuals, communities of common origin, or urbanites—we often don't look back to see the arc of our own history. Julian Castro, a former US secretary of housing and urban development under President Obama, worries that the younger generation of Latinos, which is now perched to wrest some modicum of attention on the American stage, does not really know itself. Nor does it "have much of an understanding of the sacrifice, of the political activism, of how much it took to get us where we are." His twin brother, Joaquín Castro, a current Democratic US representative from Texas, has kickstarted a one-man campaign to educate Americans—and our media, especially—about the cultural and economic contributions Hispanics have made throughout the course of US history.

Certainly, in this country's public schoolrooms, no American child is learning much about the long, hard struggle Latinos have undertaken to emerge from anonymity. We may now have sixty-two Latinos in the United States Congress (fifty-six in the House; six in the Senate) and a considerable history of state governors and lieutenant governors—plus an accumulation of six US Treasurers, sixteen chief executive officers of Fortune 500 corporations, more than five hundred college presidents, dozens of legendary baseball players, scores of Catholic bishops, more than a dozen Pulitzer Prize winners, five Academy Award winners, and even one Heisman Trophy winner—but Americans are hardly aware of the long and winding road it took for those Latinos to reach those hard-won laurels. Americans are also unaware that those numbers represent but a tiny percentage of what they could be, given the sixty-three million who might aspire to those heights.

This ignorance bespeaks a kind of numbness in the American

psyche; a lack of interest in the nation's immigrants and their stories. When I was in college, for instance, I was never asked about my Latin American background or what my life had been like in Peru. Not once. For months, my roommate misheard the word *Peru* and thought I was from Beirut. She never posed the logical, follow-up question. Decades later, at a college reunion, a sorority sister finally made reference to my heritage. She asked if I wore "Peruvian traditional dress" when I went home to visit family in Lima. She seemed bewildered when I smiled and asked which dress she could possibly mean: my mountain *pollera*? Jungle *cushma*? Desert *hojotas*? It was churlish of me to mock her, I admit, but I was stung by the ridicule inherent in her question. Did she wear pioneer boots and a wire-frame sunbonnet when she went back to her family home in Skokie, Illinois? In stints as a senior editor during the eighties and nineties for two major publishing houses in New York, no higher-up seemed interested in the fact that I might actually contribute work that reflected the country's booming population of Hispanic Americans. When I tried suggesting something along those lines at editorial meetings, I was told that Hispanics didn't read.

This is precisely the sort of neglect that Juan Sepúlveda—former director of President Obama's White House Initiative on Educational Excellence for Hispanics and a current advisor on Latino leadership to the president of Trinity University in Texas—is laboring to correct. Juan was born in Topeka, Kansas, and is a tireless optimist with curly hair and a sunny demeanor that exudes confidence and good cheer. For many years, he has dedicated himself to bringing along young Hispanics—to educating them and identifying potential leaders in their midst. In his various roles as activist, innovator, educator, and political advisor, not only has he emphasized the pressing importance of our history, but also he's been part of that history himself.

Juan is the son of Mexican Americans. His parents met in Topeka as a result of an assertive sixty-year drive to hire cheap labor to boost the city and build America's legendary Atchison, Topeka and Santa Fe Railway, an enterprise that spooled a massive and intricate web of steel from the flatlands of Kansas to the rocky shores of California. The company began to conduct hiring sweeps in Mexico as early as 1902, just as the public fury against the three-decade iron rule of General Porfirio Díaz—whose presidency was referred to as the Porfiriato, "Porfirio's reign"—had started to brew. Shrewdly, the company continued to transport migrant labor when the revolutionary fervor heightened, violence erupted, and Mexicans became desperate to leave the killing fields. So it was that workers rushed into the United States, bringing their families and launching a chain migration that brought thousands to live in abandoned railroad cars in Kansas and tens of thousands more to establish barrios alongside the seemingly endless tracks that snaked through the heart of America. Juan's grandfather had been a Mexican-born *traquero*, a laborer who lay track and pounded in the switches and connections so vital in that dizzying era of fat-cat acquisitions and mergers. Juan's father, too, was Mexico born, a bright young man with a basic education who had been hired by a Kansas state office but died in a car accident before he could realize his promise. Juan was but an infant when his mother was widowed, leaving her to manage him and his older brother alone.

She soon remarried, and Juan had the good fortune to be raised by a kind Latino stepfather—"the only father I ever knew," he says—who worked as a janitor in Topeka's Veterans Administration Hospital. The family thrived in their community of working-class Mexicans, across the tracks from their African American neighbors and across town from the more prosperous whites. "We were poor," says Juan, shaking his head, "very poor. But it never felt that way. . . . Actually, those early days were an idyllic time for me. Eventually, by the time I got to high school, I had an Anglo girlfriend. I hadn't realized how pronounced the prejudice against Hispanics was in Topeka until her parents made it clear they didn't like me: a Mexican from the bad part of town. That didn't faze me, somehow. I'd had an incredible childhood, thanks to the Catholic church and the powerful culture of mutual help in our community." Indeed, so ubiquitous was the presence of his church, Our Lady of Guadalupe, that it informed every aspect of his life: school, home, faith, sports, friends. In time, it would show the way to his future, when a radical young Hispanic priest watching the boys play basketball in the church's backyard introduced him to the critical importance of politics in American life and the door it might open for Latinos.

Juan listened. Much later, when he was well on the road to life as a political analyst and community developer, the same priest was asked what Juan was like as a kid. "Bright boy," he answered. "And we knew it. We put him through leadership training early." Juan was taken aback—leadership training? Sure, the priest and his teachers snapped back. We made you head of the altar boys, head of the basketball club, a delegate to the young people's Kansas High School Domestic and Foreign Affairs Conference, head of the *this* and the *that*. They had been enacting precisely the sort of mentorship and guidance that Juan works to develop today in promising Hispanic youth nationwide.

The priest's encouragement did not go unrewarded. Juan was a mere sixteen years old when he landed an opportunity that set the course for a long career in activism. He had been singled out and hired by the Kansas secretary of state to join a group of much older graduate students, meet the governor, and learn how the state's maze of elected lawmakers—and the art of pushing legislation—worked. Here he was, the son of immigrants with limited education, doing government work and being considered for the best colleges in the country. He soon found himself at Harvard University, where he became one of the few Latinos admitted in 1981. There Juan attended a course in Hispanic voter registration that transformed his thinking completely. It was taught by William ("Willie") Velásquez, a fiery, charismatic, and brilliant young lecturer who had abandoned the angry protests of the Chicano movement to begin the practical work of increasing the Latino electorate and ensuring Latino participation. It was Willie Velásquez who made Juan Sepúlveda the passionate game changer that he is today. And it was Velásquez who eventually would yank the entire Latino population from its slumber and transform it into the potentially powerful electorate it has become in the twenty-first century.

Naturally, this begs the question: What schoolchild in America has ever heard of Willie? As Congressman Joaquín Castro might say, How can such a transformational figure go ignored by the general public? By schoolteachers. By the media. By Hollywood, for that matter. In truth, for many Americans, the struggle of Latinos for political justice in this country does not figure in the nation's collective consciousness, much less the schoolbooks. What is it about Hispanic American heroes that they are met with such rank neglect?

Henry Cisneros, a former beneficiary of Velásquez's mentorship, has often asked the same question about the fog of disregard that eclipses his mentor and other groundbreaking Latinos like him. Cisneros, mayor of San Antonio from 1981 to 1989, was the first Latino to preside over a major American city in the twentieth century; he also served as secretary of HUD during the Clinton administration's first term. Velásquez, he says, had a burning idea to which he dedicated his entire life force and energy. "He had decided that we Latinos wouldn't be represented until the number of registered voters equaled the numbers in the population. It was a patriotic idea. An *unassailably* patriotic idea."

Indeed, few Americans in modern times have had as much influence over electoral participation and minority representation in this country as Willie Velásquez. Despite the mistrust that Latinos had long harbored about American fairness to the darker races—despite more than a century of institutionalized exclusion—Willie's skills as a political organizer and community builder eventually helped elevate Latino voter participations to a level commensurate with their growing numbers. Before him, Latino citizens were regularly harassed at the polls, their districts gerrymandered and fractured so that their candidates could not possibly win. Heads of businesses brazenly instructed their Hispanic employees to vote a certain way or lose their jobs. Willie once commented, "It was like old Texas law: 'If you know what's good for you, boy, you'll be out of town by sundown.'"

In Willie's birthplace of San Antonio, especially, discrimination was so flagrant that armed Texas Rangers circled the polling places to intimidate anyone who looked remotely Mexican. Whenever Hispanics were asked why they didn't vote, they'd respond, *"Pa' qué?"* "What for?" Their votes only stood to be blocked, manipulated, erased. But Willie understood that Latinos' burgeoning numbers were their best ammunition. Enough of a crowd, and no force could keep them away. *"Tu voto es tu voz!"* became his motto and battle cry: "Your vote is your voice!" That's what for.

"His work probably had more long-term impact on minority politics in the United States than any other person of his generation," says Cisneros. "Today, largely because of Velásquez's efforts, Hispanic Americans comprise one of the most important voting blocks in US electoral politics, with growing and increasingly significant impact on elections in virtually every major US city and state, and ever-growing strategic influence on the nation's quadrennial presidential races."

In other words, Willie is one of Latino history's titans, perhaps the single greatest force to rallying the sleeping colossus to its feet. Young Juan Sepúlveda fell under his spell immediately. During summers away from Harvard, Juan volunteered to assist Willie's campaign to educate Latinos about the importance of their vote, not only for the good of Latino communities but also to force American democracy to live up to its promise. Juan joined a band of Hispanic students who holed up in Willie's San Antonio garage and worked to create a national army of activists that would get out the word and persuade fellow Latinos to show up and be counted.

Willie's campaign turned out to be even more ambitious and radical than that of Cesar Chavez and Dolores Huerta, who had co-founded the National Farm Workers Association in 1962 and mobilized Chicano field laborers to demand more equitable pay and safer working conditions. Groundbreaking activists to be sure, Chavez and Huerta had kindled an awareness of the injustices experienced by thousands of Latino war veterans who had returned home from heroic service in World War II only to find that they were third-class citizens: forbidden from eating at American lunch counters, barred from using whites' bathrooms, denied entry at their local movie theaters, and paid a fraction of the minimum wage. But it was a sudden and drastic shift of policy for farmworkers that had incited Chavez and Huerta to action. In 1964 the US government abruptly terminated the Bracero Program, which, over the course of twenty-two years, had brought four million Mexicans to work on contract for very cheap wages. Stoop laborers were suddenly left to endure growers' harsh conditions and meager pay without the support of a US government contract. Enraged by the inequities, Chavez and Huerta set out to foment a strike. For all the historic advances they made in winning better overall conditions for their fellow farmworkers, that segment was but a fraction of the greater Hispanic population, and the bullying and intimidation of voters only continued.

In contrast, Willie's campaign was massive in scope, nationally directed, far more informed by a new, college-educated generation of rising, middle-class Latinos, and it touched every Hispanic in the nation. Inspired by the African American civil rights movement, the antiwar crusades of the Vietnam era, and the Chicano fervor for authentic, spirited representation, Willie set out single-handedly to animate the voting muscle of the Latino masses. He started by mobilizing the Chicano base he knew so well in his hometown of San Antonio, and, once he established the Southwest Voter Registration Education Project (SVREP), his efforts spread through Latino neighborhoods like fire through tinder. Soon there were Latino high school and college students across the country, knocking on doors and posting signs to let families know that the racist poll tax had been eliminated, that each vote was crucial, that they could actually impact themselves, their neighbors, their circumstances, their school board, their government, and this new-won power wouldn't cost them a cent. The results were phenomenal. From SVREP's conception in 1974 to Willie's untimely death of cancer in 1988 at the age of forty-four, the organization doubled the Latino electorate, registering almost four million voters. In years since, it has registered many more times that number and initiated a virtual avalanche of politically engaged citizens. As a result, the Latino body politic today numbers thirty-five million and represents the fastest-growing race or ethnic group in the United States electorate. We have Willie Velásquez to thank for that.

•   •   •

In the end, the American dream is not a sprint, or even a marathon, but a relay. Our families don't always cross the finish line in the span of one generation. But each generation passes on to the next the fruits of their labor.

—Mayor Julian Castro, Democratic National Convention, 2012

When I ask Juan Sepúlveda what inspired him to take this route, not only to follow Willie and learn from him but also to nudge the model one step further—to pluck young, talented, potential ringleaders from that newly energized electorate and show them the way to leadership—he answers: "It's just the way we grow up in our Catholic, Latino communities. We're taught to stick together, work hard, give back." He recalls an exchange about this very subject with Robert Putnam, a Harvard professor and author of *Bowling Alone: The Collapse and Revival of American Community*, a groundbreaking book that argues that Americans don't know their neighbors anymore, that we've lost our sense of community, and that we're headed for trouble as a result. According to Putnam, solidarity is social capital, and everyone who partakes in it gains valuable life skills. Those who don't are sure to spin into an increasingly solitary, aloof spiral that erodes the very spirit of society; or, for that matter, democracy.

In 1997, after Juan had completed his tenure as a Rhodes Scholar, attained a law degree from Stanford University, and begun a Hispanic initiative for the Rockefeller Foundation, Putnam invited him to join a panel of thirty scholars from different fields (including then civil rights lawyer Barack Obama) and—within the span of three years—produce a coherent plan to address this grave American disconnect. The outcome was the *Better Together* report, issued in 2000 and meant to restore America's lost sense of unity.

In the course of the panel discussions, Putnam explained his fears: "You know," he told them, "the way Americans used to work together? Worship together? Try to solve problems together? That stuff's all gone now." Juan's hand shot into the air and he piped up: "Not in my community!" The group bristled with incredulity. Could it be? A place in America where bonds of fellowship and mutual responsibility still existed? A place where ordinary citizens really knew one another and looked out for one another's interests? Juan assured them that it did indeed exist, and did so in his old neighborhood of Mexican Americans, across the tracks from everyone else in Topeka, Kansas. To prove it, he organized and hosted a number of trips so that panel members could see it for themselves. There, in northeast Topeka, among the Latino working class, was a model of old-fashioned American teamwork. Juan introduced them to the tightly knit, dynamic community that clustered around Our Lady of Guadalupe Church and had since burgeoned to almost 16 percent of the city's population. At the time, families were hard at work readying for the renowned Mexican Fiesta, a community-organized, weeklong, annual extravaganza that, for three-quarters of a century, had been bringing Kansans together for authentic barbacoa, mariachi, and dance.

Over more than three generations, the Fiesta's principal goal has been to raise money to support Our Lady of Guadalupe's school and educate the barrio's children. But it has become a banner event for the entire Latino population of Topeka—one around which families build vacations, engage young and old alike, and celebrate community ties. To panel members observing the preparations, it seemed as if every Mexican American in town, from schoolchild to grandparent, had something to contribute. And it wasn't only Latinos who looked forward to La Fiesta. As Juan quipped, not entirely in jest, "It's the one week of the year that people from the other side of town feel safe coming to my neighborhood."

Putnam and his Better Together panelists were astonished. So there still are pockets like this in America! Indeed, there are. They exist in Paterson, New Jersey, among Dominicans, Puerto Ricans, and Cubans who patronize one another's restaurants and build lasting collaborations. Or in Rockville, Maryland, where Peruvians from the sierra don their boldly colored garb to dance, organize competitive sports events, and—while they're at it—sell home-cooked tamales to raise money for incapacitated neighbors. Or in the tenements of Chicago, where, in their limited spare time, Latinas who scour out the city's kitchens and lavatories help one another care for their children. Or in a tiny Salvadoran grocery in San Diego, where notes pinned randomly onto a cork board alert customers to neighborhood gatherings, upcoming anniversaries, English language classes, college application tutorials, prayer circles, or a pending quinceañera. Indeed, those circles of support may exist even in the toniest neighborhoods of northwest Washington, DC, where Latina professionals from a dozen origin countries gather to hold *tertulias*—salons, whose subjects might range from current events to nineteenth-century composers—even as they help one another mentor their children, secure domestic services, keep abreast of business and cultural news, and advance to the next lofty rung in their careers.

Ask an ordinary Latino on the street what he or she wants—how he or she thinks—and the answer from one to the next is bound to be much the same, no matter the class or color: We want to fit in, have our children thrive as full-fledged Americans. We want to participate, work, be counted as citizens. But we also want to retain our customs, our language, our cultural idiosyncrasies, our motherland senses of identity. And we want to be valued and respected for it. This, then, is the core Latino mind-set as I see it. It may seem contradictory: How can I hope to be a fully assimilated member of an Anglo-dominant culture if I hold fast to my Peruvian identity? How can I expect to be seen as a red-blooded American if I cling stubbornly to speaking Spanish? It is no easy enterprise, and some—like the Mexican American Republican Linda Chavez, whose family has been in North America for almost a half millennium and who counts herself white—believe the process of full assimilation may take a little longer in Latinos than in Europeans. But, she adds, it is bound to happen all the same. "I am certain Hispanics will go the way of other immigrants," she says, "and dissolve into the larger population of Americans. . . . There is that aspirational sense of wanting to be in the mainstream."

Sure enough. Why would you want to linger in a population that is virtually invisible? As former HUD secretary Julian Castro has lamented, young Latinos simply do not see their history reflected in the mainstream.

Their ancestor stories go largely untaught and unappreciated. Naturally, there are those who will lose their Spanish, their connection to their origin country, their affiliation to another culture—especially if, like Linda Chavez, they and their children can pass for white. It is an eventuality we think about as our children disappear into the powerful, all-consuming, ready-to-wear American culture around us. "So, you've become an American now," my father said to me once with a wistful sigh, congratulating me even as he broke my heart into little pieces. "You're not a Peruvian anymore."

How can the young help from losing their Latino identities when, beyond their front doors, they are systematically deprived of learning about their heritage? This is something that preys on the mind of Joaquín Castro, whose all-out campaign to win Latinos their due attention from textbook publishers, news media conglomerates, corporate entities, teacher associations, even Hollywood is beginning to get some traction. Representative Castro believes that the more these mavens of communication can get the Latino story onto the page, into the classrooms, and onto screens, the more young Latinos—and the whole American public at large—will understand who they are and the sea change of possibility they represent. Ignorance is curable, but neglect is hard to foil. Indifference is a formidable foe.

"I had the most remarkable meeting in May 2020," Castro tells me. "I asked a publisher to name three Latinos who have made an impact on American history. Just three!" The congressman holds up three fingers and shakes them. "Three! Now, understand, this is a highly educated, accomplished publisher—a CEO!—of a textbook company, and he couldn't do it. He couldn't name three." Castro's indignation is fevered, contagious. So much so that my own pique is rising now. The inexcusable erasures of Willie Velásquez and Dolores Huerta jump to mind.

"It really struck me," Castro continues, "that if you asked the same question of the American public, ninety percent—or more!—would give you the same answer. There's a void in the narrative. Here we are, coming on seventy million, and Americans don't know what their own society is made of. They don't know who we are or where we fit. They don't *see* us." That blindness breeds misapprehension and fear, according to Castro, and those two, in turn, beget nothing so much as a dangerous bigotry. It's why Texas governor Greg Abbott's blatantly racist character-ization of Latino immigrants as "an invasion"—calling to mind the very word a white gunman used when he massacred twenty-three Latinos in the infamous 2019 El Paso shooting at a neighborhood Walmart—is so inflammatory, so frightening, so unacceptable, so un-American that it is hard to believe that any government official of an immigrant nation would resort to such a slur. In the end, it bespeaks a rank ignorance of history as well as a deep-seated, hard-bitten racism. In such a view, white immigrants like Abbott's English and German ancestors are a resource, while immigrants of color are malign parasites. "Abusive stereotypes like that are dangerous," says the impassioned Castro. And not only for in-nocent immigrants. They are ahistorical, defamatory. "They inflict col-lateral damage on everyone."

## CONVICTIONS

> They tried to bury us. They did not know we were seeds.
> —Slogan on banners, graffiti on walls, DACA supporters

The attempt to erase Latino history from the nation's psyche—and cer-tainly from the nation's textbooks—is nothing new. It begins with the notion that we shouldn't be part of the American landscape in the first place, as was certainly the thinking when Americans invaded Mexican territory, drove out the locals, and began calling that land their own. Or when the United States appropriated Puerto Rico and granted Puerto Ricans citizenship in order to send them to the front lines of war, yet refused them the right to be represented in Congress or vote in presi-dential elections. The attempt to eradicate Latino culture continued into the twentieth century with demands of "English only!" even in districts where Hispanics were the majority and the Spanish language, ubiqui-tous. And it persists when a state board of education rejects books about Latino history—or bans classics by literary giants such as Isabel Allende,

Sandra Cisneros, and Elizabeth Acevedo—as Texas has been doing for years. There is, too, the blatant indifference. In the Houston area, for example, where 62 percent of the entire population and more than half of all schoolchildren are Hispanic, to date there are no prepared instructional materials to teach Hispanic history. Sometimes there is outright denigration, as happened recently when a textbook proposed for Texas public school classrooms not only cast Mexican Americans as responsible for the country's drug and crime crisis but also described them as bent on the destruction of Western civilization.

The effort by some public officials to muzzle Latinos is precisely what has inspired numerous gifted historians and scholars—Kelly Lytle Hernández, Geraldo Cadava, Ilan Stavans, and Ed Morales among them—to produce resounding contributions to the Hispanic American canon. Hernández has written a groundbreaking book about this country's role in the Mexican Revolution of 1910; Cadava writes about Hispanic Republicans and the half century of American history that explains them; Ilan Stavans records the literature that represents us; and Morales has written about Latinos' five-hundred-year romance with *mestizaje* and the mixed-race culture it has bred. But producing work that informs readers about this massive population of Americans is a Sisyphean, sometimes thankless task. Often it gets relegated to the periphery of American consciousness. Whereas, by every right, the story of Latinos in this country belongs on a main shelf with "United States History," it gets shoved in a corner with "Latin American Studies."

The scant material offered to Americans in public institutions is precisely what propelled the historian-activist Mariana Barros-Titus, a thirty-year-old researcher at Washington's DC History Center, to unearth the long-buried story of Hispanics in the nation's capital. Her goal, she tells me with emphatic conviction, is to shine a very bright light on this drastically underrepresented group and render a more nuanced understanding of how the metropolitan area of Washington, DC, grew and how Hispanics contributed to that growth. Too often, she explains, Latino narratives can go ignored in the larger, black-white preoccupations of "Chocolate City." In rare instances when Latino stories do bubble up, they are told by non-Hispanic voices that have not seen the population from the inside. "The words may be about us, but they are not *from* us," she says. "It falls to us, the younger generation, to dig out the stories from those who have genuinely experienced Latino life. We need to expand the lens."

Mariana is a Colombian American whose parents had to flee their comfortable home in the green valley of Valledupar after Communist guerrillas targeted her father, a skilled surgeon, for his political affiliations. Terrified, destitute, the family arrived in Scranton, Pennsylvania, to take a bottom rung in the American Dream. "My father, a brown-skinned, highly educated medical professional whose vernacular happened to be black," she recounts, "had to reinvent himself as a driver and a handyman in the United States of America." Eventually, with enough English language classes, he was able to find work in the medical sphere, but not at his previous level. He became a surgical assistant—and a very valuable one at that, given that he often exhibited more experience than the attending surgeons. "My family had made a huge sacrifice, a backward slide, a regression, and we had done so from one day to another, instantly, on little more than a slender hope." Along the way, as can happen to Latinos in our highly racialized culture, young Mariana was made aware of her African features and the reduced status they signified. She was, at once, radicalized by that sudden otherness and transformed into an acute observer of the American underclass. "We had arrived right before September 11, just in time to see Mayor Rudy Giuliani put the city's immigrants to work cleaning up the rubble. Even as a kid, I understood that it was Latinos who had brought New York City back to life." Since then, as a transplant to Washington, she has vowed to exhume the many layers that undergird the capital's complicated history. "My goal is to bring attention to that untold story, complicate the conversation. I mean to delve into the neglected details. There's a lot of in-between here that gets missed."

•   •   •

It happened in high school. . . . I had two options at that point: assimilate or do the opposite—cling to my roots, dig deeper, look at the
history, discover it in myself.

—Calista Correa, educator, Chilean American, 2023

Mariana is not alone in her passion to set history straight in the larger
American consciousness. According to government reports, a full
30 percent of the Latino population in the United States is engaged in
some way in the civic life of their communities, trying to correct the
way Latinos are thought of and understood. A similar conviction for
setting things right drives Calista Correa, a young Chilean American
who has thrown herself into the business of schooling Washington's
underserved youth: the Black, Latino, and special needs children who,
generation after generation, are stunted by flawed strategies and low
expectations. Calista is diminutive—black hair, fair olive skin, a doll's
hands—with a quiet beauty that ignites when her eyes surrender to a
radiant smile. Her determination, like Mariana's, comes from an intensely lived sense of injustice and marginalization. She was born in
Fairfax, Virginia, the child of Chilean Americans whose families had
decided to emigrate during the dictatorship of Chilean general Au-
gusto Pinochet in the 1980s. Calista's parents met in the United States
when they were teenagers.

Calista's father was a highly intelligent boy, but he became frus-
trated by a system that kept shunting him into remedial classes. Within
a few years, he dropped out of high school entirely to take a job as a
menial worker. Calista's mother, on the other hand, had white-collar
ambitions and, upon graduation, pursued a career as a bookkeeper.
When they married, the only things they seemed to have in common
were their origins. But as compelling as these congruities were, they
began to fade over time. "My mother and her mother are white, blue-
eyed, Chilean-European, conservative," Calista says, "and very racist.
My father's side, on the other hand, is dark complexioned, part Mapuche." And indeed, when Calista tested her DNA, it turned out to be

41 percent indigenous. Her life changed dramatically one afternoon in her seventeenth year when she came home from school to learn that her father had walked out of the house, never to return. He had left his scolding, querulous wife in order to move in with—and eventually marry—his wealthy, liberal Anglo lover. No words were ever spoken about this. No apologies or excuses made. It simply became a new reality in Calista's adolescence. Not long after that, to her dismay, her mother moved in with a man whose ultraconservative convictions cemented her own.

By then, Calista's views on social justice were firm, if not resolute. They had revealed themselves sometime before, in the first grade, when she began to question everything that seemed unfair, including her mother's bad temper—her inclination to shout, complain, deride. Eventually Calista reported to a teacher that her mother had screamed at her, used harsh words, frightened her, even whipped her with a belt, and that there was something very wrong about that. Within hours, Fairfax's social services were at the Correas' door, accusing her mother of physical and psychological abuse, checking her baby sister for injuries. Young Calista had made up her mind: she would oppose, resist, and scrap her way to fairness if she had to—call out the bad actors, the bad system, the entropy. Adults simply shook their heads and clucked their tongues at the diminutive rebel. "When you're older, Calista," they told her, "perhaps you'll understand."

But she never did. She continued to protest any conduct that struck her as unprincipled. And her schoolmates began to see her as a leader. By the sixth grade, Calista was identified as a highly gifted student and singled out to take a placement test for a coveted spot in Fairfax's highly competitive Thomas Jefferson High School for Science and Technology, often rated the best public high school in the nation. Two years later, when she scored at the top of her class and was ushered into Quest, Fairfax County's grooming arm for high-achieving minority students, one of her friends grumbled, "How come you get to do Quest, and there's no program like that for us white kids?" It was the first time she had ever encountered a blatantly racist affront, and she immediately sensed the wrongness of it, the violation. Such was the start of a determined, activist mind-set that runs like a steel beam through everything Calista has done since.

At Thomas Jefferson, research labs and robotic hardware were plentiful, and its STEM-focused curriculum had no peer, but Latinos were chronically in short supply. Even today, the school is criticized, even sued, for being slow to admit blacks and Hispanics. Nevertheless, over the years, the scant Latinos who were there managed to cobble together the Hispanic Alliance, a tiny group meant to bolster minority confidence. In the Alliance, Latinos shared their common culture, engaged in mentorships with younger children, organized dances and celebrations. By junior year, Calista was leading the group. In time, she encouraged it to forge an affiliation with the school's Black Student Union. "I had always felt an immediate closeness to blacks," she reflects. "Of course, they had experienced a sharper racism than I had, but I could relate. Even in the ninth grade, I was passionate about social justice of all kinds—against racism, sure, but against any and all -isms—and I was especially interested in the power of numbers." "My little Socialist," her mother called her. One night while her mother was cooking, Calista announced she wanted to go to a meeting of LGBTQ students in her high school and learn how she might support them or even enlist them in her cause. That did it. Her mother slammed her pan on the stovetop, demanded to know whether Calista was a lesbian, and forbade her from having anything to do with the group.

Much later, as an alumnus, when the Black Lives Matter movement came into full flower, Calista decided to try persuading "TJ," as the school is sometimes called, to change its admission policy, be more inclusive. Even with Quest paving the way for minority representation, by 2019, the school still had not come close to reflecting the county's demographics: whereas Hispanics represented approximately 30 percent of the county's students, they comprised less than 6 percent of Thomas Jefferson's incoming class. As for African Americans, their numbers were so few that an asterisk was attached, meaning they were too insignificant to count statistically. All the same, when Calista organized a band of alums to complain about those low numbers, she soon got a taste of partisan politics. "It got nasty fast. The right-wing groups fought back, and they were very well funded. They were paying people to argue against us. No one was paying us." Unable to deal financially or emotionally with the lawsuits thrown at her from the opposition, Calista eventually backed away. Today, although the number of Asian students at TJ has skyrocketed, bitter complaints about the paucity of Latino and black students continue to cast a shadow on the school's successes.

Upon graduation from high school, Calista had some decisions to make about her passion for minority activism. "I had two options at that point: assimilate or do the opposite—cling to my roots, dig deeper, look at the history, discover it in myself." But she needed to learn how to do that. The "how" was answered when she enrolled as a freshman at Duke University, where she majored in liberal arts. Duke had a healthier representation of Latinos than her high school did, but an even more richly diversified community of Hispanics attended the state universities around her. She set her mind to engaging them, bringing like-minded students together, making them more politically aware, more capable of effecting real and lasting change.

Calista joined Mi Gente, Duke's leading Latino organization. Its mission is to emphasize—by its own description—"Latinx cultural, political, educational, and social issues." It seemed the sort of wide-ranging, broadly welcoming, aspirational group she'd been hoping for all along. She had big dreams for Mi Gente and pushed it to be more political, more goal driven, but the divisions were too great. "There was such economic disparity between those born abroad [who likely were rich] and those born here [who likely were not]," she says. It ended up being more of a social circle than she had hoped for. Instead, she found a more comfortable niche as co-chair of Unidos, an umbrella organization that unites the Latinos of Duke, North Carolina State University, and the University of North Carolina. There she found others like her: children of working-class Latinos, who thought as she did and had a clear sense of mission, a passionate resolve. From random fantasies, they began making policy. What if we started a scholarship for undocumented students? Calista asked. Within days, they launched a series of festivities to raise funds to help pay for college tuitions. This was the sort of brisk, bold, group-driven change she had wished for.

And yet, for all the expanded opportunities Duke offered after Thomas Jefferson, it was not the welcoming place she had expected. The Latino organizations she joined did not have the respect of the majority white student body; indeed, the whites seemed blind to the Latinos among them, indifferent to their needs or the issues that vexed them. Worse, a pronounced racism seemed to simmer just under the surface of collegial life. "Go back to Mexico!" students barked and then burst into derisive taunts as Calista passed. Standing in front of a notoriously racist fraternity, a white student threw a drink in her face.

One student became so infuriated by the growing presence of Hispanics on campus that he claimed he wanted them all dead. When he shouted this to a gathering of Calista's friends, he turned and pointed at her, insisting he was going to "get" her. Perhaps it was because of her leadership status, perhaps it was because of her confident manner, but so virulent was his animus that, more than once, he threatened to kill her, kicking or punching anyone who would so much as mention her name. Given Calista's acute sense of justice, she got the police involved, but when the report came around, the university demurred, not wanting to expel the boy, shame him, and risk the violence that had just taken place at Virginia Polytechnic Institute and State University, where a humiliated student went on a shooting spree, wantonly murdering dozens of people. There always seemed to be a reason not to set matters right when it involved aggrieved Latinos.

Upon graduation and after a short stint as a paralegal, she accepted an offer to teach mathematics in a school in a rural, poverty-stricken corner of North Carolina. She had always been good at math, fascinated by numbers—comfortable in all the sciences, given her superb exposure to them at Thomas Jefferson. From there, she went on to positions in Washington, DC public schools. At least she could change lives day by day and, possibly, by the roomful. She became a middle school STEM teacher and, eventually, a founding staff member at the city's first Montessori high school. Along the way she made another decision: she married her boyfriend, an African American.

As far as her ultra-conservative grandmother was concerned, she might as well have committed a crime. The woman had long made her racist views known, but now she did not hide her disgust. Why would "you marry one of *them*," she asked, full of indignation, "in a country full of nice white men?" Calista rode out the family storm and tried to make a life for herself despite the ostracism. It hadn't been a good match, contracted too soon after a traumatizing relationship, but she tried to make it work. She had always felt a keen affiliation with black culture, so that was never the obstacle. As years went by and two baby girls were born—and as she began to feel trapped in a loveless marriage—she finally did what her father had done fifteen years before: she broke it off, never went back.

Today Calista is a young, single mother to two bright, lively, inquisitive Afro-Latina girls. Ever the believer in effecting positive change through the power of numbers, she has left the classroom for a job that stands to serve the larger student population of Washington, DC. She currently studies, designs, and directs STEM curricula for special education classes in the DC public school system, finding ways to make science and mathematics spark neurons in youngsters who might not otherwise imagine they have capacities in that direction.

In this, her mind is firm. Calista will move generations forward. For all her studies in elite American classrooms, she may never have stumbled across the name of Willie Velásquez—the changemaker who did more than anyone to ensure that Latinos are part of the American democratic process—but her convictions most assuredly align with his. Like Willie, Calista is certain that numbers do make a difference, that sleeping giants should be awakened, that voices need to be heard and represented. More than anything, they both share the notion that Latinos need to be given the opportunity to open doors for themselves, prompt change, make better futures for their children. When you get down to it, according to Willie, inspiring change is "all about the pavement." It's about giving people the tools they need, education they can stand on, progress that feels as real as the concrete beneath their feet. The moment Latinos stand up and say, "'Vote for me, and I'll pave your streets,'" as Willie liked to say, "that's when the revolution begins." And indeed, that is precisely what Mariana Barros-Titus and Calista Correa have in mind to do: gather the numbers, lay the pavement, spark a revolution.

# 10

# MUSCLE

You have to work harder. In every position I've been in, there have been naysayers who don't believe I'm qualified or who don't believe I can do the work. And I feel a special responsibility to prove them wrong.

—Sonia Sotomayor, Supreme Court justice,
Puerto Rican American, 2014

Hispanics are here to work. They have worked this land, built its cities, traded its riches, marshaled its armies, and defended it on land and sea since long before the first ships set sail from England to bring a new breed of conqueror to these shores. In fact, the first English colony—attempted in 1585 and abandoned a year later when Spain was already well established on the North American continent—was not meant to be a haven for religious freedom or a base for commercial ventures so much as a fort from which Queen Elizabeth I's rapacious mercenaries could intercept Spain's galleons and plunder their treasures for a backward and beggared England. Even then, Spanish America was an exuberant fount of productivity—a capitalist model for the future—whereas the British heroes of the day, Sir Walter Raleigh and Sir Francis Drake, were pirates in service of a queen, stealing from Spain what Spaniards had stolen from the indigenous.

The New World collision had produced a vast and profitable empire, with Spain bearing the whip and natives furnishing the muscle. Since then, American Latinos, descendants of that upheaval—children of master and toiler alike—have never ceased to be industrious. For most, work is a lodestar, and generational progress, a pressing imperative. Indeed, the sweat of Latinos has contributed to every aspect of American life since this nation's inception, yet textbooks seldom tell of their role in founding and shaping the United States. Latinos often say that our history can be traced to more than a half millennium ago when places that now seem quintessentially American—California, Florida, Texas, New Orleans—were dominated entirely by Hispanic culture. But being hijacked by history can hardly be called contributing muscle. True Hispanic agency in the American story dates instead to the Revolutionary era, to the pugnacious 1770s, as British Americans grew increasingly prosperous and rich plantation owners, weary of predatory overlords, began to imagine their independence. Here, in that early hubbub of rebellion, Hispanics played a spirited hand and helped birth the new republic.

## WARRIORS

> Ten thousand unknown Latino patriots fought in the American Revolution! Cuban women in Virginia sold their jewelry to feed patriots! Latino General Gálvez sent weapons to George Washington!
> —John Leguizamo, actor, Colombian American,
> Fourth of July, 2019

Large-scale Hispanic participation in United States history began when the 1st Viscount of Galveston, Bernardo de Gálvez, decided that Spain could profit from assisting the plucky Americans who had risen up to rebel against England's parasitical taxes. Like them, Gálvez was a subverter capable of imagining alternate futures. When he was made governor of Louisiana in 1777—and subsequently Florida—for his heroic military service to Spain, he decided to dedicate himself to modernizing the colony under his command. He reformed the legal system, established public education for all, and worked to grant blacks and in-digenous full inclusion as citizens. Like any good Spanish warrior, he also dreamed of foiling the brash interloper in the Americas: Spain's archenemy, the English. Little by little, England had nibbled at the New World that Spain had made. It had started with English pirates plunder-ing Spain's shipments of gold, continued with England's appropriation of the entire East Coast of the American continent, and then escalated with its settlements along Nicaragua's Mosquito Coast and Hondu-ras. These were rapidly proliferating thorns in Spain's dominion that the Spanish king was loath to accept. To top it off, the English were already encroaching on the Mississippi River and crossing over it, to the ne plus ultra beyond which they were not supposed to go. Spanish ani-mus against them grew to such a degree that even the baby-faced, good-natured, family-loving governor of Louisiana was provoked to put aside his more peaceful duties and go back to a full-frontal war.

From the very beginning of his appointment, Gálvez displayed great sympathy for General George Washington and his fellow insurgents, who, by then, were struggling to keep their revolution alive. By now, all ports on the Atlantic Seaboard had been blockaded by the British, reducing the American general's supply chain to gridlock and his will to incertitude. The revolutionaries soon decided there was only one way to break the impasse: by shifting their movements to the Mississippi and Ohio Rivers. When George Morgan, the commander at Pittsburgh's Fort Pitt, sent a flotilla downriver to New Orleans, carrying a letter to Gálvez that requested aid, Gálvez didn't hesitate. "I will extend whatever assistance I can," he responded, "but it must appear that I am ignorant of it all." The flotilla returned to Fort Pitt filled to the brim with Spanish arms, ammunition, and provisions.

That brisk, generous response began a close alliance between Spain and the American Revolutionary forces without which the destiny of the United States might have been entirely different. Of course, it wasn't long before the British realized that Gálvez was not at all ignorant of the riverine successes the patriots began to enjoy. Gálvez had made a con-certed effort to disrupt England's incursions into the Gulf of Mexico as

well as block any English ship that dared venture up and down the Ohio
or Mississippi. He had allowed American ships to fly the Spanish flag and
thus elude attack or capture. He had sent vital supplies to General Washington's army in Virginia, as well as financed George Rogers Clark's audacious expedition through ice and storm to secure Illinois as a western
front against British-led Indian invasions. Eventually he contributed vast
sums of his own personal fortune to the American cause and persuaded
Madrid to commit millions of Spanish *reales* in financial aid, as well as
countless ships and guns. It was here, as many historians will agree, that
Gálvez began to feel himself more American than Spanish—more a man
of the New World than the Old. After all, he had spent much of his life
in the Americas and would go on to wed happily on this continent and
raise children on its soil.

At Gálvez's encouragement, a prodigious army of 7,500 men, including Spanish, French, black Africans, Mexicans, and Cubans, coursed
into Louisiana and upriver to assist the patriots in what, until then, had
seemed a losing war with England. Sympathies against England were
running so high in the hemisphere's Spanish and Caribbean territories
that Gálvez found it easy to win soldiers to the rebel side. These hastily
cobbled regiments, which freely committed body and soul to American
independence, represented a full 15 percent of the Revolutionary forces.
We can imagine the Babel of languages Gálvez needed to commandeer
in order to carry out the historic maneuvers that followed. But Gálvez's
greatest gift was his own valor in leading troops into major battlefields
of the Revolution. It is no exaggeration to say that without Gálvez's victories at the Battles of Pensacola, Baton Rouge, Natchez, and Mobile,
independence might not have been won in 1776. That, at least, was the
message given more than two centuries later, in 2014, when Congress
passed a bill posthumously proclaiming Gálvez an honorary American
for playing "an integral role" in the struggle and for being, in George
Washington's estimation, "a deciding factor" in securing the nation's liberty. So it is that Bernardo de Gálvez—for whom the city of Galveston,
Texas, is named—can be called the most influential Latino citizen in the
history of the United States.

Two hundred years after the viscount's extraordinary efforts on behalf of American independence, Juan Carlos I, the king of Spain, traveled to Washington, DC, to celebrate the nation's bicentennial and dedicate a statue of Gálvez, which now stands on Liberator Square, not far from the State Department. "My ancestor, King Carlos III," the king recounted, "who kept up correspondence and exchanged gifts with your first president, gave Gálvez the right to use a coat of arms bearing the heraldic motto 'I alone.'" *Yo solo*, one man: which is to say that a single human will had changed the course of history. And that, the king said in closing, can be said of every Hispanic in America, every individual of Latino heritage who has put another brick in the ever-evolving architecture of this nation.

Some might argue that being given honorary citizenship does not a Hispanic American make. But there are only eight honorary American citizens in all of history—Winston Churchill and Mother Teresa among them—and I would contend that Gálvez, who went on to govern Cuba as well as New Spain, did a great deal more than the other seven to secure a firm foothold for the country.

•    •    •

Latinos who fought in the American Civil War represent another heroic story, one that involves more than the will of one man. By the late nineteenth century, there was a modest representation of Hispanics in the United States. Numbering more than a hundred thousand—a mere 0.5 percent of the overall American population—they were largely naturalized Americans in former Mexican lands who had been granted citizenship after the Mexican-American War. Conveniently, these fledgling citizens then became subject to the military draft. Once called to arms by either side, they were joined by a natural cohort: volunteers and mercenaries from Spanish-speaking nations. By the end of the hostilities between the Union and the Confederacy, twenty thousand Hispanics— Americans as well as foreigners—had served in either army, entering the fray for any number of reasons, from an urgent need to improve their lots in life to a passionate desire to eradicate slavery. Some were well-to-do slaveholding Latinos with considerable stakes in the cotton and tobacco trades, who, like others of the Southern gentry, rose up to defend their family businesses. The more humble, however, were simply swept into the abattoirs of that grisly war by virtue of their availability.

By far, the most celebrated Hispanic warrior of the Civil War, though seldom recognized for his Hispanic roots, was the very first admiral of the US Navy, David Glasgow Farragut. His father was Jorge (Jordi) Ferragut Mesquida, the only known Spanish volunteer to fight under the American flag in the American Revolutionary War. A merchant marine born on the Spanish island of Menorca, Jordi Ferragut had become so enamored of the spirit of American liberty that he changed his name to George Farragut, joined South Carolina's navy as a first lieutenant, and began supplying Charleston with cannons, firearms, gun powder, and cannonballs that he smuggled from Port-au-Prince, in what would soon become Haiti, a notorious source of arms for the patriot army.

Jordi effectively equipped the Revolutionary army for the Battle of Sullivan's Island and the Capture of Savannah, culminating in the Siege of Charleston. Along the way, he married a North Carolinian with family roots in Scotland, hence their son's middle name, Glasgow. By the time the younger Farragut was born, the elder had lost an arm in conflict, become a foot soldier and an artillery gunner, saved the life of Colonel William Washington (a distant cousin of General George Washington) at the Battle of Cowpens, and served under Francis Marion, the Swamp Fox. But in the course of those frantic events, his wife died suddenly and left him a widower, and the bereaved Jordi Ferragut was forced to entrust his seven-year-old boy to an American family, powerless as he was to fight a revolution and care for a child at the same time. Years later, he would go on to commandeer a gunboat in Mississippi during the War of 1812, even as his now eleven-year-old son was serving as a midshipman under his foster father, sailing along the coast of Chile in hunt of British ships. Eventually, after three hard decades of warfare, Jordi returned to civilian life utterly debilitated, a shadow of the intrepid warrior he had once been. "The peace for which I fought," he said wistfully, "left my country free and independent, but me without a penny." He died before his son's twelfth birthday.

Little could the Spaniard have imagined as he lay dying that his or-
phaned boy would become a highly decorated American admiral—the
very first of the nation—and go on to play an equally dramatic yet far
more resplendent role in history. Indeed, young David Farragut would
cut his teeth on a flurry of decisive conflagrations, including skirmishes
with the British and a tour of duty in the Mexican-American War. But
his valor would see its florescence in the Civil War, when he defended
the Union in masterful shows of naval grit at the Battle of New Orleans,
the Siege of Vicksburg, the Siege of Port Hudson, and the Battle of Mobile Bay, among other conflicts. It was he who would utter one of the
most colorful and memorable lines in American battle lore as he led his
squadron into the mine-riddled waters of the Gulf of Mexico, "Damn
the torpedoes, full speed ahead!"

Yet for all the glory he might have brought Hispanics then and now,
Admiral Farragut's Latino roots were swept into the dustbin of history,
as neglected and forgotten as the Revolutionary heroics of his father. Instead, Civil War annals tend to anoint him with the ethnicity of his foster
father, Commodore David Porter. There is a reason for that: during the
War of 1812, the boy took Commodore Porter's first name as a tribute
to his guardian. Today the thoroughly Anglo name that endures is emblazoned on many a US Navy ship, military academy, postage stamp,
city square, even state park—and the Latino Admiral Farragut is rarely
acknowledged.

Indeed, nine blocks from where I live in Washington, DC, a statue
of this brave Hispanic American stands on Farragut Square, fixing a keen
gaze in the direction of the White House, only a few blocks away. It is a
massive and fierce likeness, forged from a melted-down propeller of the
USS *Hartford*, Farragut's Civil War flagship, a vessel he lived on for much
of those perilous years and loved dearly. In planning for that monument,
a full study of Farragut's life and formidable battle prowess was undertaken, all of it painstakingly recorded for prosperity; a similar study was
made when Augustus Saint-Gaudens designed and produced the statue
of David Farragut that now stands in New York City's Madison Square.
Yet nowhere on either monument is there any mention of his origins.

He is not alone. Hispanic military heroes who have served honorably are often overlooked if not recast as something other than Hispanic.
For Admiral Farragut, that assignation is Scots. Indeed, the best-known
children's biography of Farragut refers to the admiral throughout as
"Glasgow," and transforms his father, Jordi Ferragut Mesquida, into a
seemingly full-blooded Anglo-American.

The same invisibility has been imposed on Brigadier General Stephen Vincent Benét, another Hispanic commanding officer of considerable stature in the Civil War. A grandson and nephew of prominent
Spaniards in Saint Augustine, Florida, Benét graduated with honors
from West Point Military Academy where he became one of its most
distinguished specialists in ordnance. The assumption in many history
books is that the general was an Anglo through and through, although
he was born in Saint Augustine only a few years after Florida was acquired from Spain, and both his father (Pedro Benét) and mother (Juana
Hernández) were natives of the island of Menorca, as—coincidentally
enough—was Jordi Ferragut. Benét's grandson, also called Stephen Vincent Benét, would become one of the great American poets of the early
twentieth century, winning a Pulitzer Prize for his epic poem about the
Civil War, *John Brown's Body*. No wonder that Representative Joaquín
Castro finds it maddening that so many Americans cannot name three,
or even one, illustrious Hispanic, when men such as these are hiding in
plain sight.

Two years before succumbing to a heart attack, Admiral David
Glasgow Farragut made a victory trip across the Atlantic on the USS
*Franklin*, brandishing the American flag as well as his own and being received and celebrated by royals from Madrid to Saint Petersburg. In the
course of that yearlong voyage, he decided to accept an invitation to visit
Ciutadella, the seaside town where his father had been born. Springing
onto those shores on the day after Christmas, December 26, 1867, the
admiral was received by a throng such as the island had never seen. Vis-
ibly moved, he surveyed the multitudes as they surged down the streets,
straining to see their prodigal hero. No one suspected that the strapping,
sixty-six-year-old lion of the seas had a weak heart. He was erect and

energetic as ever, silver hair combed neatly to one side, dark brown eyes piercing under a furrowed brow. His Spanish—learned in childhood and reinforced during his service in Mexico and the Caribbean—was courteous, idiomatic, issued at a fair clip. Indeed, he had always enjoyed a distinct skill for languages and could exchange pleasantries in at least four of them, all of which served him well on this last, triumphant, valedictory tour.

The island's luminaries were dispatched in twenty carriages to greet him, and they ferried him ceremonially from landmark to landmark: ushering him through the cathedral where his father had been baptized more than a century before, whisking him away to meet the only living descendant of his father's godmother, presenting him with a gold-embossed history of his Spanish and Catalan origins, and showing him breathtaking views of the Balearic Sea that had inspired his forebears to set out for the horizon in the first place. From his quarters on board the *Franklin*, Admiral Farragut telegraphed his superior, the American secretary of the navy, to report that he intended to do no official business in Menorca; the visit was to be strictly personal, entirely sentimental. Spanish historians report the sojourn with more dramatic flourish: to them, he was a hero of that island soil, a seaman whose "greatness of character and goodness of heart" at long last had led him home. One historian goes so far as to suggest that the admiral came specifically to lay his hard-won American laurels before the memory of his Menorcan father.

•    •    •

When my Confederate ancestors heard the call to arms [in Cuba], they went. You see, my friends, my entry from Cuba into the United States in 1971 was paid a long, long time ago with their blood.
                —John O'Donnell-Rosales, historian, Cuban American, 2002

To be clear, the inventory of Hispanics who fought valiantly in the Civil War is much longer than those two names: Admiral Farragut and General Benét. Among the twenty thousand, the list numbers whole battalions of foreigners. Take, for example, John O'Donnell-Rosales, the historian quoted above, who makes the claim that America is his birthright, even though he emigrated from Cuba to the United States in 1971. His rationale? His ancestors sailed here from Cuba in the 1860s, fought for the Confederacy, and died on this soil one hundred years before he stepped foot on it. His ancestors were not alone. As much as one-quarter of the troops who fought for the Union were citizens of other countries: Mexicans, Spaniards, Cubans, Germans, Poles, Irish. Hispanics were heavily represented among them; the overwhelming majority of them Mexican Americans who were enlisted, at Abraham Lincoln's urging, to the Union side.

Perhaps the most famous were the four regiments of New Mexico Volunteers: four thousand combatants whose families had inhabited Mexican terrain for hundreds of years and understood each twist and turn of their contested land. Fierce in battle, prized on the open scrublands for their horsemanship, the Volunteers had honed their abilities in wars against the Comanche, Navajo, Apache, and Ute, but they were scorned and abused by Anglo officers, who dismissed them as "greaser soldiers." Mustered by Henry Connelly, an antislavery governor with an aristocratic Mexican wife, the Volunteers rose to the occasion nevertheless and fought long and hard for the Northern cause, although much of the Southwest had pledged itself to the Confederacy. Despite the rabid racism and low pay—despite the shabby supplies issued to them—they soon proved indispensable to the Union's victory at the decisive Battle of Glorieta Pass.

Lore has it that Confederate soldiers were lily white, predominantly Scotch-Irish, and Protestant. But the truth was very different. A vast number were *caribeños* from the Caribbean, or *Mexicanos* from the coasts of Mexico; there were also Canary Islanders from the west of Spain and rugged seamen who hailed from the Balearic Islands, as did the ancestors of Farragut and Benét. There was good reason for this. They were sailors in lively international ports that had strong, daily ties to foreign harbors. And, in the South—particularly in the ports of Louisiana—in lieu of turf and mountain, the war's focus was on waterways: the rivers, bays, and the Gulf of Mexico. To protect the city of New Orleans, its harbor, and vast commercial interests, nearly one thousand Hispanics of every hue, foreigners as well as citizens, joined the European Brigade, a highly effective Confederate fighting force, many of its ranks from aristocratic families invested in the slave economy of the South.

Hispanics also served in the Confederacy's famed Louisiana Tigers, a shaggy company of disparate nationalities lured from the wilds of that unruly territory. They were a rough-and-ready ten thousand, most of them foreign born—largely Irish, though many were Spaniards, Cubans, Mexicans, Nicaraguans—an ungodly combination of "wharf-rats to cutthroats to thieves," as one writer has put it. Despite their lack of formal training, the Tigers made for scrappy guerrilla fighters, willing to undertake any task and defeat any foe, but their rampant misdeeds also made for the notorious image throughout the North that came to be associated with Louisiana fighting men. Unlike the aristocrats of the European Brigade, most were rank newcomers to the American idea: humble men, laborers who made their living on the levees, or wharves, or doing backbreaking work on plantations. But they also fought loyally and made momentous advances for the South.

Among the more unexpected soldiers were the Latinas who secretly donned uniforms, impersonated men, and took up the banner for both North and South. One was Loreta Janeta Velázquez, a fourteen-year-old schoolgirl from Cuba who abandoned her aunt's sumptuous New Orleans home to elope with an officer in the Texas army. When Texas seceded from the Union in 1861, her husband joined the Confederate army. Loreta begged him to let her join him. Unfazed by his refusal, she disguised herself as a man, enlisted against his wishes, and fought valiantly for the Confederacy in numerous battles. Registered as a very youthful Lieutenant Harry Buford, she took up arms at Manassas, Ball's Bluff, and Fort Donelson. In truth, in those years before stringent protocols were put in place, it wasn't difficult for a woman to pass as male, since the armies of either side were so desperate for fresh troops that unshaved young boys were often admitted to the ranks. Moreover, uniforms were so ill-fitting that they handily cloaked the female body. Generally, the women who fought as soldiers went undiscovered unless they

were wounded, became ill, were taken prisoner, or—as happened with
quite a few—gave birth in the encampments.

On Loreta's return to New Orleans, however, her gender was revealed, and her superiors immediately reprimanded and discharged her.
Undaunted, she took off again and reenlisted in Tennessee to fight in the
bitter conflict at Shiloh, the largest, most costly battle in American history at that point. Unmasked for a second time, she ended her wartime
career by operating as a Confederate spy. Eventually Loreta penned a best-
selling memoir revealing the extent of the presence of Hispanic women
on the front lines of the Civil War, although the army vehemently denied
it. Even the more prudent Latinas who stayed home and out of harm's
way ended up serving the war effort in one way or another: as nurses,
water bearers, runners, and intelligence operatives. Many offered food,
shelter, and medical care to the soldiers who knocked on their doors.

In every military engagement that followed for the next 150 years,
Latinos proceeded to contribute mightily to the American war effort.
They served by the thousands in the Spanish-American War; they rode
with Theodore Roosevelt as part of his famed Rough Riders. Two battalions of Puerto Rican volunteers formed a regiment that then served
with distinction in whatever zones of conflict emerged, including the
Boxer Rebellion in China. But the largest recruitment of Hispanics would
take place during the spring of 1917 when some two hundred thousand
Hispanics, the great majority of them Mexican Americans, were mobilized to fight in World War I. Because they were legally counted as white
Americans, they were integrated into the regular forces and scattered
throughout the fighting fronts. But eighteen thousand Puerto Ricans,
lacking that racial distinction, were fed instead into segregated infantry
regiments that guarded key installations in the Caribbean and the Panama Canal Zone, holding their fire until they were allowed to deploy for
battlefields. That time never came: before they were allowed to ship out
to Europe, an armistice was reached on November 11, 1918, bringing all
fighting to an end.

•    •    •

AMERICANS ALL! Let's fight for victory!

AMERICANOS TODOS! Luchamos por la gloria!

—Leon Helguera, poster artist, Mexican American, 1942

Come World War II, by which time the Hispanic population had ballooned considerably, more than a half million Latinos served in the
United States military effort overseas. Sources reported that 60 percent
of all American-born Hispanic males between the ages of sixteen and
twenty-two were serving on the war's battlefields. And yet many who
were willing to fight were never called to colors: take, for instance, the
350,000 Puerto Ricans, all of them American citizens, who reported
to wartime conscription offices, although only 65,000 of them were
admitted to the ranks. On the mainland, millions more Latinos, including my engineer father, worked in factories producing war materiél:
turbines, bombs, parachutes, navigational instruments, cluster adapt-
ers. Indeed, the iconic image of Rosie the Riveter as a white woman is
grossly misleading; most women who worked the punishing, round-
the-clock, eight-hour shifts in America's war factories were women of
color.

The exact numbers are difficult to quantify and maddeningly inaccurate, because undercounting was rampant and because the US Census
and the military itself were more preoccupied with counting blacks (for
segregational purposes) than reckoning a wildly diverse and confounding ethnicity. The choices offered on military rosters said it all: "White,"
"Negro," and "Other." Often, Latinos checked off "White," believing
themselves to be so. Otherwise, clerks simply typed in whatever they
saw, depending on their own prejudices, now and then crossing out
"Other" and registering an arbitrarily designated "Mexican." The challenges are amply illustrated in the experiences of the Botello family:
five Texan brothers, all army or navy servicemen, whose phenotypes
were officially recorded in 1945 and 1946 as they were discharged. The
first brother was certified by the clerk as "Mexican"; the next three as
"White"; the fifth was penciled in as "Spanish." To this day, these capricious categorizations continue to bedevil demographers, public policy

makers, historians, even Hispanics themselves. As one veteran put it, "I was born American in Fort Stockton, Texas, but they called me Mexican. And when the war started, I became a white man."

For all the confusion, military records show that soldiers with Spanish surnames were amply represented in the Pacific Theater as well as in Europe. Thousands died on the killing fields of Italy or in defense of South Pacific territories. Valued for their language abilities, many ended up serving in the Philippines, where Spanish was understood. Indeed, the legendary Bushmasters (158th Infantry), a combat team that fought the Japanese in the Philippines, were mostly Mexicans and indigenous people from Arizona, trained in the Panama rainforests to battle in the jungles of Southeast Asia. They ended up being so audacious a force that General Douglas MacArthur was inspired to say of them, "No greater fighting combat team has ever deployed for battle." But there were instances, too, when diplomacy served as much as valor: for US Marine Guy Gabaldon, deployed to the Mariana Islands, the fluent Japanese he had learned in his racially diverse—partially Latino, partially Asian—neighborhood of East Los Angeles gave him a vital advantage when, with no assistance whatsoever, he lured, cajoled, and captured 1,500 Japanese soldiers with cigarettes, candy, and fictitious threats that they were surrounded by American forces, earning this eighteen-year-old the nickname the "Pied Piper of Saipan."

For Staff Sergeant Macario García, an undocumented Mexican who had done stoop labor alongside his parents in the Texan cotton fields, a sense of duty to his adopted country would earn him honors never before attained by a Latino. Despite his unofficial status, García enlisted in the army, joined Bravo Company, and was shipped off to war, but was gravely wounded on D-Day, June 6, 1944, as the Allied forces landed on the heavily defended beaches of Normandy, France, initiating the long-awaited invasion of Nazi-occupied Europe. Four months later, upon his recovery, medics urged caution, but García insisted on serving like any other soldier. When ordered to eliminate two enemy machine gun nests as his regiment crossed into Germany, he succeeded in clearing the first, but the second suddenly opened fire, riddling him with bullets. Despite those injuries, García single-handedly charged the second post, killing half the Germans in it and taking the other soldiers prisoner. For achieving his unit's objectives despite such physical hardship, President Harry S. Truman awarded him the Purple Heart as well as the Bronze Star and made him the first Mexican national ever to receive America's highest military accolade, the Congressional Medal of Honor.

When the war was over, García tried to enter a restaurant in Richmond, Texas, but was stopped and refused service. He objected to the insult, a violent brawl ensued, and the restaurant owner retaliated by bludgeoning him with a baseball bat. Seriously injured, García was carted off to the local police station, charged with assault, jailed, and released the next morning on bail. He survived the indignity, although Texas had named him the offender, and eventually shrugged off the incident as just another racist slight, became an American citizen, and went to work as a counselor for the Veterans Administration in Houston. But the humiliation stung.

Almost two decades later, García and a number of Hispanic veterans in Houston were asked to attend a fancy civil rights gala honoring John F. Kennedy. The president spoke of Hispanics' vibrant contributions to the country; First Lady Jacqueline Kennedy thanked the veterans personally in her fluent Spanish. Suddenly García found himself shaking a president's hand for the second time and being acknowledged once again for his service. He claimed he would never forget the moment, but he didn't have long to savor it: the following afternoon, Kennedy was assassinated in Dallas, and the country was plunged into mourning. García himself didn't last until old age, dying in an automobile accident nine years later. The army, which had always lauded his service, buried him with full military honors. With time—in the more enlightened 1980s—the city of Houston, whose laws had strictly forbidden the likes of Macario García from setting foot in its "public" establishments, named an unremarkable stretch of street in the old Mexican barrio after him.

· · ·

Hispanics fought on the battlefields of World War II in unprecedented numbers, and yet approximately the same numbers fought in the Korean

War, a far smaller conflict, which illustrates their continued proliferation in American war zones. There were 180,000 of them manning the
ramparts of that neglected, underreported war, and they represented
a strikingly diverse rainbow of Americans: Mexican Americans whose
families had inhabited the Southwest for hundreds of years as well as
Mexican nationals who happened to be living and working in the United
States. But there were also Puerto Ricans, Cuban Americans, and an
array of others who emerged to enlist from faraway pockets of the
country. Those of Mexican extraction made for a full 10 percent of the
entire US fighting force, although—at the time—Mexican Americans
were less than 4 percent of the country's population. Always serving in
the front lines, the Hispanics tended to bear the brunt of the casualties.
One-tenth of all American fatalities in the Korean War were endured by
Mexican American soldiers, making them the third highest group—after
South Koreans and non-Hispanic Americans—to lose their lives or suffer calamitous wounds in that brutal war. Again, it is entirely possible
that those numbers were even greater, since many Hispanics enlisted
with anglicized names—Raúl Álvarez Castillo, for instance, signed on as
Ralph Castle—and so eluded the only way that the army was counting
Hispanics at the time.

•   •   •

> During the Vietnam War, a lower-income Mexican American neigh-
> borhood of San Antonio suffered 54 casualties, one of the highest
> rates for a single school district in the country. All but three of the 54
> were Latino.
>
> —Deborah Paredez, poet, Vietnam veteran's
> daughter, Mexican American, 2018

By the outbreak of the Vietnam War in the 1960s, a mere decade after
the killing fields of Korea, it was clear that the Hispanic population of
young men had become a rich field of recruitment for the US military.
The "Vietnam Conflict," as it was called euphemistically in the beginning, was a poor man's war and a working-class war. Even as the sons of
the middle and upper classes were going to college and demonstrating

at antiwar rallies, the sons of the undocumented, the unemployed, the grape pickers, the ghetto poor, the steelworkers, the strivers, and the sharecroppers were registering at draft stations and being sent off to the rice paddies of Indochina. In general, Hispanics represented a young population, overwhelmingly low income, but, overall, the majority of American grunts on the ground in Vietnam were painfully callow, averaging barely more than nineteen, while the average age of a World War II GI was twenty-seven. It also needs to be said that most Latinos who were drafted reported for duty as ordered and did not shirk service, seek deferments, or slip across the border to Canada.

Official reports tell us that eighty-three thousand Hispanics served in every branch of the military during the Vietnam War, although that figure—given the usual difficulty of the count—turns out to be a gross underestimate. One thing we do know: the Pentagon was not bothering to count Hispanics, or document where they served, or tally how many of them were being sacrificed to the political hubris that prevailed in Washington's relentless thresher of American young. Even so, the existing numbers—as under-representative as they might be—do cite Latino soldiers suffering more fatalities than their ethnicity's share in the overall population. This is no surprise. We know now that in the 1960s and early 1970s, Selective Service boards, which were composed largely of middle-class, middle-aged white men, were inclined to send low-income males (poor whites as well as those of color) into the butchery of that faraway war. Deferments for Latinos in the Southwest, where most of these young men lived, were almost nonexistent. First, because deferments were not available for high school dropouts, which low-income Mexican Americans tended to be, but they were also unavailable to youths who were not enrolled in college.

That said, Hispanics *wanted* to serve in the Vietnam War, and they wanted to do so in the most vulnerable front lines of the war. You can call it machismo; you can call it naiveté. But they tended to seek action, the exhilaration of battle, an opportunity to test their mettle. For that reason, they often tended to enlist—as they continue to do today—in the US Marines, where the perils were more extreme. Just as American blacks believed that their willingness to serve in World War II would win them a "double victory" by gaining them the full rights of a citizen at home, Hispanics signed up for the Vietnam War willingly—enthusiastically—with the clear intent of proving their patriotism and showing just how American they could be. One Mexican soldier even reported that when any greenhorn Latino arrived on a platoon, the white draftees would laugh at him, mock him, for being such a knucklehead as to *volunteer* to serve in that perverse war.

One of the most eager to ship out to Indochina was Sergeant First Class Jorge Otero-Barreto, later known as the "Puerto Rican Rambo," the most highly decorated soldier to serve in the Vietnam War. Otero had been born in the town of Vega Baja in Puerto Rico, where he graduated from high school, and had studied biology in the University of Puerto Rico. In 1959, just before going on to medical school in Madrid, however, he changed his mind, volunteered to join the US Army, and began training at the Army Air Assault School in Fort Campbell, Tennessee. He began his service in 1961 as an advisor, training South Vietnamese troops, but his expertise and zeal eventually thrust him into the combat zone. During his five years on Vietnamese ground, from 1961 to 1966, he served a record five tours of duty, participated in two hundred combat missions, and was awarded thirty-eight medals for his valor and leadership. The man was beloved by his troops, universally acknowledged to be a brave warrior, great teacher—the sort of commander who led by example and faced hazards before ordering a soldier to step into the breach.

Sergeant "Rock," as he was also called, reached his highest achievement during the Battle of Phuoc Yen, in the spring of 1968, when he cagily devised and employed the "cordon maneuver" to encircle and trap the Ninetieth Division, the most feared and recalcitrant unit of the North Vietnamese army. Getting his machine gunners to "talk"—or fire cartridges from numerous points along the periphery of a zone to sow terror into the enemy—he backed the Ninetieth into a cul-de-sac formed by a loop in the Song Bo River. Otero-Barreto followed with artillery fire from the rear bank. A platoon of approximately fifty had gone up against a massive force of close to a thousand fighters, and, by the end of the three-day battle, Rock had overseen the largest mass surrender of Vietnamese soldiers in the history of the war. He was a Puerto Rican, after all, a Boricua, "from the land of the brave lords," as signified by the Taíno word for Puerto Rico.

To commend such extraordinary courage and cunning, veterans and politicians today are lobbying to give this eighty-seven-year-old the Medal of Honor he should have received long ago. Others have done far less to win that accolade. But Otero-Barreto dismisses the pretty words. "A warrior doesn't love himself," he says. "A warrior is somebody beyond himself, willing to give his life for his people." He pauses, then adds, "I was a *soldier*, proud of his people." *Proud of his people*. Talking to Otero-Baretto as he lies shirtless in his hammock on a hot, languid Puerto Rican afternoon is a bit like talking to a restless animal: a bird, perhaps, or a fox. He glances from side to side while his interviewer speaks, conditioned like a beast of prey to be alert to any sound, any shadow, but he is also the quintessential predator, anticipating the scent of a weaker foe. "You see? You *see* that? See what I'm doing?" he asks, suddenly aware of the disquiet that his nervous movements produce in his interlocutor. "You see my mind? Anything that moves, I move. Any sound? I hear it."

Dr. Martin Luther King Jr., a leader also infinitely proud of his people, once observed that "Vietnam was a white man's war but a black man's fight," and the military's numbers—largely accurate for blacks—prove Dr. King's claim. African Americans filled 31 percent of the ground combat battalions in the war and represented 24 percent of the fatalities, even though they made up only 12 percent of the population. It wasn't long after the killing statistics in Vietnam began to mount and the public began to notice the race differentials that Ralph Guzman, a professor at the University of California at Santa Cruz, began to suspect that the body count for Hispanics was criminally underreported, given not only the system's propensity to dismiss Mexican Americans but also the confusion about skin color among Hispanics themselves. Dr. King's dictum needed to be broadened: the Vietnam War was also a brown man's fight. A deadly roulette for Latinos as well as blacks. Three things were sure:

Mexicans were being lumped in with whites, Afro-Latinos were being conflated with blacks, and the truth about their fatality rates was being relegated to oblivion. Professor Guzman set out to prove that a more scientific and thorough accounting might reveal the genuine sacrifices American Latinos were making.

By 1969, he had reckoned some truths. On October 8 of that year, Edward R. Roybal, a Mexican American congressman from California, entered Guzman's research into the *Congressional Record*. The representative explained that, with no credible, official reports available, Guzman had set out to gather the facts meticulously himself. Focusing on areas where Mexican Americans, the majority of Latinos at the time, were most densely concentrated—Arizona, Colorado, New Mexico, Texas, and California—(precisely as the Census Bureau would begin to do a year later), Guzman and his team of researchers had calculated the number of casualties reported in those states against the states' population of Hispanics. The findings were finalized in 1970 and, in 1971, were published by the National Council of La Raza, which had been founded four years before to fight discrimination against American Hispanics and improve their circumstances. What Professor Guzman's research revealed was something very different from what the Pentagon was telling us.

Professor Guzman's report indicated that, between 1961 and 1969, Vietnam War casualties among Mexican Americans were more than 50 percent greater than the ratio Mexican Americans bore to the overall American population. This was something Latino neighborhoods in Southwest neighborhoods knew all too well already. Their young were being killed in disproportionate numbers. They could see it for themselves in their communities: the constant knocks on the doors, the wailing parents, the flag-draped coffins. At the time, Latinos constituted a mere 12 percent of the US population but, according to Guzman, their sons accounted for 20 percent of the fatalities—far exceeding the Pentagon's claim. Four times higher, in fact. Guzman had revealed that in America's tragic, unwinnable standoff with North Vietnam, blacks and Latinos were being mowed down at far greater rates than that of any other Americans. They were the battlefront targets, the fodder, the expendable ones, sacrificing far more than their ratios of the population. Whites, on the other hand, were contributing less than their share.

It is a sorry state of affairs when one needs to prove what seemed so obvious to Hispanic families, but, as Roybal was now telling Congress, Guzman had proven it. He had compiled the numbers, shown the discrepancies. And yet no one seemed to pay either man—Roybal or Guzman—any mind. Almost thirty years later, in 1995, a history of military statistics in Indochina would refer to the obviously disproportionate share of American fatalities in Vietnam as being sustained by blacks "and other minorities." The Latino dead had been entirely erased. That deletion is summed up in the final pages of Michael Herr's iconic, prizewinning 1977 account of the war, *Dispatches*. As Herr closes the book, he describes sitting in the main hall of the Tan Son Nhat Airport in Saigon, waiting to head out from an excruciating tour of duty reporting the war. He glances up to see a departing soldier's graffiti scrawled on the wall in front of him. It reads: "Mendoza was here. 12 Sept 68. Texas." And next to it: "Color me gone." It is Herr's only reference to a Hispanic in that otherwise perceptive portrait of the war.

• • •

Today nearly 20 percent of all military personnel in the country identify as Latino; and among female soldiers, Latinas represent an even larger ratio. Eighteen percent of the US Marine Corps are Hispanic. The rise in representation has been especially dramatic since the wars in Afghanistan and Iraq, which saw all the military services avidly recruiting Latino personnel. Their efforts were rewarded. Hispanics eagerly signed up for tours of duty, starting in Operation Desert Storm, which engaged twenty thousand Latino fighters in 1990. Ten years later, after the galvanizing effect of Al Qaeda's attack on US soil, the Marine Corps commissioned a report on its strategic plan to engage more soldiers from this segment of the population. The results, shared with the workforce training staff throughout the corps, was explicit about its enthusiasm for the Latino soldier:

As the Hispanic population has grown, so has its representation in the military—particularly in the Marine Corps. Data show that young Hispanic men and women have higher active duty propensity (i.e., they say they are interested in joining the military) than non-Hispanic youths. . . . Hispanics' interest in military service and strong enlistment behavior have been good for the Marine Corps. We find that Hispanic recruits are more likely than recruits of other races or ethnicities to complete bootcamp and the first term of service—even after controlling for other differences. Although we have not investigated Hispanic recruits' success in the other Services, we would not expect their behavior to differ significantly from Hispanics in the Marine Corps. Thus, expected increases in the Hispanic youth population should be good news for all the Services.

It certainly was good news for the recruiters. By 2004, only one year into the "Global War on Terror" and shortly after celebrating the Fourth of July, President George W. Bush was able to declare to a largely Hispanic audience, "Some eighty-five thousand Latinos have served in Operation Enduring Freedom and Operation Iraqi Freedom. More than one hundred have given their lives. Over four hundred have been injured in combat. Our nation will never forget their service and their sacrifice to our security and to our freedom." A few years later, in 2007, with the military-industrial complex's recruitment engine huffing away in full force, there were almost two hundred thousand Hispanic soldiers serving the country in some corner of the world and almost a million and a half Hispanic veterans still living, having fought in a multitude of wars and skirmishes since the Second World War. And still, fourteen hapless members of the 110th Congress were lamenting that the country was lagging in its appreciation of the Hispanic soldier, "Whereas the contributions of Hispanics to the United States Armed Forces have been largely unrecognized in American history," the congressional resolution asserted. "Now, therefore, be it *Resolved by the House of Representatives (the Senate concurring).* . . . [that] Congress recognizes Hispanic servicemembers for their courage on the battlefield throughout the history of the United States, as well as their determination, discipline, selfless service, and patriotism."

But the military's eye continued to be trained on fodder, not on bringing Latinos up the chain of command. It seemed no one was looking for leaders among the hordes of Hispanics entering the services, even though, by then, dozens of Congressional Medals of Honor had festooned Hispanic chests. No. Even as Congress lauded the valor, dedication, and excellence of the Latino serviceperson, there were but four Hispanic senior officers in any segment of the armed forces. Between 1995 and 2016, only one was promoted to three-star general, even as the number of Hispanic officers doubled to many thousands during the same period. At this book's writing, almost two decades after that congressional resolution, there is not one active-duty four-star Hispanic general. There are only four Hispanic officers in the top echelons of the US Army. And, below that, at the most senior level of the rest, we represent a paltry 2 percent.

Why is that? Some will argue that not enough have a bachelor's degree—a requirement for the appointment and advancement of most officers. Others will insist that those who occupy the highest posts in the chain of command constitute a "good old boy network" and tend to bring along their own kind. Statistics don't lie: the Olympians of the military are overwhelmingly white. In truth, almost 97 percent of the leadership of the armed services is white, even though non-Hispanic whites represent little more than half the population of the United States. It should be of some concern to every American that it took 246 years of history before the first nonwhite officer of the US Marines would be given a fourth star. That honor finally arrived in late 2022, when the highly accomplished black Marine general Michael E. Langley reached that landmark achievement. Today, among the nearly one thousand American soldiers who have reached four-star stature in every arm of the US military throughout history, we can count fewer than twenty blacks. Only one Hispanic since the very dawn of this country has been granted that honor: US Army general Richard E. Cavazos, who earned two Distinguished Service Crosses for his heroics during the Korean and

Vietnam Wars and became head of the US Armed Forces Command (FORSCOM) upon his promotion to four-star status in 1982. He retired two years later.

Yet another argument is that the myth of the dim-witted, idle Hispanic imposed throughout Hollywood's history lives on in the American mind. It was certainly frighteningly present in my lifetime, during the Vietnam War. One decorated Latino colonel—the first US pilot to be shot down over Vietcong territory, a navy man who was subsequently held prisoner for more than eight years in the brutal "Hanoi Hilton"— recounts that he made a point of championing exceptionally bright, young, talented Latinos whom the more senior, white airmen had refused. My own observation is that, among soldiers I've interviewed for this book, the very attributes that make Latinos useful to the military— their loyalty, their willingness to fight in the front lines and accept their assigned duties—too often are obstacles to their own elevation. "It's part of the macho mind-set, I think," says retired general Albert Zapanta, a former Special Services soldier in Vietnam. "We are a warrior culture. We never want to be viewed as weak," so, as a group, Latinos are more focused on action than on climbing up the ranks. "We jump out of airplanes," says Zapanta, "we do Ranger, we do all the tough stuff, but at the end of the day, that's not how you become a general."

In short, Latinos do not join the military for self-aggrandizement or personal gain. They may long to elevate their station in the great American Dream, make better lives for their families, take their children to the next rung, prove their loyalty to their country, but—perhaps to their own detriment—they are not inclined to strategize a rise through the intricate, highly political labyrinth of the military complex. Their numbers alone may change that.

# GROWERS

> The overarching narrative is that we're taking jobs, space, education, etcetera. In fact, we are *givers*. We gave our land. We give work. We contribute. We gave names to much of this country. We are the opposite of what you think we are.
>
> —Mónica Ramírez, rights activist, Mexican American, Ohio, 2021

Latinos and Latinas are the most highly employed people in the United States. Work is the air we breathe, the creed we live by. That doesn't mean we hold the enviable jobs or earn the highest incomes. Quite the reverse. We have the highest employment rate—higher than any other race or ethnicity in the nation—precisely because many of us are willing to do the work that no one else wants to do. Half of all farmworkers and seafood employees in this country are Hispanic, as are the construction workers, cleaning and maintenance crews, domestic workers, and miners. We fill more than a quarter of the ranks of kitchen labor, service jobs, and transport operations. In California, the state that purveys more fresh produce than any other state in America, 92 percent of all workers are Latinos and Latinas. We put food on the table, feed the nation, build the cities, and scour out all the pots.

It wasn't always so. In 1990 the Latino workforce numbered a modest eleven million people. By 2020, it had tripled to almost thirty million. Political upheaval in Latin America certainly contributed to that influx, as it had since the days of the Mexican Revolution, but the demand for affordable labor in America's fields and cities has been a mighty magnet—gargantuan, irresistible, ravenous. Even as the pool of white, Asian, and black Americans willing to do stoop labor and backbreaking construction diminishes, the Latino appetite for that work continues to explode, pulling in aspiring toilers from the Sonora Desert, the faraway canyons of the Peruvian Colca Valley, or the scattered exile communities of Venezuelans. That trend only promises to grow. By 2030, it is projected that Hispanics will account for 80 percent of all new workers in the country, their representation in the labor force ballooning to nearly forty million.

All the same, though Latinos may represent a massive, highly employed American labor force—some even hyper-employed, taking on more than one job to make ends meet—they are not as employed as they could be or want to be. It may seem contradictory, but within the last decade, many Latinos registered higher unemployment rates than non-Hispanic whites. There are reasons why: mainly, because the population is constantly multiplying (just in the last decade, Latinos have represented more than half the country's overall population growth); second, the overwhelming majority of Hispanics who are not in the workforce *want* to work, and very possibly *are* working in a hazy, informal sector of transient, underreported menial jobs. One thing is sure: it is a young population, averaging twenty-five to thirty years old, the optimal childbearing age. One out of every four American children is a Hispanic; considerably more than half of all Texans and Californians under eighteen years old is Hispanic. Not only is it a mammoth agglomeration of human beings, but also its numbers are ever mounting. It is a future workforce without parallel.

Much of the population toils on farmlands. Latinos represent half of all agricultural laborers in the country. That simple fact is largely lost on the American consciousness, but it has enormous implications for the nation. Historically, we have been a republic that can feed itself, a vital attribute in a world where, overnight, political ruptures can render a population hungry. Witness how Russia's twenty-first-century assault on Ukraine spurred food shortages around the globe, and how the United States—thanks to its Latino farmworkers—was able to spring instantly to feed the hungry masses. This bounty of food is, in many ways, a pillar of America's strength and resilience, but too often that abundance and its vast population of custodians are taken for granted. Clearly, the humble stoop laborer is long overdue for a healthy round of recognition. As *Foreign Policy* magazine recently declared, the farmworkers of this country—whatever their citizenship—are America's "unsung heroes."

Dependency on their labor was established firmly during World War II, when the United States drew up a bilateral agreement with Mexico, allowing Mexicans to enter freely, replace Americans who had gone off to war, and relieve the work shortages that were crippling US agriculture as well as the building industry. The Bracero "guest worker" program brought in four and a half million Mexicans over the course of the next two decades, successfully resuscitating the domestic economy and making it clear to the world that this country was not just determined to be an arsenal of democracy; it was bent on being democracy's pantry as well. The Braceros—which literally means "the arms"—were perceived as just that: limbs to be borrowed at America's whim; easily disposed of when inconvenient. The Braceros are long gone, they ceased to be allowed to cross the border legally in 1964, as passions about civil rights peaked, the Vietnam War erupted in all its bloody-minded ferocity, and the country turned its weary eyes to other concerns. Just as quickly as the agreement had been brought to life, it was brought to an abrupt close. All the same, Mexicans, who had been crossing the Rio Grande for centuries before the program was put in place, continued to come; and they—and their descendants—continued to be the mainstay of American abundance and provender.

Even as the sun was setting on those Bracero days, the country's farmworkers were mostly heads of families and largely legal. Today they are uniformly young and largely undocumented. Most are Mexican nationals, Northern Triangle refugees, or Latinos who have inhabited the Southwest for generations. Such is the cohort that feeds America and the many nations it sustains. Even so, farmhands and domestic workers continue to endure an animus that goes back to the 1930s, when, for blatantly racist reasons, the New Deal's labor laws explicitly excluded them from protection. The prejudice has rattled down the decades to haunt the present day, despite all evidence of Latinos' vital importance to the American table.

The bigotry was made glaringly obvious in 2017, when President Donald Trump abruptly slammed shut the border to asylum seekers. His antipathy began to look foolish and shortsighted once the COVID-19 pandemic was upon us, however. Trump was then forced to declare

that farmworkers (and sanitation workers) were part of America's "critical, essential infrastructure," although no mention was made that most
of them were migrants and undocumented. The forty-fifth president
unleashed an anti-immigrant wave unlike any other in recent memory.
"Whose country is this anyway?" seemed to be its operative anthem.
And yet, that phrase might have been sung long ago in 1885, when one
out of every six residents in the United States was an immigrant. Today
the percentage of foreign-born on this land is actually less than it was
then, but it's not about the numbers. It's about skin color. Latinos, except for a very few, do not look like Northern Europeans—the hordes,
including Trump's grandfather Friedrich Heinrich—who stormed our
gates in 1885. And yet Latinos are doing the very work, and more, that
those immigrants did then.

We should know by now that it was Latino workers who kept going
out into the world during the COVID pandemic to keep the country fed
and served, even as the rest of us shuttered ourselves at home and visited
the food banks when grocery shelves ran empty. Facing a raging virus,
a scourge of pesticides, diminished work crews, and heightened work
hazards, Hispanic laborers kept a full-blown food crisis at bay. Hispanic
orderlies and aides kept the hospitals, clinics, and vaccination units humming. And they paid the price for it, dying of the virus in unprecedented
numbers. By any measure, those workers have proved themselves as essential to national security today as the Braceros were in 1942, and yet,
to date, they have not received the recognition they merit.

Instead, the image most associated with Mexicans in the popular
imagination is the ubiquitous "sleeping man," who dozes under a som-
brero with an empty bottle at his feet. But he can also be the heavily
accented, fugacious cartoon character, the unreliable rodent Speedy
Gonzales; or the gold-toothed, stubble-faced Frito Bandito, who robs
people of food at gunpoint. One needn't even ask about the stock-
Hollywood Mexican female, who is either an oversexed vamp or the aged
frump on her knees, scrubbing the floor. Never mind that these popular
fabrications are in direct counterpoint to the hardworking, upstanding
Mexican American who, throughout history, has been America's source

of sustenance. Food guru Anthony Bourdain, in a blog post before his untimely death, summed up this decidedly two-faced American attitude:

> We consume nachos, tacos, burritos, tortas, enchiladas, tamales and anything resembling Mexican in enormous quantities. Despite our ridiculously hypocritical attitudes toward immigration, we demand that Mexicans cook a large percentage of the food we eat and grow the ingredients we need to make that food. As any chef will tell you, our entire service economy—the restaurant business as we know it, and food in most American cities—would collapse overnight without Mexican workers.

## BUILDERS

*They worked / They were never late /*
*They never spoke back / when they were insulted /*
*They worked / They never took days off /*
*They worked . . . They worked / and they died/*
*They died broke / They died owing / They died never knowing*
—Pedro Pietri, poet, Nuyorican, 1973

The theme of the unsung hero continues in the American construction industry, where one out of three workers is Hispanic. Between 2010 and 2020, as the world emerged from the global financial crisis, the number of Latinos employed in the building trade grew by more than half, expanding so exuberantly that today a construction worker in the United States is likely to be male, Hispanic, and born south of the Rio Grande. He is also more likely to be bilked of his wages or die on the job.

By the beginning of this decade, there were almost four million Latino men and women—largely undocumented—lending their muscle and risking their lives to forge America's cities and suburbs, highways and country roads. In cities from coast to coast, and especially in the Southwest, residential areas and skyscrapers built by Latino hands seemed to mushroom overnight. But predators have emerged with them. Like farmworkers, construction workers tend to be undocumented and therefore susceptible to victimization, wage theft, and poor working conditions. In Texas alone, of the half million who labor in the trade, the majority lack papers. To put this into perspective, of the twenty-one million immigrants of Hispanic origin newly arrived in the country today, about one-third are undocumented.

Most of the undocumented have been living and working here for more than fifteen years, but they are loath to complain and afraid to apply for legal status, since for them to identify themselves, even on an application, can be cause enough for deportation. So it is that the phenomenon of the paperless Latino menial worker persists. Some are active in their communities, have children in local schools, and find steady work with established contractors. Others find stints through networks of middlemen. Still others are picked up arbitrarily on street corners where they gather to make themselves available as day laborers; these workers are often untrained and raw, vulnerable to accidents, and too often subject to abuse or exploitation. But all who remain paperless live in a legal limbo, with little access to protection. When things go wrong, they have precious little recourse to set them right.

Any resident of a major American city is witness to these laborers, if one takes the time to look. You can see them down the street, unloading cement blocks from towering cranes, pressing themselves into leaping jackhammers, shouldering heavy timber like modern-day Atlases, inching their way along a high-rise's planks. In the nation's capital, where I live, I'm often struck by the insect-like hierarchies so evident in these scenarios: the Hispanics, newly arrived and operating in Spanish, are the ones doing the heavy labor; the African American foremen give the orders; and the white engineers, with their clipboards, pencils, and shiny hardhats, check the work. Come midday, the bosses go off to the local eateries; the Hispanics huddle around the trunk of a car, where a cluster of enterprising Latinas are selling warm tamales and ladling soup from an oversize pot.

As contradictory as it seems, it is not uncommon for the more seasoned workers among these to live comfortably in middle-income neighborhoods. One out of every three undocumented Hispanics in the United States owns his or her own home. Collectively, they pay $12 billion a year in local and federal taxes and have a net-zero effect on government budgets—which is to say that they pay as much in taxes as they consume in benefits, often more. Yet their fear of deportation is such that they are shy to protest if an unscrupulous employer refuses to pay their wages, or if a woman is sexually abused on a job, or if a family member suffers a casualty—even a fatal one—because of workplace negligence. And yet Hispanic workers on these shores have faced injustices through history, from the early days of the twentieth century, when Mexicans were brought by the tens of thousands to labor in American fields or as *traqueros*, laying track to build the nation's railways. The current-day version of the undocumented construction worker's predicament is portrayed masterfully in Chelsea Hernandez's powerful, Emmy Award–nominated documentary *Building the American Dream* (2019), which trains a resolute eye on lives that continue to be imperiled—financially and mortally—by the work they do.

The film begins with Roendy Granillo—a strapping, twenty-five-year-old laborer—as he is being sped to the hospital with a 110-degree temperature, his organs in acute failure. He had been lifting heavy beams in the extreme heat of a Dallas summer when, a few hours into his ten-hour work shift, he told his foreman that he wasn't well. He was paid no attention. By the end of this story, he will be dead, his devastated parents left with a burning desire to serve his memory, set things right.

A few weeks later, along with a group of activists, the Granillos beg the Dallas City Council to legislate what would seem the bare minimum in a humane work environment: a ten-minute water break every four hours. But the "Texas Miracle" is afoot—a massive building boom in which corporations rule and the state offers them a hands-off, nonregulatory playing field. That pro-corporate, to-hell-with-the-worker strategy pays off handsomely for Texas: the state has become home to four of the five fastest growing cities in the nation. In the course of Mr. and Mrs. Granillo's appearance before the city council, the couple makes an impassioned plea to not let what happened to their son befall even one more

Latino; to do something to fix Texas's heinous record of burying a dead construction worker every two days. In response, without a hint of compassion, a council member accuses the stunned Mr. and Mrs. Granillo of being "charlatans" and argues instead on behalf of the billionaires bringing in the cash: "Stop saying no to business!" he scolds the grieving parents and the social justice organizations that support them.

Later, we meet Claudia Golinelli, an undocumented electrician from El Salvador who, with her husband, Alex, works as a contractor, installing entire electrical systems in new residential constructions near Roanoke, Texas. They pride themselves on their meticulousness, and, indeed, over the course of many years, they are able to find plenty of work, live in a pleasant neighborhood, and provide for their two growing American children. But trouble surfaces when a building supervisor refuses to pay them $11,000 in back wages. As time grinds on, the Golinellis find themselves three months behind in mortgage payments and at risk of losing their home. When the supervisor finally responds to their entreaties and suggests a meeting, the Golinellis go off to join it happily, thinking they will receive their hard-won payment at long last. But on arrival, they are met by accusations of robbery, the Dallas police, and agents of the US Immigration and Customs Enforcement (ICE). The company's supervisors had been counting on turning them in all along.

Even the most harrowing accounts of those ordeals, however, cannot compare to the shattering abuses that unaccompanied migrant children suffer in the United States today. A full quarter million Hispanic child laborers, mostly from the Northern Triangle and driven by desperation, entered this country from 2020 to 2022 and toil today in field and factory, feeding what the *New York Times* calls America's "new economy of exploitation." These minors are the product of a heartless, patently dysfunctional immigration system that has not understood this country's history and hasn't faced its injustices in almost forty years. Their suffering is in plain sight, with no real legislation to stop it; it's as if the country had turned a blind eye to the influx of wretched humans, the caravans of despair, the caged children. Between 1986—the last time an immigration law was passed—and today, the Hispanic population has increased by forty-five million souls, almost 300 percent, which is akin to adding a completely new state the size of California. And still no action. How can we think that the laws that were in place two generations ago can possibly address the magnitude of the problem today?

As a result, we have Cristián, fourteen years old, who has worked construction in North Miami since he was twelve. When he walked across the Texas border alone, he presented himself to the authorities, then was shunted to a shadowy sponsor in Florida who put him to work immediately. We have Kevin, age thirteen, who arrived in Grand Rapids, Michigan, with his seven-year-old brother and was hired onto the night shift crew at a local factory, making parts for Ford and General Motors. We have Carolina, fifteen, who works on an assembly line in a food factory in the Midwest, packing Cheerios. In the cavernous concrete labyrinth where she labors, the conveyor belt's gears and pulleys have been known to amputate limbs, rip off fingers, tear open a woman's scalp. Other children are there with her, and they slog away alongside gigantic ovens, making Chewy and Nature Valley granola bars, or stuffing bags with Lucky Charms and Cheetos—churning out profits for companies such as Frito-Lay, General Mills, and Quaker Oats. In hundreds of interviews conducted across the country, investigative reporters found Hispanic children laboring in factories that supply some of America's most beloved brands, including J. Crew, Walmart, Target, Whole Foods, Fruit of the Loom, Ben & Jerry's, Hyundai, Kia, as well as the slaughterhouses of JBS Foods, the world's largest meat processor.

By now, the number of unaccompanied immigrant children who work on construction sites, in manufacturing plants, poultry factories, and farms in order to send money home has reached record numbers. You see them loitering in front of workplaces—the young boys muscled, their torsos developed well beyond their years, the girls hunched with exhaustion. In 2022 alone, 130,000 of them entered the United States on foot. The federal government knows they are here; the Department of Health and Human Services is responsible for ensuring that the youngsters have sponsors, are supported, and are not exploited by traffickers or unscrupulous handlers. But recent arrivals, nearly half of them from Guatemala, have been rushed out of shelters, released to random adults and, inevitably, they end up in the sawmills of South Dakota, the kitchens of Palm Beach, Florida, the dairy farms of Vermont, roofing operations in Florida, paint crews in Virginia, landscapers in Tennessee, automotive factories in Alabama. "It's the new child labor," declares a public school teacher in Michigan who has witnessed these children, some as young as eleven, fall asleep on their desks or simply drop out of school, unable to keep up with their studies. We are "taking children from another country," she says in a voice filled with outrage, "and putting them in almost indentured servitude."

Ironically, given the government's involvement, this army of lone child laborers may have more of a chance of staying in the United States than undocumented families who run the daily and terrifying risk of being deported. They may spend the rest of their lives as cogs in America's underclass, but their offspring—given some grit and determination—may well enter the American wheel of chance to arrive at the American Dream.

Certainly there are many examples of successful Latinos who have come from communities of menial workers who have built, made, and fed this country. You have read some of their stories in this book: Ralph de la Vega, the high-level Cuban executive who arrived as a boy on a Pedro Pan airlift, was the son of shoe factory workers. The celebrated Chicana writer Sandra Cisneros was the daughter of an upholsterer. The Dominican American novelist Esmeralda Santiago was the child of a hotel maid. The hilariously funny stand-up comedian George Lopez was raised by his grandmother, a Mexican American factory worker, and his stepfather, a construction worker. One of the greatest players in golf history, Lee Trevino, a Mexican who had worked in the Texan cotton fields as a child, was raised by his grandfather—a gravedigger. The successful Ecuadorian American memoirist Karla Cornejo Villavicencio is the daughter of a deliveryman for a coffee shop in Manhattan. The great baseball Hall of Fame hero Roberto Clemente was the son of a cane cutter in Puerto Rico. And then there is Alejandro, a top honors student in a Maryland public high school—an eighteen-year-old boy with a promising future in science—who is the child of Tanita, a housecleaner from El Salvador.

## SELLERS

From the moment that Juan Rodriguez, the first Dominican to arrive in Manhattan, opened his traveling gun-and-knife emporium in 1613, Latino businesses have thrived on this continent. Whether it's behind ramshackle *pupusa* stands or polished desks of America's major corporations, resourceful Latinos participate at every level of the economy, eager to make or sell whatever the public demands. Much of that mercantilism has been spirited for centuries, starting perhaps when Mexican vaqueros, America's first cowboys, began to sell saddles, ten-gallon hats, chaps, and reins to a nascent culture of white buckaroos. But one hundred years later, when Cubans and Puerto Ricans began to arrive by the tens of thousands in the 1960s and 1970s, bodegas, *paladares*, and Latino specialty shops sprang up on the East Coast, creating a vibrant national commerce.

Within a generation, the growth of Latino businesses was so exuberant that Wall Street analysts—and an American president—began to take note. In 2004 George W. Bush, in a speech to a Hispanic activist organization, made the White House's attention abundantly clear. "According to the most recent data," he said, "Hispanic-owned companies employ about 1.4 million Americans and carry a payroll of nearly thirty billion dollars. And what I'm here to tell you today is our economy is stronger, our society is better off because those businesses are thriving and creating jobs all across America." The explosion of Latino commerce that followed in the next twenty years has been astonishing. Just within the last decade, Hispanic-owned businesses have multiplied by 44 percent (compared to 4 percent in the non-Hispanic sector). Which is to say that, despite inadequate access to capital—despite having to establish themselves with their own funding—Latino-owned enterprises have been growing at a rate that outpaces every other ethnic group: black, white, Asian, and everybody else. Surprisingly, almost 90 percent of these ventures are owned by millennials (under the age of forty) who came to the United States as children. In 2020 alone, Latino businesses generated almost $500 billion for the US economy. That is a phenomenal increase from the successes Bush noted at the dawn of the twenty-first century. No other entrepreneurial group in the United States has experienced as much growth.

Today there are nearly five million Hispanic-owned businesses in the country—a half million of which employ five to five hundred people—and they contribute more than $800 billion to our economy every year. But that doesn't tell the whole story. Those small businesses—the little housecleaning operations, construction companies, trucking enterprises, beauty shops, and ethnic restaurants that now proliferate from Manhattan to Los Angeles—employ millions of Latino workers, with an annual payroll of more than $100 billion. Add that to the millions of Hispanics who work for non-Hispanic-owned companies, and it's little wonder that, over the last few years, this segment of America has one of the lowest percentages of unemployed. Economists project that, by 2050, Latinos could add a mammoth $1.4 trillion to the US economy—a difficult number to imagine, but it is equivalent to 40 percent more *in one year* than Microsoft has made since its founding in 1975. It is more than the gross domestic product of every country in the world below the top ten. It currently contributes far more to the US economy than America's much-touted entertainment business or the vast agriculture and food service industry, and nearly as much as the vaunted American tech trade.

## THE *TALENTOSO* TENTH

> A remnant continually survives and persists, continually aspires, continually shows itself in thrift and ability and character.
>
> —W. E. B. Du Bois, "The Talented Tenth," 1903

The American intellectual W. E. B. Du Bois referred to "the talented tenth": individuals within a cohort who excel and become a model for their race; those "yeasty" few who shine by example, force open the doors, rise to the top of their professions, lead. So it is that Latinos have their own talented tenth: the contingent that directs and manages crews, businesses, or entire institutional enterprises, and so joins the wonderland of American success.

We see that penchant for leadership in Cuban refugee Desi Arnaz, who went from living in a Miami garage in the 1930s to comic stardom with his wife Lucille Ball in the 1940s. In 1950, Arnaz was made president of Desilu Productions, which became a more powerful Hollywood entity than Metro-Goldwyn-Mayer or Twentieth Century-Fox. Or Ralph de la Vega, who arrived in this country as an unaccompanied minor, began his career sweeping floors in a Miami garment factory, and rose by dint of determination to become a leading executive officer of the communications giant AT&T. We see it, too, in Carlos Gutierrez, the Havana-born son of a Cuban pineapple merchant, who became the chairman of the board and chief executive officer of the Kellogg Company as well as secretary of commerce under George W. Bush and, as such, the first Hispanic to occupy such a senior government position. There is also Oscar Muñoz, a Mexican American from Southern California, the eldest of nine children of a supermarket butcher, who became the first Hispanic chief executive officer of a major airline when he took over the command of United Airlines in 2015.

Only a precious few Latinos reach those hyaline heights. Most struggle in the mid to lower rungs of the business world; only 5 percent have mentors or sponsors to guide them through the maze of corporate life. To date, despite their continual entry and progress in every field of business, there are fewer than twenty Hispanics who occupy the C-suite—the chief executive's office—of Fortune 500 companies.

There are any number of reasons for this paucity of Latinos at the very top of large corporations, but when all is said and done, they boil down to one: prejudice—a general mistrust inculcated over the generations by Hollywood, the media, politicians, white supremacists, and any number of urban legends. The myth is that we are poor, undocumented, unemployed, hypersexual, unreliable. News organizations amplify those images every day. Nothing could be more inaccurate. The median annual income for a Latino nationally hovers at about $60,000—well above the poverty level (in certain cities it can be as high as $108,000); and half of all Latino families have owned their homes for at least eight years. One in five of all Hispanic adults has a college or postgraduate degree, and 25 percent hold managerial or professional positions. Of course, the range of educational accomplishments among Hispanics reflects staggering disparities, given the spectrum of backgrounds our vast numbers represent: one out of every three has never finished high school (whereas the ratio for whites is one out of sixteen).

In sum, we are a constantly evolving, buoyant, wide-ranging, and protean agglomeration of colors and classes. Often, the humblest among us produce children who are better off, better educated, and more ambitious; this engine of upward mobility has made Latinos the fastest growing population of high-income households in America. For all the myths that are broadcast about us, we are not an alien, undocumented breed. We occupy high-level jobs and high-income households in unprecedented numbers. The great majority—70 percent—are American born and bred, some of us reaching back into this country's history for dozens of generations. Almost 90 percent are citizens or legal residents.

Then why are there so few Latinos in the very highest places of the business arena? By 2004, the corporate boardrooms of all American companies (not just the Fortune 500) were still, as one Latino activist put it, "a sea of white," and only 9 percent of all chief executive officers in that stratosphere were Hispanic. But the overall diversity picture began to change in 2012: since then, Americans of Asian or East Indian descent have shot up dramatically to occupy 45 percent of those CEO slots. The number of Hispanics at the helm is nowhere near that count, even though it has doubled to 21 percent. The African American presence, however, has remained static at 7 percent. And yet, although Latino representation may be growing in the C-suite, it falls wretchedly behind every other gender, racial, and ethnic group when it comes to company boardrooms; Hispanics represent but 1 percent of those august ranks. Blacks represent 28 percent.

The glass ceilings that lead to the C-suites of major corporations are even more impenetrable for Latinas. As of this writing, there have only been three Latina chief executives in the history of corporate America, all of them within the last five years: the first was appointed in 2017, when Cuban-born refugee Geisha (Jiménez) Williams became the CEO of Pacific Gas and Electric Company—California's largest utility—before she stepped down two years later, bringing the number temporarily back to zero. In 2019 Cheryl Miller, whose mother is Puerto Rican, rose past an overwhelmingly male staff to lead AutoNation—the country's largest automotive retailer—before financial troubles began to rock the company, her health suffered, and she eventually resigned. She was replaced by a white male who was paid more than seven times her salary. Most recently, Priscilla Almodovar, who grew up in a working-class, Puerto Rican neighborhood of Brooklyn, was named chief of the Federal National Mortgage Association (Fannie Mae for short), the largest mortgage company in America. And yet Hispanics account for a mere 4 percent of large companies' most senior executives. We are simultaneously the most dynamic yet underpromoted workforce in the United States of America.

The disconnect of Latinos to corporate power is especially jarring given that Latinos are driving growth in every consumer market segment and adding Herculean muscle to the American marketplace. Just as the number of Latinos has increased by more than thirty million souls since 2000, dwarfing any other race or ethnicity on the American landscape, Latino buying power has rocketed from $500 billion to $2 trillion within the same period. It is projected to reach $2.6 trillion by 2025, outpacing all other consumer segments in the nation. The implications for the American economy are stupefying. Financial analysts tell us that, if LatinoLand were an independent country, its gross domestic product would be the fifth largest in the world.

It seems a grave and foolish miscalculation, if not shortsighted, not to welcome promising Hispanics to executive positions of corporations that ultimately will have to deal with this vast and promising sector of American consumers. That adjustment should have been made more than fifty years ago, but it has yet to be addressed fully, despite all the evidence. Having been a Hispanic manager within a large, powerful institution, I understand the frustration of witnessing the burgeoning importance of this segment of America but being helpless to draw attention to it. Working as a lone representative of a race or ethnicity in a large company can be an unsettling enterprise.

When I was vice president and senior editor at Simon & Schuster and Harcourt Brace Jovanovich publishers in New York in the 1980s and 1990s, I was the only Hispanic sitting on "editorial row," if not within the entire trade publishing division. And when I went on to become the editor in chief of Book World at the *Washington Post*, I was the only Hispanic division head of the newspaper. As years passed and the Hispanic population mushroomed, the situation in those offices remained relatively the same. By the time, ten years later, that I became the inaugural literary director of the Library of Congress, I was the only Hispanic at a senior level in the Librarian's Office; indeed, Hispanics represented a mere 8 percent in all US government offices, and, even then, 6 percent were largely custodial staff. There was no higher Latino executive to mentor me, much less anyone coming along beneath me in my line of work; no Latinos or Latinas to bring along. Even though the Librarian of Congress, James H. Billington, insisted that I take the office next to his and advise him on Latino affairs as well as literary matters, the wheels moved so slowly that the Hispanic working group I formed was never truly recognized by the rest of the organization and was abandoned when Billington retired. There is still no serious, forceful, organized effort to hire, promote, and mentor Latinos in any of the important cultural institutions in the capital, and, as a result, Hispanic representation in Washington's power grid is drastically low.

To improve representation in a workplace requires agency. My most enthusiastic champion at the *Washington Post* in the early 2000s was actually an African American assistant managing editor who was deeply committed to making the paper look like the city it served. The heart of Washington, DC, may be overwhelmingly African American, but the metropolitan area is 17 percent Latino and growing. When Leonard Downie Jr., the executive editor of the *Post*, learned that I was a native of Peru and fluent in Spanish, he asked if the features editor could send me out to report on Latino communities from time to time in addition to my duties as head of the book review section. I was already past forty, and yet it was the first time that any of my supervisors had asked if I spoke Spanish and was willing to represent my people. I readily agreed and wrote a number of front-page features on Hispanics in the capital as well as the migrant workers in the agricultural fields that surround the city, which set me on the course I've taken ever since: writing books about the world of Latinos. I have the *Washington Post* and Jim Billington to thank for finding the Latina in me.

•  •  •

The world has since changed. There is more than one Latino or Latina editor in New York book publishing today, and there are certainly more of our voices in the general media. But Latinos are still woefully under-represented in American culture and business. From 2000 to 2008, when Hispanics barely made up 17 percent of the population, the chance of seeing a Latino face in any form of mainstream media was 5 percent. Even then, those you were likely to catch fleetingly on a screen were negative stereotypes. A 2000 study titled *Latinwood and TV: Prime Time for a Reality Check* found that most Latino protagonists portrayed on television or Hollywood screens were nannies, gardeners, or servants—usually villains or secondary walk-ons—and totally irrelevant to the plot. Now, a generation later, even as we comprise 20 percent of the American population and promise to represent a full quarter by 2030, our presence in films is a miserable 5 percent. On popular media it has improved only slightly to 12 percent. An uptick, to be sure, but nowhere near our proportional slice of the American pie.

Fortunately, there are strong-minded, ambitious entrepreneurs among our talented tenth who combine business savvy with participation at a high level and do what Du Bois expected the exceptional to do: break the mold, rise, be models and inspirations for the rest of us. One Latina who has done just that is the Peruvian American Hilda Quispe, whose penniless father made his way north from Cabanaconde—that remote little Andean village tucked into the Colca Canyon—to Rockville, Maryland, and found a job as a janitor in a Catholic school. Today Hilda, who is a native-born citizen and boasts a law degree from the University of Massachusetts, is an immigration lawyer with her own practice—an enterprising, social minded American who understands well the legal labyrinth that her clients confront.

Also embodying the spirit of progress is Suhaly Bautista-Carolina, an Afro-Indigenous-Dominican known as "Earth Warrior," who—along with her wife, Naiema—owns Moon Mother Apothecary, a Manhattan herbal shop that features traditional Afro-Quisqueyan cures. Suhaly is an organizer, educator, herbalist, and visual artist. Born in New York City and the recipient of two degrees from New York University, she learned rudimentary Taíno herbalism from her Dominican mother, who always had a pot of plant medicinals bubbling on the stove, alongside the stew and the beans. Apart from running a business that prescribes potions for anything from migraines to heartbreak, Suhaly has produced cutting-edge events for New York's Metropolitan Museum of Art, where she has served as the museum's senior managing educator of audience engagement. Suhaly is the epitome of irrepressible creativity—a Latina who is valued for her ability to attract an entirely new audience to one of the cornerstone cultural institutions in this country. "Somewhere along the way, people became secondary to objects," she tells me about her work in the museum. "There are ancient Taíno objects here. Why no contemporary? When did it become a storage closet without people? We descendants of the Taíno are living proof of that indigenous culture, but we don't exist today. Who erased us? Who gave the colonizer the mic? My value is to be disruptive, ask those questions. Interrogate what it is that a museum should do." Today she is the program director of the newly established American LGBTQ+ Museum in New York City, which will open its doors in 2024. Like other Latino changemakers who are propelling Latinos to the forefront of American business and culture, Suhaly lives at the nexus of the three forces—innovation, ingenuity, and hard work—that will transform the way we think of America.

# PART V

# HOW WE SHINE

*Si se puede!* Yes, we can!

—Dolores Huerta, labor organizer, Chicana, 1972

# 11

# CHANGEMAKERS

Any time you have an opportunity to make a difference in the world
and you don't, then you are wasting your time on earth.
            —Roberto Clemente, baseball player and
                                humanitarian, Puerto Rican

My father, Jorge Arana Cisneros, was a doer. An engineer. Un *in-genioso*—a genius by definition, since the word *engineer* in Spanish, *ingeniero*, means just that: ingenious one. He couldn't understand why someone might not be inclined to change his or her circumstances for the better. Even if that person had to improvise, make do, scrounge whatever resources available, and go out into the world and get it done. He was sure people had it in them to do these things, even if they didn't know they did. I watched him coax roads, schoolhouses, factories, whole towns from people with less ambition—humble villagers who thought his aspirations too lofty for the crimped world they inhabited. When they looked back and saw what they had done, he was the happiest I'd ever seen him. Their delight was his reward.

I imagine that the landmark advances made by Dolores Huerta and Cesar Chavez in the 1960s emerged from that same impulse. Something had to be done. Changes needed to be made. Life had to be better for the multitudes of farmworkers who labored alongside Huerta and Chavez. Who will correct the injustices if not you? they asked. Their families were stooped over in the fields, seeding the rows, pulling down fruit, harvesting the bounty, feeding a hungry nation, but they were made to work in feudal conditions; live in hovels; and fall victim to pesticides, poverty, scorn, and disease, with no legal recourse to correct the inequities. If an owner decided to spray his fields with DDT (a carcinogenic insecticide since banned in the United States), exposing workers to birth defects, cancers, and disabling chemical burns, they had no way to stop it. If a mechanical thresher crushed their fingers, there was no medical coverage to treat the wounds. If a corrupt boss called the authorities and had his workers deported after a season's labors so that he wouldn't have to pay them, too bad. In a land of plenty, they were less than human— their young herded into dilapidated classrooms, subjected to rates of cancer 800 percent above the norm—their contributions to the mill of American bounty unheralded, unremunerated, unseen.

We can credit Cesar Chavez and Dolores Huerta for focusing the American gaze on these abuses. During the 1960s, grape pickers were earning little more than $1 an hour. They were helpless in the face of predatory employers and vulnerable to bullying, arrest, even deportation. They didn't imagine that they could change things for the better, catalyze progress, until Chavez and Huerta organized a strike that spurred seventeen million Americans to sympathize, stop purchasing grapes altogether, and bring abusive growers to their fiscal knees.

Cesar Chavez, a young navy veteran from Arizona whose forebears had been in this country for almost a century, was picking apricots in the San Joaquín Valley in 1952, when Fred Ross—a consummate organizer some have called "America's social arsonist"—approached him to organize Hispanic farmworkers toiling in punishing, menial jobs like his. A small, shy man with piercing black eyes and less-than-stirring speaking abilities, Chavez soon found that his monastic, self-abnegating, Gandhi-like manner inspired trust and galvanized followers. He had never graduated high school—he could count sixty-five elementary schools he had attended for a day, a week, perhaps only a month, as his family had traveled the migrant trail. By the time he and Huerta established what would become the United Farm Workers union, he was known as an ascetic, a disciplined vegetarian, whose $5-a-week salary represented a virtual vow of poverty. But with that aura of frugality and incorruptibility, he mustered the requisite charisma to lead thousands of farmhands to turn power on its ear, demand better work conditions, and get their due.

Huerta, his equal partner in this quest for justice, had been born in New Mexico, the child of a farmworker and a miner whose failed marriage landed her in her grandfather's house when she was three. A naturally bright, highly articulate youngster—a reader—she was stung to the core by a bigoted teacher who accused her of cheating because her vocabulary seemed too sophisticated for a Hispanic child. Twice divorced and a mother of seven by the time she turned twenty-five, Huerta tried to redress that bitter classroom experience by becoming a schoolteacher herself. But after seeing so many children come to her classroom sick and hungry, she decided she could serve them better by organizing their parents to demand better pay.

Huerta, whose name literally means "farm" or "garden," would become the lead negotiator in the farmworkers' contract that emerged from the strikes she planned with Chavez. Throughout the 1970s and 1980s, she dedicated herself to lobbying on behalf of field laborers, winning groundbreaking legislation that would bring real change. But by the 1980s, when Chavez suddenly died in his sleep in a hotel room in Arizona, his dream of forging a strong, nationwide organization had already begun to falter. Today in these United States, there are fewer than seven thousand members in the United Farm Workers union, a tiny percentage of the overall population of two and a half million that tends our farmlands. And still the stoop laborers who go on refilling the American horn of plenty continue to moil in shockingly primitive conditions. Some now earn less than their predecessors did in the 1970s, when Chavez and Huerta were at the apogees of their careers.

All the same, these two occupy a singular place in the pantheon of Latino changemakers: In 1968 Senator Robert F. Kennedy of New York called Chavez "one of the heroic figures of our time." Almost thirty years later, President Bill Clinton posthumously awarded him the highest civilian honor, the Presidential Medal of Freedom. In 2012, a half century after Chavez and Huerta sat across from each other at her kitchen table and masterminded their workers' union, Barack Obama honored Huerta at the White House with her own Medal of Freedom, confessing that he had stolen his presidential campaign slogan—"*Sí, se puede!*" "Yes, we can!"—from her legendary movement. "Knowing her, I'm pleased that she let me off easy," Obama joked to the capacity crowd in the White House, "'cos Dolores does not play." Huerta, a flinty, diminutive woman who had endured a career of being edited out of her own story and having others take credit for her accomplishments, was finally getting her due. She was eighty-two.

When my father was about the same age, just past his eightieth birthday, I took him on a long, eight-hour car ride from Lima; up the desert coast to visit some of the factories he had conjured from sand dunes fifty years before. One was especially strong in memory, a mill I had visited often as a little girl. Suddenly, there it was, the colossal iron heart of Paramonga, still beating, still huffing away, making paper from heaping dregs of crushed sugarcane. One of his former coworkers, an old, retired foreman—also in his eighties—who had walked miles from another village to greet him, stood at his side as they looked out at the steel beast they had built together. "*Señor ingeniero*"—mister engineer— the man said, his chest held high, "*su obra sigue igual.*" Your work lives on. "*No, señor,*" my father replied. "What you see is *your* work. Your hands. It exists thanks to you."

## THE ACTIVISTS

> I reject the notion that we don't have power. Every one of us has inherent power. Positionality is what we need—to position people to have power.
>
> —Mónica Ramírez, rights activist, Mexican American, 2021

The United Farm Workers union may have dwindled in numbers, its force greatly diminished by workers' fears of making too many demands, attracting official attention, and inviting deportation. But that doesn't mean activists have halted efforts on their behalf. Indeed, scores of Latino activist groups have cropped up to do the work that unions used to do. Mónica Ramírez is a case in point. She is a civil rights attorney with a passion for seeing that the nation's farmhands get what they deserve: a decent wage, their basic rights, and recourse to legal protection. Mónica, who hails from a family of farmworkers in Fremont, Ohio, is the founder and president of Justice for Migrant Women, an organization that strives to educate officials and lawmakers about the issues that migrant women face—the barriers that prevent them from reaching their full potential. "Migrant farmwork is a universe unto itself," she tells me. "We come, we have no means to go home, we lose connection to our countries of origin, we have American children, we never go back. We move with the work, not firmly rooted anywhere. We're taken advantage of constantly. It takes a certain kind of resilience to find joy, peace, and love from that way of life. But, somehow, we do."

Mónica is a third-generation Mexican American in a long line of migrant workers. Her people eventually settled in Ohio, but they were so firmly embedded in the migrant life, so comfortable in their element, that she never experienced prejudice until one day in high school, when, in a fleeting disagreement, a schoolmate spat out a derogatory name. "That was the car wreck in my life. The pivotal moment," she says. She was supposed to go back to Mexico? She had never been there in her life. Her great-grandparents had come to this country almost a century before. She didn't belong anywhere but here. The insult wormed into her very being, igniting a fierce desire to change things, make others understand just how American her people were, what they had contributed to the United States, and what they had endured. "The overarching narrative is that we're taking all the jobs, the space, the desks in school . . . taking this, taking that!" she argues with all the intensity of a courtroom defender. "In fact, we are the *givers*. We *gave* our land. We *give* our work. We are the opposite of what you think we are."

As a young woman, Mónica excelled in her schoolwork, went on to study at Loyola University in Chicago, and eventually took a law degree from The Ohio State University's Moritz College of Law. Upon graduation, she decided to focus on the sexual harassment of female migrant workers. She had witnessed those abuses firsthand in the most horrific manner, when, as a child, she had been forced to watch someone in her family be raped by a gang of men. The problem was rampant, she knew, and few understood its magnitude.

Growing up, she became aware that women and girls who worked the fields were constantly exposed to victimization; they still are. Assault is simply a fact of life for Latinas in the farmlands. For some bosses, it seems, a sexual favor is a perquisite of employment, a *droit de seigneur*—an employer's privilege. Then, too, there are the aggressions by men who work alongside women in the fields, men who outnumber the females by twenty to one. In Salinas, California, migrants refer to a certain farm company as *"el fil de calzón"*—a veritable field of panties—because supervisors are so brazen as to rape women by the full light of day. In Florida, some women call the fruit farm where they work "El Motel Verde," because they are expected to lie down and offer themselves between rows of green. A worker involved in a class action suit in Iowa was so numb to the abuse she had endured at her workplace that she told a lawyer, "We thought it was normal in the USA that you had to have sex to keep your job."

Mónica Ramírez decided something needed to be done about this normalized exploitation—this vicious cycle of flagrant lechery and resigned acquiescence. Earning an additional master's degree in public administration at Harvard University's John F. Kennedy School of Government, she set to work. Now in her mid-forties, Mónica has founded no fewer than a half dozen organizations whose charge it is to weed out these abuses and raise public awareness of the fact that the women who help feed America are being victimized and violated on American farms.

Mónica has gone on to lead a number of migrant organizations in the United States as well as Mexico and co-found the National Farmworker Women's Alliance. In 2017 she sparked the famous "Dear Sisters" letter, signed by seven hundred thousand female farmworkers and published in *Time* magazine. That letter, which immediately went viral, offered solidarity with Hollywood employees who had come forward to tell their stories of sexual harassment in the wake of the Harvey Weinstein scandal. "Your job feeds souls," the farmworkers told the mavens of the silver screen, whereas "our job nourishes the nation." Then they explained how, for all the differences, a grape picker's workaday world might have something in common with a film star's:

> Even though we work in very different environments, we share a common experience of being preyed upon by individuals who have the power to hire, fire, blacklist, and otherwise threaten our economic, physical, and emotional security. Like you, there are few positions available to us, and reporting any kind of harm or injustice committed against us doesn't seem like a viable option. Complaining about anything—even sexual harassment—seems unthinkable because too much is at risk, including the ability to feed our families and preserve our reputations.

In 2021, just after Mónica raised millions of dollars to aid essential farmworkers who were laboring grueling hours during the COVID pandemic, she was named one of *Time* magazine's "100 Most Influential People." From her humble beginnings as a third-generation migrant worker in Fremont, Ohio, she was now being hailed as a person whose work was "changing the world," the sort of paladin who had recognized injustice, seized the moment, challenged the status quo, and improved lives by her moral example.

• • •

> *No tenemos tiempo para división.* I have no time for that crap. Get access, get in the door. You think you can count on someone else to do it for you? Get real. That someone else is *us*.
>
> —J. Walter Tejada, activist and politician,
> Salvadoran American, 2022

Even as Mónica was becoming aware of the extent of abuses against hundreds of thousands of Latinas laboring in America's fields of green, a Salvadoran soccer player turned his passion to the growing hordes of Hispanics in his neighborhood who had no representation, no voice with which to call out their rights as citizens or their contributions to the public good. His name is J. Walter Tejada, and, unlike Mónica, he is a political activist less engaged with national issues than the immediate needs of his community. The old 1932 aphorism that "all politics is local" could easily be his creed. "I'm pushing for civic participation by the Latinos around me. We are not Texan Latinos. We are *Virginia* Latinos. There's a very big difference there. We have different demands, different ways of life, different challenges."

For the past thirty years, Tejada has been a fighter for immigrant, civil, and human rights, all of them in his beloved county of Arlington and his adopted state of Virginia. He was born in 1958 in San Luis Talpa, a tiny but beautiful seaside village inhabited largely by Pipil fishermen, on the Pacific coast of El Salvador. The Pipil tribe, which originated in Mexico and migrated south in the twelfth century, was known for its social cohesion and fierce determination—traits that came to the fore when they resolutely opposed the Spanish conquest—characteristics altogether present in Tejada's stubborn commitment to his constituents.

Although he is now a powerful force in the politics of Northern Virginia—the first Latino in the state to be elected to public office—few would have foreseen that future in the thirteen-year-old boy who migrated to a rough neighborhood of Brooklyn in 1971, just as the great wave of Latino immigration skyrocketed in this country. He didn't speak English; he had never traveled far from San Luis Talpa. His mother, a single parent, had left her three children behind to be raised by their grandmother as she went off to earn a living as a housemaid in Tucson, Arizona. But when she had raised enough money, she gathered up her children and moved to the bustling, immigrant streets of New York City. Young Walter took an after-school job in a local factory, read the *New York Times* out loud in order to learn English, and followed his passion: playing soccer in the crime-riddled, drug-addled streets of

Bedford-Stuyvesant. "There was only one other Salvadoran boy in all of the United States that I knew of at the time," he tells me, "and he lived, like, ten miles away." His friends were largely black, Puerto Rican, or Jewish, "and so different, we couldn't understand what each other was saying. But we got along. Mostly, we just laughed at each other." And, so, soccer became his life.

Things began to fall apart for Walter when his mother decided to move to Trenton, New Jersey, in the middle of a school year. Suddenly he was far from his soccer buddies, making do in a cramped one-room apartment hung with curtains to create the illusion of privacy. He attended Trenton High reluctantly and took a job at the nearby Ocean Spray factory, working from three in the afternoon until eleven o'clock at night, which forced him to consider dropping out of school entirely. But all that changed when a Latino friend whose family had moved to Scranton, Pennsylvania, persuaded him to come live with them, attend high school there, join its champion soccer team, and perhaps get lucky enough to break into the professional game. Although Walter took up his friend's offer, the dream of playing sports for a living never became a reality. Fate would sweep him in another direction: the team's coach encouraged him to apply to college.

Walter was unsure. No one in his family had ever had ambitions beyond the eighth grade. But as he struggled to support himself, sweeping floors at Dunkin' Donuts after school and picking up trash at a McGraw Hill bookstore, he understood there was no future in menial work; a university education was the right next step. He applied to nearby Keystone College as a student-athlete and got in on a scholarship. It was there that another life-changing factor emerged: her name was Robin. She was a pretty gringa with high ambitions. Not only was she surpassingly bright, but also she was headed for a career in international affairs. She was fluent in Spanish, too. It was clear to him that if he had any illusions of winning her, he had to stay in school.

He and Robin continued to see each other, even after graduation, when she went off to New York and Walter took a job as a bilingual

Spanish translator for a public defender's office. The work was fascinating, a real glimpse into the inner workings of American civic life. But, as he looked around at his fellow translators, Walter began to be troubled by differences among their skills—disparities that could be crucial in judging and convicting Hispanics. One day, while translating for a highly charged capital punishment case, negotiating the intricacies in both languages, he became convinced of these doubts. Something needed to be done to better serve Latinos who were being funneled willy-nilly—and with little comprehension of what was happening to them—through the American judicial system. Grave injustices needed to be addressed. Before long, he was advocating to certify Spanish translators and furnish the courts with qualified, proficient professionals. Eventually he helped set up an association to do just that.

Later, noticing how many young Puerto Ricans and Cuban Marielitos were being tried in criminal cases, he became interested in tracking how anti-Hispanic sentiment was possibly affecting those outcomes. Soon he was working as a criminal defense investigator and seeing how systemic prejudices did, in fact, underlie many of the judgments. It was exciting work, precisely the sort of civic involvement he could throw himself into, believe in. At the same time, his romance with Robin was deepening. When she went off to complete her master's degree at George Mason University in Arlington, Virginia, he began visiting her there.

The area took an immediate hold on Walter. It was 1987, the civil war in El Salvador had been raging for eight years, and an immense population of Salvadorans had settled in or near the American capital. Almost 20 percent of Arlington County's residents were just like him, refugees who had fled a crumbling homeland for a chance at a better life. The fragrance of Salvadoran *pupusas* filled the air. Salvadoran chatter issued from the verandas. It was 1992, and the Washington Metropolitan area, including Arlington, held the third largest population of Salvadorans in the world outside El Salvador. Given the food, the welcoming ambience, and the woman he loved, he soon made Arlington his home.

It wasn't long before Walter's sense of justice and his highly honed watchdog faculties fixed on the obvious: for all their vibrant contributions to the area, the Salvadoran people—the whole Latino and immigrant community, for that matter—had no voice in their government. They had been rendered invisible and mute by a county that was profiting from their muscle, their taxes, their ingenuity, but paying their needs little mind. He felt an urgent need to voice an objection, correct the disregard. How could something like that happen within five miles of the legislative heart of the nation, from the very halls where the Constitution and the Bill of Rights—proclaiming the equality of every American citizen—were housed? He had been bitten by the political bug.

When he complained about the neglect to Eduardo Bretón, the Argentinian head of the Virginia chapter of LULAC (the League of United Latin American Citizens), Bretón simply trained his piercing blue eyes on Walter and said, "If you care about it so much, Walter, join the board. *Tienes que involucrarte!*" You need to get involved! Walter did just that. He joined LULAC, the oldest and largest institution fighting to advance the civil rights of Latinos in the United States. He was soon working for the Civilian Complaint Review Board of Washington, DC, scrutinizing the way the police force dealt with Hispanics in the course of any interaction: the many instances of discriminatory language, racial harassment, or outright violence.

Walter quickly became known as the person who could get things done, the one who asked the difficult questions, dug deep, shattered barriers, and seemed to be able to recruit everyone around him to the task. In 2003, when he became the first individual of Latino heritage ever to be elected to the Arlington County Board of Supervisors (or to any board of government in Virginia, period), he began shaping his message to Virginia's immigrants, which has never wavered since: Get your citizenship. Register to vote. In a county where the average detached, single-family dwelling costs more than $1 million, raise your voice, insist on affordable housing. In a building frenzy in which commercial projects threaten to raze your children's playing fields, turn out, make demands, defend the turf, do right by your children. In a time when immigrants are demonized, immigration reform is needed, and Latinos remain tacitly ignored, ask your county to distinguish itself as a model of democracy and serve those who make the community work. And yet, for all the muscle he dedicates to lifting up Latino people, it is his unfailing respect for his constituents—no matter who they are—that is Walter's greatest instrument.

He tells me of the time when he was readying an area park for the annual Salvadoran Festival and suddenly received word that two rival gangs were on their way there to hold a shoot-out at the event. Walter didn't fret over it. There was too much to be done. He turned instead to the volunteers, the setup, the sheer physical challenge of lugging supplies from here to there. Seeing a gaggle of youths walk by, he shouted to them to help move the equipment. He didn't notice their tattoos, he didn't much care who they were, except that they looked like young, strong, well-muscled Salvadoran boys. Soon they were helping out, shouldering the boxes, hauling the festival supplies, joking and carrying on like any youths with a big party ahead. "I learned only after the fact that they were the gang members everyone was so worried about," he recounts. "I have to give them credit. They worked. They were there just like the rest of us. They had become part of the festival."

That brief anecdote, which he tells with gusto, speaks volumes about Walter Tejada. It is that abiding belief in treating every single human in his ambit fairly, giving people a leg up, a running chance—guiding his constituents to their potential civic power—that has carried him through an extraordinary career of leadership. Over the years, he has led or founded a myriad policy- or influence-making organizations that have given Latinos, and immigrants in general, an increasing voice in their government. "If I had one wish for Latinos," he says, "it would be for us to stop wanting to be off the radar. So many say to me, 'Oye, I just want to put my head down and work. Someone else can do the speaking up.' And I say back to them: 'That someone has to be you! You need to be participating. You need to be the face in their face. *You*.'"

•　　•　　•

Sometimes those who take Walter Tejada's challenge to heart (if not me, then who?) don't count themselves as activists—they may not even be aware that they are amplifying Latinx power—but they are activists all the same. The Colombian-American actor John Leguizamo is one of these. "I'm a history addict," he says. "It's my thing, my passion, and I try to smuggle it wherever I can." To prove the point, he created a television series called *Leguizamo Does America*, a travel show that celebrates the many diverse layers of Latin culture and history that permeate this country. If only the rest of America would see it. It's the first time in the history of television that a major travel series has been developed and hosted by a Hispanic. The only reason it passed muster at NBC, according to Leguizamo, is because Cesar Conde, the chairman of NBC Universal, is Latino himself. Conde understood the need to raise the profile of this colossal yet culturally neglected segment of America.

"I live in New York City, where we're equal to whites in the population," Leguizamo grumbles, "and yet we're less than one percent of the journalists at the *New York Times*, less than one percent of the stories being told in the *New York Times*, the *New York Post*, the *New Yorker*, the *New York* magazine. This is *our* city, and still it's like a cultural apartheid." That, he adds, is the sort of erasure that can happen when there aren't enough Hispanic media executives or powerbrokers to champion Latin culture—push it. Though Leguizamo doesn't call himself an activist, he is always defending the culture, promoting it, *pushing* it. What is an activist, if not a television star who argues for his *gente* in a medium that reaches 93 percent of the American people?

There are hundreds of thousands of Latinos across this nation—and, incidentally, not always Latinos—like John Leguizamo or Walter Tejada or Mónica Ramírez, who work to give the Latinx muscle. They may not be publicly known; they may not be seeking the limelight. They are simply those who move the needle slowly, patiently for their communities, or for the millions like them who need their rights preserved, their grievances minded, their presence acknowledged. They may be civic leaders such as Julissa Gutierrez, the Colombian American daughter of a maid and a chauffeur, who became the first Latina diversity chief of the state of New York, where she dedicates herself to protecting Latino small businesses; or Julissa's former roommate from college, the Afro-Dominican Wendy García, who looks out for the city's Hispanics as deputy commissioner for equity and inclusion in the New York City Police Department (NYPD). Indeed, the first Latino commissioner in the history of the NYPD, Edward A. Caban (of Puerto Rican descent), was sworn into office in July of 2023.

And then there is Arturo Griffiths, a lifelong activist whose West Indian father and Panamanian mother fled bigotry in the Canal Zone to bring him to America as a teenager. If they were hoping to elude racism, they would find themselves squarely in the heart of it. Landing in the increasingly Latino neighborhoods of northwest Washington, DC, Arturo came of age just a few years before Martin Luther King Jr. was assassinated and the capital erupted in a ferocious race riot. As an Afro-Latino raised in the Panama Canal's very white-dominant *Leave It to Beaver* culture, Arturo grew up sensing affiliation to all sides; he seemed to have special antennae for racial sensibilities. Even as a seventeen-year-old, he began to be known as a mediator, celebrator, the person who could mend fences and make radically different constituencies feel good about themselves. Perhaps his crowning moment came in 1991, when he was in his mid-forties and his neighborhood seemed a cauldron of simmering antipathies. It was a nervous age: the country was struggling to emerge from a financial crash, whole populations had slipped back into poverty, a crack epidemic was afoot, and racial tensions seemed to electrify the air, ready to ignite. It was then, on Cinco de Mayo—May 5, 1991—that a very different kind of race conflagration erupted in his neighborhood. It began with a single act: an African American rookie policewoman shot an intoxicated Salvadoran as he and his friends careened drunkenly down the street.

The Mount Pleasant Riots were a portentous moment in the life of the capital. They began on an otherwise serene Saturday evening in the spring when people were out and about, enjoying the Mexican American party spirit. Two cops were walking the beat. When they came upon the merrymaking Salvadorans stumbling along Mount Pleasant Street, bottles in hand, one of the police shouted at them to put down the alcohol. But the men didn't speak English and didn't understand the officers' demand. A ruckus ensued. The eyewitness accounts vary. Some claim that the Hispanic, already handcuffed, lunged forward clumsily, pleading in Spanish to be released. Others have him with his hands free, reaching to take off his belt—a common enough response in Central America, where men often fight with their belts. The police report, highly contested, has him wielding a knife. Whatever the case, the policewoman, clearly rattled by his motions, shot him point-blank in the chest.

The outrage was swift, catastrophic. For three days and nights, Latinos, provoked by the stark brutality of the police response and honed by the violence they had fled in their own countries, stormed down those streets in avenging fury. Blacks, too—roused by the sight of one thousand heavily armed, largely white police officers, not to mention a stampeding horde of Latinos—fought back. Bottles flew, weapons were improvised, rocks met their mark, and gunfire responded in kind. Young Hispanics rushed out of their homes and onto the scene, flipping over police cars, setting vehicles ablaze with their own gasoline. As José Suero, the editor of the Spanish-language newspaper *El Diario* recounted, "The cops were like 'Whoa! What the hell is this?' The kids had organized an army in about an hour . . . and they knew more about urban guerrilla warfare than the police did." By the second day, the disturbances had spread into the Adams Morgan sector of the city, gutting whole businesses, provoking looting, growing more dangerous by the hour. In the end, when the tear gas wafted into the night sky and dawn crept over the city, dozens of police cars, buses, and storefronts had been reduced to ash and rubble. More than fifty people were injured, some catastrophically. And the nation's capital was shaken, consumed by rage. As the African American mayor Sharon Pratt put it later, the Latino rioters were not looked upon sympathetically in "Chocolate City":

Many Washingtonians, black and white, were resentful and expected
me to handle the situation with brute force. They wanted DC police
to check rioters for green cards. They wanted rioters deported. The
thinking was clear: Why should citizens of a majority-black city—
a city without a vote in Congress and ravaged by riots, poverty, and
HIV—step aside for anyone?

But for all the bitterness, a door had opened: the rampant discrimination, the stifling lack of opportunity, the unequal access to government services—all these prompted the US Civil Rights Commission to
hold a hearing on the status of Hispanics in the greater Washington,
DC, area. Its final judgment was clear, scathing, and it cited evidence
upon evidence of an "appalling" denial of basic civil rights. Despite
complaints from non-Hispanics, the District of Columbia began publishing documents in two languages; it directed the police to open two
branches of Latino community relations offices; it supported the Latino
task force that emerged from the Commission's report. It was as if a
wake-up call had been issued and the city had opened its eyes, looked
around, grown up.

Arturo was in his element, in the midst of things. He stepped forward as a representative of both sides—as a black and as a Hispanic—to
organize a healing conference that represented every color of immigrant
in his city. He had been applying this sort of balm for communities since
he was seventeen years old, and he would do it for fifty more. It takes
a powerful belief in the promise of change—the possibility of forward
movement, the wild hope for a new and gentler world, the capacity to
build something better—to shuck obstacles and work toward a more
just future, but that is precisely what an activist will do. It is an optimist's
vocation.

# THE EDUCATORS

I have a cousin who works four jobs. I have family that is undocumented. I have family that has been split, separated, deported back to
Colombia. Being an optimist is a discipline.

—Julissa Gutierrez, diversity chief, state of New York

It takes a positive thinker—a dreamer—to be an activist, to be sure,
and the most effective kind of activism comes from those who have
the capacity to imagine that whatever is best for you is what's best for
me. And best for everyone else. It is the basis of most world religions,
the foundation of democracy, the bedrock of environmentalism, and
the bright, shining light that guides a truly public-minded education.
Can there be a greater agent to change—a greater promoter of better
outcomes—than education itself?

Which is to say that much activism that benefits Latinx communities comes from educators, teachers, promoters of learning. It can
come from individuals one might never suspect of having anything in
common with Latinos, except that they understand that education is a
central pillar of democracy and that public education demands total inclusion. Nothing less. Promoters of education offer agency to Latinos
not because they have family or friends who are Latinos—nor because
they have commercial interests in the Latinx world—but because they
have no choice. Because they believe it is the right thing to do. Such is
the case for Donald E. Graham, former publisher of the *Washington Post*.

Don Graham is a scion of one of the most influential media families in the world. Son of legendary Katharine Graham, the *Post*'s steely
publisher during the harrowing days of the civil rights movement, the
Vietnam War, the Watergate Scandal, and the Pentagon Papers, Don is
also a grandson of Eugene Meyer, who bought the failing newspaper
in a bankruptcy sale in the midst of the Great Depression after leaving
his duties as chairman of the Federal Reserve. Don was raised as media
royalty: he was educated at the renowned St. Albans School as well as
Harvard University. He went on to become president of his college

newspaper, the *Harvard Crimson*, and intern to the most powerful journalist of his generation: James "Scotty" Reston of the *New York Times*. To be sure, Don had every privilege a member of America's East Coast cultural elite could boast. Yet when he graduated from Harvard in 1966, he didn't go on to a job in a fancy law firm, or a bank, or publishing, as would have been expected at the time. Instead, he chose to enlist as a private in the US Army and serve during two of the most harrowing years of the Vietnam War.

Given his family connections, he might have avoided those killing fields with minimal effort—obtained a deferral, landed a cushy spot in the National Guard. But he headed for those faraway jungles with no little conviction. When he returned, he joined the Washington, DC, Police Department as an ordinary patrolman—this, during a time when rioters on the angry streets of America were shouting "Off the pigs!" and the country was feeling the ripple effect of Lyndon B. Johnson's "War on Crime," which had sent militarized police into poor neighborhoods. All the same, with his open, amiable face, ruddy cheeks, imposing stature, and rolling gait, Don certainly looked the part of the good cop. His intent, he told his mother at the time, was to better understand the city that the family newspaper served. In 1971 he joined the *Post* as a city reporter.

Thirty years later, after a steady climb up the management ladder—from print room to newsroom to fulfillment, and finally to the publisher's office—he stepped aside to become chairman of the Washington Post Company. In September 2013, pummeled by seven consecutive years of declining revenues and a fevered recession that had forced dozens of American newspapers to shutter their doors, Don finally sold the family business to Amazon titan Jeff Bezos. Five months later, he founded a national movement to provide scholarships for underserved, undocumented, promising young people. He called it TheDream.Us.

So, what could possibly have inspired Don Graham to leave newspapers behind only to plunge wholeheartedly into an issue that, by far, impacts Latinos more than anyone else? The catalyst, it turned out, was DACA: Deferred Action for Childhood Arrivals, a program introduced by President Obama on June 15, 2012, to shield undocumented children from deportation and allow them access to the basics that allow a resident to work: a Social Security number, a guarantee of safety from exile, and a state-issued photo identification or driver's license. DACA, as Joe Biden's White House has since described it, promises to allow such children—the "Dreamers"—to live and work in peace, and to do so "in the only country they know as home." It was clear that Don may have intended to support DACA for some time, but hadn't been free to do so, being part of the dynasty that ruled the news in the American capital and claimed absolute neutrality to partisan politics.

That he would care about the plight of millions of young Latinos came as a surprise to me. I had worked for Don for seventeen years at the *Washington Post* and never imagined that he would be interested in undocumented children—the vast majority of them immigrants from Latin America—who live in official limbo, forbidden from participating in the most rudimentary aspects of American life. From time to time when I worked at the *Post*, Don would drop into my office for an amiable chat—as he tended to do with everyone in every corner of that building, whether you were a college intern sorting the daily mail or a big-foot executive dealing with major financial issues. Our conversation would either be about a review I had published or a good book he had read, but it always centered on work, which, for me, was books. In all that time, Don never referred to my being Latina or to my experience as an immigrant. Indeed, for as long as I'd worked for him, he had been admirably apolitical, mindful of the optics, wary of supporting any institution that might be suspected as "outcome based." Fast-forward twenty years, and I find myself sitting in his living room, asking him, "What made you interested in the Dreamers, Don?" His answer is simple and to the point: "They are the kids most discriminated against in the United States right now."

He is a force field of energy when describing his new and abiding passion. It has been more than a decade since he founded TheDream. Us, but the wave of youth coming through the application process— with their manifold stories of how they arrived, what they endured, and how ardently they believe in the future—keeps it fresh for him. Before I can pepper him with questions, he insists I hear out his pitch about TheDream.Us, which he delivers with signature calm and clarity. But the emotion is palpable in his face, in its heightened pink, in the fierce intensity of his eyes. His is an activism of an almost messianic order, paid for out of his own family fortunes. He is deeply proud, if not in awe, of the thousands of undocumented young he puts through college every year. He wonders how these children, who have come so far with so little—who arrived at the average age of three and a half, with no safety net whatsoever, and with the system firmly stacked against them—can have such fortitude, work so diligently, and show such promise. "How do they do it?" he marvels. "The motivation is so strong it is almost absurd."

TheDream.Us puts more than a thousand promising DACA and undocumented students through college every year. Its recipients are sprinkled across the country, ranging from southwest Texas to northern New Jersey, from Mexicans to Dominicans to Vietnamese. Nine in ten are Latinos. By the time this book publishes, ten thousand more will have received their degrees through Don Graham's graces. They will have done so with full support—tuition, room, and board—and no debt whatsoever. Furthermore, his bet on them will prove well founded: these students consistently outperform their peers. The statistics he cites are impressive: 92 percent of all recipients complete their first year of college; 82 percent flip their tassels at the end of four years with at least a 3.3 grade average. Those who graduated in 2023, for instance, did so with a 3.5 average, dozens of them as valedictorians or salutatorians. When they receive their degrees, 93 percent either find work right away or go on to graduate school—as opposed to the 84 percent national average—and the great majority become essential workers: in STEM, health, or medical jobs. A third head for work in business, education, or social science.

But they have no rights. Now that DACA is faltering, its future in question, the majority of these youths who have grown up here for most of their lives cannot get a driver's license. They cannot apply for federal grants for financial assistance, even if they are at the top of their class, top of their school, rocket science geniuses. In effect, they are barred from college, consigned to a life of menial work and pauperism—like their parents. In some states, universities are prohibited from admitting them. Worse, they cannot apply for citizenship. Joining the US Army or marrying an American will not win them that prize; that is forbidden, too. Some have won Rhodes scholarships but remain undocumented. Hundreds have gone on to become doctors or medical students, but not citizens. They are in a virtual trap; an existential stalemate. And yet ninety-eight thousand of them graduate from high school every year. "It baffles me why everyone doesn't understand what we as a country are doing to these children," Don tells me. "There is *nothing* they can do to change their status." Nothing.

Moreover, they live in constant fear of deportation. They dare not enroll in health, nutrition, financial assistance, or job training programs; nor do they dare complain about victimization or crimes against them in their schools or workplaces. Furthermore, in some ideological precincts, they will find little sympathy—they will even be spurned, told to go home to a place they do not know. Told to go back to a country in which more than two-thirds of them no longer have relatives.

In 2017 the Trump administration announced that DACA would be phased out, killed. One of President Joe Biden's first actions as president in 2021 was to direct the secretary of homeland security to overturn that directive and fortify the program; a few months later, a federal judge in Texas ruled DACA illegal and blocked all new applicants in his state. When Republican Kevin McCarthy became Speaker of the House of Representatives in 2023, he made it clear that he would work to quash any amnesty bill to come his way, and, of course, that meant DACA. Today, as I write this, the program to protect undocumented children is in peril—on the verge of strangulation—although a new Dream Act, which Congress continues to bat around tirelessly like a cat with a wounded mouse, would allow almost two million eligible Dreamers, including the roughly half million young whom the original bill shields, to receive permanent protections to live and work in the United States, the nation to which they feel most allegiance. Of course, it needs to be said: the country desperately needs to secure its borders, prevent illegal immigration, and enforce our laws. But as Don makes abundantly clear, it also should value its immigrants and safeguard the children who are already here.

The irony is that we need these children. As Don came to write on the opinion pages of his old newspaper:

> Our country needs the dreamers. We desperately need nurses; since 2005, more than 180 rural hospitals have closed. Among our [The Dream.Us] scholars, the No. 1 major is nursing and health care. Education majors make up another large group, and the United States also desperately needs teachers. . . . Another important employer in need of help is the army, which has missed its recruiting goals this past fiscal year by 25 percent—even after offering citizens $50,000 to enlist. Why not allow young immigrants educated since first grade in American schools to enlist as a path to citizenship? The military would fill its ranks with willing and able young people who love this country.

A number of Don's high-profile donors—Bill Gates, Jeff Bezos, MacKenzie Scott—would agree. But perhaps it's the experiences of the "dream-dot" youngsters that say it best. When Don invites me to drive out to Virginia and visit a few of them, I jump at the chance. There, in the decorous halls of a local Catholic university, I meet the preternaturally poised Abby from Honduras, who toddled across the border sixteen years ago when she was four, and is now her college's student body president, headed for a career in medicine. I meet the no-nonsense Andrea of El Salvador, a high achiever with a passion for politics, who worked as an intern for Representative Jamie Raskin (D-MD), was courted by eighteen colleges, and yet suffers panic attacks every day about her precarious status.

And then there is Carlos from Mexico, a pale, whip-thin young man with kind eyes, soft hands, and a resolute handshake. His mother, a kitchen and sanitation worker for a nearby hotel, sits in a corner of that handsome administrative lobby, watching the young ones with a tired gaze. When I approach her, she slides over with an amiable smile to make room on the couch. She tells me how proud she is of Carlos: a straight-A physics student, *"muy exitoso y inteligente, pero más que todo una muy buena persona"*—very successful and intelligent, but more than anything, a very good person. I ask how long she's been in this country. Seventeen years, she answers. She swam Carlos across the Rio Grande when he was three. Today they live in a two-room apartment, and here she points out two more "dream-dot" students sitting nearby—young women, huddled in quiet conversation, comparing notebooks. "We live with them." The young women look up, startled as deer. "It has been hard, very hard for us," the mother goes on to say—*"muy duro"*—shaking her head. "But, just look at him. I know he will do great things. For him, *señora*, it's been worth every minute." She leans in, grabs my hand, and urges me to write about her son. I can't help but note the roughness of her palms.

## BETTING ON EXCELLENCE

> In the end, the American dream is not a sprint, or even a marathon, but a relay. Each generation passes on to the next the fruits of their labor. . . . My mother fought hard for civil rights so that instead of a mop, I could hold this microphone.
>
> —Julian Castro, mayor of San Antonio, Mexican American, 2012

If I have learned anything from the years of research and hundreds of interviews I've undertaken for this book, it is that there is a massive cohort of Americans working tirelessly to support Latinos—no matter their race or class—and lift them up, educate them, study their ways, bring them into the mainstream. Which is to say: there are many Don Grahams in this country. The overwhelming majority of them are Latinos themselves.

Unfortunately, in recent years, to be Latinx is to be the victim of much misinformation and blame. Most famously—and alarmingly— the slings and arrows have come from the highest office in the land.

Campaigning in 2016 (and echoing the falsehoods again in his run-up to the 2024 election), Donald Trump characterized the people of Mexico—the origin nation of most Hispanics, including "dream-dot" Carlos, the young physics prodigy—as being wanton, depraved criminals. "When Mexico sends its people," he said, "they're not sending their best. . . . They're sending people that have lots of problems, and they're bringing those problems with us. They're bringing drugs. They're bringing crime. They're rapists. And some, I assume, are good people." His followers believed him. They believe him still. And yet, the opposite is true. Hispanic crime is actually proportionately less than the Hispanic share of the population. In fact, Latinos are more likely to be the victims of crime than its perpetrators. Far more Latinos have been killed by American gun violence in the past twenty years—seventy-five thousand dead, to be exact—than the number of Americans killed in Vietnam during the nearly two decades of that misguided war.

Happily, the army of changemakers addressing the calumnies against Latinos is formidable. Rather than fill the wind with objections, they are at work in classrooms, research offices, science labs, proving the reverse. Among educators, they can be found at every level of the pedagogical system. As a result, young Latinx are nothing if not upwardly mobile. While less than half of all Americans believe their children will be better off than they are, more than two-thirds of the Hispanic population are confident that their next generation will thrive in ways they could not.

When I visit Elise Heil, the principal of the only bilingual Catholic elementary school in Washington, DC, she is outside on the playground along with the entire student body—kindergarten through eighth grade. It is a bright, warm September day and I stroll up to the almost century-old School of the Sacred Heart (Escuela del Corazón Sagrado) to find that a fire drill has spilled all the children into the sunshine. In their crisp white shirts and navy-blue trousers and plaid skirts, they are a diverse lot—brown, white, black, Asian—a true mirror of all the phenotypes a Latino can embody. The boys are playing kickball; the girls are huddled on the steps, sharing secrets; the kindergartners are singing. The teachers look on, chatting with one another in Spanish or English, bursting into laughter from time to time, but with a firm eye on their charges. The children are so comfortable in both languages that they mix them freely, sometimes within a single sentence. They are largely Salvadoran-, Honduran-, or Guatemalan-American youngsters—the great majority of them US-born citizens, although, every year, the school adds two or three recent immigrants to each class. But there is also a sprinkling of Vietnamese, Ethiopians, and towheaded whites, a true reflection of the congregation that worships at Father Emilio Biosca's church down the street.

Principal Heil was a fledgling math teacher in a nearby school when she took a walk with her mother one day and passed the imposing Shrine of the Sacred Heart, where Father Emilio now presides over his congregation of multicultural faithful. Their curiosity piqued, the women went inside. Elise was immediately enchanted by the loyal, urban, hardworking population the church served, especially the bright-eyed, well-behaved children. When she pointed out a notice announcing that the companion school down the street was hiring teachers, her mother turned to her and said, "Why don't you apply?"

Elise taught at the school for four years before she was made principal at the age of twenty-seven. Being a white monolingual American—and so young—her election to the position raised eyebrows, but she dutifully learned Spanish and proved her abilities to lead this historic establishment and its largely Latino staff. In the twelve years of her tenure, Sacred Heart has consistently won awards for being one of the best schools in the capital; as a result, it is generously supported by church and federal grants, which means that two-thirds of its students receive financial aid. One hundred percent go on to the most prestigious high schools in the city and study at universities throughout the country. Over the years, they have entered careers in business, medicine, education, the arts, and the law. Analysts ranging from Harvard University professors to visiting nuns from the Vatican have come to study the school's remarkable triumphs—the main fascination centering on its tightly interwoven Spanish-English curriculum, designed to produce high functionality in either language. Sometimes even the principal is surprised: "We have students who speak Vietnamese at home and English and Spanish at school," says Elise. "It blows your mind." But mainly Sacred Heart can chalk up its successes to a highly involved community and its commitment to teaching children to value communicating across languages—to being a cultural bridge.

That cultural fluidity is what David Bowles, a Mexican American author of young adult books who grew up in the Rio Grande Valley, wishes he could have had as a child. "I didn't realize who I was until college," he says. "Not until I took a class in world literature and I was presented with Sandra Cisneros and *The House on Mango Street*. I was Latino, both sides, but I had never read anything by a Latino." A further college class in anthropology revealed more about the people from whom he had descended but did not really know: he became immersed in the myths and legends of Mesoamerican civilizations—tales told by the Olmec, Zapotec, Maya, Toltec, and Aztec peoples. "Even though I was Mexican American—even though I had been raised on the border, so close to Mexico, even though I loved and had studied the legends of other lands—I had never read about the legends of my own ancestors. My culture had been erased. I was fascinated by what I was learning and infuriated at the same time."

David is nothing if not passionate about the result of that youthful rage. "It got me thinking," he tells me. "We needed to get back what others had worked so hard to stamp out. I decided to try to undo that de-indigenization, reclaim the pan-indigenous undercurrent that connects us all: Peru, Mexico, you, me." David went on to become a professor of literature at the University of Texas, but his mission as a writer has been to educate the very young about the real America, the one that has existed all along, below the mainstream's gaze. His subject is the origin world that colonization has tried mightily to rub out, ever since the Church marched with the conquistadors and founded all the schools; ever since the first American textbook, the *New England Primer*, promulgated the notion that this land belongs—by God's volition, English exceptionalism, and the majority will—to Christian whites, and that it was free for the taking.

By now, David Bowles has produced dozens of prizewinning books for Americans from toddlers to teens. Each one is meant to create that cultural bridge that was so absent in his own early instruction. From Aztec-inspired stories about *naguales*—human shapeshifters who wondrously transform themselves into their spirit animals—to Mayan trickster tales, to thrillers about underworld demons and hummingbird gods, he guides schoolchildren into the magical story-world in which his ancestors, and possibly theirs, were steeped. It is as much a resurrection as an education.

Although they are separated by almost two thousand miles, author Bowles and high school teacher Topher Kandik would agree on the principle that in order for education to engage, the stories it tells need to speak to a child. Topher is an award-winning educator in Washington, DC, who found himself lured to the classroom by a passing encounter on the subway. He had been working for the American Film Institute, riding to work one day, when a towering African American man he did not recognize stopped him, shouting "Topher! Topher Kandik!" Kandik did not recognize him at all, but the man was insistent, "Topher, it's me! From the Southeast Projects!" As a younger man, when Topher had worked as a publicist for the Shakespeare Theatre Company, he had volunteered to create after-school programs for sixth graders. The children would write plays; Topher would find professional actors to act them out. The smiling face in front of him on the DC Metro was one of those little kids, all grown up, happily employed, and remembering his schooldays fondly. There and then, Topher decided he wanted to go back to that child-molding milieu; a place where you could really make a difference. He wanted to be a teacher. He found work as an English instructor at SEED, a charter school that served mostly African American children.

"You can imagine," he says now, "the absurdity of it. A white boy from Toledo, Ohio, teaching African Americans about literature." He knew right away that he wanted them to read important books by black writers. As a child in an all-boys Jesuit school, he had grown up seeing himself in the classic "dead white male" curriculum. His students deserved nothing less, an ability to see themselves in a curriculum of their own. "But I was uncomfortable being seen as someone who was 'bringing' African Americans their own culture. I opted to take the position of *learner* as opposed to *teacher*." He decided he would learn alongside his students, observe the ways they responded to great African American works they read together, and reflect those observations back to them in class.

As years went by, and Topher won awards for excellence in teaching, he took a position at the E. L. Haynes Public Charter School across town. There he was presented with a different challenge: the school, which had been founded by E. L. Haynes, purportedly the first Black American woman to earn a doctorate degree in mathematics, had begun as an African American institution, but over the years the faces behind the desks had changed. In the course of a single decade, the number of Hispanics had doubled. Haynes was now largely Latino—almost 60 percent, to be exact—and yet it was continuing to hire black teachers and teach a black curriculum for its majority Spanish-speaking student body. Topher immediately saw what David Bowles had seen as a deficit in instruction: an erasure. With a difference. Whereas in Texas, Bowles had sat in a largely Latino classroom and been taught a white curriculum with not a thought to diversity and not a drop of Latino content, Topher's Hispanic students were being taught great black American literature in a school dedicated to diversity, and *still* they were being denied any reference to their own culture. In other words, although the school counted itself a model of urban sensitivity—and it was—Latino children were experiencing the very same cultural neglect Bowles had run up against two generations before. Haynes's enlightened "multicultural" approach was not factoring its Latinos at all. Topher decided to set the situation right: he would teach Hispanic authors—Junot Díaz, Sandra Cisneros, Jennine Capó-Crucet, Luis Alberto Urrea, Carmen María Machado, Javier Zamora, Karla Cornejo Villavicencio, Valeria Luiselli—and he would do so in the same way he had undertaken to teach African Americans at SEED: by learning alongside them.

•   •   •

Sadly, even with well-meaning teachers and writers like Topher Kandik and David Bowles, the numbers don't speak well for the majority of Hispanic students. More than a quarter—quickly approaching one-third—of all seats in American classrooms are filled by Latinos, and yet those students often go unmonitored, passed over, relegated to failure. And though Hispanics come to the United States with high expectations for their children's educations—87 percent say they hope their children go on to college—they remain among the least educated group in the country. Certainly there are not enough Hispanic teachers to teach them: whereas almost 80 percent of all American teachers are white, only 9 percent are Hispanic, a meager fraction of what the percentage should be—and the great majority of those teachers are clustered in the Southwest and West.

Even so, and remarkably, there have been notable gains: within the past ten years, the high school graduation rate for Latinos has risen more than 10 percentage points to 82 percent. The number of Hispanic students enrolled in college has skyrocketed almost 400 percent as a result, reaching four million. (It is very possible that the enrollment numbers will shrink, however, given the 2023 Supreme Court decision banning race-based affirmative action and race-based admissions in American colleges.) Lastly, the number of Latinx immigrants with at least a bachelor's degree has risen to 26 percent, thanks to recently heightened immigration from countries with higher rates of educational attainment: Spain, Argentina, Venezuela, Colombia.

According to Janet Murguía, the head of UnidosUS, the nation's largest Hispanic civil rights and advocacy organization, there may be great asymmetry among Latinos when it comes to education, but there are also many traits that unite us. To name a few: 94 percent of all Latino schoolchildren under eighteen are born in the United States. Many are fluent in Spanish and familiar with their origin traditions, promising an abundance of Americans in the future workforce who will be able to negotiate across languages and cultures. A remarkable share of that youth also represents a range of racial and ethnic identities, including three million who self-identify as black and, so, promise to give us human bridges such as Arturo Griffiths, the Afro-Latino community activist who identifies amply with both sides of his heritage. Fortifying that notion of diversities within a diversity, Murguía informs us that an increasing share of Latino young adults—one out of five millennials—also consider themselves LGBTQIA+, which is to say that a growing proportion of young American Latinos are shattering the age-old, macho taboo against gender fluidity.

As the bracingly intellectual Ed Morales of Columbia University tells us, the very fact that Latinx are not monolithic—that we cannot be boxed and sold as a single flavor—is our greatest gift to America. What Hispanic children ultimately bring to the American table is a fresh perspective. We are past masters at border thinking, bi-thinking, multi-positioning, and so—because we are practiced in logic that is more pro-tean than rigid—we are uniquely equipped to flip the binary and fuse America as it has never been fused before. We are, as Morales describes us, like the long-lost relative who visits your house, sits by your fireplace, tells you a thing or two, and changes your life forever by turning every-thing you knew on its ear.

## THE CUTTING EDGE

> I am an optimist. I am positive. It's possible to do the necessary changes [to fix our environment], but it's not going to be easy. It will take a lot of hard work. I have a lot of trust in the children.
>
> —Mario Molina, scientist, Nobel Prize
> winner, Mexican American

It is heartening to hear Don Graham tell of the legion of aspiring young Latinos who come to his organization, intent on pursuing careers in sci-ence, technology, engineering, and medicine (STEM). These are the op-timists, our future changemakers, über-educators—the ones who will ask questions, pore over answers, and find a better way. But, like every-thing else in LatinoLand, Latinx scientists are hardly noticed; even the lu-minaries are barely visible. I can just hear Joaquín Castro fussing: "When I say to people, 'Name me some famous Latinos,' why don't they shout back, 'Mario Molina'? The *ingenioso* who proved that man-made chemi-cal compounds are destroying the ozone layer, for heaven's sake!" And, sure enough, Molina is one of the foundational names of environmental science, "a trailblazing pioneer of the climate movement," as Al Gore tagged him; a Mexican-born American who, as a little boy, did wacky experiments in his parents' spare bathroom and went on to win a Nobel Prize in Chemistry.

It was Molina who showed that chlorofluorocarbons (CFCs) used in hair spray and refrigerators, among the many other common products we humans use, were wreaking irreversible damage on the ozone layer, the sliver of stratosphere that keeps us from being fried by ultraviolet rays. In Molina's 2020 obituary, the *New York Times* called the chemist's findings dire: "Without the protective ozone, an increase in ultraviolet radiation would put the health of many species, including humans, at risk." Those discoveries, which were attacked by big-foot industry—even accused by one corporation of being "orchestrated by the Ministry of Disinformation of the K.G.B."—led to a landmark international treaty to phase out the manufacture of ruinous substances. When President Obama awarded Molina the Presidential Medal of Freedom in 2013, the gratitude was real. "Thanks to Mario's work," Obama said, we leave the planet "safer and cleaner for future generations."

But there are plenty of other Latinos who have thrown open the doors to progress: Albert Baez, for instance, a man probably best known for fathering folk-music sensations Joan Baez and Mimi Fariña, and yet it was he who gave us two inventions that would transform the way we think of earthly life as well as the universe as a whole. He was born in Puebla, Mexico, and immigrated to the United States at the age of two with his Methodist minister father. In time, Albert married a Scotswoman, converted to Quakerism, and pursued physics at Stanford University. There, in 1948, he was credited with co-developing the first X-ray reflection microscope that is still used today in doctor's offices to examine living cells; eventually the same technology would be used in telescopes that photograph entire galaxies. During the Cold War, the American defense industry offered Baez vast sums of money to develop similar devices for use in the nuclear arms race, but Albert refused those overtures, claiming that his vows as a Quaker and pacifist prevented him from creating instruments of war or weapons of mass destruction. Instead, he devoted his energies to education or humanitarian work—teaching physics at prestigious universities, working on peace initiatives for the United Nations Educational, Scientific, and Cultural Organization (UNESCO), fashioning dozens of educational films for encyclopedias—and winning awards along the way.

Peruse any field of science, from plant life to human cell division to space optics, and you are bound to find prominent Latinx like Baez and Molina in the vanguard. Take Ynés Mexía, for example, a fiercely independent twentieth-century Mexican American botanist who, despite confronting considerable opposition from male chauvinists, traveled the Americas largely alone—from ice-bound mountains of Alaska to belching volcanoes of Colombia. Along the way, she discovered five hundred new plant species as well as two entirely new plant genera. Feisty, willful, meticulous, Ynés was an extraordinary force in documenting the hemisphere's plant life. Today more than fifty species are named after her.

Or consider Dr. Alfredo Quiñones-Hinojosa, the neurosurgeon known as "Dr. Q," who was born into a destitute family in Baja California, began work in these United States as a nineteen-year-old undocumented grape picker in Fresno, and went on to scrape his way through community college, the University of California at Berkeley, and graduate with honors from Harvard Medical School. The desperate young man whose hands were once raw from ripping out scrub in the vineyards is now the nimble-fingered "samurai" of metastatic brain tumors—a pathbreaking neurosurgeon, the Mayo Clinic's dean of research—with more than a dozen patented surgical innovations to his name.

Or Ellen Ochoa, the granddaughter of immigrants from the Sonora Desert, whose father was so determined to protect her from the prejudice he'd experienced as a boy that he refused to teach her Spanish. Ellen soared through school, excelling in the sciences, setting her sights high—so high, in fact, that she became a space engineer, developing optics innovations for space travel. In 1993 she became the first Latina astronaut at NASA, flying numerous missions aboard the space shuttle *Discovery* and studying the effects of the sun on Earth's environment as well as the damage humans had inflicted on the ozone layer. In 2013 she was made director of NASA's Johnson Space Center—that hub of all human spaceflight—becoming the first Latinx to hold that position. Seven years later, she was elected chair of the National Science Board, which advises Congress and the American president on all things science.

If you don't recognize those names, it's not surprising. They're not often taught, or publicized, nor commemorated. Indeed, Latino scientists—and their Latin Americans forebears—are distinctly unrecognized for their groundbreaking inventions. Even the Maya, Aztec, and Inca, from whose cultures so many Latinx descend, were great chemists, engineers, and astronomers. But is that taught to the American young? It's very doubtful. We all know that Orville and Wilbur Wright invented, built, and flew the airplane; that Dr. Christiaan Bernard performed the first human-to-human heart transplant, and that Benjamin Franklin invented the bifocals and the Franklin Stove. But does anyone remember that Luis Miramontes developed the birth control pill from a variety of Mexican yam growing in the wild and, so, revolutionized women's lives as well as the entire world economy? Or that Julio Palmaz, using a scrap of metal from his garage floor, invented the stent and completely transformed cardiac care? Or that Guillermo González Camarena, at the age of twenty-four, received the first United States patent for the color television? That Angela Ruiz Robles created the forerunner of the e-book decades before an American would be credited for its invention? That Victor Ochoa invented the electrical brake and made transportation history?

Then there are those who take science a step further. Eliseo Pérez-Stable, for one: a physician who studies the cultural factors—the peculiar stresses, discomforts, habits, vices—that can skew the human biome, alter people's biology, and impact their well-being. He means to show how socioeconomic conditions of the poor and marginalized can affect their health. Pérez-Stable is the director of the National Institute on Minority Health and Health Disparities (NIMHHD)—a division of the National Institutes of Health that is doing pioneering work on the intersection of race, ethnicity, and wellness.

He was born in Cuba just before Castro's revolution. His parents, fearful of their country's future, sent him off to Miami at the age of eight to live with his grandparents. A year later, he still hadn't learned English. Rendered a virtual mute, Eliseo was bullied, ridiculed. Only the mumps could save him from the indignities of the schoolyard; even as he recovered, he did all he could to delay his healing and to avoid having to return to school. Eliseo's experiences as a tongue-tied immigrant child proved decisive as he grew up. Mathematics and science became his languages, and he never lost his sympathy for the humiliations that immigrants face. Eventually he chose his father's profession: medicine.

His research in racial and ethnic disparities began in the 1980s, when he was a professor at the University of California at San Francisco. The city's racial makeup interested him immediately; this was no empowered, upwardly mobile Latino community like the one he had known in Miami. It was poor, struggling, and, in many cases, trapped. Stymied. Some had never seen a physician of color. The experience had a profound effect on him. As Eliseo tells me, "When John Ruffin—the former African American director of the NIMHHD—retired, I found myself thinking a lot about the question of representation, and so I applied. I saw right away that there seemed to be an Eastern bias at the institute. When people think of race and health here in the East, they immediately think about African Americans. I had come from directing a clinic in San Francisco, where Latinos were the majority. Here in the East, Latinos were not being acknowledged. Naming me director was a statement, I think."

According to Pérez-Stable, his division doesn't really do science. Not the test-tube variety, in any case. What it does is take science to another level. How do social and psychological pressures, poverty, education and its lack, work conditions, and ethnic fads and customs, affect the wellness of minorities in America? For Eliseo, getting the US Congress to think about how Latinos have been physically altered by their environment was an accomplishment in itself; for so long, the scrutiny had been fixed on African American issues. Not that those issues weren't urgently important, too, but as director of the NIMHHD, Eliseo felt the institutional embrace had to be larger, more robust. Both groups were suffering a pervasive racism that had much in common; there was much to study in that confluence. And much of what the NIMHHD was discovering might also apply to East Asians, continental Africans, East Indians. How does racism affect the heart? How does it invite diseases? How does it influence puberty? Infant health? Mental soundness? Obesity? And more to the point: Should race be considered at all in clinical care? Is it racist to do that? Is this science?

It has turned out to be. What the NIMHHD is finding, under Pérez-Stable's direction, is that the impact of living conditions, ethnic diets, even generational stress—along with everything else—can have real, measurable repercussions on Latino health. "A lot of social scientists get very nervous when we talk about genetic determinism," says Eliseo, but if you study the population, he says, the evidence is there. You can see it, feel it, predict it, document it, by observing the way people live. Or the way they are made to live.

Back in 1915, when Mexicans building our railroads were being persecuted as typhus carriers—vessels of disease, the anathema of the nation—no one bothered to consider that they were being herded into cramped quarters like animals, prey to insect and rodent infestations, not to mention mortal infections, exposed to chemicals and raw sewage, given food laden with carrion. That they would become afflicted with typhus was obvious. It was simple science. It was their masters' abuses that were causing their disease.

Later, during the Bracero Program that flourished during World War II until the 1960s, Mexican workers faced much the same. Although the program was put forth by the United States government as humane, promising a good life and a steady living for the workers, the conditions in Bracero camps were harrowing. Men were stripped naked, hosed, and sprayed with insecticides—their hair, faces, and groins shot with toxic white powder. Throughout, the American public worried about the scourge that Mexican workers presumably were bringing. The truth was that hard work and a hard life were crippling an entire ethnicity. As the *American Journal of Public Health* reported in 2011, "It is striking that these concerns [about the Braceros] involved a government program, carried out by the very same government that was enacting laws and policies dedicated to eradicating the diseases that were spawned by conditions in which they were forcing the workers to live." If basic, public-spirited health programs had been put in practice, they might have curtailed those diseases and abated the cruelties of bigotry.

Today is no different. During the COVID pandemic, Mexicans were cravenly judged by the Trump administration to be the source of the virus's spread, and they were treated much the same as the early-twentieth-century railroad workers or the mid-century Braceros. Many were rounded up in the hospitals and deported. This, even though they were feeding the nation, caring for the sick, disinfecting the hospitals, and laboring in industries that kept essential services and products available. This, even though COVID affected Latinos disproportionately more than other minorities in the country. According to veteran *New York Times* journalist Deborah Sontag, America's knee-jerk, racist, deeply undemocratic response derives from the age-old "collision of two deeply flawed American systems: immigration and health care." Eliseo Pérez-Stable would go one step further and call it structural racism. Over the years, according to him, it has had a marked effect on the health of tens of millions. Latinos are especially vulnerable to type 2 diabetes, hypertension, cancer, largely because of their diet and lifestyle. But studying the habits that help people thrive—that keep them alive—is important, too, says Eliseo. Our culture of blending races, for instance, and strengthening the species. The energy we take from the richness of our imaginations—the music, the art, the stories, the dance. Our strong family bonds. Our resilience. Our capacity for faith. These are balm, medicine, and should be studied as impacting our biology as well.

· · ·

"Science has eliminated distance," Melquiades proclaimed. "In a short time, man will be able to see what is happening in any place in the world without ever leaving his own house."
—Gabriel García Márquez, *One Hundred Years of Solitude*, 1967

For all the Latinos we can point to who have made groundbreaking advances in science—or the thousands of "dream-dot" students pursuing a

STEM education—what worries activists is why more young Hispanics are not rushing to take up careers in STEM. Latinos are well represented in some health-related professions, especially nursing, but less so in the physical sciences, life sciences, mathematics, computer and engineering jobs—and, certainly, they are rarely seen in the upper echelons inhabited by the likes of Eliseo Pérez-Stable. For a population that represents almost 18 percent of the adult workforce, a meager 8 percent hold a job that requires these skills in science. In short, although Latinos are growing in numbers at a rate seldom seen in modern American demographics, they are glaringly underrepresented in science's most consequential ranks.

The reasons for this are several: schools have often been shown to harbor deep-seated prejudices and low expectations for Latino students, and counselors are inclined to shunt them to professions in manual labor; this certainly happened to Ralph de la Vega, who decided to ignore his high school advisor, study engineering, and go on to become a chief executive officer of AT&T. In addition, there is a distinct lack of role models for young people, since few Hispanic teachers specialize in STEM. When inspiring Latino educators do appear, results can be striking: we saw this with the famous teacher memorialized in the 1988 film *Stand and Deliver*, Jaime Escalante, who miraculously transformed a school of low-performing Mexican American teenagers given up for lost in the sprawling, broken neighborhoods of East Los Angeles into one of the most impressive engines of STEM the city had ever known. "The Mayan Indians invented the concept of zero!" Escalante would shout gleefully to his students. "You burros have math in your blood!" When the kids of Garfield High shrugged and didn't believe him—when they saw calculus as beyond their capabilities—Escalante would tell each one, "I'll make a deal with you. I'll teach you math, and that's your language. With that you're going to make it. You're going to go to college and sit in the first row, not in the back, because you're going to know more than anybody."

And so they did. Escalante created what he called his Pipeline, working with junior high schools to prepare students firmly in algebra, so that they could proceed to higher and higher math in his classes. Within a few years, Garfield was outpacing the prestigious Beverly Hills High

School in advanced-placement calculus scores. One by one, Escalante's students went on to win scholarships to MIT, Harvard, Yale, UC-Berkeley, University of Southern California, or UCLA to further their studies in STEM. When Escalante finally retired from Garfield in 1991, the program withered, and the number of Hispanic students passing the AP calculus exams dropped by 80 percent.

The most obvious reason for a hesitancy to pursue science as a life pursuit is the all-too-apparent absence of Hispanic faces at the front of the class—the fact that Latino youths simply don't see themselves represented there. Models and mentors such as Jaime Escalante are scarce; and Hispanic innovators who have made impressive scientific advances—Mario Molina, for instance, or Ynés Mexía—are not taught in American schoolrooms. Research also shows that Latinos are not made to feel particularly welcome in science classrooms, or labs, or institutions. In the list of professions in which Latinx feel wholly *unwanted*—business executives, lawyers, and military officers—science comes in at a close fourth. So, even though Hispanics may now be enrolling in college in unprecedented numbers, and even though they may aspire initially to careers in science, many end up feeling unsupported, out of place, and ultimately move on to other disciplines.

Coming from a family of at least five generations of men and women passionately engaged in science, I understand the role that models and mentors can play in encouraging the young. My grandfather Victor Manuel Arana Sobrevilla—who, at fifteen, traveled to Notre Dame University to enroll in the science curriculum—became an engineer as well as an engineering professor in Peru. He also became my father's teacher at the Colegio de Ingenieros—the College of Engineers—in Lima. From the start, my grandfather had his firstborn doing experiments, often alarming ones, in their house on Avenida La Paz. It began with simple lessons: dropping eggs from different levels of the house, for instance—the roof first, a second-floor window next—to time the relative lengths of those falls; thrusting live electric wires into salt water to test conductivity. At the age of six, my father was pounding nails into his parents' handsome wood floor, building miniature railway tracks that ran from the front door all the way to the kitchen. His father did not stop him. His mother was appalled.

In turn, when my father became a civic engineer, he took my brother and me on jaunts to his factories, where we would bob down the aisles with our outsize hard hats, the roar of heavy machinery shaking our knees. Or he would ask us to assist him in his workshop, where together we would make what seemed like wondrous things: Christmas trees out of hula hoops. Whole miniature cities—with houses, train stations, and parks—out of scraps of balsam wood. Colorful sheets of paper from dried plants. Tidy little boxes with brass hinges and our names carved into them. Along the way, we would learn mathematics, the marvels of the man-made world, the importance of precision. Later, in his garage in Maryland, my father would pass along his enthusiasms to my eight-year-old son, making time every Thursday afternoon to create elaborate, moving contraptions out of pistachio shells, or popsicle sticks, or random bits of copper, to teach him the laws of physics, mechanics, and the science of flow. My son would go on to become an innovation engineer in a major multinational technology corporation.

With time, my brother, who became a physician and hospital administrator, would convey his passion for science to two of his daughters, one a cardiologist and the other an emergency room doctor. From all this passing of the baton—from one America to the other—my grandson has decided to study cyber intelligence with an eye to a military career. We have been fortunate. It takes support, enthusiasm, and, most of all, opportunity to create generations of Latino scientists. Scores of determined institutions, from TheDream.Us, to the Hispanic Heritage Foundation, to UnidosUS, are working to ensure that the paucity in STEM is corrected as the years unwind. Juan Espinoza, president of a support network for Latinos at Virginia Tech, puts it this way: "It's a matter of surrounding students with people who look like them, talk like them—Latinos—but successful ones, passionate ones. Build that confidence. At first, the kids think they can't afford it, don't have the necessary background, don't have the documentation. By the end of our program, fifty percent want to go on to pursue a doctorate."

# 12

# LIMELIGHT

Give your time, give your heart, give your service. Give someone
something you made.

—Lin-Manuel Miranda, actor, composer,
playwright, Puerto Rican

The same reports that have American Latinos feeling uninvited and
unwanted in fields of science have them feeling welcomed and
embraced—even celebrated—in athletics and music. Little wonder, since
there are legions of exemplary Hispanics for them in those arenas, from
baseball legend Roberto Clemente—who won more Gold Gloves than
any other right fielder in history—to Bad Bunny or Gloria Estefan, whose
irresistible rhythms have galvanized generations of young musicians.

Hispanic romance with baseball begins at the turn of the century in
1902, when Luis Manuel Castro—known variously as Lou, Louis, Judge,
or "the president of Venezuela"—was signed by the Philadelphia Athletics to replace Napoleon Lajoie, known to baseball scholars as "the first
superstar in American League history." Lou Castro had been born into a
well-to-do banking family in Medellín, Colombia, in 1876, and was sent
to private school in New York eight years later, just as political upheaval
began to roil the Colombian landscape. By thirteen, he had fallen in love
with baseball and started training for the sport. By twenty, he was playing for semiprofessional teams and, in 1902, caught the eye of Athletics

manager Connie Mack. He never did match the caliber of Lajoie's heroics for the club, but his career marked a threshold for American baseball.
He was the first Latino to play for a major league baseball team. But he
also played a pointed role in baseball's troubled history with race.

Lou Castro was liked immediately and received warmly by the baseball public. Early on, he was described as "a quiet, reserved fellow on or
off the baseball field, one whose gentlemanly demeanor has made him
friends wherever he has gone." But he was also witty, something of a
court jester. According to the *Atlanta Constitution*:

> There is no player in the Southern (Association) today more univer-
> sally liked than Count Louis Castro, the Atlanta shortstop, and this
> popularity is due in a great measure to the never-ceasing flow of good
> humor which he is fortunate enough to possess. . . . Castro is one
> of the most brilliant fielders in the league, and gets away with some
> sensational work in every game. He is a consistent player, never lets
> down, and is a great man for a baseball team, with his abundant sup-
> ply of ginger, and an overflowing line of talk while in action. . . . He is
> the comedian of the league, and hardly a day passes that he does not
> pull off some funny performance on the coaching lines or on the field.

He was also something of an enigma. One couldn't be sure whether
his moniker as "president of Venezuela" was a joke. He played along
that he indeed might be a nephew of Cipriano Castro, "the Lion from
the Andes," a military despot who ruled Venezuela for nine remarkably
corrupt years, embezzling enormous amounts of money and living a
debauched life until he was unseated by an even more ruthless dictator.

But so many facts about Lou Castro seemed wobbly and uncertain.
His death certificate names his birthplace as New York City, which he
sometimes claimed, but his naturalization papers report it as Medellín,
which matches records in Colombia. He changed his name at will—
sometimes "Louis Michael," other times "Luis Manuel," and even "Jud"
or "Judge" or "Count." We do not know, in fact, whether America's first

Hispanic major league player was Colombian or Venezuelan, since he claimed both nationalities publicly.

There were good reasons for the uncertainty, and those reasons point to a deeper problem within baseball: the color line. After the Civil War, African Americans were free to play on white baseball teams and did so in good numbers, but all that stopped when, in an "old gentlemen's agreement" of 1890, team owners decided jointly to bar black players from professional and minor leagues, and they did so on blatantly racist grounds. As a result, sports entrepreneurs in Cuba, Mexico, Puerto Rico, and elsewhere in Latin America recruited first-rate African American baseball players for their national teams, even though those Americans were not allowed to play in their own native country. Latino players, however, inhabited a more fluid situation, given that their place in the racial hierarchy was inconclusive. Team officials began to allow Latinos to play as long as they looked white enough not to be confused with blacks. As one sportswriter explained it, officials "possessed the power to construct whatever racial categories they deemed necessary," as long as those categories held fast to "a color line that excluded African Americans."

And so, Lou Castro proceeded to spend his career in a limbo of racial ambiguities. He was light skinned, a descendant of his country's elite, and passed sufficiently to attend a white private school and college. But he was also cast into that hazy middle zone of nonwhiteness, where, in these United States of the one-drop rule, any white might be your judge. What color are you, really? Identity for Lou Castro had become an addled question. It was no surprise that he took so many names, claimed so many histories. Eventually whatever financial fortunes he possessed were lost irretrievably to the Great Depression. He died a derelict in the psychiatric ward of the Manhattan State Hospital days before America entered the Second World War.

•   •   •

Lou Castro's racial fluidity—his ability to deflect uncomfortable questions about his color—prefigured the discomfitures of another, much more talented and darker-skinned player, the extraordinarily gifted

Puerto Rican superstar Roberto Clemente. For all Clemente's legendary heroics in his career with the Pittsburgh Pirates—his .317 lifetime batting average, the twelve Gold Gloves, a National League Most Valuable Player, a World Series MVP, and the four NL batting championships, finishing with exactly three thousand hits—it was his public profile that set him apart. His Hispanicity. He was brilliant, invariably outspoken, as irrepressible with his commentary as he was with his play on the field, voicing strong opinions about racism and justice.

He was also a humanitarian who devoted countless hours to helping children and Latin Americans in dire need. "He had about him a touch of royalty," according to Bowie Kuhn, the baseball commissioner of his day—a nobility of the soul. And yet, for all the posthumous veneration that has portrayed him as a benign do-gooder, he was "no gentle giant," according to biographer David Maraniss, so much as "a fierce critic of both baseball and American society." His sharp tongue could be as dazzling as his wrecking-ball arm.

Roberto Clemente was born in Carolina, Puerto Rico, a municipality known today as Tierra de los Gigantes—land of the giants—in honor of its most famous natives: the celebrated poet Julia de Burgos; Jesús Piñero, the first Puerto Rican to be named its governor; Don Felipe Birriél Fernández, the tallest Puerto Rican in recorded history (who measured seven feet, eleven inches); and, not least, the outsize hero Clemente himself. His father was a cane cutter, later a foreman in the sugar fields that run west and embrace the capital of San Juan. His mother had been a widow with several children when she married his father. It was a family touched by heartbreak, suffering the tragic losses of four of its seven children, but a strong faith was its bulwark. The Clementes began every morning with a *bendición* for one another, a blessing, a custom Roberto would maintain for the rest of his life.

Young Roberto was a thoughtful child, nicknamed "Momen" for always replying *"momentito, momentito"*—wait, wait, just a moment!— whenever he was told to hurry; he was not one to be pressured, determined as he was to do things his own way. He grew up obsessed by baseball, showing prodigious physical prowess even as a boy. It wasn't long before North American scouts found him; he was signed up first by the Brooklyn Dodgers, but assigned to the International League, playing for the Montreal Royals before being snatched away by the Pittsburgh Pirates. Less than four months before his debut with the Pirates, he was driving home from visiting his terminally ill brother in Puerto Rico, when a car slammed into him, damaging his spine and leaving him with lifelong pain and a debilitating case of insomnia. But a different sort of irritant would follow.

He hadn't known about racism, Clemente once said, until he got to Pittsburgh. He had always been proud to be Puerto Rican, never thinking twice about the color of his skin. But arriving in 1955 after a stint in the US Marine Reserves, he was shocked by the segregation he saw in America. He made a point of sounding off when he was told to wait on a team bus, hungry, while white players went in to eat leisurely at all-white establishments, where the darker-skinned were not allowed to set foot. He demanded that blacks and Latinos be given their own vehicle and be driven to places where they could enter freely and eat with dignity. He became, in a way, the moral voice of his people, the defender of his tribe. He was a listener, as alert to any poor Puerto Rican kid with big baseball dreams as he was to the egalitarian vision of Dr. Martin Luther King Jr., who became his friend. A one-man civil rights movement—a living echo of the first African American to play in the major leagues, Jackie Robinson—Clemente was one of those players whose sociological impact transcended the sport itself.

He bristled over the way journalists wrote about him, not because they criticized his game, but because they belittled him as a Hispanic: they called him lazy and insinuated he was faking his injuries; they used his ethnicity to project the age-old trope of Latino indolence. And they did this even though, between 1955 and 1972, Clemente was playing more games than anyone in Pirates history. "Mickey Mantle is God," Clemente observed about the New York Yankees' often-injured slugging center fielder, a golden boy from Oklahoma. Mantle was never accused of malingering, Clemente pointed out, "but if a Latin or black is sick, they say it is in his head." The racism extended to names sportswriters used for him—Bobby or Bob—when he had made it clear to them that his name was Roberto. He was still learning English when he began playing for the Pirates, but broadcasters felt free to mock him all the same. They made fun of his accent. His flawed grammar. They rolled their eyes when he stopped to search for the right word. When white players used bad grammar, Clemente's defenders noted, editors corrected them before it was published in the papers; when Latinos did it, they became objects of media derision.

He was often criticized for being brash and moody, for giving those sportswriters a piece of his mind. But prejudice was coming in hard and fast in those days, the slurs against blacks and Latinos flung freely by media and public alike. "You writers are all the same!" he finally shouted at a reporter who was chiding him about his origins. "You don't know a damn thing about me." It was the double standard that angered him. Whites were always given a pass, not asked rude questions; blacks and Latinos had to earn their way, and then some. "I believe every human being is equal," he said near the end of his life, "but one has to fight hard to maintain that equality. Always, they say you have to be like Babe Ruth. But Babe Ruth was an American player. What we needed was a Puerto Rican player they could . . . look up to." He would become that person. By 1970, half the Pirates roster was black, Latino, or Spanish speaking. Clemente had accomplished that, too.

There was much about him to admire. "He walked a little taller than most men," declared his fellow Pirate and Hall of Famer Willie Stargell. "He was like an artist," a broadcaster wrote after his death. "His body was his cathedral." That body, which one writer compared to Michelangelo's *David*, was graced by his unique stance, his ebony skin, his large hands, and a broad, handsome face that would never be grizzled with white. On December 31, 1972, days after Nicaragua suffered a catastrophic earthquake that killed or maimed thirty thousand souls, Clemente left his home in Puerto Rico and boarded a small airplane to take food and supplies to the victims. He did not trust anyone but himself to deliver it; the Nixon administration was too comfortable with the corrupt regime of dictator Anastasio Somoza Debayle, which was looting any aid coming into the country. Within minutes of takeoff, Clemente's plane plunged into the sea off the coast of San Juan, his body never to be recovered. He was thirty-eight years old.

The Pirate of the Caribbean went suddenly, in the full flush of his glory. Months later, he became the first Latino inducted into the Baseball Hall of Fame; Nixon posthumously awarded him the first-ever Presidential Citizen's Medal; and George W. Bush bestowed on him the Presidential Medal of Freedom. He may or may not have appreciated the hands from which these last two came, but he would have been ecstatic about the hands that took up the bat after him—the close to two thousand Latinos who have graced the big-league rosters ever since, most likely inspired by his example. Today they constitute almost a third of the talent in the Major Leagues.

## THE ARTISTS

> My mother lived with guts and heart. That's how I play guitar.
> —Carlos Santana, musician, Mexican American

Ask Latinos on the street how they would describe Latino music, and you're bound to get a different answer every time: if you're in New York, you'll hear "Salsa! Merengue! Dembow! Bachata! Hip-hop! Reggaeton!" Which makes sense because those musical styles are as markedly Caribbean as the Puerto Ricans and Dominicans who live there. The legendary singers who made salsa famous—Celia Cruz, Willie Colón, Rubén Blades, and Marc Anthony, among others—actually represent a mash-up of Caribbean countries, which also makes sense, because salsa is a great saucepan of ingredients, just like the word itself: sauce. *"Échale salsita!"* as the classic Cuban song commands you to do—Pour on a little hot sauce!—so that dancers will pick up the tempo. And dance you must, if you're anywhere within earshot.

If you're in Miami, on the other hand, ask the same question, and you're bound to hear a few other styles in response: Mambo! Rumba! Bembé! Son! Cha-cha-cha! Or guaguancó!" Because these are the Cuban

genres, heavily infused with African rhythms, and most familiar to the
*cubanos* who reside in Florida. But ask the question in Texas or Southern California, where the population is predominantly Mexican, and
the music you'll hear about is entirely different. If it's traditional, you
won't necessarily hear bongos, congas, or timbales, the Afro-Latino
instruments indispensable for a Caribbean beat. Here, as conventional
wisdom has it, you're more inclined to sing your heart out than dance.
The time-honored Mexican American music is a *ranchera*, or a *corrido*,
or *mariachi*—the sort of music singer Linda Ronstadt grew up with in
her Sonoran family—and it is played with violins, trumpets, and guitars.
Filled with passion and heartbreak and hard-won lessons, this music suggests that Mexicans might prefer to have a good cry than spring out of
their chairs and boogie.

That, at least, is the assumption. The truth about *música latina*, however, is far richer and more complicated than any overview can portray.
Cubans may well shake up the dance floor, but they've also produced
romantic, heartrending, by-now classic boleros. In addition to singing,
Mexicans also have foot-stomping polkas, *tapatías*, not to mention *la
bamba*—and no one should ever suggest that a Mexican can't dance. As
much as these genres seem unique to their cultures, they are products of
more than five hundred years of fusion, starting with Spain and Portugal's colonization of the hemisphere.

As history unfolded—as conquest, slavery, and migration proliferated—musicians of various cultures came together to discover instruments they had never heard played: the indigenous brought their reed
flutes and dried-gourd maracas; the Spanish, their guitars and violins;
Africans, a prodigious array of drums; Germans, their distinctive *ban-
doleón*; Chinese, the high-pitched horn they called the *suona*. Combining
those sounds even as they co-mixed their races, Spain's colonies developed genres that began to typify their regions. Even the instruments mutated: indigenous Andeans made a diminutive guitar, the *charango*, out
of the shells of armadillos; in the Pacific ports of Peru, the *cajón*, or box
percussion, was fashioned by African slaves out of fruit crates. In America, we are surprised today when bluegrass mingles with heavy metal,

but this is the sort of radical amalgamation Latin Americans have forged since Jesuit monks wended their way down the Amazon in the 1630s. By now, Latinos in the United States have crossbred and merged their music to such an extent that the highly original rock-and-roll wonder Carlos Santana freely blends his signature electric guitar with congas, bongos, and African batá to create an entirely new, transporting sound that is unmistakably Latino. Just listen to "Smooth," "Black Magic Woman," or "Put Your Lights On," and the Caribbean is suddenly very present in the streets of Los Angeles.

Latinos, in other words, come with a soundtrack. We live and breathe music. Singing and dancing are in our nature. Just as the Andeans who come here from Cabanaconde do the *huititi*, the Porteños from Buenos Aires do the tango, and the *paisas* from Cartagena do the *cumbia*. And they all do it on these shores, played by Hispanic artists. Good, professional wedding musicians and disc jockeys know to have every one of these dance rhythms in their repertoire, and those musicians won't be hard to find. One out of every eight professional musicians in this country is Latinx.

Like sports, music is a profession so broad in its appeal and so accessible that any youth from any barrio can aspire to its pantheons. Sometimes, what looks like a mash-up of cultures is actually plumbing something deeper. The way Latino jazz was born in 1947, for instance, when Dizzy Gillespie was looking for a drummer and was introduced to Chano Pozo, the swaggering Yoruba master of the conga drums, who had just arrived from Cuba. The meeting was nothing short of providential, spawning a blazing new art form that would inspire saxophonist Paquito D'Rivera, composer Chico O'Farrill, and trumpeter Arturo Sandoval. When Dizzy was asked how he and Chano, two monolinguals, could possibly communicate with each other, he answered, "I don't speak Spanish, and Chano don't speak English, but we both speak African." Which actually makes a lot of sense. There are lots of jazz purists who don't want to admit it, says Chico O'Farrill, but "jazz and Latin are the same trunk of the same tree." That tree may have come from an African seed, but it couldn't have taken root anywhere but the Americas.

Sometimes the musicians who excel most are those who have come from different disciplines: the exceedingly charismatic Panamanian American Rubén Blades, for instance, who received a doctorate in international law from Harvard University before he became one of the greatest salsa composers and singers of all time; so great, that he even went back to Panama to run for president in 1994. Or Tito Puente, the Puerto Rican king of mambo, who served in the US Navy during World War II and then went to the prestigious Juilliard School on the G.I. Bill to study classical conducting before he picked up the beat and made music history with *"Oye Como Va."* There are hundreds of famous Latinos in popular music, to be sure, but there are also conductors of classical music, stars of opera as well as rap, composers of chamber music as well as composers for film. It is a tapestry so large and various that it defies facile summary.

## CLASSICAL MUSIC

My mother and my grandmother were maids when they were eight-year-olds. . . . Under all these bells of celebration, there is still a kind of struggle.

—Tania León, Cuban American composer,
on winning the Pulitzer Prize, 2021

In 1862, fourteen years after the United States appropriated half of Mexico, María Teresa Carreño, an eight-year-old musical prodigy whose family had fled the chaos of civil war in her native Venezuela, made her debut on a New York stage. Soon after, she performed for President Abraham Lincoln at the White House. She was a diminutive virtuoso with a furrowed brow, decked out in her frilly white dresses—a genius freak, a near carnivalesque sensation—molting later into "the Valkyrie of the Piano," a bantam-chested grande dame who played under the baton of many a distinguished composer, including Edvard Grieg and Gustav Mahler. That she was a cousin of Simón Bolívar's wife, María Teresa Rodríguez del Toro, whose tragic death at twenty-one—according to Bolívar—left the Liberator with little choice but to pursue revolution, gave the pianist a certain allure. She had even been given the dead woman's name.

As a child, Teresa was the pupil of the dazzling New Orleans creole musician Louis Moreau Gottschalk, composer of "Bamboula!," who rarely took students, but found the girl's artistry compelling; in turn, when Teresa was an adult, she became the teacher of the quintessentially romantic American composer, Edward MacDowell. A British conductor, besotted with her transcendent talents, wrote of her: "It is difficult to express adequately what all musicians felt about this great woman who looked like a queen among pianists—and *played* like a goddess. The instant she walked onto the platform her steady dignity held her audience. . . . Her masculine vigour of tone and touch and her marvellous precision on executing octave passages carried everyone completely away." In time, she turned her formidable skills to composing, and her famous waltz, "Mi Teresita," written for her daughter, became a staple of Hispanic repertory. In 1916, President Woodrow Wilson, a fan of her music, invited her back to the White House for a second performance, half a century after her first.

Throughout the nineteenth and twentieth centuries, Latino classical music, which had enjoyed a rich tradition in its origin countries, from Mexico's composer Manuel Ponce to Argentina's Astor Piazzolla—began to seep into the American consciousness with gifted immigrants such as Teresa—many of them the human chaff of war. Ernesto Lecuona, the great Cuban composer, who wrote his wildly successful "Malagueña" and "Siboney" in Havana in the 1930s, was forced by Castro's revolution to leave his beloved country. Sick with sadness, he immigrated to Tampa in the 1960s and proceeded to write gorgeous, Cuban-tinged themes for American film and radio. Much of his richly melodic music was introduced to Americans by his fellow émigré Desi Arnaz, the bandleader husband of comedienne Lucille Ball.

Political turmoil also brought Afro-Panamanian Roque Cordero to our shores. Cordero was a former plumber whose majestic ode to his country—the "Second Panamanian Overture"—premiered in

Minneapolis in 1946, even as two thousand Latin Americans of Japanese descent were released from US internment camps in Panama and sent home to uncertain futures. Cordero was fiercely loyal to his native land and highly aware of the ways the United States had defined it, but, because he could find little support for his music in Panama, he was forced to spend the rest of his days in America, composing groundbreaking compositions that combined popular Caribbean dance rhythms of *cumbia, tamborito,* and *pasillo* with a hyper-modern, twelve-tone technique. Clearly, he was trapped in an all too familiar Hispanic bind: he needed this country for work, but was hesitant to give up his native citizenship. As a result, he bounced from one midwestern university faculty to another—from Indiana to Illinois to Ohio—as he spooled an extraordinary body of Afro-Latino classical works.

Another Hispanic pioneer pushing the frontiers of American music was Pauline Oliveros, one of the most innovative voices in modern composition—an openly queer *tejana* from Houston, who died in 2016 at the age of eighty-four, leaving behind a remarkable trove of music and an institution to support its state-of-the-art science. Oliveros, a master of avant-garde electronic compositions, began her musical adventures when she received a child's accordion from her parents at the age of nine. She had always been a curious youngster, attuned to the lush music of the natural world around her in Texas. "I was hearing all these insects and birds and animals. . . . It was almost like a rainforest. So that *that* became the overall sound that I was interested in. I was fascinated with listening as far back as I can remember." And so, she began trying to capture those random sounds on her accordion, on different musical instruments, on the sonic possibilities of a tape recorder. If she couldn't reproduce a sound on the instrument in hand, she invented another. After a long, distinguished career in experimental music, and after many plaudits and awards, Pauline founded the Center for Deep Listening at Rensselaer Polytechnic Institute, where she focused on the healing, meditative qualities of sound.

From the nimble-fingered wizardry of Teresa Carreño in the nineteenth century to the auditory genius of Pauline Oliveros in the twenty-first, Latino composers have made an indelible mark on American classical music: Ernesto Lecuona was a lifelong friend of George Gershwin; and Mexican composer Carlos Chávez may well have inspired Aaron Copland's masterwork "El Salon México." But this country's classical musical stage has hardly been a welcoming terrain for Latinos in general. Only 4 percent of America's orchestra chairs are taken by blacks or Hispanics, a natural eventuality, one supposes, given that so few are lured to or trained for the field. There are, nevertheless, notable exceptions to that rule. One glorious aberration was Martina Arroyo, an Afro-Latina native of Harlem, who ventured into the rarefied halls of opera to become one of the first black Hispanics to prosper there. Martina's Puerto Rican parents had been well-off enough to send her to a flurry of music lessons as a child—first in piano, then ballet—until 1958, when she found her calling in her capacious and thrilling voice. Arroyo became the first of a generation of modern-day black female opera singers who would take prominent positions on the international stage: the superstar African American divas Leontyne Price, Grace Bumbry, Jessye Norman, and Denyce Graves.

Even so, classical music has proved difficult to navigate, especially for Hispanic women. Dominated for so many years by white males—more than 80 percent of all jobs in music continue to be taken by them—the field leaves little room for an aspiring Latina. When one manages to crash through the glass ceiling, it seems a victory for all. A case in point is Lina Gonzalez-Granados, a Colombian who immigrated to this country in 2008 to study at the Juilliard School. She had started her foray into music as a five-year-old girl, singing and dancing in folkloric groups in her native city of Cali, taking up piano, and finally reaching her true calling when, as a university student in Bogotá, she stepped onto a podium and conducted a youth orchestra. It was then she decided to dedicate herself fully to that pursuit. Lina arrived in the United States looking for opportunity, as any aspiring laborer might. Her calculus had been simple: here, there was work a female conductor could live on; in Colombia, there was none. That decision proved to be the right one. In 2020, Lina was granted American citizenship. In 2023, when she was named conductor of the Los Angeles Opera, a great roar of approval greeted her from that very Latino city.

Angelenos admire Lina for her passion and precision, her absolute command of the operatic craft, but they appreciate her perhaps even more for her pluck and spirit. This newly minted American dominates her perch with absolutely no doubt that she has every right to be there. I'm Hispanic, she tells us, and I'm a woman, take good notice. "This is how America looks."

## ROCK AND ROLL

It's like, "He's not black enough. He's not white enough. He doesn't speak Spanish. Who are we selling this to? Are you making urban music? Pop music? What kind of music you making?"

—Bruno Mars (born Peter Hernández),
rock musician, Puerto Rican / Filipino

By now, the Latino rock star is a familiar figure, but it wasn't always that way. At least in the American consciousness, the story begins with a sunny-faced boy from Pacoima, California, called Ritchie Valens, and it culminates with a "double-A-side" best-selling 45 RPM record, "La Bamba" and "Donna."

Ritchie had been born Richard Steven Valenzuela in 1941, the son of two Mexican American laborers who, at the time, were working for the war effort in a nearby munitions factory. When he was three, his parents separated, leaving him with his father, who worked a litany of random blue-collar jobs—farmworker, tree surgeon, miner, horse trainer—although he managed to inculcate a single, focused passion in his son: song.

Joseph Valenzuela loved the guitar and he loved to sing, especially Mexican folksongs. Little Ritchie grew up plucking at a tiny ukulele while his father sang, soon taking up the guitar, harmonica, Mexican trumpet, and drums. When his father died of complications due to diabetes, Ritchie was only eleven years old. His mother moved back into the modest family home with her third husband and three other children, and Ritchie mourned his father by losing himself in his music. By high school, he was known in his neighborhood for his sweet face, tough nature, strong voice, and catchy songs. Along with his teen band, the Silhouettes, he worked up a spirited tune, "Come On, Let's Go," and set about persuading his mother to hold back her monthly mortgage payment and rent the local Pacoima Legion Hall so that they could perform it live. Somehow, she agreed. Whether she reneged on her mortgage payment or actually sold tickets to pay it off is one of the details in question, but the rest is rock and roll history. Bob Keane, the owner of what would become Del-Fi Records, dropped in on the performance and, knowing a good thing when he heard it, signed him up. Ritchie was all of sixteen years old.

Keane changed the boy's name to Valens, fearing that Americans wouldn't be able to pronounce a name so foreign as Valenzuela, hired professional sidemen, and recorded "Come On, Let's Go," which was received well enough in early 1958. For summer, he planned the release of a more carefully promoted single. One side—the "A" side, meant to be the "hit" side—would be a slow, dreamy love song, "Donna," which Ritchie had composed and sung to his girlfriend over the phone. The other song, which Keane decided to put on the "B" side—the throwaway side—was an up-tempo rendition of an eighteenth-century Mexican wedding song, "La Bamba," sung in Spanish, a language Ritchie could pronounce well enough but didn't really speak. Keane suspected no one would pay attention to that one.

The record was released on November 15, 1958. The adulation was immediate, as were sales, skyrocketing the fledgling record to the top of the charts. Overnight, Ritchie Valens became the first Latino rock star and, to Keane's amazement, "La Bamba" was a runaway million-record sensation. *"Bai-la-la, baila la bamba!"* Americans across the nation were suddenly singing it, dancing it. Even those who didn't know a word of Spanish, had never seen a Mexican, bounced joyfully to the irrepressible wedding song, babbling the words. In the full fizz of that elation, a major concert tour was planned. Ritchie was to pack up, join other rock stars for the greatly anticipated Winter Dance Party—a barnstorming, twenty-four-day sweep of the Midwest—and start his first national tour just weeks later, in January.

On February 3, 1959, on a frigid, predawn morning in Mason City, Iowa, instead of boarding the tour's chartered bus, which was having mechanical problems, Ritchie Valens boarded a small plane with Buddy Holly and J. P. "Big Bopper" Richardson, hoping to spend a full night in clean clothes and a warm hotel bed rather than rattle down the road to Minnesota all night long. Waylon Jennings was supposed to be on board that airplane, but a coin toss won Ritchie his seat. And his fate. The plane went down no more than three minutes after takeoff, crashing into a cornfield, killing everyone on board and scattering debris across the snow. The Big Bopper was twenty-eight, Buddy Holly was twenty-two, Ritchie was seventeen. Twelve years later, in his epic song "American Pie," Don McLean would memorialize that grim February morning as the day the music died.

•   •   •

Ritchie Valens's name would live on as the Latino kid who kicked open the door and birthed a new breed of American rock star. One who could borrow from his heritage freely—one who might even sing in Spanish, if so inspired. Even if he didn't speak it all that well. Talented musicians began to be welcomed to the profession—first, as a trickle; then in a healthy rush—some reveling in their Latinidad, others simply performing as gifted Americans. Two musicians who embodied that range were the pan-Hispanic twosome Jerry Garcia of the Grateful Dead—who never spoke or sang in Spanish, although his ancestors had immigrated to California from northern Spain—and Enrique Iglesias—born in Madrid but raised in Miami—who began his career exclusively in Spanish and went on to sing in English and embrace a fully bilingual career, certainly one of the most successful Latino crooners of our day.

But there was more to come. Apart from the rich Mexican and

Spanish idioms that were present in the American southwest for half a millennium, new infusions began to enter America's musical bloodstream with the Caribbean influx of the sixties and seventies. The Cuban and Puerto Rican rhythms that began to flourish in the cities to which those immigrants were drawn—New York, Philadelphia, Miami—opened American auditory pathways to an altogether new sound.

Into that musical efflorescence came Gloria Estefan, a Havana-born dance-pop phenomenon whose father, José Manuel Fajardo, had been a personal bodyguard to Marta Fernández Miranda—wife of the infamous dictator Fulgencio Batista. Gloria was fourteen months old when Castro's rebel forces swept into the capital in 1959 and her father, tainted by his association to the presidential family, was forced to flee Cuba and settle in Miami. Fajardo went on to serve as a tank-division commander in the CIA-funded militia that, two years later, attempted the failed invasion of the Bay of Pigs. Captured on Cuba's beaches—quite providentially—by his own cousin, a communist soldier, Fajardo was imprisoned in Havana for two years. When released, he briefly rejoined his family in Miami only to volunteer as an Army infantryman in the Vietnam War. Shortly after his return from duty, he began to manifest symptoms of multiple sclerosis, probably as a result of exposure to Agent Orange. It is here that Gloria Estefan's story truly begins, for—from age eleven to sixteen—even as she minded her bedridden father and cared for her younger sister so that their mother could work, Gloria threw herself into her music. "I would lock myself up in my room for hours and just sing," she says. "I wouldn't cry—I refused to cry. Music was the only way." When, as a teenager, she met Emilio Estefan, leader of the Miami Latin Boys, and sang for him, he immediately recognized the power of her voice. The Miami Sound Machine (MSM) was the result, and Gloria its star attraction. She also became Emilio's wife.

The passage to stardom is never easy, and it certainly wasn't then. Again and again, the Estefans were told their band was not Latin enough for Latinos, not American enough for the *gringos*. The band persevered, nevertheless, eventually surprising even themselves by bringing out one hit after another: "Conga," "Rhythm Is Gonna Getcha," "Don't Wanna Lose You Now," alternating a driving, emphatically afro-Cuban beat with starry-eyed, romantic ballads and featuring Gloria's inimitably rich contralto voice at every turn. No one knew quite how to label what they were doing. Why are you mixing bongos with trumpets? industry professionals wanted to know. Why are you combining English and Spanish in a single show? Who is your audience, anyway? But the Estefans persisted defiantly with what they knew. When Gloria was booked as the opening act for the American Music Awards in 1988—the first Latin artist to be admitted to those giddy heights—directors tried to talk her into wearing fruit on her head. "Like Carmen Miranda?" she shot back. Like Chiquita Banana? She refused. I'm not who you think I am, she told them. *Yo sé quien soy.*

When all was said and done, the Estefans were simply following their instincts: mixing languages freely, blending *bembé* with conga, featuring heartbreakingly beautiful ballads alongside high-spirited dance. The amalgamation became so popular the world over that, come 2015, President Obama decided to honor Gloria and Emilio with Presidential Medals of Freedom. By bringing a distinctive Latin American idiom to American audiences, the White House citation told the Estefans, they had proved that "the power of music transcends cultural, social and economic boundaries." In other words, Cuban American music—with all of its insistence, spontaneity, and danceability—had become part of American song.

• • •

The Puerto Ricans, too, hewing to their rich Afro-Indigenous roots have had an equal impact on American popular music. Perhaps the most emblematic musician of the Boricua sound is Nuyorican singer Marc Anthony, who was born in Spanish Harlem in the 1960s, started out as a hawker of rodeo tickets, and today is known throughout the world as the top-selling salsa singer of all time.

Anthony came into the world as Marco Antonio Muñiz; his father, a hospital cafeteria worker by day and guitarist by night, had named him after the most famous Mexican balladeer of the day. The youngest of eight children, little Marco learned how to sing by clambering onto the kitchen table and performing for the rest of the family, understanding very early on that his future would be in music. By the time he was an adolescent, he had changed his name to Marc, dropped his surname, and began working as a "house" vocalist in clubs specializing in "freestyle," or hip hop, a form of electronic dance music that was taking New York City and Philadelphia by storm, particularly among blacks and Hispanics. Anthony became well enough known in hip hop circles that by 1992, he was part of the opening act for the legendary Puerto Rican musician Tito Puente at Madison Square Garden. Yet he was still unwilling to dedicate himself entirely to Latin music, at least not professionally. And then, on a taxi-ride through Manhattan one day, he heard a wistful ballad by Mexican singer-songwriter Juan Gabriel on the radio and was instantly persuaded to try the song himself. He decided to sing it up-tempo. In a salsa beat. A few months later, he featured *"Hasta Que Te Conocí"* on his debut studio album, *"Otra Nota."* The recording was an entirely new, thoroughly buoyant interpretation of the sentimental love song. It became an instant bestseller.

Indeed, everything seemed to change when he began to sing salsa; especially when he sang it in Spanish. "Salsa opened up a whole new world for me," he claims, "and I wanted to learn about it. My Spanish was horrible. In some of my early interviews, I couldn't conjugate a verb. But I plowed through it, and I taught myself. It was like seeing light for the first time. Salsa gave me a voice, and it gave me a platform, and it gave me an identity. I had found my culture, and I was not about to let go." With a remarkably versatile voice that could veer suddenly from an achingly romantic timbre to an electrifying salsa beat, Marc Anthony quickly became the global music legend his father always hoped he would be. In 2000, 2002, and 2013, he earned Guinness World Records for producing "the most year-end best-selling albums" in the Latin world by a solo artist.

As a result, he rose from humble roots to become one of America's wealthiest musicians, even after a number of expensive divorces from his ex-wives, including the Hollywood superstar Jennifer Lopez. Most important in his career, perhaps, Marc Antony has been a unifier. This is an artist who succeeds in attracting a wildly diverse Latino audience—as willing to promote Cuban rapper "Pitbull" Pérez as he is to perform with Colombian reggaeton artist Maluma, or Spanish opera star Placido Domingo, or fellow Boricuan rocker Bad Bunny. Beloved of three generations of *Boricuas*, *cubanos*, and *mexicanos* alike, Marc Anthony has become known the world over, from Rio de Janeiro to Tokyo. "It was bizarre," he said, when he was asked how he felt about performing for fans in such faraway places. "You do these festivals, and there's 40,000 people out there singing along with you. How did my music reach all the way over here?"

·   ·   ·

From the mid-1960s onward—that is, from Ritchie Valens to Marc Anthony and Gloria Estefan—as the number of Latinos in the United States mounted, the "Latin Music" sections of record stores began to grow to meet that population, and the Latin influence spread to genres across the music industry, even to those that ostensibly had nothing to do with Latinos. All at once, there was a samba and bossa nova rage, led by Brasil '66, with Sérgio Mendes at the helm and Antônio Carlos Jobim at its heart, inspiring the towering talent Stan Getz to new saxophone heights. But he was hardly the only one under the influence: the offshoots seemed endless. Rockabilly crooner Freddy Fender (whose real name was Baldemar Garza Huerta), took "Before the Next Teardrop Falls" to number one on the charts in 1975, and suddenly *música latina* was country music, too. The Latin beat seemed to permeate distant crannies of that exuberant era. Even trumpeter and producer Herb Alpert, a son of Ukrainian Jews, climbed aboard to astounding effect. He had grown up in East Los Angeles, after all, absorbed the Mexican vibe, and was welcomed to the fold readily along with his distinctly Mexican-sounding, all-horn band, the Tijuana Brass. Herb certainly *looked* Latino, and, so, for millions of fans, he passed as one. Come 1966, the Tijuana Brass would outsell the Beatles, moving more than thirteen million albums and winning legions to the "sound."

What is it about that half-Mexican, half-African sound—that Latino beat—that drives you? a journalist once asked Carlos Santana, possibly the most creative Latino rocker of our time, an artist credited with "giving voice to the invisible ones." "Because it's one hundred and fifty percent spirituality," he answered without hesitation. "It is meant to tame the beast in us. Glorify the light in you. That's what I love about it: the intensity of spirit. And the joy."

## THE SILVER SCREEN

> Latinos make up one of the largest demographics in the box office [25 percent of all box office sales]. . . . The fact that we're not seen on screen despite the vast contributions is devastating.
> —Gina Alexis Rodríguez, film actress, Puerto Rican

As for film and television, Latinos continue to await a representation that corresponds to their presence on American ground and their influence on the wider culture. The numbers are so anemic as to be in cardiac arrest. Only 5 percent of Hollywood's lead actors are Latino; the same can be said for co-leads. Only 3 percent of all screenwriters are Hispanic, which says something about the lack of Latino stories being told in film; there are even fewer directors. Although Latinos make up almost a quarter of the frequent movie-going public, only forty of the 1,335 directors employed in this country are Hispanic—and only one of those is a woman. The head of the inclusion initiative doing this research in 2019 was flabbergasted by the results. In all areas of the film industry, she concluded, "Latinos are vastly unrepresented." Worse, even as the Hispanic population has burgeoned in the last ten years, those percentage numbers haven't budged; if anything, they have slipped. Perhaps that is because there is not one Latinx executive chairman, senior executive, or unit head in the entire industry—a business that continues to be among the largest, most influential in America and the world. The situation is not much better in mainstream American television, where a mere 3 percent of lead actors are Latino, and a paltry 1 percent are showrunners—executives who have control over an entire series. The shortages are dire.

According to a professor at UCLA who has studied this travesty of inclusion, the reason for the neglect is because industry executives view

Latinos—as well as Asian Americans—as foreigners. "There's this misunderstanding of who the community is and what the audience wants
to see," she says. It begs the question of whether that prejudice wouldn't
prompt any Latino actor to concede they'd be better off changing their
name and calling themselves white or black. The chicano cartoonist Lalo
Alcaraz would argue that this is a problem throughout the arts, not just
the film business: "I get a lot of hate mail," he confided in his acceptance
speech for the prestigious Herblock Prize for excellence in editorial car-
tooning, because "there is still this American societal attitude that we
are foreign." Another scholar points out that if you do see a Hispanic
onscreen, it's likely *because* of his or her race or apparent "foreignness."
It's the ethnicity that gets the part, in other words, not the actor. Why,
asks the professor, don't they "just let them be people?"—the man on the
street, the kid playing ball, or the female executive?

The Hispanic relationship to Hollywood is a long, fraught story, and
its dysfunctionality stretches back to the beginning of the twentieth century. America's earliest silent films, released in the full flower of the Mexican Revolution, portrayed the Mexican as the most vile character on the
screen: a villain who robbed, murdered, pillaged, raped, cheated, gambled,
lied, and personified every vice imaginable. The "greaser" films followed—
*Tony the Greaser* (1911) and *The Greaser's Revenge* (1914) among them—and
all too soon the word *greaser* became America's synonym for "Mexican"
or "Latin." Mexico objected vociferously to this slander, causing industry
minders to issue warnings about these flagrantly racist characterizations,
but rather than change its ways, Hollywood stuck with its essential prejudice. Scriptwriters and directors began to set films in imagined Mediterranean lands that conjured an unmistakeable Mexican atmosphere and
characters that smacked of the old racist tropes: one character went so far
as to call himself "the bes' damn caballero" in town. No one was fooled.

Later, Hollywood tempered its portrayals, but only slightly. *Border-
town* (1935) featured Paul Muni (whose real name was Meshilem Meier
Weisenfreund) as a young Latino law school graduate whose true sav-
age Latino nature erupts in a violent courtroom scene causing him
to be disbarred, rejected, and spit out into the districts where Latinos

actually belong: the sleazy gambling halls. In fact, Paul Muni became Warner Bros.'s resident Latin, along with Ricardo Cortez (whose real name was actually Jacob Krantz). The pseudo-Latins were getting all the parts, and the growing Mexican American population was left to reap the prejudice. Things did improve slightly before the Second World War, when US government agents persuaded Hollywood to ease up; America needed the goodwill of its South American neighbors. But the image remained, vivid and unshakable. When my father traveled from Peru to enter MIT as a graduate student during that war, his American landlord would chide him: so do you wear feathers and stomp around barefoot?

During the 1950s, however, there was a brief glimmer of hope. A number of Hispanics began taking Hispanic roles and making no secret of their ethnicity. For every Marlon Brando playing in *Viva Zapata!*, there was a Ricardo Montalbán or Fernando Lamas turning in solid performances. Montalbán's first leading role was in *Border Incident* (1949), a film noir about a Mexican who sets out to foil a criminal gang that is smuggling farmworkers into the country. Montalbán made such an impression that he became the first Hispanic actor to appear on the cover of *Life* magazine. "I was king for a week," he commented later. "I thought the offers would flood in, but after a week—nothing." It has been that way for seventy more years. Any advances that were made in the 1950s were wiped away as the stereotypes came roaring back with films such as *The Good, the Bad, and the Ugly* (1966) and *Bring Me the Head of Alfredo García* (1974). Even real efforts to lure Hispanics to the cinema with *Walk Proud* (1979) or *Boulevard Nights* (1979) backfired when Hispanics noted that the focus was on urban gang violence.

Some would say those stereotypes were reinforced with Leonard Bernstein's *West Side Story*, which premiered on Broadway in 1957 to great acclaim and continued to grip American audiences for decades once the film version was released four years later. The musical had not helped with its raw portrayal of knife-toting, hyper-tribal, highly strung Puerto Ricans. As the *Los Angeles Times* pointed out, the plot, music, and script had been conjured by four Jewish men, after all (Leonard Bernstein, Stephen Sondheim, Jerome Robbins, and Arthur Laurents), and one even admitted he was totally unfamiliar with the culture. "I've never been that poor!" Sondheim exclaimed. "And I've never even known a Puerto Rican!" As a result, the characters rendered were an offensive cliché: thick accents, dark skin, and a dagger-quick propensity for violence. On top of that, there was only one Puerto Rican actor in the cast, Rita Moreno, and to her consternation, she was painted brown. When she objected and told the makeup artist that Puerto Ricans came in all colors, she was called a racist. The other Latino characters were played by a random assortment of non-Hispanic actors in uniform brownface: Russian-American Natalie Wood, Greek-American George Chakiris, and Filipino José De Vega. Little wonder that Puerto Ricans were furious.

All the anger came slamming back with *Fort Apache, the Bronx* (1981), starring Paul Newman as the good cop who is making his way among the impoverished Puerto Ricans of the South Bronx, all of them criminals, prostitutes, and murderers. Even his Latina girlfriend is a dope addict. Forty years after the uproar that film caused, little has improved. "White Hollywood does not want to tell the real stories of Latinos," veteran actor Edward James Olmos told a US Senate Judiciary Committee hearing in 2020. In fact, Latinos "are in a worse place now," he claimed, than they were in 1964 when he began his career—when stars such as Raquel Welch (Jo Raquel Tejada) were being made to feel they had to purge every vestige of their Latinidad from their actors' resumés. Or when television networks made no mention that Lynda Carter, the actress who breathed life into Wonder Woman, was half Mexican and proud of it. "Just because there are several successful Latino actors does not mean that Latinos are making it in Hollywood," Olmos added, hammering the point home. By now, the slight of omission is more than a sensitive point with Hispanics; it provokes passionate outrage.

Indeed, in 2022, when Hollywood released Lin-Manuel Miranda's and Quiara Alegría Hudes's *In the Heights*, about a largely Dominican neighborhood in New York, Afro-Latinos complained that the film misrepresented the true reality of the place by using actors who were either African Americans or light-skinned Hispanics when, in fact, a large portion of the population in the Heights is like them: not Black exactly, nor white Hispanic, but

Spanish-speaking Afro-Latinos. Even Miranda and Hudes, Puerto Ricans themselves—even the star of the racially conscious, runaway Broadway hit *Hamilton*—couldn't get the ethnicities right. Why? Some might say that it all goes back to the lack of Latinos at the top of the film industry, the dearth of representation in the director's chair; but here was Miranda, an example of a Latino at the very apogee of his trade who, according to his own Caribbean cohort, was getting things wrong. We are complicated, Hispanics seemed to be saying; don't reduce us to generalities, don't depict us as "white-passing Latinx people." Get the neighborhood right.

In the end, the underrepresentation and vilification is damaging, not only to Latinos but also to Americans as a whole. As an art form, the movie is a powerful instrument; perhaps the most powerful of all. "Nothing attacks the subconscious more," says Olmos. "You sit down before a theater screen, a dark room, with no peripheral vision. Everything goes into the subconscious, and it stays there." The compound effect is staggering: we are, as far as America's most powerful media is concerned, greasers, liars, thieves, criminals, and even when you clean us up and send us to law school, we are liable to trip and go haywire. That is the image of Latinos that former president Trump has used to pernicious effect. "That's why our children are in cages," one activist has commented. That's why a white supremacist with an assault rifle and a mind to kill Mexicans can stride into a Walmart in El Paso and kill twenty-three of them, injuring two dozen more. The smearing and neglect of American Hispanics is, the *Los Angeles Times* agreed, "one of Hollywood's biggest open wounds."

## WRITERS

One press account said I was an overnight success. I thought that was the longest night I've ever spent.

—Sandra Cisneros, poet and novelist, Chicana

As a Latina who has made a comfortable life in the world of media and books, it's easy for me to be deluded into believing that all's well in this corner of America. They hired me, after all. They published me, too. So many of my friends, in fact, have ended up happily published and enthusiastically received.

The truth is that this tiny, relatively new population of writers has been painfully difficult to accumulate. The late, great Chicano novelist Rudolfo Anaya, whose *Bless Me, Última*—now widely considered to be the first major Latino novel—was rejected by a slew of mainstream publishers before it was released to great acclaim in 1972 by a tiny, brief-lived Chicano outfit at the University of California at Berkeley, Quinto Sol. Anaya was later joined by the prodigiously talented Mexican American writer Cecile Pineda, whose searingly brilliant, hallucinatory *Face* was the first novel by a Latina to win a mainstream publisher's attention. It was an extraordinary achievement, as powerful as Franz Kafka's *Metamorphosis* or Albert Camus's *The Stranger*, and yet, sadly, Pineda is hardly known to American readers outside the academy.

Nevertheless, a door had opened. Soon Richard Rodriguez was shattering assumptions about our ethnicity with his bracing memoir *Hunger of Memory*, which ripped the roof off the false narrative that all Hispanics—or even all Mexican Americans—are alike and neatly definable. Affirmative action was an insult, said Rodriguez, and bilingual education an injury. He was as American as anyone else, according to him, assimilation had made him so, and he refused to play into anybody's expectation of what a Hispanic should be. Not much later, in 1985, the Chilean supernova Isabel Allende took American readers by storm with her international blockbuster *The House of the Spirits*. Here was Latin America in all its explosive glory, and she proceeded to bring it to us again and again in Spanish, imagining all the rest of her books in her native language and writing them on our shores. Within a few years, Allende was granted US citizenship, allowing us to claim her many bestsellers as part of the Latino literary canon.

The late 1980s also brought us the Cuban American novelist Oscar Hijuelos, whose vibrant, rhythm-infused Pulitzer Prize–winning *The Mambo Kings Play Songs of Love* painted a profoundly realistic portrait of lost hopes and squandered fortunes in this land of American Dreams.

His novel was the first to win a Hispanic the Pulitzer Prize. It garnered a legion of readers and went on to box-office success as a film, but it wasn't long before there were complaints about the cast: Hijuelos's characters, unforgettably Cuban in his book, had been played by an Italian and a Spaniard in the movie, and the accents were all wrong, the body language off mark. Once again, the Pooh Bahs of American culture hadn't understood what a variegated tribe we could be.

All the same, by the 1990s, publishing houses were beginning to awaken to Hispanic writers, if only because a few seemed to be attracting the limelight. None of it had been easy. Even the trailblazers could tell stories about the struggles they encountered in their efforts to get published, much less be allowed through a New York editor's doors. But little by little, the ranks grew. I have been fortunate to watch this germination in the course of my publishing career. Indeed, many of the authors mentioned here are my friends and have contributed their thoughts generously to this book. Surrounded by such a glorious accumulation of talent, I could be fooled into thinking that all is well in the field of Latino letters.

But I would be wrong: between 1972, when Rudolfo Anaya, son of a New Mexican sheepherder, published *Última* and founded the canon, and 2008, when Junot Díaz, son of the Dominican Republic as well as the mean streets of New Jersey, published his lyrical, bumptious, at once sublime and profane novel *The Brief Wondrous Life of Oscar Wao*, success was actually restricted to a privileged few. There were no Latino editors in mainstream publishing, much less heads of houses, and books by Hispanics—even those that managed to climb onto the covers of book review sections—were considered to have little sales potential; what editors called having "no legs." Those were, in fact, the very words used at editorial meetings during my years in publishing whenever a book by a Latino author was brought to the table. Who in the world was going to buy it? The Latino population was considered indigent, linguistically challenged, not a natural target market for books. With their immigrant stories, American Latino writers seemed totally unlike the dazzling Latin American boom, the "exotic" stars coming to us from abroad: Gabriel

García Márquez, Jorge Luis Borges, Mario Vargas Llosa, Carlos Fuentes. Which is to say that, for most Hispanic Americans who harbored writing aspirations, things had changed very little by the turn of the twenty-first century. The publishing houses were overwhelmingly white, and so were their tastes. The few editors interested in "Hispanic" books seemed to prefer stories about Spanish speaking people abroad, translated from Spanish. Certainly not those that were being written in English, by Latinos. In the meantime, by 2005, the Latino population of this country had exploded to forty-two million. One out of seven people walking American turf was Hispanic, and likely proficient in English.

It took more than a decade and then some, but by 2018, the mood—if not the landscape—began to improve. One by one, a few Latinos were brought into the publishing fold. Pressured by arguments about "social capital" as well as a stern hectoring by the mounting diversity, equity, and inclusion movement (DEI), which originated in the 1960s civil rights era, but started in earnest in 2019—publishers began to do the counting: How many in their ranks were Latinos? And how much of the reading population out there was Latino? What was the potential market and how best to approach it, develop it, serve it, profit from it? Hopes on all sides began to run high. At the same time, there was a great deal of looking over one's shoulder. The rush of enlightenment about inclusion also meant representation by African Americans, Native Americans, South Asians, Middle Easterners, East Asians, black Africans, LGBTQ+, and people with disabilities. DEI meant everybody, and it was difficult to avoid a sense of competition in the hires.

Today, for all the brouhaha about diversity, equity, and inclusion, the needle has hardly moved at all. According to a report by the US Government Accountability Office, Latino numbers in American media have moved up by a mere 1 percent in the course of the last ten years. All the fine journalism about Latinos being done by Ray Suarez, formerly of public television, or María Hinojosa of *Latino USA*, or the efforts of highly charismatic Spanish-language broadcasters such as María Elena Salinas and Jorge Ramos, seem to amount to naught as far as the vast American media machine is concerned. The advances have been minuscule. Today, only 8 percent of the media industry is Hispanic; and, in the whole of book publishing—a gargantuan business that sold 800 million print units last year—only 7 percent of its workers (all authors, editorial staff, and publicists taken together) are Latino. "This invisibility," declared Representative Joaquín Castro, "means that Americans don't know who Latinos are or how we have contributed to the success of our nation." What is clearly needed, he added, is a call to action to enable the Latino to finally be part of the larger American narrative. It is, by any measure, a sad state of affairs when such a demand needs to be made for one-fifth of the nation's people—a population that, in itself, equals the size of sovereign countries. Indeed, we are a population larger than all of Colombia, all of Argentina, and more than half of Mexico.

And yet, despite the scarcity of representation, a small, but determined army of Latinx authors continue to contribute to the narrative, telling penetrating stories—fact or fiction—about our invisible Americans.

Perhaps the most revelatory are those about queer life by Cheríe Moraga, Gloria E. Anzaldúa, Benjamin Alire Sáenz, and Carmen Maria Machado, reflecting the strong presence of LGBTQ+ among our number. Indeed, 7 percent of all Hispanics identify with this label—more, if we only count those under twenty-five years old. Nearly 12 percent of Generation Z Latinos (born between 1997 and 2012)—which means more than twice the number for whites or blacks—have declared themselves LGBTQ+. The reason is likely because the entire population of Latinos skews young, and "coming out" is clearly a young phenomenon. Or perhaps it is because they were always there among us and an overpowering macho culture muzzled them. Whatever the case, it is the writers who are bringing us this news. We would do well to pay attention.

Unlike Lou Castro, the first American Latino baseball player who had countless aliases and identities and claimed few concrete facts, we are generally less afraid to tell the truth about ourselves. Authors such as Mexican American Reyna Grande and Ecuadorian American Karla Cornejo Villavicencio have stepped forward to describe the excruciating—alternately humiliating and exhilarating—experience of crossing the frontier to a new, undocumented American life. The vast majority of Americans over the centuries have actually come via this route—helter-skelter, stepping onto the gangplanks, bearing no papers—whether or not this is part of their collective memory. At ports of entry, they were inspected and admitted, unless they fell into one of the excluded categories: Asians, polygamists, paupers, anarchists, the "feebleminded," the debauched, the insane, or those with "a loathsome, contagious disease." Yet, when it comes to Latinx, we are made to believe that entering without documentation is something new, something for which we should take the blame.

When all is said and done, perhaps we are best served by writers like the Peruvian American Carlos Lozada, the brilliant editorial commentator for the *New York Times*, who, by focusing on America in general—reveling in its glories and eccentricities, fixing a gaze on the American experiment—will insure that we become part of the broader American story. Mexican American Linda Chavez, former White House advisor, insists that the best thing that could happen in LatinoLand—indeed, what is surely bound to happen—is that we will all ultimately knit ourselves quietly, confidently, into the fabric of America. That we will become that man on the street, that kid playing ball, that female executive. It may take concerted agency. It may take a sudden revelation on the part of our fellow Americans that we are a population good and true. It may require historians to argue that this is a land where we have always belonged.

• • •

Few Latinos have done more to capture the American imagination than the writer Sandra Cisneros, whose *The House on Mango Street*, released in 1983, represented a milestone in the country's literary canon. It was one of the very first books by a Chicana to be published by a mainstream publisher; the first to win millions of readers and become required reading in classrooms across the nation. Cisneros went on to publish more works that resonated with fellow Hispanics and spoke powerfully to the marginalized, among them *Woman Hollering Creek*, *A House of My Own*, and *Caramelo*. Today, more than forty years after the appearance of that first seminal work, she is considered a paragon of Latino identity and a *curandera* (healer) of the Latino soul. Struggling with how to close this book—which she helped me name—I am suddenly drawn to recall a telephone conversation we had not long ago.

In it, we spoke of some pressing subjects: The shock of thousands of unaccompanied minors clamoring at the border. The dangerous echo chamber of hate-mongering social media. *La falta de amor, cariño, y ternura*—the lack of love, warmth, and tenderness—here, in El Otro Lado. The vacuum of leadership among Latinos (*nos falta un Gandhi, un Jesse Jackson, un Martin Luther King, Jr.*). Who will be brave enough to stand and deliver us from this fog of invisibility?

"I'm an amphibian," she told me in that conversation—as comfortable in water as I am on land—"a creature of *las Americas*, north and south." She is the granddaughter of immigrants, a second-generation American born in Chicago, and it is the dance between cultures that interests her most. She recalled for me the endless tap, tap, tap of her father's upholstery hammer as he labored to put something on the table, feed her and her six brothers. It seems she has taken to recording sounds that might resemble it—sounds of the every day. The decisive clack of a closing door, for instance. The whir of the *cuchillero*, village knife sharpener, as he makes his way past her window. The brisk *plic-plic-plac* of paws crossing the floor. A natural listener, she can train her ear on the commonplace. But she has moved so often in her life that she feels most affiliation with that which intrudes on the customary: the interrupters, the recent arrivals, the immigrants who never quite emerge from *nepantla*—that realm of the in-between.

Now, having settled in San Miguel de Allende, a picturesque village nestled deep in the mountains of Mexico, she lives in a sun-drenched house filled with colorful relics, copious green plants, and four yappy little dogs, just a few kilometers from the *ranchería* her grandparents left behind almost a century ago. The inspiration to return to those ancestral lands came all of a sudden in her then-home in San Antonio, Texas, when she awoke in the middle of the night with a voice ringing in her head. It said: You are not in your house. "It was clear immediately what that message meant," she says. "I understood that I needed to trust my intuition, go back, learn something more about who I was."

And so this seminal writer of the Latino experience is there, in the vertiginous, cobblestoned streets of that tiny, sixteenth-century town, listening for sounds of a long-ago past, "trying to understand my multiplicity."

*My multiplicity.* Somehow that phrase encompasses everything I'm trying to say. How do we hope to understand the *indio* in us; the *africano* in us; the *europeo* in us; the Asian, Jew, Spaniard, and Arab of us? The tall and short? The dizzying kaleidoscope of us? It is a lifetime quest unto itself. "Pay attention," we say to each other. We can do this.

# EPILOGUE

## Unity

Let us hope we have the courage to stand alone and the audacity to band together.
> —Eduardo Galeano, Uruguayan author and journalist, 2010

There are those who believe that LatinoLand is a mythical construct, not a real place with real people who share a strong identity and a sense of belonging. I certainly would have been among those skeptics more than a half century ago when I arrived in northern New Jersey and saw no LatinoLand beyond the four walls of my house. There are also those who not only doubt LatinoLand, but also doubt the very existence of Latin America as a place of origin, arguing that it is too nebulous a concept, a region with no rigorous logic or concrete parameters. It is most assuredly not continental or geographical, because then where is Brazil, or Haiti, or Jamaica? It is not linguistic, because how about Quechua, or Nahuatl, or Guaraní? Nor can it be described in any scientific or thorough way. To those doubters, Latin America is a bogus notion, not a bona fide region with a clear civilization or a well-demarcated, unique culture. It is, if anything, a confounding expanse somewhere south of this very real America; and so, as a result, LatinoLand, its supposed offspring, is little more than a limbo of random, provisional souls hoping to molt some day into genuine Americans.

Raul Yzaguirre, the founder and former president of the National Council of La Raza (NCLR)—one of the largest national organizations dedicated to promoting policies that serve Latino interests—once described Hispanics as "a national community with a shared past, a common agenda, and a united future." To depict a vast multitude of tens of millions of America's Latinos as a constituency of common interests is a powerful conceit, even if there are glaring internal contradictions within the assertion. How can one possibly conflate the interests of white, conservative, largely well-to-do Florida Cubans with the brown, liberal, largely low-income Mexicans of South Texas and the struggling, urbanite Afro-Caribbeans of New York? How can one claim to represent the hopes and ambitions of educated South American professionals as well as those of Northern Triangle refugees who live by dint of their sweat and brawn?

Indeed, La Raza's aspirations appeared to make more sense back in 1968 when the council was small, southwestern, and the great majority of nine million "Spanish Americans" in this country were of Mexican ancestry. By 2004, however, almost forty years later, when Janet Murguía took over the organization, there were more than forty million— almost five times as many—and great waves of newcomers had come from countries other than Mexico. Murguía led La Raza for thirteen years before she decided in 2017—in her mission to represent all Latinos, whether or not they consider themselves part of "the race"—to change the organization's name to UnidosUS. And, so, unity became her credo and trademark. During Murguía's tenure alone, the Latino population has doubled yet again, meaning that UnidosUs in now charged with serving and unifying every color and culture of this colossal throng.

Much the same has happened with the League of United Latin American Citizens (LULAC), the oldest Latino-serving organization, founded in 1929 to "advance the economic condition, educational attainment, political influence, housing, health, and civil rights" of Mexican Americans. Favoring strong immigration laws, the repudiation of any residual loyalty to Mexico, and total, absolute assimilation, the league's goal in an increasingly racist nation was to hammer home that its constituents were white and, therefore, deserved full equality. The organization's influence proceeded to swing between bad and good years, unable to establish a firm financial footing, with some Mexicanos seeing LULAC as a band of *vendidos*—spineless flunkies who had sold out to the very Anglos who had stolen their lands. Finally, in 1970, as immigrants from other countries began to arrive in greater numbers, LULAC changed its focus from Mexican Americans to "Hispanics," and then to "Latinos." Today, under the leadership of a feisty, fearless, politically astute politician, Domingo García, it boasts 135,000 employees in forty-eight states. Like UnidosUS, LULAC has been obliged, by virtue of the population's ever evolving nature, to fling open its doors to a variety of cultures. And yet, being an organization faced with a booming miscellany, the challenge has been how to define it. Labels we never chose for ourselves— Hispanic, Latino, Latinx, Latine—have been adopted and rejected and adopted again willy-nilly, one after the next, causing grave doubts about their validity and reflecting the extent of our identity crisis. All of this, mind you, in an effort to portray us as a strong and unified whole.

There were objections along the way. Sociologists scoffed at the notion of conflating so many disparate identities, insisting that a single descriptor could not possibly capture us all. To one of them, the label "Hispanic" was a flawed statistical concoction that "has hardly any relation to the real world." She went on to say, "To speak about 'Hispanic' fertility, child-rearing habits, health, subculture, migration patterns, etc., is to engage in empty talk at best, or in stereotyping." To her, in other words, the department of study that Eliseo Pérez-Stable would come to head at the National Institutes of Health—a group of dedicated researchists committed to analyzing the shared medical issues that Latinos face—was bunk.

As the twenty-first century ground ahead and the ideological divide in the United States deepened, the burgeoning Latino population became a plum to be relied on or courted, depending on whether the political suitor was liberal or conservative. Counting allegiances became of paramount concern and the Latino National Political Survey was formed to do just that. In 1992 it set out to collect basic data on the political values, attitudes, and behaviors of Mexican, Puerto Rican, and Cuban Americans in the far points of the triangle they inhabit. According to researchers, the results were surprising. On the whole, "Latinos did *not* view themselves as having common concerns." Fewer than 14 percent in any one group considered themselves having anything in common with the others. They might be "somewhat similar" in some aspects, the respondents conceded, but the differences outweighed the similarities. Moreover, they broadly preferred to be identified by their national origin, not by any artificially imposed label; many insisted on being called, quite simply, "an American."

Additionally, perhaps because of a lack of contact between the subgroups—they lived on opposite sides of the continent, after all—there were startling revelations about how little they knew about one another. Mexican Americans said they felt more kinship to Anglos or African Americans than they did to Cubans or Puerto Ricans. Not that they held any negative perceptions about those populations, they simply didn't know them. Mexicanos had more regular contact with Anglos or blacks than they did with supposed Latino siblings. Similarly, Cubans reported they were closer to whites and elite South Americans than they were to their purported southwestern or northeastern kin. The reports concluded that no presuppositions could be made about the larger cohort; Latinos simply did not constitute a communal or political bloc. But the 1992 survey's final judgment also made it very clear that its researchists considered Latinos a *potential* community. It might very well be that as the twenty-first century unfolded, Latinos would come to embrace the identity and be persuaded that they had common values, linked histories, and a shared fate. But the message for the moment was crystal clear: the idiosyncrasies were too compelling. Unity was a distant mirage.

Murguía—daughter of a Mexican American steelworker as well as a sister to six who, like her, grew up in cramped quarters, went on to postgraduate educations, and excelled in their respective fields—is not cowed by those conclusions. "We are *together*," she tells me with no little conviction. "Together doesn't mean we are the *same*." She points out that other Americans—German Americans, Anglo Americans, African Americans—are not asked if they are a political bloc, why should we be expected to produce one? She continues the argument undaunted, determined, as if I need convincing. "We are like-minded. We have our commonalities: a powerful work ethic, a deep appreciation for family, faith, patriotism, culture, food, music, art."

If Janet Murguía is obsessed with the Holy Grail of unity—with gathering our unruly flock under the banner of UnidosUS—Mark Hugo Lopez of the Pew Research Center is sticking fast to the numbers. Lopez describes himself as a Chicano, from a family that has inhabited this country for generations. The division he leads at Pew has dedicated years and considerable manpower to locking down what census reports cannot hope to deliver: how we raise our children, where we worship, what we earn, what we've learned, how we dance, how we feel, where we're headed. According to Lopez's calculus, the "potential" unity mentioned fleetingly in the 1992 survey and passionately pursued by the likes of Murguía, is actually coming to pass.

As we advanced into the new century, as the media riveted its attention on our growing presence—as the community began to be more aware of its nascent power—a sense of affiliation emerged. It was almost as if the media attention alone had fired something in the Latino subconscious. In a recent "pan-ethnicity" report, Pew found that almost 40 percent considered Latinos from different countries to have "a lot in common," while another 40 percent agreed that they share at least "some" traits. Which is to say that a whopping eight out of ten Latinos feel a kinship to the larger group. Of these, Salvadorans were the most enthusiastic about our commonalities; Puerto Ricans, the least. Those who speak Spanish at home agree broadly that Latinos, no matter where they're from, have much in common. There is also no doubt that immigrants from Latin America's educated white elite population, no matter the country, feel very much at home with one another.

And yet, as Lopez points out cautiously, there is also the phenomenon of ethnic attrition: as generations pass, descendants of Latinos may no longer feel a part of the community. This can happen with breathtaking speed, especially if those descendants are products of intermarriage. Indeed, my sister, who was born in Lima, Peru, does not check the Hispanic/Latino box on questionnaires. As far as she is concerned, she is a white American. And so, although we were raised under the same roof, with the same parents, we have opposing notions of who we are. When, at a casual meal, I venture the question "How many Latina friends do you have, Vicky?," to my great surprise, she answers, "None," and then she pauses. "Apart from you."

I am so taken aback by her answer that I can hardly swallow. That absence—that deprivation—galvanizes something in me. Here is a woman who speaks perfect Spanish, reads avidly in her father tongue, paints compelling landscapes of her Peruvian childhood, and is so accomplished in her scholarly career that Latino rosters would be proud to count her. And yet she names me as her only Latina friend. Suddenly I want her to meet everyone I know. I live in a capacious, happy world of Latinidad, populated by many colors and breeds of friends who share my Latin American heritage. Now, at our advanced ages, I worry for my big sister.

But soon enough I find that her reluctance to count herself Hispanic is even more magnified in our children. They are all adults now, largely married to non-Hispanics, hard at work in demanding professional careers. When I ask this younger generation the same questions—Do you identify yourselves as Latinos in any documentation? In the voting booth, your place of work, or the doctor's office? Do you have close Latino friends? Do you still speak Spanish?—my nieces and nephew answer in negatives. No, no, and no. Of course, as doctors, lawyers, and architects facing a public world, they encounter plenty of Latinos in their work, but no, they no longer identify themselves as Latinos in documentation. They may have claimed Hispanicity once upon a time—in school applications, for instance—when they were living at home with a strongly affiliated Latino parent. But not as adults. Not in their own homes. They feel that doing so would be presumptuous, bordering on a lie; it would be appropriating an identity they no longer feel is theirs. My daughter, married to an Irish Slavic American, agrees. My son, married to a Mexican American who has never spoken Spanish and is from a family that has lived in Texas for generations, says the same. This, it suddenly strikes me, is an uncounted, undocumented population of a different kind.

Ethnic attrition is very real. The problem, according to the National Academy of Sciences, is that we can't simply use statistics from US-born citizens who self-identify as Hispanics and hope to form an accurate picture of the whole, nor—if the response patterns are so patchy—can we measure in any scientific way the process of assimilation. Science can account for random answers, but it can't account for selective ones. Any poll would eventually run up against a family like mine, in which some of us choose to identify strongly, proudly, fiercely as Latinos, and some of us don't register our ethnicity at all. If we are unable to count ourselves accurately, with rigor, how can we expect to measure the population? And so, Latinidad becomes a slippery, elusive condition. But ask those same family members whether they think there is such a thing as unity for Latinos, and the overwhelming answer is *yes*. There is unity, they say—it is out there. Is there potential power in that unity? Another resounding *yes*. The business of identity may be complicated, the political affiliation shifty, but, as contradictory as it sounds, Latino unity is surprisingly hale and strong.

I see that this is so when I take my cohort's pulse in this book of a thousand voices. "Yeah, we're all different," says the prize-winning Dominican American novelist Junot Díaz. "Latinidad is aspirational. Maybe even a futurity. But say one bad word about a Mexicano, and just watch us all fall into line." No one, perhaps, has united Latinos more than Donald Trump when, in his 2016 campaign to win the White House, he loosed a litany of vile accusations against Mexicans. Just as there are no atheists in the trenches, there are no Latino fence-sitters when we are under attack. As the great Uruguayan writer Eduardo Galeano once wrote, it takes audacity to band together.

Sometimes this reflex is prompted when we least expect it. Antonio Tijerino, a Nicaraguan American who directs the Hispanic Heritage Foundation—a group committed to nudging talented young Latinx up the ladder to leadership—tells of an incident that flipped his normally affable nature into a white-hot fury. He is strolling down the garden path of a fancy country club in suburban Maryland, headed toward the tennis courts to pick up his son, when suddenly he is pulled out of his reverie by the sound of angry shouting: "Hey, you! What do you think you're doing?" He spins around to see an older gentleman, shaking a furious finger. "What am I doing?" Antonio says. "I'm taking a walk."

"Well, get to work!" the white shouts back. Now it is Antonio whose indignation rises. He roars back at the man, "See over there? That's my kid taking a lesson there. I wouldn't belong to your shitty club if you paid me!"

No sooner does he say this than the club's manager emerges and hurries toward them. When he hears out Antonio and understands that this is a father with a son in the club's summer camp, he apologizes. The older man does, too. But Antonio is not so easily mollified; he is livid at the arrogance, the affront, the barefaced racism. He points to the Hispanic gardener who is toiling in the dirt in the distance. "See him?" Antonio bellows. "That's the person you should be apologizing to. He works harder than you or I have ever worked in our lives." When I ask Antonio where the gardener was from, he answers, "I have no idea. El Salvador? New Mexico? Bolivia? It didn't matter even for a moment to me. That man was *us*."

There is no one more focused on the question of "us" right now than the Latino entrusted with imparting our collective identity in the future National Museum of the American Latino, due to open on the National Capital Mall in 2035. He is Jorge Zamanillo, a Miami Cuban who thought he would grow up to be a trumpeter in a salsa band until he toured Washington as a high schooler and—trudging through two feet of snow, visiting one museum after another—fell in love with archaeology. Today, charged with fashioning a comprehensive portrait of a people and their history, he is unshrinking, resolute. "We're not that different!" he says, unvexed by my question. "Hard as that 'us' may be to describe, we share a common bond." It might be embedded in the past: in Spain's colonization of the Americas, in the rawness of our culture clash, in our habit of race mixing, in the influence of Catholicism, the shock of immigration, the sharing of an ancestral language; or it may be in blood itself. Like a true archaeologist, Zamanillo talks about the way his ancestry tests have allowed him to dig down though the centuries to reveal that, while he may have thought of himself as Cuban American, he has DNA relatives in Mexico, Argentina, Colombia, Peru. I nod vigorously when he tells me this: I, too, have found I have living DNA relatives in Mexico, Nicaragua, Cuba, Chile, and Spain. He goes on to say that we may not recognize, or even perceive the bond that unites us; the one that is buried deep in our history. "But you feel it in your bones. You taste it in the food. You feel it in the music."

Just go to a fiesta. It is there.

# ACKNOWLEDGMENTS

I owe this book to hundreds of voices—gathered in the course of a lifetime as well as during the three intense years it has taken me to research and write this book. There are two hundred and thirty-seven interviews reflected on these pages. Sometimes those voices arrive unexpectedly, serendipitously, when I least expect them. I have learned to pick up my ears, stop in my tracks, and listen.

One of those voices came in a telephone call not long ago, as I careened down Sixth Avenue in a Manhattan taxi, hurrying to a meeting. My cellphone did not reveal the caller, but I took the call anyway and a familiar voice greeted me in Spanish. It was Harold Forsyth Mejía, the tall, amiable, distinguished Peruvian politician and diplomat, ambassador to a handful of countries including the United States. He was calling to ask if he could introduce me to a journalist. I agreed. He then asked what I was working on. "Really? The Latino population of the United States!" he exclaimed when I told him, not hiding his delight. And then he told me this story.

It was 2014. A seasoned diplomat for thirty-seven years, Harold had been the ambassador to the United States for three of them, all during the presidency of Barack Obama. In the course of his tenure, it had been announced that the Latino population of the United States had surpassed fifty million and was climbing vertiginously to greater heights. It was an astounding revelation, Harold tells me, a watershed moment. At a gathering of Latin American CEOs organized by the Mexican embassy, Harold told the president, Do you know what those fifty-five million signify, Mr. President? And then he carefully explains it. "Of course, the country where Spanish is spoken most is Mexico," he says, recounting the conversation. "It is the largest Spanish-speaking country in the world. The *numero uno*. But can you guess which is the second? The second is the United States." Here, he pauses to let that sink in.

And it does. What sinks in as I fly down the avenue, tossing about in my New York cab with my phone firmly against my ear, is that even a decade ago—even at fifty-five million—the Latinos of this country already represented a population larger than Colombia, Argentina, or Peru, even Spain. Now, with almost ten million more, what we have is a mind-reeling multitude. A whole country unto itself. A monumental nation. Like any nation, it has its liberals, its conservatives, its spectrum of colors, its panoply of traditions, its inevitable contradictions. But it is an entity, nevertheless, bound by language and history. "What strikes me as most important," the ambassador adds, punctuating his message, "is that the United States has yet to wake up to that reality. I said that at the time. It has yet to look around and develop that potential. You know what harboring such a majority of Latinos means? It can only mean that the United States has become part of Latin America." Here I could almost see the twinkle in the ambassador's eye, the playful smile, the sheer delight in the topsy turvy worldview he was offering the American president.

It is from such snapshots of perspective that this book was born. To list all the book's forebears—every voice that gave it another slant, a different nuance—would be impossible. Nevertheless, I am indebted to those who, like Harold, informed me, yet may not appear in this very personal portrait of LatinoLand. Those people know who they are.

Apart from my generous interviewees who are specifically mentioned in these chapters, I want to thank the following, either for their indispensable works, our conversations, their referrals, or our simple friendship: Rolena Adorno, Daniel Alarcón, Isabel Allende, Noé Álvarez, Cecilia C. Alvear, Quique Avilés, Irma Becerra Hernández, Geraldo Cadava, Ángel Cano, Francisco Cantú, Marta Casals Istómin, Patricia Cepeda, Raquel Chang-Rodríguez, Milton Coleman, Benji de la Piedra, Roxane Dunbar-Ortíz, Isabel and Ricardo Ernst, Kali Fajardo-Anstine, América Ferrera, Gabriela Flores, Eduardo Galeano, Cristina García, Domingo García, Mildred García, Henry Louis Gates, Dagoberto Gilb, Debra Gittler, Laura E. Gómez, Clara and Stephanie González, Juan González, Donald Graham, Greg Grandin, Micael Guzmán, John Hemming, Cristina Henríquez, Daisy Hernández, Juan Felipe Herrera, María Hinojosa, Sandra Jordan, Luz Lazo, John Leguizamo, Mirella and Daniel Levinas, Ada Limón, Carlos Lozada, Kelly Lytle-Hernández, Clara Martínez, Rubén Martínez, Juan Matéo, G. Cristina Mora, Ed Morales, Luis Alberto Moreno, Moisés Naím, Hilda Ochoa-Brillembourg, Ismael (Smiley) Ortíz, Alejandra Pizarro-Romann, Don Podesta, Maricel Quintana-Baker, Erika Quinteros Lucas, Jorge Ramos, Andrés Reséndez, Tomás Rivera, Ana Patricia Rodríguez, Richard Rodríguez, David Rubenstein, María Elena Salinas, Suzanne M. Schadl, Lacey Schwartz, Natalia Sobrevilla, Ray Suarez, Mauricio Tenorio-Trillo, Héctor Tobar, Sergio Troncoso, Luis Alberto Urrea, Patricia Veliz Macal, Marcela Valdes, Mario Vargas Llosa, Helena María Viramontes, Jorge Zamanillo, and the bilingual reading circle of the Literary Gypsies.

Institutionally, I owe an enormous debt of gratitude to Mark Hugo López, director of Hispanic Research at the Pew Research Center, who gave me raw graphs early on in this project and led me through the maze of ever-evolving statistics he oversees at Pew; Kevin Butterfield, director of the John W. Kluge Center, and his colleagues Daniele Turello and Travis Hensley, who offered me a much needed sanctuary in their offices at the Library of Congress; Jeffrey Walsh, founder and CEO of sooth.fyi, who allowed me early access to his formidable engine of research, which focuses on strictly reliable sources of internet information; the hundreds of families of CabanacondeCityColcaUSA, who welcomed me warmly into their close community in Montgomery County, Maryland; and, lastly, the many organizations committed to raising us up, among them

UnidosUS, the Hispanic Heritage Foundation, the Congressional Hispanic Caucus Institute, the Museum of the American Latino, and the League of United Latin American Citizens (LULAC).

I could not have written *LatinoLand* without the steady and stalwart support of my dear friend and agent, Amanda (Binky) Urban, who, for almost thirty years, has led me through the writing business like a sure-footed sherpa and plied me with invaluable, razor-sharp insights and observations along the way. I owe her the moon.

This represents my third book for veteran publishing executive Bob Bender, who was my colleague at Simon & Schuster before he became my editor. His encyclopedic brain, unerring pen, and Job-like patience have been a godsend for this humble writer. I am grateful, too, to my publisher Jonathan Karp for his unfailing support, and to all the staff at Simon & Schuster who stand behind Jon and Bob, especially Bob's assistant of many years, the gifted Johanna Li, my wonderful publicists Julie Prosser and Cat Boyd, and my keen-eyed copyeditor, Philip Bashe. Thanks also go to Phil Metcalf, Simon & Schuster's production editor, as well as talented designers Jackie Seow and Ruth Lee-Mui.

I have been fortunate to have family members with vividly idiosyncratic views of Latinidad. They have given me the benefit of much wisdom over the years. To wit: my late father and mother, Jorge Enrique Arana Cisneros and Marie Elverine Campbell Clapp, who had opposing views on how to be in this world, yet were my greatest life teachers; my deeply thoughtful and brilliant siblings, Rosa Victoria Arana-Robinson and Dr. George Winston Arana, who temper my memories with their own; and my beloved, hugely perceptive children, Hilary (Lalo) Brooks Walsh and Adam Williamson Ward.

Once again, for his many contributions to my labors, I owe my loyal husband, Jonathan Yardley, a mountain of good dinners, months of cheery conversation about H. L. Mencken and American jazz, and another twenty-five years of joy.

# NOTES

vii *"I know who I am, and what I might be"*: Miguel de Cervantes Saavedra, *Don Quijote de la Mancha* (Leipzig: F.A. Brockhaus, 1866), 21. "Yo sé quien soy," respondió D. Quijote, "y sé que puedo ser no solo los que he dicho, sino todos los doce Pares de Francia."

vii *"You mind your own business"*: Pedro Pietri, "Ode to a Grasshopper," *Selected Poetry* (San Francisco: City Lights, 2015).

## AUTHOR'S NOTE: WE OF NO NAME

xi *"We are not a race, a nation"*: This is a paraphrase of José Carlos Mariátegui from the first issue of the journal *Repertorio Hebreo*, edited in Lima in 1929. Mariátegui was a Peruvian philosopher and radical thinker who understood and appreciated the transformational contributions of Jewish thought (Freud, Marx, Einstein, and so on). The original quote refers to Israel, but the words are so apt in describing the American Latino/Hispanic/Latinx that I am taking the liberty of lending it that meaning and giving it precedence here. With great thanks to Claudio Lomnitz and his magnificent memoir, *Nuestra América: My Family in the Vertigo of Translation,* which quotes this passage in its original form, but translated into English (New York: Other Press, 2021), 21.

xii *for the next thirty-five years:* Jie Zong, "A Mosaic, Not a Monolith: A Profile of the U.S. Latino Population, 2000–2020," UCLA Latino Policy and Politics Institute online, last modified October 26, 2022, https://latino.ucla.edu/re search/latino-population-2000-2020/.

xiii *When I ask . . . Cheríe Moraga:* Cheríe Moraga, author interview, June 14, 2021.

xiii *A good number of us choose not to use:* Of US adults with Hispanic ancestry, 89 percent identify as Hispanic or Latino; 11 percent do not consider themselves either of those labels. Mark Hugo Lopez, Ana Gonzalez-Barrera, and Gustavo López, *Hispanic Identity Fades Across Generations as Immigrant Connections Fall Away*, Pew Research Center online, last modified December 20, 2017, https://www.pewresearch.org/hispanic/2017/12/20/hispanic-identity-fades-across-generations-as-immigrant-connections-fall-away/.

xiii   *"We have yet to find a name"*: Junot Díaz, author interview, June 18, 2021.

xiii   *we number sixty-three million:* 62.6 million, according to the US Census Bureau, "Hispanic Heritage Month 2022," press release CB22-FF.09, September 8, 2022, https://www.census.gov/newsroom/facts-for-features/2022/hispanic-heritage-month.html.

xiii   *19 percent of the United States whole:* 18.9 percent as of 2021. Census Bureau, "Hispanic Heritage Month 2022."

xiii   *the US Bureau of the Census predicts that, by 2060, Americans of Hispanic descent will total 111.2 million:* and 27.5 percent of the greater population. US Census Bureau online, "Projections for the United States: 2017–2060," last modified September 2018, https://www.census.gov/data/datasets/2017/demo/popproj/2017-popproj.html. Larger projections are found elsewhere. The organization Hispanic Star, for instance, projects the number to be 132 million by 2050, or 30.2 percent of the overall population. "Hispanics in the U.S. 2022," Hispanic Star, 5, online, accessed July, 13, 2023, https://hispanicstar.org/wp-content/uploads/2022/04/2022-Hispanics-in-the-US-30-MIN-.pdf.

xiv   *"the enormous condescension of posterity"*: The phrase is taken from Edward P. Thompson's *The Making of the English Working Class* (London: Victor Gollancz, 1963), 12. The full phrase is: "I am seeking to rescue the poor stockinger, the Luddite cropper, the 'obsolete' hand-loom weaver, the 'utopian' artisan . . . from the enormous condescension of posterity."

## PART I: ORIGIN STORIES

1   *"Origin stories matter":* Annette Gordon-Reed, "Estebanico's America," *Atlantic*, June 2021.

## CHAPTER 1: ARRIVALS

3   *"We are on the bus now":* Juan Felipe Herrera, "Borderbus," *Notes on the Assemblage* (San Francisco: City Lights, 2015), 59.

3   *It was the first of my arrivals:* The scene is described briefly in my memoir. Marie Arana, *American Chica: Two Worlds, One Childhood* (New York: Dial Press, 2001), 172–74.

3   *There were a scant four million Latinos:* "Hispanics in the United States, 1850–1990," Brian Gratton and Myron P. Gutmann, *Historical Methods* 33, no. 3 (Summer 2000): 137, http://latinamericanstudies.org/immigration/Hispanics-US-1850-1990.pdf. In 1950 there were 3,558,761 Hispanics, or 2.36 percent of the total US population. In 1960, due largely to the Puerto Rican and Cuban migrations, there were 5,814,784, or 3.24 percent. This influx of Puerto Ricans became known as their "Great Migration."

4   *three-quarters of a million Puerto Ricans:* Terrence Haverluk, "The Changing Geography of U.S. Hispanics, 1850–1990," *Journal of Geography* 96, no. 3 (May-June 1997): 139–40.

4   *soar to more than sixty-three million:* Jens Manuel Krogstad, Jeffrey Passel, Mohamad Moslimani, and Luis Noe-Bustamante, "Key Facts About U.S. Latinos for National Hispanic Heritage Month," Pew Research Center online, September 22, 2023.

4   pishtacos, *white ghouls:* Growing up in Peru, far from Lima, I was well acquainted with stories of the *pishtacos* (literally, "beheaders" in Quechua) from the locals in our vicinity. I had heard them whisper that my mother—who was fair, blonde, with very light blue eyes—was a *pishtaco,* or *kharisiri,* a white-skinned ghoul who marauds the streets and murders Indians in order to steal their fat to grease their machinery. More detailed information can be found in Andrew Canessa, "Fear and Loathing on the *Kharisiri* Trail: Alterity and Identity in the Andes," *Journal of the Royal Anthropological Institute* 6, no. 4 (May 30, 2003).

6   *As major waves of Chinese poured into the continent:* "The Chinese Community in Latin America," Observatorio Parlamentario, Asia Pacifico, Biblioteca del Congreso Nacional de Chile online, last modified November 11, 2008, https://www.bcn.cl/observatorio/asiapacifico/noticias/chinese-community-latin-america.

6   *"Our people are nothing like Europeans or North Americans":* Simón Bolívar, "An Address of Bolívar at the Congress of Angostura," February 15, 1819 (repr., Washington, DC: Press of B. S. Adams, 1919). Quoted in Arana, *Bolívar: American Liberator* (New York: Simon & Schuster, 2013), 223.

7   *a "one-drop rule":* In the South, the "one-drop rule" meant that a single drop of "black blood" makes a person black. It is also known as the "one black ancestor rule." Courts call it the "traceable amount rule." Anthropologists call it the "hypo-descent rule," which means that racially mixed people are automatically assigned the status of the subordinate group, or the darkest quotient in their mix. It is a rule accepted by blacks and whites, and found only in the United States—nowhere else in the world. See F. James Davis,

*Who Is Black? One Nation's Definition* (Philadelphia: Penn State University Press, 1991).

7   *a chart of possible race admixtures:* The most famous of these is probably the *Las Castas* painting by an anonymous eighteenth-century artist; oil on canvas, Museo Nacional del Virreinato, Tepotzotlán, Mexico, https://lugares .inah.gob.mx/es/museos-inah/museo/museo-piezas/8409-8409-10-241348 -cuadro-de-castas.html?lugar_id=475.

9   *it included an African conquistador shipmate:* This was Juan Garrido, born on the coast of West Africa circa 1487. He joined the Spanish conquest as a soldier and served under Poncé de León for many years before he took part in Hernán Cortés's conquest of Mexico. See Ricardo E. Alegría, *Juan Garrido: el conquistador negro en las Antillas, Florida, México, y California* (San Juan: Centro de Estudios Avanzados de Puerto Rico y el Caribe, 1990), 12.

9   *In 1524 Giovanni da Verrazzano, the intrepid Italian explorer . . . famously crawled up the coast:* Edwin G. Burrows and Mike Wallace, *Gotham: A History of New York City to 1898* (New York: Oxford University Press, 1999), 11.

## The First White (and Black) Inhabitants of America

10   *"All of them are archers":* Álvar Núñez Cabeza de Vaca, *Rélacion de Naufragios y comentarios*, ed. Roberto Ferrando Pérez (Madrid: Dastin, 2000), 70.

10   *It was April 12, 1528:* Cabeza de Vaca, *Naufragios*, 53. All details of this section are taken from Cabeza de Vaca's own account in this chronicle, written for Holy Roman Emperor King Charles V (referred to as Charles I in Spain).

10   *"Tierra!": "Tierra a la vista!"* or "Land ahoy!" The standard cry of sailors in the Age of Discovery.

10   *"White King" and a vast empire of silver:* Marie Arana, *Silver, Sword, and Stone: Three Crucibles in the Latin American Story* (New York: Simon & Schuster, 2019), 75, 80.

11   *A Franciscan friar, spreading the word of Jesus:* This was Marcos de Niza, the first explorer to claim to have seen the Seven Cities of Cíbola. He traveled to what is now New Mexico with Estebaníco, the slave who survived the Narváez expedition with Cabeza de Vaca. "Marcos de Niza," in *Encyclopedia Britannica* online, last modified March 21, 2023, https://www.britannica.com/biogra phy/Marcos-de-Niza.

11   *the beaches of Sanlúcar de Barrameda:* Cabeza de Vaca, *Naufragios*, 53.

11   *Narváez's charge from the king:* Milagros del Vas Mingo, *Las Capitulaciones de Indias en el siglo XVI* (Madrid: Instituto de Cooperación Iberoamericana, 1986). Quoted in Andrés Reséndez, *A Land So Strange* (New York: Basic Books, 2007), 44.

12  *a rivalry and envy that stretched back many years:* Hernán Cortés, *Hernán Cortés: Letters from Mexico,* trans. and ed. Anthony R. Pagden (New York: Grossman, 1971), 113–27. Narváez had been charged with chasing down Hernán Cortés when Cortés disobeyed his governor and sailed for Mexico without approval. Narváez landed on the coast of Mexico with an army meant to take Cortés under arrest, but Cortés put up a battle and repulsed the operation. When Cortés was victorious, the insubordination was forgotten. Narváez, foiled in his efforts to reprimand Cortés, harbored a bitter resentment against the conquistador ever after. So, there was much irony (and incentive on Narváez's part) when he was engaged to conquer the lands north of Cortés's realm of influence. I wrote about this in *Silver, Sword, and Stone,* 67–70.

12  *the nine hundred miles it took to reach it:* Reséndez, *Land So Strange,* 77–81.

13  *from the Calusa, Muskogee, and Seminoles in the east:* Roberto Ferrando, introduction to Cabeza de Vaca, *Naufragios,* 20–27.

13  *the detachment reached the Apalachee:* Cabeza de Vaca, *Naufragios,* 67–72.

13  *the reality was inescapable:* I owe much of the following interpretation of the events to Andrés Reséndez's splendid account in Reséndez, *Land So Strange,* 96–106.

14  *waded through chest-deep waters:* Reséndez, *Land So Strange,* 103.

14  *build crude rafts from surrounding pines:* Cabeza de Vaca, *Naufragios,* 72–75.

14  *The very argument that Catholic Spain had used:* Arana, *Silver, Sword, and Stone,* 139.

14  *As fate unfolded:* I owe this colorful image to Reséndez, *Land So Strange,* 131.

15  *overpower them, enslave them:* Cabeza de Vaca, *Naufragios,* 91–106.

15  *surprising shamanic powers:* Cabeza de Vaca, *Naufragios,* 107–18.

16  *an Indian wearing a necklace:* Cabeza de Vaca, *Naufragios,* 139–40.

16  *chained Indians shuffled alongside:* Reséndez, *Land So Strange,* 208.

16  *beard that hung to his chest:* Ibid.

### Native Born

16  *"And when Columbus discovered America . . . ?":* Ronald Wright, *Stolen Continents: The Americas Through Indian Eyes Since 1492* (Boston: Houghton Mifflin, 1992), 48. Ignacio Ek is identified as a Maya.

17  *slave trade that eventually displaced five million:* Andrés Reséndez, *The Other Slavery: The Uncovered Story of Indian Enslavement in America* (Boston: Houghton Mifflin Harcourt, 2016).

17  *in 1990 almost ten million American Latinos:* In 1990, 9,721,221 Latinos identified as mestizo (other) or Native American out of a total population of

22,354,059 (43 percent). In 2020, 48,001,278 Latinos identified as mestizo or Native American out of 62,080,044 (77 percent). For 1990: US Census Bureau, *Population by Race and Hispanic or Latino Origin for the United States: 1990 and 2000*, report PHC-T-1, last modified April 2, 2001, https://www.census.gov /data/tables/2000/dec/phc-t-01.html. For 2020: Nicholas Jones et al., "2020 Census Illuminates Racial and Ethnic Composition of the Country," US Census Bureau online, last modified August 12, 2021, https://www.census.gov /library/stories/2021/08/improved-race-ethnicity-measures-reveal-united -states-population-much-more-multiracial.html.

17 *No one calls us Native Americans:* Roxanne Dunbar-Ortiz argues in her book *Not an Immigrant Nation* (Boston: Beacon Press, 2021), 113: "Racializing identity to be about blood quantum is another way of eliminating Indigenous nations whose indigeneity is not based in genetics but in their citizenship in a Native nation based on ancestry, not race. . . . Tribal citizenship is a legal category." Of course, in the Latino world, where the original people were largely rooted in the land, not in nomadic tribes, we think of our indigenous very differently.

18 *carries the blood of the original peoples:* A complete report on the Latino descendants of the original peoples of Latin America can be found in: Kim Parker, Juliana Menasce Horowitz, Rich Morin, and Mark Hugo Lopez, chap. 7, "The Many Dimensions of Hispanic Racial Identity," in *Report: Multiracial in America,* Pew Research Center online, last modified June 11, 2015, https:// www.pewresearch.org/social-trends/2015/06/11/chapter-7-the-many-di mensions-of-hispanic-racial-identity/.

19 *"miscegenation":* I put this word in quotes, as it is now considered to have white supremacist overtones. Although used by scholars freely in the past, it is now seen as a pejorative—and therefore racist—term. I employ it with that caveat, and only in contexts that seem appropriate to that usage.

19 *one of the most violent assaults:* José Manuel García Leduc, in his brief history of Puerto Rico, *Apuntes para una Historia Breve de Puerto Rico* (San Juan: Editorial Isla Negra, 2007), 122, makes this point about the indigenous in the larger hemisphere and their inability to propagate the race in that first century of the Spanish conquest.

19 *slashed the indigenous population by as much as 90 percent:* Alexander Koch et al., "Earth System Impacts of the European Arrival and the Great Dying in the Americas After 1492," *Quaternary Science Review* 207 (March 1, 2019): 13–36.

20 *slave trade that brought more than ten million:* A total of 12.5 million slaves were shipped from Africa by (in order of magnitude) Portuguese, English, French, Spanish, Dutch, American, and Danish ships in more than thirty-six

thousand crossings. Only 10.7 million of the captives survived the journey. All but the 388,000 destined for North America were delivered to what is now Latin America. Henry Louis Gates Jr., "How Many Slaves Landed in the U.S.?," *The African Americans: Many Rivers to Cross*, PBS, accessed July 13, 2023, https://www.pbs.org/wnet/african-americans-many-rivers-to-cross/history/how-many-slaves-landed-in-the-us//. Posted originally on the Root. See also "Trans-Atlantic Slave Trade—Estimates," SlaveVoyages, accessed July 13, 2023, https://www.slavevoyages.org/assessment/estimates.

20   *Nearly two-thirds of us are mixed race:* Francisco Lizcano Fernández, "Composición étnica de las tres áreas culturales del continente americano," *Revista Argentina de Sociología* 38 (May–August 2005): 218. See also Parker et al., "Many Dimensions of Hispanic Racial Identity," which claims that more than half of Latinos identify as multiracial.

20   *Nowhere else on earth:* J. L. Salcedo-Bastardo, *Bolívar: A Continent and Its Destiny,* ed. and trans. Annella McDermott (Richmond, UK: Richmond, 1977), 16.

20   *la raza cósmica—the cosmic race:* This term was coined by the Mexican philosopher-politician José Vasconcelos in his famous 1925 essay "La Raza Cosmica."

20   *"To gaze idly at a crime":* José Martí, *Cuba*, vol. 2 (Habana: Gonzalo de Quesada, 1901), 182. *"Ver en calma un crimen, es cometerlo."*

20   *as Argentina did when it instigated—even institutionalized—white supremacy:* Article 25 of the 1853 Constitution of Argentina (reinstated in 1983) states: "The Federal Government shall foster European immigration; and may not restrict, limit or burden with any tax whatsoever, the entry into the Argentine territory of foreigners who arrive for the purpose of tilling the soil, improving industries, and introducing and teaching arts and sciences." This is explained in Austin F. MacDonald, "The Government of Argentina," *Hispanic American Historical Review* 5, no. 1 (February 1922): 52–82. See also G. Romagnolli, *Aspectos jurídicos e institucionales de las migraciones en la república argentina* (Geneva: International Organization for Migration, 1991), 4.

21   *Or as Chile did in the nineteenth and twentieth centuries:* The largest influxes were from Switzerland, Germany, England, and Yugoslavia. "On average, over 52.5 percent of total foreigners residing in Chile between 1865 and 1920 were Europeans." Quoted from Cristián Doña and Amanda Levinson, "Chile: Moving Towards a Migration Policy," Migration Policy Institute online, last modified February 1, 2004, https://www.migrationpolicy.org/article/chile-moving-towards-migration-policy.

21   *Or, for that matter, Uruguay:* The desirable immigrant population was drawn

largely from Basques, Italians, Swiss, Russians, Jews, Armenians, and Lebanese. Felipe Arocena and Sebastián Aguiar, eds., *Multiculturalismo en Uruguay* (Montevideo: Trilce, 2007).

21  *the ghosts live on:* The phrase in Mapuche is *"la chi mapuche mongelekakei,"* or, translated literally, "the Mapuche who dies, goes on living." Tomás Guevara, "Folklore Araucano" (Santiago de Chile: Imprenta Cervantes, 1911), available online, in Spanish, at https://benmolineaux.github.io/bookshelf/Refranes .html.

22  *If twenty thousand years of human history were collapsed into a week:* Computing years into weeks, the Beringians arrived approximately 1,040,000 weeks (or 20,000 years) ago. The conquistadors arrived 26,000 weeks ago. The English pilgrims, 12,792 weeks. Converted to hours and collapsed into a single week, the percentages work out to: one week, four hours, and less than two hours, respectively.

## The Ancients Who Walk Among Us

22  *"What shall I be called?":* Julia de Burgos, "Poema para mi muerte" ("Poem for My Death"), *Amor y soledad* (Madrid: Ediciones Torremozas, 1994). For a good summary of de Burgos's life, see Maira Garcia, "Overlooked No More: Julia de Burgos, a Poet Who Helped Shape Puerto Rico's Identity," *New York Times,* May 2, 2018, https://www.nytimes.com/2018/05/02/obituaries/over looked-julia-de-burgos.amp.html.

22  *At least this was so for Sandra:* Sandra Guzmán, interviewed via telephone by the author May 27, 2021.

23  *"Color was the elephant in the room":* Lori L. Tharps, *Same Family, Different Colors: Confronting Colorism in America's Diverse Families* (Boston: Beacon Press, 2016), 78.

23  *Some had wide, Nubian noses:* Tharps, *Same Family, Different Colors.*

24  *"There can be no question to perplex any reasonable mind":* Amos K. Fiske, "Puerto Rico as a Permanent Possession," *New York Times,* July 11, 1898, 6. See also Carmen Teresa Whalen, "Colonialism, Citizenship, and the Making of the Puerto Rican Diaspora: An Introduction," in *The Puerto Rican Diaspora: Historical Perspectives,* eds. Carmen Teresa Whalen and Víctor Vásquez-Hernández (Philadephia: Temple University Press, 2005), https:// web.archive.org/web/20131105195921/http://www.temple.edu/tempress /chapters_1400/1523_ch1.pdf.

25  *make the world safe for democracy:* "The world must be made safe for democracy," President Thomas Woodrow Wilson, "April 2, 1917: Address to Congress

Requesting a Declaration of War Against Germany (Transcript)," University of Virginia Miller Center online, accessed July 13, 2023, https://millercenter.org/the-presidency/presidential-speeches/april-2-1917-address-congress-requesting-declaration-war. By the time the United States entered the conflict, the war in Europe had been raging for three years. On March 2, 1917, Wilson had signed the Jones-Shafroth Act, granting statutory citizenship to Puerto Ricans and thereby making them subject to compulsory military service. In his April 2 speech, he asked Congress to send troops against Germany. "1917: Puerto Ricans Become U.S. Citizens, Are Recruited for War Effort," History.com, last modified April 26, 2023, https://www.history.com/this-day-in-history/puerto-ricans-become-u-s-citizens-are-recruited-for-war-effort.

25  *are subject to US military service*: The Boricuas, as they call themselves, have served in every war since World War I and in every branch of the service.

25  *consider Puerto Rico a sovereign nation*: Sandra Guzmán, author interview via email, December 14, 2021.

25  *Puerto Rico's governor, craving a stronger relationship*: This was Governor Luis Muñoz Marín. The industrialization's effects on migration are studied in José Vasquez Calzada, *La poblactón de Puerto Rico y su trayectoria histórica* (Rio Piedras, Puerto Rico: Escuela Graduada de Salud Pública, Recinto de Ciencias Médicas, Universidad de Puerto Rico, 1988), 286. See also "Puerto Rican Emigration: Why the 1950s?," Lehman College, CUNY, online, accessed July 13, 2023, https://lcw.lehman.edu/lehman/depts/latinampuertorican/latinoweb/PuertoRico/1950s.htm.

25  *ended up bringing twice as many Puerto Ricans*: As of 2018, there were almost six million Puerto Ricans in the United States, whereas the population of Puerto Rico is three million. Pew Research data files, "Latino Population by Nativity and Origin, 2018" and "Puerto Rico Island Population Change, 1910–2019."

26  *Its municipal systems were in free fall*: Andrew Jacobs, "A City Whose Time Has Come Again; After Years of Deprivation, Jersey City, an Old Industrial Powerhouse, Is Remaking Itself," *New York Times*, April 30, 2000, sec. NJ, 14.

26  *Nature reclaimed construction sites*: Photos of Jersey City by Andy Blair document the decay. An example: *Abandoned Factories and Wild Sunflowers*, 1977, Flickr, https://www.flickr.com/photos/wavz13/32579111090/in/photostream/.

26  *She knew through her paternal uncle, an elder griot*: Sandra Guzmán, author interview, December 14, 2021.

27  *Sandra, a features editor for the* New York Post, *had been assigned to be one of four subjects*: Guzmán, author interview, December 14, 2021.

27  *mitochondrial DNA indicated*: According to a study funded by the National

Science Foundation, 61 percent of all Puerto Ricans have Amerindian mitochondrial DNA; 27 percent have African; and 12 percent, Caucasian. Rick Kearns, "Indigenous Puerto Rico: DNA Evidence Upsets Established History,"
Indian Country Today (ICT), last modified September 13, 2018, https://indi
ancountrytoday.com/archive/indigenous-puerto-rico-dna-evidence-upsets
-established-history.

27   *as many as nine thousand years ago:* From studies conducted by geneticist Juan
Martínez-Cruzado, quoted in Kearns, "Indigenous Puerto Rico." See also
J. C. Martínez-Cruzado et al., "Mitochondrial DNA Analysis Reveals Substantial Native American Ancestry in Puerto Rico," *Human Biology* 73, no. 4 (August 2001): 491–511.

27   *the current population may contain more of this ancient DNA:* According to ge-
neticists, the Caribbean's current population of forty-four million contains
more Taíno DNA than it did in pre-Columbian times. Carl Zimmer, "Ancient
DNA Shows Humans Settled Caribbean in 2 Distinct Waves," *New York Times,*
December 23, 2020, sec. D, 4. Archeologist Ricardo Alegría calculated that in
1508 there were about 33,000 Taíno on the island of Boriken. By 1520, the
Taíno presence had almost vanished. Governor Francisco Manuel de Lando's
census in 1530 reports the existence of only 1,148 remaining. See Russell
Schimmer, "Puerto Rico," Yale University: Genocide Studies Program online,
accessed July 13, 2023, https://gsp.yale.edu/case-studies/colonial-genocides
-project/puerto-rico.

27   *before the genocide unleashed by the conquest:* Koch et al., "Earth System Impacts
of the European Arrival," 13–36.

28   *the great cacique Agüeybana:* Gonzalo Fernández de Oviedo y Valdés, *Historia
general y natural de las Indias,* vol. 1, ed. José Amador de los Ríos (Madrid: Imprenta de la Real Academia de la Historia, 1851), 467, 474.

28   *planted placentas deep in the earth:* Sandra Guzmán, "Rituals in the Time of the
Rona," Shondaland, Hearst Young Women's Group, last modified August 12,
2020, https://www.shondaland.com/live/body/a33566305/rituals-in-the
-time-of-the-rona/.

## CHAPTER 2: THE PRICE OF ADMISSION

29   *"The question of where we began":* Octavio Paz, *El laberinto de la soledad* (México,
DF: Fondo de Cultura Economica, 1981), 84. My translation.

31   *Ralph de la Vega, a Cuban boy:* All information about Ralph de la Vega and his
family was taken from interviews (in person or via email) conducted between
September and December 2021 or from his memoir: Ralph de la Vega with

Paul B. Brown, *Obstacles Welcome: How to Turn Adversity into Advantage in Business and in Life* (Nashville: Thomas Nelson, 2009).

32 *"the brothel of the Western hemisphere"*: Quoted in "American Comandante, Pre-Castro Cuba," *The American Experience*, PBS, 2005, https://www.pbs.org/wgbh/americanexperience/features/comandante-pre-castro-cuba/.

32 *the voluble, peremptory Colorado senator*: This was Republican Henry Moore Teller, a former secretary of the interior who authored the 1898 Teller Amendment preventing the annexation of Cuba. The historian who claims the sugar beet industry was a driving factor in the decision is Gregory Bart Weeks, *U.S. and Latin American Relations* (New York: Pearson, 2008), 56.

32 *it would own 90 percent . . . one-quarter of all Cuban wealth*: US Department of Commerce, Bureau of Foreign Commerce, Investment in Cuba (Washington, DC, 1956), 10. Also Leland L. Johnson, "U.S. Business Interests in Cuba and the Rise of Castro" (monograph, RAND Corporation, Santa Monica, CA, 1964).

32 *"We are fighting for the beautiful ideal"*: Fidel Castro, "Sierra Maestra Manifesto," July 12, 1957, available at Latin American Studies, accessed July 13, 2023, http://www.latinamericanstudies.org/cuban-rebels/manifesto.htm.

33 *"Our hardest fight is against North American monopolies"*: Che Guevara, quoted in the *New York Times*, February 2, 1960, 1. Cited in Johnson, "U.S. Business Interests in Cuba."

33 *"We'll take and take"*: Fidel Castro, quoted in the *New York Times*, August 21, 1960, sec. 3, 1. Cited in Johnson, "U.S. Business Interests in Cuba."

## Dissidents

33 *"Look David. How the last few horses fret"*: Maria Elena Cruz Varela, "El Ángel Caído" ("The Fallen Angel"), my translation, from the collection *El Ángel Agotado* (Havana, Cuba: Fundación Liberal José Martí). Also available at: https://adncuba.com/noticias-de-cuba-cultura/literatura/los-prohibidos-seleccion-de-poemas-de-maria-elena-cruz-varela.

33 *Castro announced that he would nationalize*: Alistair Cooke, "Castro in Control of Cuba: President Urrutia Declares General Strike," *Guardian* (UK edition) online, last modified January 3, 1959, https://uploads.guim.co.uk/2016/12/05/Castro_in_control_-_3_Jan_1959.jpg.

34 *herded into fortresses or stadiums and summarily shot*: Alistair Cooke, "Fading Legend of Castro the Idealist: Rebels Taking Their Revenge," *Guardian* (UK edition) online, last modified January 15, 1959, https://uploads.guim.co.uk/2016/12/05/Castro_-_fading_legend_-_15_Jan_1959.jpg.

34 *Airplanes were suddenly filled with frightened members of the clergy:* María de los Angeles Torres, author interview, January 10, 2022; and María de los Angeles Torres, *The Lost Apple: Operation Pedro Pan, Cuban Children in the U.S., and the Promise of a Better Future* (Boston: Beacon Press, 2003) 161–62. I owe much of the information about Operation Pedro Pan that follows to the excellent research conducted over many years by Illinois University professor María de los Angeles Torres and published in *The Lost Apple.*

34 *perhaps sent to the Soviet Union:* Torres, *The Lost Apple,* 55. Catholic organizations referred to this as "coercive regimentation," 62.

34 *"We will create the man of the twenty-first century":* "Che Guevara Living Presence Beyond a Symbol," Representaciones Diplomáticas de Cuba en el Exterior, October 8, 2020, http://www.cubadiplomatica.cu/en/articulo/che-guevara-living-presence-beyond-symbol. Also, Torres, *Lost Apple,* 255.

34 *he was ordered to report to his teacher:* de la Vega with Brown, "Ninety Miles to Advantage," in *Obstacles Welcome,* 6.

35 *"the revolution betrayed":* de la Vega with Brown, "Ninety Miles to Advantage," in *Obstacles Welcome.*

35 *On the morning of Monday, July 1, 1961:* de la Vega, author interviews and de la Vega with Brown, *Obstacles Welcome.*

## Flying

36 *"Mothers of Cuba!":* Radio Swan reports, 1960, from the personal archives of Ramón Torreira Crespo. "La Operación Peter Pan en la memoria histórica del pueblo cubano" (Miami: University of Miami, Cuban Historical Collection). The original Spanish follows: "¡Madre Cuba, escucha esto! ¡La próxima ley del gobierno sera quitarte a tu hijo! Es la nueva ley del Gobierno quitártelo . . . y cuando te devuelvan serán unos monstruos del materialismo. ¡No te dejes quitar a tu hijo!" Note: *materialismo* refers to dialectical materialism, the theory most closely associated with Karl Marx and Friedrich Engels.

36 *Operation Pedro Pan (Peter Pan), as it would eventually become known:* Torres, *Lost Apple,* especially chapters 3, 5, and 7.

36 *James Baker, principal of the Ruston Academy:* This was the Ruston Academy, established in 1920 by Hiram and Martha Ruston, and considered the premiere American college preparatory school in Latin America. See James D. Baker, *Ruston: From Dreams to Reality* (Palmetto Bay, FL: Ruston-Baker Educational Institution, 2007), available online at https://www.rustonacademy.net/bakerbook.pdf.

37 *One had helped resettle one thousand unaccompanied teenagers:* This was

Monsignor Bryan Walsh, who was central to the work of Operation Pedro Pan. Baker, *Ruston*.

37 *in the brilliantly conceived and executed Kindertransport:* Torres, *Lost Apple*, 4.

37 *had evacuated four thousand Basque children:* Ibid.

37 *Britain's conservative government was none too pleased:* Daniel Vulliamy and Simon Martinez, "The Reception of Basque Refugees in 1937 Showed Britain at Its Best and Worst," letters to the editor, *Guardian* (US edition) online, last modified May 22, 2017, https://www.theguardian.com/world/2017/may/22/the-reception-of-basque-refugees-in-1937-showed-britain-at-its-best-and-worst.

37 *a pet project for Central Intelligence Agency (CIA) personnel:* Torres, *Lost Apple*, 43, 47, 89–92, 136, 138, 179, 242. See also Rick Jervis, "Operation Pedro Pan: DePaul Prof's Personal Journey," *Chicago Tribune*, August 15, 2003: "Midway through her research [María de los Angeles Torres] filed a lawsuit against the intelligence agency to try to declassify documents. The case was ultimately dismissed, but the suit awarded her three documents, with some parts blacked out, she says were good pieces to the [CIA] puzzle." See also Deborah Shnookal, "The Dark Side of Neverland," in *Operation Pedro Pan and the Exodus of Cuba's Children* (Gainesville: University of Florida Press, 2020).

37 *"My name is Carmen Gómez":* Jean Marbella, "Quiet Cuban Airlift Altered 14,000 Lives," *Baltimore Sun*, January 23, 2000.

38 *the plight of children had been put to potent political use:* Torres dedicates her first chapter in *The Lost Apple* to the political philosophy behind shaping children to suit regimes, especially as relates to the Cold War contest for young minds.

38 *"underground railway in the sky":* Torres, *Lost Apple*, 8.

38 *a high-level airline executive:* This was Tony Comellas, who had the power to issue visa waivers to the children. Torres, *Lost Apple*, 132.

38 *Pan American World Airways agents in Havana:* Torres, *Lost Apple*, 81.

38 *Many parents believed the new Cuban government might imprison, even execute:* Silvia Pedraza, "Cuba's Revolution and Exodus," *Journal of the International Institute* 5, no. 2 (Winter 1998).

39 *separated from their families for as many as eighteen years:* One example of this is Eduardo Rabel, who was age sixteen when he arrived at Camp Matecumbe in Miami and was sent on to an orphanage in Kentucky. It would be eighteen years before he was reunited with his mother and brothers; his father had died in the interim. See Glenda Meekins, "'Pedro Pan' Documentary Debuts in Central Florida," *Florida Catholic*, Archdiocese of Miami, March 1, 2018, www.miamiarch.org/CatholicDiocese.php?op=Article_pedro-pan-documentary-debuts-in-central-florida.

39   *never see their parents again:* María de los Angeles Torres recounts that in a re-
     union of fifty Pedro Pans in 2001, six had never seen their parents again. *Lost
     Apple,* 223.

39   *in far corners of the United States:* The Catholic Welfare Bureau (Catholic Chari-
     ties) worked with foster families in two hundred cities throughout forty-eight
     states. Meekins, "'Pedro Pan' Documentary Debuts."

39   *some were treated like chattel:* Torres, *Lost Apple,* 163–65.

39   *some were sexually abused:* One example is Dulce María (Candi) Sosa, who was
     transferred from the receiving facility in Miami to a foster home in California
     at the age of twelve. The father of the family abused her. When she reported
     the abuse, the social workers in charge did not believe her and refused to re-
     move her from his care. Dulce María (Candi) Sosa, interviewed by the María
     de los Angeles Torres, June 6, 1996; Torres, *Lost Apple,* 175–77.

39   *Many who were sent off to orphanages:* Torres, *Lost Apple,* 163–65.

40   *wandering the city streets:* Joint report of James Hennessey, INS, Al McDer-
     mitt, Department of Labor, John Hurley, "Cuban Refugee Situation in Dade
     County," Miami, November 8, 1960. Eisenhower Presidential Library, Confi-
     dential Files, box 42, Subject Series, Mutual Security Assistance, 1960–1963;
     cited in Torres, *Lost Apple,* 61.

40   *One thirteen-year-old was bounced:* This was Rafael Ravelo, a young seminary
     student who left Cuba in May 1961 and returned in 1982. His parents were di-
     vorced by then, his family almost unrecognizable. Torres, *Lost Apple,* 118–19,
     162–63, 223–26.

40   *248,100 Cuban immigrants:* Jorge Duany, "Cuban Migration: A Postrevolution
     Exodus Ebbs and Flows," Migration Policy Institute, migrationpolicy.org,
     July 3, 2017.

40   *successful, outstanding leaders in their fields:* Numbering among the children most
     notably are: Senator Mel Martinez of Florida, Ambassador Eduardo Aguirre,
     artist Ana Mendieta, president of Miami Dade College Eduardo Padrón, Na-
     tional Institutes of Health Dr. Eliseo Pérez-Stable, singer-songwriter Willy
     Chirino, Miami real estate developer Armando Codina, Florida judge Margarita
     Esquiroz, Sunshine Gasoline founder Maximo Alvarez, author and Yale profes-
     sor Carlos Eire, and, of course, AT&T chief executive officer Ralph de la Vega.

40   *a virtual list of Cuba's dissidents:* Torres, *Lost Apple,* 50.

40   Escoria, *he called them:* "Boat People, Launched," editorial, *New York Times,*
     May 18, 1983, A-26.

41   *Cubans were considered loud, pushy:* María de los Angeles Torres, *In the Land of
     Mirrors* (Ann Arbor: University of Michigan Press, 1999), 182.

41 *"No children. No pets. No Cubans"*: María de los Angeles Torres, author interview, January 10, 2022. Also in Torres, *Land of Mirrors*, 73.

41 *"changing the complexion of the city"*: The quote is from Arthur Patten, Dade County commissioner, reporting to the US Congress: "Cuban Refugee Problem," Hearings Before the Subcommittee to Investigate Problems Connected with Refugees and Escapees of the Committee on the Judiciary, United States Senate, part 1, December 6, 7, 13, 1961, 49. Also Torres, *In the Land of Mirrors*, 73.

42 *a number of newspapers began to report*: Jean Abroad, "No te dejes quitar a tu hijo!: Operation Pedro Pan and the Cuban Children's Program" (PhD thesis, Duke University, Department of History, Durham, NC, April 2008).

42 *eventually opened a furniture shop*: All information here about the Báezes and Ralph's grandmother are taken from the author's interview with Ralph de la Vega, September 1, 2021.

43 *was made a top executive of one of the most dynamic*: Roger Cheng, "AT&T Vice Chairman Ralph de la Vega to Retire December 31," December 8, 2016, cnet .com. Ralph de la Vega took on the CEO and vice chairman positions in February 2016. He retired eleven months later. One of his most notable achievements was working with Steve Jobs to make AT&T the official carrier of the iPhone.

### Devil's Highway

43 *"I thought I was done with borders"*: Reyna Grande, "Crossing Borders," November 17, 2021, reynagrande.com/crossing-borders.

43 *Julia Mamani is not entirely sure of the name*: For obvious reasons, given her undocumented status, I've given this informant an alias to protect her identity. The details about her voyage to the United States and her arrangements with countless individuals are taken from numerous personal interviews and telephone conversations with her. The information was corroborated by the informant's daughter and members of Cabanaconde City Colca USA.

43 *ten million undocumented immigrants*: Jeffrey S. Passel, "Unauthorized Migrants: Numbers and Characteristics," Pew Research Center online, last modified June 15, 2005, https://www.pewresearch.org/hispanic/2005/06/14/unau thorized-migrants/. Also, Mark Hugo Lopez, Jeffrey S. Passel, and D'Vera Cohn, "Key Facts About the Changing U.S. Unauthorized Immigrant Population," Pew Research Center online, last modified April 13, 2021, https://www.pewresearch.org/short-reads/2021/04/13/key-facts-about-the-chang ing-u-s-unauthorized-immigrant-population/.

44 *the 1970s, just as the glaciers began to disappear:* Astrid B. Stensrud, "Harvesting Water for the Future: Reciprocity and Environmental Justice in the Politics of Climate Change in Peru," *Latin American Perspectives* 43, no. 4, Climate Change in Latin America (July 2016): 64–65.

44 *fled first to Peru's coastal towns: Transnational Fiesta: Twenty Years Later,* documentary produced by Wilton Martinez and Paul H. Gelles, 2014.

44 *principle of mutual assistance and reciprocity, or* ayni: Bruce Mannheim, "The Language of Reciprocity in Southern Peruvian Quechua," *Anthropological Linguistics* 28, no. 3 (Fall 1986): 267–73.

45 *If one Cabanacondino:* Information on Cabanaconde City Colca USA is taken from the author's three interviews between November 15 and November 30 with the president of the organization, Ángel Cano, as well as with three other officers of his executive committee.

45 *They called themselves Cabanaconde City Colca USA (CCC-USA):* The organization's Facebook page is at https://www.facebook.com/ccc.usa.oficial /?ref=page_internal.

45 *burgeoned to well over a thousand:* Ángel Cano, author interviews.

46 *a picturesque, million-square-foot parcel:* BlockShopper, Maryland, Montgomery County: https://blockshopper.com/md/montgomery-county/poolesville /property/3-001-03449993/18450-cattail-road.

47 *fissure twice as deep as the Grand Canyon:* Brendan Sainsbury, "Exploring Peru's Epic Colca Canyon," BBC Travel online, last modified October 15, 2012, https://www.bbc.com/travel/article/20121012-exploring-perus-epic-colca -canyon. The Colca Canyon's depth is second only to the nearby Kutawasi Canyon, also in Peru.

47 *"The gringos are swarming our old stomping grounds": Transnational Fiesta.*

47 *Julia's story begins in the slums of Lima:* Mamani, author interviews.

49 *"We leave after I've had my dinner":* Mamani, author interviews.

49 *all in the service of the infamous Gulf Cartel, alias "La Mano":* See "Mexico Cartels: Which Are the Biggest and Most Powerful?," BBC News online, last modified October 24, 2019, https://www.bbc.com/news/world-latin-amer ica-40480405. See also Seth Harp, "The Coyote Cartel," *Rolling Stone,* June 14, 2021.

50 *billion-dollar business:* Investigators have projected, for instance, that a million unauthorized migrants arrived in the United States in 2021. If each was able to pay a minimum of $7,000 to the smuggling network, that's $7 billion of black-market cash. Harp, "Coyote Cartel."

50   la carretera de la muerte: Diana García, "Familiares de desaparecidos en 'carretera de la muerte' no frenan su lucha," La Voz, azcentral.com, Ciudad de
México, November 18, 2021, https://www.azcentral.com/story/noticias
/2021/11/18/familiares-de-desaparecidos-en-carretera-de-la-muerte-no-fre
nan-su-lucha/5456978001/.

50   *easy prey for the drug cartels:* See the following, especially for the situation in
2005, when Julia Mamani was making her voyage: Ginger Thompson, "Rival
Drug Gangs Turn the Streets of Nuevo Laredo into a War Zone," *New York
Times*, December 4, 2005. Also, in reference to the rivalries, see "Mexico Cartels."

50   *are known to regularly beat, hold captive, or starve itinerants:* Thompson, "Rival
Drug Gangs Turn the Streets of Nuevo Laredo into a War Zone."

50   *US Border agents peeked into an empty tanker trailer:* Ibid.

50   *burned bone fragments that lay scattered in the brush:* Associated Press, "Mexican
Government Says It Found Body Disposal Site Near Border," BorderReport
.com, last modified September 30, 2021, https://www.borderreport.com
/regions/mexico/mexican-government-says-it-found-body-disposal-site
-near-border/.

50   *disappearances had been so common:* There were more than eleven thousand
reported disappearances on the Monterrey–Nuevo Laredo Highway since
1964. Diana García, "Familiares de desaparecidos," azcentral.com.

51   *the foul, sewage-laden river:* Neena Satija, "Despite Efforts, the Rio Grande Is
One Dirty Border," Special Series: 20 Years of NAFTA, *All Things Considered*,
NPR, October 22, 2013.

51   *"Run when the field is dark":* Mamani, author interviews.

52   *Militias from as far away as Wisconsin:* Patrick Strickland, "The U.S.-Mexican
Border Has Long Been a Magnet for Far-Right Vigilantes," *Time*, February 17,
2022.

## CHAPTER 3: FORERUNNERS

56   *"I live al reves, upside down. Always have":* Sandra Cisneros, "Jarcería Shop," in
Sergio Troncoso, *Nepantla Families* (College Station: Texas A&M University
Press, 2021).

56   *forty indigenous tribes continue to straddle the existing border:* Michelle Chen, "Defying US Borders, Native Americans Are Asserting Their Territorial Rights,"
*Nation*, February 22, 2019.

57   *even before the founders dreamed of independence:* Greg Grandin, *The End of the*

*Myth: From the Frontier to the Border Wall in the Mind of America* (New York: Metropolitan Books, 2019), 3.

57 *"insatiable appetite, or Bulimia, of enlarging dominion":* Thomas Hobbes, *Leviathan* (Cambridge: Cambridge University Press, 1904), 242.

57 *Jefferson imagined that his infant nation:* Jefferson to Archibald Stewart, Paris, January 25, 1786, *The Works of Thomas Jefferson,* vol. 4, ed. Paul Leicester Ford (New York: G. P. Putnam & Sons, 1904–5), 4; quoted in Arana, *Bolívar,* 74.

58 *a treaty negotiated at gunpoint:* John S. D. Eisenhower, "Occupation," in *So Far from God: The U.S. War with Mexico 1846–1848* (New York: Random House, 1989).

58 *It wasn't until 1904 that fifty mounted guards:* The Chinese Exclusion Act, passed in 1882, made Chinese immigration illegal in the United States. The "mounted guards" were also known as Chinese Inspectors. Bill Broyles and Mark Haynes, *Desert Duty: On the Line with the U.S. Border Patrol* (Austin: University of Texas Press, 2010), 5.

58 *And it wasn't until 1924 that immigration laws:* The US Border Patrol was founded by Congress on May 28, 1924. The modern-day Immigration and Naturalization Service (INS) was founded in the same year. Broyles and Haynes, *Desert Duty,* 8.

58 *"stupidity, obstinacy, ignorance, duplicity, and vanity":* This was Charles Bent, the first civil governor under American rule in the newly claimed territory of New Mexico. William H. Wroth, "Charles Bent, Biographical Sketch," New Mexico History online, accessed July 13, 2023, https://newmexicohistory .org/2012/06/28/charles-bent-bio/.

58 *"The meanest looking race of people I ever saw":* Captain Lemuel Ford of the First Dragoons, US Army, quoted in Charles Kenner, *A History of New Mexico–Palins Indian Relations* (Norman: University of Oklahoma Press, 1969), 83. Also Roxanne Dunbar-Ortiz, *Not a Nation of Immigrants* (Boston: Beacon Press, 2021), 88.

59 *my own grandfather crossed into the United States:* I tell this story briefly in my memoir, *American Chica,* 22, 41.

59 *Its vice president, Reverend John Augustine Zahm:* Brendan O'Shaughnessy, "Way Out Front," *Notre Dame* online, Spring 2018, accessed July 13, 2023, https:// magazine.nd.edu/stories/way-out-front/.

60 *Almost a half century later, in December 1941:* O'Shaughnessy, "Way Out Front."

### The In-Between People

61  *"Mexicans who live in the borderlands"*: This is paraphrased from the introduction of Sergio Troncoso's *Nepantla Familias: An Anthology of Mexican American Literature on Families in Between Worlds* (College Station: Texas A&M University Press, 2021), 1–3. Nepantla is the Nahua concept of living in a space in which you belong to neither one side or the other—literally in-between. Modern-day writers such as Gloria E. Anzaldúa, Sandra Cisneros, Reyna Grande, and others have been eloquent on the subject.

61  *Americans balked at the prospect of including Mexicans:* This was President Herbert Hoover's announcement of a national program of "American jobs for real Americans." See Phillip B. Gonzales, Renato Rosaldo, and Mary Louise Pratt, eds., *Trumpism, Mexican America and the Struggle for Latinx Citizenship*, School for Advanced Research Seminar Series (Albuquerque: University of New Mexico Press, 2021), xiv.

62  *rounded up and deported nearly two million Mexicanos:* The most recent figures put it at 1.8 million. Alex Wagner, "America's Forgotten History of Illegal Deportations," *Atlantic*, March 6, 2017. For the two million figure, see Ramón A. Gutiérrez, "Mexican Immigration to the United States," *Oxford Research Encyclopedias*, July 29, 2019. See also Francisco E. Balderrama and Raymond Rodríguez, *Decade of Betrayal: Mexican Repatriation in the 1930s* (Albuquerque: University of New Mexico Press, 2006), 149, 195, 334.

62  *One Idaho farm family was just sitting down:* Francisco E. Balderrama told this story on NPR's *Fresh Air with Terry Gross*, September 10, 2015. It was an anecdote from his and Rodríguez's *Decade of Betrayal*, 149, 195, 334.

62  *"We all know about the internment of 145,000 Japanese":* Former senator Joseph Dunn (D-CA), quoted in Diane Bernard, "The Time a President Deported 1 Million Mexican Americans for Supposedly Stealing U.S. Jobs," *Washington Post*, August 13, 2018.

62  *Four and a half million workers streamed across the border:* Ramón A. Gutiérrez, "Mexican Immigrants."

62  *the Eisenhower administration implemented Operation Wetback:* Gonzales, Rosaldo, and Pratt, *Trumpism*, 61–62.

62  *1.3 million people—once again:* Ramón A. Gutierrez, "Mexican Immigration." See also José Angel Gutiérrez, *FBI Surveillance of Mexicans and Chicanos, 1920–1980* (Lanham, MD: Lexington Books, 2020), 245–46. Also Erin Blakemore, "The Largest Mass Deportation in American History," History.com, last modified June 18, 2019, https://www.history.com/news/operation-wetback-eisenhower-1954-deportation.

63  *"It was about the color of their skin":* Dunn, quoted in Bernard, "The Time a President Deported."

63  *Puerto Ricans in the United States numbered one million:* Carmen Teresa Whalen and Victor Vásquez-Hernández, *The Puerto Rican Diaspora: Historical Perspectives* (Philadelphia: Temple University, 2005), 3.

64  *Cubans, on the other hand, amounted to a mere 163,000:* Pew Research files and notebooks, "Latino Population by Nativity and Origin in, 2021." For 1980 figure, see Silvia Pedraza-Bailey, "Cuba's Exiles: Portrait of a Refugee Migration," *International Migration Review* 19, no. 1 (Spring 1985): 4–34.

64  *a population equal to that of Virginia:* Virginia's population on July 1, 2021, was 8,642,274. US Census, QuickFacts, Virginia, accessed February 18, 2022.

64  *almost half of all Puerto Ricans in the United States:* Sharon R. Enis, Merarys Ríos-Vargas, and Nora G. Albert, "The Hispanic Population: 2010," table 6, 2010 Census Briefs, US Census Bureau online, https://www.census.gov/prod/cen2010/briefs/c2010br-04.pdf. In the 2004 US census, 86 percent of all Cubans in the United States claimed to be white. "Cubans in the United States: Fact Sheet," Pew Research Center online, last modified August 25, 2006, https://www.pew research.org/hispanic/2006/08/25/cubans-in-the-united-states/.

64  *"I do not think there was ever a more wicked war":* Ulysses S. Grant to journalist John Russell Young (1879), quoted by Young in *Around the World with General Grant* (Baltimore: John Hopkins University Press, 2002), 376–77.

64  *treacherous Anglo-American incursion across their borders:* Two good (and very different) sources for the Mexican-American War in general are Peter Guardino, *The Dead March: A History of the Mexican-American War* (Cambridge, MA: Harvard University Press, 2017), and Eisenhower, *So Far from God.*

65  *killed thousands of Mexicans along the way:* Taking the sum of the casualties from numerous battles as Major General Scott made his way west toward the capital, Mexican casualties counted more than four thousand. "The Conquest of Mexico City," encyclopedia.com.

65  *Congressman Abraham Lincoln of Illinois:* Guardino, *The Dead March,* 205.

65  *there were twenty-five thousand dead Mexicans:* Micheal Clodfelter, *Warfare and Armed Conflicts: A Statistical Encyclopedia of Casualty and Other Figures, 1492–2015,* 4th ed. (Jefferson, NC: McFarland, 2017), 249. In contrast, almost 90 percent of American deaths in the war were due to dysentery.

65  *one hundred thousand Mexican survivors:* Enrique Krause, "Will Mexico Get Half of Its Territory Back?" *New York Times,* April 6, 2017; see also Richard L. Nostrand, "Mexican Americans Circa 1850," *Annals of the Association of American Geographers* 65, no. 3 (1975): 378–90.

65 *home to three and a half million:* Arnoldo de León, "Mexican Americans," Texas State Historical Association Handbook of Texas, December 3, 2020. Also "Persons of Spanish Surname," Subject Report, US Census of Population: 1960, Final Report PC(2)-1B, US Department of Commerce, 1961, and Campbell Gibson and Kay Jung, "Historical Census Statistics on Population Totals by Race and Hispanic Origin, 1790 to 1990" (working paper no. 56, US Census Bureau, September 2002), https://www.census.gov/content/dam/Census/library/working-papers/2002/demo/POP-twps0056.pdf.

**To Have and Have Not**

66 *"We took the liberty of removing his right foot":* Cited in Roxanne Dunbar-Ortiz, *Not a Nation of Immigrants* (Boston: Beacon Press, 2021), 112.

66 *Among Linda Chavez's earliest memories:* Much of the material on Linda Chavez is taken from interviews with the author (particularly on September 6, 1921), her memoir *An Unlikely Conservative: The Transformation of an Ex-Liberal (Or, How I Became the Most Hated Hispanic in America* (New York: Basic Books, 2003), and my decades-long acquaintance with Linda.

67 *They were speeding down a highway:* Chavez, *An Unlikely Conservative,* 38–39.

67 *Ambrosio Chavez, hauled away in handcuffs and chains:* Chavez, *An Unlikely Conservative,* 36–37.

68 *she had fled a husband before Rudy:* Chavez, *An Unlikely Conservative,* 34–35.

68 *Velma moved in with Rudy, Cecily:* Chavez, author interview. Also Chavez, *An Unlikely Conservative,* 37–38.

68 *Her ancestral line, the Chavez and Armijo families:* Chavez, *An Unlikely Conservative,* 36–39.

69 *Chaves—had joined the Oñate expedition:* All information on the Oñate expedition is taken from George P. Hammond, "Don Juan de Oñate and the Founding of New Mexico," *New Mexico Historical Review* 1, no. 4 (October 1, 1926): 459–62, and Carrie Gibson, *El Norte* (New York: Grove Press, 2019), 64–69.

69 *"a well-built" midlife widower:* "About Don Pedro Gómez Durán y Chávez," Geni entry, last modified July 25, 2020, https://www.geni.com/people/Don-Pedro-Gomez-Duran-y-Chavez.

69 *the clan would drop the name Durán and change the s:* "About Don Pedro Gómez Durán y Chávez."

70 *"[T]he families of Armijo, Chávez":* George F. A. Ruxton, *Adventures in Mexico and the Rocky Mountains* (New York: Harper & Brothers, 1848), 186–87. See also Janet LeCompte, "Manuel Armijo's Family History," *New Mexico Historical Review* 48, no. 3 (July 1, 1973): 252.

70  *"I've always been proud of [Armijo's] role":* Chavez, *An Unlikely Conservative*, 36–37.

70  *According to her mother, the family has spoken English primarily:* MacArena Hernandez, "Conservative and Hispanic, Linda Chavez Carves Out Leadership Niche," *New York Times*, August 19, 1998.

70  *"Every immigrant who comes here":* This was made in a statement to the *Kansas City Star* in 1918, not long before he died; quoted in Michael Cronin, *Translation in the Digital Age* (Abingdon, UK: Routledge, 2013), 141. Other sources date it to January 3, 1919; see K. L. Katz, "Did Theodore Roosevelt Really Say That?," *Patriot-News* (Harrisburg, PA) online, last modified, March 3, 2007, https://www.pennlive.com/americanhistory101/2007/03/did_theodore _roosevelt_really.html.

71  *the highest-ranking woman in the Reagan White House:* Steven Ginsburg, "Linda Chavez, Formerly the Highest-Ranking Woman in the Reagan White House," March 5, 1986, UPI, available at UPI Archives online, https://www.upi.com /Archives/1986/03/05/Linda-Chavez-formerly-the-highest-ranking -woman-in-the-Reagan/4871510382800/.

71  *Bush selected her to be his secretary of labor:* Steven A. Holmes and Steven Greenhouse, "Bush Choice for Labor Post Withdraws and Cites Furor of Illegal Immigrant Issue," *New York Times*, January 10, 2001.

71  *sheltering an undocumented Guatemalan:* Holmes and Greenhouse, "Bush Choice for Labor Post Withdraws." See also Eric Schmitt with Renwick McLean, "Onetime Illegal Immigrant Sheltered by Chavez Recalls Painful Past," *New York Times*, February 8, 2001.

71  *she feels little attachment to the Latino population of this country:* Chavez, author interview.

71  *"Hispanics as permanently disadvantaged victims":* Chavez, *An Unlikely Conservative*, 224–25.

71  *forbidden him "to play with Mes'cans":* Ibid., 40–41, and author interview.

71  *"I don't feel affiliated to the Latino community":* Chavez, author interview.

72  *Henry Louis Gates Jr.'s genealogical PBS series:* Linda Chavez's genealogical roots are featured in *Finding Your Roots*, season 1, episode 10, aired on May 20, 2012.

72  *Spanish documents from the returning colonial army:* These are the records of Governor Diego de Vargas, assigned with task of reconquering New Mexico for Spain in 1691. *Finding Your Roots*, May 20, 2012.

### The Boomerang of History

73   *"The U.S.-Mexican border [is an open wound]":* Gloria Anzaldúa, *Borderlands/ La Frontera: The New Mestiza* (1987, 4th ed. repr.: San Francisco: Aunt Lute Books, 2012).

73   *little more than a string of agreed-upon lies:* Attributed to Napoléon Bonaparte, "l'histoire est une suite des mensonges sur lesquels on est d'accord." Purportedly, this line was said to Emmanuel, Comte de las Cases in an interview, but it is not recorded in *Mémorial de Sainte Hélène: Journal of the Private Life and Conversations of Emperor Napoleon at Saint Helena*, which was translated into English in 1823.

73   *"not for money, not for possessions or fame":* David McCullough, *The Pioneers: The Heroic Story of the Settlers Who Brought the American Ideal West* (New York: Simon & Schuster, 2019), 258.

73   *"No myth in American history has been more powerful":* Grandin, *End of the Myth*, 2.

73   *"a horizon where endless sky meets endless hate":* Ibid.

74   *Dr. George Gilson Clapp, a colorful individual:* Dr. Clapp and his descendants are listed in Ebenezer Clapp, *The Clapp Memorial: Record of the Clapp Family in America* (Boston: David Clapp & Sons, 1876), 283–314.

74   *"great experiment of liberty":* John L. O'Sullivan, "Annexation," *Democratic Review*, July/August 1845. The full sentence is as follows: "And that claim is by the right of our manifest destiny to overspread and to possess the whole of the continent which Providence has given us for the development of the great experiment of liberty and federated self-government entrusted to us."

75   *known for offering Native Americans his services free of charge:* I refer to his Indian patients in my memoir, *American Chica*, 186–87.

75   *full sting of racist venom:* Arana, *American Chica*, 192.

75   *Arturo García, an undocumented Mexican laborer:* Given this informant's undocumented status, I use a pseudonym here. García is indeed currently in Texas, born in Veracruz, Mexico, and a descendant of Acoma Pueblo Indians. The information here is taken from the author's multiple interviews on June 8 and 9, 2021, and April 3, 2022.

76   *So dark is his skin:* I owe this description and the comments on Arturo's physical bearing to my friend Mexican American writer Dagoberto Gilb, who has known him for many years.

76   *an unholy bond between the government and the cartels:* Veracruz: Fixing Mexico's State of Terror, Report no. 61/Latin America & Caribbean, International Crisis Group, February 28, 2017, https://www.crisisgroup.org/latin

-america-caribbean/mexico/61-veracruz-fixing-mexicos-state-terror. See also
"'A Brutal Complicity': The Roots of Violence in Veracruz," Mexico Violence
Research Project online, last modified September 22, 2020, https://www
.mexicoviolence.org/post/a-brutal-complicity.

76   *"In Veracruz, an alliance between criminal groups"*: *Veracruz: Fixing Mexico's State
     of Terror.*

76   *almost 95 percent of all unreported crimes in Mexico*: Ibid.

76   *most lethal area for journalists*: Ibid.

77   *a massive amphibious invasion of Veracruz*: K. J. Bauer, *The Mexican War, 1846–
     1848* (New York: Macmillan, 1974), 233.

77   *a devastating civil war that was catalyzed, in part, by American interference*: "The
     Mexican Revolution and the United States in the Collections of the Library
     of Congress: U.S. Involvement Before 1913," Library of Congress online, ac-
     cessed July 14, 2023. See especially "U.S. Arms Trade with Villa Prior to World
     War I," www.loc.gov/exhibits/mexican-revolution-and-the-united-states/us
     -involvement-before-1913.html#obj013.

77   *the repressive and corrupt military regime he'd helped install*: "Officials in Wash-
     ington, D.C., met with Huerta, and supported the Reyes-Díaz rebellion,
     because US Ambassador Henry Lane Wilson believed Huerta could better
     protect U.S. interests in Mexico," "U.S. Arms Trade with Villa Prior to World
     War I."

78   *"Sonny" Falcon, "king of the Austin fajita"*: Michael Barnes, "1938–2019: Aus-
     tin's 'Fajita King,' Juan 'Sonny' Falcon Has Died," *Austin (TX) American-
     Statesman*, December 20, 2019.

78   *a butcher in Lupe's parents' popular Latino food market*: Sonny and Lupe Falcon's
     store, which was originally Lupe's parents', was Guajardo's Cash Grocery
     & Market. See "Zoning Change Review Sheet," City of Austin online, ac-
     cessed July 14, 2023, https://www.austintexas.gov/edims/document.cfm?id
     =202613.

79   *the classic Austin fajita*: Michael Barnes, "Austin's Fajita King," *Austin (TX)
     American-Statesman*, September 25, 2019.

80   *two-thirds of the country's unauthorized immigrants have been travelers*: Imelda
     García, "As Illegal Border Crossings Drop, the Face of Unauthorized Im-
     migration in the U.S. Has Changed," *Dallas Morning News*, April 27, 2021.
     See also Robert Warren, "US Undocumented Population Continued to Fall
     from 2016 to 2017 and Visa Overstays Significantly Exceeded Illegal Cross-
     ings for the Seventh Consecutive Year," *Journal on Migration and Human*

*Security* 7, no. 1 (March 2019): 19–22, https://journals.sagepub.com/doi/full/10.1177/2331502419830339.

80    *Analysts for the Pew Research Center estimate:* Jens Manuel Krogstad, senior editor, Pew Research Center, quoted in García, "As Illegal Border Crossings Drop."

80    *1.2 percent of all fifty-six million visitors:* In 2015 Homeland Security reported 44,928,381 visitors; of that number, 482,781 (or 1.07 percent) overstayed their visas, "Entry/Exit Overstay Report, Fiscal Year 2015," iv. In 2021 those figures were: 55,928,990 legal entries and 676,422 (1.21 percent) people who stayed, ignoring their expiration dates. García, "As Illegal Border Crossings Drop."

80    *The great majority of them were Canadians:* There were 99,906 Canadians who overstayed their visas that year as opposed to 45,272 Mexicans. "Entry/Exit Overstay Report," 14.

## PART II: TURF AND SKIN

### CHAPTER 4: WHY THEY LEFT, WHERE THEY WENT

83    *"I'm going to sing America!":* From Julia Álvarez's unpublished poem "I, Too, Sing America." See "Dominican-American Author Julia Álvarez Reading from Her Work" (audio recording, 31:57), Archive of Hispanic Literature on Tape (Library of Congress), 2015, https://www.loc.gov/item/2016686124/.

83    *the first non-Indian:* Sam Roberts, "Honoring a Very Early New Yorker," *New York Times*, October 2, 2012.

83    *born of an African woman and a Portuguese sailor:* A comprehensive description of Juan Rodriguez (also known as Jan Rodrigues) can be found in Anthony Stevens-Acevedo, Tom Weterings, and Leonor Álvarez Francés, *Juan Rodriguez and the Beginnings of New York City* (New York: CUNY Dominican Studies Institute, 2013).

84    *learned her Munsee tongue:* Most Lenape spoke Munsee, a dialect of the Delaware language. Edwin G. Burrows and Mike Wallace, *Gotham: A History of New York City to 1898* (New York: Oxford University Press, 1999), 5.

84    *richly endowed Manahatta:* Burrows and Wallace, *Gotham*, 3.

85    *Juan and his cohort, became the first free "African American":* "Juan Rodriguez, an Original New Yorker," janos.nyc. https://janos.nyc/history/juan-rodriguez-an-original-new-yorker/.

85    *Thirteen thousand of them:* Hansi Lo Wang, "New York City Bodegas and the Generations Who Love Them," *All Things Considered*, NPR, March 10, 2017.

## Dominican Americans

85 *"We are a Dominican-ass family"*: Elizabeth Acevedo, "How to Keep Stirring," *Bon Appetit*, December 2021–January 2022, 47.

86 *Comfortable in black neighborhoods*: Lance Freeman, "A Note on the Influence of African Heritage on Segregation: The Case of Dominicans," *Urban Affairs Review 35*, no. 1 (1999): 137–46.

86 *"It's possible to be too white"*: Julia Álvarez, author interview, May 17, 2021.

87 *"We Dominicans in the United States have the highest rate"*: Junot Díaz, author interview, May 14, 2021.

87 *a lowly sugarcane plantation guard*: Michele Wucker, *Why the Cocks Fight: Dominicans, Haitians and the Struggle for Hispaniola* (New York: Hill & Wang, 1999). See Wucker's article, "The River Massacre," *Tikkun*, November 1998.

88 *Trujillo ordered a mass genocide*: Robert Crassweller, *The Life and Times of a Caribbean Dictator* (New York: Macmillan, 1966), 156.

88 *"pigmentocracy"*: Jeremy Tarbox, "Racist Massacre in the Dominican Pigmentocracy," *Eureka Street* 22, no. 19 (October 1, 2012).

88 *pressing known criminals into service*: Richard Lee Turrets, "A World Destroyed, a Nation Imposed: The 1937 Haitian Massacre in the Dominican Republic," *Hispanic American Historical Review* 82, no. 3 (2002): 589–635.

89 *The killing was rampant, merciless*: Turrets, "A World Destroyed, a Nation Imposed."

89 *Dominicans of all walks—be they intellectuals, politicians, businessmen*: René Fortunato, *Trujillo: El Poder del Jefe*, documentary, Edison Rivas, producer. Dominican Republic: 1991.

89 *nearly thirty thousand blacks had been slaughtered*: Fortunato, *Trujillo*. The documentary cites as many as fifty thousand. Generally, the figures cited a range from fifteen thousand to fifty thousand. See also Philip L. Martin, Susan Forbes Martin, and Patrick Weil, *Managing Migration: The Promise of Cooperation* (Lanham, MD: Lexington Books, 2006), 163.

89 *"I know he is an SOB, but at least he is our SOB"*: George Lopez and Michael Stohl, *Liberalization and Democratization* (New York: Greenwood, 1987), 258. This quote is variously attributed to Secretary of State Cordell Hull about Trujillo, or to Franklin D. Roosevelt about Nicaragua's Anastasio Somoza. It is also claimed to have been said by FDR about Generalissimo Francisco Franco of Spain. The conjecture by many historians and journalists is that it was probably a phrase used generally in the day about dictators and strongmen whom the United Sates supported. Kevin Drum, "But He's Our Son of a Bitch," *Washington Monthly*, May 16, 2006.

89  *CIA, finally, due to pressure from Washington:* James Wilderotter (associate deputy attorney general), memo for the file, January 2, 1975, "skeletons in closet," item (11), "CIA apparently 'plotted' the assassination of foreign leaders, including Trujillo," https://nsarchive2.gwu.edu/NSAEBB/NSAEBB222/family_jewels_wilderotter.pdf.

90  *"the exercise of an international police power":* This is known as the Roosevelt Corollary to the Monroe Doctrine. See Mark Neocleous, "Under the Sign of Security: Trauma, Terror, Resilience," in *War Power, Police Power* (Edinburgh: Edinburgh University Press, 2014). See also Salvador E. Gomez, "The US Invasion of the Dominican Republic: 1965," *Sincronía* 2, no. 2 (Spring/Primavera 1997) online, accessed July 14, 2023, http://sincronia.cucsh.udg.mx/dominican.html.

90  *that grand "American Lake":* Ransford W. Palmer, ed., *U.S.-Caribbean Relations: Their Impact on Peoples and Culture* (Westport, CT: Praeger, 1998), 11.

90  *Johnson ordered twenty-two thousand US Marines:* McNamara cites at least twenty-one thousand. Robert McNamara, US secretary of defense, to Lyndon Johnson, president of the United States, "Draft Memorandum: Courses of Action in Vietnam," November 3, 1965, available at US Department of State Office of the Historian online, accessed July 14, 2023, https://history.state.gov/historicaldocuments/frus1964-68v03/d189. See also Glenn Hastedt, *Encyclopedia of American Foreign Policy* (New York: Facts on File, 2004), 134. Other sources cite as many as 42,000 marines and airborne troops.

90  *"their independence destroyed":* William R. Shepherd, "The Caribbean Policy of the United States," *Journal of International Relations* 11, no. 1 (July 1920): 87–108, https://www.jstor.org/stable/29738383.

90  *"You'd be surprised!":* Lou Cannon, "Latin Trip an Eye-Opener for Reagan," *Washington Post*, December 6, 1982.

91  *soared from a mere twelve thousand immigrants to seven hundred thousand:* Ralph Salvador Oropesa and Leif Jensen, "Dominican Immigrants and Discrimination in a New Destination: The Case of Reading, Pennsylvania," *City & Community* 9, no. 3 (September 1, 2010): 274–98, doi: 10.1111/j.1540-6040.2010.01330.x.

91  *Álvarez's father, a physician:* Julia Álvarez, author interview. See also Julia Álvarez Biography, Chicago Public Library, www.chipublilib.org/julia-alvarez-biography/.

91  *"I had a father who was in the post-Trujillo military apparatus":* Olga Segura, "Junot Díaz Talks Dominican Identity, Immigration and the (Complicated) American Dream," *America: The Jesuit Review* online, last modified, May 4,

2017, https://www.americamagazine.org/arts-culture/2017/05/04/junot
-diaz-talks-dominican-identity-immigration-and-complicated-american. See
also Jordi Gassó, "Dominican author displays depth," *Yale Daily News*, January 26, 2010. "Díaz . . . involves himself in liberal causes like immigration
reform, which he accredits to growing up with a 'fascist, trujillista, right-wing
lunatic of a father.'"

92   *"fought on the side of the Americans":* Nicholas Wroe, "Junot Díaz: A Life in
Books," *Guardian* (US edition) online, last modified August 31, 2012, https://
www.theguardian.com/books/2012/aug/31/life-in-books-junot-diaz.

92   *a midsize city of tough-guy Puerto Ricans, Cubans, and blacks:* There were hardly
any Dominicans in Paterson at the time. Díaz, quoted in Segura, "Junot Díaz
Talks Dominican Identity."

92   *more than one-third of Paterson's residents:* Jayed Rahman, "Paterson's Largest
Hispanic Community Celebrates Renaming Park Avenue to Dominican Republic Way," *Paterson (NJ) Times*, October 8, 2016. See also "Paterson, New
Jersey, Population 2023," World Population Review online, https://world
populationreview.com/us-cities/paterson-nj-population.

92   *are less likely to be educated:* Max J. Castro, *The Dominican Diaspora Revisited:
Dominicans and Dominican Americans in a New Century* (Miami: Dante Fascell
North-South Center, 2002).

93   *"Fundamentally, almost no one coming from the Dominican Republic":* Senator
Jeffrey Sessions, quoted in Sam Stein and Amanda Terkel, "Donald Trump's
Attorney General Nominee Wrote Off Nearly All Immigrants from an Entire Country," Huffington Post, last modified November 19, 2016, https://
www.huffpost.com/entry/jeff-sessions-dominican-immigrants_n_582f9d1
4e4b030997bbf8ded. Sessions became attorney general of the nation under
President Trump, tendered his resignation at Trump's request for recusing
himself from any legal investigation into Trump's Russian dealings, then ran
to reclaim his old Senate seat in 2020, but lost.

93   *Take Shirley Collado:* Shirley Collado, author interview, June 10, 2021.

93   *bastion of whiteness:* Lisa Benavides, "How VU Tackles Tough Job of Lassoing
More Diversity," *Tennessean* (Nashville), Metro, November 19, 1995.

94   *Mario is a genial, round-faced young man:* Mario Álvarez, author interview, August 9, 2021, and April 22, 2022.

94   *"We relieved ourselves in the backyard":* Álvarez, author interview, August 9,
2021, and April 22, 2022.

94   *The idea of Prep for Prep was to be disruptive:* Vinson Cunningham, "Prep for
Prep and the Fault Lines in New York's Schools," *New Yorker*, March 9, 2020.

95 *"The rich white kids laughed"*: Mario Álvarez, author interviews.

95 *"I could have joined the majority"*: Álvarez, author interviews.

**Honduran Americans**

96 *"The history of Honduras"*: Roberto Sosa, "Secreto Militar," my translation, https://circulodepoesia.com/2010/06/la-trayectoria-poetica-de-roberto-sosa/.

96 *Raymundo Paniagua is a marine biologist*: Because of this individual's status as an undocumented resident of the United States and because of the obvious dangers to him, I have given him and his brother (Alex) pseudonyms. His story is based on more than a dozen personal and telephone interviews from June 2021 through June 2023.

98 *Matta Ballesteros, the most notorious narco-trafficker in Honduras*: Steven Dudley, "Honduras Elites and Organized Crime: Juan Ramón Matta Ballesteros," April 9, 2016, insightcrime.org, Honduras.

99 *Brother Tony would be sentenced to life in prison*: United States Drug Enforcement Administration (DEA), "DEA Announces Arrest of Former Honduran Congressman and Brother of Current President of Honduras for Drug Trafficking and Weapons Charges," press release, November 26, 2018.

99 *from congressman to president*: Hernández was first elected to the Honduran Congress in 1997, the year of Raymundo's car accident involving his brother. United States Department of Justice, "Juan Orlando Hernández, Former President of Honduras, Indicted on Drug-Trafficking and Firearms Charges, Extradited to the United States from Honduras," press release, April 21, 2022, https://www.justice.gov/opa/pr/juan-orlando-hern%C3%A1ndez-former-president-honduras-indicted-drug-trafficking.

100 *Environmentalists and journalists*: Olivia Le Poidevin, "Environment Activists: 'I Got Death and Rape Threats,'" BBC News online, last modified September 17, 2020, https://www.bbc.com/news/av/science-environment-54165868.

100 *Berta Cáceres, an indigenous activist*: "Berta Cáceres: Ex–Dam Company Boss Guilty of Planning Honduran Activist's Murder," BBC online, last modified July 5, 2021, https://www.bbc.com/news/world-latin-america-57725007. See also "The Death of the Guardian," Revistazo, Asociación para una Sociedad Más Justa, November 30, 2018.

100 *Alex, and a cohort of civil rights lawyers*: Poder Ejecutivo: Decreto Ejecutivo Número PCM-059-2015. The $5 million suit was brought on behalf of the Asociación de Ex Trabajadores Bananeros de Norte de Honduras (ASEXTBANH), claiming that Standard Fruit had inflicted harm by employing

dibromocloropropane (DBCP), a potent pesticide that had caused severe and extensive psychological, physical, and genetic damage to its Honduran workers. "Alex" is a pseudonym used to protect his brother "Raymundo," given Raymundo's current unauthorized status in the United States.

100   *Alex ended up dead:* Paniagua, author interviews.


## The Northern Triangle

100   *H.R. 3524, A Bill:* 116th Congress, "H.R.3524 - Northern Triangle and Border Stabilization Act," Sponsor: Representative Zoe Lofgren (D-CA), introduced June 27, 2019, https://www.congress.gov/bill/116th-congress/house-bill /3524/text?r=3&s=1.

101   *grew exponentially in the first decade:* "The Hispanic Population: 2010," 2010 Census Briefs, census.gov/history/pdf/c2010br-04-092020.pdf.

101   *highest murder rate in the world:* Amelia Cheatham, "Central America's Turbulent Northern Triangle," Council on Foreign Relations, last modified July 1, 2021.

101   *a traffic that represents more than $150 billion annually:* Beau Kilmer, "Americans' Spending on Illicit Drugs Nears $150 Billion Annually; Appears to Rival What Is Spent on Alcohol," RAND Corporation, news release, August 20, 2019, https://www.rand.org/news/press/2019/08/20.html#:~:text =Researchers.

101   *exceeding the GDPs of the vast majority of countries:* worldometers.info lists the GDP of 189 countries the world over; 138 of them have GDPs less than $150 billion.

101   *power of a drug lord:* Michael Sinclair, "The Wicked Problem of Drug Trafficking in the Western Hemisphere," Brookings online, last modified January 15, 2021, https://www.brookings.edu/blog/order-from-chaos/2021/01/15/the -wicked-problem-of-drug-trafficking-in-the-western-hemisphere/.

101   *The region swings from drought to deluge:* Sarah Bermeo and David Leblang, "Climate, Violence, and Honduran Migration to the United States," Brookings online, last modified April 1, 2021, https://www.brookings.edu/blog /future-development/2021/04/01/climate-violence-and-honduran-migra tion-to-the-united-states/.

101   *one out of every six migrants who fled the Northern Triangle:* To be precise, 116,280 of the nearly 684,000 migrants. "Central American Migration: Root Causes and U.S. Policy," In Focus, Congressional Research Service, Updated March 31, 2022. See also Nick Miroff, Andrew Ba Tran, and Leslie Shapiro,

"Hundreds of Minors Are Crossing the Border Each Day Without Their Parents. Who Are They?," *Washington Post*, March 11, 2021.

101  *Of the two million souls who headed for the United States:* Cheatham, "Central America's Turbulent Northern Triangle."

102  *US Border Patrol apprehended an average of 240,000 unauthorized migrants:* "Southwest Land Border Encounters," US Customs and Border Protection, accessed July 5, 2023, https://www.cbp.gov/newsroom/stats/southwest -land-border-encounters.

102  *although only a half million:* 460,000, to be exact. D'Vera Cohn, Jeffrey S. Passel, and Ana Gonzalez-Barrera, "1. Recent Trends in Northern Triangle Immigration," in *Rise in U.S. Immigrants from El Salvador, Guatemala and Honduras Outpaces Growth from Elsewhere,* Pew Research Center online, December 7, 2017, https://www.pewresearch.org/hispanic/2017/12/07/recent-trends-in -northern-triangle-immigration/.

102  *migrants sent home $16 billion:* "Remittance Flows Worldwide in 2017," Pew Research Center online, last modified April 3, 2019, https://www.pewre search.org/global/interactives/remittance-flows-by-country/.

103  *boosted El Salvador's GDP by nearly 22 percent:* Piotr Plewa, "Migration from El Salvador to the U.S.: A Background Brief," Duke University Center for International & Global Studies, April 14, 2021.

103  *"I feel no bond with a Cuban or an Argentine":* Dagoberto Gilb, author interview, June 7, 2021.

## Salvadoran Americans

104  *"I am what comes after the civil war":* Yesika Salgado, "Diaspora Writes to Her New Home," *Hermosa* (Los Angeles: Not a Cult, 2019).

104  *Tanita is a small, energetic Salvadoran:* Tanita, author interviews, May 13, 20, 27, June 3, 10, 17, 2021. The informant has elected to use her first name only. I use the same approach with her family.

105  *the average wage of a local schoolteacher:* "Salaries San Miguel (El Salvador)," BDEEX, accessed July 14, 2023, https://bdeex.com/el-salvador/san-miguel/.

105  *not least the United and Standard Fruit companies:* Much has been written about the predatory practices of these companies in Latin America, not least by journalist-novelist Gabriel García Márquez and diplomat-poet Pablo Neruda. For a more comprehensive history, see Steve Striffler and Mark Mobler, eds., *Banana Wars: Power, Production and History in the Americas* (Durham, NC: Duke University Press, 2003).

105   *had even reached, by every rational definition, semicolonial status:* John Weeks,
      "An Interpretation of the Central American Crisis," *Latin American Research
      Review* 21, no. 3 (1986): 35.

105   *in all five, at least one government had been removed or installed:* Ibid.

105   democracias de fachada: Ibid., 40.

105   *"I used to believe in democracy":* Paniagua, author interview, April 16, 2021.

106   *a brutal retaliation by American-trained soldiers of the Atlácatl Battalion:* For a har-
      rowing, meticulous description of these events, see Mark Danner, *The Mas-
      sacre at El Mozote* (New York: Alfred A. Knopf, 1994).

107   *one quarter of the population of Nicaragua:* "Displacement in Central Amer-
      ica," The United Nations Refugee Agency, https://www.unhcr.org/en-us
      /displacement-in-central-america.html.

107   *genocide of the Mayan people:* Billy Briggs, "Secrets of the Dead," *Guardian* (US
      edition) online, last modified February 1, 2007, https://www.theguardian
      .com/theguardian/2007/feb/02/features11.g2.

107   *Honduras was now a staging area:* Julia Preston, "Honduras: Sandinistas
      Bombed," *Washington Post*, December 8, 1986.

107   *"Not us! We lived under the ire of a volcano":* Tanita, author interviews.

107   *to force boys as young as twelve into service:* Jocelyn Courtney, "The Civil War
      That Was Fought by Children: Understanding the Role of Child Combatants
      in El Salvador's Civil War, 1980–1992," *Journal of Military History* 74, no. 2
      (2010): 525.

108   *seventy-five thousand Salvadorans were dead:* Mike Allison, "El Salvador's Brutal
      Civil War: What We Still Don't Know," *Al Jazeera*, March 1, 2012.

108   *Chapultepec Peace Accords:* United Nations Security Council, *Report of the UN
      Truth Commission on El Salvador*, S/25500, April 1, 1993, 192, http://www
      .derechos.org/nizkor/salvador/informes/truth.html.

108   *"criminal aliens":* Jennifer M. Chacón, "Whose Community Shield?: Examin-
      ing the Removal of the Criminal Street Gang Member," *University of Chicago
      Legal Forum*, vol. 2007, Article 11, 324.

109   *homicide rate that is 500 percent higher:* "Central American Youth Programs
      Threatened as Department of Labor Funding on the Line," Catholic Relief
      Services, El Salvador, April 13, 2017. See also "The Central America Migration
      Crisis," Catholic Relief Services: www.crs.org. For 700 percent, see *"Global
      Study on Homicide,"* United Nations Office on Drugs and Crime (UNODC),
      Vienna, 2019.

109   *nearly four hundred thousand aspirants:* "Central American Migration: Root

Causes and U.S. Policy," Congressional Research Service, updated March 31, 2022.

109 *classification called Temporary Protective Status:* "Temporary Protective Status: An Overview," American Immigration Council, May 20, 2022.

110 *TPS is not a legal status:* Carolyn Gallaher, "This Region Has One of the Largest Salvadoran Communities. A Federal Program Puts That in Jeopardy," Greater Greater Washington online, last modified August 23, 2017, https://ggwash.org/view/64531/dc-has-one-of-the-nations-largest-salvadoran -communities.-a-federal-program.

110 *there are almost four million—forty-four times:* Erin Babich and Jeanne Batalova, "Central American Immigrants in the United States," Migration Policy Institute, Migration Information Source, August 11, 2021.

**The Department of Second Chances**

111 *"This country is the mother of second chances":* Jorge Ramos, in "Jorge Ramos, Time's 100 Most Influential People, Keynote Speech at UCLA Graduation," UCLA Extension video, June 19, 2015.

111 *Paniagua finally managed to find a room:* Paniagua, author interviews.

**CHAPTER 5: SHADES OF BELONGING**

113 *"Imagine having to constantly tell people that you're made of two colors":* Cindy Y. Rodriguez, "Which Is It, Hispanic or Latino?," CNN online, last modified May 3, 2014, https://www.cnn.com/2014/05/03/living/hispanic-latino -identity/index.html.

113 *in the 1850s, Mexicanos:* "Until 1930, Mexicans, the dominant Hispanic national origin group, had been classified as white." Kim Parker et al., "Race and Multiracial Americans in the U.S. Census" (1790–2010), *Report: Multiracial in America,* Pew Research Center online, last modified June 11, 2015, https://www.pewresearch.org/social-trends/2015/06/11/chapter-1-race-and-multi racial-americans-in-the-u-s-census/.

114 *when Disney unveiled Lin-Manuel Miranda's:* Aja Romero, "The Backlash Against In the Heights, Explained," Vox, last modified June 15, 2021, https://www.vox.com/culture/22535040/in-the-heights-casting-backlash-colorism -representation.

115 *bizarre loophole allowing a mulatto to purchase "whiteness":* This was the ability, granted by Spain's *Cedulas de Gracias al Sacar* for mulattos or mestizos with influence and money to buy rights granted to whites that were unavailable to

the colored races. See James F. King, "The Case of José Ponciano de Ayarza: A Document on Gracias al Sacar," *Hispanic American Historical Review* 31, no. 4 (November 1951): 640–47.

116 *"According to family legend, I was one hundred percent white"*: Javier Lizarzaburu, "Quién diablos soy?," BBC Mundo, Lima, 1 julio 2013. Although I have known Javier Lizarzaburu for decades and we have spoken of this often, all material on him recounted here is taken from his series for BBC, which ran from July 1–5, 8–12, 19, 2013, https://www.bbc.com/mundo/noticias /2013/07/130701_serie_adn_quien_diablos_soy_1_historias_sacadas_de _un_cajon.

118 *the fierce anti-Spanish Black Legend:* According to scholar George Mariscal of the University of California, the Black Legend represents 450 years of European writings that have "cast Spain as the cruel, arrogant, irrational southern neighbor of the continent." Mariscal, "The Role of Spain in Contemporary Race Theory," *Arizona Journal of Hispanic Cultural Studies* 2 (1998): 7.

118 *"Of all nations under heaven"*: Edmund Spenser, "A View of the Present State of Ireland," http://www.luminarium.org/renascence-editions/veue1.html.

118 *"Africa begins in the Pyrenees"*: This phrase is often attributed to Alexandre Dumas, but historians agree it was probably French ambassador Dominique Dufour de Pradt who said essentially the same in his 1816 account of the Peninsular War. K. Meira Goldberg, *Sonidos Negros* (New York: Oxford University, 2019), 92.

### Shades of Invisibility

119 *"We didn't cross the border"*: This was a popular activist chant in protests throughout the American southwest and elsewhere in the United States. It was thought to have been inspired by the Chicano Movement of the 1960s. See Neil Foley, *Mexicans in the Making of America* (Cambridge, MA: Belknap Press, 2014), 147.

119 *Mexican Americans became white via the law:* Cybelle Fox and Irene Bloemraad, "Beyond 'White by Law': Explaining the Gulf in Citizenship Acquisition between Mexican and European Immigrants, 1930," *Social Forces* 94, no. 1 (September 2015): 183.

119 *They'd had no such ambitions before:* Brandon Morgan, "The Border Crossed Us," section of chapter 8, "U.S. Conquests of New Mexico," in *The History of New Mexico* (Albuquerque: Central New Mexico Community College, 2015).

120 *an 1839 article in* La Luna, *a Chihuahua newspaper:* Quoted in Anthony Mora,

*Border Dilemmas: Racial and National Uncertainties in New Mexico, 1848–1912* (Durham, NC: Duke University Press, 2011), 47.

120  *reverse one-drop rule had long operated among Mexicans:* Laura E. Gómez, *Inventing Latinos: A New Story of American Racism* (New York: New Press, 2020), 151.

120  *They were demanding whiteness:* Neil Foley, "Mexican Americans and the Faustian Pact with Whiteness," in *Reflexiones, 1997: New Directions in Mexican American Studies,* ed. Neil Foley (Austin, TX: Center for Mexican American Studies, 1998), 53–70. Also Laura E. Gómez, *Manifest Destinies: The Making of the Mexican American Race* (New York: New York University Press, 2007).

120  *Anglos began to blame:* I am using the definition Brandon Morgan uses in his digital notes for *The History of New Mexico,* but applying it to Mexican Americans in general: "Although the term 'Anglo' broadly refers to anyone of British or Anglo-Saxon linguistic descent, in New Mexico history the term refers to people from the Eastern United States who first migrated to the area in the 1820s. Following the US-Mexico War, more and more Anglo Americans arrived in New Mexico in search of economic and political power during the territorial period."

120  *blame Mexicanos for taking their jobs:* Erin Blakemore, "The Brutal History of Anti-Latino Discrimination in America," History.com, last modified September 27, 2017.

120  *forcibly removed as many as two million people of Mexican descent:* Gómez, *Inventing Latinos,* 29.

120  *the word* Mexican *suddenly appeared on the census:* Julie Dowling, quoted in Gene Demby, "On the Census, Who Checks 'Hispanic,' Who Checks 'White,' and Why," *Code Switch,* NPR, June 16, 2014.

121  *true assimilation was little more than a hollow hope:* I am using Laura E. Gómez's characterization here. Gómez, *Inventing Latinos,* 179.

121  *the 1930 census was used to round up Japanese Americans:* Dowling, in "On the Census, Who Checks 'Hispanic,' Who Checks 'White,' and Why."

121  *The story of Rubén Aguilar:* "Drafted to Fight for the Country That Hurt Him," *Morning Edition,* NPR, April 5, 2013.

121  *"What I remember":* Ibid.

121  *"Right around the corner":* Ibid.

121  *"going to places like Medicine Bow, Wyoming":* University of Arizona professor David Taylor and Mexican artist Marcos Ramirez set out in July of 2014 to mark the original US border with Mexico (that is, the one with the Viceroyalty of New Spain before 1821 and the subsequently independent republic). See "Delimitations: A survey of the 1821 border between Mexico and the

United States, https://delimitationsblog.tumblr.com/. Also: Carolina Miranda, "Why two artists surveyed the U.S.-Mexico border . . . the one from 1821," *Los Angeles Times*, July 22, 2016.

122   *more than one in nine Americans are of Mexican extraction*: There are more than 40 million people of Mexican origin in this country. Against a population of 330 million, they represent 12 percent.

122   *by 1940, the lion's share of Mexican Americans were native born*: Mario T. García, quoting the U.S. Census, *The Latino Generation* (Chapel Hill, NC: University of North Carolina Press, 2014), 14.

122   *more than 70 percent of Mexican Americans*: US Census, B05006, "Place of Birth for the Foreign-Born Population in the United States, 2019 American Community Survey 1-Year Estimates." United States Census Bureau, July 1, 2019.

122   *full third say they face racism every day*: T. H. Chan, "Poll finds one-third of Latinos say they have experienced discrimination in their jobs and when seeking housing," Harvard School of Public Health Press Release, November 1, 2017.

122   *backlash in the Chicano movement*: Marita Hernandez, "Chicano Movement: Generation in Search of Its Legacy," *Los Angeles Times*, August 14, 1983.

122   *"We were driven by a hot, passionate anger"*: Ibid.

123   *William C. Velásquez, who, after years of leading protest marches*: For the full story of Willie Velásquez, see Juan A. Sepúlveda Jr.'s excellent biography, *Life and Times of Willie Velásquez* (Houston: Arte Publico Press, 2006). Also useful is Hector Galán's documentary on Velásquez, "Willie Velásquez: Your Vote Is Your Voice," which premiered on PBS in 2016.

123   *greatly advanced the full, activist embrace of Latinidad*: Marlene Santos, "How the Roots of the Chicano Movement Are Present Today," Nueva Verdad Publicación (NUVE), November 7, 2019.

## The Census and Latinidad

124   *"The Constitution's original sin"*: Gómez, *Inventing Latinos*, 143.

124   *massacre as many as three hundred*: Myles Hudson, "Wounded Knee Massacre," *Encyclopedia Britannica*, https://www.britannica.com/event/Wounded-Knee-Massacre. There would be more skirmishes after Wounded Knee; the Indian Wars began in 1622 with the Jamestown Massacre and lasted until 1924.

124   *proclaimed the "unsettled" frontier to exist no longer*: US Census, "Following the Frontier Line," 1880s, 1890s, September 6, 2012, https://www.census.gov/dataviz/visualizations/001/.

124 *In 1850, a landmark year, clerks began to register:* US Census figures, 1850.

125 *the census began to tally Indians:* US Census figures, 1860.

125 *"a form of surveillance":* Naomi Mezey, "Erasure and Recognition: The Census, Race, and the National Imagination," *Northwestern University Law Review* 97 (2003): 1730.

125 *in 1860 recorded a mere forty thousand Native Americans:* US Census figures, 1860.

125 *the more accurate number was almost ten times greater:* 340,000 to be exact. James P. Collins, "Native Americans in the Census, 1869–1890," *Prologue* 38, no. 2 (Summer 2006), https://www.archives.gov/publications/prologue/2006/summer/indian-census.html.

126 *afraid of how the information might be used:* Richard Reid, "The 1870 United States Census and the Black Undernumeration," *Histoire sociale/Social History*, York University, Canada, file://Users/aranam/Downloads/admin,+hssh28n56_reid%20(4).pdf.

126 *Indian, Chinese, Hindu, Korean, and Japanese:* This was the 1890 census. US Census figures, 1890.

126 *By 1900, when there were already a minimum of a half million:* James Gregory, "Latinx Great Migrations," *America's Great Migration Project*, Civil Right and Labor History Consortium, University of Washington, https://depts.washington.edu/moving1/latinx_migration.shtml.

126 *It began when the League of the United Latin American Citizens:* Dowling, in "On the Census, Who Checks 'Hispanic,' Who Checks 'White,' and Why."

127 *propelled anywhere from six hundred thousand to more than a million Mexicans:* For six hundred thousand: "Immigration and Relocation in U.S. History: A Growing Community," Library of Congress online, https://www.loc.gov/classroom-materials/immigration/mexican/a-growing-community/.

127 *more than a million:* "Revolution and War, 1910 to 1921," *Mexican Emigration to the United States 1897–1931: Socio-Economic Patterns*, https://open.uapress.arizona.edu/.

127 *an America that was 90 percent white:* The exact figure was actually 89.8 percent. D'Vera Cohn, "The 1940 Census: A Few FAQs," Pew Research Center online, last modified April 3, 2012, https://www.pewresearch.org/social-trends/2012/04/03/the-1940-census-a-few-faqs/.

127 *"It would of course be an exaggeration":* Kenneth Prewitt, "A Nation Imagined, A Nation Measured: The Jeffersonian Legacy," in *Across the Continent: Jefferson, Lewis & Clark, and the Making of America*, ed. Douglas Seefeldt, Jeffrey L. Hantman, and Peter S. Onus (Charlottesville: University of Virginia Press, 2004), 152.

127   *In 1960 the official number of people "of Spanish surnames":* "Table 1. Nativity, Parentage, and Country of Origin of White Persons of Spanish Surname, by Sex, for Five Southwestern States, Urban and Rural: 1960," US Census online, https://www2.census.gov/library/publications/decennial/1960/population -volume-2/41927938v2p1a-1ech04.pdf.

127   *they, too, marked "white" on the census:* Camilo Vargas and Marlon Bishop, "The Invention of Hispanics," *Latino USA,* Futuro Media, May 22, 2015.

**Birth of "The Hispanic"**

128   *"Nixon found us. He made us known and famous":* Henry M. Ramirez, *A Chicano in the White House: The Nixon No One Knew* (self-pub., Maryland, 2014), 19.

128   *"I know who you Mexicans are":* Quoted by Henry Ramirez, director of the Cabinet Committee on the Opportunities of Spanish Speaking People, "Nixon Now Podcast—Henry Ramirez on Richard Nixon and the Mexican Diaspora," Nixon Foundation, May 19, 2018, nixonfoundation.org.

128   *"The Hispanic culture is one to which this nation":* President Richard M. Nixon, Proclamation, September 12, 1969, quoted in "Richard Nixon and Hispanic Heritage," Richard Nixon Foundation, September 15, 2014.

129   *Count us. Invest in us:* Henry Ramirez, "Nixon Now Podcast."

129   *Let's do it. All of it. Start the paperwork:* Ibid.

130   *Mexican American bishop Patricio Flores:* Flores was consecrated on May 5, 1970. Adrian Chavana, "Flores, Patricio Fernández," *Texas State Historical Association,* TSHA handbook online.

130   *a run of Latina treasurers would follow:* After Nixon appointed Romana Acosta Bañuelos, Latina US treasurers would be appointed by presidents from both parties: Katherine Davalos Ortega, appointed by Ronald Reagan and then by George H. W. Bush; Catalina Vasquez Villalpando, a George H. W. Bush appointee; Rosario Marin, appointed by George W. Bush; Anna Escobedo Cabral, appointed by George W. Bush; Rosie Rios, appointed by Barack Obama; and Jovita Carranza, appointed by Donald Trump.

130   *Nixon selected more Hispanics to high positions:* Jessie Kratz, "President Nixon and the Hispanic Strategy," National Archives, Pieces of History, October 3, 2014.

130   *White House began immediate pressure:* Cristina Mora, author of *Making Hispanics: How Activists, Bureaucrats, and Media Created a New American,* in an interview with Shereen Marisol Meraji, "Who Put the 'Hispanic' in Hispanic Heritage Month," *Code Switch,* podcast, NPR, September 23, 2017.

130   *the first comprehensive campaign to win the "Hispanic vote":* Mora, in Meraji, "Who Put the 'Hispanic' in Hispanic Heritage Month?"

130  *Viva Kennedy clubs:* See Ignacio M. García, *Viva Kennedy: Mexican Americans in Search of Camelot* (College Station: Texas A&M University Press, 2000).

130  *And even though Lyndon Johnson was acutely aware:* Julie Leininger Pycior, "Mexican Americans and Lyndon Johnson in 1967," *Western Historical Quarterly* 24, no. 4 (November 1993): 469–94.

131  *increased his Hispanic vote from 5 percent to 40 percent:* Kratz, "President Nixon and the Hispanic Strategy."

131  *bill to grant amnesty to two million undocumented Mexican Americans:* Ramirez, "Nixon Now Podcast."

131  *the "Nixon Hispanic Strategy":* Kratz, "President Nixon and the Hispanic Strategy."

131  *population of Latinos had more than doubled from nine million to nineteen million:* 18.9 million, to be exact. C. Denavas and M. A. Hall, *The Hispanic Population in the United States, Current Population Reports* (series P-20, Population Characteristics) 434 (December 1988): 1–89, https://pubmed.ncbi.nlm.nih .gov/12158799/.

## Up from a Steel-Town Basement

132  *"She made history this afternoon":* President Bill Clinton, speech on affirmative action at the National Archives, July 19, 1995, quoted in US Department of State Archive (2001–2009), Biography: Carolyn Curiel, Ambassador to Belize.

132  *Carolyn Curiel, a third-generation Mexican American:* Carolyn Curiel, author interviews, both in person and via email, June 2–12, 2021 and May 22–28, 2023.

132  *"In East Chicago, Indiana, where my father worked":* For background on East Chicago, the Rust Belt, and Latinos, see Emiliano Aguilar, "East Chicago's Failed Utopian Visions," *Belt Magazine*, July 1, 2021.

132  *"We were treated as inferior":* A good source on Mexican schools in general can be found in Vicki L. Ruiz, "South by Southwest: Mexican Americans and Segregated Schooling, 1900–1950," *OAH Magazine of History* 15, no. 2 (Winter 2001): 23–27.

133  *famine and deadly cycles of typhus:* There were twenty-two large-scale typhus epidemics in Mexico between 1655 and 1918. For more information on this, see Jordan N. Burns, Rudolfo Auna-Soto, and David W. Stahle, "Drought and Epidemic Typhus, Central Mexico, 1655–1918," *Journal of Emerging Infectious Diseases* 20, no. 3 (March 2014): 442–47.

133  *Between 1900 and 1930, tens of thousands:* "The History of Kansas Railroads," Kansas Department of Transportation, https://www.ksdot.org/bureaus/bur Rail/rail/railroads/history.asp.

135  *the largest employer of Mexicans in the nation:* Benjamin Turpin, "Inland Steel," *Clio: Your Guide to History,* May 4, 2020, accessed July 5, 2022, https://www.theclio.com/entry/98191.

135  *"When I hire Mexicans at the gate":* Ibid.

136  *who had leased a nearby vegetable farm:* Mendez had leased a farm from a Japanese family who was being sent off to an internment camp. Laura E. Gómez describes the Mendez case amply in *Inventing Latinos,* 107–8, 125.

136  *California laws expressly allowed the segregation of certain racial groups:* The *Mendez* case would have unexpected blowback, however. Arguing that it was unlawful for Mexican children to be barred from white schools because they were not listed as one of the undesirable races—and thus maintaining that they were legally "white"—would thrust Latino-black relations into an awkward position. Gómez, *Inventing Latinos,* 94–96, 100–103.

136  *Similar cases fighting this hidebound racism:* For an excellent summary of these cases see Ruben Donato and Jarrod Hanson, "Mexican-American resistance to school segregation," *Phi Delta Kappan* 100, no. 5 (January 21, 2019): 39–42.

138  Mendez v. Westminster *was entirely different:* Caitlin Yoshiko Kandil, "Mendez vs. segregation: famed case isn't just about Mexicans. It's about everyone coming together," *Los Angeles Times,* Daily Pilot, April 17, 2016.

138  *"foster antagonisms in the children":* This was Judge Paul J. McCormick, as quoted in "BRIA 23 2 c *Mendez v Westminster*: Paving the Way to School Desegregation," *Bill of Right in Action* 23, no. 2 (Summer 2007), https://www.crf-usa.org/bill-of-rights-in-action/bria-23-2-c-mendez-v-westminster-paving-the-way-to-school-desegregation.

139  *Governor Earl Warren:* "BRIA 23 2 c *Mendez v Westminster.*"

### The Virus of Latino Colorism

140  *"When we understand that none of us is pure":* Carlos Fuentes, *The Buried Mirror* (New York: Houghton Mifflin, 1992), 193.

140  *we are not just the race we see in the mirror:* The difference is called racial identity versus street race. Luis Noe-Bustamante et al., "4. Measuring the Racial Identity of Latinos," in *Majority of Latinos Say Skin Color Impacts Opportunity in America and Shapes Daily Life,* Pew Research Center online, last modified November 4, 2021, https://www.pewresearch.org/hispanic/2021/11/04/measuring-the-racial-identity-of-latinos/.

140  *"We are all men of La Mancha":* Fuentes, *The Buried Mirror,* 192.

140  *We are people of the stain:* A direct quote from my book *Silver, Sword, and Stone,* 345.

140 *in 2010 more than 50 percent of all Latinos:* Noe-Bustamante et al., "Measuring Racial Identity of Latinos."

140 *80 percent even described their skin:* Yadon/Ostfeld Test Scale, quoted in Noe-Bustamante et al., "Measuring Racial Identity of Latinos."

140 *serious data-processing consequences:* Hansi Lo Wang, "1 in 7 People Are 'Some Other Race' on the US Census. That's a Big Data Problem," *Weekend Edition Sunday*, NPR, September 30, 2021.

141 *Suddenly only 20 percent of us were white:* "Hispanic or Latino Origin by Race: 2010 and 2020," Table 4. United States Census, https://www2.census.gov /programs-surveys/decennial/2020/data/redistricting-supplementary-ta bles/redistricting-supplementary-table-04.pdf.

141 *a third major category had emerged: "two or more races":* "Hispanic or Latino Origin by Race: 2010 and 2020," Table 4.

141 *increased by almost 600 percent:* Ibid.

141 *"Until I came to New York, I didn't know I was black":* Chiqui Vicioso, as quoted in Earl Shorris, *Latinos: A Biography of the People* (New York: W. W. Norton, 1992), 146.

141 *"The internet was bypassing blacks and some Hispanics":* Michel Marriott, "Digital Divide Closing as Blacks Turn to Internet," *New York Times*, March 31, 2006.

141 *"Achievement gaps between white and black":* Fox News, as quoted in Amitai Etzioni's "Don't 'Brown' the Hispanics," *Nieman Reports*, September 15, 2006.

142 *Marco A. Davis, now the president of the Congressional Hispanic Caucus Institute:* Marco A. Davis interview, July 19, 2021. Davis's father is a Cuban-born Jamaican; his mother, a Mexican, was born in Guadalajara.

142 *Hispanics vanish from the picture entirely:* This point is made very firmly in Etzioni's piece "Don't 'Brown' the Hispanics."

142 *"We're here to forge a new path, fight the binary":* Junot Díaz, author interview, June 18, 2021.

142 *"will inevitably change America from within":* Ed Morales, *Latinx: The New Force in American Politics and Culture* (New York: Verso, 2018), 26.

143 *When José Vasconcelos:* The argument, written and published in Mexico in 1925 before Vasconcelos ran for the presidency in 1929, can be read in translation: Juan Vasconcelos, *The Cosmic Race* (Baltimore: Johns Hopkins University Press, 1997).

143 *"It will not take long for the population to be completely unified":* Argentina, Second National Census 1895, 48.

### The Color of Language

143 *"My father made the decision to deprive me of a language"*: Cecile Pineda, in "Imagining a Community: An Interview with Cecile Pineda, Francisco Lomeli, Mission Beach, California, February 23, 1996, from Cecile Pineda, *Face* (San Antonio, TX: Wings Press, 2013), 166.

144 *Not only do Latinos begin to lose their Spanish language proficiency:* Two interesting articles on the loss of centuries-old dialects or the creation of peculiar varieties of Spanglish: Simon Romero, "New Mexico is Losing a Form of Spanish Spoken Nowhere Else on Earth," *New York Times*, April 9, 2023; and Richard Luscombe, "'Get Down from the Car': Unique Miami Dialect Traced to Cuban Influence," *Guardian*, June 19, 2023.

144 *By the fourth generation, only half:* Mark Hugo Lopez, Ana Gonzalez-Barrera, and Gustavo López, *Hispanic Identity Fades Across Generations as Immigrant Connections Fall Away*, Pew Research Center online, last modified December 20, 2017, https://www.pewresearch.org/hispanic/2017/12/20/hispanic-identity-fades-across-generations-as-immigrant-connections-fall-away/.

144 *Whereas in the 1980s and 1990s Latino numbers were rising:* Jens Manuel Krogstad and Mark Hugo Lopez, *Hispanic Nativity Shift*, Pew Research Center online, last modified April 29, 2014, https://www.pewresearch.org/hispanic/2014/04/29/hispanic-nativity-shift/.

144 *Between 2000 and 2010, almost ten million Hispanic births were recorded:* To be exact, it was 9.6 million Hispanic births and 6.5 million immigrant arrivals during that decade span. Krogstad and Lopez, *Hispanic Nativity Shift*. See also Lopez, Gonzalez-Barrera, and López, *Hispanic Identity Fades Across Generations*.

144 *The overall immigrant numbers are still falling:* Ibid.

144 *A full 40 percent of Latinos:* Gretchen Livingston and Anna Brown, "1. Trends and Patterns in Intermarriage," in *Intermarriage in the U.S. 50 Years After Loving v. Virginia*, Pew Research Center online, last modified May 18, 2017, https://www.pewresearch.org/social-trends/2017/05/18/1-trends-and-patterns-in-intermarriage/.

144 *half of all Hispanics with a bachelor's degree:* Livingston and Brown, "1. Trends and Patterns in Intermarriage."

144 *And the overwhelming likelihood:* Brittany Rico, Rose M. Kreider, and Lydia Anderson, "Growth in Interracial and Interethnic Married-Couple Households," United States Census, July 9, 2018.

145 *although almost 20 percent of all people in this country:* Lopez, Gonzalez-Barrera, and López, *Hispanic Identity Fades Across Generations*.

## CHAPTER 6: THE COLOR LINE

146 *"There are green-eyed Mexicans":* Sandra Cisneros, *Caramelo* (New York: Alfred A. Knopf, 2003), 353.

### Whiteness

146 *"The perennial question I face": "You're Hispanic?":* Don Podesta, "When Language and Culture Are More Telling Than Race," *Washington Post,* May 16, 1997. The quote is edited for clarity.

146 *Valeria Meiller was still outraged:* Valeria Meiller, author interview, September 16, 2021.

147 *"Argentinian Taylor-Joy is the first woman of color":* I cite the original quote from *Variety,* February 28, 2021, before the article was pulled and edited. "Anya Taylor-Joy Classified as Woman of Color in *Variety* Magazine," *Marca: Cinema* (English version), Madrid, March 3, 2021. The edited version and its note: "Taylor-Joy is the first Latina to win in this category. Updated: This story has been updated. A previous version identified Anya Taylor-Joy as a person of color. She has said she identifies as a white Latina." Danielle Turchiano, "Queen's Gambit Wins Golden Globes for Best Limited Series, Actress for Anya Taylor-Joy," *Variety,* February 28, 2021.

147 *"I'm aware of the fact I don't look like a typical Latin":* Anya Taylor-Joy, quoted in Perez Hilton, "Variety Calls Anya Taylor-Joy the 'First Person of Color' to Win That Golden Globe Since Queen Latifah," https://perezhilton.com /anya-taylor-joy-variety-golden-globes-person-color-latina/.

148 *six million Europeans would pour into Argentina:* Figures run anywhere from 5.8 to 6.6 million. Benjamin Bryce, "Paternal Communities: Social Welfare and Immigration in Argentina," *Journal of Social History* 49, no. 1 (Fall 2015): 215–16.

148 *ordered a cold-blooded genocide:* Rory Carroll, "Argentinian Founding Father Recast as Genocidal Murderer," *Guardian,* January 13, 2011.

148 *fewer than five hundred thousand Latinos from these countries:* Argentine, 278,240; Chilean, 173,787; Paraguayan, 24,217; total 476,244. Pew Research Center figures, 2020.

148 *"whitewashed country":* Valeria Meiller, interviews.

148 *97 percent of her fellow Argentinians are white:* "Argentina: Demographics Profile," Index Mundi, July 2021, https://www.indexmundi.com/argentina/de mographics_profile.html.

148 *blacks represented one-third:* Lyman J. Johnson, "The Afro-Argentines of Buenos Aires, 1800–1900," *Hispanic American Historical Review* 61, no. 4 (November 1,

1981): 731–33, https://doi.org/10.1215/00182168-61.4.731. See also Cristina Olulode, "Argentina's Forgotten African Roots," *Buenos Aires Times*, June 13, 2020.

149 *"Our relationship as Latinos to whiteness":* Hector Tobar, *Our Migrant Souls: A Meditation on Race and the Meanings and Myths of "Latino"* (New York: Farrar, Straus and Giroux, 2023), 89.

149 *"It's a win-win situation":* Francisco Perdomo, interview, January 4, 2022.

149 *brown Hispanics have watched the prize jobs:* "Majority of Latinos Say Skin Color Impacts Opportunity in America and Shapes Daily Life," Pew Research Center, November 4, 2021, https://www.pewresearch.org/hispanic/wp -content/uploads/sites/5/2021/11/RE_2021.11.04_Latinos-Race-Identity _FINAL.pdf.

149 *"Of course Yale accepts Hispanic Americans":* Nelson Agelvis, international edu- cational consultant and college counselor, *Quora*, #551078153, November 27, 2018.

149 *Antonio Banderas, who is Spanish and white:* Lucía Benavides, "Why La- beling Antonio Banderas a 'Person of Color' Triggers Such a Back- lash," NPR online, last modified February 18, 2020, https://www.npr .org/2020/02/09/803809670/why-labeling-antonio-banderas-a-person-of -color-triggers-such-a-backlash.

149 *"the only other Latino at the table was a blond":* Curiel, author interviews.

149 *Carolina Santa Cruz, a successful, white Latina businesswoman:* Carolina Santa Cruz, interviews for a front-page feature: Marie Arana, "Three Marielitos, Three Manifest Destinies," *Washington Post*, July 19, 1996.

150 *border officers processing incomers gave white Cubans special privileges:* All that stopped in January 2017. During the very last days of his presidency, Barack Obama announced an abrupt end to the policy. Cubans began to be turned away at the Mexican border and treated like any other immigrant without a visa. It didn't mean they didn't come in anyway—illegally—to cast their fortunes among the undocumented. President Trump did not change the policy, although Cuban Americans—who largely supported him—thought he would. At this writing, President Biden has taken a more lenient stance. Mariakarla Nodarse Venancio, "The Biden Administration Takes Construc- tive First Steps on Cuba Relations," WOLA: Advocacy for Human Rights in the Americas, May 19, 2022, https://www.wola.org/analysis/biden-adminis tration-takes-positive-steps-on-cuba/.

150 *Immigration officials would hurry them past:* Julia Preston, "Cuban Migrants Cross into the U.S.," *New York Times*, February 12, 2016.

150   *Lissette Méndez's American beginning:* Lissette Méndez, interviews, July 22, 2021.

151   *"We were poor":* Méndez, interviews, July 22, 2021. All the quotes that follow are from these interviews.

152   *a full 85 percent of Cuban Americans in Miami are white:* Arturo Dominguez, "Anti-Blackness in the Cuban Diaspora," *Latino Rebels*, July 30, 2021, latinorebels.com.

152   *The Cuba that has remained:* Arturo Dominguez, "Anti-Blackness in the Cuban Diaspora." The four migrant waves from Cuba are as follows: 1959–1962, flight by upper- and upper-middle class Cubans of high economic station; 1965–1974, in orderly migrations known as the "freedom flights"; 1980, with the helter-skelter arrival of the Marielitos; 1989 to the present, in *balseros* (improvised rafts), border crossings from Mexico, and a visa lottery system organized by both countries.

152   *Cuba is two-thirds black:* US Department of State, Archive, "Cuba: Country Information," People, Ethnic groups: 51 percent mulatto, 11 percent black, 37 percent white, 1 percent Chinese. Information released January 20, 2009 to present. See also Julia Cooke, "Amid sweeping changes in US relations, Cuba's race problem persists," Al Jazeera America, August 13, 2015.

152   *probably closer to 72 percent:* Esteban Morales Domínguez, *Desafíos de la problemática racial en Cuba* (The Challenges of the Racial Problem in Cuba), (Havana: Fundación Fernando Ortiz, 2007). See also "Cuba Briefing Sheet," afrocubaweb.com/cuba-racial-talking-points.pdf.

152   *Even the postapartheid white abandonment of South Africa:* Since 1995, some eight hundred thousand whites have left South Africa out of a population of four million. At more than double that number, the Cuban exodus has been vastly greater. Scott C. Johnson, "South Africa's New White Flight," *Newsweek*, February 13, 2009.

152   *As the historian Ada Ferrer has documented:* I owe a debt of gratitude to this clear-eyed book, which won the Pulitzer Prize in 2022. Ada Ferrer, *Cuba: An American History* (New York: Scribner, 2021), 416. For information on blackness of Marielitos, see Monika Gosin, "The Mariel Boatlift, Haitian Migration, and the Revelations of the 'Black Refugees,'" *Anthurium: A Caribbean Studies Journal* 17, no. 2 (2021): 7, doi: http://doi.org/10.33596/anth.457.

154   *two and a half million residents of Cuban origin:* "Latino Population by Nativity and Origin: Total Cuban-Origin Population," Pew Research Center raw Excel charts, 2018 figures.

154   *more than a quarter of the population of Cuba:* The population of Cuba in 2021 was approximately eleven million.

154   *almost 80 percent speak Spanish at home:* Gustavo López, "Hispanics of Cuban
Origin in the United States, 2013," Pew Research Center online, last modified
September 15, 2015, https://www.pewresearch.org/hispanic/2015/09/15
/hispanics-of-cuban-origin-in-the-united-states-2013. Also Brittany Blizzard
and Jeanne Batalova, Migration Policy Institute, June 11, 2020, and "Profile: Hispanic/Latino Americans," US Department of Health and Human
Services Office of Minority Health, https://minorityhealth.hhs.gov/omh
/browse.aspx?lvl=3&lvlid=64.

154   *a higher percentage than most segments:* Only the Central Americans register as
higher use of Spanish language at home, and that is because they are more
recent immigrants. "Profile: Hispanic/Latino Americans."

154   *own more businesses:* Miguel Angel Centeno, lecture notes, "Sociology 338:
Latinos in the US, Cubans in Miami," Princeton University.

154   *40 percent of those born here:* López, "Hispanics of Cuban Origin in the United
States, 2013."

155   *Sammy Davis Jr.:* Davis claimed all his life that he was Puerto Rican, but his
biographer Will Haygood wrote that his mother was born in New York City
to Cuban parents. Davis may have feared that anti-Cuban sentiments would
hurt his record sales. Will Haygood, *In Black and White: The Life of Sammy
Davis Junior* (New York: Alfred A. Knopf, 2003), 516.

**Black Like Us**

155   *"According to media by us or for us":* Karla Cornejo Villavicencio, "The Spectacle of Latinx Colorism," *New York Times,* July 30, 2021.

155   *When Antonio Delgado was sworn in:* Jeffery C. Mays and Luis Ferré-Sadurni,
"Hochul's Lt. Governor Pick Says He is Afro-Latino. Some Latinos Object,"
*New York Times,* May 21, 2022.

156   *"I find it curious that those of us with black skin":* Mays and Ferré-Sadurni, "Hochul's Lt. Governor Pick."

157   *"We've been laboring too long under 'elite capture'":* Junot Díaz, author interview,
May 14, 2021.

157   *six million identify as Afro-Latino:* Ana Gonzalez-Barrera, "About 6 Million US
Adults Identify as Afro-Latino," Pew Research Center online, last modified
May 2, 2022.

157   *These* hermanos *and* hermanas*:* Gonzalez-Barrera, "About 6 Million US
Adults Identify as Afro-Latino." Also: Gustavo López and Ana Gonzalez-
Barrera, "Afro-Latino: A Deeply Rooted Identity Among U.S. Hispanics," Pew
Research Center, March 1, 2016.

157   *"Double discrimination"*: Gonzalez-Barrera, "About 6 Million US Adults Identify as Afro-Latino."

157   *the great majority describe themselves as white:* López and Gonzalez-Barrera, "Afro-Latino."

157   *Only one in four Afro-Latinos:* Gonzalez-Barrera, "About 6 Million US Adults Identify as Afro-Latino."

157   *2 percent of the entire American population:* Gonzalez-Barrera, "About 6 Million US Adults Identify as Afro-Latino."

157   *frightening specter of erasure:* Grace Asiegbu, "Blackness in Puerto Rico," *Medill Reports*, Medill School, Northwestern University, Winter 2020.

158   *"Based on the current rate"*: Christopher Rodriguez, "Statistical Genocide in Puerto Rico," "Sobre el proceso de blanqueamiento en PR," *Colectivo-Ilé*, posted on January 7, 2008. See also: Natasha S. Alford, "Why Some Black Puerto Ricans Choose 'White' on the Census," *New York Times*, February 9, 2020.

158   *The organization Colectivo Ilé:* "Sobre Ilé," Colectivo Ilé, https://colectivo-ile.org/?page_id=8.

158   *in 2020, despite the aggressive campaign:* Natasha S. Alford, "Why Some Black Puerto Ricans Choose 'White' on the Census."

158   *the black count dropped dramatically:* Associated Press, "Surprised by Census Results, Many in Puerto Rico Reconsider Views on Race," NBC News online, last modified October 15, 2021, https://www.nbcnews.com/news/latino/surprised-census-results-many-puerto-rico-reconsider-views-race-rcna3101.

158   *"When I'm in the Dominican Republic, I'm white"*: Mario Álvarez, author interview, August 9, 2021.

158   *Of the ten million captives who survived the journey:* "Trans-Atlantic Slave Trade—Database, Year Range 1501–1875," https://www.slavevoyages.org/voyage/database#tables.

159   *"What brought me to the New World was my blackness"*: Junot Díaz, author interview, May 14, 2021.

159   *"The United States is so obsessed with labels"*: Esmeralda Santiago, author interview, June 1, 2021.

159   *"The conquest of America was cruel"*: Mario Vargas Llosa, Nobel Prize acceptance speech, December 7, 2010, nobelprize.org.

## Asian Latinos

160   *"Sometimes Asians feel free to say derogatory, racist"*: Isabella Do-Orozco, author interview, December 2021.

160   *Isabella Do-Orozco, born in Wichita:* All information on the Do and Orozco
      families are taken from the author's interviews and correspondence with Isa-
      bella Do-Orozco (December 4, 2021, August 16, 2021, and August 2–9, 2022),
      and Sylvia Orozco (August 16, 2021).

160   *mostly white New Englanders:* "Robert R. Taylor: First Black Student at MIT,"
      MIT Black History, https://www.blackhistory.mit.edu/story/robert-r-taylor.

160   *three out of four MIT undergraduates are nonwhite:* "Enrollment Statistics," MIT
      Facts, 2021–2022, https://facts.mit.edu/enrollment-statistics/.

160   *one out of six is Hispanic:* "Enrollment Statistics," MIT Facts. See also "MIT
      Racial/Ethnic Diversity of Undergraduates," College Factual, Massachusetts
      Institute of Technology, accessed August 2, 2022, https://www.collegefac
      tual.com/colleges/massachusetts-institute-of-technology/student-life/di
      versity/.

160   *amounting to a scant six hundred thousand people:* The last time the US Census
      Bureau counted Asian Latinos appears to have been in 2010, and their figure
      was 598,000. UnidosUS confirms that they amount to 3 percent of the total
      Asian American population (22 million total), which is 660,000. "Understand-
      ing the Diverse Origins and Experiences of Asian Latinos," Progress Report,
      UnidosUS, August 22, 2021. Also see "Overview of Race and Hispanic Origin:
      2010," 2010 Census Briefs, March 2011, 14, https://www.census.gov/con
      tent/dam/Census/library/publications/2011/dec/c2010br-02.pdf. It cites
      the figure as 1.2 percent of the total US population.

160   *"write off South Vietnam as a bad investment":* This was Major General John E.
      Murray in a cable, George Veith, *Black April: The Fall of South Vietnam, 1973–75*
      (New York: Encounter Books, 2012), 59.

161   *More than a million desperate souls were abandoning South Vietnam:* See Nghia M.
      Vo, *The Vietnamese Boat People, 1954 and 1975–1992* (Jefferson, NC: McFarland,
      2006), 193.

161   *the rusty boats became easy targets for Thai pirates:* Vo, *The Vietnamese Boat People*,
      146–47.

161   *As many as four hundred thousand Vietnamese died:* Estimates range from 250,000
      to 400,000 dead; others say as many as 70 percent of the 2 million who fled
      Vietnam between 1975 and 1990 died at sea. Vo, *The Vietnamese Boat People*,
      167; also R. J. Rummel, "Statistics of Vietnamese Democide: Estimates, Cal-
      culations, and Sources," "Statistics of Democide," Table 6.1B, http://www
      .hawaii.edu/powerkills/SOD.CHAP6.HTM.

161   *Vietnamese who were found adrift on the high seas:* The rules of rescue can be
      found in the "International Convention on Maritime Search and Rescue,

Adoption: 27 April 1979; Entry into force: 22 June 1985," International Maritime Organization, imo.org.

163 *The prevailing American myth:* Andrew Van Dam, "Today's Immigrants Rise Right on Par with Ellis Island Arrivals," *Washington Post* online, July 10, 2022, accessed July 12, 2022, https://www.washingtonpost.com/business /2022/07/01/ancestry-genealogy-immigration/. I owe some of the phrasing to this excellent article.

163 *At the very top of the prosperity charts:* Census Bureau via IPUMS, Leah Boustan (Princeton University) and Ran Abramitzky (Stanford University); Van Dam, "Today's Immigrants Rise Right on Par with Ellis Island Arrivals."

163 *"Mexicans today are just as upwardly mobile":* Quotes are from Leah Boustan and Ran Abramitzky; Van Dam, "Today's Immigrants Rise Right on Par with Ellis Island Arrivals."

164 *The first Asians to inhabit the New World were Filipino:* This history is amply described in Erika Lee's fine book *The Making of Asian America* (New York: Simon & Schuster, 2015).

164 *a proliferation of chino-cubano restaurants:* Robert Sietsema, "New York Just Lost La Caridad 78, One of Its Last Cuban-Chinese Restaurants," Eater New York, August 3, 2020.

164 *Today there are more than six million Latin Americans of Asian descent:* Spanish speaking Latin America has more than four million. See "Los 10 países con más población Asiática de América Latina," Intercambio Cultural, *Bendito Extranjero*, April 12, 2021. Brazil Has 1.9 million Japanese Brazilians; see Gabriel Leão, "I Fear for Asian Communities in Brazil," Al Jazeera, April 2, 2021.

164 *the only nation outside the Far East that has elected an Asian president:* Alberto Fujimori, a Japanese Peruvian, was president of Peru from 1990 to 2000 and was convicted for human rights abuses and embezzlement in 2009. His daughter Keiko has since run for the presidency more than once.

164 *the family of Kelly Huang Chen:* "Understanding the Diverse Origins and Experiences of Asian Latinos."

165 *Or Amalia Chamorro, a Chinese Peruvian:* "Understanding the Diverse Origins and Experiences of Asian Latinos."

165 *the descendants of Valentina Álvarez and Rullia Singh:* Benjamin Gottlieb, "Punjabi Sikh–Mexican American Community Fading into History," *Washington Post*, August 13, 2012.

165 *"to preserve the ideal of American homogeneity":* "The Immigration Act of 1924 (The Johnson-Reed Act)," Milestones 1921–1936, Office of the Historian, Department of State, history.state.gov.

165 *"subversive" or "loathsomely diseased":* Felipe Fernández-Armesto, *Our America: A Hispanic History of the United States* (New York: W. W. Norton, 2014), 246.

165 *Thind's case went all the way to the Supreme Court:* Sidin Vadukut, "Déjà View: Aryans in America," *Mint* online magazine, July 10, 2015, https://www.live mint.com/Opinion/xXujja7aZkNg5XSc8w8jJL/Aryans-in-America.html.

165 *a "white person of good character":* H. R. 40, Naturalization Bill, March 4, 1790, Records of the US Senate, National Archives and Records Administration.

165 *"great body of our people instinctively":* United States vs. Bhagat Singh Thind, January 11, 1923–February 19, 1923. Justia, U.S. Supreme Court, https://su preme.justia.com/cases/federal/us/261/204/.

166 *the country's first illegal immigrants:* Lee, *Making of Asian America.*

166 *the largest mass lynching in American history:* Seventeen Chinese men were killed by a mob of five hundred, purportedly instigated by city leaders and unstopped by the Los Angeles police. John Johnson Jr., "How Los Angeles Covered Up the Massacre of 17 Chinese," *LA Weekly,* March 10, 2011.

166 *agents known as "Chinese catchers":* Karan Mahajan, "The Two Asian Americas," *New Yorker,* October 21, 2015.

166 *the problem of the color line:* The phrase is taken from Du Bois's writings: "the problem of the Twentieth Century is the problem of the color-line." W. E. B. Du Bois, *The Souls of Black Folk* (New York: Oxford University Press, 2007), 3.

166 *plea to correct this "historic mistake":* "Repeal of the Chinese Exclusion Act, 1943," Milestones: 1937–1945, Office of the Historian, history.state.gov/milestones.

167 *a nation contaminated by race hatreds:* I owe these insights to the novelist Karan Mahajan, "Two Asian Americas."

167 *Racism became the unifying factor in the Asian American experience:* Mahajan, "Two Asian Americas."

167 *If there is any unity among Asian America today:* Ibid.

167 *the repeal of the exclusion laws:* Franklin Roosevelt was the impetus behind Congress's reform in 1943. The laws weren't truly abolished until the 1965 Immigration Law, which loosened the strictures for Asian and Latin American immigrants. Nor did Congress acknowledge or apologize for the US government's blatantly racist views until Senate Resolution 201 (October 6, 2011), in which the US Senate expressed regret for the discriminatory practices against Chinese immigrants in the various acts.

167 *Executive Order 9066:* Entered February 19, 1942; General Records of the United States Government; Record Group 11; National Archives.

167 *1,800 Peruvians:* "Hearing before the Subcommittee on Immigration, Citizenship, Refugees, Border Security and International Law," Committee on

the Judiciary, House of Representatives, 111th Congress, March 19, 2009, Serial No. 111-13, testimony of the witness Daniel M. Masterson, US Naval Academy.

167 *Citing "hemispheric security"*: Erika Lee, "The WWII Incarceration of Japanese Americans Stretched Beyond U.S. Borders," *Time,* December 4, 2019.

167 *where 120,000 Japanese Americans had been corralled*: Ibid.

167 *burned down their houses, schools, and businesses*: According to Stephanie Moore, a scholar at the Peruvian Oral History Project, six hundred Peruvian houses, schools, and businesses were torched in the anti-Asian racism provoked by the war. Jaime Gonzalez de Gispert, "The Japanese-Peruvians interned in the US during WW2," BBC Mundo, Los Angeles, February 22, 2015.

167 *The five-year-old Japanese boy*: Two Alberto Fujimoris, both father and son, are cited in the Masterson testimony, "Hearing before the Subcommittee on Immigration."

168 *half of those hapless Latin American families were refused reentry*: Gispert, "Japanese-Peruvians interned in the US during WW2."

168 *offered $20,000 for his or her trouble*: Gispert, "The Japanese-Peruvians interned in the US during WW2."

168 *"I'm proud of my Mexican heritage," says Amelia Singh Netervala*: Gottlieb, "Punjabi Sikh–Mexican American Community Fading into History."

169 *"Visiting my mother's intensely Mexican family"*: Author's interviews and correspondence with Isabella Do-Orozco, December 4, 2021, August 16, 2021, and August 2–9, 2022.

169 *"People take one look at me and assume I am Asian"*: Author's interviews and correspondence with Isabella Do-Orozco.

169 *"As an Asian Latina, I've struggled"*: Mekita Rivas, "5 Asian Latines Open Up About Their Cultural Identity," Remezcla, August 20, 2021.

170 *"I'm not gonna lie"*: Lisa Murtaugh, quoted in Rivas, "5 Asian Latines Open Up About Their Cultural Identity."

170 *the two largest and fastest growing immigrant groups in the United States*: "By race and ethnicity, more Asian immigrants than Hispanic immigrants have arrived in the U.S. in most years since 2009." Abby Budiman, "Key Findings About U.S. Immigrants," Pew Research Center online, last modified August 20, 2020, https://www.pewresearch.org/short-reads/2020/08/20/key-findings-about-u-s-immigrants/.

170 *fastest growing immigrant groups in the United States*: Abby Budiman and Neil G. Ruiz, "Asian Americans Are the Fastest Growing Immigrant Group in the U.S.," Pew Research Center online, last modified April 9, 2021, https://www

.pewresearch.org/short-reads/2021/04/09/asian-americans-are-the-fastest
-growing-racial-or-ethnic-group-in-the-u-s/.

## PART III: SOULS

171 *"The Latina in me is an ember that blazes forever"*: Sonia Sotomayor, in a speech
to law students at Long Island's Hofstra University in 1996, as reported by the
*Washington Post* and cited by Jolie Lee, "Sotomayor Said It: Notable Quotes
from Supreme Court's First Latina Justice," *USA Today*, August 8, 2014.

## CHAPTER 7: THE GOD OF CONQUEST

173 *"God exists. And if not, it ought to"*: Octavio Paz, *Primeras letras, 1931–1943* (Madrid: Seix Barral, 1988), 96. My translation.

173 *the majority of Latinos will say they are religiously observant:* Paul Taylor et al.,
"V. Politics, Values and Religion," in *When Labels Don't Fit: Hispanics and Their
Views of Identity*, Pew Research Center online, last modified April 4, 2012,
https://www.pewresearch.org/hispanic/2012/04/04/v-politics-values-and
-religion/.

173 *more likely to declare a faith:* Taylor et al., "V. Politics, Values and Religion." See
also chap. 1, "Report: Exploring Catholic Identity," in U.S. Catholics Open to
Non-Traditional Families," Pew Research Center online, last modified September 2, 2015, https://www.pewresearch.org/religion/2015/09/02/chap
ter-1-exploring-catholic-identity/.

174 *claimed that religion was Latin America's glue:* See Arana, *Silver, Sword, and Stone*, 6.

174 *may choose not to be affiliated with religion at all:* According to Taylor et al., "Politics, Values and Religion," almost 70 percent of foreign-born Latinos identify
as Catholic. By the second generation, that figure drops to almost 60 percent.
By the third generation, only 40 percent of Latinos identify as Catholic.

174 *"I was raised Catholic"*: Numerous interviews with youths in college as well as
high schoolers from Latino immigrant homes, 2021–2022. These same sentiments were expressed, interestingly enough, in R. Stephen Warner, Elise
Martel, and Rhonda E. Dugan, "Islam Is to Catholicism as Teflon Is to Velcro:
Religion and Culture Among Muslims and Latinas," in *Sustaining Faith Traditions*, ed. Carolyn Chen and Russell Jeung (New York: New York University
Press, 2012), 50.

175 *"My mom's really Catholic"*: Olga is a pseudonym for a student at the University of Illinois. See also Warner, Martel, and Dugan," "Islam Is to Catholicism," 51.

## How the Catholic Church Conquered the New World

175 *"With the faith, the scourge of God came into the country"*: Francesco G. Bressani, *Jesuit Relations* (1653), vol. 39, no. 141 (New York: Pageant 1959).

176 *Spain had emerged from centuries of foreign domination*: Much of this is taken from my own work and research in Arana, *Silver, Sword, and Stone*, 280–82.

176 *Saint Teresa of Avila, the famous Carmelite mystic*: Alonso Cortés, "Pleitos de los Cepeda," *Boletín de la Academia Española* 25 (1946): 85–110.

176 *ancestors of Miguel de Cervantes*: Marion Fischel, "Did Cervantes's Family Have Jewish Roots?," *Jerusalem* Post, July 11, 2013. See also Jean Canavaggio, "Acerca de Cervantes," *Cervantes* (Madrid: Casa de Velázquez, 1997), "Miguel de Cervantes (1547–1616): Life and Portrait," Texas A&M University, tamu.edu. Cervantes was the "son of a surgeon who presented himself as a nobleman, although Cervantes's mother was a descendant of Jewish converts to Christianity."

176 *the forebears of Christopher Columbus*: Aron Hirt-Manheimer, "Did Columbus Have Jewish Roots," *Reform Judaism*, October 8, 2015, reform judaism.org.

176 *Cardinal Tomás de Torquemada was born into a Jewish family*: His grandmother was a Jew, according to James Reston, *Dogs of God: Columbus, the Inquisition, and the Defeat of the Moors* (New York: Doubleday, 2005), 19.

177 *"to serve God and His Majesty"*: Bernal Díaz del Castillo, *The Conquest of New Spain* (1632), trans. John Ingraham Lockhart, vol. 1 (London: J. Hatchard & Son, 1845), Project Gutenberg online, accessed July 15, 2023, https://www .gutenberg.org/files/32474/32474-h/32474-h.htm.

177 *the Catholic Church had morphed into a bureaucracy*: Arana, *Silver, Sword, and Stone*, 303–306.

177 *sale of two thousand church offices a year*: Pope Leo X was Giovanni de' Medici, "Pope Leo X," Klemens Loffler, "Pope Leo X," in *Catholic Encyclopedia*, available on Catholic Answers, accessed July 15, 2023, https://www.catholic .com/encyclopedia/pope-leo-x.

178 *Church in the New World joined the invaders' routine*: Arana, *Silver, Sword, and Stone*, 280.

178 *"If you do not comply"*: El Requerimiento. (Ficción jurídica: Texto completo), Monarquía Española, 1513, redactado por Juan López de Palacios, Scribd, accessed May 21, 2023, www.scribd.com/document/125487670.

179 *bishops were appointed by kings*: John Crow, *The Epic of Latin America* (Garden City, NY: Doubleday, 1971), 164.

179 *within a century of Columbus's having dropped anchor in Hispaniola*: The Cathedral of St. Augustine (Florida) was begun in 1565, only sixty-seven years after Columbus's landing; the one at Córdoba (Argentina) in 1582.

179  *five million Indians were baptized in Mexico:* Germán Arciniegas, *Latin America: A Cultural History* (New York: Alfred A. Knopf, 1967), 139–41.

179  *Mohammedans did not force conversion:* Guadalupe Carrillo, "Stanford fellow delves into archival materials that shed new light on the early days of Islam," *Stanford News*, March 3, 2015.

180  *the humbler classes repudiated the religion on its face:* Kyle Hagelden, "Death of a Myth," in *Protestantism and Latinos in the United States* (New York: Arno Press, 1980), 22.

180  *Christian saints had corresponding native deities:* Arciniegas, *Latin America,* 50.

180  *the single most important institution:* John F. Schwaller, "The Church in Colonial Latin America," *Latin American Studies*, March 31, 2016.

181  *the principal educator of the masses:* Arciniegas, *Latin America,* 50–53.

181  *the preeminent source of capital, the banker:* Ibid. See also Roger A. Kittleson, David Bushnell, "History of Latin America: Capitalism and Social transitions," *Encyclopedia Britannica,* https://www.britannica.com/place/Latin-America/New-order-emerging-1910-45.

181  *Alexander von Humboldt remarked:* Alexander von Humboldt, Book II, Chapter VII, in *Political Essay on the Kingdom of New Spain* (London: 1811), 22.

183  *an aspirant had to prove that more than three-quarters of his ancestors:* Felipe Fernández-Armesto, *Our America* (New York: W. W. Norton, 2014), 118.

183  *with flagrant contempt:* J. E. Officer, *Hispanic America, 1536–1856* (Tucson: University of Arizona Press, 1987), 41. Quoted in Fernández-Armesto, *Our America,* 246.

183  *the Church decided to recognize "Indians as peoples":* This was in a pastoral letter issued by Catholic bishops in advance of the canonization. Richard Boudreaux, "Latin America's Indigenous Saint Stirs Anger, Pride," *Los Angeles Times,* July 30, 2002.

183  *the portrait of Juan Diego that was unveiled was infuriating:* Ibid.

183  *reproduce that white man's likeness on millions of posters:* Ibid.

183  *not one of Mexico's 132 bishops was indigenous:* Boudreaux, "Latin America's Indigenous Stirs Anger, Pride."

183  *Until 1960, more than 90 percent of all Latin Americans:* Alan Cooperman, quoted in "Religion in Latin America," Event Transcript, Pew Research Center online, last modified November 20, 2014, https://www.pewresearch.org/religion/2014/11/20/event-transcript-religion-in-latin-america/.

183  *only slightly more than 50 percent Catholic:* "Latin America Is Becoming More Secular," *Economist* online, last modified April 16, 2022, https://www.economist.com/the-americas/2022/04/16/latin-america-is-becoming-more-secular.

## The Soul Drain

184 *"Latin America is a Catholic region":* Statement by a church growth planner, as quoted in David Stoll, *Is Latin America Turning Protestant?: The Politics of Evangelical Growth* (San Francisco: University of California Press, 2023), 1.

184 *Newly minted Mexican Americans:* Julio Moran, "Latinos Renewing Bonds with Religion," *Los Angeles Times,* August 8, 1983.

184 *"By every rational standard, they should have left":* Father Virgilio Elizondo, quoted in "Latinos Renewing Bonds."

185 *Mexican army, which United States arsenals:* Jean A. Meyer, *The Cristero Rebellion: the Mexican People Between Church and State, 1926–1929,* E-book (Cambridge: Cambridge University Press, 2008), 18–20.

186 *Tens of thousands of displaced laborers:* Julia Young, *Mexican Exodus: Emigrants, Exiles, and Refugees of the Cristero War* (New York: Oxford University Press, 2019), 5–8.

186 *Six out of ten say they hold strong ties to the Church:* Jens Manuel Krogstad, "Mexicans, Dominicans Are More Catholic Than Most Other Hispanics," Pew Research Center online, last modified May 27, 2014, https://www.pew research.org/short-reads/2014/05/27/mexicans-and-dominicans-more -catholic-than-most-hispanics/.

187 *"Come on in, friend":* I wrote about this sign, which I saw for myself, in my book *Silver, Sword, and Stone,* 337. Assemblies of God is a Pentecostal church.

187 *from 1960 to 1970, Evangelical churches:* David Stoll, *Is Latin America Turning Protestant?,* 80.

187 *beloved Archbishop Óscar Romero was gunned down:* Holly Solar, *Washington's War on Nicaragua* (Cambridge, MA: South End Press, 1988), 51.

187 *A sharpshooter emerged from a red Volkswagen:* Juan José Dalton, "Una bala en el corazón de monseñor Romero," *El País,* 23 mayo 2015. See also "Salvador Archbishop Assassinated By Sniper While Officiating at Mass," *New York Times,* March 24, 1980.

187 *"Romero's sin":* Dalton, *El País.*

187 *five Salvadoran National Guard soldiers kidnapped and raped:* Stephanie M. Huezo, "The Murdered Churchwomen in El Salvador," *Origins: Current Events in Historical Perspective,* December 2020, osu.edu.

188 *had been trained and armed by the United States:* See Lesley Gill, *The School of the Americas: Military Training and Political Violence in the Americas* (Chapel Hill, NC: Duke University Press, 2004), 137–62.

188 *In Nicaragua three nuns and a bishop:* The nuns killed were Sister Maureen

Courtney of Wisconsin and Sister Teresa Rosales, a Miskito Indian from Guatemala. The wounded cleric was Bishop Paul Schmitz of Wisconsin, and the wounded nun was Sister Francisca Colomer, also a Miskito Indian. Mark Uhlig, "2 Nuns, One from U.S., Are Slain in Raid Tied to Nicaraguan Rebels," *New York Times*, January 3, 1990.

188 *In Bolivia, an activist priest:* This was Luis "Lucho" Espinal—a Catalan priest, poet, journalist, and filmmaker. "El cuervo de Espinal tenía 17 orificios de bala," *El Deber* (Bol.), January 1, 2017. See also Arana, *Silver, Sword, and Stone*, 334.

188 *Efraín Ríos Montt, was a Reagan:* Douglas Farah, "Papers Show U.S. Role in Guatemalan Abuses," *Washington Post*, March 11, 1999. President Reagan met with Montt in 1982, offered him support, called him "a man of great personal integrity," and claimed he was "getting a bum rap on human rights." Lou Cannon, "Reagan Praises Guatemalan Military Leader," *Washington Post*, December 5, 1982. Montt was later tried and convicted of genocide against the Ixil, a Mayan people who were almost entirely exterminated in the wars. See also Stephen Kinzer, "Efraín Ríos Montt, Guatemalan Dictator Convicted of Genocide, Dies at 91," *New York Times*, April 1, 2018.

188 *military descended on the leftist Guerrilla Army of the Poor:* "El caso de genocidio en Guatemala," *The Center for Justice & Accountability*, online, cja.org. For the general persecution of the church in Guatemala, see also Sergio Palencia-Frener, "Memory and Forgetting in Guatemala," Open Democracy, June 6, 2021.

188 *626 villages were destroyed:* Truth Commission Report (United Nations, Historical Clarification Commission), reported by Mireya Navarro, in "Guatemalan Army Waged Genocide, New Report Finds," *New York Times*, February 26, 1999. The report also confirmed that the CIA aided the Guatemalan military. See also "Genocide in Guatemala," Holocaust Museum Houston, https://hmh.org/library/research/genocide-in-guatemala-guide/.

188 *In Quiché, a death squad murdered three Spanish activist priests:* "Los beatas mayas y el juicio político." See also Frener, "Memory and Forgetting in Guatemala." See also "Ten Martyrs of Quiché Beatified in Guatemala," *Vatican News*, April 23, 2021.

188 *millions of dollars in military aid from Washington:* Farah, "Papers Show U.S. Role." "As the Cold War raged in the 1960s and '70s, the United States gave the Guatemalan military $33 million in aid even though U.S. officials were aware of the army's dismal track record on human rights, the documents show."

188 *assassination techniques at the School of the Americas:* See Gill, *School of the Americas*. See also Clinton Fernandes, "Remembering US-Funded State Terror in Central America," Crikey News Service, November 22, 2019.

189 *no "authentic development":* Fr. Gustavo Gutierrez, *A Theology of Liberation*, quoted in Michael Novak, "The Case Against Liberation Theology," *New York Times*, October 21, 1984.

189 *In 1989, when an elite commando unit butchered six Jesuit priests:* Associated Press, "Salvadoran Court Reopens Inquiry into Killing of Six Jesuit Priests," *Los Angeles Times*, January 6, 2022. See also "30th Anniversary Commemorative Gathering at Fort Benning, November 15–17, 2019," *School of Americas Watch*, Memoria y Resistencia (founded by Fr. Roy Bourgeois, Maryknoll), October 17, 2019.

190 *Brazil's Catholic population plunged: Report: Brazil's Changing Religious Landscape*, Report, Pew Research Center online, last modified July 18, 2013, https://www.pewresearch.org/religion/2013/07/18/brazils-changing-religious-landscape/.

190 *Brazil is projected to be a majority Protestant nation:* Mariana Zilberkan, "Evangelicos devem ultrapassar católicos no Brasil a parter de 2032," *Veja news*, Brasil, February 4, 2020.

190 *Guatemala inaugurated the first democratically elected Evangelical president:* Jorge Serrano Elías, a leader in the neo-Pentecostal Elim church, won the presidential election with 67 percent of the vote. "Historical Overview of Pentecostalism in Guatemala, Origins and Growth," in *Spirit and Power—A 10-Country Survey of Pentecostals*, Pew Research Center online, last modified October 5, 2006, https://www.pewresearch.org/religion/2006/10/05/historical-overview-of-pentecostalism-in-guatemala/. President Efraín Ríos Montt, who was also an Evangelical, was never elected. (He was a member of the Iglesia El Verbo, affiliated with the Gospel Outreach Church in Eureka, California.) Montt was part of the three-man military junta that assumed rule via a coup in March 1982; by June of that year, Montt had forced the other two members to resign, becoming the de facto head of state.

190 *Guatemala had effectively become a majority Protestant nation:* "Religion Affiliation in Guatemala as of 2020, by Type," survey time period October 26–December 15, 2020, based on 1,000 respondents, Statista, 2021, https://www.statista.com/statistics/1067082/guatemala-religion-affiliation-share-type/#statisticContainer. Protestants total 44.7 percent; Catholics, 41.2 percent; no affiliation or atheist, 13.7 percent. (Protestants consist of: Evangelists, 41.5 percent; Mormon, 1.5 percent; Adventist, 0.7 percent; Protestant,

0.6 percent; Jehovah's Witness 0.4 percent; Methodist evangelist 0.2 percent.)
41.5 percent of the total population of Guatemala (about 16,860,000 in 2020)
is seven million.

190  *nearly 40 percent of all Pentecostals are estimated to live in Latin America:* "Christian Movements and Denominations," in *Global Christianity: A Report on the
Size and Distribution of the World's Christian Population,* Pew Research Report
online, last modified December 19, 2011, https://www.pewresearch.org/re
ligion/2011/12/19/global-christianity-movements-and-denominations/.

191  *that figure is more than 30 percent:* As of this writing, 31.9 percent of the world's
Christians are Pentecostals. "Status of Global Christianity—2022," *Center for
the Study of Global Christianity,* Gordon-Conwell Theological Seminary, gordon
-conwell.edu.

191  *Today the majority of Christians on this planet:* Evangelicals represent 19.2 percent of the world's Christians; Pentecostalists, 31.9 percent. Between them,
they account for 51.1 percent of the Christian population of the globe. "Status of Global Christianity—2022."

191  *less than half (47 percent) of the entire Latinx population in the United States is
Catholic:* "Report: Exploring Catholic Identity," https://www.pewresearch
.org/religion/2015/09/02/chapter-1-exploring-catholic-identity/.

191  *25 percent of all Hispanics in this country have converted: Report:* "Changing Faiths:
Latinos and the Transformation of American Religion,*" Pew Research Center
online, April 25, 2007, https://www.pewresearch.org/hispanic/2007/04/25
/changing-faiths-latinos-and-the-transformation-of-american-religion/;
and *Report: The Shifting Religious Identity of Latinos in the United States,* Pew
Research Center online, May 7, 2014, https://www.pewresearch.org/re
ligion/2014/05/07/the-shifting-religious-identity-of-latinos-in-the-united
-states/.

191  *"If you left Washington, DC, and drove all the way to LA":* Richard Land, quoted
in Elizabeth Dias, "The Rise of Evangélicos," *Time* online, last modified
April 15, 2013, https://nation.time.com/2013/04/04/the-rise-of-evangeli
cos/. This statement may seem an exaggeration, but might not be for long.
Just recently, *Christianity Today* reported a nationwide campaign to plant Hispanic Baptist churches throughout North America. Of ten thousand new
churches across the country, more than one thousand are Hispanic. But even
the regular churches are hosting Spanish language services. Livia Giselle
Seidel, "More than 1 in 10 New Southern Baptist Churches Are Hispanic,"
*Christianity Today,* October 28, 2022.

192 *"don't look or sound anything like the megachurches":* Seidel, "More than 1 in 10 New Southern Baptist Churches Are Hispanic."

192 *One out of five Latinos:* Jens Manuel Krogstad, Joshua Alvarado, and Besheer Mohamed, "Among U.S. Latinos, Catholicism Continues to Decline but Is Still the Largest Faith," Pew Research Center, April 13, 2023.

**A Friar's Tale**

192 *"As my Father hath sent me":* John 20:21, King James Bible.

193 *Father Emilio is a Cuban American who first saw:* The information on Father Emilio Biosca's life and work is taken from a number of interviews with him and his colleagues in Washington's Shrine of the Sacred Heart (Santuario del Corazón Sagrado), September–October 2022.

193 *Come 1964, Dr. Biosca secured the necessary counterfeit documents:* Ashleigh Kassock, "Dentista jubilado ahora repara estatuas," *Arlington Catholic Herald en Español,* March 18, 2022.

194 *only 8 percent are men of Hispanic descent:* Mary L. Gautier and Thu. T. Do, "The Class of 2019: Survey of Ordinands to the Priesthood, Report to the Center of Clergy, Consecrated Life & Vocations, United States Conference of Catholic Bishops," Center for Applied Research in the Apostolate, Georgetown University, Washington, DC, March 2019, 12. See also "Hispanic/Latino Ministry in the United States: Media Kit" Secretariat for Cultural Diversity, Subcommittee on Hispanic Affairs, V Encuentro, Missionary Disciples: Witnesses of God's Love, 2020, vencuentro.org.

198 *by more than 70 percent of the island's residents:* Kirsten Lavery, "The Santería Tradition in Cuba," *Factsheet: Santería in Cuba,* United States Commission on International Religious Freedom, February 2021.

198 *intimidating, threatening, criminalizing:* Lavery, "The Santería Tradition in Cuba."

198 *received an open fire hose of Salvadorans:* Wilson Chapman, "Why Certain Immigrant Communities Thrive in Washington, D.C.," *U.S. News & World Report,* August 26, 2019.

199 *"garlic eaters":* Mark Rotella, "It's a Wonderful (Italian-American) Life," Pop Culture Happy Hour, NPR, December 20, 2012.

199 *"rum, Romanism, and rebellion":* Peter Roff, "1884, Grover Cleveland defeats James G. Blaine," Constituting America, Essay 52, constitutingamerica.org, 2016.

200 *Spanish-speaking members of Washington's international diplomatic corps:* "The

Shrine of the Sacred Heart," Grace Meridian Hill, October 20, 2011, grace meridianhill.org.

201    *the parish's leader—a much loved Capuchin priest:* Elise Heil, director, Sacred Heart School, interview, September 19, 2022.

201    *friar accused of molesting girls:* This was Father Urbano Vazquez, a four-year veteran of the church. A woman claimed he had groped her breasts and asked inappropriate questions during confession; two schoolgirls accused him of kissing them on the mouth during church services; an eleven-year-old claimed he had touched her inappropriately for years; and a fifteen-year-old accused him of touching her thigh in the confessional. Michelle Boorstein, Marisa Iati, and Peter Hermann, "Three Teens Allege Abuse by Catholic Priest in D.C., Court Papers Say," *Washington Post,* November 8, 2018. See also Natalie Delgadillo, "Columbia Heights Catholic Priest Arrested on Two Additional Counts of Sexual Abuse," *DCist,* December 12, 2018. Also Margaret Barthel, "D.C. Priest Convicted of Sexually Abusing a Woman During Confession, *DCist,* November 30, 2021, dcist.com.

201    *groping of "private parts":* Paul Duggan, "Girl Testifies She Was Repeatedly Kissed and Groped by D.C. Catholic Priest," *Washington Post,* August 7, 2019.

201    *relocated to Puerto Rico: Yo Soy Capuchino,* Facebook entry, "Fray Moisés Villalba, OFM Cap., sacerdote salvadoreño que sirve en Puerto Rico," April 21, 2020, 3:16 p.m.

202    *a kind of order emerged:* "Statement on Child Protection Matter at Shrine of the Sacred Heart Parish," Press Release, Media Portal, Roman Catholic Archdiocese of Washington, November 7, 2018.

202    *Mario Andrade, a Guatemalan:* Andrea Acosta, "Santuario del Sagrado Corazón cumple cien años cobijando a inmigrantes," *El Pregonero,* June 14, 2021.

202    *Nobody left the fold:* Elise Heil, interview.

202    *"The people have made this house":* Fr. Emilio Biosca Aguero, interview, September 17, 2022.

### CHAPTER 8: THE GODS OF CHOICE

203    *"If there are two religions in the land":* Voltaire, quoted in Ernest Dilworth, *Philosophical Letters* (Upper Saddle River, NJ: Prentice-Hall, 1961), 22–26.

### Born-Again Latinos

205    *"He said to me, 'Selena hold on'":* Selena Gomez, Twitter, October 22, 2019, 10:10 p.m. Gomez was a faithful member of Hillsong Church, an Evangelical Pentecostal church that began in Australia and has proliferated in the United

States. According to *Christian Post*, Gomez and her ex-partner Justin Bieber were close to the co-founder of Hillsong, Brian Houston. She left the church when Pastor Lentz was accused of cheating on his wife. Jeannie Ortega Law, "Selena Gomez Describes What Jesus Said to Her After Releasing Her Latest Song," *Christian Post*, October 25, 2019. See also Natasha Reda, "The Real Reason Selena Gomez Is Leaving Hillsong Church," *Nicki Swift*, updated, August 24, 2021.

205 *almost half of all Latino seminarians:* Edwin I. Hernández et al., "A Demographic Profile of Latino/a Seminarians," *Latino Research ND* 4, no. 2, March 2007.

205 *by 2030, half of the entire population of American Latinos will identify:* Mark T. Mulder, Aida I. Ramos, and Gerardo Martí, *Latino Protestants in America: Growing and Diverse* (Lanham, MD: Rowman & Littlefield, 2021). See also Terry Mattingly, "Axios looks at the hot political (of course) trend of Latinos becoming evangelical voters," *Get Religion*, August 11, 2022.

205 *a people of faith, first and foremost:* Jennifer Medina, "Latino, Evangelical, and Politically Homeless," *New York Times*, October 11, 2020.

205 *these newly minted Protestants are millennials or Generation Xers:* "Latinos Who Are Evangelical Protestant," in *Religious Landscape Study*, Pew Research Center online, accessed on July 15, 2023, https://www.pewresearch.org/reli gion/religious-landscape-study/religious-tradition/evangelical-protestant /racial-and-ethnic-composition/latino/.

206 *They don't necessarily care to assimilate:* Medina, "Latino, Evangelical, and Politically Homeless."

206 *Samuel Rodriguez, the galvanic, high-profile CEO:* The information on Pastor Sam's life and beliefs is from my interview with him, September 16, 2022.

207 *white offshoots of an African American church:* The Church of God in Christ in Memphis was founded by bishop Charles Harrison Mason, the son of former slaves, after he returned from the Azuza Revival (1906–1915) speaking in unknown tongues. When the white contingent of the congregation split off from the CGC's group of churches, those members formed the Assemblies of God. Associated Press, "Bishop Mason: Founder of Largest Pentecostal Denomination," NBC News online, last modified September 16, 2019, https://www.nbcnews.com/news/nbcblk/bishop-mason-founder-largest -pentecostal-denomination-n1054946.

207 *In 1980 only 6 percent of the world's Christians were Pentecostalist:* Elle Hardy, "How Pentecostalism Took Over the World," *London Times*, November 14, 2021. See also Richard Vijgen and Bregtje van der Haak, "Pentecostalism:

Massive Global Growth Under the Radar," Pulitzer Center, March 9, 2015, https://pulitzercenter.org/stories/pentecostalism-massive-global-growth-under-radar. See also *The Shifting Religious Identity of Latinos in the United States*, Pew Research Center online, last modified May 7, 2014, https://www.pewresearch.org/religion/2014/05/07/the-shifting-religious-identity-of-latinos-in-the-united-states/.

207    *Today, every twenty-four hours, the Pentecostal church adds another thirty-five thousand:* Vijgen and van der Haak, "Pentecostalism."

207    *one out of every three Latinos who leaves the Catholic Church: Shifting Religious Identity,* https://www.pewresearch.org/religion/2014/05/07/the-shifting-religious-identity-of-latinos-in-the-united-states/.

208    *"We have all heard the old song":* Samuel Rodriguez, "America: It's Time for a New Song," sermon, 2016 National Hispanic Christian Leadership Conference.

208    *"You can't do that in Catholic churches":* Samuel Rodriguez, author interview.

209    *Hollywood stars such as pop rock singer Selena Gomez:* Kenzie Bryant, "Hillsong Is Reportedly Losing Selena Gomez, Prominent Member of Its Flock," *Vanity Fair,* December 15, 2020.

209    *"I'm literally just laying down":* Selena Gomez, Twitter, October 22, 2019, at 10:10 p.m., @selenagomez.

209    *Selena has counted Hillsong's pop rock band:* Jeannie Ortega Law, "Selena Gomez Opens Up About First Time Leading Worship at Hillsong Concert to Perform 'Nobody,'" *Christian Post,* March 29, 2016.

210    *movement has emerged as a slick, highly commercial:* Hardy, "How Pentecostalism Took Over."

212    *leads a network of more than forty-two thousand Evangelical churches:* "Rev. Samuel Rodriguez," National Hispanic Christian Leadership Conference (NHCLC) online, nhclc.org/rev-samuel-rodriguez/.

212    *more than one hundred million:* Taylor Berglund, "Rev. Sam Rodriguez: How a Prophetic Word Launched a Major Miracle Film," *Charisma News,* May 2019, 20.

213    *The* Wall Street Journal *identified him:* "Samuel Rodriguez," The Oak Initiative, Board Member—Bio, theoakinitiative.org.

213    *In 2013* Time *magazine nominated him:* "Time Magazine Cover Story Features Rev. Samuel Rodriguez," CISION, PR Newswire, April 10, 2013.

213    *He has produced films:* Rodriguez has been executive producer of several inspirational feature films, among them *Breakthrough* (2019), *My Brothers' Crossing* (2020), *A Walking Miracle* (2021), and *Flamin' Hot* (2023).

213 *Since the age of sixteen he has been preaching:* Samuel Rodriguez, author interview.

213 *"My conversion came in an entirely nonreligious setting":* Samuel Rodriguez, author interview.

214 *"White supremacists were marching through the streets of Pennsylvania":* Samuel Rodriguez, author interview.

214 *"I have always refused to see us as victims":* Ibid.

214 *"My church looks like heaven to me":* Berglund, "Rev. Sam Rodriguez," 22.

215 *40 percent white, 40 percent African American:* Berglund, "Rev. Sam Rodriguez," 22.

216 *"Wherever you see a wildfire of spirituality":* Berglund, "Rev. Sam Rodriguez." Quote edited for grammar and confirmed.

216 *by 2060, Hispanics will number 111 million:* "Projections for the United States: 2017–2060," US Census Bureau, revised September 2018. See also Meaghan Winter, "The Fastest Growing Group of American Evangelicals," *Atlantic,* July 26, 2021.

216 *"We Latinos are not extending our hand":* Winter, "Fastest Growing Group." Quote edited for grammar and confirmed. See also Samuel Rodriguez, "The Latino Transformation of American Evangelicalism," *Reflections,* Yale University Divinity School, Fall 2008.

216 *you would be looking at half the entire Latino population:* Berglund, "Rev. Sam Rodriguez."

217 *"We are people of the Holy Spirit":* Cited originally in Berglund, "Rev. Sam Rodriguez." Quote edited for grammar and approved for this book.

**The Mormons**

217 *"I know that a lot of people coming here from Latin America":* Saul Bramasco, author interview September 21, 2022.

218 *Saul Bramasco was born into a family of eleven children:* Bramasco, author interview.

218 *"I can't believe any of them":* Ibid.

219 *"It was like a spiritual rebirth":* Ibid.

219 *"Papi, I have found the true church":* Ibid.

220 *due to the general "crucial need":* Robert D. Knight, "A Study of the Role of the Episcopal Diocese of Los Angeles in Meeting the Psychosocial Needs of Hispanics" (MA thesis, University of California, Long Beach, 1989), and Enrique Zone-Andrews, "Suggested Competencies for the Hispanic Protestant Church Leader of the Future" (PhD diss., Pepperdine University, 1996).

See also Jorge Iber, *Hispanics in the Mormon Zion: 1912–1999* (College Station: Texas A&M University Press, 2000), 25.

220  *Mormons believe that until all remaining Lamanites are converted:* Tyler Balli, "LDS Hispanic Identity and Laminates," Brigham Young University Religious Studies Center, *Religious Educator* 19, no. 3 (2018).

220  *"I see the Lamanites coming into this Church":* This was the Mormon church's elder Spencer W. Kimball of the Council of Twelve in a speech to Spanish-speaking members in 1947. Eduardo Balderas, "Northward to Mesa," *Ensign,* Church of Jesus Christ of Latter-Day Saints, September 1972.

220  *that rail against "the dark skins" of the Lamanites:* Alma 3:6, Book of Mormon, quoted in Iber, *Hispanics,* 37–38.

221  *60 percent of all Mormons in the world:* Brittany Romanello, "Mormon Church's Celebration of Latino Cultures Puts Spotlight on Often-Overlooked Diversity," *The Conversation,* November 4, 2022.

221  *There are almost six million:* Facts and Statistics, Church of the Latter Day Saints, https://newsroom.churchofjesuschrist.org/facts-and-statistics.

221  *a "bastion of Mormons":* Interviews with Bishop Barry Slaughter Olsen, Church of Jesus Christ of Latter Day Saints, McLean, VA, August 23 and October 15, 2022.

222  *"It is my plan of salvation":* Bramasco, author interviews.

222  *what Bishop Barry Olsen of Virginia calls "sacred funds":* Bishop Olsen, interviews, August 23 and October 15, 2022.

222  *stock the shelves of a "Bishop's Storehouse":* Julieta Olsen, author interview, Church of Jesus Christ of Latter Day Saints, McLean, VA, October 26, 2022.

222  *Her father's family in Mexico:* Ibid.

223  *church experienced a historic split:* Ruth Wariner, "History Behind the Sound of Gravel," a memoir about growing up in a polygamist Mormon colony as her father's thirty-ninth child, https://www.ruthwariner.com/the-sound-of-gravel/history/.

223  *Miles Romney:* Nick Miroff, "In Besieged Mormon Colony, Mitt Romney's Mexican Roots," *Washington Post,* July 23, 2011.

223  *Republic of Mexico now boasts 220 Mormon "stakes":* Facts and Statistics: Mexico, Newsroom, Church of Jesus Christ of Latter-Day Saints, retrieved November 14, 2022.

223  *the number of Spanish-speaking wards:* Kim Bojorquéz, "The Rise of Latino Latter-Day Saints," Axios, August 25, 2022, axios.com.

223  *One in ten Mormons:* The total population of Mormons in the USA as of November 2022 was 6,763,019, newsroom, Church of Jesus Christ of Latter-Day

Saints, November 14, 2022, churchofjesuschrist.org; the population of Latino Mormons is roughly calculated at about 675,000.

223 *boasts but one—in Santa Ana, California:* New Stakes and Stake Presidencies Announced in August 2020, newsroom, Church of Jesus Christ of Latter-Day Saints, August 31, 2020.

224 *white-to-brown hierarchy that nettles the church:* There is much written about this, but see, for instance, Armando Solórzano, "Latino Education in Mormon Utah, 1910–1960," *Latino Studies* 4, no. 3 (Autumn 2006): 282–301.

224 *"Mormonism has always had a way out of its racial dilemmas":* Ignacio M. García, "Thoughts on Latino Mormons, Their Afterlife, and the Need for a New Historical Paradigm for Saints of Color," *Dialogue* (Winter 2017), https://www.dialoguejournal.com/wp-content/uploads/sbi/articles/Dialogue_V50N04_12.pdf.

224 *Quorum of the Twelve Apostles:* Leadership and Organization, newsroom, Church of Jesus Christ of Latter-Day Saints, accessed November 14, 2022.

225 *"We don't track race":* Email correspondence with Irene Caso, media manager at the Church of Jesus Christ of Latter Day Saints, Salt Lake City: November 14–28, 2022.

## Latino Jews

225 *"Living, as many of them do":* Harry O. Sandberg, "The Jews of Latin America: Including South and Central America, Mexico, the West Indies, and the United States Possessions," *The American Jewish Year Book* 19 (September 17, 1917, to September 18, 1918), 39.

226 *Lomnitz writes in one especially moving passage:* Lomnitz, *Nuestra América*, 3.

226 *Some, like Pedro Arias Dávila (Pedrarias):* Seymour B. Liebman, "Sephardic Ethnicity in the Spanish New World Colonies," *Jewish Social Studies* 37, no. 2 (Spring 1975): 141–62.

226 *Pedro Arias Dávila:* Norman Roth, *Conversos, Inquisition, and the Expulsion of the Jews from Spain* (Madison: University of Wisconsin Press, 1995), 123.

226 *Other conversos, such as the Chaves and Montoya families:* See the patrilineal records of Elijo Chaves and Pedro Duran Chaves (ancestors of Linda Chavez), Linealist: New Mexico History and Archive Projects, linealist.wordpress.com/patrilineal.

227 *Genetic research shows that almost a full quarter:* Ashley Perry, "Genetic Research: Almost 25 percent of Latinos, Hispanics Have Jewish DNA," *Jerusalem Post*, March 8, 2020.

227 *the truest version of himself:* Rebecca L. Davis, "'These Are a Swinging Bunch

of People': Sammy Davis Jr., Religious Conversion, and the Color of Jewish Ethnicity," *American Jewish History* 100, no. 1 (January 2016): 26–27.

227   *"If you look at me":* Lucas Cantor Santiago, author interview, June 8, 2021.

228   *94 percent were from Eastern Europe:* Laura Limonic, *Kugel and Frijoles: Latino Jews in the United States* (Detroit: Wayne State University Press, 2019), 28–30.

228   *"Jews of color":* Ilana Kaufman and Ari Kelman, "Jews of Color and Who Counts in the Jewish Community," *Times of Israel,* May 21, 2019.

228   *(In Argentina, Jews are called* rusos*):* "Argentina Virtual History Tour," Jewish Virtual Library: A Project of AICE, https://www.jewishvirtuallibrary.org /argentina-virtual-jewish-history-tour.

229   *One survey concluded that 67 percent of Latino Jews:* Two-thirds of Latino Jews earn $100,000 a year or more, whereas the median American income is $31,000. Only 30 percent of total American Jewish households reach that salary level. "AJC Survey of Latino Jews in the United States," AJC/Global Voice, American Jewish Committee, April 7, 2016.

229   *"We are no longer":* Ilan Stavans quotes, BrainyMedia, BrainyQuote.com, 2022, accessed November 27, 2022, https://www.brainyquote.com/quotes /ilan_stavans_770036.

229   *"I went to a Jewish school in Mexico City":* Ilan Stavans, author interview, June 22, 2021.

229   *"Indeed, for many Ashkenazis":* "Ilan Stavans, a Mexican-Born Descendent of Shtetl-Dwellers," interview with Lesley Yalen, Wexler Oral History Project, Yiddish Book Centers, May 31, 2013.

230   *"I grew up as a Mexican Jew":* Sarah F. Gold, "PW Talks with Ilan Stavans," *Publishers Weekly,* July 2, 2001.

230   *he intended to taste what it meant to be "a happy Jew":* Stavans, author interview.

231   *"In Mexico, I was a Jew":* Ibid.

231   *questioning the fame of Sandra Cisneros:* Lynda Richardson, "How to Be Both an Outsider and an Insider; 'The Czar of Latino Literature and Culture' Finds Himself Under Attack," *New York Times,* November 13, 1999.

231   *of producing "cheap Red propaganda":* Ezra Glinter, "Seduced by Stavans," *Forward* online, December 9, 2009, https://forward.com/culture/120549 /seduced-by-stavans/.

231   *dismissed Gabriel García Márquez as an "outrageous" political activist:* Ilan Stavans, "The Master of Aracataca," *Michigan Quarterly Review* 34, no. 2 (Spring 1995): 149–71.

231   *an outsider who "doesn't come from within the culture":* This is Tey Diana Re-
      bolledo, a professor of Spanish at the University of New Mexico at Albuquer-
      que, in defense of Sandra Cisneros. See also Richardson, "How to Be Both an
      Outsider and an Insider."

231   *"Why Oxford University Press, which used to pride itself":* Richardson, "How to
      Be Both an Outsider and an Insider."

231   *"I think you can know enough":* Ibid.

232   *"It is a backward notion of identity":* Ruth Behar, author interview, Decem-
      ber 7, 2022.

232   *An estimated five thousand to ten thousand people become Jews by choice:* Roberto
      Loiederman, "Latinos Discover a Deep Affinity for Judaism That Leads Them
      to Convert," *Jewish Journal*, December 3, 2009.

232   *The rate is even higher for Latino Muslims:* These numbers are from the Pew
      Research Center, reported in Aqilah Allaudeen, "U.S. Latino Muslims Speak
      the Language of Shared Cultures," *U.S. News & World Report* online, last
      modified July 2, 2020, https://www.usnews.com/news/best-countries/ar
      ticles/2020-07-02/numbers-of-us-latino-muslims-growing-rapidly.

233   *Such is the case for Rabbi Eli Rafael de la Fuente:* Rafael de la Fuente is a pseud-
      onym for a Latino professional who converted from Catholicism to Judaism
      in the 1980s and then became a rabbi thereafter. For personal family reasons,
      he has chosen to remain anonymous here. Based on author interviews, No-
      vember 10, 2022, and May 26 and 28, 2023. All facts are accurate except for his
      name, his son's name, and his current location.

233   *"I've never identified with Latino culture":* de la Fuente, author interview, No-
      vember 10, 2022.

233   *"Judaism is not based on dogma":* Ibid.

234   *"I now work with human beings in dire situations":* Ibid.

234   *"Could any of this have happened in Peru?":* Ibid. In fact, conversion to Judaism is
      alive and well in Peru. Graciela Mochkofsky's recent book, *The Prophet of the
      Andes*, tells of a group of mestizo and indigenous Peruvians from a village in
      the wilds of the hills that surround Cajamarca who became fascinated with
      the story of Moses, the Old Testament, and the Torah, and decided to convert
      to Judaism. Being of the humble classes, they were turned away by the Jewish
      temple in Cajamarca. But one Sephardic rabbi listened. Eventually their faith
      was so strong and their own proselytizing message so effective that a group
      of families formed their own Orthodox temple and named themselves the
      Beni Moshe ("Children of Moses"). In 2003, they emigrated to Israel, where

they joined a small settlement near Nablus. Hundreds of Peruvian Jewish converts—"Inca Jews"—followed. They are still coming. See Graciela Mochkofsky, *The Prophet of the Andes* (New York: Alfred A. Knopf, 2022).

235  *Paco de la Fuente, one of the rabbi's children*: Francisco (Paco) de la Fuente is a pseudonym. To protect his identity, his father, Eli de la Fuente, has chosen to give him anonymity in this book. The rabbi's son was interviewed numerous times in 2021 and 2022 as a potential subject himself.

## PART IV: HOW WE THINK, HOW WE WORK

237  *"You are the storyteller of your own life"*: Isabel Allende, quoted in Kiko Martínez, "'Spectacular in Her Simplicity': Actress Daniela Ramírez Reflects On Portraying Isabel Allende," Remezcla, last modified April 9, 2021, https:// remezcla.com/features/film/interview-actress-daniela-ramirez-hbo-max -miniseries-isabel-allende/.

## CHAPTER 9: MIND-SETS

239  *"If we are to be heard and, more importantly, be effective"*: Raul Yzaguirre, foreword from National Council of La Raza's *State of Hispanic America, 2004*, iii.

241  *"I'm a heart liberal, but a mind conservative"*: Hillary Clinton, president of the Wellesley College Young Republicans in 1965, quoted in "The Crist Switch: Top 10 Political Defections" *Time*, https://content.time.com/time/specials /packages/article/0,28804,1894529_1894528_1894517,00.html.

241  *As Manny Díaz, the former mayor of Miami*: "The Latino Vote," a conference hosted by the National Council of La Raza in Miami on July 24, 2002, featuring Lisa Navarrete, Alex Penelas, Manny Díaz, Orlando Sánchez, Antonio Villaraigosa, and Fernando Ferrer, https://www.c-span.org/video/?171448-1 /latino-vote.

241  *In 1960 John F. Kennedy received the vast majority*: 85 percent, to be exact. John P. Schmal, "Electing the President: The Latino Electorate (1960–2000)," *La Prensa San Diego*, April 30, 2004.

241  *90 percent of the Mexican American and 86 percent of the Puerto Rican vote*: For these percentages and for all that follow, Schmal, "Electing the President."

242  *many a Latino Republican changed course*: Mark Hugo Lopez and Paul Taylor, *Latino Voters in the 2012 Election*, Pew Research Center online, last modified November 7, 2012, https://www.pewresearch.org/hispanic/2012/11/07 /latino-voters-in-the-2012-election/.

242  *Gallup polls indicate that we are weak Democrats and shaky Republicans*: Frank

Newport, "Hispanic Americans' Party ID: Updated Analysis," Gallup News, January 27, 2022.

### The Myth of the Latino Vote

243 *"Hispanics are Republicans. They just don't know it"*: Ronald Reagan, quoted by his Hispanic advisor, Lionel Sosa, in Stacey L. Connaughton, *Inviting Latino Voters: Party Messages and Latino Party Identification* (New York: Routledge, 2005), 42.

243 *"political elites"*: This is a term used often by Cristina Beltrán in her excellent scholarly inquiry into the question of Latino homogeneity: *The Trouble with Unity* (New York: Oxford University Press, 2010), 7.

243 *In some counties in Texas:* Voter turnout in Tom Green County was 16.9 percent in 2012, to be exact. Shawn Morrow, "Causes of Low Voter Turnout of the Hispanic Population in Southwest Texas" (PhD diss., Walden University, August 2015), 11.

243 *only half of all eligible Hispanic Americans went to the polls:* According to the Brennan Center for Justice, in 2020, 70.9 percent of white voters cast ballots while only 58.4 percent of nonwhite voters did. The nonwhite numbers: 62.6 percent of Black American voters, 53.7 percent of Latino American voters, and 59.7 percent of Asian American voters cast ballots. Kevin Morris and Corn Grange, "Large Racial Turnout Gap Persisted in 2020 Election," Brennan Center Analysis, August 6, 2021, brennancenter.org.

244 *Latinos added five million voters to their ranks:* Anusha Natarajan and Carolyne Im, "Key Facts About Hispanic Eligible Voters in 2022," Pew Research Center online, last modified October 12, 2022, https://www.pewresearch.org/short-reads/2022/10/12/key-facts-about-hispanic-eligible-voters-in-2022.

244 *(74 percent of Latino voters are pro-choice):* "Latino Voters Hold Compassionate Views on Abortion," Lake Research Partners for National Latina Institute for Reproductive Justice, November 30, 2011. Figures on this can vary wildly. Some polls place this percentage as high as 84 percent: "Comprehensive National Survey of Latino Voters Finds Widespread Support for Reproductive Freedom," prochoiceamerica.org, Press Release, October 11, 2022. On the other hand, a survey of Hispanic millennials (ages eighteen to thirty-five) conducted by the Public Religion Research Institute in 2015, revealed that 54 percent said abortion should be illegal in most or all cases.

244 *(The average age of a Hispanic voter today is thirty-nine):* Natarajan and Im, "Key Facts About Hispanic Eligible Voters in 2022."

244   *"Don't just pray"*: Samuel Rodriguez, quoted in Cindy Carcamo, "Latino Evangelicals Used to Shun Politics. Will They Now Become a Right-Wing Force?," *Los Angeles Times*, March 4, 2022.

244   *"It's not that I embrace the values of the Republican Party"*: Samuel Rodriguez, quoted in Carcamo, "Latino Evangelicals."

245   *Latino voter registration climbed from 50 percent to more than 60 percent*: "Latino Voter Registration Rates Reached an All-Time High in the 2020 Presidential Election," The Center for Latin American, Caribbean, and Latino Studies, City University of New York, clacls.gc.cuny.edu, May 7, 2021. The point is also made here that 88 percent of the 61 percent (of registered Latino voters) went to the polls in 2020.

245   *As the distinguished scholar Geraldo Cadava describes*: Geraldo Cadava's *The Hispanic Republican* (New York: Ecco, 2020) is essential reading for anyone who would understand the diverse politics of Latinos in different corners of this country.

245   *A century ago, when Hispanic Americans numbered little more than a million*: "We the American . . . Hispanics," US Bureau of the Census Report, Ethnic and Hispanic Statistics Branch, September 1993.

245   *like most African Americans of the era, almost entirely Republican*: Cadava, *The Hispanic Republican*, x.

246   *have seldom strayed from the Democratic flock*: In fact, three of the most prominent Puerto Ricans in Washington, DC, are Democrats—Supreme Court Justice Sonya Sotomayor, Representative Nydia Velázquez, and Representative Alexandria Ocasio-Cortez—all of them from New York.

246   *"criminals, drug dealers, and rapists"*: Donald Trump, interview on *Media Buzz*, Fox News, July 5, 2015.

246   *he racked up almost 30 percent of the "Latino vote"*: Cadava, *Hispanic Republican*, xiii.

247   *almost two million rallied to Donald Trump's support*: 12.65 million Latinos voted in the 2016 election. However, 16.6 million voted in the 2020 election. Trump's support went from 28 percent of 12.65 million in 2016 to 32 percent of 16.6 million in 2020. The difference is 1.77 million people. See "Latino Voters Were Decisive in 2020 Presidential Election," UCLA Latino Policy and Politics Initiative, January 19, 2021, newsroom.ucla.edu. The 12.65 million number is from Jens Manuel Krogstad and Mark Hugo Lopez, "Black Voter Turnout Fell in 2016, Even as a Record Number of Americans Cast Ballots," Pew Research Center online, last modified May 12, 2017, https://www.pewresearch.org/short-reads/2017/05/12/black-voter-turnout-fell-in-2016-even-as-a-record-number-of-americans-cast-ballots/. See also Julio

Ricardo Varela, "New Census Data Says 2016 National Latino Voter Turnout Did Not Increase," Latino USA, May 15, 2017.

247   *that same vote also helped Joe Biden flip states:* Cadava, *Hispanic Republican,* xi.

## What Do Latinos Want?

247   *"Overall, these groups do not constitute a political community":* Latino National Political Survey, University of Texas, 1992.

247   *a sleeping Leviathan:* Beltrán, introduction to *The Trouble with Unity.*

248   *stark differences of opinion:* Rodolfo O. de la Garza et al., "Latino National Political Survey," Inter-University for Latino Research, Ford Foundation, New York, December 1992, https://files.eric.ed.gov/fulltext/ED354281.pdf.

249   *cardinal concern of Latinos:* Jens Manuel Krogstad, Khadijah Edwards, and Mark Hugo Lopez, "3. Latinos and the 2022 Midterm Elections," in *Most Latinos Say Democrats Care About Them and Work Hard for Their Vote, Far Fewer Say So of GOP,* Pew Research Center online, last modified September 29, 2022, https://www.pewresearch.org/race-ethnicity/2022/09/29/latinos-and-the -2022-midterm-elections/.

249   *"practical rather than ideological":* Ritchie Torres, quoted in Bret Stephens, "New York's Superstar Progressive Isn't AOC," *New York Times,* September 21, 2021.

249   *"I don't know how anyone of Hispanic heritage":* Stephanie Condon, "Conservatives Blast Harry Reid for Remark About Hispanic Voters," CBS News online, last modified August 11, 2010, https://www.cbsnews.com/news /conservatives-blast-harry-reid-for-remark-about-hispanic-voters/.

249   *"They all think alike, right, Senator Reid?":* "They All Think Alike, Right?," Opinion, *Las Vegas Review-Journal,* August 11, 2010.

249   *"Hispanic voters don't have a 'herd mentality'":* Condon, "Conservatives Blast Harry Reid."

250   *"People here have grown up believing that the Democratic Party":* Oscar Pollorena, quoted in Story Hinckley, "The New Swing Vote: More Latino Voters Are Joining the GOP," *Christian Science Monitor,* October 21, 2022.

250   *"guided by an app powered by i360":* Marcela Valdes, "The Fight to Win Latino Voters for the GOP," *New York Times Magazine,* November 23, 2020.

251   *According to Daniel Garza:* In the ongoing information on Libre, I have relied especially on Valdes's excellent portrait of Garza in "The Fight to Win Latino Voters for the GOP."

251   *Libre, which claims to be nonpartisan:* Valdes, "The Fight to Win Latino Voters for the GOP."

251 *"'There's no such thing as a free lunch'"*: Catherine Cortez Masto, US senator from Nevada, "Kochs' Dark Web of Money Flows Through the Libre Initiative to Deceive Latinos," press release, April 24, 2018, https://www.cortezmasto .senate.gov/news/press-releases/cortez-masto-kochs-dark-web-of-money -flows-through-the-libre-initiative-to-deceive-latinos.

252 *"We need to quit taking a policy book"*: Political strategist Chuck Rocha, quoted in Geraldo L. Cadava, "Latino Voters Are Key to 2024, and They're Not Always Buying What Democrats Are Selling," *New York Times*, January 18, 2022.

**History Lessons**

253 *"My greatest strength is knowing who I am"*: Oscar de la Renta, 2002 interview in *World Investment News*, as quoted in Isabella Herrera, "Oscar de la Renta y la transnacionalidad: lo que significa hoy ser inmigrante y celebridad, y el impacto de Oscar en esa definición," *Acento*, República Dominicana, 24 de marzo, 2022.

253 *worries that the younger generation of Latinos:* Julian Castro, in the documentary *Willie Velásquez: Your Vote Is Your Voice*, PBS, September 8, 2016.

253 *Joaquín Castro:* Representative Joaquín Castro, author interview, July 6, 2021.

253 *sixty-two Latinos in the United States Congress:* In the 118th Congress, there are fifty-six Latino members of the House of Representatives (thirty-eight Democrats and eighteen Republicans), six Latino senators (four Democrats and two Republicans), including two delegates and a resident commissioner. These numbers include two House members who are also of Asian descent, and two House members who are also of African ancestry. Nineteen are women. "Membership of the 118th Congress: A Profile," Congressional Research Service, updated June 6, 2023, https://crsreports.congress.gov/product/pdf/R /R47470#. See also Katherine Schaeffer, "U.S. Congress Continues to Grow in Racial, Ethnic Diversity," Pew Research Center online, last modified January 9, 2023, https://www.pewresearch.org/short-reads/2023/01/09/u-s-con gress-continues-to-grow-in-racial-ethnic-diversity/.

253 *a considerable history of state governors:* Currently there is only one: Michelle Lujan Grisham, the Democratic governor of New Mexico. But over the years, there have been more than forty. A basic outline of the numbers over the years and corresponding ethnicities can be found on Wikipedia, "List of minority governors and lieutenant governors in the United States."

253 *six US Treasurers:* "Treasurers of the United States," US Department of the Treasury, home.treasury.gov.

253    *sixteen chief executive officers:* Michael Volpe, "Meet the 16 Hispanic CEOs of
       Top S&P 500 Companies," *Al Día*, February 3, 2021.

253    *more than five hundred college presidents:* There are 3,667 presidents of colleges
       or universities in the United States. Fourteen percent are Hispanic. For the
       number of presidents, see Inside Higher Ed and Gallup's 2019 Survey of Col-
       lege Presidents, nit.edu/university-council/reports, 9. For the number of
       Hispanics, see Zippia, "College President Demographics and Statistics in the
       U.S.," https://www.zippia.com/college-president-jobs/demographics.

253    *one Heisman Trophy winner:* This was quarterback Jim Plunkett of Stanford
       University (1970), the son of two Mexican Americans. Paul Goldberg, "Spot-
       lighting Jim Plunkett in Honor of National Hispanic Heritage Month," Heis-
       man Trophy Trust online, last modified September 21, 2022, https://www
       .heisman.com/articles/spotlighting-jim-plunkett-in-honor-of-national-his
       panic-heritage-month/.

253    *the long and winding road:* It's worth noting that there is also a Latino at the
       head of the infamous Proud Boys, the male chauvinist group with ties to
       white nationalism that was charged with instigating the January 6, 2021, riots
       at the nation's Capitol. That Latino is Enrique Tarrio, the Proud Boys' Cuban
       American chairman. Tarrio uses his Afro-Latino heritage to dismiss accusa-
       tions that his organization advocates for white supremacy. Fidel Martinez,
       "Latinx Files: The Proud Boys Hispanic Face," *Los Angeles Times*, June 16,
       2022.

254    *Juan is the son of Mexican Americans:* Juan Sepúlveda, author interview, Au-
       gust 20, 2021.

255    *company began to conduct hiring sweeps:* Jan Biles, "Mexicans Who Worked at
       Santa Fe Among Topics at Ancestor Fair," *Topeka (KS) Capital-Journal*, Octo-
       ber 5, 2014.

255    *"the only father I ever knew":* Juan Sepúlveda, author interview, January 17,
       2023.

255    *"We were poor," says Juan:* Sepúlveda, author interview, January 17, 2023.

256    *"Bright boy," he answered. "And we knew it":* Ibid.

256    *As Congressman Joaquín Castro might say:* Joaquín Castro, author interview,
       July 6, 2021.

257    *"He had decided that we Latinos wouldn't be represented":* Henry Cisneros, in the
       documentary *Willie Velásquez: Your Vote Is Your Voice.*

257    *"It was like old Texas law":* Willie Velásquez, in *Willie Velásquez: Your Vote Is
       Your Voice.*

257   "Pa' qué?": Jane Velásquez, in *Willie Velásquez: Your Vote Is Your Voice*.

258   *"His work probably had more long-term impact"*: Henry Cisneros, in *Willie Ve-lásquez: Your Vote Is Your Voice*.

258   *terminated the Bracero Program . . . brought four million Mexicans to work:* "1942: Bracero Program," *A Latinx Resource Guide: Civil Rights Cases and Events in the United States*, Library of Congress.

259   *the organization doubled the Latino electorate:* Juan A. Sepúlveda, Jr., *The Life and Times of Willie Velásquez: Su voto es su voz* (Houston: Arte Publico Press, 2003), location 154 Kindle edition.

259   *the Latino body politic today numbers thirty-five million:* 34.5 million in October 2022, to be exact. Natarajan and Im, "Key Facts About Hispanic Eligible Voters."

259   *the fastest-growing race or ethnic group in the United States electorate:* Natarajan and Im, "Key Facts About Hispanic Eligible Voters."

259   *"In the end, the American dream is not a sprint":* Julian Castro, at the Democratic National Convention, 2012, quoted in Kevin Cirilli, "Julian Castro's 5 notable lines," Politico, last modified September 4, 2012, https://www.politico.com/story/2012/09/julian-castros-5-compelling-lines-080709.

260   *"It's just the way we grow up in our Catholic, Latino communities":* Sepúlveda, author interview, January 17, 2023.

260   *Putnam invited him to join a panel of thirty scholars:* Robert D. Putnam's Saguaro Conference led to the "Better Together" panel. See: *Better Together: The Report of the Saguaro Seminar*, reprint of the 2000 report, http://robertdputnam.com/wp-content/uploads/2016/04/bt_1_29.pdf.

260   *"You know," he told them:* Juan Sepúlveda, recalling Putnam's words, author interview, January 17, 2023.

261   *"It's the one week of the year":* Sepúlveda, author interview, January 17, 2023.

261   *Putnam and his Better Together panelists were astonished:* Ibid.

261   *in Rockville, Maryland, where Peruvians:* See chapter 2, where I describe Julia Mamani and this very unified community of Maryland Peruvians from Caba-naconde, a tiny village in the remote canyons of the Colca Valley.

261   *quinceañera:* This is a pan–Latin American tradition, celebrating a girl's fif-teenth birthday and her passage into womanhood.

262   *where Latina professionals from a dozen origin countries gather:* I'm fortunate enough to belong to one of these—Las Gitanas Literarias (The Literary Gyp-sies) of Washington, DC—a bilingual book club, founded by economist Hilda Ochoa Brillembourg and the late art collector Mirella Levinas.

262   *"I am certain Hispanics will go the way of other immigrants":* Linda Chavez, au-thor interview, September 6, 2021.

262 *Julian Castro has lamented:* Julian Castro, former Secretary of Housing and Urban Development, in *Willie Velásquez: Your Vote Is Your Voice.*

263 *Joaquín Castro, whose all-out campaign:* Joaquín Castro, author interview, July 7, 2021. See also David Remnick, "Joaquin Castro: 'Americans Don't Know Who Latinos Are,'" *The New Yorker Radio Hour,* September 24, 2021.

263 *"I had the most remarkable meeting in May 2020":* Joaquín Castro, author interview, July 7, 2021.

263 *word a white gunman used when he massacred twenty-three Latinos:* Associated Press, "El Paso shooting suspect said he targeted Mexicans, police say," published in *Los Angeles Times,* August 9, 2019.

264 *"Abusive stereotypes like that are dangerous":* Joaquín Castro, author interview, July 7, 2021.

## Convictions

264 *"They tried to bury us. They did not know we were seeds":* This is variously thought to be a Mexican proverb and a line from a work by the Greek poet Dinos Christianopoulos. It has been used often in protests defending the rights of Dreamers and DACA. See Mairead McArdle, "Protesters demanded Congress find a legislative fix for Dreamers," *National Review,* March 5, 2018.

264 *refused them the right to be represented:* Charles R. Venator-Santiago, "Yes, Puerto Ricans are American citizens," *Encyclopaedia Britannica,* updated February 4, 2020. See also "Statutory Citizenship," Puerto Rico Citizenship Archives Project, University of Connecticut.

264 *state board of education rejects books about Latino history:* Aliya Swaby, "Texas education officials reject another Mexican-American studies textbook," *Texas Tribune,* November 8, 2017.

264 *or bans classics by literary giants such as Isabel Allende, Sandra Cisneros:* Angela Bonilla, "Books Written by Latino Authors Among Those Banned in Texas, Nationwide," KWTC, Waco, Texas, September 22, 2022.

264 *where 62 percent of the entire population:* Mary Tuma, "SBOE Passes Mexican-American Studies, but Whitewashes the Name," *Austin (TX) Chronicle,* April 13, 2018.

264 *there are no prepared instructional materials to teach Hispanic history:* Instead, teachers are given lists of related books, rather than any textbook or concrete course. Cameron Langford, "Outrage Over Anti-Latino Textbook in Texas," Courthouse News Service, May 26, 2016.

265 *described them as bent on the destruction of Western civilization:* Yanan Wang,

"Proposed Texas Textbook Says Some Mexican Americans 'Wanted to Destroy' U.S. Society," *Washington Post*, May 25, 2016. See also Langford, "Outrage Over Anti-Latino Textbook in Texas."

265 *Kelly Lytle Hernández, Geraldo Cadava . . . and Ed Morales:* Hernández's books, *Bad Mexicans* and *City of Inmates*, are indispensable histories, as are Cadava's *Hispanic Republicans*, and Morales's *Latinx* or *Living in Spanglish*. There are many other notable historians and chroniclers of the Hispanic experience I could name here, including Gloria Anzaldúa, Eduardo Galeano, Carrie Gibson, Laura E. Gómez, Juan González, Greg Grandin, María Hinojosa, Cherríe Moraga, Paul Ortíz, and Ray Suarez.

265 *Mariana Barros-Titus, a thirty-year-old researcher:* Mariana Barros-Titus, author interviews, August 20, 2021, and October 28, 2022.

266 *"We had arrived right before September 11, just in time":* Barros-Titus, author interviews, August 20, 2021, and October 28, 2022. Barros-Titus is certainly entitled to her opinion on this, and there is some corroboration of her claims. Regarding the 9/11 cleaning crews being largely peopled by immigrants: "These mostly Latino crews cleaned up after Sept. 11," Associated Press, September 9, 2021. Regarding Latinos bringing the city back to life: Diane Ciro et al., "Acculturation, coping and PTSD in Hispanic 9/11 rescue and recovery workers," *Psychological Trauma* 13, no. 1 (January 2021), 84–93. Also: "NYC Latino 9-11 Collecting Initiative: September 11, 20 Years Later," National Museum of American History Behring Center, Smithsonian Institution, September 11, 2021, https://americanhistory.si.edu/topics/september-11/pages/nyc-latino-9-11-collecting-initiative.

266 *It happened in high school:* Calista Correa, author interview, January 24, 2023.

266 *a full 30 percent of the Latino population:* Louis DeSipio, "Demanding Equal Political Voice . . . and Accepting Nothing Less," American Latino Theme Study: Struggles for Inclusion, National Park Service, July 10, 2020.

267 *Calista Correa, a young Chilean American:* Calista Correa is a pseudonym. Given the intimate details of my subject's life and family relationships revealed here, she has chosen to keep her identity private. All facts about institutions and places, however, are real.

267 *Calista's father was a highly intelligent boy:* Calista Correa, author interview, April 6, 2022.

267 *"My mother and her mother":* This quote and all others that follow from Correa are from my 2022 and 2023 interviews with her.

268 *"When you're older, Calista"*: Correa, author interview.

268 *often rated the best public high school in the nation*: "Thomas Jefferson High School for Science and Technology, #1 in National Rankings," *US News and World Report*, 2022. According to US News, "Thomas Jefferson High School for Science and Technology uses a STEM-focused curriculum that culminates with a technical lab project for seniors. The school offers courses like DNA science, advanced marine biology, automation and robotics, architectural drawing and design, research statistics and AP calculus. TJHSST boasts 15 specialized research labs, ranging from astronomy and astrophysics to oceanography and geophysical systems."

268 *the school is criticized, even sued*: Emma Brown, "Jefferson H.S., Fairfax Schools, Shut Out Blacks and Latinos, Complaint Alleges," *Washington Post*, July 23, 2012; "Thomas Jefferson High School for Science and Technology Hit with Civil Rights Discrimination Suit," HuffPost, last modified July 25, 2012, https://www.huffpost.com/entry/thomas-jefferson-high-sch_n_1700247. See also Amy Howe, "Court Allows Elite Virginia High School to Keep Admissions Policy While Legal Challenge Continues," SCOTUSblog, April 25, 2022.

269 *whereas Hispanics represented approximately 30 percent of the county's students*: *2005 Fairfax County Youth Survey*, Fairfax Country, Virginia and Fairfax County Public Schools, June 13, 2006.

269 *less than 6 percent of Thomas Jefferson's incoming class*: Tyler Currie, "The Quest," *Washington Post*, August 7, 2005. Curiously enough, by 2020, the Thomas Jefferson School had supposedly addressed its problem by building up to an almost 70 percent Asian student body, but the African and Hispanic representation remained grievously low.

270 *Its mission is to emphasize*: "Mi Gente," Duke University, sites.duke.edu/mi gente/.

272 *"all about the pavement"*: Burt A. Folkart, "Obituaries: Willie Velásquez; Leader of Latino Political Movement," *Los Angeles Times*, June 16, 1988.

**CHAPTER 10: MUSCLE**

274 *You have to work harder. In every position I've been in*: Sonia Sotomayor, as quoted in an interview with Terry Gross, *Fresh Air*, NPR, January 13, 2014.

274 *the first English colony—attempted in 1585 and abandoned a year later*: Michael Farquhar, "The Lost Colony of Roanoke," *Washington Post*, April 9, 1997.

## Warriors

275  *Ten thousand unknown Latino patriots fought in the American Revolution!:* John Leguizamo, American actor, in a tweet on July 4, 2019, https://twitter.com/JohnLeguizamo/status/1146856069416783872. Leguizamo makes the error of calling the weapons provider General Valdez. It should be General Gálvez. But his enthusiasm is very real.

275  *Hispanic participation . . . began when the 1st Viscount of Galveston, Bernardo de Gálvez:* He was not given this title until 1783, just before the signing of the Treaty of Paris, which ended the American Revolutionary War. For information on Gálvez, see Erick Trickey, "The Little-Remembered Ally Who Helped America Win the Revolution," *Smithsonian,* January 13, 2017. Also "Bernardo de Gálvez y Madrid: What Do the American Revolution, a Spanish Governor, and Cattle Drives Have in Common?," Galveston, Texas: History Guide, *Galveston Unscripted,* 2023.

276  *settlements along Nicaragua's Mosquito Coast and Honduras:* Gonzalo M. Quintero Saravia, *Bernardo de Gálvez: Spanish Hero of the American Revolution* (Chapel Hill: University of North Carolina Press, 2018), 14.

277  *Gálvez began to feel himself more American:* "Read the Revolution: Bernardo de Gálvez," Museum of the American Revolution, September 8, 2021. See also Saravio, *Bernardo de Gálvez,* 7.

277  *a prodigious army of 7,500 men:* Trickey, "The Little-Remembered Ally."

277  *Sympathies against England were running so high:* Manuel Cencillo de Pineda, *David Glasgow Farragut: Primer Almirante de los Estados Unidos de América e hijo de un menorquín* (Madrid: Editorial Naval, 1950), 27.

277  *in 2014, when Congress passed a bill posthumously:* House Joint Resolution 105, Conferring honorary citizenship of the United States on Bernardo de Gálvez y Madrid, Viscount of Galveston and Count of Gálvez. Representative Jeff Miller (R-FL-1), sponsor; 113th Congress Public Law 229. US Government Publishing Office, 2014.

277  *in George Washington's estimation, "a deciding factor":* The following are the exact words in House Joint Resolution 105: "Whereas Bernardo de Gaalvez's [sic] victories against the British were recognized by George Washington as a deciding factor in the outcome of the Revolutionary War," House Joint Resolution 105.

278  *"My ancestor, King Carlos III":* Juan Carlos I, King of Spain, Bernardo de Gálvez, Foreword, in *Yo Solo: The Battle Journal of Bernardo de Gálvez During the American Revolution,* trans. E. A. Montemayor (New Orleans: Polyanthos, 1978), ix.

278   *there are only eight honorary American citizens in all of history:* House Joint Resolution 105.

278   *Numbering more than a hundred thousand:* James Gregory, "Mapping the Latinx Great Migration," America's Great Migrations Project, Civil Rights and Labor History Consortium, University of Washington.

278   *twenty thousand Hispanics:* "Hispanics and the Civil War: From Battlefield to Homefront," National Park Service booklet, US Department of the Interior.

279   *(Jordi) Ferragut Mesquida, the only known Spanish volunteer:* He fought under the American flag, as opposed to those who fought alongside Bernardo de Gálvez under Spanish colors. Jaume Sastre Moll, "George Farragut: The Epitome of an American Colonial," Patriots, People, the War Years (1775–1783), *Journal of the American Revolution*, last modified June 18, 2019, https://allthingsliberty.com/2019/06/george-farragut-the-epitome-of-an-american-colonial/. Jordi Ferragut was a descendant of Don Pedro Ferragut, a thirteenth-century nobleman who had fought under King Jaime I of Aragon to expel the Moors from the island of Mallorca as well as the citadel of Valencia.

279   *merchant marine born on the Spanish island of Menorca:* "David Farragut, Primer Almirante Estadounidense," *Revista Española de Defensa* 345, diciembre 2017, https://www.defensa.gob.es/Galerias/gabinete/red/2017/red-345-farragut.pdf.

279   *saved the life of Colonel William Washington:* This is claimed by Loyall Farragut, biographer and son of Admiral David Glasgow Farragut, who lays out Jordi Ferragut's career as well as the names and careers of many generations of Ferraguts in Spain. Loyall Farragut, *The Life of David Glasgow Farragut, First Admiral of the United States Navy: Embodying His Journal and Letters* (New York: D. Appleton, 1879), 5. See also Marshall DeLancey Haywood, "Major George Farragut," *The Gulf States Historical Magazine* 2, no. 1 (July 1903): 89.

279   *sailing along the coast of Chile in hunt of British ships:* For more on this, see Frank Donovan, *The Odyssey of the Essex* (New York: McKay, 1969), David F. Long, *Nothing Too Daring: A Biography of Commodore David Porter, 1780–1843* (Annapolis, MD: Naval Institute Press, 1970), and Frances B. Robotti and James Vescovi, *The USS Essex and the Birth of the American Navy* (Holbrook, MA: Adams Media, 1999).

279   *"The peace for which I fought":* Jordi Ferragut Mesquida (George Farragut), as quoted in Cencillo de Pineda, *David Glasgow Farragut*, 30.

280   *"Damn the torpedoes, full speed ahead!":* The actual wording, according to biographers, is: "Damn the torpedoes! Four bells! Captain Drayton, go ahead.

Jouett, full speed!" Loyall Farragut, *Life of David Farragut*, 416–17. Also John Randolph Spears, *David G. Farragut* (Philadelphia: G. W. Jacobs, 1905), 359.

280   *a full study of Farragut's life and formidable battle prowess was undertaken:* "Stick to the Flag: Saint-Gaudens' Farragut Monument," Saint-Gaudens National Historical Park, National Park Service, nps.gov. Saint-Gaudens was the sculptor, but Stanford White was the architect and codesigned the pedestal on which the description of the man, his background, and his accomplishments are inscribed.

281   *the best-known children's biography of Farragut:* Jean Lee Latham, illustrated by Paul Frame, *David Glasgow Farragut: Our First Admiral* (Champaign, IL: Garrard, 1967.)

281   *refers to the admiral throughout as "Glasgow":* David Porter, his adoptive father, apparently addressed him as Glasgow, too. See David Porter to David Glasgow Farragut, St. Stephano de Constantinople, June 20, 1835, in Loyall Farragut, *The Life of David Glasgow Farragut*, 121.

281   *his father (Pedro Benét) and mother (Juana Hernández):* "Counting down to the 450th Anniversary of St. Augustine: Jan. 22, 1827, Benet Birth," St. Augustine Historical Society, *St. Augustine Record*, January 21, 2015.

281   *Benét's grandson, also called Stephen Vincent Benét:* The poet Stephen Vincent Benét (a namesake of his grandfather) published *John Brown's Body*, a book-length narrative poem memorializing the Civil War, in 1928. He was also the author of the famous short story "The Devil and Daniel Webster" (1936).

281   *brandishing the American flag as well as his own:* Mark Grossman, "David Glasgow Farragut," *World Military Leaders: A Biographical Dictionary* (New York: Facts on File, 2007).

281   *Springing onto those shores on the day after Christmas:* The entire account of his time in Menorca relies on Cencillo de Pineda, *David Glasgow Farragut*, chapter 7.

282   *could exchange pleasantries in at least four:* Farragut was tutored in languages by the famous educator Charles Folsom—librarian of Harvard University, editor at Harvard's university press, and noted linguist—who spent years as a chaplain aboard the USS *Washington*, where Farragut served as a young midshipman. Kenneth E. Carpenter, "Charles Folsom," *American National Biography*, February 2000. By his own claim, Farragut could speak Spanish, Italian, and French, apart from English. Farragut to James Dobbin, secretary of the navy, Norfolk, Virginia, April 12, 1854, in Loyall Farragut, *The Life of David Glasgow Farragut*, 166. It is mentioned elsewhere that he had a passing familiarity with Arabic and Turkish as well ("David Glasgow Farragut," www.nndb.com).

282   *telegraphed his superior, the American secretary of the navy:* This was Gideon

Welles, who was appointed by President Lincoln and served as a cabinet member from 1861 to 1869.

282 *"greatness of character and goodness of heart"*: Cencillo de Pineda, *David Glasgow Farragut*, 80.

282 *One historian goes so far as to suggest*: Cencillo de Pineda, *David Glasgow Farragut*, 86.

282 *"When my Confederate ancestors heard the call"*: John O'Donnell-Rosales, "Preface," *Hispanic Confederates* (Baltimore: Clearfield, by Genealogical, 2002), v.

283 *As much as one-quarter of the troops who fought for the Union*: "Who Fought?" American Battlefield Trust, https://www.battlefields.org/learn/articles/who-fought.

283 *at Abraham Lincoln's urging*: In 1861, Mexican Americans in California, New Mexico, and Texas responded to President Lincoln's call for seventy-five thousand volunteer fighters. Zaragosa Vargas, *Crucible of Struggle: A History of Mexican Americans* (New York: Oxford University Press, 2010), 127.

283 *four regiments of New Mexico Volunteers*: Colonel Gilberto Villahermosa, "America's Hispanics in America's Wars," *Army Magazine*, September 2002, https://valerosos.com/HispanicsMilitary.html.

283 *"greaser soldiers"*: Vargas, *Crucible of Struggle*, 129.

283 *Mustered by Henry Connelly*: This was Governor Henry Connelly of New Mexico, who rallied thousands of Hispanics to the Union cause. His wife, Dolores Perea, was the widow of Don Mariano Chaves, who, as it happens, was a descendant of Pedro Durán y Chaves, the ancestor of politician Linda Chavez, who is profiled earlier in this book.

283 *rabid racism and low pay—despite the shabby supplies*: Vargas, *Crucible of Struggle*, 129.

284 *"wharf-rats to cutthroats to thieves"*: Terry L. Jones, "Wharf-Rats to Cutthroats to Thieves," *Louisiana History: The Journal of the Louisiana Historical Association* 27, no. 2 (Spring 1986): 147–65.

284 *One was Loreta Janeta Velázquez*: "Loreta Janeta Velázquez," American Battlefield Trust, https://www.battlefields.org/learn/biographies/loreta-janeta-velazquez. See also *The Woman in Battle: The Civil War Narrative of Loreta Velazquez, Cuban Woman & Confederate Soldier* (Madison: University of Wisconsin, 2003), reprint of the 1876 edition.

285 *largest, most costly battle*: David J. Eicher, *The Longest Night: A Military History of the Civil War* (New York: Simon & Schuster, 2001), 230.

285 *two hundred thousand Hispanics, the great majority of them Mexican Americans*: Villahermosa, "America's Hispanics in America's Wars."

285  *eighteen thousand Puerto Ricans, lacking that racial distinction:* Ibid.

286  *"AMERICANS ALL! Let's fight for victory":* The poster from which these words came was created for the Office of War Information, the agency responsible for wartime propaganda in World War II. The artist, Leon Helguera (1899–1970), born in Chihuahua, Mexico, was a naturalized US citizen working as a commercial artist at a Manhattan agency. In 1942 he joined with other artists to offer their talents to the government on behalf of the war effort. Daniel Dancis, "Americans All by Leon Helguera: Appealing to Hispanics on the Home Front in World War II" *The Text Message* (blog), National Archives, October 11, 2018.

286  *more than a half million Latinos:* Villahermosa, "America's Hispanics in America's Wars." Also: approximately 350,000 Mexican Americans and 53,000 Puerto Ricans, according to the US Army numbers, although many with more ambiguous names or whiter features were not counted at all. *"Los Veteranos*—Latinos in WWII," National WWI Museum, New Orleans, los -veteranos-fact-sheet.pdf.

286  *60 percent of all American-born Hispanic males:* Karl Eschbach and Maggie Rivas-Rodriguez, "Preface: Navigating Bureaucratic Imprecision in the Search for an Accurate count of Latino/a Military Service in World War II," in Maggie Rivas-Rodriguez and B. V. Olguín, eds., *Latina/os and World War II: Mobility, Agency, and Ideology* (Austin: University of Texas Press, 2014), ix–xix.

286  *350,000 Puerto Ricans, all of them American citizens:* Villahermosa, "America's Hispanics in America's Wars."

286  *image of Rosie the Riveter as a white woman is grossly misleading:* Patricia Portales, "Tejanas on the Home Front: Women, Bombs, and the (Re)Gendering of War in Mexican American World War II Literature," in Rivas-Rodriguez and Olguín, *Latina/os and World War II*, 178.

286  *the experiences of the Botello family:* Eschbach and Rivas-Rodriguez, in Rivas-Rodriguez and Olguín, *Latina/os and World War II*, ix–xi.

287  *"I was born American in Fort Stockton, Texas":* Eschbach and Rivas-Rodriguez, in Rivas-Rodriguez and Olguín, *Latina/os and World War II*, xi.

287  *the legendary Bushmasters (158th Infantry):* General Paul E. Funk II, *Army History and Heritage,* monograph (Washington, DC: Center of Military History, United States Army, 2022), 44. Also: Jim Lankford, "158th Infantry Regiment," *On Point* 23, no. 3 (Winter 2018): 23–26. Note that the Bushmasters were largely Mexicans and Native Americans.

287  *"No greater fighting combat team has ever deployed for battle":* General Douglas MacArthur, as quoted in Funk, *Army History and Heritage.*

287   *Guy Gabaldon, deployed to the Mariana Islands:* Collin Hoeferlin, "Guy Gabaldon," MarineParents: Life in the Marine Corps, September 1, 2016, https://marineparents.com/marinecorps/guy-gabaldon.asp. See also Gregg K. Kakesako, "'Pied Piper' returning to Saipan," Honolulu *Star Bulletin*, June 6, 2004, star bulletin.com.

287   *For Staff Sergeant Macario García:* Jen S. Martínez, "Soldier, Mexican Immigrant Earned Medal of Honor During WWII," US Army, September 6, 2018, https://www.army.mil/article/210759/soldier_mexican_immigrant_earned_medal_of_honor_during_wwii.

288   *named an unremarkable stretch of street in the old Mexican barrio after him:* Honoree record, "CSM Marcario García," Medal of Honor Recipient, World War II, Military Hall of Honor, militaryhallofhonor.com. Unfortunately, García's first name, Macario, is often misspelled, as it is here. To this day, it is wrong on this Congressional Medal of Honor website.

289   *There were 180,000 of them:* Alejandra V. Contreras, "'Estaba seguro de que me iban a matar': mexicano recuerda paso en Guerra de Corea," *El Universal*, December 7, 2020, https://www.eluniversal.com.mx/mundo/estaba-seguro-de-que-me-iban-matar-mexicano-recuerda-paso-en-guerra-de-corea/.

289   *Those of Mexican extraction made for a full 10 percent:* Bruno Figueroa and Martha Barcena, "Mexicans: Forgotten Soldiers of 1950–53 Korean War," *Korean Times*, June 22, 2020.

289   *One-tenth of all American fatalities in the Korean War:* Villahermosa, "America's Hispanics in America's Wars."

289   *Raúl Alvarez Castillo, for instance:* Secretaría de Relaciones Exteriores (1951). Expediente III/580.2(73)/19221-A-20 CASTLE, Ralph A (Acervo Histórico).

289   *"During the Vietnam War, a lower-income":* Deborah Paredez, "Vietnam '67: Soldiers in la Guerra," *New York Times*, January 5, 2018. Edited slightly for clarity.

289   *Even as the sons of the middle and upper classes were going to college:* I owe much of this phrasing to Micheal Clodfelter, *Vietnam in Military Statistics: A History of the Indochina Wars, 1772–1991* (Jefferson, NC: McFarland, 1995), 243.

290   *averaging barely more than nineteen:* Ibid.

290   *most Latinos who were drafted reported for duty:* Freddie Valenzuela, *No Greater Love: The Lives and Times of Hispanic Soldiers* (Austin, TX: Ovation Books, 2008), 4–5, 40. For more general information, see also Adam McGlynn and Jessica Lavariega Monforti, *Proving Patriotismo: Latino Military Recruitment, Service, and Belonging in the US* (Lanham, MD: Lexington Books, 2021).

290 *the existing numbers—as under-representative as they might be:* The official numbers claimed that Latinos represented 4.5 percent of the US population and 5.5 percent of the soldiers killed in Vietnam. The true figures, as reported by Ralph Guzman in the study put before the US Congress on October 8, 1969, were as follows: Latinos represented 11.9 percent of the overall population and 20 percent of the Vietnam fatalities.

290 *Selective Service boards, which were composed largely of middle-class:* Valenzuela, *No Greater Love,* 65.

290 *Deferments for Latinos in the Southwest:* Ibid., 126.

290 *You can call it machismo:* Charley Trujillo, quoted in "The Chicanos of Vietnam," YouTube, posted by The Daily Chela, 2019.

290 *they often tended to enlist:* Tom Philpott, "Marines Begin to Reverse Sharp Drop in Black Recruits," Philadelphia Veterans Multi Service and Educational Center, October 25, 2007.

291 *would win them a "double victory":* "Double Victory: The African American Military Experience," National Museum of African American History, nmaahc.si.edu.

291 *One Mexican soldier:* This was Charley Trujillo, a Mexican American from Corcoran, California. "The Chicanos of Vietnam," YouTube.

291 *Sergeant First Class Jorge Otero-Barreto, later known as the "Puerto Rican Rambo":* Henry Howard, "Compassionate Rambo," American Legion, October 20, 2016. Also Bryce Mallory, "The Real Rambo SFC Jorge Otero Barreto, Vietnam War Medal of Honor Petition," YouTube, posted by Blue Falcon 420, November 26, 2022.

291 *reached his highest achievement during the Battle of Phuoc Yen:* Jon Simkins, "'Puerto Rican Rambo' Went On over 200 Combat Missions in Vietnam," *Military Times,* July 26, 2019.

292 *"A warrior doesn't love himself":* Jorge Otero Barreto, interviewed by Bryce Mallory in "The Real Rambo SFC Jorge Otero Barreto, Vietnam War Medal of Honor Petition."

292 *"I was a soldier, proud of his people":* Ibid.

292 *"Vietnam was a white man's war":* Martin Luther King, Jr., quoted in "American Minority Groups in the Vietnam War: A Resource Guide," Library of Congress, September 12, 2022.

292 *African Americans filled 31 percent:* "American Minority Groups in the Vietnam War" Library of Congress.

292 *Ralph Guzman, a professor at the University of California at Santa Cruz:* Paradez, "Vietnam '67."

293 *On October 8 of that year, Edward R. Roybal:* "Mexican American Casualties in Vietnam," entered by Hon. Edward R. Roybal of California, House of Representatives, October 8, 1969, "Extensions of Remarks," 29292.

293 *published by the National Council of La Raza:* The organization founded in 1968 was actually called the Southwest Council of La Raza. In 1970, it moved its offices to Washington, DC, and claimed a national membership. In 1973 it changed its name to the National Council of the La Raza.

293 *far exceeding the Pentagon's claim:* The Department of Defense claimed that Hispanics represented only 5.5 percent of the fatalities, whereas Guzman put that figure at 20 percent. See "American Minority Groups in the Vietnam War," Library of Congress.

294 *Whites, on the other hand:* The ratio of whites in the population at the time was 88.6 percent. "1960 Census of the Population: Supplementary Reports: Race of the Population of the United States, by States: 1960," US Census, Report Number PC(S1)-10, September 7, 1961. The ratio of white fatalities in the Vietnam War was 86 percent: "American Minority Groups in the Vietnam War," Library of Congress.

294 *"Mendoza was here. 12 Sept 68. Texas":* Michael Herr, *Dispatches* (New York: Alfred A. Knopf, 1977), 250. Deborah Paredez makes reference to the irony of the graffiti in "Vietnam '67."

294 *nearly 20 percent of all military personnel:* 21.39 percent of active-duty enlisted women are Hispanic; 17.9 percent of the men are Hispanic. "Distribution of active-duty enlisted women and men in the U.S. Military in 2019, by race and ethnicity," Statista, statista.com, 2019. An online recruitment service counted 19 percent of military personnel as Hispanic in 2021, "Military Jobs, Demographics," Zippia.

294 *especially dramatic since the wars in Afghanistan and Iraq:* "Hispanics in the U.S. Army," United States Army, https://www.army.mil/hispanics/history.html.

294 *Operation Desert Storm, which engaged twenty thousand Latino fighters:* "Hispanics in the U.S. Army."

295 *"As the Hispanic population has grown":* Anita U. Hattiangadi, Gary Lee, and Aline O. Quester, *Recruiting Hispanics: The Marine Corps Experience, Final Report* (Alexandria, VA: Center for Naval Analysis, January 2004).

295 *"Some eighty-five thousand Latinos have served in Operation Enduring Freedom":* George W. Bush, "Satellite Remarks to the League of Latin American Citizens Convention," as archived in The American Presidency

Project, University of California, Santa Barbara, July 8, 2004, presidency .ucsb.edu.

295   *almost two hundred thousand Hispanic soldiers serving:* "FY 2007 Population Represented in the Military Service," Executive Summary, Department of Defense, 2007, prhome.defense.gov.

295   *fourteen hapless members:* The fourteen members of Congress who sponsored the bill were: Charles B. Rangel (D-NY), Joe Baca (D-CA), Xavier Becerra (D-CA), Jim Costa (D-CA), Luis Fortuño (NP-Puerto Rico), Raúl Grijalva (D-AZ), David Ortíz (D-CO), Ed Pastor (D-AZ), Ciro Rodriguez (D-TX), Silvestre Reyes (D-TX), José E. Serrano (D-NY), Hilda Solis (D-CA), Albio Sires (D-NJ), and Nydia Velázquez (D-NY).

295   *"Whereas the contributions of Hispanics":* Hispanic American Heroes Resolution, H. Con. Res. 253, 110th Congress (2007–2008).

296   *by then, dozens of Congressional Medals of Honor had festooned:* Of the sixty Hispanics on the current list of Medal of Honor recipients, fifty-three had received the medal (either living or posthumously) by 2008. Hispanic Medal of Honor Society, http://hispanicmedalofhonorsociety.org/recipients.html. See also Raul A. Reyes, "Military Veterans: We Need to Recognize Latinos' Long History of Service," NBC News online, last modified November 11, 2022, https://www.nbcnews.com/news/latino/latinos-military-role-history -veterans-day-rcna56434.

296   *there were but four Hispanic senior officers in any segment of the armed forces:* "FY 2007 Population Represented in the Military Service," 26.

296   *Between 1995 and 2016, only one was promoted:* Rafael Bernal, "Latinos Aren't Reaching Top Military Positions, Study Shows," *Hill,* July 22, 2018.

296   *there are only four Hispanic officers in the top echelons:* "Active Component Demographics," data as of June 30, 2022, US Army, api.army.mil, 4.

296   *we represent a paltry 2 percent:* This is the percentage for general/flag officers. Table 6, "Race and Ethnic Representation in the Active Component and U.S. Population," *Diversity, Inclusion, and Equal Opportunity in the Armed Forces,* Congressional Research Service, Library of Congress, June 5, 2019, https:// sgp.fas.org/crs/natsec/R44321.pdf, 21. In the following, the figure is 3 percent: Carlos E. Martinez, "The US Military Has Failed Latinos," *Hispanic Executive,* September 27, 2022.

296   *Some will argue that not enough have a bachelor's degree:* "While Hispanics Represent 18 Percent of the U.S. Population, They Account for Roughly 8 Percent of all Post-Secondary Degree Holders," "Race and Ethnic Representation in the Active Component and U.S. Population," 20.

296 *"good old boy network":* This claim is made by Major General Alfred A. ("Freddie") Valenzuela in his book *No Greater Love,* 65. It is repeated by retired army general Albert Zapanta and Edward Cabrera, president of Casaba Group, a Hispanic veterans organization, in Bernal, "Latinos aren't reaching top military positions." Also Christopher S. Chivvis, "Diversity in the High Brass," Carnegie Endowment for International Peace, September 6, 2022.

296 *almost 97 percent of the leadership:* 96.5 percent, to be exact. Chivvis, "Diversity in the High Brass."

296 *non-Hispanic whites represent little more than half the population:* "Race and Hispanic Origin," QuickFacts, United States," US Census, 2023.

296 *Marine general Michael E. Langley reached that landmark:* Helene Cooper, "After 246 Years, Marine Corps Gives Four Stars to a Black Officer," *New York Times,* August 6, 2022.

296 *we can count fewer than twenty blacks:* "The Commanders: Admirals and Generals in the United States Military, 1940–," African American History, BlackPast, blackpast.org/special-features.

296 *Richard E. Cavazos:* For more information on the general, see "Richard E. Cavazos," Biographies, National Museum, United States Army, thenmusa .org.

297 *the first US pilot to be shot down over Vietcong territory:* This is Colonel Everett Alvarez, Jr. of the US Navy, as told in the film *Hispanic American Veterans Share Their Experiences in Vietnam,* The United States of America Vietnam War Commemoration, YouTube video, PBS KVIE, 2019.

297 *"It's part of the macho mind-set, I think":* General Albert Zapanta, quoted in Bernal. "Latinos aren't reaching top military positions."

297 *Latinos do not join the military for self-aggrandizement:* This is certainly the argument that Major General Valenzuela makes in *No Greater Love,* 64. It is repeated by Zapanta, in Bernal, "Latinos aren't reaching top military positions."

## Growers

298 *The overarching narrative is that we're taking jobs:* Mónica Ramírez, author interview, September 10, 2021.

298 *the most highly employed people in the United States:* Rose Chatter, Jessica Vela, and Lorena Roque, "Latino Workers Continue to Experience a Shortage of Good Jobs," fig. 1, Center for American Progress, July 18, 2022. See also "Employment rate in the United States in 2021, by ethnicity, Economy & Politics," *Statista,* statista.com, accessed March 14, 2023.

298　*In 1990 the Latino workforce numbered:* Kevin Dubina, "Hispanics in the Labor Force: 5 Facts," US Department of Labor Blog, September 15, 2021, blog.dol .gov.

298　*Hispanics will account for 80 percent of all new workers:* Hispanics in the Labor Force: 5 Facts."

299　*many Latinos registered higher unemployment rates:* The highest unemployment numbers are being registered by Dominicans, Puerto Ricans, Hondurans, Salvadorans, Mexicans, and Paraguayans. Chatter, Vela, and Roque, "Latino Workers Continue to Experience a Shortage of Good Jobs."

299　*Latinos have represented more than half:* Hispanics made up 52 percent of total US population growth from 2010 to 2021.

299　*hazy, informal sector of transient, underreported menial jobs:* For more information on this, see Michael J. Pisani, "New Age Informality: Hispanics and the Sharing Economy," *Administrative Sciences* 11, no. 1 (March 1, 2021), https:// doi.org/10.3390/admsci11010023.

299　*a young population:* The average age of Latinos is thirty, as compared to thirty-five for blacks, and forty-three for whites. But it is also a highly multiracial population, and the multiracial are the youngest population of all, with an average age of twenty-five. Zong, "A Mosaic, Not a Monolith," fig. 6. See also Jens Manuel Krogstad, Jeffrey S. Passel, and Luis Noe-Bustamante, "Key Facts About U.S. Latinos for National Hispanic Heritage Month," Pew Research Center online, last modified September 23, 2022, https://www.pewresearch .org/short-reads/2022/09/23/key-facts-about-u-s-latinos-for-national-his panic-heritage-month/.

299　*One out of every four American children is a Hispanic:* Latino children (ages eighteen and under) numbered 18.6 million in 2019, making up 26 percent of the nation's total child population. While Latino children reside disproportionately in the Southwest, they comprise a sizable share of the child population in all fifty states—and at least 25 percent of the child population in twelve states. Yiyu Chen and Lina Guzman, "Latino Children Represent Over a Quarter of the Child Population Nationwide and Make Up at Least 40 Percent in 5 Southwestern States," National Research Center on Hispanic Children & Families, September 15, 2021. The five states are California, Texas, New Mexico, Nevada, and Arizona.

299　*more than half of all Texans and Californians under eighteen years old:* For California, the exact figure in 2020 was 51.6 percent; 2020 Census Profiles, California, Naleo Educational Fund, naleo.org, 4. For Texas, it's 49.3 percent; Alexa

Ura, "Hispanic Texans may now be the state's largest demographic group, new census data show," *Texas Tribune*, September 15, 2022.

299 *its numbers are ever mounting:* Zong, "A Mosaic, Not a Monolith," fig. 14.

299 *Much of the population toils on farmlands:* "Hispanics and Latinos in industries and occupations," TED: The Economics Daily, Bureau of Labor Statistics, US Department of Labor, October 9, 2015, https://www.bls.gov/opub/ted/2015/hispanics-and-latinos-in-industries-and-occupations.htm.

299 *This bounty of food is, in many ways, a pillar of America's strength:* I owe this insight and language to Antonio De Loera-Brust, "Mexican Farmers Are U.S. Heroes," *Foreign Policy*, October 18, 2022.

299 *America's "unsung heroes":* De Loera-Brust, "Mexican Farmers Are U.S. Heroes."

300 *The Bracero "guest worker" program:* "1942: Bracero Program," A Latinx Resource Guide: Civil Rights Cases and Events in the United States, Library of Congress Research Guides, guides.loc.gov.

300 *the New Deal's labor laws explicitly excluded them from protection:* "The Road to Sacramento: Marching for Justice in the Fields—Thirty Years of Farmworker Struggle," National Park Service, accessed March 6, 2023, nps.org.

301 *Facing a raging virus, a scourge of pesticides:* More information on the dangers Hispanic farmworkers face can be found in Federico Castillo et al., "Environmental Health Threats to Latino Migrant Farmworkers," *Annual Review of Public Health* 42 (April 2021): 257–76.

301 *dying of the virus in unprecedented numbers:* "Hispanics are disproportionately affected by COVID-19, experiencing significantly higher rates in positive cases and increased mortality from the virus than other ethnicities." Quoted in "COVID-19 Impact on Agricultural Workers," National Center for Farmworker Health, updated May 2022, ncfh.org.

301 *as essential to national security today:* De Loera-Brust, Mexican Farmers Are U.S. Heroes."

302 *"We consume nachos, tacos, burritos, tortas":* Anthony Bourdain, "Under the Volcano," *Anthony Bourdain, Parts Unknown,* blog on Mexico, May 3, 2014; "Mexico City," Season 3, Episode 4, May 4, 2014.

302 *"Mexicans cook a large percentage of the food we eat":* In fact, they provide our daily bread. The owners of the largest baked goods company in the United States, Bimbo, are Mexican. Among the products this multibillion-dollar corporation owns: Arnold, Brownberry, Freihofer's, Stroehmann, Weston, Sara Lee, Entenmann's, Thomas's, and Lender's.

## Builders

302   *"They worked / They were never late"*: Pedro Pietri, excerpt from "Puerto Rican Obituary" from *Selected Poetry* (San Francisco: City Lights, 2015), 3. Permission granted by City Lights.

302   *construction industry, where one out of three workers is Hispanic:* Bureau of Labor Statistics, US Department of Labor, 2015. See also Na Zhao, "One in Three Workers in Construction is Hispanic," *Eye on Housing*, June 23, 2022. See also Lynda Lee, "Minority Business Ownership Differs by Sector," United States Census Bureau Library, January 4, 2023.

302   *number of Latinos employed in the building trade grew by more than half:* "Construction Statistics," National Institute for Occupational Safety and Health (NIOSH), accessed March 7, 2023.

302   *or die on the job:* Samantha Brown et al., "Fatal Injury Trends in the Construction Industry," Center for Construction Research and Training (CPWR) Data Bulletin, February 2021.

302   *almost four million Latino men and women:* Brown et al., "Fatal Injury Trends in the Construction Industry."

302   *cities from coast to coast:* Samantha Sharf, "Building Is Booming in These 30 Cities, but Don't Expect It to Last," *Forbes*, March 15, 2019. See also Associated Press, "Latino Construction Workers Have Enabled Construction Boom, but at a Cost, Documentary Shows," NBC News online, last modified September 14, 2020, https://www.nbcnews.com/news/latino/latino-construction-workers-have-enabled-construction-boom-cost-documentary-shows-n1240027.

302   *of the twenty-one million immigrants:* Jeffrey S. Passell and D'Vera Cohn, *Unauthorized Immigrant Population: National and State Trends,* 2010 (especially "II. Current Estimates and Trends"), Pew Research Center online, last modified February 1, 2011, https://www.pewresearch.org/hispanic/2011/02/01/unauthorized-immigrant-population-brnational-and-state-trends-2010/. Also, for 2021: Evin Millet and Jacquelyn Pavilon, *Demographic Profile of Undocumented Hispanic Immigrants in the United States,* Center for Migration Studies online, last modified October 14, 2022, https://cmsny.org/wp-content/uploads/2022/04/Hispanic_undocumented.pdf. To be precise, in 2022 the number was seven and a half million undocumented.

303   *living and working here for more than fifteen years:* Millet and Pavilon, *Demographic Profile of Undocumented Hispanic Immigrants in the United States.*

304   *owns his or her own home:* Frank Gogol, "Can an Illegal Immigrant Buy a

House?," *Stilt* (blog), last modified May 26, 2023, https://www.stilt.com/blog/2018/08/can-illegal-immigrants-buy-house.

304 *$12 billion a year in local and federal taxes:* $3 billion alone is collected from undocumented Hispanics in California. "Undocumented Immigrants' State & Local Tax Contributions," Institute on Taxation and Economic Policy, March 1, 2017, itep.org.

304 *a net-zero effect on government budgets:* Alex Nowrasteh, "The Most Common Arguments Against Immigration and Why They're Wrong," Cato Institute, as quoted in "15 Myths About Immigration Debunked," Carnegie Corporation of New York, September 27, 2021.

304 traqueros, *laying track to build the nation's railways:* See Jeffrey Marcos Garcilazo, *Traqueros: Mexican Railroad Workers in the United States, 1870–1930* (Denton: University of North Texas Press, 2012).

304 *Roendy Granillo—a strapping, twenty-five-year-old laborer:* Chelsea Hernandez, *Building the American Dream*, a PBS "Voces" documentary. See: "Building the American Dream": Film Review/ SXSW 2019, *Hollywood Reporter*, March 11, 2019.

305 *Texas's heinous record of burying a dead construction worker:* The precise statistic is one dead construction worker every 2.5 days. In 2007 alone, 142 construction workers were killed in Texas. Michael King, "Three More Casualties of Austin's Growth," *Austin Chronicle*, June 19, 2009.

305 *Later, we meet Claudia Golinelli, an undocumented electrician:* Hernandez, "Building the American Dream."

305 *A full quarter million Hispanic child laborers:* Hannah Dreier, "Alone and Exploited, Migrant Children Work Brutal Jobs Across the U.S.," *New York Times*, February 25, 2023. Photographs by Kirsten Luce. See also Hannah Dreier, "Migrant Children Worked as U.S. Ignored Warnings," *New York Times*, April 18, 2023.

305 *"new economy of exploitation":* Dreier, "Alone and Exploited."

305 *the Hispanic population has increased by forty-five million souls:* The Hispanic population in March 1985 totaled about 17 million; today it is 62.5 million. The difference is 45.5 million. Carmen DeNavas, "The Hispanic Population in the United States: March 1985," *Current Population Report*, no. 422 (March 1988), 1.

306 *As a result, we have Cristián, fourteen years old:* Most information that follows on Hispanic child migrant labor in the United States today is taken from Dreier, "Alone and Exploited." Also useful: Mica Rosenberg, Kristina Cooke, and

Joshua Schneyer, "Child Workers Found Throughout Hyundai-Kia Supply Chain in Alabama," A Reuters Special Report, December 16, 2022.

307 *"It's the new child labor":* This is Rick Angstman, a social studies teacher at Union High School in Grand Rapids, Michigan. Dreier, "Alone and Exploited."

## Sellers

308 *Juan Rodriguez, the first Dominican to arrive in Manhattan:* See Rodriguez's story, as told in chapter 4 of this book. Also: Stevens-Acevedo, Weterings, and Álvarez Francés, *Juan Rodriguez.*

308 *starting perhaps when Mexican vaqueros:* "Vaqueros: Teaching the World to Rope and Ride," The Story of Texas, Bullock Museum, Austin, TX, www .thestoryoftexas.com.

308 *"According to the most recent data . . . Hispanic-owned companies":* George W. Bush, in a speech to the League of United Latin American Citizens (LULAC), "LULAC Celebrates 75th Anniversary in San Antonio," *LULAC News,* July/ August 2004, 27. Bush was the first US president to publicly congratulate Hispanic Americans for their contributions to the economy.

308 *Hispanic-owned businesses have multiplied by 44 percent:* Neil Hare and Arturo Cazares, "New State of Latino Entrepreneurship Report Shows Strong Growth in Tech Sector," *Forbes,* April 14, 2022.

308 *almost 90 percent of these ventures are owned by millennials:* Kerry A. Dolan, "What's Fueling Latino Entrepreneurship—and What's Holding It Back," Stanford Business online, last modified February 7, 2018, https://www.gsb .stanford.edu/insights/whats-fueling-latino-entrepreneurship-whats-hold ing-it-back. See also J. Jennings Moss, "By the Numbers: Latinx-Owned Small Businesses Show Rapid Growth," *Silicon Valley Business Journal,* April 1, 2022.

309 *Today there are nearly five million Hispanic-owned businesses:* "Hispanic-Owned Small Businesses Are Starting at Record Rates, but Access to Funding Remains a Stark Challenge," CISION, PR Newswire, September 15, 2022. See also "The SBA Looks to Help Hispanic-Owned Small Businesses Build on Their Historic Momentum," US Small Business Administration, September 13, 2022.

309 *one of the lowest percentages of unemployed:* The unemployment rate of Latinos has gone from lowest to median; it is 4.0 percent at this writing. The other sectors are more volatile: Blacks are 5.9 percent. Asian are 2.5 percent, Whites are 3.3 percent. "Unemployment rate 3.6 percent in June 2023," TED: The Economics Daily, U.S. Bureau of Labor Statistics, July 12, 2023.

309 *by 2050, Latinos could add a mammoth $1.4 trillion:* "Latino-Owned Businesses May Be the U.S. Economy's Best Bet," J.P. Morgan Chase, accessed March 14, 2023.

309 *contributes far more to the US economy:* It is projected that the Hispanic business industry will contribute 8 percent to the US economy by 2050. The entertainment industry contributes 6.9 percent; the agriculture and food industry (including food services), 5.4 percent; the tech industry, 10 percent. Sources: For entertainment, Zippia Team, June 28, 2022. For agriculture and food, "Ag and Food Sectors and the Economy," US Economic Research Service, US Department of Agriculture, accessed March 14, 2023. For tech, "Industry Overview, Software and Information Technology Industry," SELECT USA, trade.gov, accessed March 14, 2023. A very good overview of the Hispanic labor force can be found in "Table A-3. Employment status of the Hispanic or Latino population by sex and age," Economic News Release, U.S. Bureau of Labor Statistics, modified on August 4, 2023.

## The *Talentoso* Tenth

309 *"A remnant continually survives and persists":* W. E. B. Du Bois, "The Talented Tenth," in *The Negro Problem: A Series of Articles by Representative American Negroes of Today* (New York: James Pott, 1903), 31–75.

309 *"yeasty" few:* Du Bois, refers to them as the yeast for excellence. Du Bois, "Talented Tenth."

309 *Latinos have their own talented tenth:* Management, business, and financial leaders among Hispanics numbered about 11 percent in 2022. In professional occupations they represent about 14 percent. "Labor Force Statistics from the Current Population Survey," Household Data, Annual Averages, employed persons by occupation, race, Hispanic or Latino ethnicity, and sex. US Bureau of Labor Statistics, bis.gov/.

310 *Carlos Gutierrez, the Havana-born son of a Cuban pineapple merchant:* "Profile: Secretary of Commerce Carlos Gutierrez," ABC News, no date, https://abc news.go.com/Politics/Inauguration/story?id=289793.

310 *the eldest of nine children of a supermarket butcher:* Luc Chenier, "Oscar Muñoz—CEO, United Airlines," accessed on May 30, 2023, dad.ceo.

310 *only 5 percent have mentors:* Celia T. Before, "It Takes a Village to Make It to the C-Suite," The Center for Association Leadership (ASAE), September 27, 2021.

310 *fewer than twenty Hispanics who occupy the C-Suite:* Theresa Agovino, "Closing the Gap: As the Hispanic population booms, workers in this demographic seek better representation in C-suites and corporate boardrooms," Society for Human Resource Management, shrm.org.

310 *paucity of Latinos at the very top of large corporations:* This prejudice is tidily summarized in Suzanne Gamboa's "Americans way off on number of Latinos

they think are undocumented, poll finds," NBC News, September 30, 2021. Americans of all backgrounds incorrectly believe that the number of Latinos in the United States who are undocumented is two to three times larger than it actually is. Asians and Blacks hold most of the exaggerated views.

310  *median annual income:* The median income for white households in 2022 was $78,000, for Latinos in 2021, it was $58,015: "Income and Wealth in the United States: An Overview of Recent Data," *Annual Social and Economic Supplement (ASEC) 2022*, as quoted in Peter Peterson Foundation, November 9, 2022, pgpf.org. In certain cities—Chicago, Dallas, Gilbert (AZ)—the median income of Hispanics can be as high as $108,000. Arturo Conde, "Where Hispanics and Latinos Fare Best Economically—2022 Edition," Smart Asset, smart asset.com/data-studies/.

310  *Latino families have owned their homes:* "2022 State of Hispanic Homeownership Report," National Association of Hispanic Real Estate Professionals (NAHREPP), accessed March 18, 2023.

310  *One in five of all Hispanic adults has a college or postgraduate degree:* Lauren Mora, "Hispanic Enrollment Reaches New High at Four-Year Colleges in the U.S., but Affordability Remains an Obstacle," Pew Research Center online, last modified October 7, 2022, https://www.pewresearch.org/short-reads/2022/10/07/hispanic-enrollment-reaches-new-high-at-four-year-colleges-in-the-u-s-but-affordability-remains-an-obstacle/. See also "Labor force characteristics by race and ethnicity, 2019," *BLS Reports*, Chart 2. J. Oliver Schak and Andrew Howard Nichols, "Degree Attainment for Latino Adults: National and State trends," *The Education Trust*, accessed March 20, 2023. And "College Graduates Statistics," ThinkImpact, accessed March 20, 2023, https://www.thinkimpact.com/college-graduates-statistics/.

311  *one out of every three has never finished high school:* "Labor force characteristics by race and ethnicity," Chart 2.

311  *the fastest growing population of high-income households:* Pamela Danzinger, "Hispanic Americans Are Rapidly Accumulating Wealth: What It Means for Luxury Brands," *Forbes*, September 22, 2022.

311  *70 percent—are American born and bred:* The exact percentage is 68 percent. Zong, "A Mosaic, not a Monolith," fig. 8.

311  *Almost 90 percent are citizens:* 13 percent of Hispanics in the United States are undocumented; 87 percent are here legally. Suzanne Gamboa, "Americans way off on the number of Latinos they think are undocumented, poll finds."

311  *"a sea of white":* Jeff Green, Esther Aguilera, chief executive officer of Latino Corporate Directors Association, speaking at the Bloomberg Equality

Summit, as reported in Jeff Green, "'Sea of White': Latino Leaders Fight to Reshape U.S. Boardrooms," Bloomberg News, last modified March 22, 2022, https://www.bloomberg.com/news/articles/2022-03-22/-sea-of-white-latino-leaders-fight-to-reshape-u-s-boardrooms#xj4y7vzkg.

311 *Asian or East Indian descent have shot up:* "Crist Colder Associates Volatility Report of America's Leading Companies, 2022," July 31, 2022. See also "Share of Companies in the United States with Racially and Ethnically Diverse of CEOs from 2004 to 2022," Statista, last modified February 23, 2023, https://www.statista.com/statistics/1097600/racial-and-ethnic-diversity-of-ceos-in-the-united-states/.

311 *Hispanics represent but 1 percent:* "5 Companies with Hispanic and Latino CEOs," Resources, AboveBoard, September 14, 2022.

311 *Blacks represent 28 percent:* "Percentage of New African American Directors on Fortune 500 Boards from 2009 to 2021," Statista, accessed June 19, 2023, statista.com.

311 *there have only been three Latina chief executives:* Victoria Arena, "Why There Are So Few Latina CEOs in Fortune 500 Companies," Latinas in Business, last modified August 16, 2022, https://latinasinbusiness.us/2022/08/16/why-there-are-so-few-latina-ceos-in-fortune-500-companies/. On Geisha Williams: "FIRSTS: The Engineer: Geisha Williams, First Latina CEO of a Fortune 500 Company," *Time*, accessed March 20, 2023. On Cheryl Miller: Marcia Heroux Pounds, "How Deal-Maker Cheryl Miller Rose to Become AutoNation's New CEO," *South Florida Sun Sentinel*, August 2, 2019. On Priscilla Almodovar: "Enterprise Names Priscilla Almodovar CEO," *Real Estate Weekly*, June 19, 2019, accessed March 20, 2023. Also: Marina E. Franco, "Despite Growth, Latinos Are Missing from Boardrooms," *Noticias Telemundo*, Axios, October 6, 2022.

312 *white male who was paid more than seven times her salary:* Cheryl Miller's annual compensation at AutoNation was $2.6 million, accessed March 20, 2023, https://www.comparably.com/companies/autonation/cheryl-scully-miller. When she left, her replacement's—Mike Jackson's—compensation was $18,288,250. AutoNation, Inc., Executive Compensation, Mike Jackson, accessed March 20, 2023, salary.com.

312 *increased by more than thirty million souls since 2000:* "The 2022 Hispanic Market Report: The New American Mainstream," Claritas, 5, accessed March 20, 2023.

312 *rocketed from $500 billion to $2 trillion:* "Buying power of Hispanic consumers in the United States from 1990 to 2020," Statista, statista.com, accessed March 20, 2023. Also: Jingqiu Ren, "Hispanic consumers drive US population and spending growth," Insider Intelligence, October 6, 2022.

312 *gross domestic product would be the fifth largest in the world:* Carmen Sesin, "U.S. Latino economic output would rank 5th in world GDP, according to new study," NBC News, September 22, 2022.

313 *My most enthusiastic champion at the* Washington Post*:* This was Milton Coleman, assistant managing editor of the newspaper, known in the media industry as a force in diversity hiring and minority representation.

314 *A 2000 study titled* Latinwood and TV*:* Heidi Denzel de Tirado, "Media Monitoring and Ethnicity: Representing Latino Families on American Television" (2000–2013), *Nuevo Mundo, Mundos Nuevos*, December 16, 2013.

314 *our presence in films is a miserable 5 percent:* Allison Michelle Morris, "A History of Hispanic and Latinx Representation in Film," September 15, 2022, allison michellemorris.com.

314 *Peruvian American Hilda Quispe: Transnational Fiesta: Twenty Years Later*, documentary produced by Wilton Martinez and Paul H. Gelles, 2014.

315 *"Somewhere along the way, people became secondary to objects":* Suhaly Bautista-Carolina, author interview, August 5, 2021.

## PART V: HOW WE SHINE

317 *"Sí, se puede! Yes, we can!":* Dolores Huerta, at a 1972 farmworkers' rally.

## CHAPTER 11: CHANGEMAKERS

319 *"Any time you have an opportunity to make a difference":* Roberto Clemente, quoted in Nick Anapolis, "Clemente Elected to Hall of Fame Only Months After Crash," National Baseball Hall of Fame, accessed May 15, 2023, base ballhall.org.

319 *the landmark advances made by Dolores Huerta and Cesar Chavez:* For thorough coverage of Huerta's and Chavez's careers, see Miriam Pawel, *The Union of Their Dreams* (New York: Bloomsbury, 2010), and Stacey K. Sowards, *Sí! Ella Puede!: The Rhetorical Legacy of Dolores Huerta and the United Farm Workers* (Austin: University of Texas Press, 2019).

320 *rates of cancer 800 percent above the norm:* "Pesticides in the Fields," Walter P. Reuther Library, Wayne State University, reuther.wayne.edu/ex/exhibits /fw/pesticide.html#.

320 *Chavez, a young navy veteran from Arizona:* Robert Lindsey, "Cesar Chavez, 66, Organizer of Union for Migrants, Dies," *New York Times*, April 24, 1993.

320 *Fred Ross—a consummate organizer:* See Gabriel Thompson, *America's Social Arsonist: Fred Ross and Grassroots Organizing in the 20th Century* (Oakland: University of California Press, 2019).

321   *Huerta, his equal partner:* Jessica M. Goldstein, "Dolores Huerta Is Done Being
      Edited Out of Her Own Story," ThinkProgress, last modified September 5,
      2017, https://archive.thinkprogress.org/dolores-huerta-documentary-a68
      8e5bf1ebb/. Also Debra Michals, ed., "Dolores Huerta: (1930–), National
      Women's History Museum, 2015, accessed April 5, 2023.

321   *fewer than seven thousand members in the United Farm Workers union:* Melissa
      Montalvo and Nigel Duara, *CAL Matters*, January 18, 2022, calmatters.org.
      See also Miriam Pawel, "How Cesar Chavez's Union Lost Its Way," *New York
      Times*, September 4, 2022.

321   *the overall population of two and a half million:* "Ag and Food Sectors and the
      Economy," US Department of Agriculture Economic Research Service, ac-
      cessed April 5, 2023.

321   *Robert F. Kennedy of New York called Chavez "one of the heroic figures of our time":*
      Lindsey, "Cesar Chavez, 66, Organizer of Union for Migrants, Dies."

322   *"Knowing her, I'm pleased that she let me off easy":* Barack Obama speaking
      at the White House Medal of Freedom ceremony, May 29, 2012, "Dolores
      Huerta Receives Medal of Freedom," 23 ABC News, youtube.com.

322   *"Señor ingeniero":* These quotes are taken from my notes on a return trip to
      Peru with my father in 1998, as I was writing my memoir, *American Chica*.

**The Activists**

322   *"I reject the notion that we don't have power":* Mónica Ramírez, author interview,
      September 10, 2021.

323   *Mónica Ramírez is a case in point:* Much of the material that follows on Ramírez
      is from my interview with her.

323   *"Migrant farmwork is a universe unto itself":* Ramírez, author interview, Sep-
      tember 10, 2021.

323   *"That was the car wreck in my life":* Ibid.

323   *"The overarching narrative is that we're taking all the jobs":* Ibid.

324   *forced to watch someone in her family be raped:* Ramírez, author interview. Also:
      Rebecca Clarren, "Field of Panties: Immigrant Workers," *Marie Claire* on-
      line, accessed on July 23, 2021, https://www.marieclaire.com/politics/news
      /a1444/esperenza-sexual-assault/.

324   *constantly exposed to victimization:* Bernice Yeung and Grace Rubenstein, "Fe-
      male Workers Face Rape, Harassment in U.S. Agriculture," The Center for
      Investigative Reporting, *Frontline*, PBS, June 25, 2013.

324   *certain farm company as "el fil de calzón":* Mónica Ramírez, "Sexual Violence in
      the Workplace Against Farmworker Women: An Overview of the Problem,

the Protections, and the Movement to End It," 2nd ed., Southern Poverty Law Center, 2008, accessed on July 15, 2023, https://www.alabamapublic health.gov/alphtn/assets/042309_01.pdf. Also Clarren, "Field of Panties."

324 *Mónica has founded no fewer than a half dozen organizations:* Mónica Ramírez served as deputy director of the Centro de los Derechos del Migrante—the Center for Migrant Rights—a transnational organization based in Mexico. She returned to the United States to lead the Labor Council for Latin American Advancement and co-found the Alianza Nacional de Campesinas (the National Farmworker Women's Alliance). Even as a fledgling law student she founded a project called Esperanza (literally "hope"), a legal initiative under the Southern Poverty Center. She also founded the Bandana Project to raise awareness of the abuses that female workers were facing on American farms. Mónica is also the founder of The Latinx House, an organization that celebrates excellence in film.

325 *she sparked the famous "Dear Sisters" letter:* "700,000 Female Farmworkers Say They Stand with Hollywood Actors Against Sexual Assault," *Time*, November 10, 2017.

325 *she was named one of* Time *magazine's "100 Most Influential People":* Kinsey Schofield, "How Does Time Magazine Pick Their 100 Most Influential People—Harry & Meghan," *Time*, September 15, 2021.

325 *"No tenemos tiempo para división":* Walter Tejada, founder, Virginia Latino Leaders Council; founder, statewide Virginia Coalition of Latino Organizations; and former Arlington County Board Member, author interview, July 5, 2022.

326 *old 1932 aphorism that "all politics is local":* Byron Price, an Associated Press columnist who went on to win a Pulitzer Prize, wrote in the *Sarasota (FL) Herald*, on February 16, 1932: "In its last essence all politics is local politics, and every ward and township politician is looking for the combination which will help him at home." Congressman Tip O'Neill, Speaker of the House from 1977 to 1987, was inaccurately attributed with coining the phrase. Entry Government/Law/Military/Religion/Health, Barry Popik, June 13, 2009, https://www.barrypopik.com/index.php/new_york_city/entry/all_politics_is_local/.

326 *"I'm pushing for civic participation by the Latinos around me":* Tejada, author interview. A good introduction to the work and philosophy of Tejada can be found in the Spanish-language video "Debate with Gaspar Rivera-Salgado, J. Walter Tejada and Kate Brick: Immigration: Social and Cultural Capital, The Hispano/Latin experience in North America," Centre de Cultura

Contemporània de Barcelona (CCCB), April 16, 2009, https://www.cccb
.org/en/multimedia/videos/debate-with-gaspar-rivera-salgado-jose-walter
-tejada-and-kate-brick-immigration-social-and-cultural-capital-the-hispano
-latin-experience-in-north-america/211615.

326   *the first Latino in the state to be elected to public office:* "Oral History: J. Walter
Tejada: Community Activist," Arlington Public Library, September 23, 2021,
library.arlingtonva.us.

326   *migrated to a rough neighborhood of Brooklyn in 1971:* Most of what follows, unless specified, is taken from my four-hour interview with Tejada in Arlington,
Virginia, on July 5, 2022.

328   *Arlington, held the third largest population of Salvadorans:* "El Salvador: Salvadoran Population in the Washington, DC, and Baltimore Metro Areas," Institute for Immigration Research, George Mason University, iir.gmu.edu.

329   *"If you care about it so much, Walter":* Eduardo Bretón, quoted by Walter Te-
jada, author interview. See also "League of United Latin American Citizens
(LULAC) Virginia State Councils Hold 1993 Training and Planning Retreat,"
*El Eco de Virginia* 3, no. 12 (December 1, 1993), archive in Virginia Chronicle,
Library of Virginia.

329   *single-family dwelling costs more than $1 million:* Jeff Clabaugh, "Want a House
in Arlington?," WTOP news, January 17, 2022, https://wtop.com/business
-finance/2022/01/want-a-house-in-arlington-1-3-million-should-do/.

330   *"I learned only after the fact":* Tejada, author interview.

330   *"If I had one wish for Latinos":* Ibid.

331   *"I'm a history addict":* John Leguizamo, quoted in Jahaura Michelle, "John Leguizamo Supports the Term 'Latinx' And Doesn't Get Why It Is So 'Contentious': 'I Feel It's Inclusive,'" Yahoo!, last modified April 17, 2023, https://
www.yahoo.com/lifestyle/john-leguizamo-supports-term-latinx-144512897
.html.

331   *"I live in New York City, where we're equal":* Michelle, "John Leguizamo Supports the Term 'Latinx.'"

331   *a medium that reaches 93 percent:* According to NBC Universal's website, "The
NBCU portfolio reaches 226 million adults every month—that's 93% of
America," Reaching Audiences at Scale, together.nbcuni.com.

331   *Julissa Gutierrez, the Colombian American daughter:* Most of the information on
Julissa Gutierrez, unless noted otherwise, is taken from my interview with
her, September 19, 2021.

332   *daughter of a maid and a chauffeur:* Gutierrez, author interview.

332   *dedicates herself to protecting Latino small businesses:* Gutierrez, author interview.

See also Megan McGibney, "NYC Awarded Less Than 4% of Contracts to Minority- and Women-Owned Businesses," City & State: New York, March 15, 2022. It was increased to 30.5 percent, to be exact.

332 *Julissa's former roommate:* Raquel Batista, in video interview with Julissa Gutierrez and Wendy García, "City and State Diversity," Critica NYC, *MNN El Barrio Firehouse Presents,* www.youtube.com.

332 *deputy commissioner for equity and inclusion in the New York City Police Department:* "Equity and Inclusion: Deputy Commissioner for Equity and Inclusion: Wendy García," New York City Police Department, https://www.nyc.gov /site/nypd/bureaus/administrative/equity-inclusion.page. "Wendy Garcia, Highest Ranking Dominican-American in the NYPD," World Today News, May 24, 2022, world-today-news.com.

332 *And then there is Arturo Griffiths:* Most of the information on Arturo Griffiths comes from my personal correspondence with him, papers he provided, and a three-hour interview in Mount Pleasant, December 6, 2022. See also "Arturo Griffiths, Statehood-Green Candidate for City Council at Large, September 12, 2000 Primary," flyer July 2000, DCWatch.com.

333 *reaching to take off his belt:* The police initially claimed the intoxicated Salvadoran, thirty-five-year-old Daniel Enrique Gómez, brandished a knife, but this claim was dismissed repeatedly by witnesses on the scene of the shooting. Emily Friedman, "Mount Pleasant Riots: May 5 Woven into Neighborhood's History," WAMU radio, Local News, wamu.org, May 5, 2011. See also Bill Miller, "Jury Rejects Suit in Police Shooting," *Washington Post,* May 19, 1995, and David Nakamura, "District Officials Make 20th Anniversary of Mount Pleasant Protests," *Washington Post,* May 6, 2011.

333 *one thousand heavily armed, largely white police officers:* Rene Sánchez, "Curfew Leaves Mount Pleasant Area Quieter," *Washington Post,* May 8, 1991.

333 *"The cops were like 'Whoa! What the hell is this?'":* José Suero, editor of El Diario de la Nación, quoted in Friedman, "Mount Pleasant Riots."

333 *More than fifty people were injured:* Friedman, "Mount Pleasant Riots."

334 *"Many Washingtonians, black and white":* Sharon Pratt, mayor of the District of Columbia from 1991 to 1995, in an editorial about the 2011 London riots, "Lessons from a D.C. Riot," *Washington Post,* August 12, 2011.

334 *prompted the US Civil Rights Commission to hold a hearing:* Friedman, "Mount Pleasant Riots." Also Griffiths, author interview.

334 *began publishing documents in two languages:* Pratt, "Lessons from a D.C. Riot."

**The Educators**

335 *"I have a cousin who works four jobs"*: Julissa Gutierrez, author interview, September 19, 2021.

336 *he might have avoided those killing fields:* Hendrik Hertzberg, "Young Don Graham," *New Yorker*, August 6, 2013.

336 *His intent, he told his mother at the time:* Don Graham, author interviews, January 13 and January 23, 2023.

336 *seven consecutive years of declining revenues:* David Remnick, "Donald Graham's Choice," *New Yorker*, August 5, 2013.

336 *he founded a national movement to provide scholarships:* "Press Release: TheDream.US Launch," February 4, 2014, thedream.us/news.

336 *The catalyst:* As it happened, there may also have been a more personal stimulus. Don Graham was well aware that there had been at least one undocumented young reporter in the newsroom he had just sold. José Antonio Vargas's story of his illegal "overstay" on a childhood visit from the Philippines had been publicized widely in a cover article for *Time* magazine in the very year that DACA was announced. Indeed, just after it, Vargas had been part of the *Washington Post* team that won the 2008 Pulitzer Prize for Breaking News Reporting for their coverage of the Virginia Tech shooting. See "Breaking News Reporting," Pulitzer Prizes, retrieved on April 25, 2023. See also José Antonio Vargas, "Jose Antonio Vargas' Life as an Undocumented Immigrant," *Time*, June 25, 2012.

337 *to allow such children—the "Dreamers":* "Fact Sheet: President Biden Announces Plan to Expand Health Coverage to DACA Recipients," White House statement, April 13, 2023.

337 *"What made you interested in the Dreamers, Don?":* Graham, author interviews.

338 *"How do they do it?":* Donald Graham, "What Abolishing DACA Would Mean for Thousands of Admirable 'Dreamers,'" *Washington Post*, November 8, 2019.

338 *TheDream.Us puts more than a thousand promising DACA:* Graham, author interviews. Current statistics can be found on https://www.thedream.us/about-us/our-work/.

338 *Nine in ten are Latinos:* 89 percent, to be exact, thedream.us.

339 *Some have won Rhodes scholarships:* Donald Graham, "Congress Could Act on the Border and 'Dreamers' This Year," *Washington Post*, November 28, 2022.

339 *ninety-eight thousand of them graduate from high school every year:* "Driven, resilient, and moving our country forward: A letter from our founders," *2021 Impact Report*, thedream.us.

339 *"It baffles me why everyone doesn't understand":* Graham, author interviews.

339 *They dare not enroll in health, nutrition, financial assistance:* Tanya Border and Gabrielle Lessard, "Overview of Immigrant Eligibility for Federal Programs," National Immigration Law Center (NILC), March 2023.

339 *country in which more than two-thirds of them no longer have relatives:* As many as 75 percent don't have remaining relatives in their country of origin. Graham, author interviews.

339 *In 2017 the Trump administration announced that DACA would be phased out:* This and the information that follows in this paragraph are corroborated in the constantly updated guide, "Deferred Action for Childhood Arrivals (DACA)," Sandra Day O'Connor College of Law, Arizona State University, https://lib guides.law.asu.edu/DACA/history#.

339 *When Republican Kevin McCarthy became Speaker of the House:* Kevin McCarthy, Twitter post, 12:55 p.m., June 22, 2022.

339 *a new Dream Act:* "Bill Summary: Dream Act of 2023," National Immigration Forum, February 10, 2023.

340 *"Our country needs the dreamers":* Graham, "Congress Could Act on the Border and 'Dreamers' This Year."

340 *A number of Don's high-profile donors:* Graham, author interviews.

340 *I meet the preternaturally poised Abby:* The accounts are taken from personal conversations on January 23, 2023, with Marymount University's "dream dot" students at a meeting with about twenty DACA and undocumented individuals who are supported by TheDream.US. The conversations followed two larger meetings hosted by Don Graham and the president of Marymount, Dr. Irma Becerra. Marymount is now almost a quarter Latino, making it Virginia's first (and only, at this reckoning) Hispanic Serving Institution.

## Betting on Excellence

341 *"In the end, the American dream is not a sprint":* Julian Castro was the mayor of San Antonio when he made this keynote speech at the 2012 Democratic National Convention. Kevin Cirilli, "Julian Castro's 5 notable lines," Politico, last modified September 4, 2012, https://www.politico.com/story/2012/09/julian-castros-5-compelling-lines-080709. He became the Secretary of Housing and Urban Development under President Barack Obama in 2014.

342 *"When Mexico sends its people":* Donald Trump, quoted by Katie Reilly, "Here Are All the Times Donald Trump Insulted Mexico," *Time*, August 31, 2016.

342 *Hispanic crime is actually proportionately less:* Allen J. Beck, "Race and Ethnicity of Violent Offenders and Arrestees, 2018," Statistical Brief, NCJ 255969,

US Department of Justice, January 2021. The question is further parsed to consider the undocumented population, at least in Texas, which is the only state that keeps such records: Michael T. Light, Jingying He, and Jason P. Robey, "Comparing crime rates between undocumented immigrants, legal immigrants, and native-born US citizens in Texas," *Proceedings of the National Academy of Sciences of the United States of America (PNAS)*, December 7, 2020.

342   *Latinos are more likely to be the victims:* Allison Jordan, "Gun Violence Has a Devastating Impact on Hispanic Communities," Center for American Progress, November 1, 2022.

342   *Far more Latinos have been killed:* 74,522 Latinos died by gun violence from 1999 to 2022. In 2020 alone, 5,003 Latinx were killed in gun violence, a record number that averages thirteen people a day. In contrast, 58,220 Americans were killed in the twenty years of the Vietnam War (1955–1975), according to the Defense Casualty Analysis System (DCAS) Extract Data Files, Military Records, National Archives, April 29, 2008.

342   *While less than half of all Americans believe their children will be better off:* Paul Taylor et al., *IV: Latinos and Upward Mobility*, Pew Research Report online, last modified January 26, 2012, https://www.pewresearch.org/hispanic/2012/01/26/iv-latinos-and-upward-mobility/.

342   *When I visit Elise Heil, the principal:* Most of the following information about the school is from the author's interview with Elizabeth (Elise) Heil, Sacred Heart School, September 19, 2022.

343   *One hundred percent go on to the most prestigious high schools:* "Our Graduates," Sacred Heart School, accessed April 27, 2023, https://sacredheartschooldc.com/our-graduates.

343   *they have entered careers:* Here is an excellent article describing two 1959 graduates, African American Rohulamin Quander and Latina Carmen Torruela, who met as small children at Sacred Heart, eventually married, and went on to successful careers in law and the fine arts: Mark Zimmermann, "'One Blessing upon Another' for Trailblazing Couple Who Were Among First Students to Integrate Sacred Heart School in 1950," *Catholic Standard*, July 1, 2022.

344   *"We have students who speak Vietnamese at home":* Elise Heil, interviewed by Michael Sean Winters, "Dual Immersion Schools Put Kids Ahead of the Curve," *U.S. Catholic*, March 14, 2017.

344   *"I didn't realize who I was until college":* All the quotes that follow from David Bowles are taken from the author's interview with him, August 26, 2021.

345   *Topher is an award-winning educator:* Information on Topher Kandik as well as

his quotes are from email correspondence and the author's interview with him, August 27, 2021. See also "SEED DD Educator Topher Kandik Named DC's 2016 Teacher of the Year!" The Seed Foundation, December 16, 2015, seedfoundation.com.

345    *"You can imagine":* Kandik, author interview. For more information on the Haynes School, see Matthew S. Schwartz, "D.C. Charter School Uses Tough Love to Erase Achievement Gap," Metro Connection, American University Radio WAMU online, last modified July 3, 2015, https://wamu.org /story/15/07/03/with_tough_love_and_encouragement_dc_charter _school_seeks_to_erase_achievement_gap/.

346    *In the course of a single decade, the number of Hispanics had doubled:* Topher Kandik, "Writing Home: Text Choice and Latinx Representation in the Classroom," E. L. Haynes School, Office of the State Superintendent of Education, District of Columbia, osse.dc.gov.

346    *the numbers don't speak well for the majority of Hispanic students:* Most of the numbers cited here are from Luis Noe-Bustamante, "Education Levels of Recent Latino Immigrants in the U.S. Reached New Highs as of 2018," Pew Research Center online, last modified April 7, 2020, https://www.pewresearch .org/short-reads/2020/04/07/education-levels-of-recent-latino-immigrants -in-the-u-s-reached-new-highs-as-of-2018/.

347    *87 percent say they hope their children:* "Hidden in Plain Sight: A Way Forward for Equity-Centered Family Engagement," Learning Heroes, June 2022.

347    *whereas almost 80 percent of all American teachers are white:* "Race and Ethnicity of Public School Teachers and Their Students," Data Point, National Center for Education Statistics, US Department of Education NCES, 020-103 September 2020.

347    *clustered in the Southwest and West:* "Higher Rate of Hispanic or Latino Teachers Teach in Public School with Majority-Minority Student Body, New NCES Data Show, National Center for Education Statistics, March 3, 2022.

347    *the high school graduation rate for Latinos:* This refers specifically to the on-time graduation rate. 81.6 percent, as compared with almost 90 percent for whites; almost 80 percent for blacks; 93 percent for Asian. "Building a Grad Nation," *Civic and Everyone Graduates Center,* School of Education, John Hopkins University, October 6, 2021.

347    *skyrocketed almost 400 percent as a result, reaching four million:* Lauren Mora, "Hispanic Enrollment Reaches New High at Four-Year Colleges in the U.S., but Affordability Remains an Obstacle," Pew Research Center online, last modified October 7, 2022, https://www.pewresearch.org/short-reads/2022/10/07

/hispanic-enrollment-reaches-new-high-at-four-year-colleges-in-the-u-s-but -affordability-remains-an-obstacle/.

347  *According to Janet Murguía, the head of UnidosUS:* All the statistics in this paragraph are taken from "Latino Student Success: Advancing U.S. Educational Progress for All," UnidosUS (Washington, DC, 2022), 32 pp.

348  *As the bracingly intellectual Ed Morales of Columbia University:* As is obvious, I'm a great admirer of Ed Morales's beautifully argued *Latinx: The New Force in American Politics and Culture* (New York: Verso, 2018); here I rely on pages 296–99.

**The Cutting Edge**

348  *"I am an optimist. I am positive":* Mario Molina, as quoted in Elisabeth Alvarado, "Mario Molina: Famous Mario Molina Quotes and Biography," Spanish Mama, last modified November 11, 2021, https://spanishmama.com /famous-mario-molina-quotes-and-biography/.

349  *"a trailblazing pioneer of the climate movement":* John Schwartz, "Mario Molina, 77, Dies; Sounded an Alarm on the Ozone Layer," *New York Times*, October 13, 2020.

349  *went on to win a Nobel Prize:* Molina shared the 1995 prize with his colleague at the University of California, Irvine, F. Sherwood Rowland.

349  *New York Times called the chemist's findings dire:* Schwartz, "Mario Molina, 77, Dies."

349  *"orchestrated by the Ministry of Disinformation of the K.G.B.":* Ibid.

349  *"Thanks to Mario's work":* President Barack Obama, "Remarks by the President at Presidential Medal of Freedom Ceremony," White House, Office of the Press Secretary, November 20, 2013.

349  *born in Puebla, Mexico:* Associated Press, "Albert Baez, 94, Scientist and Singers' Father, Dies," *New York Times*, March 27, 2007. Also Peter Fimrite, "Albert Baez, Scientist, Author, Father of Joan Baez," *San Francisco Chronicle*, March 25, 2007.

350  *Ynés Mexía, for example, a fiercely independent twentieth-century:* "Ynes Mexia," National Park Service, ops.gov/people/yenes-mexia.htm, accessed May 2, 2023. See also "Ynés Mexía: Explorer Extraordinaire," World of Women in Stem, April 8, 2022, https://www.wowstem.org/post/ynes-mexia.

350  *five hundred new plant species:* "Ynés Mexía—Plant Species," World of Women in Stem, https://www.wowstem.org/post/ynes-mexia-plant-species.

350  *Dr. Alfredo Quiñones-Hinojosa, the neurosurgeon:* Alfredo Quiñones-Hinojosa, M.D., "Terra Firma—A Journey from Migrant Farm Labor to Neurosurgery," *New England Journal of Medicine* 357, no. 6 (August 9, 2007): 529–31. See also

"Alfredo Quiñones-Hinojosa: From fieldworker to brain surgeon," Haas Jr., accessed May 2, 2023, https://www.haasjr.org/perspectives/first-person-stories/dr-quinones, and Alfredo Quiñones-Hinojosa, *Becoming Dr. Q: My Journey from Migrant Farm Worker to Brain Surgeon* (Oakland: University of California Press, 2011).

350   *the Mayo Clinic's dean of research:* "Dr. Alfredo Quiñones-Hinojosa," accessed May 2, 2023, doctorqmd.com.

350   *Or Ellen Ochoa, the granddaughter of immigrants:* "Life Story: Ellen Ochoa (1958–): The story of a scientist who became the first Latina in space," New-York Historical Society: Women & the American Story, accessed May 5, 2023. Also "Ellen Ochoa: American astronaut and administrator," *Encyclopedia Britannica*, accessed May 4, 2023, britannica.com.

351   *Luis Miramontes . . . Julio Palmaz . . . Guillermo González Camarena:* All these scientists, Latino and Latin Americans alike, are listed in Christopher McFadden, "17 Greatest Hispanic Inventors That Dramatically Transformed the World," Interesting Engineering, September 27, 2022. On González Camarena, see also "Who Invented the Color TV?," July 25, 2022, Facts.net. John Logie Bard is often attributed as having invented it in 1941, but a year before, in 1940, Camarena created a color TV called the Trichromatic Sequential Field System.

351   *Angela Ruiz Robles created the forerunner of the e-book:* Michael S. Hart is often credited with inventing the e-book and founding Project Gutenberg, which made e-books freely available on the internet. But Robles, who invented the mechanical book decades before Hart's Project Gutenberg, is credited by many as the true inventor. McFadden, "17 Greatest Hispanic inventors."

351   *Victor Ochoa invented the electrical brake:* "The Electric Brake: The Inventor," Smithsonian Education, smithsonianeducation.org.

351   *Eliseo Pérez-Stable, for one: a physician who studies the cultural factors:* Much of this information is taken from the author's interview with Dr. Eliseo Pérez-Stable, October 12, 2021. See also "About the Director," National Institute on Minority Health and Health Disparities, accessed May 1, 2023, nimhd.nih.gov, and Kimbriell Kelly, "This Doctor Breaks Down Language and Cultural Barriers to Health Care," *Washington Post*, September 6, 2016.

352   *"When John Ruffin—the former African American director":* Pérez-Stable, author interview.

352   *According to Pérez-Stable, his division doesn't really do science:* Pérez-Stable, author interview.

353   *Back in 1915, when Mexicans building our railroads:* Natalia Molina, "Borders,

Laborers, and Racialized Medicalization: Mexican Immigration and US Public Health Practices in the 20th Century," *American Journal of Public Health* 101, no. 6 (June 2011): 1024–31, as accessed through the National Library of Medicine, ncbi.nim.nih.gov.

353 *Later, during the Bracero Program:* Molina, "Borders, Laborers, and Racialized Medicalization."

353 *"It is striking that these concerns":* Ibid.

354 *During the COVID pandemic, Mexicans were cravenly judged:* Antonio De Loera-Brust, "As the U.S. Exports Coronavirus, Trump Is Blaming Mexicans," *Foreign Policy* online, last modified July 14, 2020, https://foreign policy.com/2020/07/14/as-the-u-s-exports-coronavirus-trump-is-blaming -mexicans/.

354 *even though COVID affected Latinos disproportionately:* Latoya Hill and Samantha Artiga, "COVID-19 Cases and Deaths by Race/Ethnicity," Figure 1: "Cumulative COVID-19 Age-Adjusted Mortality Rates by Race/Ethnicity, 2020–2022," Kaiser Family Foundation, August 22, 2022. See also "What Is the Impact of the COVID-19 Pandemic on Immigrants and Their Children?," OECD Policy Responses to Coronavirus, Organization for Economic Co-operation and Development, October 19, 2020, oecd.org.

354 *"collision of two deeply flawed American systems":* Deborah Sontag, quoted in Molina, "Borders, Laborers, and Racialized Medicalization."

354 *call it structural racism:* Pérez-Stable, author interview.

354 *"'Science has eliminated distance'":* Gabriel García Márquez, *One Hundred Years of Solitude,* trans. Gregory Rabassa (New York: Harper & Row, 1970), 2.

355 *why more young Hispanics are not rushing to take up careers in STEM:* The question is covered superbly by Cary Funk and Mark Hugo Lopez, *Hispanic Americans' Trust in and Engagement with Science,* Pew Research Center online, last modified June 14, 2022, https://www.pewresearch.org/science/2022/06/14/hispanic -americans-trust-in-and-engagement-with-science/, esp. "5. Many Hispanic Americans See More Representation, Visibility as Helpful for Increasing Diversity in Science," https://www.pewresearch.org/science/2022/06/14 /many-hispanic-americans-see-more-representation-visibility-as-helpful-for -increasing-diversity-in-science/.

355 *a meager 8 percent hold a job that requires these skills in science:* Funk and Lopez, *Hispanic Americans' Trust in and Engagement with Science.*

355 *a distinct lack of role models:* Funk and Lopez, *Hispanic Americans' Trust in and Engagement with Science.* See also Rachelle M. Pedersen et al. "Similarity and

Contact Frequency Promote Mentorship Quality Among Hispanic Under-graduates in STEM," *CBE—Life Sciences Education* 21, no. 2 (June 1, 2022), https://www.lifescied.org/doi/10.1187/cbe.21-10-0305.

355   *Jaime Escalante, who miraculously transformed a school:* 90 percent of the student body at Garfield High School in East Los Angeles during the 1970s and 1980s was Mexican American. Escalante's story was told in the 1987 film *Stand and Deliver*, starring Edward James Olmos. In 1978 the dropout rate at Garfield was 55 percent. In 1980 there were 32 calculus students in A.P. courses, only 10 passed the final exam. In 1988, 570 A.P. students took the exam and hundreds of them passed. Jerry Jessness, "Stand and Deliver Revisited," *Reason* magazine, July 2002. Also Ron la Brecque, "Something More Than Calculus," *New York Times*, November 6, 1988.

356   *Latinos are not made to feel particularly welcome:* Funk and López, *Hispanic Americans' Trust in and Engagement with Science.*

356   *enrolling in college in unprecedented numbers:* Ibid.

357   *Juan Espinoza, president of a support network:* Juan Espinoza is the Bolivian American director of undergraduate admissions at Virginia Tech; he is also president of the Virginia Latino Higher Education Network (VALHEN), which supports numerous colleges and universities in the effort to advance the education of Latinos. Based on personal interviews with Juan Espinoza, September 17, 2021, and Maricel Quintana Baker (founder of VALHEN), July 27, 2021.

## CHAPTER 12: LIMELIGHT

358   *"Give your time, give your heart":* Lin-Manuel Miranda, quoted in quotecatalog .com, accessed May 11, 2023.

358   *"the first superstar in American League history":* Stephen Constantelos and David Jones, "Nap Lajoie," Society for American Baseball Research, accessed on July 15, 2023, https://sabr.org/bioproj/person/nap-lajoie/.

358   *Lou Castro had been born into a well-to-do:* Laura Angélica Reyes, "The First Hispanic Major League Player in History," The Hispanic Heritage Baseball Museum Hall of Fame, October 12, 2021. Also Rhiannon Walker, "On This Day in Latinx History: Louis Castro, First Latino in Major League Baseball, Dies," Andscape, September 24, 2017, andscape.com.

359   *"a quiet, reserved fellow on or off the baseball field":* This newspaper clipping, titled "South American Infielder of Portland," is probably from 1904, when Castro played for the Portland Browns; it is pictured in Reyes, "The First Hispanic Major League Player in History."

359 *"There is no player in the Southern (Association) today"*: Quote from *Atlanta Constitution*, 1907. Brian McKenna, "Luis Castro," Society for American Baseball Research, accessed May 6, 2023, sabr.org.

360 *"old gentlemen's agreement" of 1890:* "Gentlemen's Agreement," Glossary of Terms, Negro Leagues Baseball Museum, accessed May 6, 2023, nlbemuseum.com.

360 *"possessed the power to construct whatever racial categories":* Adrian Burgos Jr., *Playing America's Game: Baseball, Latinos, and the Color Line* (Berkeley: University of California Press, 2007), 85.

360 *hazy middle zone of nonwhiteness:* McKenna, "Luis Castro."

360 *died a derelict in the psychiatric ward:* McKenna, "Luis Castro."

361 *"He had about him a touch of royalty":* Bowie Kuhn, baseball commissioner, as quoted in Larry Schwartz, "Clemente quietly grew in stature," Special to ESPN.com, http://www.espn.com/sportscentury/features/00014137.html.

361 *the celebrated poet Julia de Burgos:* See "Julia de Burgos," accessed May 11, 2023, poetryfoundation.org.

361 *the first Puerto Rican to be named its governor:* See "Jesús Piñero," Hispanic Americans in Congress, Library of Congress, accessed May 11, 2023, loc.gov.

361 *the tallest Puerto Rican in recorded history:* See "Felipe Birriel Fernández: La historia memorable del Gigante de Carolina," *El Adoquín Times*, August 27, 2020.

361 *a custom Roberto would maintain for the rest of his life:* David Bennett, "'Almost a Saint': Roberto Clemente Is as Influential as Ever 50 Years After His Death," *Los Angeles Times*, December 29, 2022.

361 *nicknamed "Momen":* Scott Holleran, "Roberto Clemente in Retrospect," *Pittsburgh Quarterly*, September 27, 2021.

362 *He demanded that blacks and Latinos be given their own vehicle:* Faith Lapidus and Steve Ember, "Roberto Clemente, 1934–1972: First Latino in Baseball Hall of Fame," Voice of America News, August 27, 2006.

362 *Dr. Martin Luther King Jr., who became his friend:* Bennett, "'Almost a Saint.'"

362 *"Mickey Mantle is God":* McKenna, "Luis Castro."

363 *"You writers are all the same!":* Joe Posnanski, "A Legacy Cherished: Remembering Roberto: Hall of Fame Synonymous with Heroism Thanks to Charitable Spirit, Baseball Feats," Major League Baseball, last modified December 28, 2017, https://www.mlb.com/news/roberto-clemente-s-legacy-still-resonates-c264059654.

363 *"I believe every human being is equal":* "Beyond Baseball: The Life of Roberto Clemente," Smithsonian Institution, accessed May 11, 2023, www.robertoclemente.si.edu.

363 *"He walked a little taller than most men"*: Holleran, "Roberto Clemente in Retrospect."

363 *"He was like an artist"*: Nellie King, quoted in Holleran, "Roberto Clemente in Retrospect."

363 *one writer compared to Michelangelo's David:* Nellie King, quoted in Holleran, "Roberto Clemente in Retrospect."

363 *graced by his unique stance, his ebony skin, his large hands:* Holleran, "Roberto Clemente in Retrospect."

364 *almost a third of the talent in the Major Leagues:* Anthony Castrovince, "Overall MLB diversity up; effort to increase Black participation continues," Major League Baseball news, April 14, 2023, mlb.com.

## The Artists

364 *"My mother lived with guts and heart":* Carlos Santana, quoted in Angie Romero, "Billboard Latin Music Conference: 10 Inspirational Quotes from Carlos Santana's 'Legends Q&A,'" *Billboard*, April 29, 2015.

364 *"Échale salsita!":* The song "Échale salsita!" was written by rumba and *son* legend Ignacio Piñeiro (1888–1969) on a train to Chicago in 1930 and recorded by Cuarteto Machín in 1933. Piñeiro met George Gershwin when visiting the United States and it is said that this song influenced George Gershwin's "Cuban Overture."

366 *One out of every eight professional musicians:* "Professional Musician Demographics and Statistics in the US," Zippia: The Career Expert, accessed May 12, 2023.

366 *"I don't speak Spanish":* Dizzy Gillespie, quoted in Ed Morales, "75 Years Ago, Latin Jazz Was Born. Its Offspring Are Going Strong," *New York Times*, January 10, 2023.

366 *"jazz and Latin are the same trunk":* Chico O'Farrill, quoted in Morales, "75 Years Ago, Latin Jazz Was Born."

367 *Rubén Blades, for instance, who received a doctorate in international law:* Anthony Depalma, "Ruben Blades: Up from Salsa," *New York Times Magazine*, June 21, 1987, 24.

367 *went to the prestigious Juilliard School:* "Tito Puente: American Musician," *Encyclopedia Britannica*, accessed May 12, 2023.

## Classical Music

367 *"My mother and my grandmother were maids":* Tania León, quoted in Zachary Woolfe, "Tania León Wins Music Pulitzer for 'Stride,'" *New York Times*, June 11, 2021.

367  *Maria Teresa Carreño:* Elise K. Kirk, "Music in Lincoln's White House," White House Historical Association, accessed May 12, 2023, whitehousehistory.org.

367  *"the Valkyrie of the Piano":* "Teresa Carreño's Death Ends a Notable Career," *Musical America* 13–14 (June 23, 1917).

367  *a cousin of Simón Bolívar's wife:* Clorinda García de Sena y Rodriguez del Toro, the mother of María Teresa Carreño, was a cousin of María Teresa Rodríguez del Toro, the wife of Simón Bolívar. Violeta Rojo, *Teresa Carreño* (Caracas: Biblioteca Biográfica Venezolana, 2011).

368  *"It is difficult to express adequately what all musicians felt":* Henry Joseph Wood, *My life of music* (London: Victor Gollancz, 1949), 147–48.

368  *In 1916, President Woodrow Wilson:* "Carreño, Teresa (1853–1917)," Encyclopedia.com.

368  *introduced to Americans by his fellow émigré:* "When Cuban music hit American living rooms thanks to Desi Arnaz—a look at the music of Ernesto Lecuona," *The New Classical FM* (blog), July 31, 2019, classicalfm.ca.

368  *Roque Cordero:* Cordero's "Panamanian Overture" premiered in Minneapolis in 1946 at about the time when nine hundred out of the two thousand Japanese from Latin America were interned in the American internment camp in Panama. "Japanese Latin Americans," *Densho Encyclopedia*, accessed May 12, 2023, encyclopedia.densho.org.

369  *an openly queer tejana from Houston:* Sara Skolnick, "A Tribute to Pauline Oliveros, the Queer Tejana Who Revolutionized Experimental Music," accessed May 12, 2023, remezcla.com.

369  *"I was hearing all these insects":* Pauline Oliveros, in a radio recording, *Red Bull Music Academy,* hosted by Hanna Bächer, Montreal, 2016, accessed July 15, 2023, https://www.redbullmusicacademy.com/lectures/pauline-oliveros-lecture.

369  *Center for Deep Listening:* "About the Center for Deep Listening," The Center for Deep Listening, accessed May 12, 2023, deeplistening.rpi.edu.

370  *Ernesto Lecuona was a lifelong friend of George Gershwin:* "The Gershwin of Cuba: Ernesto Lecuona," Songwriters Hall of Fame, inducted 1997, accessed July 15, 2023, https://www.songhall.org/profile/Ernesto_Lecuona.

370  *Carlos Chávez may well have inspired Aaron Copland:* Robert L. Parker, "Copland and Chávez: Brothers-in-Arms," *American Music* 5, no. 4 (Winter 1987): 433–44.

370  *Only 4 percent of America's orchestra chairs:* Vivien Schweitzer, *The Strad,* June 15, 2021. See also Marina E. Franco, "Classical music's rising Latin American stars," Notices Telemundo for Axios, March 19, 2022, https://www.axios.com/2022/03/19/classical-music-rising-latin-american-stars.

370 *Martina Arroyo, an Afro-Latina native of Harlem:* Andrew Martin-Weber, "Martina Arroyo," Flatt Features: Made in America, accessed May 12, 2023, http://flattmag.com/features/martina-arroyo/.

371 *"This is how America looks":* Catherine Womack, "Meet Lina González-Granados, L.A. Opera's New Resident Conductor," *Los Angeles Times*, October 7, 2022.

## Rock and Roll

371 *"It's like, 'He's not black enough'":* Bruno Mars (né Peter Hernández), "Latin Music Quotes," https://quotlr.com/quotes-about-latin-music.

371 *Ritchie had been born Richard Steven Valenzuela in 1941:* Material on Ritchie Valens is based on Gregg Barrios, "Ritchie Valens' Roots," *Los Angeles Times*, July 19, 1987; David Allen, "Childhood Pal recalls Ritchie Valens as 'Sweet,' 'Tough' from Murrieta Home," *Press-Enterprise* (Riverside, CA), February 18, 2021. Also Barbara McIntosh, "The Reveries of Valens' Donna," *Washington Post*, September 4, 1987.

372 *planned the release of a more carefully promoted single:* Rolando Arrieta, "La Bamba," *All Things Considered*, NPR, July 15, 2000, https://www.npr.org/2000/07/15/1079558/npr-100-la-bamba.

373 *Ritchie Valens boarded a small plane:* Desiree Kocis, "Mysteries of Flight: The Day the Music Died," *Plane and Piloting Magazine*, February 4, 2020.

374 *Into that musical efflorescence came Gloria Estefan:* "Gloria Estefan," Biography: History and Culture, biography.com, updated September 12, 2022. Here, among other *cubano* rock singers, I shouldn't fail to add Celia Cruz, Jon Secada, and Armando "Pitbull" Pérez.

374 *personal bodyguard to Marta Fernández Miranda:* Steve Dougherty, "One Step at a Time," *People*, June 25, 1990.

374 *Captured on Cuba's beaches:* Richard Harrington, "Miami Voice," *Washington Post*, July 17, 1988.

374 *he began to manifest symptoms of multiple sclerosis:* Harrington, "Miami Voice."

374 *"I would lock myself up in my room":* Gloria Estefan, quoted in Harrington, "Miami Voice."

375 *Why are you mixing bongos with trumpets?:* A paraphrase of Gloria Estefan's words about being told that trumpets and percussion were unsuitable in Latin music, as quoted in Carolina Kucera and Maria Elena Salinas, "Gloria Estefan Says She Fought to Have 'Conga' Become a Single," 93.5/1430 WCMY, September 15, 2022, accessed on July 31, 2023.

375 *"the power of music transcends cultural, social":* Citation read at the White

House on November 24, 2015, "President Obama presents the Presidential Medal of Freedom to Emilio and Gloria Estefan," Gloria Estefan Official FAN TV, accessed on July 31, 2023.

375 *The Puerto Ricans, too:* There are myriad Puerto Rican as well as Mexican American popular musicians who deserve a fuller mention than I am able to give them. Among the Puerto Ricans: Bad Bunny, José Feliciano, Luis Fonsi, Jennifer Lopez, Ricky Martín, Daddy Yankee. Among the Mexican Americans: Joan Baez, Vikki Carr, Jimmy Crespo of Aerosmith, Zach de la Rocha of Rage Against the Machine, Trini Lopez, Dave Navarro of the Red Hot Chili Peppers, Vince Neil of Mötley Crüe, Selena (Quintanilla), Linda Ronstadt, Robert Trujillo of Metallica, and the Mexican American bands Los Lobos, the Midniters, Malo (Jorge Santana), and Maná.

375 *Marc Anthony, who was born in Spanish Harlem:* Larry Rohter, "A Master of Crossover Relives '70s Ballads," *New York Times*, June 18, 2010.

375 *top-selling salsa singer of all time:* Lea Veloso, "Marc Anthony's Net Worth Makes Him the Highest Selling Salsa Artist Ever—Richer Than His Ex J-Lo," Stylecaster, stylecaster.com, January 31, 2023.

376 *on a taxi-ride through Manhattan one day:* Enrique Lopetegui, "Marc Anthony's Putting a Real Kick in His Salsa," *Los Angeles Times*, May 1, 1996.

376 *"Salsa opened up a whole new world for me":* Leila Como, "Marc Anthony's 30-Year Odyssey: 'When Did My Life Become This Interesting?,'" January 19, 2021.

376 *"the most year-end best-selling albums":* Sofia Rocher, "Guinness World Records honors Marc Anthony with Tropical album charts title," *Guinness World Records*, February 9, 2016.

378 *"giving voice to the invisible ones":* Carlos Santana quoting rock promoter Bill Graham, in conversation with Jeffrey Brown, *PBS Newshour*, December 6, 2013, www.pbs.org.

378 *"Because it's one hundred and fifty percent spirituality":* Carlos Santana, in conversation with Jeffrey Brown, *PBS Newshour*.

## The Silver Screen

378 *"Latinos make up one of the largest demographics in the box office":* Actress Gina Alexis Rodríguez, "Gina Rodriguez: The Fact That Latinos Are Not Seen on Screen Is Devastating," *Variety*, January 24, 2018.

378 *The numbers are so anemic as to be in cardiac arrest:* Vanessa Martínez and Aida Ylanan, "Long Underrepresented in Film and TV, Latinos Are Falling Further Behind," *Los Angeles Times*, June 13, 2021.

378   *Only 5 percent of Hollywood's lead actors are Latino:* All the statistics quoted are from Inclusion Initiative reports issued by the University of Southern California's Annenberg Institute. Reported in Associated Press, "Latino Characters Only Make Up 4.5 Percent of Hollywood Speaking Roles, Study Finds," *USA Today*, August 26, 2019. The adjusted 5 percent figure comes from the *2022 Latino Donor Collaborative—Latinos in Media Report*, as quoted in Sara Fischer, "Representation of Latinos in shows and films, 2022," Axios, September 27, 2022.

378   *Only 3 percent of all screenwriters are Hispanic:* Associated Press, "Latino Characters Only Make Up 4.5 Percent of Hollywood Speaking Roles, Study Finds."

378   *"Latinos are vastly unrepresented":* USC Annenberg Inclusion Initiative founder and director Stacy L. Smith, who coauthored the study, Associated Press, "Latino Characters Only Make Up 4.5 Percent of Hollywood Speaking Roles, Study Finds."

378   *American television, where a mere 3 percent of lead actors are Latino:* Associated Press, "Latino Characters Only Make Up 4.5 Percent of Hollywood Speaking Roles, Study Finds."

379   *"There's this misunderstanding of who the community is":* Ana-Christina Ramón, director of Research and Civic Engagement of the Division of Social Sciences at UCLA, as quoted in Lara Rosales, "The Importance of Accurate Latinx Representation in the Media," USA Wire, August 10, 2022.

379   *The chicano cartoonist Lalo Alcaraz would argue:* D. D. Degg, "CRT [Caucasian Replacement Theory] Hits The Herblock Prize (Lalo Alcaraz Won)," Daily Cartoonist, May 18, 2022, accessed on July 15, 2023, https://www.dailycartoonist.com/index.php/2022/05/18/crt-hits-the-herblock-prize-lalo-alzcaraz-won/.

379   *"just let them be people?":* Charles Ramírez Berg, professor at the University of Texas and author of *Latino Images in Film: Stereotypes, Subversion, and Resistance*, as quoted in Martínez and Ylanan, "Long Underrepresented in Film and TV, Latinos Are Falling Further Behind."

379   *The Hispanic relationship to Hollywood is a long, fraught story:* I have borrowed here from an excellent and thorough article by Allen Woll, "How Hollywood Has Portrayed Hispanics," *New York Times*, March 1, 1981, sec. 2, 17.

379   *"the bes' damn caballero":* Woll, "How Hollywood Has Portrayed Hispanics."

380   *"I was king for a week":* Ricardo Montalbán, quoted in Paul Henninger, "Ricardo Montalban Quite a Character—in Many Roles," *Los Angeles Times*, January 25, 1967.

380   *As the* Los Angeles Times *pointed out:* Ashley Lee, "Spielberg Tried to Save

'West Side Story.' But Its History Makes It Unsalvageable," *Los Angeles Times*, December 12, 2021.

381 *one even admitted he was totally unfamiliar:* This was Stephen Sondheim. Quotes are from Lee, "Spielberg Tried to Save 'West Side Story.'"

381 *"White Hollywood does not want to tell the real stories":* Edward James Olmos, as quoted in Daniel Hernandez, "Hollywood's Treatment of Latinos Is an Open Wound. Healing It Requires a Reckoning," *Los Angeles Times*, June 13, 2021.

381 *stars such as Raquel Welch:* Other Latino actors who masked their identities to avoid discrimination from directors and public alike: Margarita Rita Cansino, who became superstar heartthrob Rita Hayworth; Ramón Antonio Gerardo Estévez, who became Martin Sheen; and Manuel Antonio Rodolfo Quinn Oaxaca, who became Academy Award winner Anthony Quinn. Wonder Woman's actual birth name was Lynda Jean Córdova Carter.

381 *"Just because there are several successful Latino actors":* Hernandez, "Hollywood's Treatment of Latinos Is an Open Wound."

381 *complained that the film misrepresented the true reality of the place:* Julia Jacobs, "Lin-Manuel Miranda Addresses 'In the Heights' Casting Criticism," *New York Times*, June 21, 2021.

382 *the lack of Latinos at the top of the film industry:* When Steven Spielberg tried his hand at *West Side Story* in his film released in 2021, the cast was far more representative of Latinos than the 1961 version. But the story, the lyrics, and the prejudice were still in place and Latinos, especially Puerto Ricans, continued to be offended.

382 *"white-passing Latinx people":* Jacobs, "Lin-Manuel Miranda Addresses 'In the Heights' Casting Criticism."

382 *"Nothing attacks the subconscious more":* Hernandez, "Hollywood's Treatment of Latinos Is an Open Wound."

382 *"That's why our children are in cages":* Ibid.

382 *That's why a white supremacist with an assault rifle:* Ibid.

382 *"one of Hollywood's biggest open wounds":* Ibid.

## Writers

382 *"One press account said I was an overnight success":* Sandra Cisneros, accessed on July 15, 2023, https://www.brainyquote.com/quotes/sandra_cisneros _589108.

385 *diversity, equity, and inclusion movement (DEI):* Danielle Beavers, "Diversity, Equity and Inclusion Framework," Greenlining Institute, March 2018.

385 *Latino numbers in American media have moved up by a mere 1 percent:* Workforce

Diversity report, Government Accountability Office, September 21, 2021, cited in Jalen Brown, "Latino Representation in Media Industry Grew by Only 1 Percent in the Past Decade, a New Report Finds," CNN online, last modified October 5, 2022, https://www.cnn.com/2022/10/05/us/latino-media -underrepresentation-goa-report-reaj/index.html. See also Sara Fischer, "New Report Calls Out U.S. Media for Lack of Latino Representation," Axios, last modified September 27, 2022, https://www.axios.com/2022/09/27/latino -representation-media-film-tv-study.

386  *Today, only 8 percent of the media industry is Hispanic:* The exact number of print units sold in 2022 was 788.7 million. Ella Ceron, "For Latinx Authors, How Quickly Is Change Happening?," Bloomberg, April 6, 2023.

386  *"means that Americans don't know who Latinos are":* Joaquín Castro, quoted in Brown, "Latino Representation in Media Industry Grew by Only 1 Percent in the Past Decade."

386  *7 percent of all Hispanics identify with this label:* Astrid Galván, "Poll: LGBTQ-Identity Is Higher Among Latinos Than Other Groups," Axios, last modified March 15, 2022, https://www.axios.com/2022/03/15/latinos-lgbt-poll-gen-z.

386  *Nearly 12 percent of Generation Z Latinos:* Galván, "Poll: LGBTQ-Identity Is Higher Among Latinos Than Other Groups."

386  *an overpowering macho culture muzzled them:* A prevailing prejudice against homosexuality still exists in conservative Latino households throughout the country and especially in the American South and Southwest. Author interview with Tomás Rivera, Puerto Rican-Mexican American, San Antonio, Texas, September 15, 2022.

387  *At ports of entry:* "Did My Family Really Come Legally?," American Immigration Council, Fact Sheet, August 10, 2016.

387  *writers like the Peruvian American Carlos Lozada:* I've been privileged to know Carlos since the 1990s, when he reviewed books for me at the *Washington Post*. He later became the book critic of the *Post* and, most recently, a columnist for the *New York Times*. I'm indebted to him for an excellent, insight-rich interview for this book (August 10, 2021).

387  *Few Latinos have done more:* This section on Sandra Cisneros is taken from a telephone interview with her in San Miguel de Allende, Mexico, on June 17, 2021. The conversation was resumed in person in Washington, DC, on September 15, 2022, and by email on July 13, 2023.

387  *one of the very first books by a Chicana to be published by a mainstream publisher:* *The House on Mango Street* was published in 1984 by Arte Publico but went on to be republished by Viking in 1991. The other Chicana to have this distinction

is Cecile Pineda, whose novel *Face* was published by Viking in 1985, a year after Cisneros's original publication of *House*.

## EPILOGUE: UNITY

391 *"Let us hope we have the courage to stand alone"*: Eduardo Galeano, Stig Dagerman Prize acceptance speech, Sweden, September 12, 2010. The full quote is: "Let us hope we have the courage to stand alone and the audacity to band together because nothing is more useless than a lone tooth outside a mouth, or a single solitary finger." Text in Spanish: "Homenaje a Eduardo Galeano," delenguaylliteratura.com; my translation.

391 *doubt the very existence of Latin America as a place of origin:* Mauricio Tenorio-Trillo, *Latin America: The Allure and Power of an Idea* (Chicago: University of Chicago Press, 2017), 1.

391 *not a bona fide region with a clear civilization:* Tenorio-Trillo, *Latin America*, 2.

392 *"a national community with a shared past":* National Council of La Raza, Foreword, in *State of Hispanic America 2004*, iii.

392 *the great majority of nine million "Spanish Americans":* Anna Brown, "The U.S. Hispanic Population Has Increased Sixfold Since 1970," Pew Research Center online, last modified February 26, 2014, https://www.pewresearch.org/short-reads/2014/02/26/the-u-s-hispanic-population-has-increased-sixfold-since-1970.

392 *forty million—almost five times as many:* "The American Community—Hispanics: 2004," US Census Report Number ACS-03, February 1, 2007, https://www.census.gov/library/publications/2007/acs/acs-03.html.

392 *change the organization's name to UnidosUS*: Suzanne Gamboa, "National Council of La Raza Changes Name to UnidosUS," NBC News online, last modified July 10, 2017, https://www.nbcnews.com/news/latino/national-council-la-raza-changes-name-unidosus-n781261.

392 *During Murguía's tenure alone, the Latino population has doubled:* Latinos numbered about thirty-five million in 2004 and sixty-three million in 2023. Brown, "U.S. Hispanic Population Has Increased Sixfold Since 1970," and "Hispanic Heritage Month 2022," Press Release CB22-FF.09, September 8, 2022, US Census Newsroom, census.gov.

392 *to "advance the economic condition, educational attainment":* "Mission," League of United Latin American Citizens (LULAC), https://lulac.org/about/mission/.

392 *Favoring strong immigration laws:* Benjamin Márquez, "The Politics of Race and Assimilation: The League of United Latin American Citizens, 1929–1940," *Western Political Quarterly* 42, no. 2 (June 1989): 355–75. See also Laura E.

Gómez, *Inventing Latinos: A New Story of American Racism* (New York: New Press, 2020), 106, and Cristina Beltrán, *The Trouble with Unity* (New York: Oxford University Press, 2010), 24.

393   *some Mexicanos seeing LULAC as a band of* vendidos: *Vendidos* means "sellouts." "LULAC History—All for One and One for All," League of United American Citizens, lilac.org/about/history/.

393   *a flawed statistical concoction that "has hardly any relation to the real world":* This (along with the quotes that follow) is from Beltrán, *Trouble with Unity*, 107.

394   *"Latinos did not view themselves as having common concerns":* Rodolfo O. de la Garza et al., Latino National Political Survey, Inter-University Program for Latino Research (New York: Ford Foundation, December 1992), 8; also quoted in Beltrán, *Trouble with Unity*, 114.

394   *insisted on being called, quite simply, "an American":* This was later corroborated in Mark Hugo Lopez, "4. Pan-Ethnicity: Shared Values Among Latinos," Pew Research Report online, October 22, 2013, https://www.pewresearch.org /hispanic/2013/10/22/4-pan-ethnicity-shared-values-among-latinos/.

394   *Mexican Americans said they felt more kinship to Anglos:* LNPS, 1992, Louis DeSipio, *Counting on the Latino Vote: Latinos as a New Electorate* (Charlottesville: University of Virginia Press, 1996), 177; also Beltrán, *Trouble with Unity*, 113.

394   *considered Latinos a* potential *community:* Rodolfo O. de la Garza et al., *Latino Voices: Mexican, Puerto-Rican, and Cuban Perspectives on American Politics* (Boulder, CO: Westview Press, 1992), 14–16; also Beltrán, *Trouble with Unity*, 114.

394   *"We are together":* Janet Murguía, author interview, June 9, 2021.

395   *"We are like-minded":* Ibid.

395   *Lopez describes himself as a Chicano:* Mark Hugo Lopez, author interview, September 8, 2021.

395   *"potential" unity:* López, "Pan-Ethnicity: Shared Values Among Latinos."

395   *almost 40 percent considered Latinos:* Ibid.

395   *there is also the phenomenon of ethnic attrition:* López, author interview.

396   *"How many Latina friends do you have, Vicky?":* Rosa Victoria Arana-Robinson, author interview, September 14, 2022.

396   *my nieces and nephew:* Isabel Arana DuPree, Ashley Arana Waring, Julia Arana West, and Brandon Robinson (Arana), author interviews via text messages, March 27, 2023.

396   *My daughter . . . My son:* Lalo Walsh and Adam W. Ward, author interviews via email, May 3, 2023.

397   *The problem, according to the National Academy of Sciences:* Alex Nowrasteh, "Ethnic Attrition: Why Measuring Assimilation Is Hard," *Cato at Liberty,*

CATO Institute, December 8, 2015. Also: Brian Duncan and Stephen J. Trejo, "Ethnic Identification, Intermarriage, and Unmeasured Progress by Mexican Americans," in *Mexican Immigration to the United States*, ed. George J. Borjas (Chicago: University of Chicago Press, 2007), 229–64. Nate Cohn, "Pinpointing Another Reason That More Hispanics Are Identifying as White," *New York Times*, June 2, 2014.

397  *"Yeah, we're all different"*: Junot Díaz, author interview, May 21, 2021.

398  *"Hey, you! What do you think you're doing?"*: All Antonio Tijerino quotes here are from the author's interview with him, July 28, 2021.

398  *"I have no idea. El Salvador? New Mexico?"*: Ibid.

398  *"We're not that different!"*: All Jorge Zamanillo quotes here are from the author's interview with him, April 7, 2022.

# INDEX

Page numbers beginning with 405 refer to notes.

# Also by
# MARIE ARANA

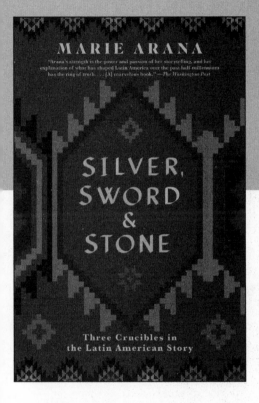

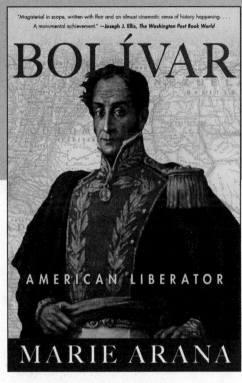

"Arana's strength is the power and passion of her storytelling.... {A} marvelous book."

—*The Washington Post*

"This book reads like a wonderful novel but is researched like a masterwork of history."

—Walter Isaacson, author of *Steve Jobs*